Date Due

6/10/74

 23-236 PRINTED IN U.S.A.

D1275139

International economics

International economics

Bo Södersten, University of Lund

Harper & Row, Publishers
New York, Evanston, London

To Astrid, Anna, Henrik, and Erika

Preface

This book's purpose is to present a modern, theoretical treatment of international economics. It builds on results published in leading journals during the last 20 years, and the author's intent has been to integrate these results with previously existing theory.

Problems of economic policy are discussed throughout the book, but the emphasis is on theory, not policy. The book seeks to provide the reader with theoretical tools that he can apply to various kinds of problems, not just certain contemporary ones. There has been no attempt at originality in developing the theory. On the contrary, the exposition follows traditional lines to demonstrate basic principles as clearly as possible and to show the logical progression of the theory. If the book differs from others in the field, it probably does so in matters of emphasis. Traditionally, textbooks in this field have been slow in incorporating theoretical advances made in the subject.

The exposition of the book is quite rigorous, and all necessary assumptions are carefully set out and explained. The stress is on geometry; almost all the mathematics used has been relegated to appendixes. Starting as it does from elementary principles and building up to more complex cases, the exposition should be fully comprehensible to undergraduates, but it should also be useful to graduate students as a summary of the main body of existing theory.

Even though good reasons may exist for treating international economics as a distinct subject area, it should be stressed that there is no single theory of international economics. International economic theory does not form one neat body of theorems. Therefore, although the structure of the models used in Parts I and II of this book is quite unified (consisting primarily of elaborations on the standard two-sector barter-trade model), the theory in Part III is of a more eclectic kind. It involves a generalization of the aggregate theory of income and employment for open economies, as well as monetary theory and general theory of economic policy. The theory of trade policy presented in Part IV is also more diversified. It includes tariff theory, which is really an elaboration on and application of standard barter-trade theory.

HOW TO USE THE BOOK

There is no one best way of organizing the subject of international economics. Some will prefer to start with macroeconomic aspects, others with microeconomic or pure-theory parts. Each part of this book has a logical structure, and it might prove difficult to break up a part, although it is unnecessary to study all the material in any one part before turning to the next. The sequence in which one chooses to cover the parts is to some extent a matter of taste and interest. For example, if one starts with pure theory, perhaps it would be logical to continue with the theory of growth and trade. But whether one wishes to take Part III next, on the balance of payments, or Part IV on trade policy is a matter of preference. The part on the balance of payments is placed before the part on trade policy because an understanding of the problems of trade policy is usually enhanced by first gaining insights into problems connected with a country's external balance. But it might also be argued that the theory of trade policy has more logical connections with the pure theory of trade, and that these parts should therefore precede Part III on the balance of payments and Part V on the international monetary system. The five parts, therefore, are intentionally self-contained.

ONE-SEMESTER COURSES

Instructors who wish to use the book in one-semester courses on international economics may find it too voluminous. For most one-semester courses, I would suggest assigning the following 14 chapters: 1–5, 8, 9, 13–16, 19, 22, and 23. But other combinations are equally possible.

ACKNOWLEDGMENTS

The conception and execution of this book have been considerably influenced by discussions with students and colleagues. I am especially grateful to the students who took my classes in international economics at the University of California, Berkeley, from 1965 to 1967. Their enthusiastic interest in the subject led me to undertake this work. I cannot mention all those who have assisted me through their written or oral evaluations, but I must thank Ronald W. Jones of Rochester, Anthony Lanyi of Princeton, and Erling Olsen of Copenhagen, who read the whole manuscript and made many valuable comments.

I am grateful to Inga Persson, who most efficiently served as my research assistant, checked the manuscript, and drew some of the figures. Ingalill Cedergren typed the manuscript several times and helped most agreeably in many ways. Sören Holm assisted me during the development of the first two parts of the book, read the manuscript critically, and drew some of the figures. I thank them all and am alone responsible for any remaining deficiencies.

I gratefully acknowledge research support during the work on this book from the Institute of International Studies at the University of California, Berkeley, and from the Swedish Social Science Research Council.

BO SÖDERSTEN

Contents

xiii

International economics

Introduction: international economics and economic theory

Today the national state is the dominant political entity. Most countries, from an economic point of view, are still intimately linked with others. A few—the United States, the Soviet Union, and China—could conceivably withdraw from the world economy without disastrous consequences to themselves. For other countries such an act would border on the unthinkable. It would bring about not only a drastic lowering of economic welfare, but also a complete change of ways of life. For practical purposes, all countries must accept the fact that they are part of a world economy. No country can escape its role in the system of interdependent trading nations.

The degree of interdependence is on the increase. World trade in commodities has increased 7 percent per year during the last 20 years. This growth rate is considerably faster than that of total world output or income.

The high degree of integration of the world economy is shown in many ways. In 1966 an estimated 128 million people traveled abroad. Capital, too, moves quite freely between countries; capital movements are more important today than they have been at any time since before World War I. International movements of technology and managerial skills, often in the form of direct investments, are now more important than ever. Considerable migration of labor also takes place.

It is sometimes argued that the world economy before 1914 was integrated to a degree not since equaled. This is debatable. True, capital movements were very important before 1914; Great Britain, for instance, invested a staggering proportion of its total savings abroad in the 40 years before World War I. At the same time, however, capital markets were not so well integrated as they are today among leading industrial nations, which is demonstrated by the fact that short-term interest-rate differentials were much larger before 1914 than they are today.

Tariffs and other trade barriers of an economic-political nature were low before World War I, especially before the 1890s. But natural obstacles in the form of high transport costs and poor communications were much more important than they are today. Furthermore, the rise of the truly international corporation is a recent phenomenon. Firms that extracted minerals, oil, or other natural resources on an international scale existed before 1914. But the multinational firm that markets industrial products on a world-wide scale and quickly responds to differing earning opportunities is of recent vintage.

Economic interdependence among nations was not unimportant before World War I. But the integration of the world economy before 1914

1

seems to have been something of an illusion. The economic interdependence among countries is more far-reaching today than it has ever been.

Another factor of relevance in this context has to do with more ambitious economic policies. Most countries are far more ambitious in their national economic policies today than they were in the decades leading up to World War I. Full employment is one of the primary goals of most governments. Considerably higher levels of unemployment were tolerated before World War I than are today; for instance, Britain accepted with equanimity a 10 percent level of unemployment in the late 1920s to defend the pound sterling under the resurrected gold standard.

Before 1914 domestic national income was deflated to save the domestic currency. Today countries are much less willing to accept such policies. This greatly complicates matters. Countries gain by trading and by taking part in international movements of factors of production. But this also entails risks of disturbances in the domestic economy. Any country that wants to reap the benefits of the international division of labor must become dependent on other nations; it will have to become integrated into the world economy. Such interdependence, however, constrains national economic policies. This dilemma is one of the important matters that we will study, both directly and indirectly.

We have so far spoken somewhat loosely about the integration of the world economy. A word of caution must be inserted. The really important integration is between parts of the world economy. There is still, for instance, a very definite dividing line between the Soviet Union and the East European communist countries on the one hand, and the United States and the Western European capitalist countries on the other. What has been said so far really applies to parts of the world economy; the world economy as a whole is not and never was integrated in any qualified sense of the word.

The areas where interdependence really counts are within the North Atlantic community, i.e., the countries belonging to the Organization for Economic Cooperation and Development (OECD), and for the communist countries cooperating with the Soviet Union within the Council for Mutual Economic Aid (COMECON).[1] Most less-developed countries are also integrated

---

[1] The members of the OECD are Austria, Belgium, Canada, Denmark, France, Great Britain, Greece, Iceland, Ireland, Italy, Japan, Luxembourg, the Netherlands, Norway, Portugal, Spain, Sweden, Switzerland, Turkey, United States, and West Germany. Affiliated members are Finland and Yugoslavia. The members

to a considerable degree into one or other parts of the world economy. Even if large segments of the economies of the less-developed countries are not dependent directly on the world economy (for instance, subsistence agriculture), trade is often critical for most less-developed countries, especially in a potential sense, as they, in their development efforts, will have to rely on imports of goods and capital.

INTERNATIONAL ECONOMICS AS A SUBJECT

Even if most people agreed that international economic relations are of great importance for most countries, it does not necessarily follow that international economics should be studied as a subject independent of other branches of economics.

International economics is often referred to as "applied economics." And there are certainly many policy problems and problems of an empirical nature within international economics that the use of economic theory can elucidate. But there are more deep-seated reasons why international economics has a long tradition as a subject in its own right.

Many theorems and insights central to economic theory have been developed by economists working within international economics. The theory of comparative advantage and the factor-price equalization theorem are examples. Both belong to the area usually called the pure theory of international trade. The pure theory of trade can be said to be part of price theory, the term used in a broad sense. But price theory or microtheory per se seldom pursues the subject to such a degree that all the aspects of the theory which are of interest to a trade theorist are revealed in its full implications. Trade theory is a distinct part of modern economic theory with a rich body of theorems. These results are not part of general economic theory as it is commonly understood and taught.

Analogous conditions hold, although perhaps to a less degree, for the macroeconomic parts of international economic theory. Some of its results,

---

of the COMECON are Bulgaria, Czechoslovakia, East Germany, Hungary, Mongolia, Poland, Rumania, and the Soviet Union. Yugoslavia is an associated member and observers are China, Cuba, North Korea, and North Vietnam.

for instance those about income determination in open economies, are quite straightforward applications of the corresponding parts of the theory for closed economies. But other parts, for instance exchange-rate theory, can hardly be obtained except from a study of the specific theory.

When it comes to the policy aspects of the subject, it is quite obvious that international economic relations give rise to problems not encountered in other fields of economics. The nation is not only a distinct political entity, it has many important economic characteristics that set it apart from the larger integrated areas that make up the world economy: The mobility of the factors of production is much larger within the nation than among nations, there are tariffs and taxes on imported goods, different currencies give rise to specific problems, etc. All this leads to international economic policy problems that are different in nature from national policy problems.

There are, therefore, from both a theoretical and a policy point of view, good reasons why international economics is dealt with as a specific branch of economics. Modern economics is a large and diversified subject. A training in general economic theory is the best background for a study of international economics. But it can be regarded only as a background. To get a real understanding of the field, the student will have to study international economics directly.

Now we shall look at some characteristics of international economics and preview some of its problems and results.

COMPARATIVE ADVANTAGE AND PURE THEORY

One of the basic questions facing international trade theory is why trade takes place. The classical economists saw labor as the only factor of production and said that differing labor productivity among countries caused trade.

A closely linked question is: Why do countries gain by trading? The classical economists said that as long as cost conditions differ between two countries, at least one and probably both will gain by trading.

These questions and answers contain the essence of the theory of comparative advantage. The first can be said to state the positive side and the second the normative side. The normative aspect is perhaps the most interesting to the modern student. It demonstrates, on very weak assumptions, that trade will be beneficial to all countries involved in trade. It is important to understand the nature of this theory. It has often been attacked and is often misunderstood. It is still frequently argued that trade is detrimental to countries, today especially in connection with less-developed countries. Right from the outset we will, therefore, enter disputed territory. Whatever the student's final opinion is, he will have to undertake a certain amount of theoretical work before he can reach an informed judgment.

One of the central assumptions of the classical economist was that factors of production were fully mobile within countries but not at all mobile between countries. Labor could move freely from New York to Arizona, but it could not cross the border into Mexico. This is an assumption that modern trade theorists have stuck to in elaborating the modern theory of trade. It might seem to be too strong. Some 4 million workers, for instance, have since World War II moved north from Portugal, Spain, southern Italy, Greece, and Turkey to France, West Germany, and Switzerland. But the movements of labor have taken place primarily within somewhat integrated areas. The movement of workers from the United States to Europe, or from Eastern Europe to Western Europe, is still insignificant.

For many purposes the assumption that labor is immobile between countries is valid. Using this (and some other fairly stringent assumptions), modern trade theory has proved some quite startling theorems. One is that trade alone will lead to a complete equalization of factor prices. Even in the absence of factor movements, if only goods can be traded freely, wages will be equalized.

A study of modern trade theory will also help the student understand one of the basic principles of economics, that of general equilibrium. While studying the Heckscher–Ohlin theory of trade or the factor-price equalization theorem, he will see how essential variables in an economy, e.g. inputs, outputs, and commodity and factor prices, are related to each other. The modern version of the pure theory of trade is perhaps the most fruitful application of general equilibrium theory that exists. By studying the pure theory, the student will gain insight into one of the most fundamental aspects of the science of economics, apart from an understanding of which basic factors explain what a country will export and import.

COMPARATIVE STATICS: THE QUESTION OF CHANGE

The pure theory of trade is fundamentally a static theory. It studies some aspects of trading economies in the setting of static equilibrium. It abstracts from one fundamental aspect, that of change.

The simplest way to study the effects of change is by the use of comparative statics. We take an economy in a given equilibrium and then introduce a change in some of the basic variables. This is done in Part II, which studies the effects of economic growth on international trade. The theory in Part II is based on the same type of model as is used in Part I for the pure theory of trade. It is the so-called two-by-two-by-two model, i.e., a model with two countries, using two factors of production, labor and capital, to produce two goods, one export commodity and one import commodity.

The theory of growth and trade is of quite recent vintage, the 1950s and 1960s. It has not so far been incorporated in a textbook. This part could therefore appear difficult and novel to some, but it has much to offer. From a methodological point of view, it demonstrates clearly how the static models used in Part I can be developed in a comparative-static way. It clearly demonstrates also some of the basic effects of economic growth on the variables in the trade model. One question it answers is the following. Let us assume that economic growth occurs in two trading economies. What will be the effects on the terms of trade (the ratio of export prices to import prices) and on national income? The answer will depend on which sectors growth occurs in and what the income elasticities are.

The effects of increases in factor endowments and technical progress are also studied. These effects can be handled clearly by the use of geometry. An understanding of this type of theory therefore does not involve very advanced or difficult methods. The effects of technical progress, for instance, are quite striking. An understanding of this kind of theory is essential also for a broad group of problems outside the field of international trade, so it seems appropriate to treat the theory of economic growth and trade rigorously and explicitly.

A study of growth and trade is also useful because it puts the static parts of trade theory (the theory of comparative advantage, for instance) into relief. It helps one understand why it can be beneficial for a country to specialize in the production of a commodity at a certain period and also why it could be detrimental for the country to increase export production of this commodity as time goes by.

MACROECONOMIC ASPECTS: DIFFERENT CURRENCIES

One of the obvious differences between trade within a country and international trade is that the latter involves different currencies. If a New Yorker trades with a Californian, they both use the same currency, but trade between a New Yorker and a Canadian involves different currencies.

One essential complication in connection with foreign trade is that the relative values of currencies change. One year, £1 sterling could be worth $2.80 U.S.; the next, $2.40. This concerns the balance of payments between countries.

Disequilibria in the external balances of countries give rise to changes in exchange rates. The policy problems surrounding disequilibria in the balance of payments and changes in exchange rates are among the most pertinent ones in the world economy. If anything, they also seem to become more important and to attract increasing attention as the years go by.

Part III is devoted to these macroeconomic aspects of international economics. The basic principles of foreign exchange markets are discussed and an explanation is given of how a country's balance of payments can be in disequilibrium and how it can be kept in equilibrium.

One of the eternal subjects of discussion in this sphere concerns flexible versus fixed exchange rates. The system prevailing in the world today is one of fixed exchange rates. Many economists argue that it is precisely because of this system that the problems connected with balance-of-payments disequilibria loom so large in the world economy. If, instead, a system of flexible exchange rates was adopted, trade between countries would automatically be in equilibrium, and economic policies could be freed of balance-of-payments constraints. The advocates of fixed exchange rates argue that such adjustments of the balance of payments would have to be bought at a high cost and that one problem would be solved at the expense of introducing new and even more awkward problems.

We can only hint at the problem here. Part III reveals that uncertainty, inflation, and unemployment all play important roles when it comes to estimating the costs and benefits of various exchange-rate systems.

TRADE POLICIES: THE INTERNATIONAL MONETARY SYSTEM

The book is based on the principle of decreasing abstraction. The most theoretical parts are in the beginning, especially in Parts I and II; then, as the exposition develops, it becomes more and more policy oriented—it assumes more of an " applied " nature. This is because theory is needed to appreciate all the facets of a policy problem. It is logical to start with theory and then proceed to policy, although it perhaps seems that policy problems are sometimes " easier " to deal with than theoretical questions.

One of the trade problems confronting less-developed countries is the stabilization of commodity prices. Together with the question of tariff preferences, this problem has dominated the two UNCTAD conferences held so far. This problem is discussed in Part IV.

The proposals for stabilization of commodity prices are of different kinds. The object of some is to stabilize terms of trade between less-developed and industrial countries; others, less far-reaching, aim at stabilizing export prices or export proceeds. To understand the true nature of some of these plans, they should be considered against the models of growth and trade developed in Part II.

These models show explicitly the basic factors that determine the development of commodity prices in international trade. Therefore, they show clearly which factors have to be controlled if international prices are to be controlled. They give an example of how recent developments in trade theory can be used to elucidate long-standing policy problems.

The problem of international liquidity is not encountered in any other branch of economics, although it is central to international economics. The questions of liquidity and of international monetary arrangements are highly topical. Most writings in this sphere are of a highly policy-oriented kind, and they are highly value-loaded; here the degree of " personal piffle " is higher than in any other area of international economics. This could be a reason for omitting the area altogether from a book devoted primarily to an exposition of the basic theoretical structure of the subject.

However, this could perhaps be going too far in theoretical puritanism; an attempt at suicide is no way to avoid death. Part V, which is devoted to the international monetary system, refrains from too much personal idiosyncracy and tries instead to analyze some of the fundamental issues underlying the problem.

A problem much discussed in recent years is that of confidence. The

American dollar is the main reserve currency. To increase liquidity the United States has to run a deficit in its balance of payments. But as these deficits continue, the rest of the world begins to lose confidence in the dollar. The nature of this conflict is discussed in Part V. It is suggested that fairly small measures, partially by the United States and partially by some central banks in Western Europe, could solve this problem.

SELECTED BIBLIOGRAPHY: INTRODUCTION

Each bibliography in this book covers the chapter or chapters that precede it. The purposes of the bibliographies are to let the reader know which works the author has especially consulted, and to guide the reader for further studies. The bibliographies are selective, but that does not imply that omitted works are not useful. The reader can easily find extensive bibliographies in survey works, especially the ones by Bhagwati, Caves, and Chipman listed below. I have been quite selective in my bibliographies because, although selectivity might in some cases be arbitrary, I find that long reading lists often tend to be inefficient: instead of giving the student real guidance, they can drown him in a multitude of works without distinguishing the important, path-breaking articles from the elaborations and repetitions.

International economics, especially in its theoretical parts, has been excellently surveyed in recent years. The most outstanding of these surveys, all containing excellent bibliographies, are:

J. Bhagwati, "The Pure Theory of International Trade," *Economic Journal*, Vol. 74, March 1964, pp. 1–84.

R. E. Caves, *Trade and Economic Structure*, Cambridge, Mass., Harvard University Press, 1960.

J. Chipman, "A Survey of the Theory of International Trade, Parts I–III," *Econometrica*, Vols. 33 and 34, July 1965, October 1965, and January 1966, pp. 477–519, 685–760, and 18–76.

When one comes to the monetary parts of international economics, no survey of the same calibre exists. The standard work in this area is still:

J. E. Meade, *The Balance of Payments*, London, Oxford University Press, 1951.

Two works that contain surveys of a more personal type are:

M. C. Kemp, *The Pure Theory of International Trade*, Englewood Cliffs, N.J., Prentice-Hall, 1964.

R. E. Mundell, *International Economics*, New York, Macmillan, 1968.

Two collections of readings published by the American Economic Association are of great interest. They are:

H. S. Ellis and L. M. Metzler, *Readings in the Theory of International Trade*, Homewood, Ill., Richard D. Irwin, 1949.

R. E. Caves and H. G. Johnson (eds.), *Readings in International Economics*, Homewood, Ill., Richard D. Irwin, 1968.

These two books will be referred to in subsequent bibliographies by the abbreviations *RTIT* and *RIE*. Two older books that contain interesting material from the point of view of the development of the subject are:

G. Haberler, *The Theory of International Trade*, London, William Hodge & Co., 1936.

J. Viner, *Studies in the Theory of International Trade*, London, Allen & Unwin, 1938.

The student who is interested in finding data can go to the statistical yearbooks and international trade statistics published by various countries and international organizations. Two standard monthly sources for data are:

International Monetary Fund, *International Financial Statistics*

United Nations, *Monthly Bulletin of Statistics*

A useful reference book is:

R. G. D. Allen and J. S. Ely (eds.), *International Trade Statistics*, New York, Wiley, 1953.

The exposition in this book builds primarily on articles published in the leading scientific journals. These journals will be referred to by the following abbreviations in the bibliographies:

AER—American Economic Review

EJ—Economic Journal

Ec—Economica

JPE—Journal of Political Economy

MS—Manchester School of Economic and Social Studies

OEP—Oxford Economic Papers

QJE—Quarterly Journal of Economics

RES—Review of Economic Studies

RE&S—Review of Economics and Statistics

SP—Staff Papers (of the International Monetary Fund)

PART I

The pure theory of international trade

The theory of comparative advantage

1

One of the basic questions that the theory of international trade has to answer is what determines trade. Put another way, why do countries gain by trading? Economics does have an answer—one that goes back more than 150 years—in the theory of comparative advantage. This theory, formulated around 1815, is usually connected with the name of David Ricardo.[1] The theory of comparative advantage, or, as it is sometimes called, the theory of comparative costs, is one of the oldest, still unchallenged theories of economics.

Before we tackle the theoretical aspects of this concept it might be worthwhile to take a quick look at its historical background—at the kind of setting out of which the theory of comparative advantage developed.

The economic doctrine that prevailed during the first two centuries of the development of the modern national state—the seventeenth and eighteenth centuries—was mercantilism. The doctrine of mercantilism had many modern features: It was highly nationalistic, it viewed the well-being of the own nation to be of prime importance, it favored the regulation and planning of economic activity as an efficient means of fostering the goals of the nation, and it generally viewed foreign trade with suspicion.

The most important way in which a country could grow rich, according to the doctrine of mercantilism, was by acquiring precious metals, especially gold. Single individuals, however, were not to be trusted; they might also like gold, but perhaps they liked other things even more. Left to themselves, they might exchange gold for satin and linen, spices from India, or sugar from Cuba, or indulge in whatever private pleasures they preferred, to the detriment of the stock of precious metals stored in the nation. To prevent such undertakings, the nation had to control foreign trade. Exports were viewed favorably as long as they brought in good, solid gold, but imports were viewed with apprehension, as depriving the country of its true source of richness—precious metals. Therefore, trade had to be regulated, controlled, and restricted, no specific virtue being seen in having a large volume of trade.

---

[1] David Ricardo (1772–1823) accumulated a fortune during the Napoleonic wars as a member of the London stock exchange. He then retired, turning to theoretical economics, and in 1819 became a Member of Parliament. In 1817 he published his main work, *Principles of Political Economy and Taxation*, which contains the first rigorous exposition of the classical theory of value and distribution; in chapter 7, "On Foreign Trade," Ricardo expounds the theory of comparative advantage.

It was against this background that English classical economics developed, for mercantilism was the credo that Adam Smith and David Ricardo rebelled against.[2] English classical economics was an offspring of liberalism and the Enlightenment—of a general philosophy that stressed the importance of the individual and viewed the nation as nothing more than the sum of its inhabitants.

For Smith, as for Ricardo, the supreme subject of economics was the consumer: Man labored and produced in order to consume. And anything that could increase consumption, or, to use Ricardo's picturesque phrase, "the sum of enjoyments," ought to be viewed with favor.

ADAM SMITH AND THE ABSOLUTE ADVANTAGE OF TRADE

Adam Smith saw clearly that a country could gain by trading. The tailor does not make his own shoes; he exchanges a suit for shoes. Thereby both the shoemaker and the tailor gain. In the same manner, Smith argued, a whole country can gain by trading with other countries.

If it takes 10 labor units to manufacture 1 unit of good A in Country I but 20 labor units in Country II, and if it takes 20 units of labor to manufacture 1 unit of good B in country I but only 10 labor units in Country II, then both countries can gain by trading.

If the two countries exchanged the 2 goods at a ratio of 1 to 1, so that 1 unit of good A is exchanged for 1 unit of good B, Country I could get 1 unit of good B by sacrificing only 10 units of labor, whereas it would have to give up 20 units of labor if it produced the good itself. Likewise, Country II would have to sacrifice only 10 units of labor to get 1 unit of good A, whereas it would have to give up 20 units of labor if it produced it itself. The implication of this is clearly that both countries could have more of both goods, with a given effort, by trading.

This was a simple and powerful illustration of the benefits of trade,

---

2 Adam Smith (1723–1790) was professor of moral philosophy at Glasgow University. The first major figure of classical economics, he introduced the theory of value and taught the blessings of the unhampered market ("the invisible hand"). His major work, *The Wealth of Nations*, was published in 1776.

and on it Adam Smith rested his plea for noninterference—for free trade as the best policy for trade between nations. Smith's argument seems convincing, but it is not very deep. It was left to Torrens[3] and Ricardo to produce the stronger and more subtle argument for the benefits of trade contained in the theory of comparative advantage.

DAVID RICARDO AND THE THEORY OF COMPARATIVE ADVANTAGE

Ricardo did not object to Smith's analysis. It is obvious that if one country has an absolute advantage over the other country in one line of production and the other country has an absolute advantage over the first country in a second line of production, both countries can gain by trading. A great deal of trade, maybe most trade, is governed by such differences. If the United States can produce tea only at very high costs and India can produce computers only at excessive costs, it surely benefits both countries to trade tea for computers.

But what if one country is more productive than another country in all lines of production? If Country I can produce all goods with less labor cost than Country II, does it still benefit the countries to trade? Ricardo's answer was yes. So long as Country II is not equally less productive in all lines of production, it still pays both countries to trade.

We will spend some time elucidating this principle, as it is of basic importance to the theory of trade. We may as well start with Ricardo's own model before going on to more modern means of demonstration.

Ricardo used England and Portugal as examples in his demonstration, the two goods they produced being wine and cloth. Being a courteous Englishman, and living in an era when no one had heard about "underdeveloped countries," Ricardo assumed that Portugal was more efficient in

---

[3] Robert Torrens (1780–1864), an officer in the British Army during the Napoleonic wars, later turned to economics and published a pamphlet in 1815, *Essay on the External Corn Trade*, which contains what seems to be the earliest formulation of the theory of comparative advantage. He also made significant contributions to classical monetary theory and policy. In 1831 he became a Member of Parliament.

TABLE 1.1

Cost comparisons

	Labor cost of production (in hours)	
	1 unit of wine	1 unit of cloth
Portugal	80	90
England	120	100

---

making both cloth and wine. In Table 1.1 Ricardo sums up cost conditions in the two countries.

According to this model, Portugal has an *absolute advantage* in the production of wine, because it takes 80 hours of labor there to produce 1 unit of wine, whereas it takes 120 hours in England to produce the same amount. Portugal also has an absolute advantage in production of cloth, because it takes 90 hours of labor there to produce 1 unit of cloth, whereas it takes 100 hours in England to produce the same amount.

But Portugal also has a *comparative advantage* in production of wine, because she can produce 1 unit of wine with only $80/120 \times 100$, or 67 percent, of the English effort while it takes $90/100 \times 100$, or 90 percent, of the English effort to produce 1 unit of cloth. Therefore, Portugal is comparatively more efficient in wine-making than in production of cloth.

Analogously, England has an *absolute disadvantage* in the production of both cloth and wine but a *comparative advantage* in the production of cloth, because, although it takes $120/80 \times 100$, or 150 percent, of the Portuguese effort for the English to make 1 unit of wine, it takes them only $100/90 \times 100$, or 111 percent, of the Portuguese effort to make 1 unit of cloth. Thus, because the absolute disadvantage of England is greater in wine-making, she has a comparative advantage in the production of cloth.

We should now further clarify the meaning of the term "comparative advantage." In order to speak about comparative advantage there must be at least two countries and two goods. We compare the ratio of the cost of production of one good in both countries (80:120) with the ratio of the cost of production of the other good in both countries (90:100). As long as these two ratios differ, one country has a comparative advantage in the production of one of the two goods, while the other country has a comparative advantage in the production of the other good. As long as this is the case, both countries will gain from trade, regardless of the fact that one of the countries might have an absolute disadvantage in both lines of production.

It was on careful reasoning about these ratios that Ricardo and the classical economists rested their argument about the benefits of trade and their plea for free trade as a cornerstone of economic policy. Let us now examine their argument about gains from trade.

RICARDO ON THE GAINS FROM TRADE

Let us assume that Portugal and England do not trade but produce and consume in isolation. The prices of cloth and wine in the two countries are then determined by their respective costs of production.

If in England it takes 120 hours of labor to make 1 unit of wine while it takes only 100 hours to make 1 unit of cloth, clearly wine must then be more expensive per unit than cloth—1 unit of wine will cost 120/100, or 1.2, units of cloth.

If in Portugal it takes 80 hours of labor to make 1 unit of wine and 90 hours to make 1 unit of cloth, cloth will be more expensive than wine—1 unit of wine will cost 80/90, or 0.89, units of cloth.

Let us now open the possibility of trade. If England could import 1 unit of wine at a price less than 1.2 units of cloth, she would gain by doing so. If Portugal could import more than 0.89 unit of cloth for 1 unit of wine, she, too, would gain. Therefore, if the international price of 1 unit of wine is somewhere between 1.2 and 0.89 units of cloth, both countries will gain by trading.

Let us assume further that in the international market 1 unit of wine exchanges for 1 unit of cloth. It is then advantageous for England to export cloth and import wine, because in the absence of trade England would have to give up 120 hours of labor for every unit of wine she wants. By trading she can, instead, with 100 hours of effort, produce 1 unit of cloth and then exchange this unit of cloth for 1 unit of wine. Under autarky—i.e., a country producing and consuming in isolation—she would have to give up 120 hours of labor for every unit of wine she wanted, whereas with trade she only needs to give up 100 hours. With each 20 hours left over she can produce more cloth and enjoy a higher level of consumption—or the workers can rest,

and trade will make possible more leisure with a given amount of consumption.

Portugal will also gain from trading. In isolation she would have to
give up 90 hours of labor to get 1 unit of cloth. Now she can make 1 unit of
wine with the effort of 80 hours of labor and exchange this unit of wine for
1 unit of cloth in the international market. Every 10 hours of labor freed by
this process can then be used for either increased production or increased leisure.

Thus trade offers each country the possibility of specializing in the line
of its comparative advantage and then exchanging these products for those
in which she has a comparative disadvantage. Both countries can reallocate
their factors of production to the line where their comparative advantage lies
and then export this product and import the other product. In short, each
country can consume more by trading than in isolation with a given amount
of resources.

This, then, is a restatement of the basic argument for gains from trade
as given by Ricardo and the English classical school of economics. It is, as
suggested, a powerful argument, and we have to regard it as basically correct.
It is built, however, on some quite drastic assumptions. It assumes only
one factor of production—labor—as creator of wealth; i.e., it is formulated
in terms of the labor theory of value. The relationship it assumes between
input and output—the production function on which it is built, to use
modern phraseology—is also quite specific and will be delineated more fully
when we come to the modern theory of international trade. Neither assumption, however drastic, invalidates the basic line of argument.

Another objection to the classical formulation of the theory of comparative advantage is that gains from trade somehow accrue to the country
as a whole. It is convenient to personalize countries (and we will go on doing
so); no great harm will result. But this is one point where we need to be
careful: A country is not a person but many persons. We have established that
a country will gain from trade, but is it true that *all* its citizens will be better
off with trade than without it?

Free trade will not guarantee such an outcome, and the classical economists can legitimately be criticized on this point by modern welfare
economics. We will, however, suspend the discussion of this point for the
time being until we have developed additional tools of analysis. For the
moment, we will merely state that a nation as a whole will be better off by
specializing according to comparative advantage and trading than it would
be in isolation.

THE THEORY OF COMPARATIVE ADVANTAGE
AS RELATING TO MANY GOODS

So far we have talked about only two goods. In much of what follows about the pure theory of trade we will also deal with a two-good model, where only two goods—one export and one import good—enter explicitly. It is, however, easy to generalize the Ricardian theory of comparative advantage to cover several goods.

Since a country that trades will export the good in which it has a comparative advantage, we can now establish the following theorem: *Country I has a comparative advantage over Country II in all its* export *commodities.*

This theorem can be proved in the following way. We start by examining how many hours of labor it takes to produce 1 unit of each good produced in the two countries and then rank them as shown in Table 1.2.

The model set up in the table assumes that in Country I it takes 100 hours of labor to produce 1 unit of each of the goods in question. We then indicate how many hours it takes to produce the same amount of each good in Country II.

We are now interested in the cost of each good in the two countries. Remember, we are still in a world where labor is the only factor of production—in other words, the only thing needed to produce a good. The cost of producing 1 unit of a good is therefore determined by the hours of labor needed and the hourly wage. Let us denote the hours of labor it takes to produce 1 unit of good A in Country I by a_1, good B by b_1, etc. In the same way, let us denote the hours of labor it takes to produce 1 unit of good A in Country II by a_2, etc. In our example from Table 1.2, $a_1 = b_1 = c_1$, etc., $= 100$; $a_2 = 200$; $b_2 = 180$; $c_2 = 160$; etc.

Let us denote the hourly wage in Country I by w_1 and the hourly wage in Country II by w_2. Let us denote the price of good A in Country I by p_{1a}, of good B by p_{1b}, etc., and the price of good A in Country II by p_{2a}, of good B by p_{2b}, etc.

Let us then assume that we live in a world without any middlemen, markups, and so on, so that the price of each good is determined solely by its cost of production. For the sake of simplicity we shall continue our model by assuming Portugal to be Country I and England to be Country II. The price of good A in Portugal is then $p_{1a} = a_1 \times w_1$; the price of the same good in England is $p_{2a} = a_2 \times w_2$. Let us further assume that the hourly wage

TABLE 1.2

Productivity ranking

Hours it takes to produce one unit of respective good in:	Types of goods									
	A	B	C	D	E	F	G	H	I	J
Country I	100	100	100	100	100	100	100	100	100	100
Country II	200	180	160	140	120	100	80	60	40	20

in Portugal is 1 escudo and in England £1 and that labor is homogeneous and completely mobile within either of the two countries. That is, 1 hour of labor in Portugal commands the same wage regardless of who the worker is or where he works, and the same applies to England.

We can then see that the price in Portugal of 1 unit of good A will be $p_{1a} = 100 \times 1$, or 100 escudos; of 1 unit of good B will be $p_{1b} = 100 \times 1$, or 100 escudos; and so on. The price in England of 1 unit of good A will be $p_{2a} = 200 \times 1$, or £200; of 1 unit of good B, $p_{2b} = 180 \times 1$, or £180; and so on.

We still have no way of comparing prices in the two countries, because we do not know how to convert Portuguese escudos into British pounds, and vice versa. This missing link is given by the exchange rate, which we will call r, r being the number of pounds sterling we can exchange for 1 escudo.

Let us assume, again for the sake of simplicity, that $r = 1$, i.e., that £1 exchanges for 1 escudo, and measure prices internationally in escudos. We can then see from Table 1.2 that the price of good A produced in Portugal will be 100 escudos, whereas it will be 200 escudos if it is produced in England; the price of good B will be 100 escudos in Portugal and 180 in England; and so on.

Therefore, in trade with England Portugal will export goods A through E. The price of good F is the same in both countries and therefore good F will not be traded. On the other hand, because the price of goods G through J will be lower if produced in England than if produced in Portugal, the goods will be exported by England to Portugal.

Thus Portugal has a comparative advantage in the production of goods A through E, and England has a comparative advantage in the production of goods G through J. The basic determinant of comparative advantage in this version of the Ricardian model is labor cost. In both countries *relative prices* are determined by labor costs, so $p_{1a} : p_{1b} : p_{1c} \cdots = a_1 : b_1 : c_1$ $\cdots$ and $p_{2a} : p_{2b} : p_{2c} \cdots = a_2 : b_2 : c_2 \cdots$. The wage rate determines the money cost of production but is of no importance for the *ranking* of the goods, and it is the ranking that is essential for the determination of comparative advantage.

If, however, the wage rate in Portugal went up 10 percent, so that the hourly wage increased from 1 escudo to 1.1 escudos (1 escudo and 10 centavos) the cost of producing 1 unit of the formerly nontraded good F would go up in Portugal while remaining the same in England. Therefore, good F will now become a traded good, exported by England and imported by Portugal. If the Portuguese wage rate increased still further, let us say up to 1.25 escudos an hour, Portugal would lose her comparative advantage in production of good E, which she would then have to import instead of export. Thus the absolute height of the wage rate is important in determining *where* the link will be broken, but it does not affect the ranking itself.

If we know that the ranking is broken at, let us say, good F, so that this good commands the same price in both countries and is therefore not traded, we can infer that Portugal will export goods A through E and import goods G through J.

The exchange rate acts in a manner analogous to the wage rate: It is important in determining where the chain of ranking will be broken, but it does not affect the ranking itself. Let us assume, for instance, that the English would like to change the exchange rate by devaluing the pound. Assume that they devalued 10 percent, so that the price of 1 escudo would be £$1\frac{1}{10}$ (£1 and 2 shillings). Then England would gain a comparative advantage in the production of good F. If they devalued even further, the line of division would be pushed farther to the left and England might gain a comparative advantage in the production of good E, which would be transformed from an import to an export good.

But England would never import good G and export good F, because the relative English labor cost as compared with the Portuguese labor cost is lower for G than for F. Therefore, if we know that the dividing line is at F, for instance, and that England exports good G, we can infer that she also exports goods H through J.

Thus we can say that the number of goods a country will export is determined by the wage rate and by the exchange rate. The lower the wage rate, the more goods a country will export. Likewise, the lower the exchange rate—that is, the more units of its own currency a country is willing to exchange for 1 unit of foreign currency—the more goods the country will be able to export. But the particular goods a country will export will be determined by comparative advantage in production.

The more goods a country can export, the better her balance of trade will be. Thus the exchange rate and the wage level, which influence the number of goods a country can export, are important variables for determining any country's balance-of-payments situation. We will discuss these issues more fully when we take up the theory of the balance of payments.

For the time being we will have to be content with the hope that we have achieved a basic understanding of the theory of comparative advantage. It is now time to introduce some geometric tools that will enable us to restate the theory of comparative advantage in modern dress and illustrate the gains from trade.

SELECTED BIBLIOGRAPHY: CHAPTER 1

Classical expositions of the classic theory of comparative advantage are contained in:

G. Haberler, *The Theory of International Trade*, especially chap. 10.

J. Viner, *Studies in the Theory of International Trade*, chap. 8.

The surveys by Bhagwati and Chipman also contain excellent parts on the theory of comparative costs. Chipman, Part I, contains the definitive exposition of this theory. Among empirical tests of the theory of comparative advantage one should especially mention:

G. D. A. MacDougall, "British and American Exports: A Study Suggested by the Theory of Comparative Costs, Parts I and II," *EJ*, December 1951 and September 1952 (Part I reprinted in *RIE*).

Supply and demand in international trade: the gains from trade

In Chapter 1 we stated the theory of comparative advantage in terms of cost ratios. We will now see how the production side of a country's economy can be illustrated by geometric means. We will begin by introducing the concept of a production-possibility curve.

THE PRODUCTION-POSSIBILITY CURVE

Let us return to the model of a country producing two goods. The quantity of each good she produces will depend on her factor endowments and on her technical knowledge. By "factor endowments" we mean the amounts of factors of production the country possesses. If we were to go on thinking in Ricardian terms, how much the country could produce would depend on how much labor she had with the production techniques available to her. But we need no longer think only in terms of one factor of production. We can think in terms of two factors—for instance, labor and capital—or of however many factors we want to.

Assume that the United States can produce either 100 bushels of wheat or 100 yards of cloth when all the factors are fully and most efficiently employed in the production of either wheat or cloth, respectively. The combinations of the two goods that she can produce can then be given by the production-possibility curve or, as it is sometimes called, the transformation curve, in Figure 2.1a.

If the United States chooses to produce only wheat, she can produce 100 bushels. If she would also like to produce cloth, she must forgo the production of some of her wheat. As the curve is drawn in Figure 2.1a, in order to produce 1 yard of cloth, she would have to give up production of 1 bushel of wheat. This illustrates what is meant by opportunity cost, which is a very important concept in economics. The opportunity cost of a particular service X in producing a particular commodity A is the benefit, or opportunity, lost if X is instead put to its best alternative use. In the case of the United States as shown in Figure 2.1a, where productive service X can produce 100 bushels of wheat or 100 yards of cloth, the opportunity cost to wheat producers for 1 bushel of wheat is 1 yard of cloth. If, however, as shown in Figure 2.1b, X can produce 50 bushels of wheat or 100 yards of

24

Supply and demand
in international trade:
the gains from trade

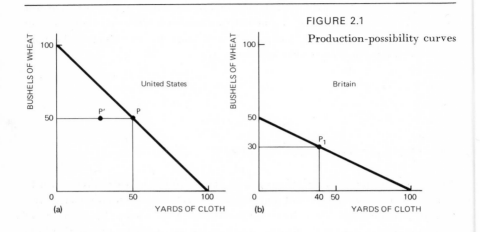

FIGURE 2.1

Production-possibility curves

cloth, the opportunity cost to wheat producers for 1 bushel of wheat is 2 yards of cloth.

If a country can produce either wheat or cloth, the opportunity cost of wheat is the amount of cloth she has to give up to gain 1 unit of wheat. When production-possibility curves are straight lines, as in Figure 2.1, the opportunity costs are constant.

In isolation, or autarky, the country ought to produce and consume at some point on the production-possibility curve. By definition, she cannot reach a point in the commodity space outside the curve. The reason for this is that with the amounts of factors of production the country has, plus her knowledge, she can only produce some combination of goods indicated by the production-possibility curve. The country can, on the other hand, produce any combination of goods represented by a point inside the curve such as point P' in Figure 2.1a. This, however, is clearly not an efficient point, because by moving out to point P on the curve, the country can produce the same amount of wheat (50 bushels) as at P' and a larger amount of cloth. Therefore, assuming as always that more of any commodity—wheat or cloth—is preferred to less of it, point P is preferable to point P'. In fact, *any* point inside the curve is less desirable than a point on the curve.

Under autarky the country does not trade and thus can consume only as much as she can produce herself—i.e., she will consume at a point on her production-possibility curve. The combination of goods the country chooses to consume—in other words, which point on the curve she picks—is determined by demand conditions. (We apply the phrase "demand conditions" in a loose sense for the time being; as we go along its meaning will be made more specific.) In our example let us assume that the United States before trade chooses to produce and consume at point P—that is, that she both produces and consumes 50 bushels of wheat and 50 yards of cloth.

In a like manner, the production and consumption pattern of the second country in our two-country model, say, Great Britain, can be established, as shown in Figure 2.1b, which shows Britain's production-possibility curve. Let us assume that in isolation she produces at point P_1, that is, that she produces and consumes 40 yards of cloth and 30 bushels of wheat.

A production-possibility curve also indicates something about comparative prices. The production-possibility curve in Figure 2.1a, which shows that the United States can produce either 100 bushels of wheat or 100 yards of cloth, also shows that to get 1 more unit of cloth at any point on the curve, the country has to give up 1 unit of wheat. From this it follows that 1 bushel of wheat will exchange for 1 yard of cloth.

Another way of stating the same fact is to say that the slope of the production-possibility curve determines the relative prices of the two goods. When the production-possibility curve is a straight line, the relative prices are obviously the same at all points.

In Britain, likewise, the relative prices of cloth and wheat are determined by the slope of her production-possibility curve. They are not the same as in the United States, because the slope of the British production-possibility curve differs from that of the United States, as we can see in Figure 2.1b. According to the figure, Britain can produce either 100 yards of cloth or 50 bushels of wheat. At whatever point on her curve she produces, in order to get 1 more unit of wheat she has to give up 2 units of cloth. Therefore, 2 units of cloth will exchange for 1 unit of wheat, and if the price of 1 bushel of wheat is £1, the price of 1 yard of cloth will be £1/2.

The relative prices under autarky differ in the two countries, and this, as we learned in Chapter 1, is the sole precondition needed in order for trade to be beneficial for both countries. The possibility of gains from trade can be easily illustrated in a geometric fashion.

26

Supply and demand
in international trade:
the gains from trade

THE GAINS FROM TRADE: A GEOMETRIC ILLUSTRATION

As we have demonstrated in Figure 2.1, wheat will be relatively cheaper in the United States than in Britain, and cloth will be relatively cheaper in Britain than in the United States. This means that the United States has a comparative advantage in production of wheat and Britain has a comparative advantage in production of cloth. Therefore, we would expect that under trade between the two countries the United States will export wheat and import cloth, while Britain will export cloth and import wheat.

Under autarky, prices for these commodities differ in the two countries. But under trade, disregarding all transport costs and impediments to trade, prices in both countries will be the same. The question is: What will this new international price be?

Let us start by assuming that Britain is a small country compared to the United States, and that her volume of trade will not influence prices; the international price will therefore be the price prevailing in the United States.

This will be very advantageous for Britain, as her new trade situation diagramed in Figure 2.2 shows. Before trade, Britain produced and consumed at point P_1. With trade she can consume at point C_1, which is clearly preferable because it represents more of both cloth and wheat. At the new price ratio it is not to Britain's advantage to produce any wheat at all, because for each unit of wheat she produces she will have to forgo the production of 2 units of cloth. Instead, by trading she can specialize completely and make only cloth, and in the international market can exchange 1 yard of cloth for 1 bushel of wheat. She should therefore produce at point P_1' and consume at point C_1 by exchanging $P_1'A$ units of cloth for C_1A units of wheat at the international exchange ratio, or the international terms of trade, shown by the line BP_1' in Figure 2.2.

We define a country's terms of trade as P_x/P_m, where P_x is the price of her export good and P_m is the price of her import good. We will have a good deal to say in coming chapters about the terms of trade. Usually the notion "terms of trade" is used to mean the quotient between an index of export prices and an index of import prices, but there is no need to limit it to that meaning. The "terms of trade" can also refer to the relative price between any two single commodities or groups of commodities.

In our first example the relative price of wheat and cloth in the United States was the same before and after trade. If this is the case, there

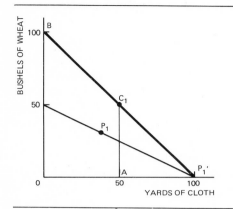

FIGURE 2.2

International trade ratio

seems to be no reason for the United States to trade with Britain because she would not gain anything by doing so.

But normally relative prices will not be the same after trade as before trade. Figure 2.1 showed that relative prices before trade were not the same in Britain as in the United States: assuming for convenience the same currency—say, the dollar—in both countries, we see that if 1 bushel of wheat cost $1 in the United States and $1 in Britain, 1 yard of cloth in the United States would also cost $1 but only $1/2 (50 cents) in Britain. What then will determine the new relative price, the new terms of trade?

The new terms of trade will be determined by both countries' joint demand and supply conditions. Let us assume that the new international price will fall between the autarky prices of both countries, that is, that 1 unit of wheat will exchange for $1\frac{1}{2}$ units of cloth. If we still assume that 1 bushel of wheat costs $1, 1 yard of cloth will cost $2/3 (67 cents) in the international market.

Figure 2.3 shows the situation before trade and after trade for each country. Before trade, the United States produced and consumed wheat and cloth at point A. After trade she will specialize exclusively in the production of wheat, producing at point B' and exchanging $B'Q$ bushels of wheat for BQ yards of cloth at the international price ratio $B'P_1$. Thereby she can consume at point B, which is obviously preferable to A as it represents larger amounts of both goods.

Figure 2.3b shows that before trade Britain produced and consumed at point A_1. After trade she will specialize exclusively in the production of

28

Supply and demand
in international trade:
the gains from trade

FIGURE 2.3

Conditions before and after trade

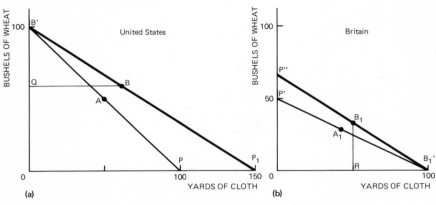

(a)

(b)

YARDS OF CLOTH

cloth, producing at point B_1'. Then trading according to the international price ratio $P''B_1'$, she will export RB_1' of cloth and import RB_1 of wheat. (The reader should observe that $B_1'P''$ in Figure 2.3b is parallel to $B'P_1$ in Figure 2.3a.) B_1 lies to the right and above A_1, so it is clear that it represents more of both goods and hence Britain's greater consumption of both goods because of trade.

We have now given a simple geometric illustration of the gains from trade and of the application of the theory of comparative advantage. If opportunity costs are constant, trade leads to complete specialization—the United States will produce only wheat and Britain only cloth. This is, however, quite a special case. Let us go on and look into the more general case where we have a production-possibility curve with variable opportunity costs.

VARIABLE OPPORTUNITY COSTS: A CONCAVE PRODUCTION-
POSSIBILITY CURVE

The economic meaning of constant opportunity costs, or a straight-line production-possibility curve, is that all factors of production are equally

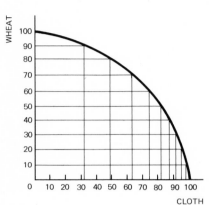

FIGURE 2.4

A concave production-possibility curve

efficient in all lines of production. This is not a very realistic assumption. If, for simplicity's sake, we think in terms of only one factor of production—labor, for example—we would expect some workers to be especially efficient in the production of wheat and others more efficient in making cloth. If this is the case, the production-possibility curve will resemble the one shown in Figure 2.4, which illustrates variable opportunity costs.

Let us say that we, as a country, start by being completely specialized in wheat, producing 100 units of wheat. If we give up production of 10 units of wheat by shifting the workers most suited for production of cloth to the cloth industry, we can produce over 30 units of cloth; by giving up still 10 more units of wheat, we can produce almost 20 additional units of cloth; and so on. We can see that the amount of extra cloth we can produce by decreasing production of wheat with a given amount is steadily decreasing as we move downward along the production-possibility curve. The *opportunity cost* of cloth in terms of wheat is therefore steadily *increasing* as we increase the production of cloth and decrease the production of wheat.

So far we have been considering only one factor of production, labor. The law of increasing opportunity cost, however, does not in any way hinge upon the number of factors of production. If we had instead three factors of production—labor, land, and capital, for example—we would still expect some factor to be more suited for production of wheat than for production of cloth. Whenever this is the case, the opportunity cost for increasing

30

Supply and demand
in international trade:
the gains from trade

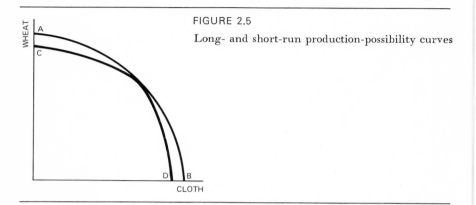

FIGURE 2.5

Long- and short-run production-possibility curves

production of a certain good increases, and the production-possibility curve will be concave to the origin, as it is in Figure 2.4.

As the shape of the production-possibility curve is determined by production conditions, the ease with which factors of production can be moved from one industry to another is one important element in determining it. In the short run, we would expect the adaptability of the economy to be low and that an increase in the production of one good from a given position on the curve would be possible only with sharply rising opportunity costs. In Figure 2.5 the production-possibility curve CD illustrates this situation. In the long run, given opportunities for retraining workers, readjusting the capital stock, etc., we would expect the substitution possibilities in the economy to be larger; the curve AB illustrates this situation. Commodity prices also play a significant part in a situation where there are variable opportunity costs, and if prices shift, the producers adjust production to obtain the greatest advantage. Figure 2.6 illustrates this interplay between shifting prices and shifting production.

Let us assume that at any given moment relative commodity prices in an economy are indicated by the line $P_0 P_0$. With these prices, producers will produce at point A, i.e., they will produce OQ of wheat and OR of cloth. This is because the price ratio $P_0 P_0$ is tangent to the production-possibility curve at A, which means that opportunity cost in production equals relative prices. If, with the same prices, the country were to produce at some other point, say, B, the opportunity cost of producing more cloth would be lower than its price, and producers could increase their profits by

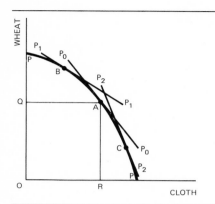

FIGURE 2.6

Role of shifting prices

making more cloth. Only at A are relative prices and opportunity costs equal and profits maximized.

If prices were to change to P_1P_1, for example, and wheat thus became more expensive, producers would again reallocate factors of production, produce more wheat, and move to point B, which is the new optimal point. Likewise, if the price of wheat fell and the new price line were P_2P_2, they would move to point C.

Figure 2.7 illustrates a country's gains from trade with a concave production-possibility curve. Assume that under autarky a certain price ratio prevails in an economy, as represented by the line P_0P_0. The country will produce and consume at the equilibrium point A, where the price line is tangent to the production-possibility curve.

In Chapter 1 we saw that the essence of the theory of comparative advantage consists of a country's being able to trade at prices that differ from those prevailing under autarky. Let us assume that the terms of trade the country faces in the international market are given by the price line P_1P_1. That means that cloth is more expensive in the international market than it is in the home market. Domestic producers will take advantage of this fact and move some factors of production from wheat to cloth, i.e., from point A to point B on the production-possibility curve where the international price line is tangent.

The country could now consume at point C by trading according to the price line P_1P_1, importing CQ of wheat and exporting BQ of cloth, as shown by the "trade triangle" QBC. Clearly, point C is better than point A

32

Supply and demand
in international trade:
the gains from trade

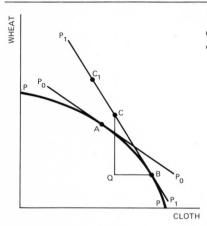

FIGURE 2.7

Gains from trade with a
concave production-possibility curve

because, as it lies to the right and above A, it represents a greater amount of both goods. This reasoning illustrates the meaning of gains from trade, that is, how a country can be better off by trading than by producing and consuming in isolation.

So far, so good. There is, however, one point that is somewhat troublesome. How do we know that the country will end up consuming at C? Maybe it will end up consuming at some other point along P_1P_1. It might, for instance, end up at C_1, a point that represents much more wheat but less cloth than the original point of equilibrium, A. Would C_1 be superior to A in that case? In order to deal with this question we have to consider demand factors, and to do this, in turn, we have to introduce the notion of indifference curves.

DEMAND FACTORS AND INDIFFERENCE CURVES

The reader is probably familiar with indifference curves from elementary demand theory. Let us start, however, by examining the meaning of an indifference curve. We shall assume that a consumer is at point P in Figure

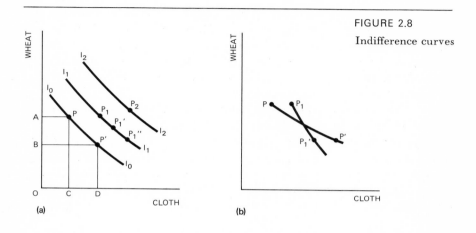

FIGURE 2.8

Indifference curves

2.8a, consuming OA of wheat and OC of cloth. If he were to move to point P', giving up AB of wheat, we would have to give him CD of cloth to make him as well off as he was at point P. In this case, the consumer is indifferent regarding point P and point P', because OA of wheat combined with OC of cloth gives him the same utility as OB of wheat combined with OD of cloth.

Point P_1 in Figure 2.8a is, however, clearly preferable to point P, because it represents the same amount of wheat as at P and more of cloth. But it is also possible to find points that are "indifferent" to P_1—for instance, P_1'—i.e., points in the commodity space that represent the same satisfaction to the consumer as does P_1.

By combining all points in the plane that give a consumer the same utility we obtain an *indifference curve*. The curves $I_0 I_0$, $I_1 I_1$, and $I_2 I_2$ are examples. The points on the first curve all give the consumer the same satisfaction as does point P; the points on the second curve all give him the same satisfaction as point P_1; and so on. By this procedure, we are able to compare points in the plane in a nontrivial fashion and to conclude, for instance, that point P_1'' is preferable to point P, even though the consumer has less of one of the goods (wheat) at P_1'' than at P.

It is important to observe that indifference curves have the property depicted in Figure 2.8a—that they are nonintersecting. Two indifference curves cannot cross, the way they are shown doing in Figure 2.8b. If they

34

Supply and demand
in international trade:
the gains from trade

did, we would get the following contradiction: P_1 would be preferred to P while at the same time P' is preferred to P_1'. But P is indifferent to P', and P_1 is indifferent to P_1'. The figure would read: P_1 is preferred to P. which is indifferent to P' which is more desirable than P_1'. But P_1' is indifferent to P_1. According to this reasoning P_1' would be both more and less desirable than P, which is obviously a contradiction.

The condition for the use of indifference curves is easily fulfilled. We might call the condition the "transitivity axiom": We assume that if P is preferred to P_1 and P_1 is indifferent to P_2, then P is also preferred to P_2.

In common-sense language, we assume that the consumer behaves in a consistent fashion, so that if he prefers a red car to a blue car but is indifferent regarding a yellow and a blue car, he will prefer a red car to a yellow car. If this condition is fulfilled, the use of indifference curves is legitimate.

COMMUNITY INDIFFERENCE CURVES

If we are referring to the demand of only one consumer, we can use indifference curves to illustrate demand factors. In international trade, however, we are concerned with a whole community or a whole nation, and things become more complicated. As it is not possible to draw an easy analogy when going from one to many, we cannot say that indifference curves can be used to illustrate the demand of a whole nation in the same way as they can be used to illustrate the demand of a single consumer unless some very restrictive assumptions are used.

Let us now see how a *community indifference curve* can be derived. We take the simplest possible example by assuming that we have a community with only two members, a and b. Each of the two consumers have been given a certain amount of wheat and a certain amount of cloth to begin with. They trade with each other until they reach the best possible point of exchange, given their initial resources. This can be called an efficient point. Such an efficient point is P_1 in Figure 2.9. At P_1, consumer a has, say, the utility level $\bar{u}_a$, and consumer b the utility level $\bar{u}_b$.

We can now ask: If we took away a certain amount of wheat from the original commodity bundle (or national incomes of a and b), how much

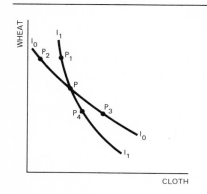

FIGURE 2.9

Community indifference curves

more cloth must we give the two consumers to make them as well off as at P_1? Doing this, we learn that P and P_4 are indifferent to point P_1. Combining these three points, we get the curve I_1I_1, which is an example of a community indifference curve.

We must observe an important fact in connection with this curve. That is that $\bar{u}_a$ and $\bar{u}_b$ have to be constant along the curve, so that the two consumers separately get the same utility, or level of satisfaction, along the curve. In other words, the distribution of utility between the two consumers has to be kept constant—i.e., the income distribution between them must be kept constant.

Let us again take the two consumers and the commodity bundle represented by point P on the indifference curve I_1I_1. But now we make an experiment: Suppose we change the income distribution. Let us assume that P is still an efficient point even with this new income distribution between a and b. We once more ask: How much less wheat and more cloth need we give the consumers to keep their respective utility levels constant? (We can call the new utility levels $\bar{u}_a^*$ and $\bar{u}_b^*$, where, say, $\bar{u}_a^* > \bar{u}_a$ and $\bar{u}_b^* < \bar{u}_b$.)

We now find that P_2 and P_3 are indifferent to P and that the new community indifference curve is given by $I_0 I_0$.

From this we can see that it is possible for community indifference curves to intersect. For an individual consumer, P_1 in Figure 2.9 would have to be preferred to P_2. If P_2 were indifferent to P, we could infer that P_1 would also have to be preferred to P. When speaking about community

36

Supply and demand
in international trade:
the gains from trade

FIGURE 2.10

Community indifference curves
based on constant income distribution

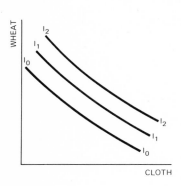

indifference curves, however, such an inference is no longer possible. The commodity bundle represented by point P in Figure 2.9 could for one income distribution be equivalent to the commodity bundle represented by P_1, but for another income distribution it could be equivalent to the commodity bundle represented by P_2. In other words, for a certain income distribution P_1 and P and P_4 could be indifferent to each other, whereas for another income distribution P_2 and P and P_3 could be indifferent. Hence it is not inconsistent to have curves that intersect. This, however, renders it impossible to compare different levels of utility, so we cannot say that one situation is better than another.

It can also be added that if all the consumers had the same preferences and if individual incomes were identical at all national income levels, community indifference curves would also be well behaved. To find a society characterized by such a degree of complete communism is not, however, an easy task.

The main point to keep in mind when using community indifference curves is that concerning the constancy of income distribution. Only if we assume a constant income distribution can we vindicate the use of community indifference curves and make meaningful comparisons. Making this assumption means that we can get community indifference curves such as those shown in Figure 2.10, which obey the same rules as ordinary indifference curves, so we can say that every point on I_1I_1 is superior to every

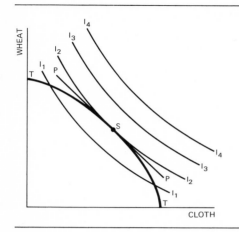

FIGURE 2.11

Equilibrium under autarky

point on $I_0 I_0$, and so on. This means that as we move along the production-possibility curve with changes in production conditions, the changes in income distribution thus induced are being neutralized by an appropriate redistribution policy.

THE GAINS FROM TRADE RESTATED

We can now restate the meaning of gains from trade, combining supply and demand factors. By combining the supply and demand sides of the economy we can illustrate how equilibrium is reached under autarky. This is shown in Figure 2.11. The optimum point is the one where an indifference curve is tangent to the production-possibility curve. This happens at point S, where the indifference curve $I_2 I_2$ is tangent to the production-possibility curve TT. Drawing the tangent line to this point on the two curves we obtain the price line PP. At point S the national income is maximized, because the marginal rate of substitution in consumption equals the opportunity cost in production. Given the shape of the indifference curves and given the production-possibility curve, S is the unique optimum point. This is demonstrated by the fact that if the society chose to produce at some other point on the

38

Supply and demand
in international trade:
the gains from trade

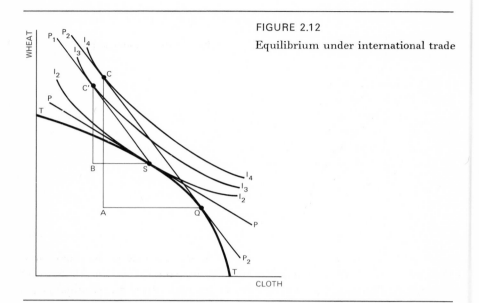

FIGURE 2.12

Equilibrium under international trade

production-possibility curve, that choice would place the consumers on an indifference curve to the left of $I_2 I_2$ (for instance, $I_1 I_1$), which represents a lower level of utility.

The possibility of trading means that the country can produce and consume at prices that differ from those prevailing in isolation. Figure 2.12 illustrates this situation. The international terms of trade are given by the price line $P_2 P_2$. The country will then reallocate its factors of production and move to point Q, where $P_2 P_2$ is tangent to the production-possibility curve. This means that the marginal rate of substitution in production equals the international terms of trade. The country will then export AQ of cloth in exchange for CA of wheat, moving to point C, where the terms of trade are tangent to the indifference curve $I_4 I_4$. Thereby the marginal rate of substitution in consumption is made equal to the terms of trade. Given the production-possibility curve and the international price ratio, point C represents the best point in the commodity space the society can achieve.

It might be useful to think of the gains from trade as consisting of two parts: one depending on the possibility for exchange, the other on the possibility for specialization in production. If the country for some reason could not change its pattern of production, it would have to continue producing at point S. It could still gain from trade by exchanging at the new price ratio, moving from S to C' (the price line $P_1 S$ is parallel to $P_2 P_2$). This would place the country on the indifference curve $I_3 I_3$, which represents a higher level of utility than does $I_2 I_2$. The gains from exchange could thus be said to consist of the movement from S to C'.

This, however, would not represent an optimal situation, because the ratio of transformation in production at S is not equal to the ratio of transformation in consumption at C'. Therefore, the country would be better off by changing its production and moving to Q, and from there to C. The move from S to Q can be said to represent the gain from specializing in production.

THE FLAW IN RICARDO'S ARGUMENT

It is important to remember that community indifference curves such as the ones in Figure 2.12 can be constructed only if the income distribution is kept unchanged. When moving from S to Q the income distribution will move in favor of the factors of production especially well suited for the production of cloth, the country's export good, while it will move against those engaged in wheat production, i.e., the wheat farmers. Somehow the wheat farmers will have to be compensated so that they are at least as well off as they were at point S. Only if this is done and something is still left over to make the cloth producers better off than at S can we say that the country gains from trade in an unambiguous sense.

This was the main point that Ricardo and the classical economists overlooked in their argument about the benefits from trade, one that has been raised by modern welfare economics. The classical economists thought in terms of each individual's utility. So does modern welfare economics. There is no guarantee that every consumer will be better off under free trade than under no trade, even though the country as a whole will be better off. Only if a policy of redistribution is pursued can free trade guarantee such an outcome. Thus free trade leads to a potential increase in welfare for everyone.

40

Supply and demand
in international trade:
the gains from trade

As we mentioned in Chapter 1, the doctrine of free trade was one of the cornerstones of economic liberalism. We have now arrived at the slightly paradoxical situation that this doctrine can be saved only if a policy of intervention is pursued concomitantly with it. Hence it follows that economic liberalism, in the sense of letting market conditions determine production and consumption, can be justified on welfare grounds without reservations only if a policy of redistribution goes with it.

OFFER CURVES

Before concluding this chapter, we should also introduce another standard tool of analysis in international economics, the offer curve, and show how gains from trade can be illustrated by the use of this tool.

We have seen how, when countries trade with each other, international terms of trade are established by the interaction of supply and demand. Another way of stating this interaction is by the use of offer curves, first used by Edgeworth and Marshall, and since then often used in international economics, especially for pedagogical purposes. Some perhaps doubt the efficacy of using offer curves, especially for direct analytical purposes. They are not very easy to derive in a clear and simple way. As they are regarded as standard tools, however, we will now show one way in which they can be derived, using the geometric tools we are familiar with.

Figure 2.13a shows a production-possibility curve and a set of community indifference curves that characterize demand in the country. In the absence of trade, equilibrium will be established at point S, where an indifference curve is tangent to the production-possibility curve. At this point, the marginal rate of transformation in production equals the marginal rate of transformation in consumption. The highest level of satisfaction that the country can enjoy under autarky is that symbolized by the indifference curve I_1I_1. The price ratio that will be ruling under autarky is given by the line PP, which is tangent to the production-possibility curve and the indifference curve at S.

In Figure 2.13a, we have depicted the relative price by the line PP, which has a negative slope. We could, however, also depict the same relative

FIGURE 2.13

Price ratio under autarky

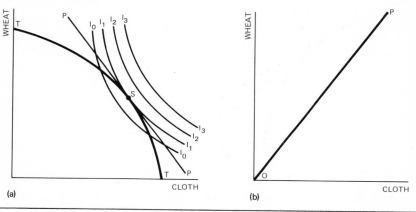

(a)

(b)

price ratio by a line with a positive slope. This is done in Figure 2.13b by the ray OP.

Suppose now that we open up the possibility of international trade. Production and demand conditions in Country I are as shown in Figure 2.13a. Which commodity Country I will export and import depends on the international terms of trade that are established. Let us suppose that Country I has a comparative advantage in production of wheat and that the new terms of trade established under trade are as shown by the line P_1P_1 in Figure 2.14. Country I will then produce at point B and consume at point C, and export AB of wheat in exchange for AC imports of cloth. By trade, Country I can move to the indifference curve I_2I_2, which represents a higher level of satisfaction than does I_1I_1, the highest one obtainable under autarky. Had the terms of trade been even more favorable, for instance such as represented by P_2P_2 in Figure 2.14, the country could have reached indifference curve I_3I_3 by trading DE of wheat for DF of cloth.

We can now show how Country I's volume of exports and imports change as the terms of trade change. This is done in Figure 2.15. On the vertical axis we have net exports of wheat and on the horizontal axis we have net imports of cloth. The triangle OAc in Figure 2.15 corresponds to the trade triangle BAC in Figure 2.14. It shows that if the terms of trade are

42

Supply and demand
in international trade:
the gains from trade

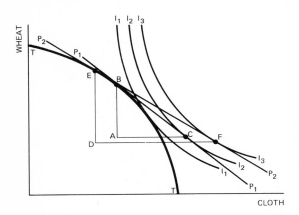

FIGURE 2.14

Trade at different
international price ratios

OA (these terms of trade are the same as those depicted by P_1P_1 in Figure, 2.14), Ow of wheat will be exchanged for Oc of cloth. If the terms of trade instead should change to OB (which corresponds to P_2P_2 in Figure 2.14), Ow_1 of wheat would be exchanged for Oc_1 of cloth (the triangle OBc_1 corresponds to the trade triangle EDF in Figure 2.14).

In this way, we can trace out a pattern of points that show how the traded volumes change when the terms of trade change. If we join together all these points for Country I, we get a curve such as OC in Figure 2.15. OC is an example of an offer curve. Thus an offer curve shows how the volumes traded change when the terms of trade change.

By analogous reasoning we can construct an offer curve for Country II. An example of such an offer curve is OD in Figure 2.15. The offer curves of the two trading countries intersect at point R. This is the only equilibrium point and the equilibrium terms of trade are given by the ray OR from the origin. Only at these terms of trade will exports of wheat (Ow_2) from Country I equal imports of wheat from Country II and imports of cloth into Country I (Oc_2) equal exports of cloth from Country II, and hence markets be cleared.

The shape of the offer curves are determined by both supply and demand conditions in the respective countries. The limits within which they will fall are given by the autarky terms of trade in the two countries (shown by the slope of the respective offer curve as it starts from the origin). With

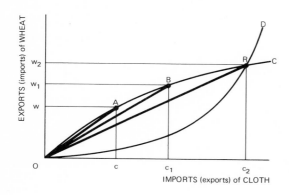

FIGURE 2.15

Offer curves

improving terms of trade, a country is willing to offer more and more of its exports for more imports. After a certain amount of trade, however, the country could become more and more unwilling to accept an increase in the amount of imports, even though they are offered at improving terms of trade. An example of this is given in Figure 2.16, where Country I's offer curve becomes inelastic after point P. After this point, Country I is willing to offer only a decreasing amount of its exports (wheat), even though its terms of trade are improving.

It is not possible to infer anything a priori about a country's offer curve. One has to study a given country's supply and demand conditions and then derive an offer curve in the way described. The exact shape of the curve depends on the given empirical conditions that prevail.

When we derived the offer curve, we argued as though the terms of trade were changing for some exogeneous reason and then derived the shape of the curve. This was a pedagogical device and must not be misunderstood. The offer curve is a general equilibrium concept. It is determined by production and consumption conditions jointly. It is more appropriate to say that these conditions determine the shape of the trading partners' offer curves, which in turn determine the terms of trade.

Offer curves might seem to be simple concepts, but they are, in fact, the result of a complicated interplay of factors. This makes them somewhat hard to deal with, as it is difficult to see how a change in more basic concepts

44

Supply and demand
in international trade:
the gains from trade

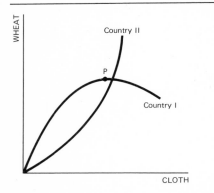

FIGURE 2.16

Inelastic offer curve

—supply and demand—exactly influences an offer curve. Some economists use offer curves extensively. We use them very sparingly. Only on one occasion, in Chapter 18, when dealing with the theory of tariffs, will offer curves be used. In the rest of the analysis we have preferred to use other types of instruments. However, by now the student should have a basic understanding of the meaning of offer curves.

Before coming to some basic theorems of international economics in Chapter 4, we will, in Chapter 3, introduce some of the geometric tools that will be used extensively throughout the book.

Production functions in international trade: the box diagram

3

In Chapter 1 we discussed the theory of comparative advantage in terms of a one-factor model, where the only factor of production was labor. What gave rise to trade was different cost ratios in production. It is now time to go a step further and look into what determines these cost ratios.

We did not dwell at any length on the causes of trade in Chapters 1 and 2. However, what determines trade in the Ricardian setting is quite obvious. If there is only one factor of production, labor, and the cost of production of any good is determined by how much labor it takes to produce a unit of the good, differences between countries in the relative productivity of labor will determine trade.

If we want to use modern jargon, we can say that different countries have different production functions and that differences in production functions are the causes of trade. This might be called the positive side of Ricardo's theory of comparative advantage, as it contains a scientific proposition about the causes of trade. The theory of comparative advantage can also be viewed as a proposition about gains from trade. This we might call its normative side, because, as we have seen, it contains a value judgment, at least by implication.

Modern trade theory, however, offers another explanation for the causes of trade. This is contained in the so-called Heckscher–Ohlin theory of trade, which says that trade is caused by the fact that different countries have different factor endowments.[1] This is a more fruitful approach than Ricardo's, as it brings factors of production explicitly into the picture and forces us to study in a detailed fashion the interrelationships between commodity and factor prices, between amounts of input and output. We will have to take a general equilibrium approach to the study of the trading relationships between countries. By so doing, we will train ourselves in the application of the first principle of economics, the notion that " everything in an economy hangs together."

---

[1] Eli F. Heckscher (1879–1952) was a Swedish economist and economic historian. In 1919 he published in the *Ekonomisk Tidskrift* a paper that contains the core of the Heckscher–Ohlin theory of trade. He is otherwise known primarily for his path-breaking studies on mercantilism and Swedish economic history.

Bertil Ohlin (1899–), a Swedish economist and politician, was a student of Heckscher's. He published his main work, *Interregional and International Trade*, in 1933. He then turned to politics and became the leader of the Swedish Liberal Party.

46

Production functions
in international trade:
the box diagram

To understand the Heckscher–Ohlin theory of trade, we need to introduce additional geometric tools. We do so in this chapter, which is primarily devoted to a derivation of different tools of analysis. We start by seeing how production functions can be illustrated geometrically.

PRODUCTION FUNCTIONS IN INTERNATIONAL TRADE

A production function states a relationship between inputs of factors of production and output of a commodity. Let us assume in the following that there are two factors of production, which we call labor and capital. By combining labor and capital we can produce varying amounts of a commodity, say cloth. The amount of labor and capital it takes to produce 1 unit of cloth is given by the production function. Thus the production function can be viewed as an engineering concept, something that is given by the state of the art.

A production function can be described with the help of isoquants, or, as they are sometimes called, equal-product contour lines. Isoquant $a_1 a_1$ in Figure 3.1 shows how much capital and labor is needed to produce 1 unit of cloth; isoquant $a_2 a_2$ shows how much labor and capital it takes to produce 2 units of cloth; and so on.

To produce 1 unit of cloth we could choose to produce at point A, for instance, where we would combine Oa of capital with Oa' of labor. Or we could produce 1 unit of cloth at any other point along the isoquant $a_1 a_1$, for instance at A_1 by combining Oa_1 of capital with Oa_1' of labor, or for instance at A_2 by combining Oa_2 of capital with Oa_2' of labor.

In an analogous fashion, at any point along $a_2 a_2$ we can produce 2 units of cloth by varying the amounts of capital and labor used in production, and at any point along $a_3 a_3$ we can produce 3 units of cloth, again by varying the amounts of capital and labor.

The production function illustrated by the isoquants in Figure 3.1 is of a neoclassical kind.[2] It is so called because labor and capital are substitutes

---

[2] The neoclassical revolution of economics occurred in the 1870s with the introduction of the marginalist concepts, which led to a complete reformulation of the theory of value. The three economists who, independently of each other, started

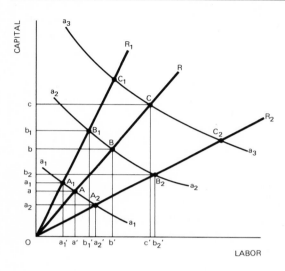

FIGURE 3.1

Isoquants

for each other. Another type of production function is the one in which labor and capital can be used only in fixed proportions. Figure 3.2 illustrates this case. With this type of production function, sometimes called a Leontief type of production function, the only efficient points of production are the ones along the ray OR.[3] At point A, 1 unit of cloth can be produced by combining Oa_1 of capital with Oa_1' of labor. Because of the production function there is no point in trying to increase the use of capital to Oa_1'', for instance, because the same amount, Oa_1', of labor is still needed to produce 1 unit of the good. Therefore, labor and capital have to be combined in fixed proportions and there is no possibility of substituting one for the other.

Experience tells us that we should expect capital and labor usually to be substitutable for each other. This being the case, a production function

---

to formulate the new theory of value were Stanley Jevons (1835–1882) in England, Léon Walras (1834–1910) in France (although a Frenchman, Walras was a professor at Lausanne), and Carl Menger (1840–1921) in Austria. Neoclassical economists usually viewed factors of production as being substitutable for each other.
[3] Wassily Leontief (1906–) was born in Russia. He left Russia during the 1920s. Since 1930 he has been Professor of Economics at Harvard University. He is best known as the originator of input–output analysis.

48

Production functions
in international trade:
the box diagram

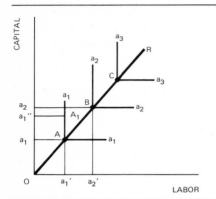

FIGURE 3.2

Leontief production function

such as the one illustrated in Figure 3.1 is of a more general nature than the one shown in Figure 3.2. Throughout this book we will assume production functions to be of a neoclassical kind.

THE MEANING OF LINEARLY HOMOGENEOUS
PRODUCTION FUNCTIONS

A production function shows the relationship between input of factors of production and output of a good (or output of several goods if we assume joint production). For many reasons it would be advantageous if we could use unspecified production functions. This means that to derive the results we wanted, to prove certain theorems, we would need to assume only that a relationship exists between inputs and outputs, but we would not have to assume anything specific about the nature of this relationship.

As a matter of fact, when we come to the effects of technical progress on international trade we will refer to results that have been derived using only this weak assumption. But for most of the theorems of trade theory a more specific relationship between inputs and outputs has to be assumed.

The standard constraint on the production function that we will have to assume is that the production function is homogeneous of the first degree, or, another way of expressing the same fact, that the production function is linearly homogeneous.[4] By this is meant that the production function is such that if the inputs are increased by a certain proportion, output is increased by the same proportion. If, for instance, both labor and capital are doubled, output is also doubled. If labor and capital are increased by 10 percent, output is also increased by 10 percent, and so on.

The reader is probably familiar with the concept of marginal productivity from elementary production theory. By marginal productivity of labor is meant the increase in output caused by an increase of 1 unit of labor, assuming that the amount of capital is held constant. Analogously, the marginal productivity of capital is defined as the increase in output we get if we increase the amount of capital by 1 unit, keeping constant the other factors of production—in our case, labor.

If we denote output with Q and labor and capital with L and C, respectively, we can write the production function analytically as

$$Q = f(L, C) \tag{3.1}$$

This shows that output is a function of labor and capital. We assume that this production function is differentiable (this is an assumption that will be used throughout the book). Differentiating equation 3.1 gives

$$dQ = \frac{\partial Q}{\partial L} \, dL + \frac{\partial Q}{\partial C} \, dC \tag{3.2}$$

The first partial derivative of Q with respect to L, i.e., $\partial Q / \partial L$, is the analytical expression for the marginal productivity of labor. Analogously, the marginal productivity of capital is expressed by $\partial Q / \partial C$.

We assume that $\partial Q / \partial L$ and $\partial Q / \partial C$ are positive. This means that if the labor force increases, with a given stock of capital, total output will increase. This is also what we would expect. If we increase labor with a given stock of machinery, we certainly would expect to be able to produce more, as we would if we were to increase the number of machines with a given labor force.

We might observe, too, that if we go on differentiating equation 3.1 we get second partial derivatives. We can take, for instance, $\partial^2 Q / \partial L^2$. This derivative shows how the marginal productivity of labor changes with a fixed

---

[4] This has to do with the fact that almost all results in trade theory have been derived using this assumption; it is also necessary if one wants to use geometry as a mode of exposition.

50

Production functions
in international trade:
the box diagram

amount of capital as we keep increasing labor. We assume that this second derivative is negative. It is easy to see the common-sense reasoning for the declining marginal productivity of labor.

The reason is that as we keep increasing labor with a given stock of capital, the workers will have relatively fewer and fewer machines to work with. Therefore, the more workers we add, the lower will be the productivity of the last added worker. By analogous reasoning it can also be shown that $\partial^2 Q/\partial C^2 < 0$.

We can also take the mixed second partial derivatives $\partial^2 Q/\partial L\, \partial C$, which shows how the marginal productivity of labor changes as we keep increasing capital. Likewise, $\partial^2 Q/\partial C\, \partial L$ shows how the marginal productivity of capital changes as we increase the labor force. Both of these partial second derivatives are positive, assuming that the production function is homogeneous of degree 1 and that the first partial derivatives are positive.

The reason is that if we add more and more machines with a given number of workers, the workers will become more and more productive. Likewise, if we add more workers to a given stock of machinery, they can tend to the machines better, and the marginal productivity of capital will go up.

It is now time to observe another important feature of a linearly homogeneous production function of which we will make repeated use: As long as the two factors of production are combined in the same proportion, the marginal productivities of the two factors stay unchanged. Another way of expressing this fact is by saying that the marginal productivities depend only on the ratios in which the two factors are combined. It is important to understand this fact, and we will illustrate it geometrically.

Refer back to Figure 3.1. Along any ray from the origin, such as OR, the two factors are combined in the same proportion. Thus Oa of capital divided by Oa' of labor at A equals Ob of capital divided by Ob' of labor at B, which also equals Oc of capital divided by Oc' of labor at C, and so on. Therefore the marginal productivity of labor is the same along all of OR, as is the marginal productivity of capital.

The same holds for OR_1, so the marginal productivity of labor is the same at A_1, B_1, and C_1, and analogously for the marginal productivity of capital. In the same vein, the marginal productivities of the two factors of production are constant along OR_2.

We can now compare the marginal productivity of labor along the isoquant a_1a_1, for instance at the three points A_1, A, and A_2. It is then immediately clear that the marginal productivity of labor is higher at A_1 than it is at A, and that it is higher at A than at A_2, because the ratio of capital to labor—the capital intensity—is higher at A_1 than at A, and higher at A than at A_2. This means that each worker has more capital, more machinery to work with, at A_1 than at A. The same holds for A as compared to A_2. The more capital-intensive the methods of production are, the higher is the marginal productivity of labor. In the same way, the more labor-intensive the methods of production, the higher is the marginal productivity of capital.

But what will determine which methods of production are used? How will labor and capital actually be combined? This cannot be inferred from Figure 3.1. To say something about this we have to know something about factor prices.

THE MEANING OF COMPETITIVE FACTOR MARKETS: FACTOR PRICES AND FACTOR INTENSITIES

Let us assume that our economy is characterized by free competition. If two goods, cloth and wheat, are produced with different production functions, a possible equilibrium situation is as shown in Figure 3.3. At points S and R the factors of production are allocated so that the ratio of marginal productivities in the two lines are equal, and both lines equal the relative factor-price ratio PP.

We know that the ratio of marginal productivities changes as we move along an isoquant. The slope of the cloth isoquant at S is equal to the slope of the wheat isoquant at R. If we combine Oa of capital with Ob of labor in cloth production, the ratio of marginal productivities in this line will be the same as the corresponding ratio for wheat production combining Oa' of capital with Ob' of labor.

We can now get a deeper understanding of the nature of our assumption about free competition. We start by having two different production functions, given by the technology prevailing in the economy. Also given is a set of factor prices. The factor-price ratio is assumed to be given by supply and demand conditions in the factor market. The point here is that because a single producer cannot influence factor prices, as far as he is concerned they are given. The question to be answered is: Given production functions and

52

Production functions
in international trade:
the box diagram

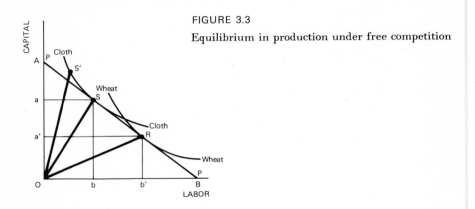

FIGURE 3.3

Equilibrium in production under free competition

given factor prices, how will the producer combine labor and capital in the two lines of production?

We assume free competition, so we find that he will have to use OS capital/labor ratio in the production of cloth and OR capital/labor ratio in the production of wheat, because only at S and R are the ratios between marginal productivities of capital and labor in the two lines of production equal to the factor-price ratio. If he were producing somewhere else, for instance at point S', using the capital/labor ratio OS' in cloth production, the marginal productivity of the last unit of capital (in value terms) would be lower than its price, and the marginal productivity of labor (in value terms) would be higher than its wage. Hence he could increase profits by employing more labor and less capital. Only at points S and R is the marginal productivity of labor equal to its price (i.e., the going wage), and the marginal productivity of capital equal to *its* price (i.e., the rental price for 1 unit of capital during the adequate time period).

The essence of the assumption of free competition is, therefore, that it is an assumption about rationality. It is not an assertion or a postulate about market forms in the real world. It is best viewed as an approximation of a reasonable behavior pattern that facilitates formulation of economic models. There is no reason to believe, a priori, that, for instance, if oligopolistic or monopolistic market forms were prevailing, the basic theorems we are about to derive would not stand up. Only a vulgar view on economic theorizing could claim such a thing. Only if we believed for some reason

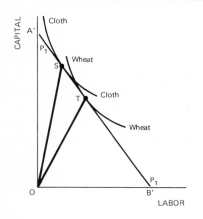

FIGURE 3.4

Factor intensity changes

that resources were systematically misallocated, or completely randomly allocated, would we have to be suspicious about the assumption of free competition. As long as this is not the case, we would expect our results on this score to hold for any type of economy, be it capitalistic, socialistic, or whatever.

If for some reason factor prices were to change, factor intensities would also change. Let us assume that the price of labor increases, compared to the price of capital. Then more capital-intensive methods of production will be used in both lines of production, as shown in Figure 3.4. We have the same type of cloth and wheat isoquants in Figure 3.4 as in Figure 3.3. The only difference is that labor is now relatively more expensive. Earlier, OA of capital exchanged for OB of labor, whereas now OA' of capital exchanges for OB' of labor. This difference is illustrated by the fact that the factor price line P_1P_1 in Figure 3.4 is steeper than the factor price line PP in Figure 3.3.

As labor is now more expensive and capital is cheaper than before, producers will use less labor and more capital by substituting capital for labor. Thus methods of production become more capital-intensive in both cloth and wheat production. This is shown by the fact that the factor ratios OS and OT in Figure 3.4 are steeper than the corresponding ratios OS and OR in Figure 3.3.

So far we have assumed that the cloth and wheat isoquants cut only once. This is a very important assumption, because if it is true, cloth will

54

Production functions
in international trade:
the box diagram

always be capital-intensive and wheat will always be labor-intensive, regardless of what the factor prices are.

This amounts to assuming that production functions differ between commodities and that there is a one-to-one relationship between factor prices and factor intensities. The reason this assumption is important is that if we can classify goods in this way, so that we can say that good A will always be capital-intensive while good B will be labor-intensive, we can show that, given some extra assumptions, trade will have some very definite effects on factor prices. We will be able to show that trade will lead either to a complete factor price equalization (so that wages will be the same in both trading countries), or else to a complete specialization in production. All this will be carefully spelled out in due course. But before that, there is some more groundwork to be done.

FACTOR REVERSALS

What if the assumption just described did not hold? What would happen if the isoquants cut twice? This situation is depicted in Figure 3.5. We can see from Figure 3.5 that the wheat isoquant W_0W_0 cuts the cloth isoquant CC twice. As both these isoquants are each members of families of isoquants, each member having the same shape, we can find another isoquant, such as W_1W_1, which at some point is tangent to the cloth isoquant CC. This happens at point R. If the factor-price ratio is represented by the line PP, that is tangent to the two isoquants at R, then R is the equilibrium point, and the factor intensity in both lines of production is OR.

But out of infinitely many factor-price ratios there is only one that gives the same factor intensity in both lines of production. If labor were more expensive (or less expensive), how would labor and capital then be combined? The answer is contained in Figure 3.6. In the figure we have the same cloth isoquant CC and the same wheat isoquant W_1W_1 as in Figure 3.5, with a common point of tangency at R.

If labor becomes more expensive than in our earlier example, the factor-price line will become steeper. The factor-price ratio P_1P_1 and $P_1'P_1'$ (these lines are parallel) illustrates this case. We know that both lines will use more capital-intensive methods of production as labor becomes relatively

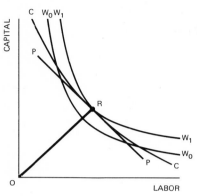

FIGURE 3.5

Isoquants cut twice: identical factor intensity

more expensive. The factor intensity used in wheat will be OS, and in cloth it will be OS'. Thus, at this price ratio, cloth will be the capital-intensive good and wheat will be the labor-intensive good. By analogous reasoning, we find that at all factor-price ratios where labor is relatively more expensive than at PP in Figure 3.5, cloth will be the capital-intensive good and wheat the labor-intensive good.

But what happens if labor is relatively cheaper than at the ratio PP? This case is also illustrated in Figure 3.6. Then the factor-price ratio has to be less steep than PP. An example is $P_2 P_2$ and $P_2' P_2'$ (they are parallel). We find that the factor intensity is OT in wheat production and OT' in cloth production. Thus wheat is now the capital-intensive line of production and cloth the labor-intensive good. By analogous reasoning, we find that at any factor-price ratio where capital is relatively more expensive than at PP, wheat is capital-intensive and cloth is labor-intensive.

From this it follows that there is no longer a one-to-one correspondence between factor prices and factor intensities. Whether cloth is the labor-intensive good or the capital-intensive good will depend on which factor-price ratio is ruling.

The economic meaning of the fact that isoquants cut twice is that possibilities of substitution differ significantly between the two industries. We can see this from Figures 3.5 and 3.6, where we find that the wheat isoquant is more convex to the origin than is the cloth isoquant. This means that the two factors of production are better substitutes for each other in cloth production than in wheat production. This is a fact derived from the shape

56

Production functions
in international trade:
the box diagram

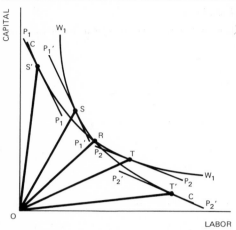

FIGURE 3.6

Differing factor intensities

of the production functions, something given to us from the state of the art.

With any change in factor prices, the two industries will substitute the relatively cheaper factor for the more expensive. But their possibilities of doing this in a profitable way depend on technological factors.

Let us assume first of all that the factor-price ratio PP is the ruling one, and hence OR is the factor intensity in both lines of production. If factor prices change and labor becomes more expensive, capital will be substituted for labor. But this is more easily done in cloth than in wheat production. Therefore, cloth will be more capital-intensive than wheat. Analogously, if capital becomes more expensive relative to labor, labor will be substituted for capital, but as this still is more easily done in cloth than in wheat production, cloth will become labor-intensive. From this it follows that the new equilibrium-factor-intensity ray in wheat will be closer to the ray OR than the new equilibrium-factor-intensity ray in cloth, regardless of the way factor prices change relative to the ratio PP.

Thus we have established the proposition that if factor reversals exist, there is no longer a one-to-one correspondence between factor prices and factor intensities. We will be able to show, however, that once we have specified the total amounts of the factors of production a country has, only a limited number of factor-price ratios are compatible with economic equilibrium. And, given that, it will turn out that there is a one-to-one correspondence between this set of possible factor prices and factor intensities, so that we will be able to classify one good as being always labor-intensive and the other as being always capital-intensive.

But the proof of this proposition involves a little bit of tricky reasoning and the need for more tools. Therefore, we will postpone it to Chapter 7, where we will give a detailed treatment of the implications of factor reversals for the effects of trade on factor prices. Before we end this chapter, however, we should introduce another important tool of analysis, the box diagram.

THE BOX DIAGRAM

So far we have not said anything about a country's total factor endowments. The box diagram permits us to study the interrelationships between production functions and total amounts of factors of production and to derive optimal factor inputs and outputs.

A box diagram is illustrated in Figure 3.7. The sides of the box measure labor and capital. In the figure we have capital on the vertical side and labor on the horizontal side. The dimensions of the box give total factor endowments, so that OA measures the total amount of capital available to the economy and OB gives the total amount of labor. The diagonal OO' gives the overall factor intensity of the economy.

Furthermore, we are producing two goods, wheat and cloth, and their production functions are illustrated by two sets of isoquants. These are of the same kind as the ones illustrated in Figure 3.3. The only difference is that we now measure wheat production from the lower left-hand corner, whereas we measure cloth production from the upper right-hand corner. We can then draw two sets of isoquants, one for wheat with the origin at O, and another for cloth with the origin at O'.

We still assume the production functions to be homogeneous of degree 1. The isoquant W_2W_2 is twice as far from the origin as the isoquant W_1W_1 and therefore represents twice as much wheat as does W_1W_1. Likewise, W_3W_3 is three times as far from the origin as W_1W_1 and therefore represents three times as much wheat. Analogous conditions hold for the cloth isoquants. For the sake of reasoning, let us assume that W_1W_1 represents

Production functions
in international trade:
the box diagram

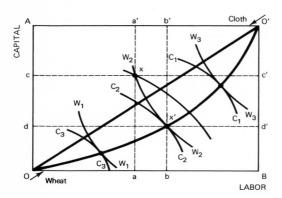

FIGURE 3.7

Box diagram

1 unit of wheat, $W_2 W_2$ represents 2 units of wheat, and so on, and that the same is true for the cloth isoquants.

Any point in the box, for instance x, represents a certain combination of outputs of the two goods. In our present example, x represents 2 units of wheat and between 1 and 2 units of cloth. But it also represents a certain input combination. To produce x of wheat we have to combine Oa of labor with Oc of capital. And to produce x of cloth we have to combine what is left of labor, $O'a'$, with what is left of capital, $O'c'$. This is an application of the assumption that the economy is fully employed, so that all labor and all capital are used up in production.

The output combination represented by x is not efficient, however. This is shown by the fact that if we move along the isoquant $W_2 W_2$ to the point x' we can still get the same amount of wheat but a greater amount of cloth, because at x' the cloth isoquant $C_2 C_2$ is tangent to the wheat isoquant $W_2 W_2$. This, then, is an efficient point because here the ratio between the marginal productivities is the same in both lines of production. Therefore, the relative efficiency of the two factors of production is the same in both lines of production and the factors of production are allocated in an optimal way. Another way of stating this is by saying that it is impossible to produce more of one commodity without decreasing production of the other commodity.

Thus by combining Ob of labor with Od of capital in wheat production and $O'b'$ of labor with $O'd'$ of capital in cloth production, the ratio

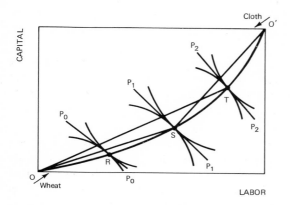

FIGURE 3.8

Box diagram

between the marginal productivities in the two lines of production are equalized. Therefore, x' is a possible equilibrium point.

If we combine all the points in the box where two isoquants are tangent to each other, we get a curve such as OO' in Figure 3.7. This curve is usually called the *contract curve*. All the points on the contract curve are efficient in the sense just described; i.e., they represent efficient output and input combinations. Any point off the contract curve can be shown to be inferior to a point on the curve by the type of reasoning we have just used. So far, however, we have no way of judging which point on the contract curve is preferred to any of the other points. This can be done only after we know something about demand conditions, and we will have to wait to introduce these. The contract curve is derived exclusively from technical conditions in production.

In concluding this chapter it might be worthwhile to make a couple of comments about the box diagram. Figure 3.8 illustrates the same kind of production conditions as did Figure 3.7. We are still measuring production of wheat from the lower left-hand corner and cloth production from the upper right-hand corner, etc.

First, it might be observed that wheat is the labor-intensive commodity and cloth is the capital-intensive one, because the contract curve is below the diagonal. If the contract curve had gone above the diagonal, wheat would have been the capital-intensive good.

Let us assume that S in Figure 3.8 illustrates the initial equilibrium

60

Production functions
in international trade:
the box diagram

position in the economy. Then we know how the factors of production will be allocated. By drawing a ray from O to S we find that OS is the factor intensity in wheat production, and by drawing a ray from O' to S we find that $O'S$ is the factor intensity in cloth production.

What would happen if the demand for wheat increased? Then the relative price of wheat would go up and more of it would be produced. That means that we would move away from S along the contract curve toward O'. A new possible equilibrium point could be T, which represents more wheat and less cloth.

At point T we find that the factor intensities in both lines of production differ from those at S. In wheat production the new factor intensity is OT, which shows that the new method of production is more capital-intensive than the old one. Likewise, we find that the new method of production in cloth, $O'T$, is more capital-intensive than the old method of production $O'S$. But how is it possible that both lines of production can become more capital-intensive when the over-all amounts of capital and labor have not changed?

The answer to this apparent paradox is that the output mix at T differs from that at S. At T, more wheat and less cloth is produced. When cloth production is decreased, both capital and labor are released. Cloth is the capital-intensive good, so relatively much capital and little labor is freed. Part of this capital will be used in wheat production, so the method of production there will be more capital-intensive. But part of it will also be re-engaged in cloth production, so the method of production will be more capital-intensive there, too.

Obviously, the movement from S to T will also have some implications for factor prices. The relative factor price ratio is shown by the slope of a line tangent to the point of tangency between two isoquants. The slopes of the lines $P_0 P_0$, $P_1 P_1$, and $P_2 P_2$ show relative factor prices at R, S, and T, respectively. We can see that these lines *become steeper and steeper* as we move along the contract curve from the lower left-hand corner to the upper right-hand corner. This means that the relative price of labor increases as we move from O to O'.

The economic explanation of this is as follows: As we move from O toward O' we increase production of wheat and decrease production of cloth. This means that the relative price of wheat is going up. But wheat is the labor-intensive commodity. To produce more wheat, the entrepreneurs need larger amounts of the factors of production, and as wheat is labor-intensive, they are especially eager to get more labor. To hire more labor they bid up the price of labor, so the relative price of labor rises. But as this occurs, producers in both lines of production try to economize on labor and to use capital instead of labor. Therefore as the wage increases, more capital-intensive methods are used in both lines of production.

THE PRODUCTION-POSSIBILITY CURVE DERIVED
FROM THE BOX DIAGRAM

In a general sense, we know already that any movement along the production-possibility curve must correspond to a movement along the contract curve in the box diagram. The time has come to spell out explicitly the connection between the two tools of analysis and to show how the production-possibility curve can be derived from the box diagram.

Figure 3.9 shows a slightly modified box diagram. On the left-hand vertical side and on the upper horizontal side we still measure factor inputs, capital and labor, respectively. Inputs into the two goods are still measured in the usual way: inputs into good A from the lower left-hand corner and inputs into good B from the upper right-hand corner. The difference that we now introduce is that we measure outputs along the two remaining sides. The right-hand vertical side $O''O'$ is used to represent an index for measuring output of good A, and the lower horizontal side $O''O$ is used to measure output of good B. The O'' corner is the origin for both the output scales.

We draw the diagonal OO' in the box. Because of the fact that the production functions are homogeneous of the first degree, we know that if an isoquant cuts the diagonal twice as far away from the origin O as a_1a_1, it represents twice as large an output as a_1a_1. Likewise, if a b isoquant cuts the diagonal twice as far away from the O' corner as another b isoquant, it represents double the output of the latter. We can therefore find where the a isoquants cut the diagonal and then project them on the vertical axis. Analogously, we can find where the b isoquants cut the diagonal and project it on the horizontal axis. In this manner the $O''O'$ axis and the $O''O$ axis can be used as output scales.

Therefore, the input combinations represented by a point, T, on the contract curve correspond to a unique output combination. We can read off

62

Production functions
in international trade:
the box diagram

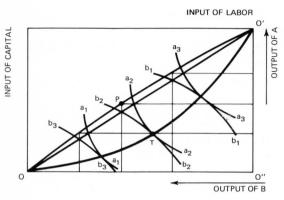

INPUT OF LABOR

FIGURE 3.9

The box diagram and the
production-possibility curve

this point in the commodity space from the respective output scales with
their mutual origin at O'', and we find that it is P. We can go on and read
off several points in an analogous fashion that correspond to input combinations on the contract curve. If we join all these points in the commodity
space we get a curve such as OPO'. This is the production-possibility curve.
Thus we find that there is a one-to-one correspondence between the contract
curve and the production-possibility curve, so that for every point on the
production-possibility curve representing an output combination there is a
corresponding point on the contract curve representing an input combination.

We will use this fact to study more closely, in Chapter 6, the relationships between commodity and factor prices, as well as the connection between the gains from trade and income distribution.

SELECTED BIBLIOGRAPHY: CHAPTERS 2 AND 3

A survey of the concept of gains from trade among the classics and early
neoclassics is found in Viner, *op. cit.*, chap. 9. A classical article is:

P. A. Samuelson, "The Gains from International Trade," *Canadian
Journal of Economics and Political Science*, May 1939 (reprinted in
RTIT).

Later contributions that can be mentioned are:

E. Olsen, "Udenrigshandelens Gevinst," *Nationalökonomisk Tidsskrift*, vol. 96, 1958.

M. C. Kemp, "The Gain from International Trade," *EJ*, December 1962.

P. A. Samuelson, "The Gain from International Trade Once Again," *EJ*, December 1962.

The two articles that introduced the use of production-possibility curves are:

A. P. Lerner, "The Diagrammatical Representation of Cost Conditions in International Trade," *Ec*, 1932 (reprinted in Lerner, *Essays in Economic Analysis*, London, Macmillan, 1953).

W. W. Leontief, "The Use of Indifference Curves in International Trade," *QJE*, May 1933 (reprinted in *RTIT*).

For a discussion of the signification of community indifference curves see:

T. Scitovsky, "A Reconsideration of the Theory of Tariffs," *RES*, Summer 1942 (reprinted in *RTIT*).

The derivation of the production-possibility curve from the box diagram was originally made in:

K. M. Savosnick, "The Box Diagram and the Production-Possibility Curve," *Ekonomisk Tidskrift*, vol. 60, September 1958.

A thorough discussion of the significance of cost and demand conditions for the theory of international trade is also found in Chipman, *op. cit.*, Part II.

Comparative advantage in the Heckscher–Ohlin trade model

4

In Chapter 1 we studied the theory of comparative advantage in terms of a one-factor model. In this setting, differences in productivity of labor were the cause of trade. It is now time to take a closer look at the Heckscher–Ohlin theory of trade. According to this theory, trade results from the fact that different countries have different factor endowments.

The Heckscher–Ohlin theory is usually formulated in terms of a two-factor model, with labor and capital as the two factors of production. We will use this model, and in the following we will be concerned only with this case. It would be possible in some instances to generalize the results to the case in which there are many factors of production. Attempts at such generalizations, however, would require the use of fairly advanced mathematics and therefore fall outside the scope of this book. The two-factor case will give us an understanding of all the essentials of the Heckscher–Ohlin theory.

As we have said, according to the Heckscher–Ohlin theory, what determines trade is differences in factor endowments. Some countries have much capital, others have much labor. The theory now says that countries that are rich in capital will export capital-intensive goods, and countries that have much labor will export labor-intensive goods.

The terms " rich in capital " and " rich in labor " are not very precise so far. Before we can get much further, we have to define our terms and give them a more precise meaning. First, however, we will comment upon and explain some of the more general assumptions for this type of analysis. Since the exposition in Chapter 3 has paved the way for us, we can do this briefly.

The following five assumptions are essential to the analysis: (1) There are no transport costs or other impediments to trade; (2) there is perfect competition in both commodity and factor markets; (3) all production functions are homogeneous of the first degree; (4) the production functions are such that the two commodities show different factor intensities; and (5) the production functions differ between commodities, but are the same in both countries; i.e., good A is produced with the same technique in both countries and good B is produced with the same technique in both countries.

What these assumptions mean should not be difficult to understand. The first assumption is an abstraction to facilitate the analysis. It implies that commodity prices under trade will be the same in both countries. The meaning of the second assumption should be clear from Chapter 3. It implies that the factors of production will be allocated in an optimal way.

64

The last three assumptions all refer to characteristics of the production functions. The meaning of a production function being linearly homogeneous was explained in Chapter 3. The fourth assumption means that different techniques of production are used in the two industries. Furthermore, we assume that there is a one-to-one correspondence between factor intensities and factor prices; another way of stating this fact is by saying that there are no factor reversals.

The fifth assumption, that production functions are the same in both countries, is quite a strong one. What it amounts to is assuming that knowledge travels freely. In other words, the best techniques of production in the world are known to everyone.

These are the assumptions used in connection with the Heckscher–Ohlin theory of trade. They are necessary to state the meaning of comparative advantage in the two-by-two-by-two model, and to prove the factor-price-equalization theorem. They are quite strong assumptions, and one might think that they are rarely fulfilled in the real world. Sometimes, however, strong assumptions are needed to prove interesting theorems. The conclusions of the theorems can still be empirically valid, even though some of the assumptions are only approximations of conditions existing in the real world. Simplifying assumptions have to be made in theoretical studies. The theorems built on such assumptions can still be important.[1] The theorems we are about to derive will give us a most useful insight into the general equilibrium character of economics. In this way, we will be able to see that a change in one variable in our trading system necessarily implies changes in all the other variables.

FACTOR ABUNDANCE DEFINED BY FACTOR PRICES

We will now try to demonstrate the proposition that capital-rich countries export capital-intensive goods and that labor-rich countries export labor-

[1] For a discussion of the role of assumptions in economic theory, see Milton Friedman, *Essays in Positive Economics*, Chicago, The University of Chicago Press, 1953; and Ernst Nagel, "Assumptions in Economic Theory," *American Economic Review*, Vol. 53, Papers and Proceedings, May 1963, pp. 211–219.

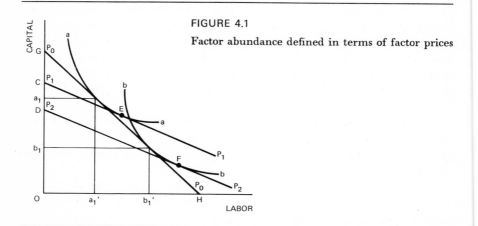

FIGURE 4.1

Factor abundance defined in terms of factor prices

intensive goods. It is, however, not yet clear what is meant by a country being rich in capital. At least two alternative definitions can be given.

One of these definitions runs in terms of factor prices. This definition says that Country I is capital-rich compared to Country II if capital is relatively cheaper in Country I than in Country II. The second definition compares over-all physical amounts of labor and capital. It says that Country I is rich in capital if the ratio of capital to labor is larger in Country I than in Country II.

These two alternative definitions are not equivalent. We will now show that the Heckscher–Ohlin proposition follows if we use the first definition but that it does not necessarily follow using the second definition. Ohlin himself defined richness in factor endowments with the help of factor prices. According to his definition Country I is abundant in capital if $P_{1C}/P_{1L} < P_{2C}/P_{2L}$, where P_{1C} is the price of capital in Country I, P_{1L} is the price of labor in Country I, and P_{2C} and P_{2L} are the prices in Country II of capital and labor, respectively. In other words, if capital is relatively cheap in Country I, the country is abundant in capital, and if labor is relatively cheap in Country II, Country II is rich in labor.

It now remains for us to show that Country I will export the capital-intensive good and that Country II will export the labor-intensive good. This is easily done, as is demonstrated with the help of Figure 4.1. We start with two isoquants, *aa* and *bb*, which characterize the production functions and are the same in both countries. According to these isoquants, *B* is the labor-intensive good and A is the capital-intensive good. Relative factor prices in Country I, where capital is cheap, are given by the line $P_0 P_0$. Let us assume that the isoquants represent 1 unit of the respective good. Then 1 unit of good A will be produced with Oa_1 of capital and Oa_1' of labor. But capital and labor can be exchanged for each other in a ratio shown by the factor-price line $P_0 P_0$. Therefore, Oa_1' of labor is worth $a_1 G$ of capital, and Oa_1 of capital is worth $a_1' H$ of labor.

We said that 1 unit of good A would be produced with Oa_1 of capital and Oa_1' of labor. But now we can view the line GH as a budget line or a cost line, and we can express the cost of producing 1 unit of A in terms of capital alone or of labor alone. Doing so, we find that the cost of producing 1 unit of A is OG measured in capital or OH measured in labor.

By applying exactly the same kind of reasoning, we also find that the cost of producing 1 unit of good B in Country I is the same as that for producing 1 unit of A; i.e., it is OG measured in capital and OH measured in labor.

The next step is to find out the cost of producing 1 unit of each good in Country II. The only information we have about Country II is that capital is relatively more expensive there than in Country I. This means that the slope of the line representing the ratio of factor prices in Country II will be less steep than the slope of $P_0 P_0$.

A possible factor-price line in Country II is $P_1 P_1$. It is tangent to the aa isoquant at E. A parallel factor-price line is $P_2 P_2$, which is tangent to the bb isoquant at F. It is obvious that $P_2 P_2$ must lie below $P_1 P_1$. From this it follows that the cost of producing 1 unit of good A in Country II is OC measured in capital, whereas it is OD measured in capital for 1 unit of good B. Thus in Country II it is more expensive to produce a given amount of good A than it is to produce the same amount of good B.

If we now compare production costs in the two countries, we find that it is relatively cheap to produce good A in Country I and relatively cheap to produce good B in Country II. From this it follows that Country I will export good A and Country II will export good B. This establishes the Heckscher–Ohlin theorem that the country abundant in capital will export the capital-intensive good and the country abundant in labor will export the labor-intensive good.

Thus, starting from the definition of factor abundance in terms of factor prices, it is easy to establish the Heckscher–Ohlin theorem. We might mention in passing that the reverse of the theorem also holds; i.e., if a country exports the capital-intensive good, capital is its relatively cheap factor of production.

One could argue, however, that stating the theorem in terms of factor prices is not very interesting, because factor prices are themselves results of a complicated interplay of economic forces. They are, for instance, not only determined by supply factors but are also influenced by demand factors. It is not possible to say anything about factor prices from the knowledge of factor endowments alone. To state the Heckscher–Ohlin theorem in terms of factor prices gives perhaps not the most interesting version of the theorem.

A more natural definition, it seems, would run in terms of physical amounts. Let us now use this definition and see what the result will be.

FACTOR ABUNDANCE DEFINED IN PHYSICAL TERMS

Defining factor abundance in physical terms, we say that Country I is rich in capital and Country II is rich in labor if $C_1/L_1 > C_2/L_2$, where C_1 is the total amount of capital in Country I, L_1 is the total amount of labor in Country I, and C_2 and L_2 are the total amounts of capital and labor, respectively, in Country II.

We will now show that if Country I is abundant in capital according to this definition, it implies that Country I has a bias in favor of producing the capital-intensive good. The nature of this bias is best illustrated by Figure 4.2. It is assumed in the figure that good A is the capital-intensive good and good B is the labor-intensive good. If both countries were to produce the goods in the same proportion, say along the ray OR, Country I would be producing at point S' on its production-possibility curve and Country II would be producing at point S on its production-possibility curve. The slope of Country I's production-possibility curve at S' is steeper than the slope of Country II's curve at S. This implies that good A would be cheaper in Country I than in Country II, and that good B would be cheaper in Country II than in Country I, were the two countries producing at the respective points. This is also illustrated by the fact that the commodity price line $P_1 P_1$ is steeper than the line $P_2 P_2$. The opportunity cost of expanding production of good A is, therefore, lower in Country I than in Country II, and vice versa

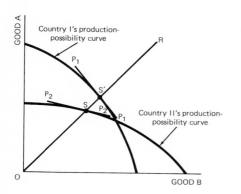

FIGURE 4.2

Factor abundance defined in physical terms

for good B. This shows that Country I, the capital-rich country, has a bias in favor of the capital-intensive good from the production side, and that the country abundant in labor, Country II, has a bias in favor of producing the labor-intensive good.

It does not follow from this, however, that the labor-rich country will export the labor-intensive good. It might be the case that demand factors more than offset the bias from the production side. Such a case is illustrated in Figure 4.3, which contains the same production-possibility curves as Figure 4.2, and good A is still the capital-intensive good and good B the labor-intensive good. The difference is that now we have taken demand into account. Demand in the two countries is characterized by two sets of indifference curves, where the curves $I_0'I_0'$, $I_1'I_1'$, etc., represent demand in Country I and the curves $I_0''I_0''$, $I_1''I_1''$, etc., represent demand in Country II. Demand in Country I is obviously biased toward the capital-intensive good and demand in Country II is biased toward the labor-intensive good. Thus in isolation good A is relatively more expensive in Country I than in Country II. This is shown by the fact that the commodity price line $P_2 P_2$ in Country II is steeper than the line P_1P_1 representing relative commodity prices in Country I.

From this it follows that when trade is opened up between the two countries, Country I will export good B and Country II will export good A. In other words, the country abundant in capital will export the labor-intensive good, and the country abundant in labor will export the capital-intensive good.

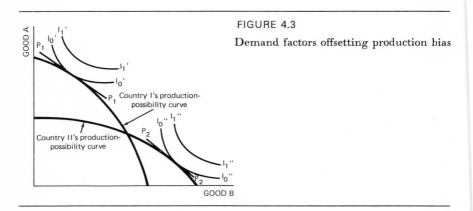

FIGURE 4.3

Demand factors offsetting production bias

To sum up: Factor abundance can be defined in two ways in the Heckscher–Ohlin trade model. The two alternative definitions are not equivalent. Only according to one of them does it follow that the country abundant in capital will export the capital-intensive good and that the country rich in labor will export the labor-intensive good. Let us, before we conclude this chapter, compare and contrast the meaning of comparative advantage in the Ricardian and in the Heckscher–Ohlin trade models.

A COMPARISON OF COMPARATIVE ADVANTAGE IN THE RICARDIAN AND IN THE HECKSCHER–OHLIN TRADE MODELS

In Chapter 1, where we treated comparative advantage in the Ricardian model, the only factor of production was labor. In the Ricardian model, comparative advantage was determined by production conditions alone. We also learned that if a country had a comparative advantage in the production of a good it would export that good.

In the neoclassical, two-factor model these two conditions are no longer met. Speaking in terms of the first definition of factor abundance, i.e., in terms of factor prices, we can see that the second condition is fulfilled and that if a country is abundant in capital it will also export the capital-intensive good. But the first condition is not met, because we cannot infer from production conditions alone anything about factor prices.

Then, going to the second definition of factor abundance—the definition in terms of physical amounts of factors of production—we find that it is the other way around. This definition takes into account only production conditions; here the first condition of the Ricardian model is fulfilled, but the second is not, because we cannot infer anything about comparative advantage. We cannot, for instance, use this definition to say that the country abundant in capital will export the capital-intensive good.

One thing which does hold, however, is that even though the country that is abundant in capital according to the second definition might export the labor-intensive good, it will still produce relatively more of the capital-intensive good than the other country. If A is the capital-intensive good and B is the labor-intensive good, and if Country I is abundant in capital and Country II in labor, we know that Country I will always produce A/B in a higher ratio than Country II. In this sense we can say that Country I has a comparative advantage in the production of the capital-intensive good and that Country II has a comparative advantage in the production of the labor-intensive good.

Another interesting comment concerns the ranking of goods. We remember from Chapter 1 that we could rank the goods produced according to the amount of labor it took to produce 1 unit of each good in each country. Ranking goods in this way amounted to ranking according to comparative advantage.

In the two-factor trade model we can rank goods in an analogous way according to factor intensities. Let us assume Country I to be abundant in capital and Country II to be abundant in labor. Then if we rank all goods in Country I according to capital intensity used in production, we rank them according to comparative advantage. This country will first export the most capital-intensive good and then go to the second most capital-intensive, and so on. And this chain can never be broken.

In a completely analogous fashion, Country II will export its most labor-intensive good first, then go on to the second most labor-intensive, and so on. The formal proof for this proposition involves some mathematics, so it is presented as an appendix to this chapter.

The proposition that ranking goods according to factor intensities is a ranking according to comparative advantage is of interest also from the point of view of development economics. Provided that all the assumptions for the analysis were fulfilled, all a developing country abundant in labor would have to do would be to rank the goods it produced according to labor intensity in production and concentrate on exporting the most labor-intensive products.

We have to remember, however, that the theory of comparative advantage is a completely static type of theory. It only gives some characteristics of an economy at a given point in time. For instance, it can give information about how to rank goods at any given moment, but it cannot give any indication about how the economy would develop if production conditions were to change.

We will have to wait for later chapters and develop first a comparative-static framework before we can say anything about how changes in the conditions of production affect the variables in the trade models.

Factor intensities and the ranking of goods according to comparative advantage

4-A

We have already asserted that ranking goods according to factor intensities is ranking them according to comparative advantage. Here is the proof of this assertion.

Let us assume that each of the two countries produces three goods, A, B, and C. All the assumptions introduced in the beginning of Chapter 4 about production functions, competitive markets, etc., are assumed to hold. We also assume that good A at any factor-price ratio uses more capital-intensive methods in production than B, which in turn is more capital-intensive than C. Hence, if $C_a/L_a = \rho_a$, $C_b/L_b = \rho_b$, and $C_c/L_c = \rho_c$, where C_a, C_b, C_c and L_a, L_b, L_c are the amounts of capital and labor used in the respective industries, it follows that $\rho_a > \rho_b > \rho_c$.

As the production functions are homogeneous of the first degree, we can write them in the following way:

$$A = L_a f(\rho_a) \tag{4A.1a}$$
$$B = L_b g(\rho_b) \tag{4A.1b}$$
$$C = L_c h(\rho_c) \tag{4A.1c}$$

Differentiating equation 4A.1a with respect to L_a and C_a, i.e., deriving the expressions for the marginal productivity of labor and capital, respectively, we get

$$\frac{\partial A}{\partial L_a} = L_a f'\left(-\frac{C_a}{L_a^2}\right) + f(\rho_a) = f(\rho_a) - \rho_a f'(\rho_a) \tag{4A.2a}$$

$$\frac{\partial A}{\partial C_a} = L_a f'(\rho_a)\frac{1}{L_a} = f'(\rho_a) \tag{4A.2b}$$

In a completely analogous manner we can get

$$\frac{\partial B}{\partial L_b} = g(\rho_b) - g'(\rho_b)\rho_b \qquad \frac{\partial B}{\partial C_b} = g'(\rho_b)$$

$$\frac{\partial C}{\partial L_c} = h(\rho_c) - h'(\rho_c)\rho_c \qquad \frac{\partial C}{\partial C_c} = h'(\rho_c)$$

Denote the price of capital and the price of labor by P_C and P_L, respectively. Optimal resource allocation then requires that the ratio between factor prices and marginal productivities must be the same in all lines of production, so that we get

$$\frac{P_L}{P_C} = \frac{f(\rho_a) - \rho_a f'(\rho_a)}{f'(\rho_a)} = \frac{g(\rho_b) - \rho_b g'(\rho_b)}{g'(\rho_b)} = \frac{h(\rho_c) - \rho_c h'(\rho_c)}{h'(\rho_c)} \tag{4A.3}$$

73

Factor intensities and
the ranking of goods
according to
comparative advantage

Let us denote the price of good A by P_a, of good B by P_b, and of good C by P_c. We know that in equilibrium the value of the marginal products must be the same in each line of production, for instance, $P_b \times g'(\rho_b) = P_c \times h'(\rho_c)$. From this follows

$$\frac{P_b}{P_c} = \frac{h'(\rho_c)}{g'(\rho_b)} \tag{4A.4}$$

The idea is now to find how relative commodity prices vary with the capital/labor ratio employed in any commodity. By differentiating equation 4A.4 we get

$$\frac{d(P_b/P_c)}{d\rho_b} = \frac{g'(\rho_b)h''(\rho_c)(d\rho_c/d\rho_b) - h'(\rho_c)g''(\rho_b)}{[g'(\rho_b)]^2} \tag{4A.5}$$

It is not possible to give a qualitative interpretation of equation 4A.5 because it contains both positive and negative terms. Therefore, we have to make a few more manipulations.

Differentiating equation 4A.3 gives

$$\frac{d(P_L/P_C)}{d\rho_b} = \frac{[h'(h' - \rho_c h'' - h') - (h - \rho_c h')h''](d\rho_c/d\rho_b)}{(h')^2}$$
$$= -\frac{h(\rho_c)h''(\rho_c)(d\rho_c/d\rho_b)}{[h'(\rho_c)]^2} \tag{4A.6}$$

In an analogous way,

$$\frac{d(P_L/P_C)}{d\rho_b} = -\frac{g(\rho_b)g''(\rho_b)}{[g'(\rho_b)]^2}$$

From this it follows that

$$\frac{d\rho_c}{d\rho_b} = \frac{[h'(\rho_c)]^2 g(\rho_b)g''(\rho_b)}{h(\rho_c)h''(\rho_c)[g'(\rho_b)]^2} \tag{4A.7}$$

Hence

$$\frac{d(P_b/P_c)}{d\rho_b} = \frac{\dfrac{g(\rho_b)[h'(\rho_c)]^2 g''(\rho_b)}{h(\rho_c)g'(\rho_b)} - h'(\rho_c)g''(\rho_b)}{[g'(\rho_b)]^2} \tag{4A.8}$$

From equation 4A.3 we get

$$\frac{g(\rho_b)}{g'(\rho_b)} = \frac{h(\rho_c)}{h'(\rho_c)} + \rho_b - \rho_c \tag{4A.9}$$

Substituting equation 4A.9 into 4A.8 gives

$$\frac{d(P_b/P_c)}{d\rho_b} = \frac{g''(\rho_b)[h'(\rho_c)]^2}{h(\rho_c)[g'(\rho_b)]^2}(\rho_b - \rho_c) \qquad (4A.10)$$

According to our assumptions, $\rho_b > \rho_c$ at any factor/price ratio. The second derivative, $g''(\rho_b)$, which denotes the change in the marginal productivity of capital as capital increases [if we write it out explicitly, $g''(\rho_b) = \partial^2 B/\partial C_b^2$], is negative, because the production function is assumed to be homogeneous of the first degree. All the other factors in equation 4A.10 are positive. Hence equation 4A.10 must be negative.

Goods B and C were picked arbitrarily. With any number of commodities, $1 \cdots n$, it follows that $d(P_i/P_j)/d\rho_i < 0$ if $\rho_i > \rho_j$. $P_{1a}/P_{1b} < P_{2a}/P_{2b}$ implies that $\rho_{1a} > \rho_{2a}$. In other words, if good A is relatively cheaper in Country I than in Country II, the methods of production of good A in Country I will be more capital-intensive than the methods of production of the same good in Country II. Thus ranking goods according to factor intensities is ranking them according to comparative advantage.

We find that there is a complete analogy between ranking goods according to labor hours used in production in the one-factor case, the way we did it in Chapter 1, and the ranking according to factor intensities in the two-factor case. If, for instance, Country I exports good H, she will also export goods A to G. Demand conditions will influence the point at which the chain of ranking will be broken, but they will not influence the order of ranking. In this sense, production conditions alone determine the goods in which a country will have a comparative advantage.

Commodity and factor
prices under trade:
factor-price equalization

5

We have studied the meaning of comparative advantage in the two-factor trade model. To get a more complete understanding of the interrelationships between the variables in a general equilibrium system, we now turn our attention to the effects that trade will have on factor prices.

We have assumed that there are no impediments to trade. Then when trade is introduced, commodity prices will be the same in both countries. But what about factor prices? What effects will trade have on factor prices?

One assumption central to the theory of international trade is that factors of production are completely immobile between countries. This has also been tacitly assumed in the preceding chapters. We have assumed that factors of production are completely mobile within each country but that they cannot cross borders. There is no cost involved for labor or capital in moving from Florida to California, but it is impossible for labor or capital to move from Florida to Cuba, or from Arizona to Mexico.

Let us for a moment give up this assumption and instead assume full mobility internationally for factors of production; that capital and labor can move freely without cost. Then it is quite obvious that factor prices would be the same in all countries: If workers on Haiti had lower wages than workers in the United States they would move to the United States, as there are no costs of transportation and no impediments to migration of labor. In this process wages in the two countries would be equalized. In an analogous manner, capital would move to the countries where returns to capital are highest. Thereby, returns to capital would be equalized and the rental price for 1 unit of capital would be the same everywhere.

We will now demonstrate that in a world where factors of production cannot move between countries but where goods can move freely, trade in goods can be viewed as a substitution for factor mobility. In a model built on the type of assumptions that we have already set out in earlier chapters we will find that free trade leads to a complete equalization of factor rewards or to a partial equalization combined with complete specialization in production.

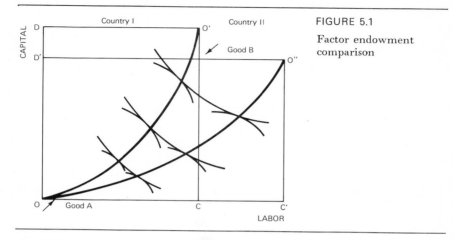

FIGURE 5.1

Factor endowment comparison

THE BOX DIAGRAM WITH THE SAME PRODUCTION
FUNCTIONS IN THE TWO COUNTRIES

We will, as usual, couch our argument in terms of the two-country, two-good model with two factors of production. We retain all the assumptions that were listed at the beginning of Chapter 4 and explained there and in Chapter 3. One of these assumptions was that production functions differ between goods but are the same in both countries.

It might be useful to give a geometric illustration of this fact (Fig. 5.1). The box $OCO'D$ represents total factor endowments in Country I, and the box $OC'O''D'$ represents total factor endowments in Country II. From this we can read that Country I is abundant in capital, measured in physical amounts as $C_1/L_1 > C_2/L_2$, and Country II is abundant in labor, using the same measure.

We measure production of good A from the lower left-hand corner and production of good B from the upper right-hand corner. As production functions are the same in both countries, the aa isoquants are identical for both countries. This can easily be seen from Figure 5.1 for good A, because production of this good is measured from the O corner in both countries. The bb isoquants are also the same, in the sense that they both illustrate the same production function, even though production of this good in Country I is measured from the O' corner and production in Country II is measured from the O'' corner.

78

Commodity and factor
prices under trade:
factor-price equalization

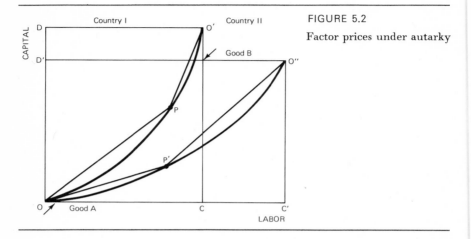

FIGURE 5.2

Factor prices under autarky

As can be seen from the figure, labor is measured on the horizontal axis of the box and capital on the vertical axis. From the ways the isoquants are drawn, it follows that good A is the labor-intensive good and good B is the capital-intensive good.

FACTOR PRICES UNDER AUTARKY

In isolation, before trade, the two countries can produce anywhere on the contract curve in their respective boxes. Figure 5.2 illustrates the same situation as Figure 5.1, but for convenience the isoquants are omitted here. Let us assume, for the sake of reasoning, that Country I produces at point P on its contract curve and that Country II produces at point P'. What will then be the implication for factor prices?

We can see immediately from Figure 5.2 that Country I uses more capital-intensive methods of production than Country II in both lines of production. Production functions are the same in both countries and they are homogeneous of the first degree. We know that the marginal productivities are determined exclusively by the factor intensities used in production. Because Country I uses more capital per unit of labor than Country II, the marginal productivity of capital at P in Country I will be lower than the marginal productivity of capital at P' in Country II. Factor prices are determined by marginal productivities. From this it follows that the price of capital will be lower in Country I than in Country II and that the return for labor; i.e., the wages will be higher in Country I than in Country II.

This holds when each country produces and consumes in isolation. Let us now introduce the possibility of trade and see what happens.

COMMODITY AND FACTOR PRICES UNDER TRADE: FACTOR-PRICE EQUALIZATION

If the equilibrium situation before trade is the one that we have depicted in Figure 5.2, it follows that $P_{1C}/P_{1L} < P_{2C}/P_{2L}$. Then we know from Chapter 4 that Country I, where capital is relatively cheap, will export the capital-intensive good when the countries start to trade and that Country II will export the labor-intensive good. This follows from a straightforward application of the Heckscher–Ohlin theorem.

Good B is the capital-intensive good and good A is the labor-intensive one. Hence, when trade starts, Country I will move along its contract curve from point P toward the O corner and Country II will move from point P' along its contract curve toward the O'' corner. Possible equilibrium points when the two countries trade are shown in Figure 5.3. The boxes and the contract curves are, of course, the same. The difference is that Country I now produces at point T and Country II produces at point T'. These are obviously production patterns which are possible under trade. What are the implications for factor prices?

Because of the assumption about constant returns to scale, the marginal productivity of labor and capital will be constant along any ray from the origin, such as OTT'. Denote the marginal productivity of labor and capital in Country I in industry A and in industry B with, respectively, MPL_{1A}, MPC_{1A}, MPL_{1B}, and MPC_{1B}. Analogously, denote the marginal productivities in the respective industries in the second country with MPL_{2A}, MPC_{2A}, MPL_{2B}, and MPC_{2B}.

We can see that labor and capital are used in the same proportions in industry A in both countries at T and T'. From this it follows that $MPL_{1A} = MPL_{2A}$ and that $MPC_{1A} = MPC_{2A}$. Furthermore, the line $O'T$ is

Commodity and factor
prices under trade:
factor-price equalization

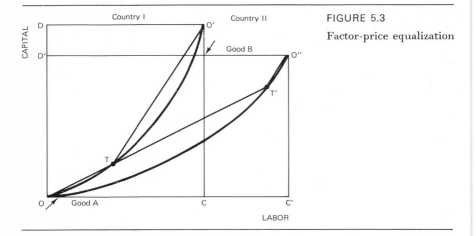

FIGURE 5.3

Factor-price equalization

parallel to the line $O'' T'$. Hence the factors of production are combined in the same proportions in both countries in industry B, too. From this it follows that $MPL_{1B} = MPL_{2B}$ and that $MPC_{1B} = MPC_{2B}$.

One of our assumptions is that factor markets are perfectly competitive and that factors of production are fully mobile within each country. This means that the payment for labor, the wage, must be the same in both industries and that the payment for 1 unit of capital also must be the same in both industries. But the factor reward equals the marginal productivity of the factor multiplied by the price of the good produced. From this it follows that $MPL_{1A} \times P_{1A} = MPL_{1B} \times P_{1B}$ and that $MPC_{1A} \times P_{1A} = MPC_{1B} \times P_{1B}$. This gives $P_{1A}/P_{1B} = MPL_{1B}/MPL_{1A}$ and $P_{1A}/P_{1B} = MPC_{1B}/MPC_{1A}$. Analogously, we get for the second country, $MPL_{2A} \times P_{2A} = MPL_{2B} \times P_{2B}$ and $MPC_{2A} \times P_{2A} = MPC_{2B} \times P_{2B}$. Hence $P_{2A}/P_{2B} = MPL_{2B}/MPL_{2A}$ and $P_{2A}/P_{2B} = MPC_{2B}/MPC_{2A}$.

But P_{1A}/P_{1B} and P_{2A}/P_{2B} are nothing but relative commodity prices in the two countries. Under trade, disregarding all impediments to trade, they must be the same, and hence $P_{1A}/P_{1B} = P_{2A}/P_{2B}$. We already know that at points T and T' $MPL_{1A} = MPL_{2A}$, $MPC_{1A} = MPC_{2A}$, $MPL_{1B} = MPL_{2B}$, and $MPC_{1B} = MPC_{2B}$. This gives $MPL_{1A} \times P_{1A} = MPL_{2A} \times P_{2A} = MPL_{1B} \times P_{1B} = MPL_{2B} \times P_{2B}$. In other words, factor prices will be completely equalized in the two countries.

This demonstration shows that as long as we can find trading points such as T and T' in Figure 5.3, the implication is that factor prices will be the same in both countries. Given our present assumptions, this means that as long as both countries are incompletely specialized—i.e., as long as both countries produce both goods—trade will lead to a complete factor-price equalization.

Let us now examine the common-sense explanation of factor-price equalization. We start out with the situation illustrated in Figure 5.2. In isolation, capital is cheap in Country I and labor is cheap in Country II. Therefore, Country I has a comparative advantage in the capital-intensive good (good B) and Country II has a comparative advantage in the labor-intensive good (good A).

When the two countries start to trade, it is obvious that Country I will export good B and Country II will export good A. To increase its production of good B, Country I has to move its factors of production from industry A to industry B. But industry B is the capital-intensive industry. To produce more of good B, the producers in Country I need, especially, more capital. Therefore, the price of capital is bid up, and the relative price of what was the cheap factor before trade rises.

In an exactly analogous manner, the producers in Country II start to produce more of good A, in order to export it. This is the labor-intensive good. As more of it is produced, more labor is needed and the relative price of labor goes up. Hence trade leads to an increase, in both countries, in the price of the abundant factor—the relatively cheap factor—until factor prices are the same in both countries.

But are we always able to find trade points such as T and T' in Figure 5.3? Not necessarily. The alternative is that one of the countries, or possibly both, might be completely specialized and produce only one good. Let us look into this case.

COMPLETE SPECIALIZATION

Figure 5.4 can be used to illustrate the conditions that must be fulfilled if trading points are to be found with production of both goods in both countries. First we draw a line tangent to Country I's contract curve. This line is OE', which meets Country II's contract curve at E'. Then we draw the diagonal OO'' for Country II's box. This line cuts Country I's contract curve

82

Commodity and factor
prices under trade:
factor-price equalization

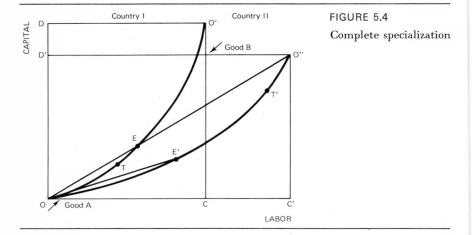

FIGURE 5.4

Complete specialization

at *E*. Then any point between *OE* on Country I's contract curve can be paired with any point between *E'O"* on Country II's contract curve. But only if both countries produce on these segments of their contract curves will we be able to find corresponding trading points and incomplete specialization, which are conditions for full factor-price equalization.

Figure 5.4 also illustrates the fact that only if the factor-endowment ratios in both countries lie between the factor intensities used in the two lines of production will there be incomplete specialization. This was obviously the case for points *T* and *T'*, for example, and therefore we had incomplete specialization at these points.

Let us assume that we have the situation depicted in Figure 5.4, so that Country I is producing at point *T* and Country II is producing at Point *T'*, and let us see how complete specialization can be brought about. This equilibrium situation might be disturbed by, for instance, an increase in the demand for good *A* brought about by a change in tastes. Both countries will then produce more of good *A*, and both will move up and to the right, Country I toward *O'* and Country II toward *O"*. This can be done only by shifting factors of production from good *B* to good *A*.

But Country II was already producing much of good *A* at *T'*. After a while the country will therefore reach point *O"*, where it will produce only good *A*. Country I will then be producing at point *E*. If the demand for *A*, and at the same time the relative price of *A*, keep on increasing, Country I will increase its production of good *A*. This means that it will be producing somewhere on the contract curve between E and O'. But Country II has already shifted all its factors of production to good A. Even if the price of A goes up, it cannot produce more of it. Therefore, the factor intensities used in the same line of production in the two countries will no longer be the same.

The implications of such a development for factor prices are easy to see. At T and T' factor prices were equalized in the two countries. When the demand for good A—the labor-intensive good—increases, the demand for labor increases concomitantly. This leads to an increase in the relative price of labor. As this happens, producers try to substitute capital for labor and go over to more capital-intensive methods of production. It can also easily be seen from Figure 5.4 that as we move up and to the right, the methods of production in both lines of production become more and more capital-intensive.

But at point O'' Country II has pulled all its factors of production out of industry B and put them into industry A, and the capital-intensity in industry A at O'' equals the over-all capital-intensity of the country. Country I, which is abundant in capital, uses the same capital intensity in the production of good A but still has enough capital to use methods even more capital-intensive in the production of good B. At points E and O'' factor prices are still equalized. If the relative price of good A goes up even higher, so does the relative price of labor in Country I. But it cannot go higher in Country II. Factor intensities will no longer be the same in the two countries, the relation between marginal productivities will no longer be the same, and factor prices will no longer be completely equalized.

However, there will still be a tendency to factor-price equalization because of trade: If capital is relatively cheap in Country I, the country will export the capital-intensive good and the price of capital will go up, and if labor is relatively cheap in Country II, the country will export the labor-intensive good and the wage will go up, because of trade.

We might now make a couple of comments on which factors determine whether countries under trade will be completely or incompletely specialized. If there was a greater difference between factor endowments than in Figure 5.4, the probability for complete specialization would increase. This can be seen from Figure 5.5. The figure shows a situation where Country II has relatively more labor than in Figure 5.4. The amount of labor $C'C''$ has been added, and Country II's new box consists of $OC''O_1''D'$. This leads to a diminution of the segments of the two countries' contract

84

Commodity and factor
prices under trade:
factor-price equalization

FIGURE 5.5

Changes in factor endowment and complete specialization

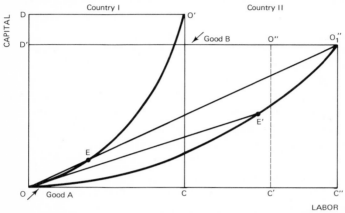

curves, OE and $E'O''$, where trading points with incomplete specialization can be found. If Country II's labor force continued to grow with a constant amount of capital, we would finally end up in a situation where the diagonal of Country II's box would coincide with the tangent to Country I's contract curve. Then no trading points could be found. The reasoning above leads to the conclusion that the more the factor endowments in the two countries differ, the larger is the probability that one country will be completely specialized and that complete factor-price equalization will not occur.

Likewise, if the techniques used in the two lines of production were more similar to each other than as shown in Figure 5.5, the likelihood of complete specialization would increase. In geometric terms, this means that the contract curves in the two countries would be closer to the diagonal. Then the segments of the contract curves where matching trading points can be found would diminish.

FACTOR PRICES, POVERTY, AND INCOME EQUALIZATION

We have now proved that given certain rather strict assumptions, trade will equalize factor prices. But we live in a world where wide divergences in wages can be observed. Does not experience contradict the results of the factor-price-equalization theorem? Before we conclude this chapter it is appropriate to make a few comments on this question.

First we must observe what the factor-price-equalization theorem does *not* say. It does not say that trade will equalize incomes. Wages are not the only source of income. Someone must own the capital, and capital also commands its factor reward. Therefore, the more capital a country has for a given amount of labor, the higher the average income will be. So even if factor rewards were completely equalized, as long as the capital stocks differ, incomes will also differ.

Second, the factor-price-equalization theorem is a completely static type of theory. It only studies some characteristics of a given equilibrium situation at a given point in time. It says only what the effects of trade will be with a given technique, with given factor endowments, and so on. But the real world is not in a given equilibrium forever; all sorts of changes occur. It could very well be the case that trade does have the effects on factor prices which the factor-price-equalization theorem predicts but that other factors, disregarded by this type of theory, work in an opposite direction.

Furthermore, of course, we have to keep in mind that the factor-price-equalization theorem builds on some very strong assumptions, all of which can hardly be expected to be fulfilled. Perhaps the factor-price-equalization theorem, and static theorizing in general, should not be viewed as directly amenable to or geared toward empirical testing. It gives us, however, indispensable tools and insights into the general equilibrium nature of economics. It is the necessary background for all further theorizing. As we go along, for instance in the section on economic growth and international trade, we will see how the theory can be developed and how testable hypotheses of considerable interest can be derived from it.

SELECTED BIBLIOGRAPHY: CHAPTERS 4 AND 5

The basic sources for the Heckscher-Ohlin theory of international trade are:

E. F. Heckscher, "Utrikeshandelns verkan på inkomstfördelningen," *Ekonomisk Tidskrift*, 1919 (reprinted in English translation in *RTIT*).

86

Commodity and factor
prices under trade :
factor-price equalization

B. Ohlin, *Interregional and International Trade*, Cambridge, Mass., Harvard University Press, 1933, especially chaps. 5–7 and 8.

There exists a vast literature about the Heckscher–Ohlin model and the factor-price equalization theorem. The following essays are but a few gleanings from the existing literature. An article that the author has found most useful and on which much of the exposition in Chapter 4 is founded is:

R. W. Jones, "Factor Proportions and the Heckscher–Ohlin Theorem," *RES*, January 1956.

The first published proofs of the factor-price equalization theorem are found in:

P. A. Samuelson, "International Trade and the Equalization of Factor Prices," *EJ*, June 1948.

P. A. Samuelson, "International Factor-Price Equalization Once Again," *EJ*, June 1949 (reprinted in *RIE*).

Another important essay by the same author is:

"Prices of Factors and Goods in General Equilibrium," *RES*, vol. 21, no. 1, 1953.

A stringent proof of the theorem was given already in 1933 by A. P. Lerner in a paper given to the Robbins seminar at the London School of Economics. But the exposition was not published until 19 years later:

"Factor Prices and International Trade," *Ec*, February 1952.

Other essays that can be mentioned are:

H. G. Johnson, "Factor Endowments, International Trade and Factor Prices," *MS*, September 1957 (reprinted in *RIE*).

K. Lancaster, "The Heckscher–Ohlin Trade Model: A Geometric Treatment," *Ec*, February 1957.

An excellent survey of the discussion about the factor-price equalization theorem is given in Chipman, *op. cit.*, Part 3.

The gains from trade and the income distribution

6

In this chapter, some of the general equilibrium aspects of the standard model will be studied more closely. We will start by looking into how a change in one variable in the general equilibrium system necessarily implies changes in the other variables. We will then go on and study the inter-relationships between gains from trade and the income distribution. But we will start by seeing how, in general equilibrium, "everything hangs together."

"EVERYTHING HANGS TOGETHER"

We demonstrated in Chapter 3 the precise relationship between the production-possibility curve and the box diagram. We will now apply this knowledge.

Figures 6.1 and 6.2 can be used to demonstrate the interrelationships between the variables in the general equilibrium system. The production-possibility curve RR in Figure 6.2 has been derived from the box in Figure 6.1 in the way that we have shown in Chapter 3. The only difference from Figure 3.9 is that we have changed it in a mirror-like fashion, so that in Figure 6.2 the origin is at O.

Let us assume that we start with an equilibrium situation with production at point S' in Figure 6.2. This means that the country produces Oa of good A and Ob of good B. This implies that relative commodity prices are as shown by the line $P_0 P_0$, tangent to the production-possibility curve at S'.

A unique point on the contract curve in the box diagram corresponds to this point on the production-possibility curve. This unique point is S. This tells us that in order to produce Oa of good A the country has to use Ol of labor combined with Oc of capital, as can be seen from Figure 6.1. It also says that in order to produce Ob of good B the country has to use $O'l'$ of labor combined with $O'c'$ of capital in industry B. It also implies that a certain relative factor price ratio, $P_0' P_0'$, corresponds to a certain relative commodity price ratio, $P_0 P_0$.

Let us now see what happens if there is a disturbance—if something happens that induces the system to move away from points S and S' to a new equilibrium. There are many factors that could disturb the system. Examples are changes in the factor endowments, innovations that change the technology, changes in demand, and so on. Some of these changes, such as

88

The gains from
trade and the
income distribution

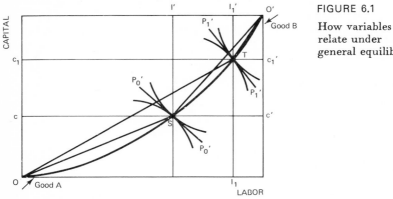

FIGURE 6.1

How variables
relate under
general equilibrium

technical progress, are so important that they deserve to be studied at length. This we will do in coming chapters, when we come to the theory of economic growth and trade. For the time being we are only interested in understanding the basic features of the general equilibrium system. Therefore, we choose the simplest possible type of disturbance as an example: a change in demand, caused, for instance, by a change in tastes.

If tastes change so that consumers want more of good A and less of good B, the relative price of A will go up. Let us say that the relative price of A increases from $P_0 P_0$ in Figure 6.2 to $P_1 P_1$. This will induce producers to produce more of A and less of B, so that they move to point T', where the price line $P_1 P_1$ is tangent to the production-possibility curve RR.

What are the implications for factor inputs? First we have to find the point on the contract curve in the box that corresponds to point T'. This point is T. As T lies to the right and above S, it implies more of good A and less of good B. We can directly read off the factor inputs and find that Ol_1 of labor combined with Oc_1 of capital is used in production of good A, and that $O'l_1'$ of labor combined with $O'c_1'$ of capital is used in production of good B. Therefore we can see that a change in relative prices induces a change in outputs, entailing a change in inputs as well.

It was the labor-intensive good that became relatively more expensive. This implies that the factor intensities in production will change. From Figure 6.1 we can immediately see that the methods of production at T are more capital-intensive in both lines of production compared to what they were at S.

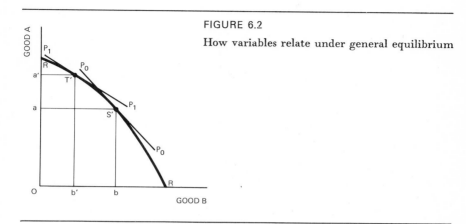

FIGURE 6.2

How variables relate under general equilibrium

The implications for factor prices are clear. We can read off directly from the box diagram that the relative price of labor has gone up, because the factor-price line $P_1'P_1'$ at T is steeper than the factor-price line $P_0'P_0'$ at S. The explanation for the rise in wages is simple. As more of good A is demanded, the demand for factors of production increases. The good is labor-intensive, so the demand for labor increases relatively much and there is an excess supply of capital as factors are released from industry B, causing an increase in the price of labor and a fall in the price of capital. The change in relative factor prices can also be inferred from the fact that the marginal productivity of labor is higher at T than at S, whereas the marginal productivity of capital is lower at T than at S.

Thus we can see that a change in one of the variables in our general equilibrium model implies a change in all other variables. Once we know which good is labor-intensive and which is capital-intensive, we can infer from a change in commodity prices the direction in which factor inputs, factor intensities, and factor prices will change.

THE GAINS FROM TRADE AND THE INCOME DISTRIBUTION

In Chapter 2 when we studied the gains from trade, we found that trade would make a country as a whole better off, but that it need not necessarily

90

The gains from
trade and the
income distribution

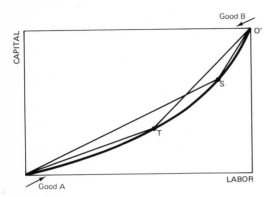

FIGURE 6.3

Gains from trade and
resource allocation

make every citizen better off. Therefore, some citizens might need to be
bribed into accepting the change from autarky to free trade, so that some
could earn much on the transition while others, by being compensated for
eventual losses, at least would not get hurt by it.

We are now equipped to study this matter in detail and to see exactly
what effect the introduction of trade will have on the income distribution.
Let us again use the box diagram and a production-possibility curve derived
from this box diagram as the means of exposition.

Figure 6.4 shows a production-possibility curve RR derived from the
box diagram in Figure 6.3. Before trade, under autarky, the country produces and consumes at point S' on its production-possibility curve. Relative
commodity prices before trade are given by the line $P_0 P_0$ tangent to the
production-possibility curve at S'. The point on the contract curve in the box
diagram that corresponds to S' is S.

Let us now assume that a possibility for trade is introduced and
that the international terms of trade are given by the line $P_1 P_1$. As good B
is relatively more expensive, the country changes its pattern of production and
produces more of good B, thus moving to point T' on its production-possibility curve, where the international price line $P_1 P_1$ is tangent to the
production-possibility curve. The country can then trade along the international price line. Let us assume that the country moves to point T'' by
trading. T'' is obviously better than point S' because it represents more of
both goods. This establishes the fact that the country as a whole can be made
better off by trading.

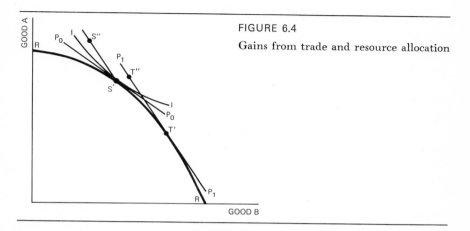

FIGURE 6.4

Gains from trade and resource allocation

But what about factor prices, and what happens with the income distribution? Can we infer anything about the income distribution from the movement along the production-possibility curve from S' to T'?

Yes, we can. With the tools we have at hand it is easy to see what happens. The point on the contract curve in the box that corresponds to point T' on the production-possibility curve is point T. We then have to compare factor prices at points S and T on the contract curve. We can easily see that at point T the methods of production are more labor-intensive in both industries than they are at S. This implies that the marginal productivities of labor are lower and those of capital higher at T than at S. Therefore, wages are lower and returns to capital higher at T than at S. Thus the income distribution has moved against labor and in favor of the owners of capital.

Another way of stating the same fact is as follows: At point T every worker in both industries has less machinery to work with than he had at point S as the methods of production become more labor-intensive. This means that the marginal productivity is lower, and because the marginal productivity determines the wage, the wage is also lower. The wage times the amount of labor employed determines the income that goes to labor. As there is full employment both before and after trade, there is no change in the volume of employment. Hence the income going to labor decreases when the country goes from autarky to free trade.

From this it follows that the ones who gain from free trade—in our example the owners of capital—will have to compensate the workers for

92

The gains from
trade and the
income distribution

their loss of income in order for us to be sure that all citizens are at least as well off at point T'' as they were at point S'. Only if this is done can we say unconditionally that free trade is better than no trade. This was the point that Ricardo and the classical economists failed to see.

It is no accident that one factor of production gets hurt, as it did in our example, when going from autarky to free trade. In the two-factor model, the factor that is used intensively in the import-competing industry will always suffer when going from autarky to free trade. Therefore, a policy of free trade will generally have to be accompanied by measures of redistribution in order to make sure that free trade will be an advantage over no trade.

But what if those who gain from free trade are not willing to compensate those who suffer? Could some degree of trade still be advantageous?

Yes, it could be. This situation, too, can be illustrated with the help of Figure 6.4. If the capital owners are not willing to compensate the workers, the workers could refuse to move into the other industry. Then we would have the same pattern of production after trade as before trade and the country would still be producing at point S' on the production-possibility curve. The country would still have the option, however, to trade according to the international terms of trade: She could trade along the price line $S'S''$ (which is parallel to P_1P_1). She would then produce at point S' but consume, for instance, at point S''. This would clearly be advantageous, as point S'' lies to the right of the indifference curve II, which is tangent to the production-possibility curve at S' and represents the highest level of utility obtainable under autarky. This shows that restricted trade is better than no trade. But restricted trade is potentially less advantageous than free trade.

Factor reversals
and factor prices:
the Leontief paradox

7

One of our assumptions in Chapters 4 and 5 was that there was a one-to-one relationship between factor intensities and factor prices, so that regardless of factor prices one good could always be classified as labor-intensive and the other good could always be classified as capital-intensive. Another way of stating this fact is by saying that the isoquants cut only once.

This is a critical assumption for proving factor-price equalization. If this condition is not fulfilled we have the case of factor reversals, as explained in Chapter 3. The meaning of factor reversals is that at a certain set of factor prices one good is labor-intensive, whereas at another set of factor prices the same good is capital-intensive. This situation is illustrated in Figure 7.1.

For a given factor-price ratio, illustrated by the price line $P_0 P_0$, both industries combine the factors in the same ratio, the λ ratio. If factor prices were to change, so that capital—for example—became relatively cheaper, both industries would go over to more capital-intensive methods of production. But as the possibilities for substitution are easier in industry B than in industry A, good A would now be labor-intensive and good B would be capital-intensive. Analogously, if factor prices changed in the opposite direction, so that labor became relatively cheaper, good A would become the capital-intensive industry and good B would become the labor-intensive industry. Again, this is because it is easier to substitute labor for capital in industry B than in industry A. Therefore, the factor-intensity ray in industry A will always be closer to the λ ratio than will the factor intensity ray of industry B.

This was already explained in Chapter 3, with the help of Figures 3.5 and 3.6.

We do not know a priori if industry A, for instance, is labor-intensive or capital-intensive. It depends on factor prices. We hinted in Chapter 3 that if factor endowments are specified, only a limited number of factor prices are compatible with economic equilibrium. And at this limited set of possible factor prices one good is always labor-intensive and the other is always capital-intensive. The time has come to establish this fact.

94

Factor reversals
and factor prices:
the Leontief paradox

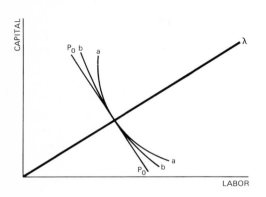

FIGURE 7.1

Factor reversal

FACTOR REVERSALS, FACTOR PRICES, AND ECONOMIC EQUILIBRIUM

We use Figure 7.2 to establish the proposition that, given factor endowments, one good is always labor-intensive and the other is always capital-intensive. We have the same kind of isoquants as in Figure 7.1—isoquants tangent to each other at the point where they are cut by the critical λ ratio. The only difference is that now we have specified the country's factor endowments. They are given by the box $OBO'A$. The diagonal of the box is the line OO'. We measure good A from the lower left-hand corner and good B from the upper right-hand corner.

  If factor prices are depicted by the $P_0 P_0$ price line in Figure 7.1, the factor intensity in industry A will be the one depicted by the λ ratio. What will then be the factor intensity in industry B?

  If, for instance, industry A were producing at point C, the factor intensity in industry B would be $O'C$. But at point C the relative factor prices must be as given by the price line $P_0 P_0$; only then can C be a possible equilibrium point, i.e., a point on the contract curve. This presupposes that factor intensities are the same in both lines of production, because we know that at this given factor-price ratio both industries use the same factor intensities. But the factor intensity OC in industry A is obviously not the same as the factor intensity $O'C$ in industry B. Hence point C cannot be on the contract curve.

  The explanation of why C cannot be on the contract curve is simple: Given that industry A uses the factor intensity shown by the λ ratio—i.e.,

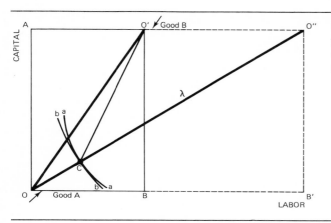

FIGURE 7.2

Factor reversal
with factor
endowment specified

uses the factor intensity OC—industry B would also have to use the same
factor intensity. But this is not possible, because the total factor endowments
do not suffice for this. It would be possible only if the country had more
labor than it has—if the box was $OB'O''A$ instead of $OBO'A$. As long
as factor endowments are what they are, C cannot be on the contract
curve.

Nor can the contract curve go below the λ ray from the origin. For
it to do so would imply that industry A could use production methods even
more labor-intensive than those illustrated by the λ ratio. Then factor prices
would be such that industry B also would use a factor intensity more labor-
intensive than the one shown by the λ ratio. But the over-all factor endowments do not suffice for this. For this reason the contract curve must be
wholly above the λ ray.

But if the contract curve goes above the λ ray, we know that factor
prices will have to be such that capital is relatively cheaper than what is
shown by the factor-price ratio $P_0 P_0$ in Figure 7.1. And at any set of factor
prices where capital is relatively cheaper than it is at the factor-price ratio
depicted by $P_0 P_0$, good B will be capital-intensive and good A will be labor-
intensive. Therefore, once the total factor endowments are specified, the set
of factor prices compatible with economic equilibrium will be restricted. At
this restricted set of factor prices one good will always be labor-intensive and
the other good will always be capital-intensive.

We have now cleared the ground for showing the effects of trade on
factor prices in the case of factor reversals.

96

Factor reversals
and factor prices:
the Leontief paradox

TRADE AND FACTOR PRICES WITH FACTOR REVERSALS

We assume that we have the situation illustrated in Figure 7.1, so that factor reversals do exist. We now have to distinguish carefully between two cases—one in which factor reversals, although existing in theory, do not play a practical role, and another in which they will destroy all the earlier results for the effects of trade on factor prices.

The first case is easy to deal with. It is the one in which the endowment proportions in both countries lie on the same side of the critical λ ratio. If, for instance, the diagonals in both countries' box diagrams lie to the left of the λ ray, the only factor-price ratios compatible with economic equilibrium in both countries will be ones with the relative price of capital lower than that shown by the price ratio $P_0 P_0$ in Figure 7.1. At this set of possible factor-price ratios good A will be labor-intensive in both countries and good B will be capital-intensive in both countries.

If, on the other hand, the endowment proportions are to the right of the λ ray, good A will be capital-intensive in both countries and good B will be labor-intensive in both countries.

From this it follows that if the endowment proportions in both countries are on the same side of the critical λ ratio, there will be the same one-to-one relationship between factor prices and factor intensities in both countries. Although factor reversals exist in theory, they will have no practical importance.

This being the case, we have the same situation in practice as when we assumed that no factor reversals existed, with the strong assumption about a one-to-one relationship between factor prices and factor intensities. Therefore, the same analysis that was used in Chapter 5 can be applied to this case, with the conclusion that trade will lead either to a complete equalization of factor prices or to a tendency to factor-price equalization combined with complete specialization in one or both countries.

The interesting case in connection with factor reversals is therefore the one in which factor endowments differ significantly between the two countries, so that the endowment proportions in the two countries are on different sides of the critical λ ratio. We will now examine this case, which is illustrated geometrically in Figure 7.3, in detail. The factor endowment of Country I is given by the box $OCO'D$, and the factor endowment of Country II is given by the box $OC'O''D'$. In terms of physical endowments Country I is capital-rich and Country II is labor-rich.

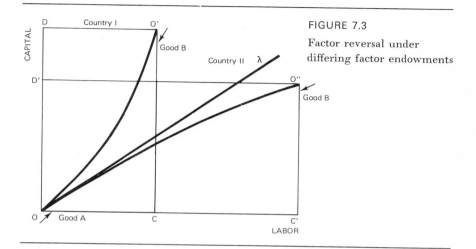

FIGURE 7.3

Factor reversal under differing factor endowments

We assume the isoquants to be of the same kind as those illustrated in Figures 7.1 and 7.2. As the diagonal of Country I lies to the left of the critical λ ratio, its contract curve has to lie wholly above the λ ratio. This implies that in Country I good A is labor-intensive and good B is capital-intensive.

The diagonal of Country II's box, on the other hand, lies to the right of the critical λ ratio. This implies that the only factor-price ratios compatible with economic equilibrium are the ones at which good A is capital-intensive. Therefore, the contract curve for Country II has to go above the diagonal of its box.

From this it follows that good A is labor-intensive in Country I and capital-intensive in Country II, and that good B is capital-intensive in Country I but labor-intensive in Country II.

The next step is to look into the interrelationships among commodity prices, factor prices, and factor intensities in the two countries. If the relative price of good A increases, Country I will move along its contract curve from the O corner toward the O' corner. As good A is the labor-intensive good in Country I, the relative price of labor will rise and producers will go over to more capital-intensive methods of production. If we use ρ_{1a} to denote the capital/labor ratio in industry A in Country I (i.e., $\rho_{1a} = C_{1a}/L_{1a}$), we find that P_a/P_b is an increasing function of ρ_{1a} in Country I.

Country II, by analogy, will move along its contract curve from the O corner toward the O'' corner if the relative price of good A goes up.

98

Factor reversals
and factor prices:
the Leontief paradox

FIGURE 7.4

Commodity prices and factor prices under factor reversal

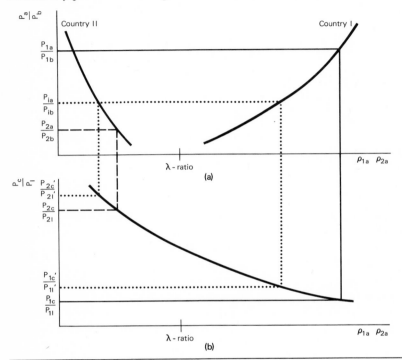

However, in Country II good A is the capital-intensive good. Therefore, the relative price of capital will increase and the producers will go over to more labor-intensive methods of production. Using the notation introduced above, we find that in Country II P_a/P_b is a decreasing function of ρ_{2a}.

These interrelationships are illustrated in Figure 7.4. On the vertical axis in Figure 7.4a we have relative commodity prices, P_a/P_b, and on the horizontal axis we have the capital/labor ratios, ρ_{1a} and ρ_{2a} in industry A. Figure 7.4a illustrates the fact that in Country I the relative price of good A is an increasing function of the capital/labor ratio in industry A, while in Country II it is a decreasing function of the capital/labor ratio in industry A.

Both Figures 7.3 and 7.4 illustrate the fact that the sets of possible capital/labor ratios in the two countries are separated by the critical λ ratio.

Using the notation just introduced, we find that the capital/labor ratios in Country I in both industries—i.e., ρ_{1a} and ρ_{1b}—are greater than the capital/labor ratios in Country II, ρ_{2a} and ρ_{2b}. It can be seen from Figures 7.3 and 7.4 that the most labor-intensive methods of production used in Country I will be more capital-intensive than the most capital-intensive methods of production in Country II. This naturally depends on Country I's being much more abundant in capital than Country II. It also implies, as can be seen from Figure 7.4, that the relative price of capital will always be higher in Country II than in Country I, regardless of what methods of production are used in the two countries.

What then will be the implications for trade patterns and factor prices when factor reversals exist? With factor reversals it is no longer possible to infer anything about comparative advantage and trade patterns from factor prices before trade. This can be shown with the help of Figure 7.4. Let us assume that before trade good A is relatively expensive in Country I and relatively cheap in Country II. This is illustrated by the solid line, showing relative commodity and factor prices in Country I before trade, and by the dashed line, showing relative commodity and factor prices in Country II before trade.

When trade is opened up between the two countries, Country I will export good B and Country II will export good A. The international terms of trade will move to P_{ia}/P_{ib} in Figure 7.4, illustrated by the dotted line. It follows that Country I, the capital-rich country, will export its capital-intensive good, and Country II, the labor-abundant country, will also export *its* capital-intensive good. Hence both countries will export their respective capital-intensive goods.

This follows from the simple fact that both countries will not export the same good. But with factor reversals, if good A is labor-intensive in one country it is capital-intensive in the other country, and vice versa. Hence it follows that either both countries export their respective capital-intensive good or else both countries export their respective labor-intensive good.

In our example, Country I, which is abundant in capital, exported its capital-intensive good. There is, however, nothing that prevents it from exporting instead its labor-intensive good. Had good B been relatively expensive in Country I before trade, the country would have exported good A, its labor-intensive good. Hence with factor reversals it is fully conceivable that the capital-rich country exports its labor-intensive good and the labor-abundant country exports its capital-intensive good. This holds true even if

100

Factor reversals
and factor prices:
the Leontief paradox

we define capital abundance and labor abundance in terms of factor prices. Hence the Heckscher–Ohlin theorem does not hold when factor reversals exist.

In a way, however, this is only a superficial objection to the Heckscher–Ohlin theorem. The theorem does not hold true in the literal interpretation given above, but it still holds in a deeper sense. It is true that the country abundant in capital might export its labor-intensive good. It is also true, however, that even in the production of this good the capital-rich country will use methods of production that are more capital-intensive than any of the methods of production used by the labor-abundant country.

In other words, even though the capital-rich country might export its labor-intensive good, its methods of production even in the labor-intensive industry will be more capital-intensive than will the labor-rich country's methods of production in its capital-intensive line of production. Analogously, the labor-rich country will always use more labor-intensive methods of production in both its industries than will the capital-rich country in either of its industries. In this deeper sense, therefore, the Heckscher–Ohlin theorem will still hold.

What about the factor-price-equalization theorem? Will it still hold? No; the factor-price-equalization theorem will not hold, given factor reversals. This can easily be seen from Figure 7.4. Country I will export good B, its capital-intensive good. This will increase the relative demand for capital, and the relative price of capital will increase because of trade. Country II will export good B, *its* capital-intensive good. Therefore, in Country II also the demand for capital will increase relatively and its relative price will go up. Hence the relative price of capital will go up in both countries.

We have no way of knowing in which country the relative price of capital will increase more. It might increase more in Country I; then there will be a tendency to factor-price equalization. But it might just as likely increase more in Country II; then there will be a tendency to increase the difference between relative factor prices in the two countries. With factor reversals, however, there is no possibility for factor-price equalization in the two countries. This can easily be seen from Figure 7.4. The relative price of capital will always be lower in the capital-rich country than in the labor-rich country, and the return for labor will always be relatively lower in the labor-rich country than in the capital-rich country.

Perhaps the most interesting empirical test of the Heckscher–Ohlin theorem that has been made so far is a study undertaken by Wassily Leontief in the early 1950s.[1] A very intensive debate followed on the publication of Leontief's somewhat paradoxical findings. One way of explaining his result is by reference to factor reversals. Before concluding this chapter and the part of the book that deals with the pure theory of trade, it might be worth while to discuss briefly Leontief's findings and some of the more important aspects of the discussion of the Leontief paradox.

THE EMPIRICAL RELEVANCE OF THE HECKSCHER–OHLIN THEOREM: THE LEONTIEF PARADOX

Leontief starts from the observation that a country will tend to export those commodities which use its abundant factors of production intensively and import those which use its scarce factors intensively. By common consent the United States is the one country that is most abundantly endowed with capital. Therefore, one would expect the United States to export capital-intensive goods and import labor-intensive ones.

Leontief tests his hypothesis with the help of an input–output table for the United States for 1947. He assumes that the United States decreases its production of exports and its imports by an equal amount, $1 million. This can be achieved, for instance, by an increase in tariffs, making the relative price of imports go up, thereby stimulating production of import-competing goods and making the relative price of exports fall, thereby curtailing production of exports.

Leontief then goes on to see what effects this change in the production pattern will have on the use of the factors of production. He only takes two factors explicitly into account, labor and capital. When exports are decreased, both labor and capital are released. When production of import-competing goods is increased, both more labor and capital are needed. According to Leontief's hypothesis, we would expect relatively much capital to be released from the export industries and relatively much labor to be needed by the import-competing industries.

---

[1] W. W. Leontief, "Domestic Production and Foreign Trade: the American Capital Position Re-examined," *Proceedings of the American Philosophical Society*, vol. 97, September 1953, pp. 332 ff.

102

Factor reversals
and factor prices:
the Leontief paradox

His finding, however, is that it is the other way around. Export industries use relatively more labor than do import-competing industries. Hence the United States exports labor-intensive goods and imports capital-intensive goods!

How are we to explain Leontief's paradoxical results—that the most capital-rich of all countries, the United States, exports labor-intensive goods?

Like all empirical findings, Leontief's paradox can be explained in a number of ways. We can in this context only touch on what we regard as some of the main contributions to the heated controversy that Leontief's findings gave rise to.

To start with, we might mention that several writers questioned the accuracy and the appropriateness of the data. N. S. Buchanan criticized Leontief's measurement of capital: He argued that Leontief's capital coefficients were "investment requirement coefficients" which did not take into account the durability of capital.[2] G. A. Loeb argued that the differences in capital intensity between the export sector and the import-competing sector were not statistically significant.[3] B. C. Swerling contended that 1947 (the year for which the input–output table was constructed) was an atypical year.[4]

Leontief refined his measurements and tried to answer this and some other criticism in a paper published in 1956.[5] This paper hardly settled all the points about measurements and the like. This was not to be expected. There are too many difficulties involved for any completely unambiguous conclusions to come forward. Renewed measurements for later years might reveal a picture other than the one given by Leontief. Until then it seems reasonable to accept Leontief's measurements as basically correct. Let us then go on to the theoretically more interesting question of what explanations can be given for the Leontief paradox, provided we are willing to accept the data on which it is founded.

---

[2] N. S. Buchanan, "Lines on the Leontief Paradox," *Economia Internazionale*, vol. 8, November 1955, pp. 791 ff.

[3] G. A. Loeb, "A Estrutura do Comércio Exterior da América do Norte," *Revista Brasileira de Economia*, vol. 8, December 1954, pp. 81 ff.

[4] B. C. Swerling, "Capital Shortage and Labor Surplus in the United States," *Review of Economics and Statistics*, vol. 36, August 1954, pp. 286 ff.

[5] W. W. Leontief, "Factor Proportions and the Structure of American Trade: Further Theoretical and Empirical Analysis," *Review of Economics and Statistics*, vol. 38, November 1956, pp. 386 ff.

Several alternative explanations of the Leontief paradox have been given, including the ones forwarded by Leontief himself. We will now briefly discuss the most interesting of these explanations.

One explanation is fully compatible with the Heckscher–Ohlin theory. We know from Chapter 5 that in the case of consistent factor intensities, differential factor endowments establish a comparative advantage in each country for the production of the good using its intensive factor. But demand conditions might offset this predisposition. If the capital-rich country, for instance, prefers capital-intensive goods, it might import these and export labor-intensive goods instead. From data relating to factor coefficients in export goods and import-competing goods alone, no inference can be made about factor endowments.[6]

There is, however, little empirical evidence to support this view. Studies made by H. S. Houthakker show that there is a considerable similarity in demand functions among countries.[7] To date there is little evidence that capital-rich countries have a disproportionate tendency to consume capital-intensive goods. This type of explanation is a theoretical possibility but it does not seem to be a very likely one in view of existing evidence; it is more a theoretical *curiosum* than a very likely empirical possibility.

Leontief himself tried to explain his findings along two different lines. The one he gave priority ran in terms of differences in labor productivity. Leontief argued that American labor could not really be compared to labor in other countries, because the productivity of an American worker is substantially higher (three times higher, suggested Leontief) than that of a foreign worker. This would be one way, according to Leontief, by which his findings could be reconciled with the Heckscher–Ohlin theorem.

If production functions are identical between countries, if factor reversals are ruled out, and if factors of production are homogeneous and identical between countries except for a multiplication constant (Leontief suggested a constant of 3 for labor in the United States), Leontief's explanation might be valid.

---

[6] The argument about the perverse demand effects as an explanation of the Leontief paradox has been proposed by Stefan Valavanis-Vail, "Leontief's Scarce Factor Paradox," *Journal of Political Economy*, vol. 52, December 1954, pp. 523 ff.

[7] H. S. Houthakker, "An International Comparison of Household Expenditure Patterns, Commemorating the Centenary of Engel's Law," *Econometrica*, vol. 25, October 1957, pp. 532 ff.

104

Factor reversals
and factor prices:
the Leontief paradox

These are quite strong assumptions to accept. Most economists might acknowledge the superior quality of U.S. labor. Leontief quotes a study by I. B. Kravis indicating that wages are higher in U.S. export industries than in its import-competing industries as supporting evidence.[8] This, however, conflicts with Leontief's assumption of labor being a homogeneous factor of production, which would imply the same wage irrespective of occupation.

Difficulties such as these are easily encountered if one is willing to accept Leontief's explanation. It is not easy to swallow the multiplicative constant 3 without further ado. This would then also have to be explained. It could be explained by the fact that skilled workers have capital embedded in them by being a product of capital-intensive educational institutions. Then it might be argued that the United States is still exporting capital-intensive goods but goods intensive in human capital.

Explanations like these, however, easily become somewhat farfetched. They are not easily compatible with the assumptions of identical production functions between countries and the homogeneity of factors of production, two assumptions that are critical for reaching the Heckscher–Ohlin result. Leontief's explanation is a little too good to be true. It is possible, but it rests on very stringent assumptions. It has a flair of being an ad hoc justification of a puzzling result.

Another explanation for which Leontief has shown a certain understanding is connected with the two-factor framework and the broad use of the term capital. The only two factors explicitly taken into account are labor and capital. But, as Leontief notes: "Invisible in all these tables but ever present as a third factor or rather as a whole additional set of factors determining this country's productive capacity and, in particular, its comparative advantage vis-à-vis the rest of the world, are natural resources: agricultural lands, forests, rivers and our rich mineral deposits."[9]

By taking into account this third factor an explanation to the Leontief paradox can be found. It might be the case, for instance, that imports require more capital to labor than exports; it is still, however, possible that imports are intensive in the third factor, say land. If capital and the third factor (land) are substitutes but both are complementary with labor, it might

---

[8] I. B. Kravis, "Wages and Foreign Trade," *Review of Economics and Statistics*, vol. 38, February 1956, pp. 14 ff.
[9] Leontief, "Domestic Production and Foreign Trade; the American Capital Position Re-examined," *op. cit.*, p. 346.

be the case that import-competing goods are capital-intensive in the United States but land-intensive abroad. By bringing a third factor into account in this way, possible explanations might be found.

The analytically most interesting explanation is perhaps the one that invokes factor reversals. We have already discussed the theoretical meaning of factor reversals in the beginning of this chapter. Let us now look into the implications of the existence of factor reversals for Leontief's results.

Leontief took only one country into account. He only computed factor requirements for marginal changes in the production of American exports and import-competing goods. In the beginning of this chapter we have, however, demonstrated that if factor reversals exist, it is fully possible for a capital-rich country to export its labor-intensive goods. The country will still use more capital-intensive methods in its export industries than any other country.

Leontief never brought a second country into the picture. Had he done so and compared, for instance, the factor intensities in American export industries with those of Japan or Western Europe, he might well have found that American exports were capital-intensive compared to Japanese or Western European exports. By invoking factor reversals we can thus explain Leontief's puzzling results.[10]

An interesting empirical study of the possibility of factor reversals has been made by B. S. Minhas.[11] Minhas has together with some other economists derived a new form of production function, the so-called C.E.S., or homohypallagic, production function.[12] When estimating this production function for different countries Minhas finds that factor reversals are quite common because the elasticity of substitution differs between industries, and that these factor reversals occur in the empirically relevant range of relative factor prices (i.e.,factor/price ratios prevailing in such diverse countries as the United States and India).[13] This result would tend to reinforce the

---

[10] This point is made by R. W. Jones in "Factor Proportions and the Heckscher–Ohlin Theorem," *Review of Economic Studies*, vol. 24, 1956, pp. 1 ff.

[11] B. S. Minhas, *An International Comparison of Factor Costs and Factor Use*, Amsterdam, North Holland Publishing Company, 1963.

[12] K. J. Arrow, H. B. Chenery, B. S. Minhas, and R. M. Solow, "Capital-Labor Substitution and Economic Efficiency," *Review of Economics and Statistics*, vol. 43, August 1961, pp. 225 ff. C.E.S. stands for constant elasticity of substitution. Homohypallagic is compounded from the two Greek words homo ("same") and hypallage ("substitution").

[13] Minhas, *op. cit.*, pp. 32 ff.

106

Factor reversals
and factor prices:
the Leontief paradox

theoretical possibility of factor reversals as an explanation of the Leontief paradox. Minhas's findings would, alas, also tend to minimize the practical relevance of the factor-price-equalization theorem and the Heckscher–Ohlin theorem about capital-rich countries exporting capital-intensive goods, as both these theorems build on the assumption of a one-to-one correspondence between factor prices and factor intensities.

Minhas's study is, therefore, of considerable empirical relevance. His findings have, however, been criticized on econometric grounds, primarily by Leontief. Leontief has recalculated some of Minhas's results using additional information. He then finds that the possibility of factor reversals is much less than Minhas suggests.[14]

Leontief's argument carries a great deal of conviction. This is not to say that the controversy is thereby closed. On the contrary, the empirical relevance of factor reversals is still a very open question. Pending further research, it seems wise not to express a firm opinion in this matter.

Another explanation to the Leontief paradox has been given by Erik Hoffmeyer. He argues that if products relying to a large extent on natural resources are excluded from Leontief's list of goods, the normally expected picture that the United States exports capital-intensive goods and imports labor-intensive goods will prevail.[15]

Hoffmeyer's conclusion is still not completely satisfactory. Some of the products that the United States imports are highly capital-intensive, e.g., petroleum, copper, and newsprint. These products are probably as capital-intensive in other countries as in the United States. At the same time production of these goods might be more efficient outside the United States and hence require a smaller quantity of inputs per unit produced.[16]

Hoffmeyer's conclusion raises some questions. Why is it that the United States does not import more of these resource-rich products if they are cheaper abroad than at home? Why should just these products be excluded? Are they the only ones in which the United States has comparative disadvantage?

[14] W. W. Leontief, "An International Comparison of Factor Costs and Factor Use: A Review Article," *American Economic Review*, vol. 54, June 1964, pp. 335 ff.
[15] Erik Hoffmeyer, "The Leontief Paradox Critically Examined," *Manchester School of Economic and Social Studies*, vol. 26, May 1958, pp. 160 ff.
[16] This point has also been made by M. A. Diab, *The United States Capital Position and the Structure of its Foreign Trade*, Amsterdam, North Holland Publishing Company, 1956.

An answer to these questions has been suggested by William P. Travis. All the discussants of the Leontief paradox have so far implicitly assumed that the law of comparative advantage determines the existing pattern of trade. Travis takes the opposite view. He wants to explain the Leontief paradox with the help of U.S. trade policy.

He refers to the fact that U.S. trade is highly protected, a fact even more true when Leontief made his study than it is today. Travis explains the Leontief paradox as merely a quirk of nature. When Leontief made his study, most competitive imports consisted of crude oil, paper pulp, primary copper and lead, and metallic ores. These products were imported because the United States simply could not produce them. These products are more capital-intensive than any other products. According to Travis, U.S. protective policies alone, therefore, are sufficient to explain the Leontief paradox.[17]

The discussion of the Leontief paradox has hardly been able to establish firm conclusions. It has provided a good deal of insight into the foreign trade position of the United States, but it has hardly helped to establish or refute the Heckscher–Ohlin theory of international trade.

It might seem strange that so much theoretical speculation has been built on such fairly limited empirical investigations. This has not only to do with the fact that many economists prefer theoretical inventiveness to painstaking empirical research. It has also, probably, to do with the fact that the pure theory of trade is quite abstract by nature. Static theories such as the factor-price-equalization theorem or the Heckscher–Ohlin theory of comparative advantage should perhaps not, as was pointed out in Chapter 5, primarily be viewed as geared toward empirical testing. They are first and foremost means of studying the general equilibrium characteristics of open economies.

SUMMARY AND CONCLUSION

In the first seven chapters of the book we have covered the static part of the pure theory of international trade in a careful manner. We have thereby

---

[17] W. P. Travis, *The Theory of Trade and Protection*, Cambridge, Mass., Harvard University Press, 1964, chaps. 3 and 4.

108

Factor reversals
and factor prices:
the Leontief paradox

been able to give an explanation to the causes of trade. We have also seen why countries will gain by trading.

By studying the trade model connected with the names of Heckscher and Ohlin we have also been able to get a good understanding of the meaning of general equilibrium. We have seen how the possibility of trade causes a change in commodity prices, giving rise to a change in factor prices, to a reallocation of factors of production, and to a change in the production structure. All these variables are intimately linked together and it is not possible to change one of them without changing all the others. We should by now have a good grasp of how the essential variables in a trading system are interrelated to each other.

Along the way we have introduced economic concepts and geometric tools. We are now familiar with the use of production-possibility curves, indifference curves, and box diagrams in the exposition of trade theory.

Having worked our way through the static part of pure trade theory, we can now continue to fresh pastures. In Part II we will study economic growth and international trade, including the effects of increases in factor endowments, of capital accumulation and population increases on trade, and of technical progress on trade. We will find that the tools developed in the first part of the book and the results achieved there will be absolutely essential in order for us to say anything more precise about growth and trade. The theory of growth and trade will then help us to cast light on the trading relationships between industrial countries and less-developed countries. We will be able to explain, for instance, why less-developed countries have suffered deteriorating terms of trade.

Then in later parts of the book we will go on to study the balance of payments, the theory of trade policy; and the problems of international liquidity. This will all be facilitated by our study of the pure theory of trade.

SELECTED BIBLIOGRAPHY: CHAPTERS 6 AND 7

An important work that should be mentioned in connection with the general equilibrium models of international trade is:

J. L. Mosak, *General Equilibrium Theory in International Trade*, Bloomington, Ind., Principia Press, 1944.

For a discussion of the role of factor reversals which has influenced the exposition in Chapter 7 see:

> R. W. Jones, " Factor Proportions and the Heckscher–Ohlin Theorem," *RES*, January 1956.

Two interesting papers that give a somewhat critical appraisal of the importance of the factor-price equalization theorem and stress the role of the restricting assumptions are:

> S. F. James and I. F. Pearce, " The Factor Price Equalization Myth," *RES*, no. 49, 1951–52.

> R. Robinson, "Factor Proportions and Comparative Advantage," *QJE*, May 1956.

For a bibliography of the discussion of the Leontief paradox the reader is referred to the footnotes in Chapter 7. An excellent summary is provided in Chipman, *op. cit.*, Part 3.

PART II

Economic
growth and
international
trade

Economic growth and international trade during the nineteenth and twentieth centuries

8

In the first seven chapters we studied the theory of international trade under static conditions. We took an economic system characterized by no trade, introduced the possibility of trade, and studied in a careful way the characteristics of the new equilibrium with trade. This part of trade theory is completely static.

Now we have to go on and see what happens to two countries' trading relationships given economic growth, i.e., provided that some fundamental variables in the trading system change. New methods will have to be used to do this. We then no longer study only the characteristics of a static, never-changing situation. The methodology that we will use is that of comparative statics. We now start from a given equilibrium situation, introduce a change in one of the variables—for instance, in the amount of capital available to an economy—and study the implications for the new equilibrium, given this change.

Before we go into the theoretical aspects of economic growth and international trade, it is appropriate to say a few words about the long-run development of the world economy.

THE GROWTH OF WORLD TRADE DURING THE NINETEENTH AND TWENTIETH CENTURIES: A BIRD'S-EYE VIEW

The nineteenth century, from an economic point of view, is remarkable. Earlier centuries had witnessed economic development, but on a slow and modest scale. The limited amount of empirical evidence that exists shows that, for instance in Great Britain, probably the most vigorously expanding country during the eighteenth century, total product grew by 5 percent per decade from 1700 to 1780, and that income per capita increased by 2 percent per decade during the same period.

This shows that an economic transformation of the British society took place during the eighteenth century, and that the change occurred at a slow pace. The nineteenth century, by contrast, showed very high rates of growth in several fields. The growth of the British economy, for instance, was spectacular: Britain's population more than trebled during the nineteenth century, despite heavy emigration, and the national income seems to have increased more than sevenfold at current prices.

Economic growth and
international trade during the
nineteenth and twentieth centuries

TABLE 8.1

World foreign trade from 1750 to 1889

	Approx. 1750	1820– 1830	1830– 1840	1840– 1850	1850– 1860	1860– 1870	1870– 1880	1880– 1889
World trade, at 1865–1885 prices (millions of £)	153	315	410	662	1058	1616	2483	3497
Rate of growth per decade (%)		10.1	30.2	61.5	59.8	52.7	53.7	43.4

SOURCE: S. Kuznets, *Modern Economic Growth: Rate, Structure, and Spread*, New Haven, Conn., Yale University Press, 1966, pp. 306–307.

Britain was not the only country to experience rapid economic growth. The United States showed an even higher rate of growth, especially during the latter half of the nineteenth century. Several European countries, and some countries overseas, too, especially those colonized by Britain, also showed rapid economic development.

The growth of world trade is an important aspect of economic development during the nineteenth century. Tables 8.1 and 8.2 summarize this development. The tables contain some important and interesting information. First, the rate of growth of world trade was quite low from around 1750 to 1820. During this period, trade seems to have increased by about 10 percent per decade, or 1 percent per annum.

Needless to say, the statistical information for this period is not too reliable. Trade between the relatively developed countries and the more isolated parts of the world could possibly have been measured inadequately. Smuggling, which at this time was not insignificant, is not taken into account, and so on. It is hardly probable, however, that factors such as these would influence the broad trend, which shows that foreign trade grew at a very moderate pace from the middle of the eighteenth century up to approximately 1820.

After the Napoleonic wars, from around 1820, world trade started to grow at a brisk pace. During the 1820s and 1830s, trade speeded up, international trade growing at an astonishingly steady rate during most of the nineteenth century. The rate of growth, by roughly 30-year periods, was

TABLE 8.2

World foreign trade from 1881 to 1913

	1881–1885	1886–1890	1891–1895	1896–1900	1901–1905	1906–1910	1911–1913	1913
World trade, at 1913 prices (billions of $)	15.69	18.13	19.97	22.54	27.52	32.88	39.07	40.50
Rate of growth per decade (%)		42.0	27.3	24.2	37.8	45.9	47.6	

SOURCE: Kuznets, *op. cit.*, pp. 306–307.

50 percent per decade between 1820–1830 and 1850–1860, and between 1850–1860 and 1880–1889.

The next 30-year period, from the 1880s to the beginning of World War I, also showed a very marked increase in world trade, although the relative rate of growth was somewhat lower: From 1881–1885 to 1911–1913, world trade grew at a rate of 37 percent per decade. For the long period as a whole, i.e., from the 1820s to 1913, the rate of growth of world trade was 46 percent per decade.

Another interesting fact is the trend in foreign trade ratios. We have seen that trade grew rapidly. For most countries, their foreign trade grew faster than their national income. This led to an increase in the foreign trade quota. Around 1840, the proportion of foreign trade to the British national product was roughly 20 percent; at the outbreak of World War I, this proportion had grown to over 40 percent.[1]

Other European countries experienced an analogous development. The foreign trade proportion of France was 21.9 in 1859; around 1910 it had risen to 35.2. Italy and the Scandinavian countries also showed a marked increase in their dependence on foreign trade. Germany is the only exception, showing a more or less stable foreign trade quota during the latter half of the nineteenth century.

---

[1] The given figures for the proportion of foreign trade measure the sum of exports and imports related to GNP. The figures are taken from Kuznets, *op. cit.*, pp. 312 ff.

116

Economic growth and
international trade during the
nineteenth and twentieth centuries

Other " new " countries which underwent a rapid economic development showed a diverse picture in this respect. Japan followed the general
European pattern and had a rapidly growing foreign trade ratio: Around
1880 it amounted to only 10 percent of GNP; at the outbreak of World
War I it had risen to 30 percent. Other " new " countries, such as the United
States, Canada, and Australia, showed a steady, or even falling, foreign trade
ratio. For Canada, the ratio showed some fluctuations, but the trend was on
the whole steady. Australia and the United States showed a slight fall in
their ratios: The United States had a foreign trade ratio of 13 percent in the
1840s; at the beginning of the twentieth century, it had fallen to 11 percent; apart from showing a declining trend, the foreign trade ratio of the
United States was remarkably small.

In a general way, the changes in the foreign trade proportions could
be regarded as the result of two competing sets of forces: On the one hand,
those that induce growth of domestic output, and, on the other, those that
induce growth of exports and imports. It is obvious that the trade generating
growth factors were very strong during the nineteenth century. For most
countries, trade grew faster than domestic output. The main European
countries, especially Britain, economically the most important, showed an
export-biased type of growth. The major exception is the United States,
which even during the nineteenth century showed an import-biased type
of growth.[2]

To explain the pattern of growth and trade is a large and involved
undertaking. This chapter presents only a broad outline of this process;
therefore we will merely point to some of the most important causes of this
development.

One is that the nineteenth century was dominated by a great revolution in transport connected with the development of railroads and ocean
transport. The railroads led to an opening up of new territories such as the
west of the United States, and of formerly underdeveloped parts of Canada,
Argentina, and Australia, which then became exporting areas of agricultural
products. In Europe, the introduction of railroads led to an increase in both
foreign and domestic trade. The development of ocean transport made
possible an increase in the trade between Europe and the countries overseas.

It seems that for the " new " countries, such as the United States,

---

2 The terms export- and import-biased growth are explained in Chapter 9, where
the theory underlying the concepts is also discussed.

Australia, Canada, and Argentina, the improvements of transport had the strongest effects on domestic trade. These countries also showed high rates of growth during the nineteenth century. In Europe, on the other hand, improvements in transport mostly favored foreign trade.

Another important aspect was the continuous absorption of previously closed areas into the network of world trade: Japan is the most conspicuous example. Apart from Japan and the "new" countries referred to above, foreign trade did not induce any strong domestic growth. The other less-developed countries remained underdeveloped and had mostly the character of trade posts of the developing countries.

Economic policy also played an important role. For most of the nineteenth century, Britain was the world's leading economic nation. It was there that the industrial revolution started in the middle of the eighteenth century, and consequently she became the center of the world economy. Britain was an island with limited resources, so it was natural for her economy to be geared to trade. The classical British doctrine of comparative advantage developed by Ricardo and others in the early nineteenth century stressed, as we have seen, the gains from trade. The doctrine of free trade was the cornerstone of Britain's economic policy, and the British economists preached the virtues of free trade.[3] At least until the last quarter of the nineteenth century, there was also a marked lowering of trade barriers. This could hardly have done other than have greatly favored the growth of world trade.

Britain's economic growth was centered around manufacturing. It was of an export-biased kind, and Britain was the main supplier of industrial products to the rest of the world. As the British economy grew, it became increasingly specialized. It depended more and more on imports, of which agricultural goods and raw materials were the most important. Britain's imports came from the United States, to some extent from Central Europe, from what have been called "regions of recent settlement"—i.e., Canada, Argentina, Uruguay, South Africa, Australia, and New Zealand—and from the Scandinavian countries. All these countries experienced a great impetus for economic growth through an increased demand from Britain for their exports. They could start to grow by exporting food products and raw material to Britain, and they could continue to grow because Britain's demand for their exports kept growing.

---

[3] See also Chapters 19, 20, and 21.

118

Economic growth and
international trade during the
nineteenth and twentieth centuries

TABLE 8.3

Percentage distribution of British imports by countries of origin

	1857–1859	1911–1913
United States	19	19
Other " new " countries[a]	8	18
Industrial Europe[b]	21	23
All other areas	52	40
	100	100

[a] Canada, Argentina, South Africa, Australia, and New Zealand.
[b] Germany, France, Italy, Belgium, and the Netherlands.

SOURCE: R. Nurkse, *Patterns of Trade and Development*, Oxford, Blackwell, 1962 (2nd pr.), p. 16.

A significant fact to bear in mind is that countries which could be classified among the less-developed at this time—the regions of recent settlement and the Scandinavian countries—especially benefited from this type of growth. Table 8.3 gives a hint of this.

We know that Britain's imports grew rapidly during the nineteenth century. Table 8.3 indicates that the " new " countries increased their share of British imports very substantially. For these countries, and for some others, such as the Scandinavian countries, trade truly served as—to use Dennis Robertson's well-known phrase—an engine of growth.

From the point of view of theory, we can observe the following. We know that international trade along the lines of comparative advantage brings about an improved allocation of existing resources and gains from trade. But static trade theory has no implications for growth; it can only tell how resources ought to be allocated at a given point in time. At a time when transport improved greatly in efficiency, when policy barriers to trade were removed and countries entered into trade with each other, static trade theory did have a great deal of relevance. But once the countries in question had started to trade and had reallocated their resources, what happened?

About this, the static theory has little to say. What happened was that the central country of the world economy, Britain, grew at a steady pace. Her imports grew even faster. Her trading partners, the " peripheral countries " to use Prebisch's phrase, saw their exports expand rapidly; they could continue to grow along a pattern suggested by the theory of compara-

TABLE 8.4

World foreign trade from 1913 to 1960

	1913	1928	1937	1950	1960
Index of volume of world exports (1913 = 100)	100	113	114	131	244
Rate of growth per decade (%)		8.5	1.0	11.3	86.0

SOURCE: Kuznets, *op. cit.*, p. 308.

tive advantage. The theory itself did not promise any growth, but it so happened that the demand for the products in which the "peripheral" countries had specialized grew rapidly.

The first half of the twentieth century did not show any comparable expansion of world trade. Trade between countries continued to grow but on a much more modest scale. Table 8.4 illustrates this. One important point to note is that trade did not increase nearly as fast during the first half of the twentieth century as it did during the nineteenth century: From 1913 to 1960, it only increased by 21 percent per decade, or about 2 percent per annum. The growth rate of world trade had been more than double that figure during the nineteenth century. Even if we allow for World War I being an abnormal interval, the growth rate for the period 1928 to 1960 is only 27 percent per decade.

Another important aspect of the development of world trade since World War I is its unevenness. During the 1920s, there was a modest growth of around 1 percent per annum; in the 1930s, there was a complete standstill. During the 1940s, there was again a modest growth; and during the 1950s, a very rapid growth, over 8 percent per annum.

Much of this development is explained by the upheavals of the first half of the twentieth century. During the 50 years since 1913, a full decade was taken up by the two world wars. Another decade was characterized by deep depression. Several years were taken up by recovery after the wars; these were painful years, especially for the countries that had suffered heavy

120

Economic growth and
international trade during the
nineteenth and twentieth centuries

damage in the wars. No comparable, long periods of disruption took place during the nineteenth century.

Because of the disruptions, it is difficult to allocate meaningful measures for the development of foreign trade proportions. It seems that most of the important industrial countries experienced a fall in their foreign trade proportions during World War I, so that their foreign trade quotas were lower in the 1920s than they were in 1913. This applies, for instance, to the major European countries and to the United States.[4]

It is quite clear that this fall in foreign trade proportions was accentuated during the following three decades. The foreign trade proportion of the United States was 10.8 in the 1920s; in the 1950s, it had fallen to 7.9. Other major countries show an analogous development during the same period: in Britain it fell from 38.1 to 30.4, in France from 51.3 to 41.2, in Italy from 26.3 to 25.0, and in Japan from 35.5 to 18.8.[5]

One important conclusion is therefore that during the first half of the twentieth century, we can witness a marked decrease in the dependence on foreign trade by the leading industrial countries. The volume of world trade continued to grow despite wars and depression. But its rate of growth was impeded much more than were the rates of growth of the national income of the leading countries.

Another important feature of the development during this period was the emergence of the Communist countries. This tended to decrease trade. The proportion of exports to national income in Russia was estimated at 10.4 percent in 1913, whereas it ranged around 2 percent in the Soviet Union in the 1950s. The foreign trade ratio of Communist China is probably also lower than that for normal times in China before the Communist revolution.

The upshot is therefore that the major changes occurring since 1913 have had a more retarding effect on trade flows than on national incomes. The world wars have impeded foreign trade more than output and capacity to produce. The effects of the prolonged depression were more harmful to trade than to domestic production; this seems to follow to a large extent from the fact that the depression induced protectionist policy measures. The emergence of Communist countries, which for different reasons pursued autarchic trade policies, also hampered trade.

---

4 See Kuznets, *op. cit.*, pp. 312 ff.
5 Kuznets, *op. cit.*, pp. 312 ff. The figures for France relate the sum of exports and imports to physical product.

We have seen that world trade and trade among industrial countries increased at a relatively slow pace during the first half of the twentieth century. This pattern also applies for the less-developed countries: The retardation of world trade was even more pronounced for them. We will return to their situation and to the development of world trade since World War II at the end of this chapter. First, we will briefly examine capital movements and take a somewhat closer look at one case where trade functioned as an engine of growth along the standard nineteenth-century pattern, the case of Sweden.

INTERNATIONAL CAPITAL MOVEMENTS

International capital movements played an important role during the nineteenth century. They provided an outlet for savings in the mature, industrial countries and helped to finance development in countries then emerging from a traditional, agricultural economy. They also helped to ease the balance-of-payments problems of the rapidly developing "new" countries.

Table 8.5 summarizes some information about the major lending countries.

Table 8.5 shows the position for only three major credit countries. These, however, had a dominating position at the time: Together, they accounted in 1913 for about three quarters of the total gross debt outstanding. Table 8.5 is therefore quite a good indicator of the amount and importance of international lending during the period in question.

The annual value of world trade in 1913 prices amounted in 1881–1885 to about $6 billions per year; it increased to about $13 billions per year in 1913. The capital outflows for the 1874–1914 period averaged between $1/2 and 1.1 billions per year. The outflow of foreign capital seems therefore to have amounted to roughly 10 percent of the trade volume. This is quite a substantial figure and shows that capital movements played an important role during the 45 years before World War I.

There was no marked rise in the annual flow of capital according to Table 8.5 (with a possible exception of the last few years before 1914). Yet the increase in the cumulative total of foreign capital invested was striking.

122

Economic growth and
international trade during the
nineteenth and twentieth centuries

TABLE 8.5

Foreign capital investments and the shares of three major countries before World War I (absolute figures in billions of dollars)

Gross foreign investment outstanding	Ca. 1874	Ca. 1880	Ca. 1890	Ca. 1900	Begin. 1914
Great Britain	4.6	5.8	9.5	11.7	19.6
France	Not available	3.0	4.0	5.6	9.0
Germany	Not available	1.2	2.8	3.4	5.6
TOTAL	6.0	10.0	16.3	20.7	34.2
Volume per year, 1913 prices		0.62	0.68	0.52	1.09
Total foreign investment, 1913 prices	4.9	8.6	15.4	20.6	35.3

SOURCE: Kuznets, *op. cit.*, p. 322.

The total amount invested rose from $4.9 to 35.3 billions (in 1913 prices) from 1874 to 1913–1914. The growth rate per decade was 64 percent, which is higher than the rates of growth of both foreign trade and national income. The explanation of this phenomenon must have been that these foreign investments earned a good return, and that these earnings were reinvested on the spot. On top of this came the net flow of capital illustrated in Table 8.5. The result of this development was that the stock of foreign capital increased in relation to the national income. This applied to both lending and borrowing countries.

Most of these capital exports seem to have gone to fairly developed countries. The available statistics relate to 1913–1914 only. Table 8.6 shows the distribution of the outstanding foreign gross investments at that time.

It shows that at least half of the foreign capital then outstanding had been invested in developed countries. Of the 28 percent invested in Europe, most had been invested in the developed parts of Europe. To this has to be added the United States, Canada, and Oceania. Then the share going to these parts of the world is well over 50 percent. If Argentina and Japan are also added, the share going to developed countries increases to over 60 percent.

It seems, however, as though the share of investments going to the less-developed parts of the world could have risen during the period 1870–1913. It seems especially as though foreign investments in Europe were

123

TABLE 8.6

Shares of debtor areas in outstanding gross investment in 1913–1914 (in percent)

Europe	28
United States and Canada	24
Oceania	5
Latin America	19
Asia and Africa	24

SOURCE: Kuznets, *op. cit.*, p. 322.

declining relatively, whereas investments in the less-developed parts of the world—both in colonies and independent nations in Africa, Asia, and Latin America—were on the increase. Figures for Britain seem to confirm this view, as shown in Table 8.7.

Around the middle of the nineteenth century and up to 1870, the bulk of British foreign investment went to Europe. During the latter part of the century and in the years leading up to World War I, British capital went instead mostly to the "new" countries, i.e., Argentina, Canada, South Africa, Australia, and New Zealand. It was investments in these countries that expanded by far the most rapidly. But there was also an increase, both absolutely and relatively, in capital going to the colonies; this was, after all, the heyday of European imperialism.

Capital movements were substantial both in absolute and relative terms during this period. The proportion of the annual outflow of capital to national output varied between 1 and 4 percent for the major credit countries. During its peak periods, in 1880–1889 and 1905–1914, Britain sent 5 and 7 percent, respectively, of its GNP as capital exports abroad. In terms of capital formation generated within the country, the share was, of course, much higher. During the peak periods, it was close to 50 percent, and during the whole period 1860–1913 between 25 and 40 percent of gross domestic savings were invested abroad, a high figure indeed. Germany and France also exported a substantial share of their savings as capital exports abroad. These figures show that the world economy had reached a high degree of integration at this time.

Viewed from the angle of the debtor countries, there is little doubt that these capital imports played a critical role for speeding up the rate of domestic investment. The United States had already at this time developed

124

Economic growth and
international trade during the
nineteenth and twentieth centuries

TABLE 8.7

Percentage distribution of total British capital invested overseas

	1870	1913
United States	20	20
Other "new" countries	10	45
Europe	50	5
All other areas	20	30
	100	100

SOURCE: Nurkse, *op. cit.*, p. 17.

a high degree of autarky, but it still financed about 10 percent of its capital formation by capital imports. Toward the end of the century, this position changed, however, and the United States, from being a debtor country became a creditor country, exporting capital, instead.

Japan, the other large country that imported capital, showed a more varied picture. During the time when it imported capital on a massive scale, from 1897 to 1906, it financed about 30 percent of its domestic investment by imported capital.

Capital imports played the largest role for a group of smaller countries. To this group belonged primarily the "regions of recent settlement," i.e., Canada, South Africa, Australia and New Zealand, the Scandinavian countries, and Argentina. Canada, for instance, financed between 30 and 50 percent of her investments by capital imports. Australia similarly, during the period from 1860 to 1900, financed between 20 and 50 percent of her domestic capital formation by imported capital. The bulk of Argentina's capital imports seem to have come during the first two decades of the twentieth century. During this period, roughly 40 percent of investments in Argentina were financed by foreign capital. The Scandinavian countries had also substantial deficits in their balance of payments, which they financed by capital imports. During 1870–1910, foreign capital financed around 20 percent of total investments in these countries.

All these countries were "peripheral" with respect to the leading European industrial nations, especially Britain. Their exports to Britain and other mature industrial nations grew, as we have seen, very rapidly during this period. They needed to invest both in the traditional export lines and in

TABLE 8.8

Foreign capital investments since World War I, all countries
(absolute figures in millions of dollars per year)

	1921–1929	1930–1938	1921–1938	1951–1955	1956–1961
Total per year, flows from all creditor countries	1547	−706	421	4279	7145
Same flows, in 1913 prices	1067	−728	170	2038	3226
Shares of major creditors, flows in current prices (%)					
Great Britain	27.7	14.1	39.1	10.5	10.2
France	21.8	1.3	38.9	2.5	6.2
Germany	Net debtor			2.2	9.2
United States	43.0	78.1	13.6	78.4	67.4

SOURCE: Kuznets, *op. cit.*, p. 323.

various forms of social overhead capital to meet the increased demand for their export products. The original increase in demand led to more investments which, in their turn, through a multiplier effect, led to higher income and a still higher increase in demand, which led to more investments, and so on. The well-known accelerator-multiplier mechanism was at work guaranteeing growth. Slowdowns and crises occurred, but the over-all world economy grew rapidly, and world trade grew even faster. Then as now, the less-developed and semideveloped countries of the era needed capital to invest in order to grow. Being poor, they had difficulties in generating enough savings by themselves. To speed up their growth process they needed to import capital. We have just seen how for several of these "peripheral" countries both trade flows and capital flows formed an integral part of their growth process.

Capital movements played a very small role during the interwar period. This is illustrated in Table 8.8.

We know that the growth of world trade was slowed down during the interwar period. The disruptive effects on the international capital market was even stronger. Before World War I, a net flow of about $1.1 billions went to debtor countries. During the period between the two world wars, only a fraction of this amount was invested abroad. During the 1920s,

126

Economic growth and
international trade during the
nineteenth and twentieth centuries

capital movements still played a role that was not unimportant. During the 1930s, the net flows completely stopped; what happened was that capital was repatriated. During the interwar period as a whole, the importance of capital movements drastically diminished.

Since World War II, capital movements have again been substantial. However, they have to a considerable extent changed their nature. They no longer consist only of private capital flows geared by market considerations. They have to a large extent consisted of government grants and loans. About 30 percent of capital exports during this period has been in the form of government grants, and another 20 percent has consisted of government loans. The major credit nation has been the United States. The Soviet Union and France have also been active in exporting capital.

Private capital flows, especially in the form of direct investments, however, have also played an important role, especially in the years since 1955. We return to this topic in Chapter 25, which is devoted to theoretical and empirical aspects of direct investments.

We have now got a general understanding of the importance of trade and capital movements, especially for the countries on the periphery during the nineteenth century. Trade during this period functioned as an engine of growth for several countries. It might now be useful to illustrate this general principle by taking a brief look into how it worked in a specific case.

GROWTH AND TRADE DURING THE NINETEENTH CENTURY: THE CASE OF SWEDEN

Sweden was, in the beginning of the 1870s, a poorly developed country with more than 70 percent of the population employed in agriculture. Certain prerequisites for growth were at hand: A compulsory school system had been introduced as early as 1842; the administration was honest and competent; and there was a tradition of manufacturing simple products from iron. Nevertheless, the country was poor and primitive in many respects, and it would have been no great surprise if it had remained so.

By the 1870s a sustained growth process had begun. The growth that took place was geared especially toward exports. The dominating export branch up to the beginning of the 1890s was timber and wood products, which made up around 35 percent of total exports. Total exports expanded fast; the export volume rose, on the average, 4 percent a year from 1870 to 1890. The terms of trade also showed a favorable development. Exports of timber and wood products went primarily to England, and the performance of Swedish exports during this period is a good example of how a country could grow by specializing in the production of raw materials that it sold in an expanding market at rising prices.

Another interesting feature of Swedish exports during 1870–1890 is the export of butter. This export group expanded most rapidly of all exports; it comprised 20 percent of the total in 1895. This reflects an important transformation that took place in Swedish agriculture during this time.

Around 1850 Swedish agriculture produced mainly grain, of which it had a considerable export surplus. During the following decades Swedish grain exports were outcompeted, especially by American and Russian producers. Swedish farmers turned instead to production of animal products, concentrating on butter, for which it found an expanding market in Britain. Some other of the traditional export branches, such as bar iron, were less lucky and underwent a drastic decline, especially in relative terms.

By the beginning of the 1890s a new export pattern emerged. Exports of timber and wood and agricultural products lost their momentum and were no longer focal in the growth process. New products took their place. For example, Swedish iron ore deposits were rich in phosphorous. Technical progress in steel production (the application of the Thomas process) made it possible to extract the phosphorous from the iron. Thereby the rich iron ore deposits in Lapland, in the north of Sweden, could be profitably mined. From the 1890s iron ore became one of the expanding export branches.

Other emerging export branches which built on the application of innovations were paper and pulp and engineering products. Innovations made it possible to use spruce and pine as raw material for the production of paper and pulp. Swedish forests provided these trees in abundance, and paper and pulp became one of the rapidly expanding export industries.

Swedish economic history shows many examples of unsuccessful ventures in the engineering industries during the latter part of the nineteenth century. By the end of the century the audacity and innovative spirit of many Swedish engineers and small entrepreneurs started to pay off, and some highly successful companies began to exploit homemade innovations.

128

Economic growth and
international trade during the
nineteenth and twentieth centuries

Examples of such innovations were a lighthouse, separators, diesel engines, some electric products, and, somewhat later, ball bearings. All this led to the engineering industry becoming one of the most expansive export industries from 1890 on.

At the outbreak of World War I the new pattern of Swedish exports was firmly established. The shift in the structure of exports that began around 1890 had matured, and by 1913 the three most expansive export industries, iron ore, paper and pulp, and engineering products, comprised roughly 40 percent of total exports. This pattern has since continued, with the engineering industry as the leading sector, so that over half of Swedish exports today consist of a well-diversified list of engineering products.

Another very interesting aspect of Swedish economic development in the period from 1870 to 1913 is the role of capital movements. Sweden had, almost without exception, consistent deficits in her balance of payments during the 40 years from 1870 to 1910. There was only a short period from 1895 to 1897 during which Swedish trade balanced. The deficits were also quite large: They amounted, on the average, to between 15 and 20 percent of total imports. This meant that a substantial part of Sweden's capital formation during the country's transformation from a less-developed to an industrial economy was provided by foreigners. A large part of this external debt, incidentally, was paid off in inflated prices during World War I.

This is an example of how, during the era of the classic gold standard, long-term capital movements on a large scale helped to speed up the economic growth for a less-developed country by increasing her capacity to invest, and also eased her balance-of-payments problems by providing much-needed foreign currency. According to the textbooks, the gold standard mechanism, given Sweden's strained balance-of-payments situation, should have forced the country to export gold and pursue a deflationary monetary policy. On the contrary, however, the capital imports led to an inflow of gold, which in turn led to an increase in the money supply and made possible an expansionary economic policy. A study of economic history could prove useful for those who are overly worried about the balance-of-payments problems of today's less-developed countries.

It would be premature, however, to treat this topic at length at this stage. We will discuss the role of capital movements in detail when we come to the parts of the book which deal with the theory of the balance of payments and with the problem of international liquidity.

The economic development of any country is a complicated and many-faceted process. It is not possible to give more than a glimpse of it in a couple of pages. Nevertheless, the exposition above should have illustrated the fact that for many of the countries which could be classified as less developed in the nineteenth century or as being on the periphery (to use Prebisch's phrase), trade functioned as an engine of growth. Sweden is a case in point, but its experience is in no way unique.

Today's less-developed countries seem faced with more difficult problems. To grow by specializing according to comparative advantage and to concentrate on promoting export industries is, to many, a dubious proposition. Let us now look into the role of trade in the twentieth century.

WORLD TRADE SINCE 1945: THE LESS-DEVELOPED COUNTRIES

We have seen that, for the twentieth century as a whole, world trade has not expanded very rapidly. But since World War II, the growth has been rapid—during the 20 years since 1945, 7 to 8 percent per annum.

This development, however, has been quite lopsided. It is primarily exports from the industrial, developed countries that have expanded. Exports from the less-developed countries have grown at a relatively modest rate. Table 8.9 gives an indication of this.

The industrial countries have benefited from the rapid increase in world trade that has taken place during the last 20 years. For them, trade has grown faster than national income. Trade in manufactured products, especially, has expanded during the postwar period. Exports of these products have grown rapidly in many developed countries. This in turn has had a favorable effect on the growth of national income in these countries.

Most underdeveloped countries have not experienced a similar stimulus from trade. They have not been able to break into the import markets for manufactured goods in industrial countries. Instead they have continued to export traditional products, such as raw materials and agricultural products, demand for which has grown at only a relatively low rate. The result has been a continual fall in their share of world exports, as indicated in Table 8.9.

How fast the national incomes of the less-developed countries have expanded is a difficult question to answer in a precise and meaningful

130

Economic growth and
international trade during the
nineteenth and twentieth centuries

TABLE 8.9

Growth and export shares, 1950–1965

	Average export growth rates (percent per annum)		Shares of total exports[a] (percent)		
	1950–1960	1960–1965	1950	1960	1965
Industrial countries	8.6	8.4	66	76	78
Less-developed countries	3.6	5.8	34	24	22

[a] Excludes trade between Communist countries; includes exports from non-Communist countries to Communist countries.

SOURCE: United Nations Conference on Trade and Development (UNCTAD), *Handbook for International Trade Statistics*, Doc E/Conf 46/12/Add. 1, February 28, 1964; United Nations, *Monthly Bulletin of Statistics*, May 1966.

way. The paucity and unreliability of data is one reason. The multitude of less-developed countries and the lack of homogeneity among them should also be kept in mind when attempting generalizations.

It seems, however, as if most of the less-developed countries would have shown a definite and positive growth rate during at least the last decade.[6] Table 8.10 gives an illustration of this.

Table 8.10 covers only a short period. If the information it contains can be taken at face value, it says that the national income grew at roughly the same rate for both industrial and less-developed countries during the period in question. The difference in the growth of per capita income is primarily caused by differences in the growth of population. It also tells us that no " pauperization " has taken place, at least not during the time in question; per capita income in the underdeveloped countries has grown, although at a modest rate.

The implication of the information contained in Tables 8.9 and

[6] Gunnar Myrdal presents a more pessimistic picture of the development of national incomes and per capita incomes since World War II in Southeast Asia in his recent book, *Asian Drama: An Inquiry into the Poverty of Nations*, London, Allen Lane, The Penguin Press, 1968, pp. 473 ff.

TABLE 8.10

GNP growth rates, 1957–1958 to 1963–1964

	Rate of GNP growth	Rate of GNP growth per capita	Rate of population growth
ALL LESS-DEVELOPED COUNTRIES	4.5	2.1	2.4
Latin America	4.1	1.3	2.8
Near East	5.5	3.2	2.3
South Africa	4.4	2.1	2.3
Far East	5.6	2.8	2.8
Africa	3.4	1.1	2.3
ALL INDUSTRIAL COUNTRIES	4.4	3.1	1.3
Europe	4.8	3.8	1.0
United States	3.7	2.1	1.6

SOURCE: John Pincus, *Trade, Aid and Development*, New York, McGraw-Hill, 1967, p. 72.

8.10, however, is that trade hardly seems to have played any propulsive role for the growth in these countries. Expansion of trade seems at best to have kept pace with the growth in national income.

For several of the developing, " peripheral " countries of the nineteenth century, trade functioned, as we know, as an engine of growth. It seems that this has not been the case to anything like the same extent for the underdeveloped countries of today. Their difficulties in this respect seem to have started with the slowdown of the growth of world trade that took place in the interwar period. Table 8.11 gives an indication of this.

A few of the less-developed countries, especially those that happen to be oil producers, have done quite well, but the majority of them have seen their share of world exports fall. This is not only a recent phenomenon. It dates back to the 1920s. Then the less-developed countries lost out at a time when world trade was stagnating, and they have been unable to recover their share at a time when trade has been rapidly expanding. This development has resulted in the overwhelming share of trade today being carried on between industrial countries. This is illustrated by Table 8.12.

One important fact that must be kept in mind is that trade among themselves is most important for the industrial countries. When formulating trade policies, it is only natural for them to be primarily interested in

132

Economic growth and
international trade during the
nineteenth and twentieth centuries

TABLE 8.11

Percentage share of nonindustrial countries in the value of world trade[a]

	Including oil-exporting countries		Excluding oil-exporting countries	
	1928	1957	1928	1957
Exports	33.8	31.3	32.2	24.4
Imports	28.0	35.0	26.9	30.4

[a] Excluding Soviet-area exports and imports.

SOURCE: GATT, *Trends in International Trade*, Geneva, 1958.

measures that concern trade in industrial products, which to them is the most important part of their trade. Although their trade with less-developed countries is by no means negligible, its value is less than one third of *intraindustrial* trade. For the less-developed countries, the reverse applies: For them, trade with industrial countries is much more important than trade among themselves.

A complaint often voiced by representatives for the less-developed countries is that the terms of trade of these countries deteriorate. We remember from Chapter 2 that the terms of trade were defined as export prices divided by import prices. Not only has the volume of exports declined relatively, but the prices for the exports of the less-developed countries have fallen relative to the prices they must pay for their imports, according to these spokesmen.

It is not easy to give adequate measures of the development of the terms of trade for large groups of countries. Differing results can usually be obtained depending upon what time periods are chosen, how countries are grouped, etc. It seems that the terms of trade went against the less-developed countries during the interwar period.[7] For the postwar period the evidence is less clear-cut. Table 8.13 shows indices for the terms of

[7] C. P. Kindleberger, *The Terms of Trade*, Cambridge, Mass., The Technology Press of Massachusetts Institute of Technology, 1956, pp. 232 ff.; and GATT, *Trends in International Trade*, Geneva, 1958, pp. 41 and 46 ff.

TABLE 8.12

Distribution of world exports in 1964

Exports	Billions of dollars	Percent of 1964 GNP
From industrial countries to industrial countries	85	7
From industrial countries to underdeveloped countries	25	2
From underdeveloped countries to industrial countries	25	10
From underdeveloped countries to underdeveloped countries	7	3

SOURCE: United Nations, *Monthly Bulletin of Statistics*, March 1966.

---

trade since 1948 for both groups of countries. The table shows no great difference in the development of the terms of trade for the two groups of countries. During the past 10 years it seems that the terms of trade of the less-developed countries have fallen compared to the terms of trade for the developed countries. But this deterioration is not very large.

The export volume of the less-developed countries has not been growing very fast, as we have seen. We might expect that these countries would have been able to sell their exports at increasing prices, but that is not the case. The result is that trade has not transmitted growth from the developed, industrial countries to the less-developed countries the way it did in the nineteenth century. The income per capita has been growing quickly in the industrial countries, but it seems not to have led to a proportional increase in the demand for primary products.

How are we to explain this development? One answer has been suggested by Ragnar Nurkse.[8] He gives the following six factors as reasons:

1. The emphasis of industrial production in the advanced economies is shifting away from " light " industries toward " heavy " industries (such as engineering and chemicals)—that is, from industries where the raw material content of finished output is high to those where it is low.

---

[8] R. Nurkse, *op. cit.*, p. 23.

134

Economic growth and
international trade during the
nineteenth and twentieth centuries

TABLE 8.13

Indices for terms of trade $(1958 = 100)$

	Developed countries	Less-developed countries		Developed countries	Less-developed countries
1948	99	93	1957	96	101
1949	—	—	1958	100	100
1950	97	108	1959	102	99
1951	93	115	1960	102	99
1952	95	103	1961	104	97
1953	98	102	1962	105	96
1954	97	108	1963	105	97
1955	96	107	1964	104	98
1956	97	104	1965	104	98

SOURCE: United Nations, *International Financial Statistics, Supplement to 1966/67*, New York, pp. xiv–xv.

2. The share of services in the total output of advanced industrial countries is rising, which tends to cause their raw-material demand to lag behind the rise in their national product.

3. The income elasticity of consumer demand for many agricultural commodities tends to be low.

4. Agricultural protectionism has adversely affected imports of primary products.

5. Substantial economies have been achieved in industrial uses of natural materials.

6. The leading industrial centers have tended more and more to displace natural raw materials by synthetic and other man-made substitutes.

It sounds extremely plausible that the factors Nurkse refers to should have played a role in causing the adverse demand conditions that many primary-producing countries have faced during recent decades. The type of explanation that Nurkse proposes, however, is not very systematic. It has too much the character of being invented on the spot, of being ad hoc in nature. We would like to develop a more systematic framework for studying the effects of economic growth upon international trade. This is now what we will set out to do. We will then be able to derive hypotheses to explain the development of the terms of trade. We will seek to state under what conditions countries can be expected to develop favorably by trading and under what conditions growth by trade will lead to an impasse. By continuing to build on the general equilibrium framework that was developed in the first part of the book we will also be able to see more clearly how the different variables are related to each other.

SELECTED BIBLIOGRAPHY: CHAPTER 8

The main source to Chapter 8 is:

S. Kuznets, *Modern Economic Growth: Rate, Structure and Spread*, New Haven, Conn., Yale University Press, 1966, especially chap. 6.

See also:

S. Kuznets, "Level and Structure of Foreign Trade: Long Term Trends," *Economic Development and Cultural Change*, 1967.

Another source of interest is:

R. Nurkse, *Patterns of Trade and Development*, Stockholm, 1959.

For a discussion of underdeveloped countries, see:

J. Pincus, *Trade, Aid and Development*, New York, 1967.

G. Myrdal, *Asian Drama. An Inquiry into the Poverty of Nations*, London, 1968.

The information about Swedish economic growth and trade is taken from the author's unpublished manuscript:

Studier över den långsiktiga utvecklingen av svensk utrikeshandel.

See also:

L. Jörberg, "Structural Change and Economic Growth: Sweden in the Nineteenth Century," *Economy and History*, vol. 7, 1965.

G. Fridlizius, "Sweden's Exports 1850–1960: A Study in Perspective," *Economy and History*, vol. 6, 1964.

Among the standard works in economic history are:

W. Ashworth, *A Short History of the International Economy*, London, 1952.

H. J. Habakkuk and M. Postan (eds.), *The Cambridge Economic History of Europe. Volume VI: The Industrial Revolutions and After*, Cambridge, 1965.

A model of economic growth
and international trade
where growth is unspecified

9

Most parts of the pure theory of international trade dealt with in the first part of the book were quite old. Some of the rigorous proofs of certain theorems may be recent, but the basic ideas had been known for a long time. The theory of economic growth and international trade, on the other hand, has been developed only in recent years.

Classical and neoclassical economists did not take much interest in the subject, at least not in its theoretical aspects. The question of the long-run development of the terms of trade had already in the early nineteenth century been posed as a problem in economic policy. We will come back to this aspect in Chapter 12. But little had been said about it on a more theoretical level. An exception was John Stuart Mill, when he formulated the strikingly modern question: What will be the effect of technical progress in the export industries? But he devoted only one page to the question in his *Principles of Political Economy* and then went on to other fields.

As the starting point for the modern theory of growth and trade, one can turn to a paper by J. R. Hicks published in 1953.[1]

HICKS ON GROWTH AND TRADE

The topic Hicks dealt with in his paper was the long-run development of Great Britain's terms of trade and balance of trade. In the late 1940s and the early 1950s, Britain, like the rest of Western Europe, had experienced persistent deficits in her balance of trade. Hicks tried to explain these deficits with reference to a change in the nature of economic growth in the United States.

Hicks couched his reasoning in terms of the standard two-country trade model. Let us assume, he said, that there are two countries, A and B, and that only A grows, while B is stagnant. What will happen?

If productivity grows uniformly in A—i.e., if all its industries expand at the same rate—the likelihood is that this will benefit B. The simplest way to see this is to assume that money incomes rise to the full extent of the productivity increase in A, while incomes remain unchanged in B, because

[1] J. R. Hicks, "An Inaugural Lecture," *Oxford Economic Papers*, N.S., V, no. 2, June 1953, pp. 117–135.

nothing has happened there. Then the cheapening of *A*-products would have been erased by the rise in incomes, and prices would remain unchanged in *A*. Prices would also remain unchanged in *B*, as nothing has happened there. Money income has not changed in *B*, so there is no reason why *B* should buy a larger or smaller quantity of *A*-products than before. But *A* income has risen and that will lead to an increase in demand for imports. This implies that the balance of trade will turn in *B*'s favor. To restore balance, the relative price of *B*'s exports would increase, and she would get improved terms of trade. This would also mean an improvement in her real national income.

Naturally, the picture becomes more complicated if incomes in *A* do not rise at the same rate as productivity increases. In that case the outcome might be different. For the present we are only concerned with the main drift of the argument and will lay these complications aside.

The case in which productivity increases uniformly in all industries might be called the *neutral* case. Let us go on and assume that the productivity increase instead is concentrated in the export sector and that we have what Hicks called an *export-biased* growth. What will happen then?

This case is extremely favorable for country *B*. Suppose that incomes remain constant in both countries. The prices of *B*'s exports will then remain constant, because nothing has happened in this country, whereas the prices of *A*'s exports will fall. The terms of trade will, therefore, turn in favor of *B*. What happens to the volume of *A*'s exports to *B* will depend mainly on demand conditions. If *B*'s demand for *A*'s exports is inelastic, it might happen that the value of *A*'s exports would fall while the volume would increase. Under such circumstances *A*'s whole productivity gain might be exported away to *B*. Export-biased growth is clearly the type of growth that is most detrimental to *A* and most favorable to *B*.

But what if the productivity increases in *A* are concentrated in the import-competing sector and *A* has *import-biased* growth? This is the case which is most favorable to *A* and least favorable to *B*, and can be demonstrated in the same manner as before. If incomes in both countries remain the same, the prices of import-competing goods in *A* would have to fall. This would mean that a larger share of the market would be taken over by goods produced in *A*, because imports would be substituted with import-competing goods. The demand for exports from *B* would therefore fall. This would create a deficit in *B*'s balance of trade, and to restore it and be able to compete, *B* would have to lower her export prices. Thus *B*'s terms of trade would

138

A model of economic growth
and international trade
where growth is unspecified

deteriorate, and A would be able to keep all her productivity gains and, on top of that, get improved terms of trade.

Hicks's analysis provided a good start by giving a rough formulation of the problem, but his analysis is of a very tentative nature. It is difficult to see how the different factors he discusses hold together. Sometimes Hicks argues in real terms, as for instance when he talks about the terms of trade, and other times in monetary terms, as when he talks about the balance of payments. How one moves from one framework to the other is not easily discernable. His argument is also very sketchy: The demand side, for instance, is virtually ignored. In order to come to grips with the problem of economic growth and international trade, we therefore have to go beyond Hicks's formulation and introduce a more formal kind of analysis.

A MODEL OF ECONOMIC GROWTH AND INTERNATIONAL TRADE: THE BASIC FORMULA[2]

In order to study the effects of economic growth on international trade in a more thorough manner than, for instance, Hicks did, we have to use a more formal approach and set out a well-specified model. We can then derive a formula that in a neat way captures the effects of growth in two trading countries on critical variables such as the terms of trade. This will also give us a more precise insight into the interrelationships among critical variables in a general equilibrium framework.

In the text of this chapter we will only set out the main formula and discuss the assumptions and results of the model in a verbal way. The formal presentation of the model and the derivation of the principal result will be presented as an appendix to this chapter. The model is, however, a simple one indeed, and the reader who is not strongly averse to the use of simple mathematics will probably find it very useful to go through the appendix. The main drift of the argument should, however, be clear from the text.

The argument is set up in terms of the standard trade model, with two countries and two goods. Both countries produce both goods so that

---

[2] The following section builds on B. Södersten, *A Study of Economic Growth and International Trade*, Stockholm, Almqvist & Wiksell, 1964.

specialization is incomplete. We know that economic growth occurs, but at this stage we do not specify the sources of it. Later on, in Chapters 10 and 11, we will study the effects of increases in factor endowments and of technical progress. But for the time being we shall simply take growth for granted: As time goes by, the productive capacity of both countries increases.

The model works roughly in the following way. Economic growth means that the productive capacity in one or both countries increases. This leads to an increase in the supply of one or both goods. But it also implies an increase in income. The increase in income will lead to an increase in demand.[3] The point is, however, that supply and demand of each good will not, in all likelihood, increase with the same amount. Therefore, relative prices will have to change in order to clear the markets. If, for instance, supply of Country I's export good increases more than the demand for it, there will be an excess supply of the good and its price will have to fall.

But a change in relative prices is, of course, nothing but a change in the terms of trade. The object of the model is to show how economic growth affects both the direction and the size of the changes in the terms of trade. We shall then also go on to show that once we know something about the effects of growth on the terms of trade, we also know a great deal about its effects on the real national income. We will discuss these effects in a verbal way, as a formal analysis would be too complicated.

It is now time to set out the basic formula that captures the effects of economic growth in the two trading countries on their terms of trade. This is done in equation 9.1:

$$\frac{dP}{dt} = \frac{(R_{1m} S_{1m} - R_1 E_{1m} C_{1m}) - (R_2 E_{2x} C_{2x} - R_{2x} S_{2x})}{\frac{C_{1m}}{P} e_1 + \frac{C_{2x}}{P} e_2 + \frac{S_{1m}}{P} s_1 + \frac{S_{2x}}{P} s_2} \tag{9.1}$$

Before analyzing the model we will explain the notations briefly (exact definitions are given in the appendix). Figures in the subscripts

---

[3] In order to give as simple a formulation of our problem as possible, we assume that Say's law holds and that everything produced is consumed. We have chosen this formulation because we want to simplify the exposition and concentrate the attention to real factors, i.e., to study the effects of economic growth on real factors such as the terms of trade and the real national income. To introduce savings and money into the model would indeed create great problems. In fact, so far no satisfactory general equilibrium treatment of the effects of economic growth on the balance of payments has been given.

140

A model of economic growth
and international trade
where growth is unspecified

stand for countries, x denotes export and m import magnitudes, C denotes consumption and S supply. Thus S_{1m} denotes supply (output) of the import-competing good in Country I. S_{2x} stands for supply of the export good in Country II. C_{1m} denotes consumption of the imported good in Country I and C_{2x} denotes consumption of Country II's export good. Economic growth is symbolized by t. P_x is the price of Country I's export good and P_m of its import good. Country I's terms of trade are given by P. $(P = P_x/P_m.)$ It is then obvious that Country II's terms of trade are equal to $1/P$.

R_{1m} denotes the growth rate of the import-competing sector in Country I, and R_1 denotes the growth rate of the national income in Country I; R_{2x} and R_2 have analogous meanings. The four symbols e_1, e_2, s_1, and s_2 denote demand and supply elasticities. Country I's elasticity of demand for its import good with respect to the terms of trade is given by e_1, its elasticity of supply of importables with respect to P is given by s_1, etc. E_{1m} denotes the income elasticity of importables in Country I. E_{2x} stands for the income elasticity of exportables in Country II.

AN ANALYSIS OF THE MODEL

Formula 9.1 indicates that the outcome for the terms of trade depends on quite a number of factors. The growth rates of the national incomes in the two countries are important. Which sector experiences growth is also very important. The development of demand, measured by income elasticities, also plays a role. These are the factors which have the stage, and they are depicted in the numerator.

The interrelationships between volumes and prices, measured by demand and supply elasticities, are important. They lay, so to speak, the frame within which the determining forces work. They are depicted in the denominator. We will start by looking at the factors pictured in the denominator.

The denominator will be positive provided that the two goods are substitutes (so-called gross substitutes) for each other in consumption in both countries. This hardly seems a very strong assumption to accept. The first elasticity, e_1, shows, as already stated, how demand for importables in Country I changes if relative commodity prices change. If P increased, it would imply that the imported good had become relatively cheaper. Then we would expect consumers to buy more of the cheaper good (importables) and substitute this good for the other good (exportables) in consumption; if this happens, e_1 will be positive.

Analogous reasoning can be applied to e_2. This elasticity measures how demand for exportables in Country II changes if the terms of trade change. If P would increase, it means that Country II's terms of trade deteriorate; i.e., the relative price of its export good falls. This implies that consumption of exportables in Country II increases. Then the sign of e_2 is positive (see the appendix). The only assumption needed for this result is that the two goods are substitutes (gross substitutes) for consumers in Country II.

The other two elasticities in the denominator are supply elasticities. The first one, s_1, shows how production of importables in Country I changes as relative prices change. Let us say that P increases. This implies that the relative price of importables falls. If the price of importables falls, its supply will also fall, because producers will transfer resources out of the sector. This means that s_1 will have a positive sign (for the exact definition see the appendix).

We assume in this model that competitive conditions prevail both in commodity and factor markets. This implies that the production-possibility curve is concave to the origin.[4] This means that producers are going to behave the way we expect them to behave; i.e., if the relative price of a good falls, they are never going to increase production of it.

For analogous reasons, s_2 is also nonnegative. This elasticity measures how production of the export good in Country II changes if relative prices change. If a change in P had a negative sign, it would mean that the terms of trade had deteriorated for Country I but had improved for Country II. As the price of exportables in Country II goes up, producers in this country will produce more of its export good. Provided that this happens, s_2 will always be positive.

If we are willing to accept the quite weak assumptions of competitive conditions in production and gross substitutability in consumption, the denominator will be positive. The magnitudes of the elasticities which make up the denominator are very important for the adaptability of the two trading economies. The direction of change in the terms of trade will depend, as

---

[4] For a discussion of the shape of the production-possibility curve, see Chapter 2.

A model of economic growth
and international trade
where growth is unspecified

we shall soon see, on the factors depicted in the numerator. But just how much the terms of trade will have to change in order to get to a new equilibrium depends critically on the supply and demand elasticities in the denominator. The larger they are, i.e., the more adaptable the two trading economies are, the less the terms of trade will have to change in order for a new equilibrium to be reached.

It is easy to see why this is true. High values on the demand elasticities suggest that the two goods are easily substituted for each other in consumption. Any change in relative prices will therefore lead to a substantial change in quantities consumed. Analogously, high values on the supply elasticities also make for an easy adjustment. The higher the values on these elasticities are, the more willing and able the producers in the two countries are to change the pattern of production if relative prices change.

Generally speaking we can say that the larger the value of the denominator, the smaller the change in the terms of trade, arising from any disturbance, and the easier the adjustment to price changes by producers and consumers in the two countries. Therefore, the elasticities in the denominator are very important, their values being a measure of the degree of the adaptability and the reallocative capacity of the two trading economies. In the extreme case, when the values of the elasticities tend to infinity, the change in the terms of trade is negligible.

If the denominator in equation 9.1 is positive, the outcome for the terms of trade depends on whether $R_{1m} S_{1m} - R_1 E_{1m} C_{1m} \gtreqless R_2 E_{2x} C_{2x} - R_{2x} S_{2x}$. If the left side of this expression is larger than the right side, the terms of trade will improve for Country I; she will then find that some gains from improving terms of trade will be added to her autonomous growth because of her participation in foreign trade. If the right side is the larger, the terms of trade will improve for Country II. If the two sides are equal, the terms of trade will not change during the growth process.

The important factors are obviously the sectoral growth rates and the income elasticities in the two countries. In them are captured the effects of economic growth on supply and demand in the two countries. In order to emphasize the implications of equation 9.1, let us for the sake of reasoning assume that Country II is stationary and that Country I is the only growing country. Then both R_2 and R_{2x} are zero and only the left part of the numerator in equation 9.1 is of interest.

Given these assumptions, the result for the terms of trade depends on whether the weighted growth rate of import production $(R_{1m} S_{1m})$ is larger or smaller than the weighted income elasticity of demand for importables ($R_1 E_{1m} C_{1m}$). If the former is larger than the latter, i.e., $R_{1m} S_{1m} > R_1 E_{1m} C_{1m}$, the terms of trade will improve for Country I. Growth under these conditions will lead to an increase in the supply of importables which is larger than the increase in demand. This will create an excess supply of importables in Country I at existing prices. In order to clear the markets, the price of importables has to fall, i.e., the terms of trade will improve. We can also think of this process as leading to a condition in which more of the home market for importables is captured by producers in Country I. The demand for imports falls. The exporters in Country II find a decrease in demand for their exports. Therefore, they have to lower their prices in order to clear the markets; in other words, the terms of trade move in favor of Country I.

If it were the other way around, i.e., if $R_1 E_{1m} C_{1m} > R_{1m} S_{1m}$, then the terms of trade would deteriorate for Country I, because in this event the demand for importables would grow faster than the supply of importables. There would be an excess demand for importables in Country I at existing prices. The exporters in Country II would find that demand for their product had increased; to clear the markets the price of Country II's exports would have to rise. In short, Country I's terms of trade would deteriorate.

We can now compare these results with the ones suggested by Hicks. His results lie in the same general direction, but because he never took demand factors into account, his analysis was, from a rigorous point of view, indeterminate. Hicks said that export-biased growth would turn the terms of trade against a country, and that import-biased growth would improve a country's terms of trade. With our terminology we interpret export bias in Hicks's sense to mean that $R_{1x} S_{1x} > R_{1m} S_{1m}$ and import bias to mean that $R_{1m} S_{1m} > R_{1x} S_{1x}$. That is, we simply compare the weighted growth rates in the two sectors, and if the growth in the supply of exportables is larger than the growth in the supply of importables, growth is said to be export-biased. If it is the other way around, growth is said to be import-biased.

It is, however, easy to see that Hicks's definitions of export and import bias do not necessarily imply a definite change in the terms of trade. It is fully conceivable to have an export-biased growth in Hicks's sense and still have improving terms of trade. According to formula 9.1, Country I will get improving terms of trade if $R_{1m} S_{1m} > R_1 E_{1m} C_{1m}$. Let us assume that the income elasticity of demand for importables, E_{1m}, is equal to zero. As

A model of economic growth
and international trade
where growth is unspecified

long as there is any growth at all in the import-competing sector, the terms
of trade will always improve for Country I. In such a case it is possible that
$R_{1x} S_{1x} > R_{1m} S_{1m}$, or that the growth is export-biased in Hicks's sense, and
that the terms of trade will still improve for the country. This is explained
by the simple fact that all the increased income caused by the economic
growth will be spent on exportables, and as long as some growth occurs in
the import-competing sector, economic growth will always give rise to an
excess supply of importables and to excess demand for exportables at existing
prices. To clear the markets and reach a new equilibrium the relative price
of importables will have to fall; i.e., the terms of trade will improve for the
country.

If we would like to use the notions of export bias and import bias and
have a definite connection between bias and a change in the terms of trade,
we will have to redefine the terms. If we define export-biased growth as one
in which the supply of exportables is increased more than the demand for
exportables, i.e., if $R_{1x} S_{1x} > R_1 E_{1x} C_{1x}$, then export-biased growth will
lead to deteriorating terms of trade. Analogously, if we define import-
biased growth as $R_{1m} S_{1m} > R_1 E_{1m} C_{1m}$, then import-biased growth will
always imply improving terms of trade.

Up to this point we have assumed Country II to be stationary. If we
instead assume that Country I is stationary and that Country II grows,
exactly analogous results hold. Export-biased growth in Country II, i.e.,
$R_{2x} S_{2x} > R_2 E_{2x} C_{2x}$, leads to a deterioration in her terms of trade, and
import-biased growth, i.e., $R_{2m} S_{2m} > R_2 E_{2m} C_{2m}$, leads to an improvement in her terms of trade.

If both countries grow, the outcome for the terms of trade will
depend on the type of growth which occurs. If both countries tend toward
import-biased growth, i.e., if $R_{1m} S_{1m} > R_1 E_{1m} C_{1m}$ and $R_{2m} S_{2m} >
R_2 E_{2m} C_{2m}$, the country with the greatest degree of import bias will get
improving terms of trade. If both countries have export-biased growth, the
country with the greatest degree of export bias will have deteriorating terms
of trade. If Country I has an export-biased growth and Country II an import-biased one, the terms of trade will always turn against Country I;
the faster the growth rates and the larger the bias (regardless of country), the
faster the terms of trade will deteriorate. This also holds, *mutatis mutandis*,
for Country II.

These are the kinds of results that can be obtained by a model with
unspecified growth. Its strength lies in the fact that we, with the help of the

model, are able to see the basic interrelationships between supply and demand factors in the growth process. We have now achieved a fundamental understanding of how economic growth affects prices and volumes of the trading countries. It is now possible to specify growth and see what the effects of increases in the factor endowments and of technical progress will be. Before doing this, however, we will say something about the effects of growth on the national income and touch briefly on some policy implications of the development of the terms of trade.

GROWTH, TRADE, AND THE NATIONAL INCOME

If the growth rate of a country's national product is 3 percent per annum and if the terms of trade do not change, the country's national income will also increase by 3 percent. If the growth is of such a kind as to make the terms of trade deteriorate, what might be called the "autonomous" growth rate—the growth rate at pregrowth prices—will be higher than the realized growth rate because some of the growth will be exported away in the form of falling terms of trade. On the other hand, if growth is of a type to improve the terms of trade, the realized growth rate will be higher than the autonomous one, because besides the home-generated growth, the country's real income will improve because of improving terms of trade.

Therefore, if one knows something about how growth affects a country's terms of trade, one also knows a great deal about its effect on national income. Analogous to the method in treating the terms of trade, a formula can be derived for the effects of growth on the real national income.[5] To do this would, however, require a more elaborate formal analysis. We will therefore be content with some verbal commentary.

If a country has its growth possibilities confined to the export sector, she might get adverse terms of trade. But this depends on the situation in the second country. If the second country also grows and if her income elasticity of demand for importables is high, demand for imports can be expected to grow quickly, and the first country is able to increase her exports at only slightly lower prices. In this way the first country can grow and prosper by concentrating on increasing production of exports.

---

[5] See B. Södersten, *op. cit.*, pp. 46 ff.

146

A model of economic growth
and international trade
where growth is unspecified

But if the second country does not grow, or if its income elasticity of demand for importables is low, the first country might be in trouble. Under these conditions the demand for imports in the second country might increase only slightly or not at all, and in order to sell an increased amount of exports the first country will have to lower its prices, which is to say, to accept falling terms of trade. Now the price elasticity of demand for importables in the second country (depicted in the denominator in equation 9.1) will be important. If this elasticity is low it may be impossible for the first country to increase its revenue from exports. In such a case, growth by means of export is a dead end.

The ultimate case on the pessimistic side is that of so-called impoverishing or immiserizing growth. This is the case in which a country ends up having a lower real income after growth because the loss due to deteriorating terms of trade has outweighed the gain due to increased production.

The possibility of impoverishing growth was first contemplated by F. Y. Edgeworth, who, upon reading John Stuart Mill's analysis of the effects of improvements of production in export industries, drew the conclusion that under certain conditions "the exporting country is damnified by the improvement; and by parity of reasoning may be benefited by a restriction of its exports."[6]

Edgeworth established the conditions for impoverishing growth with exceedingly simple reasoning. He used a model of complete specialization both in consumption and production whereby each of the two trading countries produced only one good, all of which it exported but did not consume, and whereby each country imported all of the good which it consumed. Under these very special conditions the foreign demand elasticity is all-important, and the condition for impoverishing growth is simply that this elasticity be less than unity. If the first country grows and the second country is stationary, and if the foreign demand elasticity for the first country's exports is less than unity, total export earnings will fall because of growth; and as the national income equals total export earnings, the country will become poorer because of growth.

If a less specific model than the one Edgeworth had in mind is used,

---

[6] F. Y. Edgeworth, "The Theory of International Values," *Economic Journal*, vol. 4, no. 1, March 1894, pp. 35 ff.; the quotation is from page 40. See also F. Y. Edgeworth, "On a Point in the Theory of International Trade," *Economic Journal*, vol. 9, no. 1, March 1899, pp. 125 ff.

the probability for impoverishing growth diminishes.[7] Then either production of importables has to decrease because of growth, or the sum of all the elasticities which appear in the denominator in equation 9.1 has to be less than unity.[8] These are both quite stringent conditions. There is no reason to expect the former to occur unless some nonreproducible factor is used in the production of importables. The implication of the sum of all the above-mentioned elasticities being less than unity is obviously that there are no possibilities of substitution, neither on the demand nor the supply side, in either of the trading economies.

Maybe the case of impoverishing growth should be viewed as a curiosity. But it brings in focus the factors that may make growth through trade an impasse for a country. That is, if a country is faced with sluggish demand in her export market, if her growth is confined to the export sector, and if her adaptability is low, growth by means of trade might be a fruitless venture.

Import-biased growth, on the other hand, will always be beneficial to a country. This kind of growth improves the country's terms of trade, and her national income will increase by more than the autonomous growth. The favorable effects of import-biased growth will be reinforced if the country has a high income elasticity of demand for her own export good and if the trading partner's economy has a low degree of adaptability.

We have now seen some of the basic factors that determine the effects on the national income of economic growth in open economies. Before we conclude this chapter it might be appropriate to say a few words about the policy aspects of the development of the terms of trade.

THE TERMS OF TRADE AS A POLICY PROBLEM

The interest economists have shown in the long-run development of the terms of trade has always been great, at times almost obsessive. One line of

---

[7] The case of impoverishing growth was discovered anew in the 1950s by H. G. Johnson and J. Bhagwati. See H. G. Johnson, "Economic Expansion and International Trade," and "Equilibrium Growth in an International Economy," both reprinted in *International Trade and Economic Growth*, London, G. Allen,

148

A model of economic growth
and international trade
where growth is unspecified

thought, inaugurated by the classical English economists, claimed that the development of the terms of trade would be detrimental to the industrial countries and benefit the primary producing countries. Keynes was a proponent of this school, and it has had its advocates even in our day. Another line of thought widely discussed during the 1950s and the 1960s is connected with the names of Singer and Prebisch. It claims that the development of the terms of trade for different reasons had, and would have, to be detrimental to the less-developed, primary producing countries and beneficial to the industrial countries.

These various explanations for the development of the terms of trade have been both loose and intricate. It should be clear by now that the type of theorizing set forth in this chapter can generate hypotheses for the development of the terms of trade. We know that these hypotheses are internally consistent, because they have their foundation in a general equilibrium type of theory. Because the theory on which they build is explicitly formulated, it is also easy to see what assumptions they rest on. It would be premature to evaluate and criticize the theories mentioned above now; this will have to wait until later, after we have dealt with the effects on the terms of trade of specified growth. But even at this point it should be clear that it is easy to set out a set of conditions which would lead to deteriorating or, for that matter, improving terms of trade for a country.

1958, and J. Bhagwati, "Immiserizing Growth: A Geometrical Note," *Review of Economic Studies*, vol. 25, no. 68, June 1958.
[8] See Södersten, *op. cit.*, pp. 52 ff.

A formal model
of economic
growth and
international trade

9–A

We will now set out the simple general equilibrium model that was used in the text of Chapter 9. It is a model with five equations in five unknowns (S_{1m}, S_{2x}, C_{1m}, C_{2x}, and P) and with an exogenous variable t. The model is rudimentary but it suffices for pedagogical purposes.[9]

The variables used in the model are as follows. Y_1 and Y_2 denote national income in Country I and II, respectively. S_{1m} denotes, as was stated in the text, output (supply) of the import-competing good in Country I. S_{2x} stands for supply of the export good in Country II. C_{1m} denotes consumption of the imported good in Country I and C_{2x} denotes consumption of Country II's export good. Economic growth is symbolized by t. P_x is the price of Country I's export good and P_m of Country I's import good. The import good of Country I is used as *numéraire*, and P_m equals 1. We then indicate Country I's terms of trade by P.

We can then set out the following system of equations:

$$S_{1m} = S_{1m}(t, P(t)) \tag{9A.1}$$

Equation 9A.1 shows that supply of Country I's import-competing good is a function of economic growth and of relative prices.

$$C_{1m} = C_{1m}(Y_1(t), P(t)) \tag{9A.2}$$

Equation 9A.2 shows that consumption of importables in Country I is a function of its national income and of relative prices. Equation 9A.2 is, in other words, a simple type of demand function.

We can then set out analogous functions for the second country.

$$S_{2x} = S_{2x}(t, P(t)) \tag{9A.3}$$

This equation illustrates that the output of exportables in Country II is a function of economic growth and relative prices.

$$C_{2x} = C_{2x}(Y_2(t), P(t)) \tag{9A.4}$$

Equation 9A.4 shows that consumption of exportables in Country II is a function of its national income and of relative prices.

Finally, we have the following equilibrium condition:

$$S_{1m} + S_{2x} = C_{1m} + C_{2x} \tag{9A.5}$$

Let us call Country I's import good, good I. Good I is thus also Country II's export good. Equation 9A.5 simply says that, in equilibrium, demand for good I must equal its supply.

---

[9] For a more complete version of the model see Södersten, *op. cit.*, chap. 2.

We assume the above system of equations to have a solution for t. By differentiating the equilibrium condition, equation 9A.5, with respect to t we get

$$\frac{d(S_{1m} + S_{2x})}{dt} = \frac{d(C_{1m} + C_{2x})}{dt} \tag{9A.6}$$

which gives

$$\frac{\partial S_{1m}}{\partial t} + \frac{\partial S_{1m}}{\partial P}\frac{dP}{dt} + \frac{\partial S_{2x}}{\partial t} + \frac{\partial S_{2x}}{\partial P}\frac{dP}{dt}$$

$$= \frac{\partial C_{1m}}{\partial Y_1}\frac{dY_1}{dt} + \frac{\partial C_{1m}}{\partial P}\frac{dP}{dt} + \frac{\partial C_{2x}}{\partial Y_2}\frac{dY_2}{dt} + \frac{\partial C_{2x}}{\partial P}\frac{dP}{dt} \tag{9A.7}$$

Solving for dP/dt gives

$$\frac{dP}{dt} = \frac{\left(\dfrac{\partial S_{1m}}{\partial t} - \dfrac{\partial C_{1m}}{\partial Y_1}\dfrac{dY_1}{dt}\right) - \left(\dfrac{\partial C_{2x}}{\partial Y_2}\dfrac{dY_2}{dt} - \dfrac{\partial S_{2x}}{\partial t}\right)}{\dfrac{\partial C_{1m}}{\partial P} + \dfrac{\partial C_{2x}}{\partial P} - \dfrac{\partial S_{1m}}{\partial P} - \dfrac{\partial S_{2x}}{\partial P}} \tag{9A.8}$$

Expression 9A.8 shows the effects of economic growth on the terms of trade. It might be convenient to rephrase it in terms of growth rates and elasticities. To do so we need to introduce the following definitions:

$R_{1m} = \dfrac{\partial S_{1m}}{\partial t}\dfrac{1}{S_{1m}}$: The growth rate of the import-competing sector at given terms of trade.

$R_1 = \dfrac{dY_1}{dt}\dfrac{1}{Y_1}$: The growth rate of the national income in Country I.

$E_{1m} = \dfrac{\partial C_{1m}}{\partial Y_1}\dfrac{Y_1}{C_{1m}}$: The income elasticity of importables in Country I.

$R_2 = \dfrac{dY_2}{dt}\dfrac{1}{Y_2}$: The growth rate of the national income in Country II.

$E_{2x} = \dfrac{\partial C_{2x}}{\partial Y_2}\dfrac{Y_2}{C_{2x}}$: The income elasticity of exportables in Country II.

$R_{2x} = \dfrac{\partial S_{2x}}{\partial t}\dfrac{1}{S_{2x}}$: The growth rate of the export sector in Country II at constant terms of trade.

$e_1 = \dfrac{\partial C_{1m}}{\partial P}\dfrac{P}{C_{1m}}$: Country I's elasticity of demand for its import good with respect to the terms of trade.

$$e_2 = \frac{\partial C_{2x}}{\partial P} \frac{P}{C_{2x}} \quad : \quad$$ Country II's elasticity of demand for its export good with respect to the terms of trade.

$$s_1 = -\frac{\partial S_{1m}}{\partial P} \frac{P}{S_{1m}} \quad : \quad$$ Country I's elasticity of supply of importables with respect to the terms of trade.

$$s_2 = -\frac{\partial S_{2x}}{\partial P} \frac{P}{S_{2x}} \quad : \quad$$ Country II's elasticity of supply of exportables with respect to the terms of trade.

Using these definitions we can rewrite equation 9A.8 as follows:

$$\frac{dP}{dt} = \frac{(R_{1m} S_{1m} - R_1 E_{1m} C_{1m}) - (R_2 E_{2x} C_{2x} - R_{2x} S_{2x})}{\dfrac{C_{1m}}{P} e_1 + \dfrac{C_{2x}}{P} e_2 + \dfrac{S_{1m}}{P} s_1 + \dfrac{S_{2x}}{P} s_2}$$

This, then, is the model that has been used and analyzed as equation 9.1 in the text of the chapter.

Increases in factor endowments and international trade: the Rybczynski theorem

10

In Chapter 9 economic growth was unspecified. As time went by both countries grew, but we did not try to examine the causes of growth. In this chapter we will go a step further. Two factors of production, conventionally called labor and capital, will be introduced and we will study what happens to the trading relationships of the two countries if one of the countries has an increase in the labor force or in the stock of capital.

In Chapter 9 we studied the effects of simultaneous growth in both countries. It will now suffice to take only one country explicitly into account, because we already know the basic interrelationships between the two countries as expressed by the elasticity factor in the denominator of equations 9A.8 and 9.1.

We will start by giving an exposition in geometric terms of the so-called Rybczynski theorem.[1] This theorem states that if one of the factors of production increases, the other one being constant, the output of the good using the accumulating factor intensively will increase and the output of the other good will decrease in absolute amount, provided that commodity and factor prices are being kept constant. We will then do away with these assumptions and look into the general equilibrium implications of the Rybczynski theorem. After having dealt with the effects on commodity and factor prices, we will also give a verbal treatment of the effects of increases in factor endowments on some other factors in the trade model, especially on the national income.

THE RYBCZYNSKI THEOREM

It will now be useful to apply the geometric tools developed in the first part of the book. We will make the by-now familiar assumptions that commodity and factor markets are characterized by competitive conditions and that the production functions are homogeneous of the first degree. These assumptions are necessary to establish our results. It is, however, not necessary to assume that production functions are the same in the two countries.

We begin by assuming that the two countries are trading and that Country I is in the equilibrium situation depicted in Figure 10.1. The coun-

---

[1] T. M. Rybczynski, "Factor Endowment and Relative Commodity Prices," *Economica*, November 1955, pp. 336 ff.

FIGURE 10.1

Factor growth at constant commodity prices

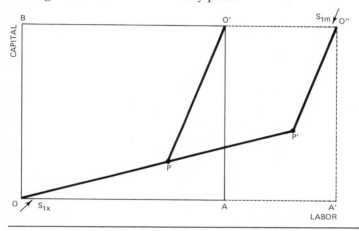

try's original factor endowments before growth are measured by the box $OAO'B$. Capital is measured on the vertical side and labor on the horizontal side. The production of the country's export good, S_{1x}, is measured from the lower left-hand corner and the production of its import-competing good, S_{1m}, from the upper right-hand corner. It follows that the export good is labor-intensive and that the import-competing good is capital-intensive.

Let us assume that Country I before growth produces at point P on its contract curve. The factor intensity used in production of exportables will then be OP and the factor intensity used in production of importables will be $O'P$. Country I now gets an increase in its labor force with a constant capital stock. The increase in the labor force is measured by the distance AA' so that the new box, after the increase in the labor force, will be $OA'O''B$. What will be the effects on volumes produced, the terms of trade, etc.?

To deal with these questions we start by assuming that commodity prices are kept constant. To keep commodity prices constant we also have to keep factor prices constant. To keep factor prices constant, the marginal productivities in each line of production have to stay fixed. Since the production functions are homogeneous of the first degree, the ratio of marginal productivities is a function only of factor intensities. As long as factor intensities do not change, the ratio of marginal productivities does not change

154

Increases in factor endowments
and international trade:
the Rybczynski theorem

either. The only point in the new box at which factors of production are combined in the same proportions as at P is P'. The factor intensity OP' is obviously the same as the factor intensity OP, and the factor intensity $O'P$ is the same as $O''P'$.

But what about point P'? Is it on the contract curve in the new box? Yes, it is, because the ray OP' cuts the isoquants of the export industry (not shown) at points where they all have equal slope. As $O'P$ and $O''P'$ are parallel they also cut the isoquants of the import-competing industry (not shown) at points where they have equal slope. Therefore, the ratios of the marginal productivities are the same at P and P'. Hence P' fulfills the optimum condition and is on the contract curve in the box $OA'O''B$.

It is now clear what the consequences of keeping commodity prices constant are for outputs. Because of the property of linear homogeneity of the production functions, the amount of a commodity produced can be measured by the distance along any ray from the origins in the box. The distance $O''P'$ is obviously shorter than the distance $O'P$. Therefore, less of the import-competing good is produced at P' than at P. Analogously, P' is farther away from the O origin than is P. Therefore, more of exportables are produced at P' than at P. This establishes the fact that if one of the factors is increased while the other is kept constant, the production of the good intensive in the increasing factor will, at constant commodity prices, increase in absolute amount, whereas the production of the other good decreases absolutely.

To see the economic implications of the above argument it might be useful to reiterate it in the following way. The assumption about constant commodity prices implies constant factor prices, which in turn implies constant labor/capital ratios in the two industries. But how can we keep the two ratios constant when the amount of one of the factors increases?

This can only be done by reallocating resources between the two lines of production. When the amount of labor increases, all the new labor has to go to the labor-intensive industry. To keep the old factor proportions, we have to release some capital from the capital-intensive industry and let it be combined with the new labor. But not only do we have to move some capital from the capital-intensive industry, we also have to move some workers from the capital-intensive to the labor-intensive industry. As long as the labor force keeps increasing, we have to move factors of production over from the capital-intensive to the labor-intensive line of production. This means that the production in the labor-intensive industry has to expand

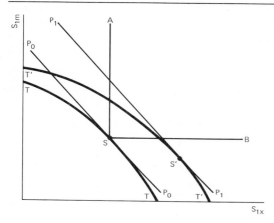

FIGURE 10.2

Equilibrium situation for terms of trade after factor growth

while production in the capital-intensive industry contracts. If this process were to continue indefinitely, the country would obviously become completely specialized.

But keeping commodity prices constant is only a device for tracing the logic of the argument; it is hardly compatible with general equilibrium. It is now time to give up that assumption and to see what the implications are for all the important variables in the general equilibrium framework.

Let us for the moment, however, ask the question: Under what conditions would point P' be a true general equilibrium point?

An increase in the labor force of Country I increases the productive capacity of the country and leads to an increase in the national income. But at point P' less of importables is consumed. In other words, an increase in income causes a fall in the demand of one of the goods. This implies, obviously, that the import good is an inferior good. P' can therefore be a possible equilibrium point only with the provision that one of the goods is inferior. If we stay with the assumption from Chapter 9 and bar inferior goods, we also rule out P' as a possible new equilibrium point. In other words, assuming constant commodity prices is not compatible with general equilibrium theorizing.

To continue the argument it is convenient to use another geometric illustration. In Figure 10.2 the production-possibility curve TT is derived from the box diagram $OAO'B$ in Figure 10.1. The international terms of trade are given by the price line $P_0 P_0$, which is tangent to TT at point S.

156

Increases in factor endowments
and international trade:
the Rybczynski theorem

What about the new production-possibility curve: What shape will it have? All we can say is that a price line such as P_1P_1, which is parallel to P_0P_0, must be tangent to the new production-possibility curve below the line SB. Because, as we have just shown, at constant prices more exportables will be produced and less importables will be produced. So if we derive the new production-possibility curve $T'T'$ from the box $OA'O''B$ in Figure 10.1 it will appear as it does in Figure 10.2.

Barring inferior goods, S' cannot be an equilibrium point. The increase in the labor force implies an increase in the national income. Demand for both goods will increase. Therefore, the new equilibrium point will lie somewhere on the new production-possibility curve $T'T'$ between where it is cut by the lines SA and SB. The slope of this segment of the production-possibility curve is not as steep as the slope of the production-possibility curve TT at S. That implies that the relative price of the import-competing good, S_{1m}, will be higher in the new equilibrium situation, or that, in other words, an increase in the labor force will lead to a deterioration in the country's terms of trade.

We have now established that factor growth leads to a deterioration in the terms of trade for that good which uses the accumulating factor intensively. Because labor increased and the country's export good was the labor-intensive good, the terms of trade deteriorated for the country. Had the import-competing good instead been the labor-intensive good, the terms of trade would have moved in favor of the country. Because in that event, assuming unchanged commodity prices, the output of importables would have increased and the output of exportables would have decreased. This would have created an excess demand for exportables at unchanged prices, and in order to clear the markets the relative price of exportables would have had to increase; i.e., the country's terms of trade would have improved.

We will now go on and make some remarks about some generalizations of the Rybczynski theorem.

MORE GENERAL REMARKS ABOUT FACTOR GROWTH AND TRADE

A critical assumption for establishing the Rybczynski theorem is that production functions are homogeneous of the first degree. Then the effects on commodity prices hinge, as we have seen, in a critical fashion on which industry is labor-intensive and which is capital-intensive. It is not possible to generalize this result to the case of less-constrained production functions. For the case of unspecified production functions no clear-cut result about the change in relative commodity prices can be established. The outcome depends on a set of second derivatives about which nothing a priori can be said.[2]

In what follows production functions are, therefore, assumed to be linearly homogeneous. The results for the volumes and for the national income again depend on which factor it is that accumulates and on factor intensities.

If, for instance, the increasing factor is used intensively in the export industry, the volume of exportables will always increase. The result for the volume of importables is not determinate. The volume of importables will probably also increase, especially if the income elasticity of demand for importables is high. The same results hold, *mutatis mutandis*, if the increasing factor is used intensively in the import-competing sector.

If the accumulating factor is used intensively in the import-competing industry, growth will have a strongly beneficial effect on the real national income. Then positive effects on the real national income will come from both sectors of the economy. If the increasing factor is used intensively in the export industry, the effects on the growth of the national income are less clear-cut. Then a negative influence will come from the export sector and the positive effects on the national income from growth might not be very large. These risks are enhanced if the share of exports in the national income is large. A large export share means that the country has a substantial amount of new exportables to offer to its trading partner. Since the terms of trade in this case go against the country, it implies a relatively strong negative influence on the growth of the real income.

Another important element in this situation is the elasticity factor (measured by the denominator in equations 9A.8 and 9.1). If its value is large, the negative influences coming from the export sector will tend to be neutralized, because the economy is sensitive to price changes and responds to

---

[2] This section of the chapter builds on the results derived in B. Södersten, *A Study of Economic Growth and International Trade*, Stockholm, Almqvist & Wiksell, 1964, chap. 3.

158

Increases in factor endowments
and international trade:
the Rybczynski theorem

them with changes in the production and demand patterns without much friction. The greater the possibilities for substitution in the two countries, the smaller the risks that the growing country will be hurt by its export-biased growth.

The effects on factor rewards are clear-cut. If capital accumulates while the labor force is constant, the real wage will always increase and the return to capital will fall. The income distribution will also usually turn in favor of labor under these circumstances. Wicksell pointed to these results in his *Lectures*, with the famous dictum:

> The capitalist saver is thus, fundamentally, the friend of labour, though the technical innovator is not infrequently its enemy. The great innovations by which industry has from time to time been revolutionized, at first reduced a number of workers to beggary, as experience shows, while causing the profits of the capitalists to soar. There is no need to explain away this circumstance by invoking "economic friction", and so on, for it is in full accord with a rational and consistent theory. But it is really not capital which should bear the blame; in proportion as accumulation continues, these evils must disappear, interest on capital will fall and wages will rise—unless the labourers on their part simultaneously counteract this result by a large increase in their numbers.[3]

Thus if one factor of production increases in amount, the reward to the other factor, which has been kept constant, will increase. This is what Wicksell meant when he pointed out that the capitalist, by saving and investing, is increasing the stock of capital: The workers have more machines to work with, the marginal productivity of labor increases and the wage goes up. As long as the workers are not reproducing themselves at a faster rate than capital accumulates, their real wage will increase in the growth process.

---

[3] Knut Wicksell (1851–1926), professor of economics at the University of Lund, Sweden, was one of the outstanding economists in the neoclassical tradition and made important contributions to many parts of economic theory. Among his main works are *Über Wert, Kapital und Rente*, 1893 (translated as *Value, Capital and Rent*, London, G. Allen, 1954), *Geldzins und Güterpreise*, 1898 (translated as *Interest and Prices*, London, Macmillan, 1936), and *Föreläsningar i national ekonomi*, 1908 (translated as *Lectures on Political Economy*, London, Routledge, 1934–1935). The quotation is from *Lectures on Political Economy*, vol. 1, p. 164.

The second part of Wicksell's statement refers to the fact that certain types of technical progress—some kinds of innovations—might have a negative effect on the marginal productivity of labor, thereby reducing the real wage. In this sense the technical innovator can be the enemy of labor. This will be made clear in Chapter 11, where we will deal with the effects of technical progress on international trade.

Technical progress and international trade

11

We have just dealt with the effects of factor growth on trade. Another perhaps more important element in modern economic life is technical progress. Innovations of different kinds—technical progress, in short—have transformed the agricultural economies of the eighteenth century into the modern industrial economy. The study of the effects of technical progress on international trade needs no justification.

Again, classical and neoclassical economists showed no great interest in the study of the effects of technical progress. It is significant that many leading classical and neoclassical economists were so preoccupied with one type of factor growth—the increase in population—that they failed completely to grasp the importance of technical progress for economic development.[1]

We shall now study how technical progress affects international trade. To do this it is convenient to illustrate geometrically how technical progress affects the production function and how technical progress can be classified into different subgroups.

THE CLASSIFICATION OF TECHNICAL PROGRESS

In order to classify technical progress we use the same type of production function used in earlier parts of the book, i.e., a production function with two inputs, labor and capital. We also assume the production function to be homogeneous of the first degree. Technical progress means that more output can be produced with a given amount of inputs—or, to use a different but equivalent formulation, that a given output can be produced with less inputs.

In the classification of technical progress we will, in this chapter, follow Hicks's way of classifying technical progress.[2] There technical progress is classified according to the effect it has on the marginal productivities of the factors of production. A neutral innovation is one which increases the

---

[1] Even a great economist like Wicksell was a sworn neo-Malthusian at the beginning of this century. No student of his at the University of Lund could get a degree in economics unless he agreed that the population question was the root of all social evil and that no economic progress could be achieved unless birth control were practiced and the increase in population curtailed.

[2] J. R. Hicks, *The Theory of Wages*, London, Macmillan, 1932, pp. 131 ff. Hicks originally used his classification for discussing the effects of technical progress on the income distribution. It should be observed that Hicks only thought in terms of

marginal productivity of both factors of production in the same proportion. Labor-saving technical progress increases the marginal productivity of capital more than it increases the marginal productivity of labor. And capital-saving innovations increase the marginal productivity of labor more than they increase the marginal productivity of capital.

We will now show how the effects of technical progress can be illustrated in a geometric fashion.[3] The effects of neutral innovations on the production function àre illustrated in Figure 11.1. Isoquant aa shows in a familiar way how labor and capital can be combined before any technical progress has taken place to produce 1 unit of good A. If factor prices are as depicted by the line $P_0 P_0$, entrepreneurs will combine factors of production along ray OR and use Oc_1 of capital combined with Ol_1 of labor. The isoquant $a'a'$ depicts the new production function for good A after technical progress has taken place. The new isoquant lies completely below the old one, which shows that less labor and capital are needed to produce 1 unit of good A after the innovation.

If relative factor prices are the same (P_1P_1 is parallel to $P_0 P_0$), it is obvious from Figure 11.1 that the factors of production even after the innovation will be combined in the same ratio as before. This is indicated by the fact that P_1P_1 is tangent to the new isoquant $a'a'$ at the point at which this isoquant is cut by the ray OR. Hence, after the technical progress has taken place, Oc_2 of capital will be combined with Ol_2 of labor to produce 1 unit of good A. This is an example of a neutral innovation. That the innovation is neutral is shown by the fact that both marginal productivities have increased in the same proportion. At constant factor prices there is therefore no reason to change factor proportions, and at constant factor prices the same capital/labor ratio will be used both before and after the innovation.

It is pure coincidence that the isoquant has changed in a neutral way

---

production functions that are homogeneous of the first degree. We will see later how the Hicksian definitions can be generalized to suit better the study of the effects of technical progress on trade.

[3] Strictly speaking, the Hicksian classifications are at constant factor inputs. This is not clearly brought out by the geometric illustration where we also want to illustrate the fact that an innovation means constant production with less inputs. For illustrative reasons, we let the latter fact take precedence over the former. Nothing substantial in the analysis is changed by this because the critical fact to illustrate is the change in relation between marginal productivities caused by the innovation.

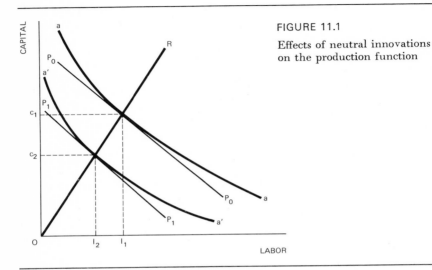

FIGURE 11.1

Effects of neutral innovations
on the production function

as in Figure 11.1. Technical progress can change the production function in
any way. The only thing we know is that more output can be produced with
constant inputs, or the same output with less inputs, i.e., that the new set
of isoquants characterizing the production function after technical progress
will be closer to the origin than was the old set of isoquants characterizing
the production function before the innovation.

Labor-saving technical progress is illustrated in Figure 11.2. We
start out with a preimprovement isoquant aa and a ruling factor price ratio
$P_0 P_0$. The capital/labor ratio used in production will then be OR. After the
innovation we get a new isoquant $a'a'$. That the innovation is labor-saving—
the marginal productivity of capital is higher relative to the marginal productivity of labor in the new situation—can be seen in either of the two
following ways. If the same factor price ratio were to prevail in the new situation, the factors of production would have to be used in the ratio OQ instead
of OR, and the production method would be more capital-intensive (P_1P_1
is parallel to $P_0 P_0$). The marginal productivity of capital is higher than
before the innovation but the relative price of capital is the same, so producers will find it advantageous to use relatively more capital than before.
If instead we assume that the same capital/labor ratio were to prevail both
before and after the innovation, the price of capital, to achieve a new equilibrium, would have to increase, compared to the price of labor, because at the

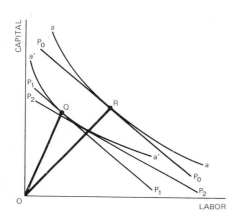

FIGURE 11.2

Labor-saving technical progress

old capital/labor ratio, capital would be more efficient and its price would be bid up. This is illustrated by the fact that the factor-price line $P_2 P_2$, tangent to the new isoquant where it is cut by OR, is less steep than the original factor-price line $P_0 P_0$.

In an analogous way Figure 11.3 demonstrates a change in the isoquants, caused by a capital-saving innovation. Here the marginal productivity of labor has increased relatively. If the factor-price ratio which existed before the innovation were to be the same after the innovation, we would get a more labor-intensive method of production, OQ instead of OR, as $P_1 P_1$ (parallel to $P_0 P_0$) is tangent to the new isoquant $a'a'$ at Q. This is explained by the fact that the marginal productivity of labor is higher than before. But the relative price of labor is the same. Hence producers try to use more labor and the methods of production become more labor-intensive, until the marginal productivity of labor is again equated to the going wage, which happens at Q.

Another way of viewing the effects of a capital-saving innovation is to assume that the same capital/labor ratio prevails both before and after the innovation. Because the marginal productivity of labor has increased relatively, labor is now more attractive to the producers and they will try to hire more labor. As they do this its relative price goes up. This is indicated by the fact that a factor-price line $P_2 P_2$, which is steeper than the original

---

FIGURE 11.3

Capital-saving technical progress

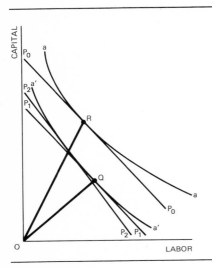

factor-price line $P_0 P_0$, is tangent to the new isoquant at the point where it is cut by the capital/labor ratio OR. This demonstrates that labor is relatively better paid than it used to be.

We have now seen how technical progress can be classified, and we should have an understanding of the meaning of the different kinds of innovations. It is now time to see what the effects of different types of technical progress will be on the terms of trade and on other variables in the trade model.

NEUTRAL TECHNICAL PROGRESS AND THE TERMS OF TRADE

To study the effects of technical progress on trade we will again use the standard trade model, with two countries consuming and producing two goods and using two factors of production. We have already studied the basic interrelationships between the two countries in Chapter 9, so we need only take one country explicitly into account in this chapter.

Let us assume that we have a country with two sectors, manufacturing and agriculture. Manufacturing is the capital-intensive sector and agriculture is the labor-intensive sector. The isoquants of the two sectors are

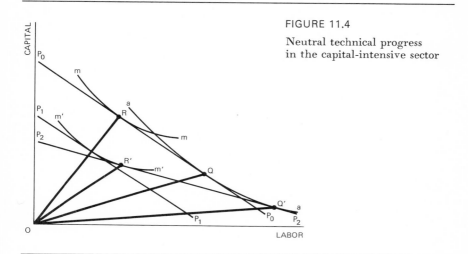

FIGURE 11.4

Neutral technical progress
in the capital-intensive sector

illustrated in Figure 11.4. We assume that they only cut once.[4] Manufacturing is supposed to be the innovating industry.

We start from an equilibrium situation in which relative factor prices are given by the factor-price line $P_0 P_0$. The preimprovement isoquants are mm for manufacturing and aa for agriculture. The capital/labor ratio used in manufacturing is OR and in agriculture it is OQ.

A neutral innovation takes place in manufacturing, so that the production function is now characterized by the isoquant $m'm'$. That the innovation is neutral can be seen from the fact that at unchanged factor prices ($P_1 P_1$ is parallel to $P_0 P_0$) the same capital/labor ratio will be used after as before the innovation.

Let us assume, for the sake of reasoning, that commodity prices are kept constant. Then what will the effect of neutral technical progress in the manufacturing sector be on outputs?

To keep commodity prices constant, factor prices will have to change. The new factor-price ratio is obtained by drawing a factor-price line that is tangent to the new manufacturing isoquant and the old agricultural

---

[4] This is, in this context, not a critical assumption the way it was when used in connection with factor-price equalization. We will comment upon this fact and upon the use of more general production functions at the end of this chapter.

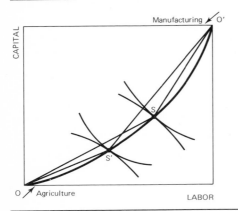

FIGURE 11.5

Effects on outputs of neutral
technical progress in the
capital-intensive sector

isoquant. This line is $P_2 P_2$ in Figure 11.4. It shows that the relative price of capital will increase because of a neutral innovation in the manufacturing sector. The economic explanation of this phenomenon is that because of the innovation, the marginal productivity of both factors of production has increased in manufacture. Producers in this sector will bid, therefore, at constant factor prices for more factors of production. Because the industry is capital-intensive they are especially eager to attract more capital, and its relative price will go up. As capital becomes more expensive, producers in both sectors will try to substitute labor for capital in production, and the methods of production in both sectors will become more labor-intensive. The new capital/labor ratio in manufacture will be OR', and the new capital/labor ratio in agriculture will be OQ'.

To study the effects on outputs, it is convenient to use the box diagram. In the box diagram in Figure 11.5 agricultural production is measured from the lower left-hand corner and manufacturing is measured from the upper right-hand corner. The contract curve is given by the curve OO'. Since agriculture is the labor-intensive sector, the contract curve goes below the diagonal.

We start from an equilibrium position at S, where two isoquants are tangent to each other before any technical progress has taken place. The capital/labor ratio used in agriculture will be OS and in manufacturing it will be $O'S$. The first question we might ask is whether point S will also be on the new contract curve which will be established after technical progress has taken place. The answer is yes, it will be.

The reason is as follows. Technical progress is of a neutral type, so the new $m'm'$ isoquant at S will have the same slope at S as the old mm isoquant. The isoquants for agriculture will, of course, be the same as before the innovation, because nothing has happened in this sector. Therefore, the two isoquants will be tangent to each other at S after, as well as before, the innovation, and S will be a point on the new contract curve.

We now have to infer what happens to outputs. We saw in Figure 11.4 that to keep commodity prices constant, factor prices would have to change and production methods would become more labor-intensive in both lines of production. This means that the new point of production will have to be somewhere on the contract curve to the left of S. A possible such point of production is S' in Figure 11.5. At S' fewer agricultural products are produced. This is because less capital and labor are used in agriculture and no technical progress has taken place in the sector. But more manufactures are produced at S', partially because more labor and capital are used in this sector, and partially because neutral technical progress has taken place, so that both labor and capital are more efficient. Neutral technical progress in manufacturing will therefore result, at constant commodity prices, in the larger production, in absolute terms, of manufactured goods, and in the smaller production, in absolute terms, of agricultural goods.[5]

Point S' is, however, not a genuine new general equilibrium point. We still assume that Say's law holds and that everything produced is consumed. Technical progress will lead to an increase in the national income. Barring the existence of inferior goods, the demand for both products will increase. This implies that at constant commodity prices there will be an excess demand for agricultural goods. In order to clear the markets, the relative price of agricultural products will go up and the relative price of manufactures will fall. If the manufacturing sector is the export sector, neutral technical progress will lead to a deterioration in the country's terms of trade. If, instead, manufactures are importables, neutral technical progress in this line of production will give the country improving terms of trade.

We can sum up the effects of neutral technical progress on the terms of trade as follows. Neutral technical progress in a country's export sector will always lead to a deterioration in the country's terms of trade, whereas

---

[5] The reader might observe the similarity between neutral technical progress and factor growth in this respect.

neutral technical progress in a country's import-competing sector will always give the country improving terms of trade.

Thus the direction in the change of the terms of trade caused by neutral technical progress is unambiguous. Just how much they will change depends on several factors. Demand factors are important. The lower the value of the income elasticity of demand for importables, the less the deterioration in the terms of trade in the unfavorable case and the more the improvement in the favorable case. The explanation for this is that if the import elasticity is low it implies that the increase in income caused by the innovation will primarily give rise to an increase in demand for exportables; this means, everything else being equal, that the export surplus at given terms of trade will be smaller in the unfavorable case and that the excess supply of importables, again at given terms of trade, will be larger in the favorable case.

The degree of adaptability of the two trading economies, as measured by the supply and demand elasticities pictured in the denominator of equations 9A.8 and 9.1, is also important. The greater the degree of adaptability, i.e., the higher the values of these elasticities, the less the change will be in the terms of trade.

We have now seen the effects of neutral technical progress. It is time to consider the effects of biased innovations.

CAPITAL-SAVING TECHNICAL PROGRESS IN THE CAPITAL-INTENSIVE INDUSTRY

The effects of a capital-saving innovation in manufacturing, the capital-intensive industry, is shown in Figure 11.6. We start out from an equilibrium situation where the isoquant mm depicts the production function for manufacturing and the isoquant aa characterizes the production function for agriculture. Relative factor prices are given by the line $P_0 P_0$. The capital/labor ratio used in manufacturing is OR, and in agriculture, OQ.

Then a capital-saving innovation takes place in the manufacturing sector, which is the capital-intensive line of production. That the innovation is capital-saving can be seen from the fact that the method of production has,

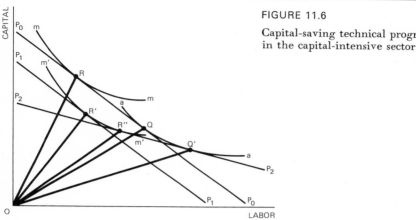

FIGURE 11.6

Capital-saving technical progress in the capital-intensive sector

at unchanged factor prices ($P_1 P_1$ is parallel to $P_0 P_0$), become more labor intensive (OR' is to the right of OR), for now the marginal productivity of labor has increased more than that of capital.

For the sake of reasoning, commodity prices are assumed to be constant. In that case, factor prices must change in favor of capital. This is illustrated by the new factor price line $P_2 P_2$, which is less steep than the original factor price line. When capital becomes relatively more expensive, more labor-intensive methods of production are used in both sectors. The new capital/labor ratio in manufacture is OR'', and in agriculture, OQ'.

To see the effects on outputs of a capital-saving innovation in manufacturing, it is convenient to use the box diagram. A box diagram illustrating the situation is set out in Figure 11.7. At the outset, the point of equilibrium is T on the preimprovement contract curve, OT being the capital/labor ratio used in agriculture and $O'T$ being the capital/labor ratio in manufacturing. We know, as was demonstrated in Figure 11.6, that at constant factor prices after the innovation, manufacturing will become more labor-intensive, while the factor intensity in agriculture will not change, of course, as long as factor prices do not change, because nothing has happened in this sector. At point T' the new capital/labor ratio in manufacture meets the original capital/labor ratio in agriculture. Because production functions in both sectors are assumed to be homogeneous of the first degree, we can conclude that one of the aa isoquants must be tangent to one of the new $m'm'$ isoquants.

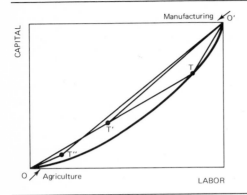

FIGURE 11.7

Effects on outputs of capital-saving
technical progress in
the capital-intensive sector

From this it follows that T' must be on the new contract curve that is established after technical progress has taken place.

At point T' the production of manufactures has increased, both because more capital and labor are used in this sector, and because at least labor
is more efficient than before because of technical progress. Fewer agricultural
products are produced, however, because fewer factors of production are devoted to this sector and because the technique of production is the same as it
was before.

We reached point T' by assuming that factor prices remained constant. But factor prices could not stay fixed. In order for commodity prices
to remain unchanged, it was necessary for factor prices to change, and thus
capital became more expensive. This would cause methods of production to
become more labor-intensive in both sectors, and we are taken farther toward the O corner, let us say to the point T''. At this point two isoquants
are again tangent to each other, and T'' is therefore on the postinnovation
contract curve.

The implication of this process for outputs is clear. At point T'' even
fewer agricultural products are produced than at T' and more manufactures
are produced. Hence, assuming constant commodity prices, capital-saving
technical progress in manufacture will lead to an absolute increase in output
of manufactured goods and an absolute decrease in the output of agricultural
products.

Keeping commodity prices constant is just a device used to trace
through the argument. It ought to be easy now to see the implication for the
new general equilibrium situation. Technical progress leads to an increase in

the national income and, if we disregard inferior goods, to an increase in demand for both goods. This implies that, at constant commodity prices, there will be an excess demand for agricultural goods, because demand for these goods has risen but supply of them has decreased. Hence the relative price of agricultural products has to go up in order to clear the markets.

The implications for the terms of trade are immediate. If manufactures are exported, the terms of trade will turn against the country; if they are imported, there will be an improvement in the country's terms of trade.

To sum up, capital-saving technical progress in the export sector will always turn the terms of trade against the country when the export sector is the capital-intensive line of production. If, on the other hand, the capital-saving innovation occurs in the import-competing sector, which is the capital-intensive sector, the terms of trade will improve for the country.

The effects of capital-saving technical progress in the capital-intensive line of production are thus unambiguous in the sense that we know in just what direction the terms of trade will change in the case of such an innovation. But the amount of this change in terms of trade depends on several factors. Demand factors and the degree of adaptability in the two countries will play a role exactly analogous to the role they played in the case of neutral technical progress. The lower the income elasticity of demand for importables is in the innovating country and the higher it is in the other country (assumed to be stationary), the better off the innovating country will be. The higher the degree of adaptability in the two countries, the less the terms of trade have to change in order to reach a new equilibrium.

We now have to treat the third and last possibility to be elaborated— that of labor-saving technical progress in the capital-intensive line of production.

LABOR-SAVING TECHNICAL PROGRESS IN THE CAPITAL-INTENSIVE INDUSTRY

The effects of labor-saving technical progress in manufacturing, the capital-intensive industry, can be illustrated in a manner analogous to that of our previous discussion of the other types of technical progress. In Figure 11.8

FIGURE 11.8

Labor-saving technical progress
in the capital-intensive sector

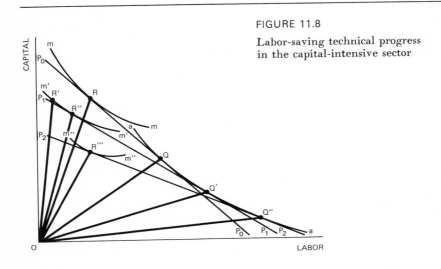

we begin with the preinnovation isoquants *mm* and *aa* and a given factor price line, $P_0 P_0$. The capital/labor ratios are then OR in manufacturing and OQ in agriculture.

A labor-saving innovation takes place in manufacturing. The new isoquant is given by $m'm'$. That the innovation is labor-saving can be seen in that, at unchanged factor prices, the new capital/labor ratio in manufacture is given by OR', as a factor-price line (not drawn) parallel to $P_0 P_0$ is tangent to $m'm'$ at R'. This shows that because of the innovation, the marginal productivity of capital has increased more than that of labor, and that producers therefore use, at unchanged factor prices, a more capital-intensive method of production, because capital is now relatively more efficient than it used to be.

We assume that commodity prices are kept unchanged and will try to infer the effects on outputs. To keep commodity prices fixed, factor prices will have to change, so capital becomes relatively more expensive. There are two reasons for this. The first is that as technical progress occurs in the manufacturing sector, costs are lowered and producers try to produce more to increase their profits. They will demand more factors of production, and because the sector is capital-intensive, they are especially eager to get capital, the relative price of which will then be bid up. The second reason is that the innovation is labor-saving, which means that the efficiency of capital has increased relatively, and this gives rise in turn to a relative increase in the demand for capital and hence to a rise in its relative price.

The next step consists of finding out what the effects of this will be on factor intensities in the two industries. The new factor-price line is given by $P_1 P_1$, which is tangent to the isoquant $m'm'$ at R'', and which is tangent to the isoquant aa at Q'. Hence the capital/labor ratio will fall in the agricultural sector. This follows from the fact that no technical progress has taken place in the sector but that the relative price of capital has increased so that more labor-intensive methods of production will be used. But in the manufacturing sector, the capital/labor ratio will rise, as OR'' lies to the left of OR. The explanation is as follows. The relative price of labor has fallen. This provides an inducement to producers to use more labor-intensive methods of production. But the marginal productivity of capital has increased relatively because of the labor-saving innovation. This provides producers an inducement to use more capital-intensive methods of production. In our case the latter tendency will be stronger than the former, so that even though capital is relatively more expensive, a more capital-intensive method of production will be used.

This is not, however, a necessary result. If the innovation had reduced costs even more and the new isoquant had been closer to the origin, the outcome would have been different. This case is also illustrated in Figure 11.8. The new, postinnovation isoquant is given by $m''m''$. Commodity prices are still assumed to be constant, and for this to be possible, factor prices will have to change in favor of capital for the same reasons as in the other case. The new factor-price line is given by $P_2 P_2$. Because capital is more expensive and no technical progress has taken place in agriculture, a more labor-intensive method of production will be used in this sector; this is shown by the fact that the new capital/labor ratio OQ'' is to the right of the original capital/labor ratio OQ. The new factor-price line $P_2 P_2$ is tangent to the isoquant $m''m''$ at R'''. The capital/labor ratio in manufacture will be OR''', which is to the right of the preimprovement capital/labor ratio OR. Hence the new method of production will be more labor-intensive in the manufacturing sector as well. This is explained by the fact that even though the marginal productivity of capital has increased relatively because of the innovation, this increase is outweighed by the fact that capital has become relatively more expensive, so the end result will be a more labor-intensive method of production.

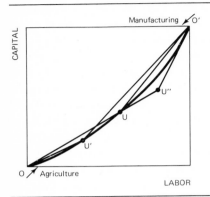

FIGURE 11.9

Effects on outputs of labor-saving technical progress in the capital-intensive sector

It is now time to infer the results for outputs. To do so we will again use the box diagram. The same type of box diagram as that used in the earlier parts of the chapter is constructed (Figure 11.9). Production of agricultural goods is measured from the lower left-hand corner, production of manufactures is measured from the upper right-hand corner, and so on. Before any technical progress has taken place, the point of equilibrium of production is at point U, with OU being the capital/labor ratio used in agriculture and $O'U$ being the capital/labor ratio in manufacturing.

We now have to study the effects on outputs of technical progress, assuming commodity prices to be constant. We start with the second case discussed above. This was the case in which the highest degree of technical progress led to the new isoquant $m''m''$ in manufacturing, as depicted in Figure 11.8. In this case the capital/labor ratio in both sectors fell, so that both lines of production became more labor-intensive. This situation is compatible with a movement from point U to point U' in Figure 11.9.

In this case the implications for outputs is clear. At point U' fewer agricultural goods and more manufactures are produced. This implies, in exactly the same manner as was the case with capital-saving technical progress, that there will be an excess demand for agricultural products at given prices. Hence the relative price of agricultural goods will increase to clear the markets. If manufactures are exported, the terms of trade will deteriorate for the innovating country; if agriculture is the export sector, the terms of trade will improve.

But this is not a necessary outcome of labor-saving technical progress in the capital-intensive industry. In the first case we dealt with, the effect of the innovation was to increase the capital/labor ratio in manufacturing but to lower it in agriculture. Labor-saving technical progress in the capital-intensive industry will always lead to an increase in the relative price of capital and to a fall in the capital/labor ratio in the labor-intensive industry. The smaller the reduction in cost caused by the innovation, the more the capital/labor ratio will increase in manufacture and the less it will fall in agriculture. Point U'' in Figure 11.9 shows a situation in which there is an unchanged capital/labor ratio in agriculture and an increasing capital/labor ratio in manufacture. This is not a possible general equilibrium point, but a point infinitesimally close to it is consistent with a new point of equilibrium characterized by a higher capital/labor ratio in manufacture and a lower one in agriculture. At such a point, output of agricultural products will have increased, and output of manufactures will have decreased, at constant commodity prices. Hence there will be an excess demand for manufactures, and their relative price will have to increase in order to clear the markets.

The implication of this is that a labor-saving innovation in the capital-intensive sector can have any effect on relative prices. Contrary to what was the case with neutral and capital-saving technical progress in this sector, the effects on the terms of trade are indeterminate.

Let us now sum up the discussion of the effects of different types of technical progress on the terms of trade. Neutral technical progress will always have a negative effect on the relative price of the good produced in the innovating sector. Neutral technical progress will improve a country's terms of trade if it takes place in the import-competing sector, and it will lead to a deterioration in the terms of trade if it is confined to the export sector.

The effects of capital-saving innovations in the capital-intensive sector, and of labor-saving innovations in the labor-intensive sector, are also clear-cut. Again, relative commodity prices of the innovating product will fall. Hence if exportables are capital-intensive, and capital-saving technical progress takes place in this sector, the terms of trade will deteriorate for the country. Analogously, if the import-competing sector is labor-intensive and if labor-saving technical progress takes place within it, the terms of trade will improve for the country.

The effects of labor-saving innovations in the capital-intensive industry and of capital-saving innovations in the labor-intensive sector, finally, are indeterminate. The relative price of the innovating product might increase or it might decrease, but no specific conclusions can be drawn from a theoretical point of view.

One of the critical assumptions for the analysis has been the assumption that production functions in the two sectors are homogeneous of the first degree. We learned, in Chapter 10, that this assumption was necessary for reaching qualitative conclusions about the effects of factor growth on the terms of trade. It is, however, not a necessary assumption for reaching clear-cut results about the effects of technical progress. Here it is possible to get results with more general, unspecified production functions. It is also easier to interpret these results in economic terms. To give a rigorous presentation of the results, a mathematical approach is needed. If the exposition is confined to the use of geometry, it is necessary to assume that the production functions are linearly homogeneous. A full-fledged mathematical exposition would take us outside the scope of the present book, so we will be content to give some verbal comments on the more general results.

REMARKS ON TECHNICAL PROGRESS AND THE TERMS OF TRADE WITH UNSPECIFIED PRODUCTION FUNCTIONS

In Chapter 3 we studied some of the characteristics of a production function with two factors of production. Technical progress leads to a shift in the production function. With given inputs a larger output will be produced. As an analytic expression for a production function with technical progress we can write

$$Q = f(L, K, t) \tag{11.1}$$

where Q stands for output, L and K for labor and capital, respectively, and t signifies technical progress. We learned in Chapter 3 that we could take partial derivatives with respect to labor and capital and get expressions for the marginal productivity of labor and the marginal productivity of capital. We could then go on and take second partial derivatives, which showed how the marginal productivity of labor changed with a constant stock of capital, etc.

In a similar fashion we can now take partial derivatives with respect to t.[6] We can take $\partial f/\partial t$, for instance. This partial derivative describes the

---

[6] This section builds on B. Södersten, *A Study of Economic Growth and International Trade*, Stockholm, Almqvist & Wiksell, 1964, chap. 4. The interested reader will find there a detailed exposition of the results reported in this section.

shift in the production function. It is a measure of the technical progress to the extent that it shows how much more can be produced with given inputs because of the technical progress. By definition, this partial derivative is always positive, because we take technical progress to mean an increased capacity to produce.

We can also take two other partial derivatives with respect to t, $\partial^2 f/\partial L\, \partial t$ and $\partial^2 f/\partial K\, \partial t$. The first shows the effect of technical progress on the marginal productivity of labor, and the second, the effect of technical progress on the marginal productivity of capital.

These three partial derivatives are very important in determining the effects of technical progress on the terms of trade and on other variables in the trade model. Once we know something about the sign of these derivatives we also know a great deal about the effects of technical progress on the terms of trade. Other factors are, of course, also important, but the sign of the second partial derivatives illustrated above determines the direction of change in the terms of trade.

Let us assume that we have technical progress only in the export sector. We know that this means that more exportables can be produced with given inputs, or, in other words, that $\partial f/\partial t$ is positive. If technical progress has a positive effect on the marginal productivity of both factors of production, it means that both $\partial^2 f/\partial L\, \partial t$ and $\partial^2 f/\partial K\, \partial t$ are positive. This implies that the terms of trade will deteriorate for the country.

It is easy to understand why this must be so. Technical progress itself, symbolized by $\partial f/\partial t$, will have a positive effect on outputs of exportables at constant prices, because more will be produced with given inputs. If the marginal productivity of labor goes up because of the innovation, more labor will be attracted to the sector and this will also have a positive effect on output. If the marginal productivity of capital increases by the technical progress, more capital will be attracted to the sector in an exactly analogous manner, and this will again have a positive effect on output. Hence all three factors will go in the same direction, and there will be an excess supply of exportables at constant commodity prices. In order to clear the markets, the price of exportables has to fall; i.e., the terms of trade will turn against the country.

Technical progress in the import-competing sector will have completely analogous effects, provided that both marginal productivities increase because of the innovation. In that case the three factors work in the same direction. More importables will be produced at constant commodity prices.

The country's own producers will capture a larger share of the market for importables. The demand for the other country's exports will fall, and in order to clear the markets, the price of the innovating country's importables will fall; i.e., its terms of trade will improve.

What is of importance, therefore, is the change in the absolute values of the marginal productivities. As long as the marginal productivity of a factor increases because of technical progress, more of this factor will be attracted to the innovating sector from the noninnovating sector. The change in the absolute value of the marginal productivities, therefore, is what is important for the reallocation of factors of production.

The Hicksian classification of technical progress concerned itself only with relative changes in the marginal productivities. To understand Hicks's classification we must take into consideration the fact that it was originally introduced to study the effects of technical progress on the income distribution. It is not difficult to understand that for the income distribution the relative change in marginal productivities is of prime importance. But for the effects on outputs, commodity prices, and allocation of factors of production, it is the absolute changes in the marginal productivities that count.[7]

Hence as long as technical progress is of a kind which increases the marginal productivity of both factors of production, the effects on outputs and relative prices are clear-cut. But there is no guarantee that innovations will have this effect. A priori it is fully possible that the marginal productivity of one, or maybe both, factors of production will fall because of technical progress.[8] If this happens, the result for the terms of trade is no longer determinate.

If, for instance, there is technical progress in the export sector, and if the innovation is of such a kind as to increase the marginal productivity of

---

[7] This suggests a reclassification of technical progress better suited to this purpose. The interested reader can consult Södersten, *op. cit.*, pp. 99 ff., on this score.

[8] If the production function is homogeneous of the first degree we know that the marginal productivity of at least one of the factors of production will increase because of technical progress. It is still, however, fully conceivable that the marginal productivity of the other factor could fall. See Södersten, *op. cit.*, pp. 103 ff. In the more general case of unspecified production functions, it is fully conceivable that both marginal productivities might fall because of the innovation. To understand this it might help to think in geometric terms: Technical progress implies an upward shift in the production function, but we do not know anything about the slope of the new production function compared to the old one, and for the marginal productivities it is the slope that matters.

labor but decrease that of capital, we will have two forces pulling in opposite directions. At constant commodity and factor prices, labor will be attracted to this section, because the marginal productivity of labor is now above the going wage. This will tend to increase output of the good. At the same time, capital will be released from the sector, because the marginal productivity of capital is below the going return to capital. This will have a negative influence on the output of the good. To this must be added the upward shift in the production function itself, symbolized by $\partial f/\partial t$, which, of course, always will have a positive effect on the supply of the good. Hence there are two positive effects and one negative effect on output of this kind of technical progress, and it is no longer possible to infer anything about the effects on outputs and relative prices.

We should now have a fairly firm grasp of how technical progress affects the terms of trade and outputs in the standard trade model. Before we conclude this chapter it might be useful to comment upon how other factors, such as the national income and the income distribution, are affected by innovations. To derive formal expressions for these effects would take us outside the scope of this book. Against the background of this chapter it should, however, not be too difficult to grasp the main drift of the argument concerning the effects on these variables.

TECHNICAL PROGRESS, THE NATIONAL INCOME, AND THE INCOME DISTRIBUTION

The effects on the real national income are closely linked with those on the terms of trade. Technical progress which improves the terms of trade has a strongly positive effect on the growth of real income. With innovations that lead to deteriorating terms of trade, the case becomes more complex. If the losses in the terms of trade are large, they might cancel out most of the prospective gains in the growth of income.

If there is technical progress in the export sector, and if this progress is of such a kind as to decrease or leave unchanged the marginal productivity of the factors of production, it is bound to have a positive effect on national income. But if the innovation (which is perhaps more likely) leads to an increase in the marginal productivities, a certain negative effect on real income will come from the export sector. This negative effect will play a larger role if the country's export share is large.[9]

Technical progress in the import-competing sector, on the other hand, will always have positive effects on real income. Thus it is of critical importance whether the progress occurs in the export- or in the import-competing sector.

The most favorable case one could construct would be that in which most technical progress would be concentrated in the import-competing industry and where any innovations in the export sector would be of a type which would lower the marginal productivity of the factors in that industry. Then all the strategic variables, i.e., the rise in the production functions and the change in the marginal productivities, would exert a positive influence on real income. In this case a large dependence on foreign trade would benefit the country. Especially if the two trading economies have small possibilities of reallocating resources and adapting demand to price changes so that the value of the elasticity factor would be low, technical progress of this kind would imply large increases in the terms of trade for the innovating country and a fast growth of real income.

In the opposite case, that in which the innovations are concentrated to the export sector and the marginal productivity of labor and capital are rising sharply because of technical progress, the contributions to real income from the innovations might easily be dispersed through trade. The chances that this will occur are especially high if the export share of the economy is large and if the adaptability of the economy is low. Technical progress of this kind might lead to a situation such as that discussed in Chapter 9, in which impoverishing growth takes place.

Thus the same general factors which tend to increase the volume of importables and to give rise to improving terms of trade will also exert a strong positive influence on the growth of national income. Those factors, on the other hand, which increase the volume of exportables and make for deteriorating terms of trade might also, under certain circumstances, cause the positive effects of innovations on real income to be comparatively weak. It should be stressed, however, that the effects depend to a large extent on

---

[9] The reader should, however, observe that technical progress in the export sector also gives rise to a potential increase in the production of importables, as the model is of a neoclassical type and the factors of production are substitutable.

the adaptability of the two economies, measured by the elasticities set out in the denominators of equations 9A.8 and 9.1. If the value of the weighted sum of these elasticities is large, the terms of trade might be said to act as an excellent steering mechanism, and small changes in relative prices will give rise to rapid and efficient reactions from consumers and producers. In these circumstances, the changes in the terms of trade might be small during the growth process, whereas the effects on volumes and incomes would be large. This should, however, not obscure the fact that it is extremely useful to know which factors influence the terms of trade in the growth process. (To say that the steering wheel of a car might not move much during a trip is not to say that it is an unimportant part of the car.)

Technical progress also affects factor rewards and income distribution. If technical progress is neutral, the effect on factor rewards depends on factor intensities in the innovating sector. If the industry is labor-intensive, neutral innovations will lead to a relative increase in the wage. If, on the other hand, the sector is capital-intensive, neutral innovations will lead to an increase in the return to capital.

The effects of biased innovations are quite clear. Labor-saving technical progress will benefit capital, because it primarily increases the marginal productivity of capital, and capital-saving progress will benefit labor, because it increases the marginal productivity of labor.

Capital-saving innovations in the labor-intensive line of production are, therefore, the type of progress most beneficial to labor. Analogously, labor-saving progress in the capital-intensive line of production should have the most favorable effects on the return to capital.

It is easy to see intuitively the economic meaning of these results. Capital-saving innovations increase the marginal productivity of labor more than they do that of capital. This gives a stimulus to producers to use more labor, because it is now relatively more efficient. If the sector in which the innovation occurs is also labor-intensive, this will reinforce the demand for labor, so the wage will be bid up even more than it would be otherwise.

Against this background it is easy to understand Wicksell's statement, given in Chapter 10, to the effect that the capitalist is the friend of the worker, whereas the innovator is not infrequently his enemy, at least in the short run. If the labor force is constant and capital accumulates, this is bound to have a positive influence on the real wage. In this sense, the capitalist-saver is the friend of the worker. But certain types of innovations can easily have a negative effect on the real wage. A labor-saving innovation of a kind which would decrease the marginal productivity of labor, especially if it were to occur in a capital-intensive line of production, could very well lead to a lowering of the real wage. In this sense the good engineer might be an enemy of the worker.

Obviously a good many cases of different effects of technical progress on income distribution can be constructed. We will satisfy ourselves for the present by merely pointing out those factors which will lead to a fast growth of the real wage and leave the task of figuring out the other cases as an exercise for the reader.

If we also take factor growth into account, it is clear that if capital accumulates faster than the population grows, the real wage will increase faster than the real rent and the income distribution will turn in favor of labor. The higher the degree of capital-saving innovations and the faster the rate of technical progress, the more the real wage will rise. This development will be further increased if the innovations occur in the labor-intensive lines of production and if the possibilities of substituting factors of production for each other are limited.

We should by now have certain insights into the theoretical aspects of economic growth and international trade. In Chapter 12 we will deal with more empirical and policy-oriented questions in this realm. We will see that many of these policy issues can be clarified by the kind of theorizing we have done in Chapters 9, 10, and 11.

SELECTED BIBLIOGRAPHY: CHAPTERS 9, 10, AND 11

The model developed in Chapter 9 was originally set out in the author's paper:

"Utrikeshandel och ekonomisk tillväxt: den marginella aspekten," *Ekonomisk Tidskrift*, no. 1, 1961. An English translation was published in *International Economic Papers*, no. 11, London, Macmillan, 1962.

Otherwise the three chapters build primarily on the author's book:

A Study of Economic Growth and International Trade, Stockholm, Almqvist & Wiksell, 1964.

Important papers on growth and trade are:

J. R. Hicks, "An Inaugural Lecture," *OEP*, June 1953 (reprinted under the title "The Long-Run Dollar Problem" in *RIE*).

H. G. Johnson, "Economic Development and International Trade," *Nationalökonomisk Tidsskrift*, vols. 5–6, 1959 (reprinted in *RIE*).

R. Findlay and H. Grubert, "Factor Intensities, Technological Progress, and International Trade," *OEP*, February 1959.

T. M. Rybczynski, "Factor Endowment and Relative Commodity Prices," *Ec*, November 1955 (reprinted in *RIE*).

J. Bhagwati, "Immiserizing Growth: A Geometric Note," *RES*, June 1958 (reprinted in *RIE*).

These articles together give a good overview of the growth and trade problem treated in a verbal and geometric way. An alternative treatment of technical progress is given in:

M. C. Kemp, *The Pure Theory of International Trade*, Englewood Cliffs, N.J., Prentice-Hall, 1964.

For a criticism of Kemp, see:

K. G. Mäler and B. Södersten, "Factor-Biased Technical Progress and the Elasticity of Substitution," *Swedish Journal of Economics*, no. 1, 1967.

Papers that aim at a dynamic treatment and deal with problems specific to the less-developed countries are:

D. M. Bensusan-Butt, "A Model of Trade and Accumulation," *AER*, September 1954.

W. A. Lewis, "Economic Development with Unlimited Supplies of Labor," *MS*, May 1952.

H. Oniki and H. Uzawa, "Patterns of Trade and Investment in a Dynamic Model of International Trade," *RES*, January 1965.

The reader can also consult:

G. M. Meier, *The International Economics of Development*, New York, Harper & Row, 1968.

The terms of trade and the national income in the growth process

12

The development of the terms of trade has, at least since the beginning of classical economics, held great sway over the imagination of economists. A case might be made for a theory about this concern being an offspring of the plague of the last two centuries: nationalism. We will, however, not go into the intricacies of the interrelationships between nationalism and the theories of the development of the terms of trade. This we will leave to the reader who is interested in intellectual history to think about in his own time. What we shall do, in this chapter, is to consider, against the background of the neoclassical theorizing developed in the last three chapters, two of the main types of theories about the development of the terms of trade which have dominated the thought of economists during the last two centuries. We will also deal with its implications for the development of the national income in real terms. At the end of the chapter we will appraise the theory of comparative advantage against the background of the theory of economic growth and international trade.

The first kind of theory we will deal with, concerning the long-run development of the terms of trade, we will call the British school, as it has been primarily the concern of British economists. This school held that the terms of trade would go against the developed, industrial nations. The other theory, or set of theories, about the terms of trade we will deal with is connected with the names of Singer and Prebisch, especially that of Prebisch. This theory maintains that the terms of trade would have gone against the less-developed countries and would continue to do so unless some specific policy measures are taken.

THE BRITISH SCHOOL

The beginnings of the British school date back to the heyday of the English classical economists. One of their firm beliefs was that of the decreasing returns of agriculture. This belief was one of the cornerstones upon which Ricardo founded his theory of income distribution. To explain the income distribution was, according to Ricardo, the main object of economics. Because of the decreasing returns to scale in agriculture, the income distribution would move in favor of the landlords: Population would increase and keep the wage at a subsistence level, the capitalists would be squeezed, and the landlords would reap an increasing land rent and live forever in leisure at the expense of the others.

The decreasing returns to scale in agriculture would also have ominous consequences for England's terms of trade. Robert Torrens wrote in 1821:

> As the several nations of the world advance in wealth and population, the commercial intercourse between them must gradually become less important and beneficial ... the species of foreign trade which has the most powerful influence in raising profits and increasing wealth, is that which is carried on between an old country in which raw produce bears a high value in relation to wrought goods, and a new country where wrought goods possess a high exchangeable power with respect to raw produce. Now, as new countries advance in population, the cultivation of inferior soils must increase the cost of raising raw produce, and the division of labor reduce the expense of working it up. Hence, in all new settlements, the increasing value of raw produce must gradually check its exportation, and the falling value of wrought goods progressively prevent their importation; until at length the commercial intercourse between nations shall be confined to those peculiar articles, in the production of which the immutable circumstances of soil and climate give one country a permanent advantage over another.[1]

This quotation indicates quite clearly that Torrens believed that the terms of trade would go against the industrial countries, of which England was the most important at the time when Torrens wrote the above paragraph. The price of manufactured goods in terms of food products and raw materials would steadily diminish, and the developed, industrial nations which exported manufactured, "wrought" goods would suffer from this development until finally the volume of trade would diminish to such an extent that every country would be self-contained.

This theory is primitive, but it is, in an odd way, complete. It builds on very narrow assumptions and drastic simplifications. From the vantage point of the middle of the twentieth century it is clear that its most crippling defect is the failure to take into account technical progress. But judged on its own terms it is quite logical. If one is willing to disregard technical progress and to assume that there are constant returns to scale in the production of

---

[1] Robert Torrens, *Essay on the Production of Wealth*, London, 1821, pp. 96 ff.

186

The terms of trade and
the national income
in the growth process

manufactures but decreasing returns to scale in agriculture, and that the prime movers in the growth process are increases in capital and labor, Torrens's result is quite likely to occur. Its chief fault lies not in defective deductive reasoning but in the narrow and unrealistic assumptions upon which the analysis is built. The emphasis put on a few strategic factors is so great that the basic model is, at least for all practical purposes, transformed from a general equilibrium to a partial model by leaving out the demand side.

The line of thought that Torrens inaugurated was virtuously upheld by English economists during all of the nineteenth century, and its remnants can be seen to this day. Its chief proponent during this century was no one else but John Maynard Keynes. As a commentary to the development of Britain's terms of trade during the first decade of this century, Keynes wrote the following in the *Economic Journal* of 1912:

> The deterioration—from the point of view of this country— shown above is due, of course, to the operation of the law of diminishing returns for raw products which, after a temporary lull, has been setting in sharply in quite recent years. There is now again a steady tendency for a given unit of manufactured product to purchase year by year a diminishing quantity of raw product. The comparative advantage is moving sharply against industrial countries.[2]

The quoted paragraph makes quite clear that Keynes adheres, on this score, to the old, classical tradition. His rebelliousness was to be saved for other causes. The notion that the terms of trade will go against the industrial countries he seems even to be willing to give the stature of a law of nature.

This line of thought was to play a great role in some of his later writings. It dominated the economic argument contained in the book which first made Keynes known to a greater public, *The Economic Consequences of the Peace*, published in 1920. The industrial nations of Europe had, before the war, relied upon imports of food and raw materials from the rural parts of Europe and from countries overseas. But they had only been able to do this at relatively increasing costs. The affluence of industrial Europe before World War I depended, according to Keynes, on an intricate and delicate balance and division of international labor:

> Much else might be said in an attempt to portray the economic consequences of the Europe of 1914. I have selected for emphasis

---

2 J. M. Keynes, *Economic Journal*, vol. XXII, no. 4, 1912, p. 630.

the three or four greatest factors of instability—the instability of an excessive population dependent for its livelihood on a complicated and artificial organization, the psychological instability of the laboring and capitalist classes, and the instability of Europe's claim, coupled with the completeness of her dependence, on food supplies of the New World.[3]

The tragedy of the Treaty of Versailles, according to Keynes, was that it disrupted the economic organization of Europe and the intricate network of international trade on which it was built. The terms at which Europe could trade were critical for her well-being. If she would have to pay too dearly for the food necessary to feed the "excessive" population, and if the raw materials needed to produce industrial goods became too expensive, the era of progress might come to an end.

There is little doubt that when Keynes wrote about Europe he had Britain primarily in mind, and that the two tended to be synonymous for him. The fear of a long-run deterioration of the terms of trade, which would cause foreign trade to be of little advantage to Europe (Britain) and would jeopardize its future economic progress, haunted his mind. The development of the terms of trade during the heyday of the British Empire (1870–1900) had not substantiated this fear, but Keynes somehow felt that this had been an abnormal period, and in *The Economic Consequences of the Peace* he again reiterated his belief in the inevitability of deteriorating terms of trade for the industrial countries:

Up to about 1900 a unit of labour applied to industry yielded year by year a purchasing power over an increasing quantity of food. It is possible that about 1900 this process began to be reversed and a diminishing yield of nature to men's effort was beginning to re-assert itself.[4]

This is not the place to make a whole-scale evaluation of all the political and economic beliefs and ideas contained in *The Economic Consequences of the Peace*. We will content ourselves with the chief idea expressed by Keynes and other members of the British school about the development of the terms of trade.

---

[3] J. M. Keynes, *The Economic Consequences of the Peace*, London, Macmillan, 1920, p. 25.
[4] Ibid., p. 10.

188

The terms of trade and
the national income
in the growth process

Keynes's main idea seems to have been that Britain's (Europe's) population would continue to grow and that this would cause a deterioration in her terms of trade. It is easy to evaluate this idea against the background of the theories developed in Chapters 9, 10, and 11.

Let us start by thinking in terms of a two-by-two-by-two model and assume that Europe is exporting industrial products which are produced with capital-intensive methods of production and that the production functions are homogeneous of the first degree. If population were to increase with other factors remaining constant, that would lead to a result opposite to that of Keynes: The terms of trade would go in favor of Europe.

The assumption about constant returns to scale is critical for obtaining this result. It might be added that this is an assumption Keynes would not have found acceptable, because he instead viewed constant returns to scale in industry but decreasing returns to scale in agriculture as being somehow embedded in nature. If this were the case, things would become more tricky; then the effects of a population increase would no longer be clear-cut but would depend on the exact shape of the production functions.[5] The general presumption would still be, however, that, given all other assumptions, the terms of trade would go in favor of Europe.

The general conclusion to be drawn seems, therefore, to be that Keynes was not very careful in theorizing about the development of the terms of trade and that he drew very far-reaching conclusions from an incomplete, weak, and intuitive type of reasoning. There is little doubt that Keynes himself in his thinking about international trade belonged to the neoclassical tradition. A consistent application of neoclassical theorizing would, if anything, have led him to conclusions quite opposite from those he drew. One might also observe that his dark prophecies were not fulfilled, at least not in a literal sense. Britain might have had difficult economic problems during the interwar period, but her terms of trade improved considerably during the 1920s.

Classical thought on the subject—the theories of Ricardo and Torrens about the development of the terms of trade—can also be elucidated by our earlier theorizing. To think in terms of two-sector models was not uncommon for these economists. They did not take technical progress into account.

---

[5] For an analytic expression for the effects of factor growth given unspecified production functions see B. Södersten, *A Study of Economic Growth and International Trade*, Stockholm, Almqvist & Wiksell, 1964.

Their case, then, seems to be best approximated by a situation in which both labor and capital increase in the industrial country but where capital is the prime mover in economic development and is the factor which increases fastest. If the manufacturing sector is the exporting, capital-intensive sector, we would expect the terms of trade to go against the industrial country, or, in other words, that even in our type of theorizing the classical result would follow from the classical assumptions.

The main criticism to be raised against the British school is that it tends to oversimplify matters. The stress on one or two factors at the expense of others made the outlook of the British school narrow and rigid. Torrens is a good example of this. The unrealistic assumptions both about the causes of growth and about production functions made the classical analysis quite sterile. Keynes and quite a few of his followers do not come off much better, even though they in principle at least had the neoclassical apparatus to fall back upon.[6] An uncritical acceptance of the classical line of thought is clearly discernible, and the dominant impression left by their writings is one of worry that things are no longer what they used to be and that somehow, as the afternoon grows late, things are not going to get better.

It is, of course, not difficult to construct examples (against the background of our earlier theorizing) which would lead to a deterioration of the terms of trade of the industrial countries. For the sake of concreteness it might be useful to give a couple of such examples. One example is the one mentioned in connection with Torrens. If the second, agricultural country is stationary, and if capital accumulates in the industrial country, her export sector being capital-intensive, the terms of trade will deteriorate for the industrial country. Another example would be the case in which the industrial country has technical progress in her export sector leading to increases in the marginal productivities of the factors of production. Such progress will also cause a deterioration in her terms of trade. A third example is the one in which the export sector, the industrial sector, is capital-intensive and capital-saving technical progress occurs in it. Again the terms of trade will go against the country.

There is obviously no difficulty in constructing hypothetical examples that will lead to a worsening in the terms of trade of industrial countries.

---

6 Some British economists took a different view. The most notable one is William Beveridge, who forcefully challenged Keynes's views, even though he did not present a more definite theory of his own. See Södersten, *op. cit.*, chap. 6.

190

The terms of trade and
the national income
in the growth process

The causes that members of the British school had in mind are by no means the only ones which might lead to a worsening in the terms of trade for industrial countries. But to prophesy the future course of the terms of trade is not our task. We have to be satisfied with having gained a certain insight into the interrelationships between the variables in the trade model in the context of economic growth.

SINGER, PREBISCH, AND THE TERMS OF TRADE

To analyze the British school in its main outline was a comparatively simple affair, because the members of this school argued within a fairly well-known and reasonably well-defined frame of reference. It was not difficult to understand what they were trying to say or to follow the logic of their reasoning. Indeed, their tendency toward oversimplification constituted one of the chief flaws in their argument. They upheld too faithfully the Ricardian tradition, with its emphasis on deduction from a few simple premises.

When we turn to the Singer–Prebisch case we move into another world.[7] The structure of the Singer–Prebisch theory of development and trade is much more complicated. The basic part of it, which refers to growth, is simple enough, it runs in terms of productivity gains, development of demand, etc. But intertwined with this basic theory are hypotheses about the influence of the business cycle on the terms of trade, the interrelation between factor rewards and the terms of trade, the effects of different market forms on the terms of trade, and so on. These different theories or hypotheses are neither clearly expressed nor rigorously formulated. Tacked on to the main

---

[7] The main sources for the Singer–Prebisch case are: H. W. Singer, "The Distribution of Gains Between Investing and Borrowing Countries," *American Economic Review, Papers & Proceedings*, vol. 40, May, 1950, pp. 473 ff., and "Economic Progress in Under-Developed Countries," *Social Research*, vol. 16, March 1949, pp. 3 ff.; United Nations Economic Commission for Latin America (written by R. Prebisch), *The Economic Development of Latin America and Its Principal Problems*, New York, 1950, and R. Prebisch, "Commercial Policy in the Underdeveloped Countries," *American Economic Review, Papers & Proceedings*, vol. 49, no. 2, May 1959, pp. 251 ff. The main partner in the Singer–Prebisch team is undoubtedly Prebisch, and the following discussion is mainly devoted to his writings.

theory, they are difficult to deal with for at least two reasons. First, it is often hard to tell what the theories really intend to say and how the interconnections are supposed to work. Second, it is often difficult to see their significance for the main line of argument: What role, for instance, can the labor unions possibly have in the development of the terms of trade?

It goes without saying that it is difficult to present an exposition and an examination of theories of this type. Maybe Singer and Prebisch would claim that we are writing about something other than the Singer–Prebisch case, but that is a risk they have taken by their implicit and incomplete theorizing.

Genetically speaking, the Singer–Prebisch case starts as an ad hoc explanation of the hardships of the South American economies and as a rationalization for certain policy conclusions. In "Commercial Policy in the Underdeveloped Countries," Prebisch begins by saying that the only way for South America to speed up its rate of economic growth is by attempting industrialization. If the South American states try to increase their primary production—their supply of raw materials and food products—they will meet falling terms of trade, because the income and demand elasticities facing them in their export markets are so low, but they need rising export incomes in the development process, because their own marginal propensities to import are so high.[8]

This is the core of the Singer–Prebisch case. If the income elasticity facing the exports of the underdeveloped (or peripheral, as Prebisch calls them) countries is low and if, furthermore, the demand and supply are inelastic with regard to price, little is to be gained from pushing these exports. However high the domestic growth rate within the export industry may be, most of the productivity gains within the export sector will be exported away through falling terms of trade. This is exactly what we would expect from our theorizing in the earlier chapters.

If this were as far as the Singer–Prebisch case were to go, it could claim a good foundation in orthodox economic theory. But in itself this proposition has to be regarded as a very simple, even trite one, and it is astonishing that such claims of novelty and revolutionary thinking could have been made for such a simple argument. However, although this is in our view the core or, to put it even more bluntly, the only meaningful part of the Singer–Prebisch case, there are also other theories or propositions attendent to it. It is now time to discuss this "superstructure" of the Singer–Prebisch case.

---

[8] Prebisch, "Commercial Policy in the Underdeveloped Countries." pp. 251 ff.

192

The terms of trade and
the national income
in the growth process

One of Prebisch's arguments is concerned with the effects of business cycles on the terms of trade. In boom times, profits, wages, and prices rise. But profits rise more than wages, and prices in the peripheral countries rise more than prices in the industrial countries, so profits among primary producers rise even more than profits in industrial countries. On the downswing, however, asymmetry enters the picture. Profits, wages, and prices now ought to fall, but because of the downward rigidity of wages there, they will not fall in industrial countries. Profits in the center (the industrial countries) will be squeezed, and entrepreneurs in these countries restore their profits from the periphery. The workers in the primary producing countries do not have strong organizations, and consequently wages and profits are squeezed more in these countries to ensure that profits in the center are kept at a level which is not regarded as abnormally low.[9]

It is hardly possible to analyze this line of argument closely. The suggested relationships are so nebulous that it is almost impossible to discern how this theory might function. Why is it that prices in the peripheral countries decrease relatively more on the downswing than they improve on the upswing, so that the end result is a deterioration in the terms of trade of these countries? How can the behavior of wages and prices hang together? This theory is very hard to fit into our frame of reference, which works with a few, well-defined variables. It can also be a relief to realize that this theory is of a typical short-run nature and consequently does not merit so much attention in the context of growth. We shall go on, therefore, and deal with a part of the Singer–Prebisch case which has attracted both more attention and more support: the theory about market forms and the terms of trade.

Prebisch stresses as an important fact that while in industrial countries monopolistic market forms are common, the export industries in most less-developed countries work under competitive conditions.[10] It is hard to say whether this assertion is right or wrong.[11] This is, however, of no great importance from our point of view, because we are primarily interested in

---

[9] United Nations Economic Commission for Latin America, *The Economic Development of Latin America and Its Principal Problems*, pp. 12 ff.
[10] Ibid., pp. 8 ff.
[11] C. P. Kindleberger gives a survey of the main investigations that have been undertaken in *The Terms of Trade, A European Case Study*, New York, Wiley, 1956, pp. 241 ff. His conclusions are quite vague and it seems not to be possible to say anything more definite about the degree of monopoly as between the Center and the Periphery, to use Prebisch's language.

the consistency of Prebisch's reasoning and in the implications of his assertion. In other words, would monopolistic market conditions tend in the long
run to improve the terms of trade for a country and would free competition
tend to worsen them?

Many economists seem to take for granted that monopoly gets better
terms of trade than competition for à country. They reach this conclusion by
applying a simple comparative-static price theory which assumes that under
unrestricted competition supply will expand faster than it would under
monopolistic conditions, because the monopolist can restrict his output to
maintain price, whereas under free competition supply will always expand
until price equals costs and profits have been competed away.[12]

Such a simple type of theory does not seem a fruitful approach to the
question at hand. What is needed is a theory of market forms and the growth
of output, or, to put it in a more general form, a theory of market forms and
economic growth. Such a theory could not take the change in productivity—
the lowering of the cost curves—as a datum and derive a result applying the
simple maximization principle; rather, it would have to offer a hypothesis
about the effect of different market forms on productivity.

There exists no such rigorous and well-established theory. Attempts
to tackle the question have, however, been made by Baumol, Galbraith,
Sylos-Labini, and others.[13] It might be worthwhile to give a short review of
the relevant aspects of these attempts.

The argument of these authors is essentially simple. They start with
the observation that the size of the firm under competitive conditions is much
smaller than under monopolistic or oligopolistic conditions. But the possibility of innovations, of introducing and applying technical progress, is intimately connected with the size of the firm. Technical progress is no longer
a matter of the ingenuity of the small man. Or, to quote Galbraith:

> Most of the cheap and simple innovations have, to put it bluntly and
> unpersuasively, been made. Not only is development now sophisticated

---

[12] We do not have to make any sharp distinction here between different types of
monopolistic markets. Prebisch *et consortes* presumedly would include under
monopolistic markets all market forms where the producer is not a simple price
taker.

[13] W. J. Baumol, *Business Behavior, Value and Growth*, New York, Wiley, 1959;
J. K. Galbraith, *American Capitalism: The Concept of Countervailing Power*,
Boston, Houghton Mifflin, 1952; and P. Sylos-Labini, *Oligopoly and Technical
Progress*, Cambridge, Mass., Harvard Economic Studies no. 119, 1962.

194

The terms of trade and
the national income
in the growth process

and costly but it must be on a sufficient scale so that successes and failures will in some measure average out. Few can afford it if they must expect all projects to pay off.[14]

This leads to the conclusion that the rate of technological progress tends to be higher under monopolistic market conditions than under competition.[15] Even if, in the short run, cost reductions might be kept within the firm and not lead to any reduction in price, output in the long run will expand, and the growth rate of supply will be higher under monopolistic and oligopolistic conditions than under free competition.[16] Only those firms that operate on a large enough scale can afford the research and development needed to introduce systematically cost reductions and new products.[17]

The implications of these arguments are clearly contrary to the hypotheses of Prebisch. What is of interest are not the market forms themselves but their influence on the growth of supply. The faster output grows, all other things being equal, the more adverse the development of relative commodity prices of the firm will be. Therefore, if one tries to isolate the effects of market forms on the terms of trade, the conclusion, according to this view, must be that the more monopolistic and oligopolistic market forms a country has in its export sector, the worse the prospects are for the terms of trade, a result which is opposite to Prebisch's assertions.

The point of our argument is not necessarily to say that Prebisch is wrong. This is an area in which no conclusive evidence is available. What can be said, however, is that the implications of what seem to be the dominant views are not on Prebisch's side. These are complicated matters, and Prebisch's slightly extravagant assertions do not stand up too well under closer scrutiny.

Another explanation of the deterioration in the terms of trade of the

---

14 Galbraith, *op. cit.*, p. 86.

15 Galbraith, *op. cit.*, pp. 84 ff.; Sylos-Labini, *op. cit.*, pp. 143 ff.

16 This point was made in 1911 by Joseph Schumpeter when he first published his *Theorie der wirtschaftlichen Entwicklung*, Munich and Leipzig, Verlag von Duncker & Humblot (2nd ed., 1926); it was on the whole absent from his treatment of short-run problems in *Business Cycles*, New York, McGraw-Hill, 1939, but appeared again in *Capitalism, Socialism and Democracy*, 3rd ed., New York, Harper & Row, 1945.

17 For a similar approach, performed at the same time in a more grand and vague manner, see F. Perroux, "Esquisse d'une théorie de l'économie dominante," *Economie Appliquée*, April–September 1948, op. 243 ff.

underdeveloped countries lies, according to Singer and Prebisch, in the fact that the industrial countries have much stronger labor organizations than the peripheral countries. In the absence of labor unions wages can be depressed, which leads to falling product prices and deteriorating terms of trade.

This argument seems to have a certain plausibility. The difficulties with institutional arguments of this sort is that they are hard to fit into a consistent theory. We want our theories to be general equilibrium in nature in order that we can have a certain confidence in their self-consistency. From a practical point of view, the variables entering a general equilibrium model must, when it is rigorously formulated, be limited. Therefore, it is almost impossible to construct a model which is consistent and at the same time takes into account the effects of different institutional arrangements.

Having said this, we may proceed to look into this aspect of the Singer–Prebisch case. A good exposition of it has been given by Werner Baer. In one of the key passages of his paper he says:

> The complications arising from an increase in productivity in the export sector can now be fully appreciated. If productivity in the domestic sector does not change, and hence the general wage level in both sectors remains the same, the fruits of this productivity increase will be transferred to the Center, since prices of exports will drop in about the same proportion as the productivity increases. But the productivity increase and the inelastic international demand will cause employment to shrink in the export sector. The resulting manpower surplus can only be employed in domestic industries if wages will shrink so that industries with a lower productivity ratio can exist (i.e., a lower international productivity ratio). This lowering of wages in order to increase employment will cause more international transfers of income through the export industries; it might also stimulate the older domestic industries into the export sector, since wages for them are now lower than productivity, but this will occur at the cost of still more international income transfers.[18]

It should, first of all, be remarked that this passage takes technical progress as the factor which sets the machinery in motion. In the context of

---

[18] Werner Baer, "The Economics of Prebisch and ECLA," *Economic Development and Cultural Change* vol. 10, Jan. 1962, pp. 169 ff.; the quotation is from page 173.

196

The terms of trade and
the national income
in the growth process

less-developed countries, one might perhaps think the origin of economic growth to be an increase in population. We shall return to this question shortly. First, we shall consider the effects of technical progress.

Technical progress will lower the cost at constant output and increase the profit. Under competitive conditions this will lead to an expansion of output. The effect on prices depends on demand conditions, which have two significant aspects. One is the growth of demand for exportables, which will be a function primarily of the growth of income in the importing country (or countries). If the incomes of the trading partners do not grow very fast or if the marginal propensity to import the product in question is very low (or perhaps zero), the demand for the products of the innovating industry will not increase very much. The second aspect is the demand elasticity. If it is small (lower than unity), it is not possible to make the demanded volume expand through price decreases. Under conditions like these it might be possible that the total income of the export industry might fall, even though output has increased. Growth under these circumstances might even become impoverishing.

A development like the one sketched above will lead to a decrease in the number of workers employed in the export sector, unless the progress is heavily biased in a capital-saving direction. The wage will fall, and the un-employed workers will hopefully find employment in other industries whose costs will now decrease, and consequently they might become export in-dustries. If the demand facing these industries is also inelastic, there might be further decreases in the terms of trade.

If this sounds like a sad story, we must keep clearly in mind that the basic reason for all these hardships is the adverse demand conditions. This is the *sine qua non* without which the difficulties described above would not occur. Trade unions would not be able to do much about the demand con-ditions in the international market, although their presence might modify the situation to some degree.

However, the presence of labor unions could conceivably make a difference. It might be useful to think in terms of a two-sector model with one capitalist, export sector where innovations occur and one domestic sub-sistence sector which uses traditional methods of production. If the workers are well informed about technical progress and have strong unions, they might be able to raise wages at the same rate as the productivity increases. This will increase the costs of the industry more than would otherwise be the case. Profits will tend to decrease, as will the rate of capital accumulation in the industry, assuming that most profits are reinvested. The growth of output of the industry will be slowed down, and if the demand conditions are analogous to the ones described above, export prices will not fall as much as they otherwise would. It should be observed that the above reasoning implies that there is a wage difference between the domestic and the export sector, which essentially amounts to assuming that the supply of labor has no effect on wages. Given the above assumptions about technical progress, this wage differential would be an ever-widening one.

It is obviously not easy to make more precise statements about how wages would behave in the long run in factor markets with and without labor unions. The influence different wage patterns would have on output and relative prices is even more difficult to establish. There is no reason to deny that labor unions might make a difference in the development of relative prices, but it is extremely difficult to have any more definite notion about what the consequences for the terms of trade would be.

We might conclude our reasoning about this aspect of the Singer–Prebisch case by saying that it is not impossible to think of cases where labor unions could affect the terms of trade in a favorable way. But it is extremely difficult to fit the possible effects of labor unions on wages into a full-fledged theory of growth and trade. In all cases we have considered, and in all the meaningful interpretations of the Singer–Prebisch argument, demand conditions are already so unfavorable that any growth of export industries can only lead to nothing. Under such conditions, an explanation of deteriorating terms of trade in less-developed countries requires no reference to the absence of labor unions.

The chief difficulty one encounters in analyzing the Singer–Prebisch approach to growth and trade is its looseness. If we take the Singer–Prebisch case in its simplest variant, i.e., as a simple statement that the terms of trade will go against the less-developed countries, it is not difficult to make a highly plausible case for it. But economists of this school are not satisfied with just that. They want also to give very special and intricate explanations for the deterioration in the terms of trade of the peripheral countries.

The reasons we are critical of these explanations have just been given. The theorizing of Chapters 9, 10, and 11 can now be used as an Occam's razor. There is no need to fall back upon highly dubious theories about the influences of market forms, of labor unions, etc. Simpler reasons can be given for why the terms of trade might go against the less-developed countries and why growth through trade might prove a fruitless venture for these

198

The terms of trade and
the national income
in the growth process

countries. If we consider this the core of the Singer–Prebisch case, there are three conditions necessary for reaching their conclusions. These are that growth must be confined to the export sector, that the degree of adaptability must be low (so that the value of the respective demand and supply elasticities will be small), and that the demand for the country's export products must only grow slowly. Usually the first two conditions—the export-biased growth and the low adaptability—are taken for granted, if only implicitly. Then the decisive circumstance is the growth of demand. If this is sluggish, the Singer–Prebisch result will follow. This is the critical condition without which no valid version of the Singer–Prebisch case can be constructed.

It might now be useful to construct a few examples which will lead to results along the Singer–Prebisch lines and view them against the background of the theorizing of Chapters 9, 10, and 11.

We can apply the two-country model and think in terms of one less-developed agricultural country and one developed industrial country. Let us start by thinking in terms of the model of unspecified growth set out in Chapter 9. If, for instance, the income elasticity facing the less-developed country is only one third of that facing the industrial country, and if the export sector is large in both countries, then the over-all growth rate of the less-developed country can be roughly only one third of that in the industrial country. If it is higher, the agricultural country will get deteriorating terms of trade. Such a development will, of course, also have implications for volumes and the real national income. The volume of exportables will grow and the country's dependence on foreign trade will increase. With export-biased growth in both countries, the factors of the greatest importance for the growth of real national income are the size of the export sector and the value of the income elasticities. The larger the export share in the agricultural ("peripheral") country, and the lower the income elasticity of importables in the industrial country, the more the terms of trade will go against the peripheral country and the less its real income will grow. How much the terms of trade will deteriorate, given these conditions, depends primarily on the demand and supply elasticities (which enter the denominator in equation 9.1). One can expect their values to be low in this case. The smaller they are, the more the terms of trade will deteriorate.

The less-developed country will, in a situation such as this one, have its possibilities of growth to a large extent determined by the development of the rich country. The faster the growth of the industrial country, the greater the possibility for growth without impediments in the agricultural country. At a certain limit, the growth rates in the two countries will match so as to yield a "balanced" development with no tendency for a change in the terms of trade. The exact conditions for this case can be found in equations 9A.8 and 9.1. If the growth rate of the poor country should fall below this rate, she will get an inducement for growth by improving terms of trade; if, on the other hand, she tries to increase her own autonomous growth rate above this level, she might find it to be a self-defeating undertaking, because the losses from her falling terms of trade will erase the gains of the extra effort.

We can then specify the source of growth and treat the case of increases in factor endowments against the background of the theorizing of Chapter 10. Here the assumption about production functions being homogeneous of the first degree is critical. The effects of an increase in labor or capital on the terms of trade depended then on factor intensities. Let us now discuss an example of a kind of factor growth that could lead to results along Singer–Prebisch lines.

Many less-developed countries have a rapidly growing labor force. Such a country, therefore, is abundantly endowed with labor, so we would expect it to export labor-intensive goods. If this is the case, an increase in the labor force will lead to a deterioration in the country's terms of trade. Again much will depend on the country's elasticity of demand for imports. If this is high, it will have a negative effect on the terms of trade, because it implies that as the country grows, more and more of its demand will be directed toward imported goods. This is a situation in which many less-developed countries find themselves, because they need to import capital goods to get their development process underway. As usual, the possibilities for substitution, both on the demand and supply sides, are important. If they are small, the negative effects on the terms of trade will be reinforced.

Export-biased growth, where the source of growth is an increase in the factor endowments, will always increase the volume of exports and lead to an increased dependence on foreign trade. The effects on the real national income will depend on the behavior of the terms of trade. If the negative influences on the terms of trade are strong, most of the prospective gains of growth will be exported away. The risk of such an outcome is enhanced if the country's export share is substantial, making the country dependent on its foreign trade.

Let us see, finally, what the effects will be if technical progress is the source of growth. We know from Chapter 11 that the effects of technical

200

The terms of trade and
the national income
in the growth process

progress depend to a large extent on which sector it occurs in. Singer and Prebisch focus their attention on the export sector; if this is the leading sector, the only " modern " sector in the economy, it is natural to regard it as being the one where innovations occur. We know from our geometric exposition in Chapter 11 that most innovations in the export sector will have negative effects on the terms of trade.

We also know that for the most general case, the one where production functions are unspecified, three strategic factors determine the upshot for the terms of trade: the upward shift in the production function associated with technical progress, the way the marginal productivity of labor changes, and the way the marginal productivity of capital changes because of the innovation. The first effect will always have a negative influence on the terms of trade. So will the other two under normal circumstances (provided, that is, that the marginal productivities increase because of the innovation). Therefore, we would expect the terms of trade to deteriorate because of technical progress in the export sector.

How much they will deteriorate depends on several more factors. The more the marginal productivities increase because of the improved technique, and the more the production function is lifted by the innovation, the more the terms of trade deteriorate. As usual, demand conditions play an important role. The larger the income elasticity of imports and the smaller the value of the elasticity factor, the less hopeful are the prospects for the terms of trade. A rapid growth of the export sector, combined with a high marginal propensity to consume importables and a low degree of response on the supply and demand side in both countries to changes in relative prices, make for a rapid deterioration of the terms of trade.

How the real national income is affected by technical progress depends to a large extent on the course of the terms of trade. If the terms of trade deteriorate heavily for the progressing country, the increments to the real income will be small. This will be the case especially if the country has a large export share. If the adaptability of the country is low, and if it is so dependent on trade that the export sector is the only progressive part of the economy, the risk is great that the country will export away most of its productivity gain. Growth in these circumstances easily becomes self-defeating.

We have, with these examples based on the theory of growth and trade set out in Chapters 9, 10, and 11, tried to substantiate the Singer–Prebisch thesis in its basic version and to show that under quite realistic conditions the terms of trade can move against a less-developed country and make growth along established lines (i.e., confined to the traditional export sector) a very frustrating undertaking. After some time there simply will be no additional gains to be made in pushing ahead in this direction. There is no need for deep and impenetrable theories to explain such a situation; nor do we have to resort to theories of conspiracy among the rich. A careful application of established, neoclassical theory will suffice.

Before we end this chapter it will be useful to take a look at the theory of comparative advantage against the background of the theory of growth and trade.

GROWTH, TRADE, AND THE THEORY OF COMPARATIVE ADVANTAGE

In the first part of the book we expounded the theory of comparative advantage and we demonstrated that countries could gain by specializing according to comparative advantage and trade. In the second part of the book we have showed that growth under trade can have quite different effects on a country's well-being and that there might be cases in which growth with trade might even be detrimental to a country. Is there not a contradiction between these two statements—between, on the one hand, the theory of comparative advantage, and, on the other hand, the case of impoverishing growth?

To resolve this apparent paradox we have to think carefully about the kind of theory the doctrine of comparative advantage is and what the theory of growth and trade says.

It is not unusual to find statements to the effect that there is something wrong with the theory of comparative advantage because it is not useful for development economics. Prebisch provides us with an example of this. Comparative advantage should not be the ruling principle; rather, one should consider marginal income increments when trying to decide which sector or industry a country should develop:

> It is not really a question of comparing industrial costs with import prices but of comparing the increment of income obtained in the expansion of industry with that which could have been obtained in export activities had the same productive resources been employed there.[19]

[19] Prebisch, "Commercial Policy in the Underdeveloped Countries," p. 255.

202

The terms of trade and
the national income
in the growth process

This statement is fallacious to the extent that it suggests that what Prebisch is saying contradicts the theory of comparative advantage. The mistake lies in imputing something to the theory of comparative advantage which is not there. The theory of comparative advantage is completely static. It only compares two countries in a given static setting and says that if prices before trade differ in the two countries, they can gain by trading. But it implies nothing whatsoever about economic development. If production conditions change—if, for instance, population were to increase, or if technical progress were to occur—there is nothing in the theory of comparative advantage which says that the same pattern of specialization ought to prevail after, as well as before, the change in production conditions. The new situation has to be assessed again after the change and the pattern of comparative advantage calculated again. The theory of comparative advantage does not imply that the same goods which were exported before the change in production conditions also ought to be exported after the change. Prebisch, in the quotation above, is therefore right when he says that the fact that a country at a certain time had a comparative advantage in exporting a certain good does not imply that she ought to expand the production of that very good, if, for instance, factor supplies were to increase. It is true that the prospective marginal income increments of different lines of production ought to be considered before any one of them is expanded. But this is no objection to the theory of comparative advantage, which was never intended to answer that kind of question.

The theory of comparative advantage does not guarantee that because a country has a comparative advantage in a certain line of production at a given time she should grow and expand along those lines. We have seen from the theory of growth and trade that economic growth can have quite varied effects on the real national income of the trading country. Certain types of growth will lead to increasing terms of trade and to strongly positive effects on the growth of the country's national income; here the country's participation in trade will bring strong advantages. But other types of growth might lead to heavily deteriorating terms of trade and to little, if any, positive effect on her national income; in these instances growth via trade in established lines is not a rewarding venture.

It may be that during the nineteenth century most national economies had durable, stable characteristics, such as the possession of specific raw materials and primary products or skills, the knowledge of which spread only slowly to other countries. Therefore, trade was grounded in typical and only slowly changing characteristics which gave rise to a situation of durable comparative advantage. A great deal of trade is of this nature even today. But it seems that comparative advantage is increasingly founded in superior technology, the possession of which can only be kept a secret for a very limited time. This leads to a more shifting pattern of comparative advantage. Only countries which are adaptable, willing, and able to develop and learn new techniques can reap the full benefits of trade.

Part I gave us an understanding of the determinants of trade and of the gains from trade. We have now seen in Part II how economic growth affects trade. We have spent a great deal of effort in studying basic theoretical aspects of international economics. It is now time to go on to more applied, policy-oriented questions and to deal with the balance of payments, trade policy, and the problem of international liquidity.

SELECTED BIBLIOGRAPHY: CHAPTER 12

The main sources for the discussion of the theories concerning the development of the terms of trade are given in the footnotes of the chapter. For empirical facts about the actual development of the terms of trade and a discussion of these facts see:

M. L. Dantwala, "Commodity Terms of Trade of Primary Producing Countries," and H. M. A. Onitiri, "The Terms of Trade," both in E. A. G. Robinson (ed.), *Problems of Economic Development*, New York, 1965.

R. E. Baldwin, "Secular Movements in the Terms of Trade," *AER*, Papers and Proceedings, May 1955.

J. Bhagwati, "A Sceptical Note on the Adverse Secular Trend in the Terms of Trade of the Underdeveloped Countries," *Pakistan Economic Journal*, December 1960.

C. P. Kindleberger, *The Terms of Trade: A European Case Study*, New York, 1956.

T. Morgan, "Trends in Terms of Trade, and Their Repercussions on Primary Producers," in R. F. Harrod and D. C. Hague (eds.), *International Trade Theory in a Developing World*, New York, 1963.

For a discussion of the Prebisch case see:

M. June Flanders, "Prebisch on Protectionism: An Evaluation," *EJ*, June 1964.

PART III

The balance
of payments

The market
for foreign
exchange

13

In Parts I and II we dealt with the " real" side of the economy. The time has now come to deal with monetary aspects of international economic relations. We have explained why countries trade with each other, and we have seen how they gain by doing so. We have also studied the effects of economic growth on international trade.

We will now deal with the monetary aspects of international economics. We will start, in Chapter 13, to study the market for foreign exchange. We will study what factors determine the demand and supply of foreign exchange in the simplest possible manner and see how the market for foreign exchange is cleared under a system of flexible exchange rates.

The ruling exchange-rate system in the world today is one of fixed exchange rates. Under such a system there is no guarantee that a country will have equilibrium in its balance of payments. On the contrary, we would expect a country's exports and imports not to balance. A wide range of goods is involved in international trade, and there is also an important international exchange of services, such as shipping, banking, insurance services, and tourism. Capital also moves quite freely between many countries, for corporations and individuals may buy property, shares, bonds, and so on, abroad. Trade in this wider sense usually does not balance between countries; some countries have a surplus in their foreign trade, others have a deficit.

Part III consists of a study of the balance of payments. To make this study in an efficient manner we have to define carefully the meaning of the balance of payments and see in what sense it will always be in equilibrium and in what sense surpluses and deficits can exist. This will be done in Chapter 14.

In Chapter 15 we shall study the determination of national income in open economies. The reader is probably familiar with the Keynesian theory of income determination for a closed economy. This theory will be generalized to open economies, foreign trade multipliers will be studied, and we will see how international business cycles are propagated. After that we will come to policy issues. In Chapter 16 we will study what policies exist for dealing with balance-of-payments problems under a system of fixed exchange rates, and discuss some of the central problems of economic policy in today's world.

We will then, in Chapter 17, take a look at a basic issue of long standing in international economics: that of the choice of exchange-rate regime. In earlier chapters we dealt with the functioning of systems of flexible exchange rates and fixed exchange rates, and in Chapter 17 we shall compare the two types of systems and try to point out and evaluate their respective advantages and disadvantages.

Chapter 18, finally, will be devoted to a discussion of aims and means in economic policy and we will see how a country jointly can achieve internal balance (full employment) and external balance under various assumptions as to what means are available to political authorities.

One of the distinguishing features of international trade is the involvement of foreign currencies. If a seller in New York sells goods to a buyer in California, he is paid in dollars. Despite the considerable regional distance between buyer and seller, they use the same currency. If a buyer in Belgium buys goods from a seller in Holland, the problem of foreign exchange occurs, because the buyer wants to pay in Belgian francs and the seller wants to receive his payment in Dutch gulden. We now look into the foreign exchange market and see how the price of one currency in terms of another currency is determined.

THE DEMAND FOR FOREIGN EXCHANGE

We shall start by treating the problem of foreign exchange in the simplest possible manner. We are interested in the question from the point of view of economic theory. We shall therefore not deal with the many technical banking aspects of the problem; readers interested in these will have to consult the specialist literature.

An importer in any one country is interested in acquiring foreign exchange with which to buy foreign goods. Figure 13.1 gives an example of the American demand schedule for Brazilian coffee. This is a very straightforward example that needs little comment. A small amount of coffee is demanded at a high price, and at a lower price a larger amount of coffee is demanded. The demand situation for coffee is especially simple, because we assume that the United States does not produce any coffee at home but imports all that it consumes.

The demand schedule for a product part of which is produced at home and part of which is imported is somewhat more complicated. An illustration of this situation is given in Figure 13.2. Figure 13.2a shows the supply and demand for shoes in the United States. At a certain price, P_1, all

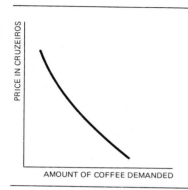

FIGURE 13.1

American demand schedule for Brazilian coffee

PRICE IN CRUZEIROS

AMOUNT OF COFFEE DEMANDED

the American demand is supplied by home producers. Only at a lower price does the United States start to import. At price P_1 the American consumers demand q_1 of shoes. If the price falls below P_1, the total increase in demand is covered by imports. At the same time, if the price falls, so does the home supply of shoes. This is also taken over by foreign exporters. To deduce the total demand schedule for imported shoes, we therefore have to add the decrease in the domestic supply of shoes to the increase in over-all demand. If this is done, we get a demand schedule for imported shoes like that of Figure 13.2b. This schedule is derived from the demand and supply schedules in Figure 13.2a.

It is important to realize that if an import-competing industry exists in a country, the country's demand schedule for imports is quite different from its demand schedule for the imported good. This fact is illustrated in Figure 13.2. Above a certain price all the country's demand is covered by home production, and nothing is imported. Then follows a range where imports start to compete with home production. In this range the demand schedule for imports is much more elastic than the demand schedule for importables. If the price falls to such a low level that all domestic import-competing production has been outcompeted, then the demand schedule for imports coincides with the demand schedule for importables. This fact is illustrated in Figure 13.2 when the price is below P_2.

From this it follows that in the range most often of interest, i.e., the range where some domestic import-competing production exists, the demand for imports is more elastic than the demand for the good itself.

If we add all the demand schedules for different imported goods for a country, we find the over-all, aggregate demand schedule for imports.

FIGURE 13.2

Supply and demand for shoes in the United States

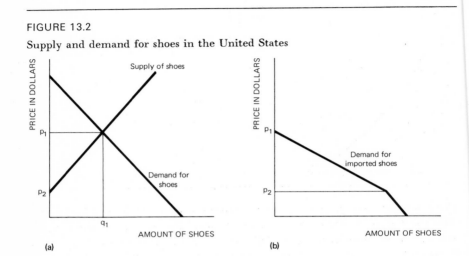

(a) (b)

Figure 13.3 shows an example of such a demand schedule, translated into terms of demand for foreign exchange. For the sake of concreteness we have chosen to take only two countries as examples, so that Figure 13.3 shows the United States demand for British pounds. If the price for £1 is high, let us say $4, the amount of British pounds demanded will be small, because an article (for instance, a sweater) which costs £1 in England will cost $4 in the United States. If the price of £1 were only $2, the American demand for British pounds would increase, because the demand for British goods would increase; the sweater would now cost only $2 in the United States. Thus it follows that we expect the demand schedule for foreign exchange to have a similar slope to that in Figure 13.3.

It is very interesting to try to deduce knowledge about the shape of the demand curve for imports so that one can remark on the elasticity of demand for imports. There are two facts of great interest in this connection. The first is the question of the elasticity of demand for importables (imported goods). If a country imports necessities and raw materials, we may expect the elasticity of demand for imports to be low and the quantity imported to be insensitive to price changes. If, on the other hand, the country imported luxury goods and goods for which suitable substitutes exist, demand elasticities for imports might be high. Whether or not the country has a domestic

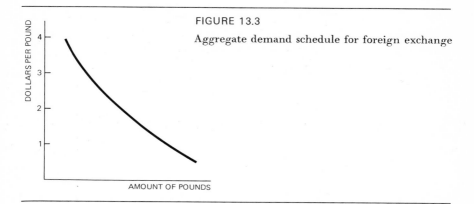

FIGURE 13.3

Aggregate demand schedule for foreign exchange

import-competing industry is the second extremely important factor. If the country has many well-developed import-competing industries, the elasticity of demand for imports most certainly is high. This is due to the fact that if the price rises, import-competing industries will come in and take a larger share of the market, and imports will fall; if the price falls, it will be the other way around.

Time is another factor to take into account. In the short run it may be difficult to react to price changes by reallocating factors of production. In the short run, therefore, elasticity of demand for imports may not be very high. In the long run, however, it is much more probable that the production pattern will alter according to price changes, and the demand for imports, therefore, will be more elastic.

If we take into account different types of countries we find that their demand for imports differs. Most well-developed, industrial countries produce and import to a large extent the same type of goods; in other words, these countries have large and well-developed import-competing industries. For these countries, the demand for imports is often very elastic. Less-developed, agricultural countries often have small, poorly developed import-competing sectors. They import necessities and the industrial goods needed for their development programs. Their demand for imports is on the whole very inelastic.

We shall find later that the question of elasticity of demand for imports has important implications for economic policy. But for the time being we shall treat the question of the supply of foreign exchange.

TABLE 13.1

Supply schedule in the foreign exchange market

(1) Price of a sweater in pounds	(2) Price of $1 in pounds	(3) Price of one sweater in dollars [col. (1) ÷ col. (2)]	(4) Quantity of sweaters demanded (elas. = 1)	(5) Amount of foreign exchange supplied (in dollars) [col. (3) x col. (4)]	(6) Quantity of sweaters demanded (elas. ≈ 2)	(7) Amount of foreign exchange supplied (in dollars) [col. (3) x col. (6)]
10	7.50	1.33	750	1000	1000	1330
10	7.00	1.43	700	1000	900	1287
10	6.50	1.54	650	1000	800	1232
10	6.00	1.67	600	1000	700	1169
10	5.50	1.82	550	1000	600	1092
10	5.00	2.00	500	1000	500	1000
10	4.50	2.22	450	1000	400	888
10	4.00	2.50	400	1000	300	750
10	3.50	2.86	350	1000	200	572
10	3.00	3.33	300	1000	100	333

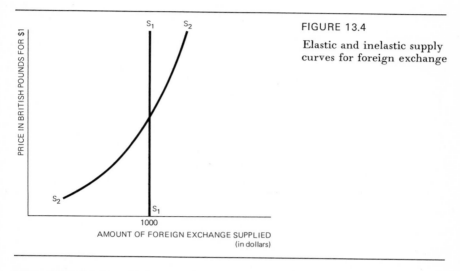

FIGURE 13.4

Elastic and inelastic supply curves for foreign exchange

THE SUPPLY OF FOREIGN EXCHANGE

We have seen that the United States demands the pound sterling in order to buy British goods. Analogously, Britain supplies pounds to receive dollars in exchange. A country's supply schedule of its own currency in the foreign exchange market is therefore best viewed as an inverted demand schedule for foreign exchange. This is illustrated in Table 13.1. The first column gives the price in Britain of a sweater made in Britain and exported to the United States. In the United States the price for this sweater depends on the exchange rate, i.e., the amount of pounds that an American may receive for $1. This is shown in column (2). If they receive £7.50 for $1, the price of the sweater in the United States will be $1.33. Let us assume that Americans demand 750 sweaters at this price. The amount of dollars supplied in the foreign exchange market in exchange for the import of this article is thus derived by simply multiplying the quantity demanded by its price, as done in column (5).

Let us assume that the exchange rate is such that $1 is worth £5; then the price of the sweater will be $2. We assume that 500 sweaters are demanded at this price. If the price changes, the amount demanded will also change. Table 13.1 gives two examples of how the supply of foreign exchange varies, depending on demand elasticity. In column (4) the demand elasticity is supposed to be 1. Thus we see from column (5) that the amount of

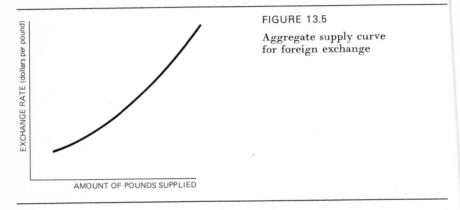

FIGURE 13.5

Aggregate supply curve
for foreign exchange

EXCHANGE RATE (dollars per pound)

AMOUNT OF POUNDS SUPPLIED

foreign exchange supplied by Americans is the same, regardless of price, because the total outlay on the good is constant. In column (6) the demand elasticity is supposed to be approximately 2. Thus we see from column (7) that the supply of dollars changes, so that if the price falls in the American market, a relatively larger quantity is demanded, and more dollars are supplied in the foreign exchange market for imports of this good. The two supply curves for dollars in the foreign exchange market that can be derived from Table 13.1 are illustrated in Figure 13.4.

We now see clearly that the supply curve of foreign exchange is derived from the demand for imports. If the demand elasticity for an imported article is 1, this gives rise to a completely inelastic supply curve, such as S_1 in Figure 13.4. If the demand for imports is elastic, we also get an elastic supply curve for foreign exchange, such as S_2 in Figure 13.4.

If we add all the supply curves for foreign exchange for all single import goods we will get an aggregate supply curve showing how much of its currency the country supplies at different exchange rates. An example of such an aggregate supply curve for foreign exchange is given in Figure 13.5.

Basically the same factors that are of importance for determining the elasticity of the demand curve for foreign exchange also determine the elasticity of the supply curve. As the value of the country's own currency increases, imports become relatively cheaper, and more is imported. As more is imported, more of the home currency is supplied on the foreign exchange market (provided the elasticity is larger than unity). When imports become relatively cheap, "new" goods (goods earlier produced only at home) will start to be imported, and domestic import-competing industries will be gradually eliminated by imports. These are two important reasons why we expect the supply of foreign exchange to be quite elastic. Furthermore, the longer the time perspective we take into account, the more elastic will be the supply.

FLEXIBLE EXCHANGE RATES

We may now put the demand and supply schedules for foreign exchange together and see how an equilibrium exchange rate is determined. This is done in Figure 13.6, where demand curve DD shows how many pounds the United States, for instance, demands, depending on the exchange rate, and supply curve SS shows how many pounds the British supply as the exchange rate varies. The supply and demand curves cut each other at point P. The equilibrium exchange rate is r_1, and Oq_1 of foreign exchange is supplied and demanded. At the exchange rate r_1 the American demand for pounds equals the British supply of pounds, and the foreign exchange market is cleared.

Let us assume that a shift occurs in the American demand curve for foreign exchange from DD to $D'D'$. There may be many reasons for such a shift. One could be a change in taste, causing American consumers to demand, at any given exchange rate, more imported goods than before. Another reason could be an increase in the national income in the United States, giving rise to an increase in imports. Whatever the reason for the shift, the result is the establishment of a new equilibrium at P', with a new exchange rate r_2 and a new amount of foreign exchange Oq_2 supplied and demanded.

We now see the implications of a system with flexible exchange rates. The exchange rate varies with varying supply and demand conditions, but it is always possible to find an equilibrium exchange rate which clears the foreign exchange market and creates external equilibrium.

The American demand for foreign exchange is based on its demand for imports. If the relative price of pounds is high, so that many dollars have to be given for £1, the demand for foreign exchange to pay for imports is small. The lower the price of sterling, the larger is the demand for British imports and hence for pounds, as can be seen from the shape of demand curve DD in Figure 13.6. The British supply curve for pounds is determined

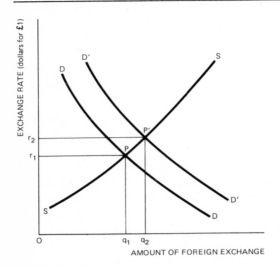

FIGURE 13.6

Determination of
equilibrium exchange rate

by its imports of goods. The higher the price of pounds in the foreign ex-change market, the cheaper will imports from abroad be in Britain and the more British pounds will be supplied, provided the elasticity of demand for imports is larger than unity. This is shown by supply curve SS in Figure 13.6. Where the supply and demand curves intersect, an equilibrium is created—at point P. If Americans import British goods to a value of Oq_1 pounds, the British will import American goods to a value of Oq_1 pounds, and trade between the two countries will balance.

If there is a shift in the demand curve from DD to $D'D'$, as illus-trated in Figure 13.6, this will imply a depreciation of the American dollar and an appreciation of the British pound. By the depreciation of a currency is meant that the relative value of the currency decreases. When the dollar depreciates it means that Americans pay more dollars for £1. Analogously, an appreciation means that the relative value of a currency increases. If the pound sterling appreciates, it means that the British will have to pay fewer pounds for $1. Increase in American demand for British imports gives rise to an increase in demand for pounds and we arrive at a new equilibrium at P' and a new exchange rate r_2, which clears the market. This implies, as we see, a depreciation of the dollar and an appreciation of the pound. Because of the shift in demand, Americans ask for a larger amount of pounds, Oq_2, which the British supply, at the higher price. American demand for foreign exchange equals British supply, and the balance of payments is in equilibrium.

Assuming that we start from a situation in which a country has equilibrium in its balance of payments, any change from this position will, under a system of flexible exchange rates, first influence the exchange rate. If a deficit in the country's balance of payments occurs, an excess demand for foreign currency is implied. This leads to a fall in the exchange rate, so the country will have to pay more units of its own currency for a unit of foreign currency. There can be many reasons for this deficit, including an increase in imports, a fall in exports, or a decrease in the inflow of foreign capital. Whatever the reason, the effect on the exchange rate will be immediate and lead to a depreciation of the currency.

Analogously, a surplus in the balance of payments will lead to an excess supply of foreign currency and hence to an increase in the exchange rate, i.e., an appreciation of the currency. This implies that imports now become cheaper, and the demand for imports increases. At the same time, exporters will receive less home currency for any one unit of foreign currency, producing a negative effect on exports. Hence imports increase, exports decrease, the surplus in the balance of payments is erased, and a new equilibrium in the balance of payments is established at the new exchange rate.

We should now have an understanding of how a system of flexible exchange rates works under ideal conditions. It is a very elegant system and seems to solve the problem of external equilibrium almost without effort. Many economists are in favor of flexible exchange rates. Despite this, the practical experiences of the system are comparatively limited. In recent times, the most interesting case is that of Canada from the 1950s; Canada had a system of flexible exchange rates from 1950 to 1961. Opinions on how well it worked are divided. It must also be added that the Canadian experience is of somewhat limited interest, as the Canadian central bank kept a close watch on fluctuations in the exchange rate and only permitted it to vary within fairly narrow limits.

The system adopted by almost all countries today is that of fixed exchange rates. We shall deal with the problems of policy that such a system entails very shortly. One has the impression that many economists believe that such a system prevails only because of human stupidity in general and the conservatism and irrationality of bankers in particular. There are, however, some important issues that should be raised in connection with flexible exchange rates and that might throw some doubts on the efficiency of such an exchange-rate system.

One is that fluctuating exchange rates might give rise to insecurity and thereby to an unnecessary limitation of foreign trade. This is especially so if speculation is of a destabilizing nature, causing fluctuations in exchange rates created by trade to be larger than they would otherwise be. Another argument is that flexible exchange rates will give rise to inflation. We will not discuss these issues here. We will first give an exposition of fixed exchange rates and treat the policy problems that such a system entails. Then, in Chapter 17, we will compare flexible and fixed exchange rates and discuss the pros and cons of the respective systems. Now we will discuss the forward market for foreign exchange.

SPOT AND FORWARD MARKETS FOR FOREIGN EXCHANGE

The foreign exchange market we have so far dealt with is the spot market. In a spot transaction the seller of exchange has to deliver the foreign exchange he has sold "on the spot" (within 2 days). Likewise, a buyer of exchange will immediately receive the foreign exchange he has bought. There is also another important market for foreign exchange, the forward market. In the forward market, when the contract is signed, the seller agrees to sell a certain amount of foreign exchange to be delivered at a future date at a price agreed upon in advance. Analogously, a buyer agrees to buy a certain amount of foreign exchange at a future date and at a predetermined price. Usually the forward contracts are on a 3-month basis, and in the following case this is assumed, although both shorter and longer contract periods exist.

Spot and forward markets are intimately linked together in at least three ways. The first way is via an interest arbitrage; the second way is by hedging or covering; the third way is by speculation.

Let us assume that the spot exchange rate is $4 for £1. This rate must be the same both in London and New York, because if the exchange rate were 4:1 in London but 3.90:1 in New York, it would pay to take dollars from New York to London and sell them there. This would continue until the rates were equalized. The forward rates might differ, however.

Let us continue to assume that the spot rate is \$4 for £1. If the forward rate is higher than 4.00, for instance 4.03, we say that there is a premium on sterling. We denote the spot rate R_s and the forward rate R_f. We then get

$R_f - R_s =$ premium on pound sterling (if $R_f > R_s$)

Analogously, we say that pound sterling is at a discount if the spot rate is higher than the forward rate. This is the case if, for instance, the spot rate is \$4.00 for £1 and the forward rate is \$3.97 for £1. We get

$R_s - R_f =$ discount on pound sterling (if $R_s > R_f$)

If the interest rates in the two countries differ, this gives rise to an interest arbitrage and a difference in spot and forward rates. Let us assume that the short-term interest rate in New York is 2 percent while it is 5 percent in London. We continue to assume that the spot rate is \$4 for £1. So \$4 in New York will yield an interest of \$0.08 per year or \$0.02 per 3 months. In London \$4.00 will yield an interest of \$0.20 per year or \$0.05 per 3 months. If the forward rate in London were the same as the spot rate, the American arbitrageurs would place their funds in London, as the yield is higher there than in New York. This would lead to an excess supply of forward pounds, and depress the forward rate until the yield on £1 in London equaled that of \$4 in New York. If we denote the British interest rate i_e, the American interest rate i_a, the discount d, and the premium p, we get the following two equilibrium conditions:

$$d = i_e - i_a \qquad \text{if } i_e > i_a \tag{13.1}$$

$$p = i_a - i_e \qquad \text{if } i_a > i_e \tag{13.2}$$

If we want to express the discount in percent per year of the spot rate, we deduce that

$$d = \frac{R_s - R_f}{R_s} 100 \times 4 \tag{13.3}$$

If the spot rate is 4.00 and the forward rate is 3.97, the discount in percent per year is $[(4.00 - 3.97)/4.00](100 \times 4) = 3$ percent.

If, analogously, the premium is expressed in percent per year,

$$p = \frac{R_f - R_s}{R_s} 100 \times 4 \qquad (13.4)$$

If the spot rate is 4.00 and the forward rate is 4.03, we see that the yearly premium is $[(4.03 - 4.00)/4.00](100 \times 4) = 3$ percent.

Let us assume that the interest rate in New York is 2 percent while it is 5 percent in London, and that there is thus an interest-rate differential of 3 percent. This will give rise to a discount on forward pounds. We assume the spot rate to be \$4.00 for £1. An interest-rate differential of 3 percent should, in equilibrium, give rise to a discount of 3 percent, and the forward dollar rate ought to be 3.97. If the discount were less, it would pay the arbitrageur to place his funds in London. If he placed \$400 in New York they would grow to \$402 in 3 months at a 2 percent interest rate. In Britain £100 would grow to £101.25 in 3 months at a 5 percent interest rate. If he had sold them in advance at the forward rate of 3.98, they would bring him $101.25 \times 3.98 = \$403$ and he would make a gain.

If the short-term interest rates between two countries differed, the country with the higher interest rate would have its forward exchange rate at a discount. Let us say that Country II has the higher interest rate. An arbitrageur in Country I can then receive a higher return on his funds if he places them in Country II. He has, however, to take into account discount on the forward rate. If the interest differential between the two countries is 3 percent, the discount on the forward rate is also 3 percent in equilibrium. If it is less, his gain on the interest-rate differential will be larger than the loss on the discount, and it is favorable for an arbitrageur to place his funds in Country II instead of Country I. This should, under normal conditions, lead to an inflow of funds to Country II which would depress the forward rate in that country until the interest-rate differential was equal to the discount.

Analogously, if the short-term interest rate in Country II is lower than the short-term interest rate in I, the forward rate in II should be at a premium. Let us again assume that the interest-rate differential is 3 percent and that the spot rate is \$4.00 for £1. Then the forward rate in Country II should be 4.03. The interest rate in I is, let us say, 5 percent, so \$4.00 in I will grow to \$4.05 in 3 months, and £1 placed in II will grow to £1.005, which equals \$4.02 at the spot rate. If the forward rate equaled the spot rate and there were no premium, it would be disadvantageous to place any funds in Country II, but if there is a premium, it has to be added. If the premium were 3 percent per annum, and therefore the forward rate were 4.03, $100 invested in II would give the same return as if they were invested in I. If the premium on the forward rate were higher than 3 percent, it would be more advantageous to place funds in II than in I. If the premium were lower than the interest-rate differential, the situation would be the opposite.

We have now set out the "theory of interest-rate parity" in its simplest form. In reality, however, we find that the premium or discount often differs from the interest-rate differential. There are several reasons for this. Depending upon his subjective risk and liquidity considerations, an arbitrageur might not find it optimal to equalize objective return on his investments in the two countries. For this reason alone the premium or discount might not equal the interest-rate differential. Interest arbitrage, however, is not the only factor influencing the forward rate.

Another important factor is hedging or covering. There is often a time difference between the signing of a contract and the delivery of the goods. An exporter, for instance, may have signed a contract to deliver goods 3 months hence. He knows that he will then receive, let us say, $1000. He may, however, fear that the exchange rate will change in the mean time. Hoping to avert a risk, he wants to know the exact sum he will receive. He is thus able to cover himself against risks by hedging. He sells $1000 forward at the going forward rate for the pound sterling. He receives no money and delivers none when he enters this contract, but 3 months hence, when he receives payment, he delivers the money that he has sold forward and he knows immediately what he will receive. Whatever the possible changes in exchange rate during the 3 months, they are of no consequence to him.

Likewise, any importer who enters a contract in the present, and knows that he will have to pay for his goods in the future, can cover himself against any exchange risks by buying forward. If the contract period is limited, 3 months, for example, he knows exactly what the price of the goods will be when delivered to him, and he can avoid any risks connected with fluctuations in the exchange rate.

Hedging will give rise to a supply and demand for forward exchange. What the supply and demand for forward exchange from this source will be depends on several factors. The volume of trade is important, and so is the risk aversion of exporters and importers. Hedging may cause the premium or discount on foreign exchange to differ from the interest-rate differential.

Hedging is important, especially in a market with flexible exchange rates, as it permits exporters and importers to protect themselves against risks connected with exchange-rate fluctuations, thus enabling them to concentrate on their pure trading functions. It should, however, be observed that the forward market is a short-run market, in which the contract period is usually 3 months. Longer contract periods exist, but these markets are not very well developed, and the upper limit for the contract period seems to be 8 months or 1 year. For many contracts the period between ordering and payment is longer. In these cases hedging does not function efficiently, and risks connected with fluctuations in exchange rates can hardly be avoided.

Speculation is a third source for the supply and demand of forward exchange. We assume that the speculation is about the development of the future spot rate and that the speculation exclusively takes place in the forward market.[1] The speculator who expects the spot rate to increase in the future buys forward in order to sell spot when he receives his delivery of the currency that he has bought forward. On the contrary, however, a speculator who expects the spot rate to fall sells forward with the intention of buying spot when he needs currency for delivery.

We have seen that there is a close link between spot and forward rates through interest arbitrage. If speculators expect the spot rate to increase, they will buy forward, putting pressure on the forward rate, so that it, also, increases. Conversely, if they expect the spot rate to fall, they will sell forward and force the forward rate down. Therefore, speculation tends to make the spot and forward rates move together.

Under a system of flexible exchange rates there are many factors which influence movements in the exchange rates. The most important factors are connected with supply and demand of imports and exports. An important question is whether speculation is stabilizing or destabilizing, i.e., whether it tends to smooth out fluctuations in the exchange rate caused by trade or make them larger than they would otherwise be.

Speculation is a very important phenomenon in connection with a system of flexible exchange rates. It could, conceivably, be of critical im-

---

[1] This assumption does not restrict the generality of the reasoning. Other forms of speculation can be viewed as a combination of interest arbitrage and forward speculation; see John Spraos, "The Theory of Forward Exchange and Recent Practice," *The Manchester School of Economic and Social Studies*, vol. 21, May 1953.

portance for the efficient functioning of a system of flexible exchange rates. We return to this question in Chapter 17 when discussing the relative merits of different exchange-rate systems.

FIXED EXCHANGE RATES

This chapter has dealt with flexible exchange rates. The system prevalent in the world today is, however, one of fixed exchange rates. One pound sterling, for instance, exchanges for $2.40 U.S., one Swedish krona exchanges for $0.19 U.S., and so on, and every country has agreed to keep currencies at these fixed exchange ratios.

Another important feature is the fact that the leading Western country, the United States, has declared that it will buy and sell gold at a certain fixed price, $35 for 1 ounce of gold. As exchange ratios are stable and the price of gold is fixed, this implies that every currency has a fixed price in terms of gold.

The present system may be called the Bretton Woods system. In July 1944 in Bretton Woods, New Hampshire, 44 countries signed an agreement establishing the International Monetary Fund. The Fund has expanded to include 102 countries. The most important countries not members of the Fund are the Communist countries and Switzerland.

Even though exchange rates are, in principle, pegged, it is possible to change them. Any member country can, after consultation with the Fund, make a change in its exchange rate of up to 10 percent. If a country wishes to bring about greater changes, it has to prove to the Fund that it has "fundamental disequilibrium" in its balance of payments. If a country can prove this to the satisfaction of the Fund, it can be permitted to change its currency with a larger percentage than 10 percent.

Most countries today, therefore, belong to a system whereby they agree to keep their currencies at a fixed, pegged rate, and to change their value only at fairly infrequent intervals, when the economic situation forces them to do so. After World War II, changes in exchange rates among the most economically important countries occurred only rarely.

The United States has not made any change in its exchange rate. Britain, France, and most other Western European countries devalued their currencies in 1949 by approximately 30 percent. In 1958 France depreciated the French franc by 18 percent. In 1961 Germany appreciated the German mark by 5 percent, and Britain devalued the pound sterling by 15 percent in 1967. Several smaller countries have also altered their exchange rates during the postwar period.

To sum up, therefore, we can say that the prevailing system is one of fixed exchange rates, in which rate adjustment occurs only at infrequent intervals. Such a system cannot guarantee equilibrium in the balance of payments. In Chapter 14 we shall discuss the meaning and significance of the concept of equilibrium in connection with a country's balance of payments. One of the most important problems in economic policy is how a country can achieve external equilibrium under pegged exchange rates. We shall devote Chapter 16 to this problem.

SELECTED BIBLIOGRAPHY: CHAPTER 13

For treatments of markets for foreign exchange, see:

> F. Machlup, "The Theory of Foreign Exchanges," *Ec*, November 1939 and February 1940 (reprinted in *RTIT*).

> J. E. Meade, *The Balance of Payments*, London, 1951, part IV.

> L. B. Yeager, *International Monetary Relations*, New York, 1966, chap. 2.

A standard work on spot and forward markets for foreign exchange is:

> P. Einzig, *The Dynamic Theory of Forward Exchange*, London, 1961.

Other excellent works in this field are:

> B. Hansen, "Kursbildningen på valutamarknaderna," *Ekonomisk Tidskrift*, no. 3, 1961.

> H. G. Grubel, *Forward Exchange, Speculation and the International Flow of Capital*, Stanford, Calif., 1966.

> J. Spraos, "The Theory of Forward Exchange and Recent Practice," *MS*, May 1953.

> S. C. Tsiang, "The Theory of Forward Exchanges and Effects of Government Intervention on the Forward Exchange Market," *SP*, April 1959.

For a discussion of international economic policy from an institutional point of view, see:

W. M. Scammell, *International Monetary Policy*, 2nd ed., London, 1961.

A thorough examination of the Canadian experience of flexible exchange rates is given in:

P. Wonnacott, *The Canadian Dollar, 1948–1962*, Toronto, 1965.

For a discussion of empirical estimates of price elasticities, see:

G. H. Orcutt, "Measurement of Price Elasticities in International Trade," *RE&S*, May 1950 (reprinted in *RIE*).

A. C. Harberger, "Some Evidence on the International Price Mechanism," *JPE*, December 1957.

The balance of payments

14

The dominant exchange-rate system in the world today is one of fixed exchange rates. The most important issue to study in this part of the book is how to reach equilibrium in the balance of payments under a system of fixed exchanges. Chapters 16 and 18, especially, will be devoted to the policy aspects of this problem. To start with, however, we will have to understand well what is meant by equilibrium and disequilibrium in the balance of payments. To do this we shall have to define carefully the meaning of the balance of payments and see in what sense there will be balance and in what way deficits and surpluses can exist. This chapter is devoted to these problems.

BALANCE OF PAYMENTS: BOOKKEEPING

In ordinary usage one speaks of countries that have a favorable balance of payments, or a surplus, and countries that have a negative or unfavorable balance of payments, or a deficit. The most important question to be dealt with in this part of the book is how a country with a deficit can cure it. At the same time the balance of payments is merely a way of listing receipts and payments in international transactions for a country. In this sense the balance of payments is an application of double-entry bookkeeping, and if we do this in a proper way debit and credit will always balance; hence in a way the balance of payments will always be in equilibrium. Our first task will be to look into this apparent paradox and understand in what way the balance of payments can be in disequilibrium and in what sense it will always be in equilibrium. The best way of treating this problem is to give a simplified example of a country's balance of payments.

The left side of Table 14.1 shows all the ways in which a country can acquire foreign currency—how it can acquire purchasing power which can be used in foreign markets. The right side of Table 14.1 shows how the foreign currency is spent and how the purchasing power over foreign goods is used. It is worthwhile to deal with each part to understand what is meant by it.

The most straightforward way in which a country can acquire foreign currency is by exporting goods. This is shown by row (1), which indicates that the country has exported goods to a value of 550. In an analogous way,

TABLE 14.1

Account of a country's balance of payments

Credit		Debit	
(1) Exports of goods	550	(5) Imports of goods	800
(2) Exports of services	150	(6) Imports of services	50
(3) Unrequited receipts (gifts, indemnities, etc., from foreigners)	100	(7) Unrequited payments (gifts, indemnities, etc., to foreigners)	80
(4) Capital receipts (borrowings from, capital repayments by, or sale of assets to, foreigners)	200	(8) Capital payments (lending to, capital repayments to, or purchase of assets from, foreigners)	70
TOTAL RECEIPTS	1000	TOTAL PAYMENTS	1000

row (5) shows that the country has imported goods to a value of 800. These two rows describe the country's visible trade.

Row (2) enumerates the receipts of the country from the sale of services to foreigners during the period in question. The most important item under this heading usually is shipping services. Exports are normally calculated fob (free on board), i.e., costs for transportation, insurance, etc., are not included, whereas imports normally are calculated cif (cost, insurance, freight), i.e., transportation, insurance costs, etc., are included. This gives rise to asymmetry, so that if we sum all countries together, the shipping services will not be canceled out but will show a positive sign; in other words, world exports will be less than world imports. Any country with a merchant fleet will therefore normally have some income from shipping services to add under the heading "exports of services." For countries with a relatively large merchant fleet, such as Norway, this can be a very substantial item; for Norway it amounts to 40 percent of the total export income. Other types of earnings under this heading are interest and dividends which citizens of the country earn on investment abroad. Such payments are regarded as payments made by foreigners for current services which they derive from the capital in question. Citizens of the country whose balance of payments we are dealing with own land, shares, bonds, etc., and the foreigners who enjoy the services of this capital will have to pay for them; these payments will be registered under row (2) as exports of services, or invisible exports, as they often are called. Income through tourism is another example under the same heading. If a foreigner, instead of consuming a country's product at home, goes to that country and consumes it as a tourist, he will still have to pay for it in his own currency. This type of consumption, and all the services that a country offers tourists, will earn the country foreign currency. Such income will be registered under row (2) as income from export of services. Other payments registered under this heading are those for banking and insurance services made by domestic firms to foreigners.

In a completely analogous way, row (6) covers payments which residents of the country in question make to foreigners for similar services, i.e., shipping, banking and insurance services, payments the residents make as tourists abroad, and payments for capital services on foreign-owned capital.

To return to Table 14.1, we see that there are four more rows to take into account. The items enumerated in these rows are referred to as transfer items, as opposed to the trade items enumerated in rows (1), (2), (5), and (6).

The items in row (3) we have called "unrequited receipts," i.e., receipts which the residents of a country receive "for free," without having to make any present or future payments in return. Examples of this kind of receipt are gifts which residents receive from foreigners. It may, for instance, be the case that emigrants send money back to relatives living in the country in question. If the country whose balance of payments we study is a less-developed country, it may receive gifts from a more-developed one. Or it may be the case that the country came out of a war morally and physically superior, and was in a position to make the foreign country (its former enemy) pay indemnities. This kind of reparation payment played an important part after World War I but has since fallen into relative obscurity. Transfer payments between developed and less-developed countries are not negligible, however, and this type of payment seems to be on the upsurge. In a purely analogous way, row (7) describes payments which the country in question makes as gifts, assistance, indemnities, etc.

Items (1), (2), (3), (5), (6), and (7) enumerate all the payments and receipts made for the current period of time; they all have a flow dimension and refer to a certain value of exports per time period. The balance of payments of a country always refers to a certain time period, usually a calendar year. Exports and imports of goods and services, and all the other items we have discussed, are flow items. They all have the dimension of an amount per day, per month, per year, or whatever the period in question may be.

Items (4) and (8) are different. They express changes in stock magnitudes and refer to capital receipts and payments. They play a most important part, and it is critical for an understanding of the balance of payments to get a firm grasp of the nature of these items. They take many forms and it may be best to start by giving some examples.

A government, a corporation, or an individual might have borrowed money abroad, and such borrowings can be of different kinds. The government of the country in question may get a loan from another government; a firm may issue stocks abroad, or a bank might float a loan in a foreign country. In all these instances the country in question will acquire foreign currency, and these transactions will be entered as items in (4).

A government, a corporation, or an individual resident may receive sums from abroad in repayment for a loan that it had previously extended to a borrowing agency in a foreign country.

Foreigners might acquire assets in the country with whose balance of payments we are concerned. These assets can be of different kinds. They may be land, houses, productive plants, shares, etc. Changes in the country's stock of gold or reserves of foreign currency are also included in row (4).

Analogously, if residents of the country in their turn were to acquire foreign assets, for instance in the form of land abroad or foreign shares, or if the government were to lend money to a foreign government, this would give rise to an outflow of foreign currency and come as a capital transfer under row (8).

We will have more to say about the capital account in the balance of payments later in this chapter and also when studying the adjustment mechanism in later chapters. To start with, we shall say something about the somewhat puzzling use of the concepts "capital imports" and "capital exports."

We have seen that if a foreign corporation buys a firm in the country we are considering, this is said to be an import of capital. One might expect it to be called an export of capital, as, after all, this firm is, so to speak, "exported" abroad, in the sense that foreigners acquire ownership of it— but this is not the case. The key factor on which to focus our attention is the fact that the country whose balance of payments we consider will get foreign currency, in other words, will acquire purchasing power abroad by selling some of its property to foreigners. Therefore, this transaction will be listed on the credit side of the country's balance of payments, as it will give rise to an inflow of foreign currency. We could say that a country can acquire foreign currency in either of two fundamental ways: by exporting goods and services or by importing capital. Therefore, exports of goods and imports of capital both have to be listed on the credit side (i.e., on the receipt or inflow side) of a country's balance of payments.

In the same way, a country can export capital by acquiring foreign assets. This means that the country puts foreign currency to the disposal of the foreign country, in which it acquires assets. Therefore, this transaction will be put on the debit side of the country's balance of payments. Again we can say that there are two fundamental ways in which a country can use its foreign currency: by importing goods and services or by exporting capital. In this sense imports of goods and exports of capital have the same effect, and therefore both have to be listed on the debit side (the outflow or payments side) of a country's balance of payments.

We said above that items (1), (2), (3), (5), (6), and (7) were flow magnitudes. Items (4) and (8) are of a different nature, because they do not have the dimensions of being flows per period of time but are instead changes in stock magnitudes during the period considered. A country has a certain capital stock consisting of land, houses, productive plants, ships, etc. If it sells part of this abroad it engages in a stock transaction which is entered on the capital account in the balance of payments. It is important to recognize the difference in nature between a flow and a stock transaction, and for the time being this remark may suffice. We should now be equipped to say something significant about the question we started with: In what sense can the balance of payments be in equilibrium, and in what sense will it always balance? We will, however, have to answer this question in a somewhat roundabout way by introducing more concepts and definitions.

THE BALANCE OF TRADE, THE BALANCE OF CURRENT ACCOUNT, AND THE BALANCE OF PAYMENTS

There are several ways in which the balance of payments can be broken down vertically. We can first be concerned only with the export and import of goods. This gives us the balance of trade. It is obvious that the balance of trade need not always balance. If the country exports more goods than it

TABLE 14.2

Three external balances

(1) BALANCE OF TRADE
    [Table 13.1 rows (1) and (5)] $550 - 800 = -250$
(2) Balance of services
    [Table 13.1 rows (2) and (6)] $150 - 50 = 100$
(3) Balance of unrequited transfers
    [Table 13.1 rows (3) and (7)] $100 - 80 = 20$
(4) BALANCE OF CURRENT ACCOUNT
    [Sum of rows (1), (2), and (3) of Table 14.2] $800 - 930 = -130$
(5) Balance of capital account
    [Table 13.1 rows (4) and (8)] $200 - 70 = 130$
(6) BALANCE OF PAYMENTS
    [Sum of rows (4) and (5) of Table 14.2] $1000 - 1000 = 0$

imports, it is said to have a favorable balance or surplus in its balance of trade. If it imports more goods than it exports, it has a deficit or unfavorable balance of trade.

Row (1) of Table 14.2 shows the balance of trade for the country from our hypothetical example in Table 14.1. This country exported goods for 550 and imported goods for 800, it had a deficit in its balance of trade of 250.

Even though the country had a deficit in its balance of trade, this might be offset by items on other accounts. We can see from our example that the country has a surplus in its balance of services of 100 and a surplus in its balance of unrequited transfers of 20. This leads us to the balance of current account, which is a larger concept than the balance of trade, as it includes the balance of trade, the balance of services, and the balance of unrequited transfers. The balance of current account need not be equal but can show a surplus or a deficit. In our example the country in question has a deficit in its balance of current account of 130.

The balance of current account is a very important concept, as it shows the flow aspect of a country's international transactions. We could say that all the goods and services produced within the country during the time period in question, and exported, are entered on the credit side of the balance of current account, and all the goods and services imported and consumed (or perhaps stored) within the country during the same period are entered on the credit side of the balance of current account. We could also say that all the international transactions entering a country's system of national accounting should be listed on the country's balance of current account.

A word of warning must be inserted here. National accounting is not completely standardized among countries; different countries use different systems. This is reflected also in the construction of the balance of payments. There is agreement on the broad features; for instance, everyone agrees that exports of goods and services should be entered on the balance of current account. Differences in detail do exist, however. Some countries include such items as gifts and indemnities on the balance of unrequited transfers in the balance of capital account instead of in the balance of current account. It is hardly meaningful to say a priori that some of these items should be counted one way or the other. To a large extent it depends on the purpose for which the analysis of the balance of payments is used. Here we can only be concerned with the broader principles. Our aim is to understand how basic questions of economic analysis and policy can be elucidated by the use of balance-of-payments statistics and what factors one has to take into account to be able to interpret a country's balance of payments in any significant sense. A student interested in studying a specific country's balance of payments closely will have to refer to the country's balance-of-payments statistics. After having read this part of the book one should be aware of the things to watch for.

In search of a helpful general definition we might say that all items of a flow nature should be included in the balance of current account and that all items expressing changes in stocks should enter the balance of capital account.

Let us now return to the general discussion. The sum of exports of goods, services, gifts, etc., need not equal the sum of imports of goods, services, indemnities, etc., and therefore there is no reason the balance of current account should be in equilibrium. The natural thing is to assume that it is not balanced, and in our example we saw that the country in question had a deficit of 130.

This deficit must be settled, because if a country has a deficit on the balance of current account, the country has spent more abroad during the period than it has earned. A way to settle this is by a transaction on the capital account. The country can deplete part of its stocks to an amount equal to the deficit on the balance of current account. This can be done, for instance, by borrowing abroad, i.e., by sending a loan instrument to the value of 130 abroad, by selling assets, or by depleting its reserves of foreign currency.

If we go back and look at our hypothetical example from Table 14.2

we can see that the country in question exported capital for 70 and imported capital for 200. Hence the country imported more capital than was necessary to cover the deficit in the balance on current account. This, however, is explained by the fact that it also exported capital to the value of 70. The net inflow of capital to the value of 130 was enough to offset exactly the deficit in the balance of current account and to equalize the two sides in the balance of payments. Before considering in what sense the balance of payments is in equilibrium, however, we should look more closely at the balance of capital account.

We have already said that the items on the capital account can take many forms. We might assume, in our example, that a corporation in one country acquired shares in a foreign corporation, and that the value of these shares amounted to 70. This explains the capital exports of the country which appear in Table 14.1. At the same time we might assume that a foreign company acquired shares to the value of 70 in the country whose balance of payments we are studying. This explains part of the total of 200 capital imports into the country. The rest, we can assume, consists of a loan which the government in this country receives from a foreign government, amounting to 130.

Is this, then, the deficit in the country's balance of payments? To answer this question it is no longer possible to look at the figures in the balance of payments and to think in bookkeeping terms. We have to start thinking in wider economic terms.

EQUILIBRIUM AND DISEQUILIBRIUM IN THE BALANCE OF PAYMENTS

In a trivial sense the balance of payments will always be in equilibrium. Let us assume, for example, that a country has a deficit of 100 in the balance of current account. If no other transactions occur in the capital account, the country has to import capital at least to the value of 100 by, for instance, borrowing abroad (exporting a loan instrument) or depleting its reserves of foreign currency. On the other hand, if the country had a surplus in its balance of current account, it would mean that the country had exported more than it had imported (exports and imports taken in a wide sense). If no other transactions took place in the capital account, the country would still have to export capital to an extent equal to its surplus on the current account, by lending money abroad, for instance. Whatever the values on other items, there will always be a residual transaction of this kind which brings the balance of payments into equilibrium. In this bookkeeping sense the balance of payments will always balance.

In what sense, then, can the balance of payments be in disequilibrium? If we return to our example from Tables 14.1 and 14.2 we can see that the country has a capital inflow of 200. The critical factor is to understand the nature of this inflow. We assumed earlier that 70 was accounted for by a foreign corporation acquiring shares in a firm in the country. This meant, in other words, that some residents in the country sold assets to foreigners, thereby creating a capital inflow. The rest, 130, can be assumed to consist of a depletion of the country's reserves of foreign currency. Is this, then, the deficit in the country's balance of payments?

The answer is yes, if we assume that the country does this unwillingly and has a scarcity of foreign reserves. If, on the other hand, the country's reserves of foreign currency were plentiful and the depletion of these reserves were a consequence of a deliberate policy, it is doubtful if we could say that the country had a deficit in its balance of payments.

The inflow of capital need not take the form of a depletion of reserves. It is possible that the country has many attractive investment opportunities to offer, and that because of this, foreign investors want to invest in the country, thus covering the capital inflow. On the other hand, it is possible that an international agency is prepared to give the country a long-term loan to cover the "deficit" of 130.

To say anything significant about a country's balance of payments, we have to study the nature of its international capital flows and also take into account its economic policy. The problem of judging the equilibrium position of a country's balance of payments becomes fairly complicated and soon takes us outside the sphere of bookkeeping. The time has come to make an important distinction concerning a country's international capital flows.

AUTONOMOUS AND ACCOMMODATING CAPITAL FLOWS

We have learned that if a country has a deficit in its balance of current account, there will always be an offsetting transaction on the capital account to bring the balance of payments into equilibrium. If, for instance, a country's importers had imported 100 more than the exporters had exported, they might have to borrow 100 from the foreign exporters to pay for their purchases, and this would be registered as an inflow of capital on the capital account. There are, however, other capital flows which have no connection with the country's balance-of-payments situation. It may be, for instance, that a foreign exporter buys an advertising agency in the country at the cost of 100, to be able to better market his products; this would also be registered as a capital inflow of 100. The significance of these two capital flows for the country's balance of payments is very different. We therefore have to distinguish between two types of capital flow.

One type we call accommodating capital movements. These are capital flows that take place specifically to equalize the balance of payments in the bookkeeping sense. The other we call autonomous capital flows; these are "ordinary" capital flows, and their distinguishing feature is that they take place regardless of other items in the balance of payments. To bring out the meaning and significance of autonomous and accommodating capital flows, it might be worthwhile to regroup the items from Tables 14.1 and 14.2 in a new way and to give some examples of the two types of capital movement.

Looking at Table 14.3, we see that the country in question exported goods and services to a value of 700. Furthermore, it received unrequited gifts and such to a value of 100. We assume, moreover, that the country had an autonomous capital inflow of 70. This could, for instance, be in the form of a foreign corporation buying up a subsidiary firm, thereby acquiring capital assets to a value of 70 in the country in question.

This autonomous capital inflow could take many other forms. It could have been caused, for instance, by a foreign firm or a foreign resident paying back a loan to a firm or a person in the country under discussion. Or it could be that a person or a company took up a loan abroad, by issuing bonds, for instance. In all these cases it is a question of private persons or firms having capital transactions with foreigners. These transactions have an effect on the country's balance of payments but they are in no way caused by balance-of-payments considerations. In fact, they are all examples of autonomous capital movements.

If we look at the debit side, i.e., the payments side, of Table 14.3, we find that the country imported goods and services to a value of 850, at the same time paying 80 to foreigners in the form of gifts, indemnities, etc.

TABLE 14.3

Autonomous and accommodating transactions

Credit		Debit	
(1) Autonomous receipts	870	(3) Autonomous payments	1000
(a) Autonomous exports (visible and invisible)	700	(a) Autonomous imports (visible and invisible)	850
(b) Autonomous unrequited receipts from foreigners	100	(b) Autonomous unrequited payments to foreigners	80
(c) Autonomous capital receipts from foreigners	70	(c) Autonomous capital payments to foreigners	70
(2) Accommodating capital receipts from foreigners	130	(4) Accommodating capital payments to foreigners	0
	1000		1000

Furthermore, the country had an autonomous outflow of capital to the value of 70. Summing this up we find that total payments to foreigners amount to 1000, whereas the inflow only amounted to 870, a difference of 130. This difference has to be settled by an accommodating inflow of capital of the same amount.

This accommodating inflow of capital can take various forms. Foreign firms might accept short-term claims on firms in the country whose balance of payments we are studying, or perhaps a foreign government extends a loan to the country. In the case of a less-developed country, it might even be possible that a foreign government is willing to ease the balance-of-payments situation of the country by making it a gift amounting to the value of the accommodating inflow. Or possibly the country in question has had to delete its reserves of foreign currency to settle its accommodating capital inflow.

In all these cases the accommodating capital movements are a direct consequence of the balance-of-payments situation. Accommodating capital flows are unforeseen capital flows, which have to be made to bring the balance of payments into equilibrium.

We are now in a position to define a surplus or a deficit in a country's balance of payments. Looking at Table 14.4, we see that the country we have used as an example had autonomous receipts of 870 and autonomous pay-

TABLE 14.4

Balance of payments

(1) Balance of autonomous trade [Table 14.3, rows (1a) and (3a)]	$700 - 850 = -150$
(2) Balance of autonomous unrequited transfers [Table 14.3, rows (1b) and (3b)]	$100 - 80 = 20$
(3) Balance of autonomous capital movements [Table 14.3, rows (1c) and (3c)]	$70 - 70 = 0$
(4) Balance of payments	$870 - 1000 = -130$
(5) Balance of foreign accommodation	$130 - 0 = 130$
(6) Balance of accommodating and autonomous transactions	$1000 - 1000 = 0$

ments of 1000. The difference comprises an accommodating inflow of 130. This is the country's deficit in its balance of payments. We therefore reach the conclusion that if a country's autonomous receipts are larger than its autonomous payments, it will have a surplus in its balance of payments. This will then be settled by an accommodating outflow of capital equal to the surplus, thereby bringing the balance of payments into equilibrium in a bookkeeping sense. In a completely analogous manner we say that a country has a deficit in its balance of payments if its autonomous receipts are smaller than its autonomous payments. This deficit will have to be settled by an accommodating capital inflow which brings the balance of payments into equilibrium. If a country's autonomous payments equal its autonomous receipts, the balance of payments will be in equilibrium and no accommodating capital movements will take place.

It is useful to take into account a time perspective and think of accommodating capital movements as unforeseen or unplanned. In the capitalist or mixed type of economy prevalent in the West, the outcome of the balance of payments depends on many atomistic decisions taken by the firms and individuals that comprise the decision units of these economies. There is little reason to expect that the result of these decisions on the balance of payments will be an equilibrium in external transactions. If this is not the case, accommodating capital movements will result. Therefore, accommodating capital flows can be regarded as a residual needed to create a bookkeeping equilibrium in the balance of payments.

Autonomous capital movements, on the contrary, can be regarded as planned capital movements. The different decision units—the individual, the firm, or the government, for that matter—may, for different reasons, plan to engage in capital transactions with the rest of the world. These autonomous capital flows have, of course, consequences on the balance-of-payments situation of the country, but firms engage in these capital flows as a matter of course, without direct regard for the balance-of-payments consequences. It may be useful to think, in planning terms, of autonomous capital flows as being planned capital flows. Using terminology of Swedish origin we can say that autonomous capital movements are *ex ante* in nature; i.e., the different decision units plan to engage in these capital movements at the beginning of the planning period in question.

Accommodating capital flows are, on the contrary, *ex post* in nature. Only at the end of the period can one discover whether accommodating movements have taken place. In this sense they are unplanned and appear as a result of the economic activity which has taken place during the period in question.

Accommodating capital movements have great political significance. If a country has a deficit in its balance of payments of the type just defined, and if this is settled by an accommodating inflow of capital, the accommodating inflow can be viewed as a warning signal. As has been stated, the deficit can be settled by a short-term loan or a depletion of reserves. Usually this condition cannot continue for long. Lenders are seldom willing to extend short-term loans forever, and reserves have a tendency to become depleted. If an accommodating capital inflow occurs, it is usually a sign that the government will have to change its economic policy to abolish the deficit in the balance of payments that has caused the accommodating inflow. The situation depends now to a large extent on the type of policy the country already pursues. If it works within the framework of a liberal trade policy, and if the general economic policy is not very restrictive, it may be easy to close the deficit by merely having a slightly tighter economic policy. It is possible, however, that the country already has a heavily controlled economy with many restrictions and that it still cannot avoid a balance-of-payments deficit. In that case, the country's predicament will be much more severe. Before finishing this chapter, we will say a few more words about the balance of payments within the framework of general economic policy.

Again, it could be that the country need not revise its economic policy, even though it has a deficit in its balance of payments and an accommodating capital inflow. If the country has many attractive investment opportunities to offer, it may be possible to convert the short-term, unplanned accommodating inflow to a long-term, planned, autonomous capital inflow by, for instance, issuing a long-term loan abroad. The country may receive a 20-year loan, thus easing its balance-of-payments problems. After 20 years of foreign investment the country will perhaps be able to turn an unfavorable balance of current account into a favorable one.

THE BALANCE OF PAYMENTS AND ECONOMIC POLICY

We should now have a basic understanding of the sense in which the balance of payments is always in equilibrium and the sense in which the balance of payments might be in disequilibrium. If accommodating capital flows take place, they always have some policy implications. If a country has a deficit and an accommodating capital inflow, it must in general try to implement policy measures aimed at reducing the deficit. An asymmetry occurs here for surplus countries. A country with a surplus in its balance of payments and an accommodating outflow of capital need not take immediate measures, because it can continue to have a surplus and accumulate foreign reserves or claims on foreigners without running into difficulty. Surpluses do not usually create great problems, so we are not specifically concerned with surplus countries. We shall continue, as we have so far in this chapter, to concentrate on the balance-of-payments problems of deficit countries.

Countries can, as we have hinted, be in very different positions concerning the balance of payments, even though their deficits and accommodating capital inflows are the same, because the general economic situation in the two countries may be very different. It is, therefore, not possible to discuss a country's balance-of-payments situation intelligently without taking into account its general economic background.

To understand the nature of a deficit one has to judge it against the background of the general economic policy of a country and the policy means a country has at its disposal. The more restrictions and controls, the less scope a country has for getting rid of a deficit. If a country is already pursuing a tight monetary and fiscal policy and has high tariffs and import controls, yet still has a deficit, it may be very difficult to get rid of the deficit. We can then talk about actual and potential deficits. The actual deficit is the deficit that appears, and the potential deficit is the deficit that would appear with a more neutral "normal" economic policy. It is, of course, somewhat arbitrary to think of a certain economic policy as "normal." However, the possibility of pursuing a restrictive policy to close a deficit in the balance of payments depends on the level of tightness and restriction existing in the economy. This is important and should be kept in mind. The more restrictive a policy at the outset, the more difficult it is to get rid of a deficit.

Another important factor is the scope of policy means available. If a government has many means at its disposal and the political situation is such that the government can use any means it chooses, it is obviously in a better position than one with few means and narrowly constrained because of political reasons. We will come back to this question in Chapter 18.

The nature of capital flows is also important. We have already said that an accommodating inflow of capital can be viewed as a warning signal. It might, however, be possible for a country to convert an unforeseen accommodating import of capital into a long-term, planned capital import. This can be achieved, for instance, by issuing a long-term-bond loan abroad. In such a case, the country need not change its economic policy but can continue to run a deficit for a long time, perhaps 20 years or so, without having to worry about the balance-of-payments situation.

Several examples of how a long-term import of capital has helped developing countries to solve their balance-of-payments problems are evident in history. Sweden had, as we mentioned in Chapter 8, an almost uninterrupted inflow of capital from 1870 to 1910, much of which seems to have been planned. In the 1870s capital was imported to finance the construction of railways. In the 1880s the rapid expansion in housing construction that took place in cities such as Stockholm and Gothenburg was also financed by bond issues on the international markets in Paris and London. This import of capital was a way of raising the rate of capital formation in a poor country with limited resources to devote to domestic savings. It was, however, also a way to solve the balance-of-payments problem and thus appears to have been, to a certain degree, a consciously planned policy.

Canada and Argentina are additional examples. These countries imported much capital during the period 1880–1913. Development was the main reason behind this import of capital: These countries were developing countries which were building export industries based on natural resources.

To do this rapidly they needed to have a higher rate of capital formation than that possible if they had been forced to rely entirely on domestic savings. This import of foreign capital also had important implications for the balance-of-payments situation. The investment, needed to open up export possibilities, led to a high level of economic activity, creating a stress on the balance of payments and causing deficits. To close the deficit one had to import capital. These countries foresaw this development to a certain degree and by planning for an import of capital were able to turn what would otherwise have been an accommodating inflow into a planned, autonomous capital import.

International capital flows play an important part in equilibrating the balance of payments. Much superstition surrounds this subject. It is often argued that capital flows can only be of a short-run nature. As often stated, countries that cover their deficits with capital imports cannot continue for long. But this depends on the general economic situation. In a monetary system such as prevails among leading industrial countries today, capital flows have an extremely important role to play as the natural complement of other forms of adjustment. We shall have more to say on this in the following chapters, but before going on to more policy-oriented questions, we must deal with some problems of analysis. First we have to understand what determines the national income in an open economy. We should now at least have a basic understanding of what is meant by equilibrium and disequilibrium in the balance of payments and of the role played by accommodating capital flows.

15

One of Keynes's main contributions to economic theory was to describe how equilibrium in national income is created. As most students are familiar with the determination of national income in a closed economy, we shall only give a brief recapitulation of it.

THE DETERMINATION OF NATIONAL INCOME IN A CLOSED ECONOMY

The sum of the goods and services produced in a country gives rise to its national product. Every productive service produces an income, and the sum of all incomes in a country is called the national income. In a closed economy, i.e., an economy without trade, the national product and the national income are two sides of the same coin, and the national product equals, by definition, the national income.

In the simplest formulation we can say that the national product can either be consumed or invested. Analogously, the national income can either be saved or consumed, giving rise to the following simple equation:

$$C + I = C + S = Y \tag{15.1}$$

where C stands for goods consumed or produced, I investment, S savings, and Y national income. From this we then deduce that in equilibrium savings must equal investment, so that we get

$$I = S \tag{15.2}$$

The economic meaning of this is that if producers plan to invest the same amount as consumers plan to save, the national income is in an equilibrium position. The meaning of equilibrium here is simply that there are no forces which tend to move the national income from its given equilibrium. The total value of the goods planned for production equals the value of all planned consumption, and both producers and consumers are able to pursue their intentions as planned. A geometric illustration of this simple idea is given in Figure 15.1.

We have already said that consumers can spend their income in only two ways: They can consume it or save it. In Figure 15.1 we take only

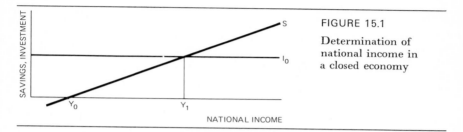

FIGURE 15.1

Determination of
national income in
a closed economy

savings explicitly into account. From this we see that savings are a function
of income; in mathematical terms,

$$S = S(Y) \tag{15.3}$$

At a certain low national income, nothing is saved; all income is consumed.
Savings are zero at the point where the savings schedule, S, in Figure 15.1
cuts the horizontal axis, denoting national income. This happens at Y_0. If
the national income falls below this point, savings are negative. This implies
that the country is consuming part of its stock of capital. Only at a national
income larger than Y_0 will positive savings occur. The larger the national
income, the more the country saves. Thus savings are an increasing function
of national income. The savings schedule, shown here as a straight line,
indicates that marginally a constant fraction of the national income is saved.

Let us, for the sake of reasoning, start by assuming that investment
is independent of the level of national income, so that producers invest a
constant amount, regardless of how small or how large the national income is,
or, in mathematical terms,

$$I_0 = \text{constant} \tag{15.4}$$

Equilibrium in the national income is reached at the point where the savings
schedule, denoting planned savings, cuts the investments schedule, denoting
planned investment. This happens at Y_1, the national income equilibrium.

To understand the notion of equilibrium in national income and to
discover what determines the level of national income, let us assume that the
behavior of the producers or consumers changes. Let us start by assuming
that producers plan to invest more. There can be many reasons for such a
change in plan, e.g., a wish to take advantage of innovations or a belief that
a boom is coming. Such a change in investment plans is illustrated in
Figure 15.2. When producers decide to invest more, we get a once-and-for-
all upward shift in the investment schedule. The increase in investment we

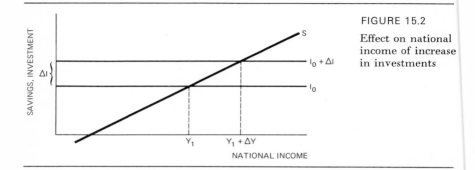

FIGURE 15.2

Effect on national
income of increase
in investments

can denote ΔI, and the new investment schedule is therefore $I_0 + \Delta I$. This causes the national income to expand, increasing by ΔY from Y_1 to $Y_1 + \Delta Y$. The intuitive reason for this is as follows.

Let us assume that a shipping line decided to increase its investment by ordering a new ship, giving rise to an increase in orders and income to the shipyard. The shipyard needs materials with which to build the ship and so orders more steel, sheets, machinery, etc., and tries to hire more workers. All this in its turn gives rise to new incomes and increased consumption. Hence an autonomous increase in investment produces general expansionary effects on the national income and an increase in the national income larger than the increase in investment, which started the procedure. This we can see from Figure 15.2, where obviously the increase in national income ΔY, is larger than the increase in investment, ΔI.

The next item we have to discover is the size of the increase in national income. To determine this, we have to invoke the well-known multiplier.

Let us start by defining the marginal propensity to save, s. It measures how much of an increment in income is saved. Let us say that the national income increases from 1000 to 1100. If 20 of this income increment of 100 is saved, the marginal propensity to save, s, is 0.2. The marginal propensity to consume is defined analogously as the fraction consumed of an income increment. As, by definition, the income can only be consumed or saved, the sum of the marginal propensity to save and the marginal propensity to consume equals 1. In our example, 20 of an income increment of 100 was saved; therefore, 80 was consumed and the marginal propensity to consume was 0.8.

We have already stated that for the national income to be in equilibrium, S must equal I. We now have an autonomous change in investment

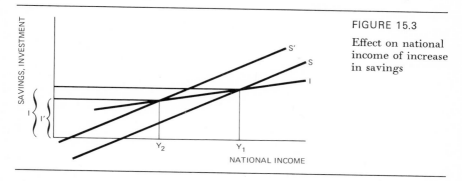

FIGURE 15.3

Effect on national
income of increase
in savings

with ΔI. The change in savings needed to bring about a new equilibrium is ΔS. The increase in savings is measured by the marginal propensity to save multiplied by the increase in national income, ΔY. Hence we evolve the following condition for a new equilibrium:

$$s \, \Delta Y = \Delta I \tag{15.5}$$

from which it follows that

$$\Delta Y = \frac{1}{s} \Delta I \tag{15.6}$$

The expression $1/s = k$ is called the multiplier. As s varies between zero and unity, we see that the multiplier $k \geq 1$. If s is 0.2, as in the example, the multiplier will be 5. An autonomous increase in investment of 100 will in that case lead to an increase in the national income of 500.

Instead of an increase in investment, let us assume that we get an increase in savings. What, then, will happen to the national income? This case is illustrated in Figure 15.3. The figure shows a change in the savings schedule from its original position S to a new position S'. This shift implies that the consumers at all levels of national income save more than they did before. The increased thriftiness may have many causes: a feeling of saturation in consumption, worry about old age, etc. We may also note a difference in the investment schedule in Figure 15.3 as compared to Figures 15.1 and 15.2. We now assume investment to be an increasing function of the national income, with the result that the investment schedule also has a positive slope.

The upward shift in the savings schedule obviously gives rise to a contraction in the national income, as the new savings schedule cuts the investment schedule vertically above Y_2, indicating that the national income must, to reach a new equilibrium, fall from Y_1 to Y_2. This movement is explained in the following way.

When the consumers start to save more they consume less. As consumption falls, producers find that they can no longer sell as much as before and that they will have to cut back production and lay off workers. The unemployed workers will thus receive less income, and consumption will fall even more. Finally, a new equilibrium will be reached at the lower national income Y_2, where, again, planned savings and planned investment equal each other. The decision to save more thus starts a contractive process, which in the end causes a drop in savings, as savings and investment are seen to be smaller at the income Y_2 than at the income Y_1. This is an example of what is often referred to as the savings paradox.

This might do as a repetition of the elementary theory of income determination in a closed economy. We now have to see how this mechanism works in an open economy.

THE IMPORT FUNCTION

In a closed economy consumers could spend their incomes on consumption goods or they could save them. Total consumption could then be viewed as a function of the national income. This functional relationship can be expressed in the following way:

$$C = C(Y) \tag{15.7}$$

Savings (see equation 15.3) and consumption are both increasing functions of the national income.

In an open economy consumers will also demand imported goods, and imports can be expressed as a function of national income. We write the import function as

$$M = M(Y) \tag{15.8}$$

Imports are also an increasing function of income. We can illustrate the import function graphically as shown in Figure 15.4. The figure shows that even at zero national income, something would be imported (by exporting part of the country's capital stock or by borrowing abroad).

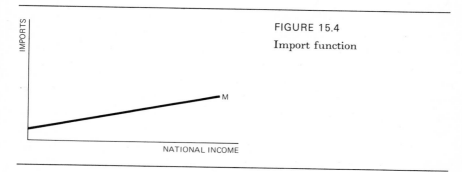

FIGURE 15.4

Import function

As the national income increases, so do imports. A country's average propensity to import is defined as the total imports divided by the total national income, i.e., M/Y. The average propensity to import varies greatly between countries. A large country such as the United States, well endowed with resources and whose dependence on foreign trade is very small, has a low average propensity to import, 0.03; i.e., only 3 percent of its national income is imported. The average propensity to import has fallen in the United States over the years. Early in the nineteenth century it was over 10 percent, at the end of the century it fell to 7 percent, after World War I it was 5 percent, and now it is down to 3 percent, even though a slight tendency to increase has been discernible during recent years. Another large country, the Soviet Union, also has a very low average propensity to import, between 0.02 and 0.03; and so has a country such as India, which in national-income terms, is not a large country. As far as India is concerned, its low propensity to import seems to be the result of an economic policy directed toward autarky.

Smaller countries are usually more dependent on foreign trade and have a larger average propensity to import. Great Britain, for instance, has an average propensity to import of about 0.2 and Holland one of 0.4.

The marginal propensity to import measures how much of a change in the national income is spent on imports. Using algebraic terms it is defined as $\Delta M/\Delta Y$. If imports increase by 10 when the national income increases by 100, the marginal propensity to import will be 0.1. If the marginal propensity to import is divided by the average propensity to import, we deduce the income elasticity of demand for imports. Expressed in algebraic terms this becomes $(\Delta M/\Delta Y):(M/Y)$. The income elasticity of imports is defined under the assumption that all other things are equal, for instance that there are no changes in prices. If the demand for imports increases by 5 percent when the income increases by 10 percent, the income elasticity of imports equals 0.5. If a country's average and marginal propensities to import are equal, its income elasticity of demand for imports is 1. This implies that as the country's income increases, a constant proportion of the increasing income is spent on imports, and the share of its national product which is traded is constant. If the marginal propensity to import is larger than its average propensity, this tends to increase the country's dependence on foreign trade, and if the opposite is the case, its foreign trade quota will fall.

This way of defining the propensities to import and the import elasticity should not lure the reader into thinking that these concepts are constants that do not change. A country's marginal propensity to import, for instance, is influenced by many economic factors and usually changes from year to year.

THE DETERMINATION OF NATIONAL INCOME IN AN OPEN ECONOMY: THE FOREIGN TRADE MULTIPLIER

We will now show how the national income is determined in an open economy. The difference between a closed and an open economy is that in the latter we have the possibility of foreign trade, i.e., of exports and imports. In an open economy we can write the national income identity as

$$Y + M = C + I + X \tag{15.9}$$

where the left side of the expression shows the total supply, i.e., the sum of total domestic supply (Y) and imports (M), and where the right side shows the three ways total output can be used, i.e., as consumption (C), investment (I), or exports (X).

In a closed economy we know that savings have to equal investment in equilibrium. In an open economy we have to take into account that there can be a net inflow or outflow of capital. In an open economy we can therefore write the equilibrium condition as

$$S = I + X - M \tag{15.10}$$

or

$$S + M = I + X \tag{15.10a}$$

If there is a change in any of the four variables, the change in the left side of expression 15.10 must equal the change in the right side, as a condition for reaching a new equilibrium. Hence

$$\Delta S + \Delta M = \Delta I + \Delta X \tag{15.11}$$

Using the definitions of marginal propensity to save, s, and of marginal propensity to import, m, we can write $\Delta S = s\,\Delta Y$ and $\Delta M = m\,\Delta Y$. Then we can rewrite equation 15.11 as

$$(s + m)\,\Delta Y = \Delta I + \Delta X \tag{15.12}$$

Hence we get

$$\Delta Y = \frac{1}{s + m}\,(\Delta I + \Delta X) \tag{15.13}$$

We can now view the changes in investment and exports as the autonomous variables and see what the effects of a change in, let us say, exports will be on the national income. From equation 15.13 we see that the effect of a change in exports on the national income equals the change in exports multiplied by the expression $1/(s + m)$, which in our formulation is the foreign trade multiplier, which we shall call k_f.

Let us for a moment assume that there is no change in investment, and see what the effect of an increase in exports will be. Assuming that the marginal propensity to consume is positive, we see that k_f will always be larger than unity and that hence the increase in exports will have some secondary effects on the national income, so that the increase in the national income will be larger than the original increase in exports.

The foreign trade multiplier, or the export multiplier as it is sometimes called, works in exactly the same way as the ordinary investment multiplier. An increase in exports gives rise to an increase in income for the exporters and those employed in the export industries. They, in turn, spend more of their increased incomes. How much more they spend on domestic goods depends on two leakages: how much they save and how much they spend on imports. The savings do not create any new incomes. An increase in import spendings does not create new incomes in the country itself, only in those foreign countries with which the first country trades. And it is the effect on the country's own national income with which we, for the moment, are concerned.

It is now easy to see that the larger the marginal propensities to save and import, the smaller will be the value of the multiplier. If the marginal

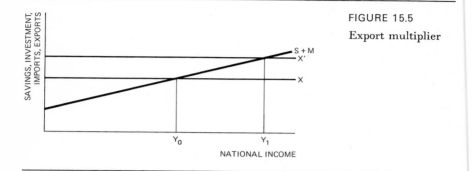

FIGURE 15.5

Export multiplier

propensity to save is 0.2 and if the marginal propensity to import is 0.3, the value of the multiplier will be $1/(0.2 + 0.3) = 2$; i.e., an autonomous increase in exports of 100 will lead to an increase in the national income of 200.

The reason for the original increase in exports may be one of many. It could be, for instance, that a change in tastes among foreign consumers in favor of imported goods has occurred. This gives rise to increased orders to producers of export goods. To start with, exporters may sell their stocks and receive increased incomes; in the next period they will then try to increase production and hire more workers. This creates new incomes among food and textiles producers, and so on. When the whole process has worked itself out, the increase in the national income becomes larger than the original increase in exports. How much larger depends on the value of the export multiplier, which depends in itself in a critical fashion, on the values of the marginal propensities to save and import.

Figure 15.5 illustrates the export multiplier diagrammatically. The figure shows a savings–imports schedule, i.e., how much consumers plan to save and import at different values of the national income. This is arrived at by adding an import schedule to the savings schedule. We assume, furthermore, to simplify the reasoning, that there is no net investment, so that exports are the only autonomous variable. To start with, we have an equilibrium national income, Y_0, where savings plus imports are equal to exports. We now get an increase in exports, so that the export schedule rises from X to X'. This produces an expansionary effect on the national income, which increases from Y_0 to Y_1, where again we have a state of equilibrium with savings plus imports equal to exports. How large the expansionary effect on national income will be from a given increase in exports depends on

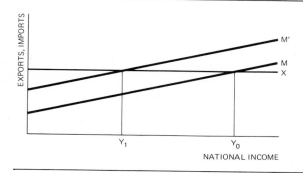

FIGURE 15.6

Effect on national income
of increase in imports

the slope of the savings–imports schedule. This slope depends on the marginal propensities to save and import. The smaller the sum of these propensities, the smaller will be the slope of the schedule and the larger the expansionary effect of an increase in exports on national income.

In the same way as an autonomous increase in exports will have an expansionary effect on the national income, an increase in imports will have a contractive effect. This is illustrated in Figure 15.6. For the sake of reasoning, we assume that there are no net savings and no net investment. The reason for the increase in imports can be one of many. The most simple explanation could be to assume that it depends on a change in tastes. The consumers consume as much as before but fewer home-produced goods and more imports. This leads to a decrease in orders for the domestic industries. Sooner or later domestic producers will have to decrease production and lay off workers. This will lead to a decrease in income for those employed in these domestic industries, and the total income will fall even more through the multiplier effect, until finally a new equilibrium is reached at a lower national income.

This process is illustrated with the help of geometry in Figure 15.6. We start from an equilibrium position at Y_0, where imports and exports are equal and where we show the original equilibrium of the national income. We then see an upward movement in the import schedule, leading to a contraction in the national income and finally to a new equilibrium at the lower national income Y_1. We might observe that this process is of exactly the same nature as the one connected with the savings paradox.

In a closed economy we had the equilibrium condition

$$I = S \qquad\qquad (15.2)$$

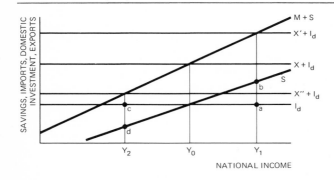

FIGURE 15.7

Effect on national
income of
changes in exports

In an open economy, investment can be broken down into two parts: domestic investment, I_d, and foreign investment, I_f. The equilibrium condition can be written

$$I_d + I_f = S \qquad (15.14)$$

Foreign investment is the difference between exports of goods and services and imports of goods and services. Hence we get

$$I_f = X - M \qquad (15.15)$$

Substituting equation 15.15 into 15.14 gives

$$I_d + X = S + M \qquad (15.16)$$

Again it may be useful to give a geometric illustration. In Figure 15.7 we start from a situation where S is the savings schedule and $M + S$ is the added imports and savings schedule. I_d is the domestic investment schedule and $X + I_d$ denotes the schedule for exports and domestic investment. This schedule cuts the savings–import schedule vertically above Y_0, which is the equilibrium national income. At this level of income there is also equilibrium in the balance of current account, because savings equals domestic investment and exports equal imports.

Let us then assume that there is an autonomous increase in exports so that the combined export-investment schedule rises to $X' + I_d$. This produces an expansionary impetus on the national income, increasing it to Y_1, where again exports plus domestic investment equals savings plus imports. This is the new equilibrium in the national income, but we no longer have an equilibrium in the balance of current account because the total savings is now larger than domestic investment. The difference between savings and domestic investment at Y_1 is given by the distance $a\text{-}b$. This implies that exports are larger than imports by the same amount, and that the country exports capital.

If, on the other hand, exports fell, so that the schedule for exports plus investment fell to $X'' + I_d$, this would have a contractive effect on the national income, which would fall from Y_0 to Y_2. At this level of income domestic investment would be larger than savings by the distance $c\text{-}d$. This implies that imports are larger than exports by the same amount, that the country has a deficit in its balance of current account, and that an import of capital is needed to cover the given, autonomous domestic investment program which takes place.

NATIONAL INCOME AND THE BALANCE OF PAYMENTS

We have just demonstrated in Figure 15.7 that there may be an internal equilibrium, i.e., that the national income may be in equilibrium, but that there is no external equilibrium, i.e., that there is no equilibrium in the balance of payments. The time has come to see how this can occur and to discern the effects of income changes on the balance of payments.

First we must understand clearly what is meant by equilibrium in the national income. The condition of equilibrium is for planned savings (*ex ante* savings) to equal planned investment (*ex ante* investment). This being the case, consumers will be able to carry out their plans to consume and save and producers will be able to fulfill their plans regarding production of consumer and investment goods. Production of consumer goods will equal their consumption, and savings and investment will be equal. Then there will be no change in the national income from its given equilibrium value.

In an open economy the equilibrium condition has only to be re-formulated so that it takes into account the possibility of a country's not having to rely only on domestic savings but also on foreigners to provide part of the total savings by their exporting capital. Also, a country need not only invest at home but can invest abroad by exporting capital.

It is often said that the two main aims of a country's economic policy are to maintain full employment and an external balance. We shall return to the question of the aims and means in economic policy in later chapters. For the time being, we must only observe that equilibrium in a country's national income, according to the Keynesian definition just given, does not necessarily imply that the economy is fully employed. This definition says only that total planned demand equals total planned production. This equilibrium can be at any capacity level. If it happens to be at 100 percent capacity, the economy is fully employed. If it is at a lower level of capacity utilization, there will be some unemployment in the economy, and if it is at a 110 percent of the economy's capacity level, this will have definite implications for the balance of payments.

In this connection we must also define the way we use the terms inflation and deflation. By inflation, or an inflationary pressure in the economy, we mean simply that planned total demand is larger than planned total production, that is, that investment *ex ante* is larger than savings *ex ante*. This does not necessarily imply rising prices, but it will, in many instances, lead to a rising price level. With deflation, or a deflationary pressure in the economy, we mean, analogously, that total production is larger than total demand, in other words, that planned savings are larger than planned investment.

Let us first assume that during the previous period of time a country achieved internal balance at a full employment level and that the balance of payments was in equilibrium. We now get an increase in total demand. There can be many causes for such an increase. Perhaps consumers wish to save less and consume more from a given income. Or it can be a change in a policy variable, for instance, a decrease in interest rates, which encourages investment. Whatever the reason, there will be an inflationary pressure in the economy. In an open economy, such pressure need not usually lead to rising prices but to a deficit in the balance of payments; it can, of course, lead to both. Consumers will consume more than before, and producers will continue to invest as much as they used to. As the economy, however, is already at full employment, there is no possibility of increasing domestic production in the short run. Exports will not change, but imports will increase to satisfy the increase in demand for consumer goods. At the end of the period, the country will find that it has a deficit in its balance of payments and that, in fact, a part of its domestic investment has been financed out of capital imports.

It is of no consequence for this process how the internal production pattern has been influenced—how the composition of goods has been affected. It may be that exports and home production of investment goods remain unchanged and that imports, only, increase. Or perhaps production of exports fall, and factors of production from this sector are drawn into domestic sectors to meet the increase in demand for consumer goods. Whichever way the production pattern changes under inflationary pressure, the main thing for us to observe is the fact that domestic investment is larger than domestic savings and that imports are larger than exports.

It is is important to realize that an increase in the national income, generated on the demand side in the way just described, often leads to a deficit in the balance of payments. An inflationary pressure within the economy does not necessarily lead to rising prices but instead gives rise to a deficit in the balance of payments, which has to be covered by an unforeseen accommodating inflow of capital. This accommodating capital inflow can then be seen as a warning signal, as described in Chapter 14. This case is a classical example taken from Keynesian analysis. The policy implications in this case are also quite clear, but we shall return later to a fuller discussion of these.

Let us now assume, instead, that starting from an equilibrium with full employment, a decrease in exports occurs. This produces a contractive effect on the national income, which, through the multiplier effect, will be larger than the original decrease in exports. Imports will also fall as national income falls, but the decrease in imports will be smaller than the decrease in exports, so the country will simultaneously fall into a situation of unemployment and a deficit in balance of payments.

This is a tricky situation to escape from. An inflationary policy can return the country to full employment but only at the cost of a deterioration of the deficit in the balance of payments. A simple Keynesian policy, which works by deflating or inflating the national income, cannot alone cope with this situation.[1]

A simpler situation is one in which, again starting from equilibrium with full employment, the country receives an autonomous upward impetus in its savings schedule. As the consumers wish to save more and consume less, deflationary pressure on national income is evolved. Income falls, resulting in some unemployment. As national income falls, so does the demand for imports, but there is no reason to expect a change in exports. Demand for exports depends primarily on incomes abroad, and these, at least to start with,

---

[1] This problem will be discussed at length in Chapters 16 and 18.

have not changed. At the same time, exporters at home will be, if anything, in a better competitive position than before, as unemployment will create a downward pressure on wages, so that exporters obtain their factors of production more cheaply than previously. The country, therefore, will have a surplus in its balance of payments and be put into a situation where unemployment is combined with a favorable balance of payments.

This situation is comparatively simple to deal with. An inflationary policy will lead the country back toward equilibrium in national income at the full employment level. This will lead to an increase in demand for imports at an unchanged level of exports, but as the country has a surplus in its balance of payments, there is little cause to worry.

We have now set out several cases of how changes in the national income affect the balance of payments. There is an intimate connection between income changes and the balance of payments, and any change in the national income will have some effect on it. To sum up, we can say that in general an inflationary change in national income will have a negative effect on the balance of payments, and a deflationary change in national income will have a favorable effect on the balance of payments. There are, however, exceptions to this general rule. An autonomous decrease in exports will have both a deflationary effect on the national income and lead to a deficit in the balance of payments. Analogously, a shift in consumption away from imports to domestically produced goods will have both an inflationary effect on the national income and lead to a surplus in the balance of payments.

The policy implications of income and balance-of-payments changes will be discussed more fully in later chapters, where we will deal with the question of how to achieve both internal and external equilibrium.

THE INTERNATIONAL PROPAGATION OF BUSINESS CYCLES

We have demonstrated how a change in a country's exports or imports will affect the country's national income. Countries are linked together by trade with each other, however, and a change in one country's national income will have repercussions on the income of its trading partners.

A recession in the United States which leads to a fall in its national income will also lead to a fall in American imports and thus lead to a fall in exports from its trading partners. Countries such as Britain, France, and

Canada will be affected by the American recession through a fall in their exports, which in turn, through a multiplier effect, will have a deflationary impact on national income in these countries. In this way all trading countries are linked together, and no country can be completely isolated from others. In a large country such as the United States, whose national income comprises approximately 40 percent of the world's income, a change in national income will have important repercussions, even though its marginal propensity to import is small. The larger a country's marginal propensity to import, and therefore the more dependent on foreign trade it is, the more sensitive to foreign repercussions the country will usually be.

A geometric illustration of the foreign repercussions, and of how national incomes of countries are connected through trade, is given in Figure 15.8. We start off in stage 1 with an increase in domestic investment in Country I, which increases from I_d to I'_d. This gives rise to a vertical upward shift in the combined investment plus exports schedule and to an expansionary effect on the national income, which increases from Y_0 to Y_1. As national income increases, so does the demand for imports. For the country's trading partners, here symbolized by Country II, this means an increase in exports. We also see from the figure over stage 2 how Country II receives an upward shift in its export schedule, leading to an expansion of its national income, which increases from Y_0 to Y_1. As Country II's income increases, its demand for imports also increases, which in turn leads to a repercussion back to Country I in the form of an increase in the demand for Country I's exports. This is illustrated in stage 3, where we see that Country I receives another upward shift in the $I_d + X$ schedule, so that the national income increases even more, from Y_1 to Y_2.

In this way we see how national incomes hang together and how a change in one country's national income affects another country. A disturbance in one country will, through rebounding repercussions, affect the incomes in all trading countries until a new equilibrium is achieved.

The international propagation of business cycles was once a very important problem. During the period between World Wars I and II it even constituted *the* economic problem. After the Great Depression hit the United States in the late 1920s it spread rapidly and began to be felt in the rest of the world. The most important factor was the fall in demand for imports in the United States, a result of the fall in national income. To this has to be added a drastic decline in American investment abroad. As a result, the number of dollars made available to the rest of the world decreased by 68

FIGURE 15.8

International propagation of business cycles

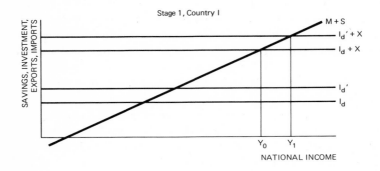

Stage 1, Country I

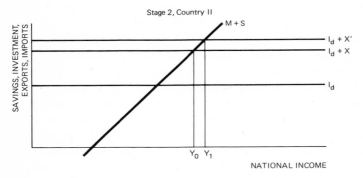

Stage 2, Country II

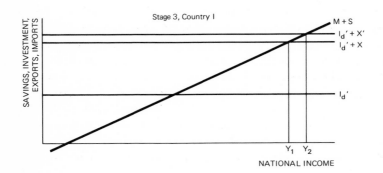

Stage 3, Country I

percent between the end of the 1920s and the bottom of the depression in 1932–1933. Within a short period of time, most countries began to feel the depression, and many were soon in as bad a situation as the United States itself.

Since World War II, the world economy has not undergone a deep depression of the type that, with periodic certainty, occurred in capitalist economies from the beginning of the Industrial Revolution to World War II. It seems that Keynesian economics has provided policy makers in capitalist economies with tools to avoid major fluctuations. Economic fluctuations still occur, however, although of a milder type. This still creates important problems of policy for countries which aim both to trade as much as possible to benefit to the highest degree from gains from trade, and simultaneously to avoid unemployment, which they might have to import because of recessions abroad. We shall return to these policy questions later on.

One way of characterizing the interrelationships among countries and the sensitivity in these relationships is by means of foreign trade multipliers. In the appendix to this chapter we have derived expressions for foreign trade multipliers in a more formal way than we have done previously.

We should now have a basic understanding of how the national income is determined in an open economy and how fluctuations in one economy spread to others. It should be stressed, however, that only basic principles have been discussed. In order to derive fairly uncomplicated expressions for the foreign trade multiplier, we have assumed simple functional relationships and have often added assumptions that investment and exports are independent of changes in the national income. In reality this is not the case, and things become more complicated than they appear in this simplified version.

Another important factor is that if we introduce time into the models, the relationships become even more complex. We have then to take time lags into account, admit that some functional relationships might change in time. The savings functions may not be of the simple linear type which we have assumed but may be nonlinear and change in a fashion hard to predict; wealth must be taken into account to determine the consumption functions; etc.

We should, therefore, keep in mind the fact that the dynamic world in which we live is more complex than the simple comparative-static models that we have used might lead us to believe. This should not cloud the fact that even simple theorizing can be very useful and that simple Keynesian models have proved very powerful tools for economic policy.

Derivation of some foreign trade multipliers

15–A

We have seen that national incomes of different trading countries are closely interrelated. One normally expects that a change in one country's income will have some effects on the incomes of other countries. In an attempt to be more precise about these interconnections and the factors important for determining the strength of these interrelations, we shall derive two more intricate multipliers.

We shall start by setting out the following equation of the national income in Country I:

$$Y_1 = C_1 + G_1 + I_1 + M_2 + \alpha \tag{15A.1}$$

where Y_1 denotes national income in Country I and C_1, G_1, and I_1 denote consumption, government expenditure, and investment in Country I, respectively. M_2 represents imports into Country II ($=$ exports from Country I). Finally, α is a parameter used to express a shift in any one of the expenditure schedules.

Analogously, we shall write for Country II,

$$Y_2 = C_2 + G_2 + I_2 + M_1 - \lambda\alpha \tag{15A.2}$$

The variables in this equation are analogous to the ones used in equation 15A.1, and λ denotes an arbitrary constant relating a shift in spending in Country II to a shift in Country I.

C_1, G_1, C_2, etc., are assumed to be functions of the national income in the respective countries. We assume furthermore that they are continuous and differentiable. We may now differentiate equations 15A.1 and 15A.2 totally with respect to α. This gives

$$\frac{dY_1}{d\alpha} = \frac{\partial C_1}{\partial Y_1}\frac{dY_1}{d\alpha} + \frac{\partial G_1}{\partial Y_1}\frac{dY_1}{d\alpha} + \frac{\partial I_1}{\partial Y_1}\frac{dY_1}{d\alpha} + \frac{\partial M_2}{\partial Y_2}\frac{dY_2}{d\alpha} + 1 \tag{15A.3}$$

$$\frac{dY_2}{d\alpha} = \frac{\partial C_2}{\partial Y_2}\frac{dY_2}{d\alpha} + \frac{\partial G_2}{\partial Y_2}\frac{dY_2}{d\alpha} + \frac{\partial I_2}{\partial Y_2}\frac{dY_2}{d\alpha} + \frac{\partial M_1}{\partial Y_1}\frac{dY_1}{d\alpha} - \lambda \tag{15A.4}$$

Let us now rewrite this system of two equations with a matrix notation, using "primes" for the first partial derivatives, so that $\partial C_1/\partial Y_1 = C_1'$, etc.:

$$\begin{bmatrix} 1 - C_1' - G_1' - I_1' & -M_2' \\ -M_1' & 1 - C_2' - G_2' - I_2' \end{bmatrix} \begin{bmatrix} \dfrac{dY_1}{d\alpha} \\ \dfrac{dY_2}{d\alpha} \end{bmatrix} = \begin{bmatrix} 1 \\ -\lambda \end{bmatrix} \tag{15A.5}$$

Solving this system for $dY_1/d\alpha$, using, for instance, Cramer's rule, gives

$$\frac{dY_1}{d\alpha} = \frac{1}{\Delta}\left[(1 - C_2' - G_2' - I_2') - \lambda M_2'\right] \tag{15A.6}$$

where Δ is determinant of the coefficient matrix;

$$\Delta = (1 - C_1' - G_1' - I_1')(1 - C_2' - G_2' - I_2') - M_2' M_1'$$

This is the general multiplier formula.

The formula contained in equation 15A.6 is somewhat difficult to interpret. The main reason for this is that the expression $(1 - C_2' - G_2' - I_2')$ appears both in the denominator and numerator of equation 15A.6. This implies that the effects of different values of marginal propensities to consume, and so on, in Country II have a somewhat ambiguous effect on Country I's export multiplier. One general comment we can make, however, is to assume that the sum of the marginal propensities to consume, spend for the government, and invest in Country I, i.e., $C_1' + G_1' + I_1'$, is less than unity. Thus the larger the sum of these propensities, the larger will be the export multiplier. This is easy to understand: It simply states that the smaller the leakages in Country I, the larger will be the secondary, tertiary, etc., income increments and multiplier effects of an increase in exports.

In order to interpret expression 15A.6 and study the multiplier effects, it is best to introduce some limiting assumptions which will permit us to re-write equation 15A.6 in more manageable forms.

We shall, for the sake of simplicity, start with the assumption that there are no foreign repercussions but that the two countries are isolated from each other, so that a change in the national income in one country does not affect the other. This amounts to the assumption that $dY_2/d\alpha = 0$. We can then solve for $dY_1/d\alpha$ directly from equation 15A.3 and we get

$$\frac{dY_1}{d\alpha} = \frac{1}{1 - C_1' - G_1' - I_1'} \tag{15A.7}$$

This expression is simple to interpret. The amount the country itself spends of an income increment is the one important matter. Again assuming that the sum of the marginal propensities to spend for consumers, government, and investors is less than unity, making the situation stable, then the more they spend, the larger will be the export multiplier. The reason for this is outlined above. If we assume that government expenditures and investment are independent of changes in the national income, the expression for the multiplier becomes even simpler. Falling back on our earlier assumption that consumers can dispense of their incomes in three ways—on consumer goods, imports, or savings—we deduce that $C_1' + s_1 + m_1 = 1$. Hence equation 15A.7 simplifies to $dY_1/d\alpha = 1/(m_1 + s_1)$, which is the simple expression for the export multiplier, in equation 15.13, already shown, assuming that $G_1' = I_1' = 0$.

We shall now continue to treat a more intricate case, where foreign repercussions exist. We can start by assuming that $\lambda = 1$. This means that an initial increase in Country I's income will be matched by an equal decrease in Country II's income. The reason for this could be, for instance, that Country II has to make a reparations payment to Country I. In this case formula 15A.6 becomes

$$\frac{dY_1}{d\alpha} = \frac{1}{\Delta}\left[(1 - C_2' - G_2' - I_2') - M_2'\right] \tag{15A.8}$$

Assuming that investment and government expenditures are independent of changes in the national income in both countries, so that $G_1' = I_1' = G_2' = I_2' = 0$, and that $1 - C_1' = s_1 + m_1$, and $1 - C_2' = s_2 + m_2$, we deduce that

$$\frac{dY_1}{d\alpha} = \frac{s_2 + m_2 - m_2}{(s_1 + m_1)(s_2 + m_2) - m_1 m_2} = \frac{1}{s_1 + m_1 + (s_1 m_2/s_2)} \tag{15A.9}$$

We see from expression 15A.9 that the smaller s_1 and m_1 are, the larger will be the positive effect on Country I's national income. The marginal propensities to save and import play the same role here as in the simpler versions of the foreign trade multiplier, which we dealt with earlier. The smaller these propensities are, the smaller will be the leakages and the larger all the secondary effects, and so on, on the national income. The marginal propensity to import in Country II, m_2, plays an analogous role: The smaller it is, the larger will be the effects on Country I's income. The reason is that we have assumed here that the initial increase in Country I's income will be matched by a decrease in Country II's income. This decrease also leads to a decrease in demand for exports from Country I, but the smaller m_2 is, the smaller this fall in demand for exports from Country I will be. The marginal propensity to save in Country II, s_2, will, on the other hand, have an opposite function. The smaller it is, the smaller will be the positive effect on Country I's income. The smaller s_2 is, the larger will be the "home" multiplier in this country and the larger will be the deflationary effects in Country II of its initial decrease in income. The larger the deflationary effects in Country II, the larger will also be the unfavorable effect on Country I of a decrease in income in Country II.

The case just treated, where an initial increase in income in Country I is matched completely by an equal decrease in Country II, is one extreme. Let us now continue with the opposite extreme, where the initial increase in Country I is not matched by any initial change in Country II, so that $\lambda = 0$. The two countries still influence each other, however, as all the subsequent changes in income in the two countries are interrelated.

The basic formula, 15A.6, is now transformed to

$$\frac{dY_1}{d\alpha} = \frac{1}{\Delta}(1 - C_2' - G_2' - I_2') \tag{15A.10}$$

Assuming that $G_1' = I_1' = G_2' = I_2' = 0$, and using the same notation as before, we deduce that

$$\frac{dY_1}{d\alpha} = \frac{s_2 + m_2}{(s_1 + m_1)(s_2 + m_2) - m_1 m_2} = \frac{1 + (m_2/s_2)}{s_1 + m_1 + (s_1 m_2)/s_2} \tag{15A.11}$$

Again we see that s_1 and m_1 perform their ordinary function: The larger they are, the smaller will be the positive effects on Country I's national income. The marginal propensities to import and save in Country II, m_2 and s_2, now play a more ambiguous role, as they appear both in the denominator and numerator of expression 15A.11. On the whole, however, we may say that the larger m_2, the more expansionary will be the effect on Country I's national income, and the larger s_2, the less expansionary that effect will be.

We have now treated two cases, where the first case can be said to constitute that of the pure export multiplier, where the initial cause is a shift in demand in Country II away from home consumption to imports. The second case is an example of an increase in investment at home (in Country I) in a trading economy; i.e., it is an example of the workings of the traditional investment multiplier in an open economy. There can, of course, be many different sorts of intermediate cases, where a change in one country is partially, but not wholly, matched by a change in the other—where, to use technical language, the value of λ is somewhere between zero and unity.

SELECTED BIBLIOGRAPHY: CHAPTERS 14 AND 15

A standard work in this field is:

> J. M. Meade, *The Balance of Payments*, London, 1951.

Chapter 14 follows Meade's chaps. 1–3 rather closely. The reader should observe, however, that the use of the concepts of autonomous and accommodating capital movements does not coincide completely with Meade's use of the terms. Chapter 15 contains an exposition of income formation in an open economy, founded on Keynesian analysis. The pioneering work in this field is:

> J. M. Keynes, *The General Theory of Employment, Interest and Money*, London, 1936, especially chap. 21.

For early generalizations and elaborations of the Keynesian theory in this field, compare:

> F. Machlup, *International Trade and the National Income Multiplier*, Philadelphia, 1943.

> L. M. Metzler, "Underemployment Equilibrium in International Trade," *Econometrica*, April 1942.

This is a field where existing textbooks give a relatively good exposition. For example, see:

> C. P. Kindleberger, *International Economics*, 3rd ed., Homewood, Ill., 1963, chaps. 10–11.

The method used for the derivation of multipliers in the Appendix to Chapter 15 was originally used by Jaroslav Vanek. Compare Kindleberger, *op. cit.*, p. 659. For empirical estimates of marginal propensities to import and foreign trade multipliers, see:

> J. H. Adler, "U.S. Import Demand during the Interwar Period," *AER*, June 1945.

> H. Neisser and F. Modigliani, *National Incomes and Foreign Trade*, Urbana, Ill., 1953.

> J. J. Polak, *An International Economic System*, London, 1954.

International economic policy and the adjustment mechanism

16

The price of foreign exchange will, under a system of flexible exchange rates, fluctuate in such a way that the demand for foreign exchange equals the supply and the balance of payments is in equilibrium. There is no comparable mechanism that will keep the balance of payments in equilibrium under a system of fixed exchange rates. The normal situation is that the export of goods and services will not equal their import but that a surplus or a deficit will arise. A surplus in the balance of payments generally causes no problems; therefore, we will not deal with its implications at any length. A deficit in the balance of payments often entails difficult problems of economic policy. How an economy can adjust to a situation with a deficit is an important question. In this chapter we shall discuss the main policy means by which to achieve equilibrium in the balance of payments and the workings of the adjustment mechanism. Before doing this, it is, however, appropriate to briefly touch on some factors that may cause a deficit in the balance of payments.

CAUSES OF DISEQUILIBRIUM

A country's exports can, in brief, be said to be a function of the national income of its trading partners, of tastes, and of relative prices. An increase in income abroad will have a favorable effect on the country's exports; so will a change in tastes abroad in favor of imports. If the prices of import-competing goods abroad increase, the home country's exports will benefit.

Analogously, a country's imports are a function of its national income, of tastes, and of relative prices. An increase in the country's national income will lead to an increase in imports; so will a change in relative prices, which make import-competing goods relatively more expensive.

Hence a country's exports and imports are influenced by different factors. There is little reason for a country's balance of trade to be in equilibrium at pegged exchange rates during any longer period of time. Factors affecting exports and imports change continuously, and even if the balance of payments has been in equilibrium for some time, this could easily change.

Let us assume that a country has a deficit in its balance of payments. A natural question to ask is: What has caused this deficit? The most obvious cause to think of is inflation. The Keynesian model stressed imports as a function of income. If a country has an increase in its national income in money terms, this will usually boost imports. There may be many reasons for the increase in income. One could be an increase in investment, giving rise to an increase in total demand; another could be an increase in consumption caused by a downward shift in the savings schedule. If the country is already at full employment, any change of this nature will cause an inflationary pressure that will give rise to an increase in imports.

Inflation as a cause of a disequilibrium in the balance is the obvious thing to look for in the context of the Keynesian model. There may, however, also be other reasons. In 1958 the United States started to have a fairly large deficit in its balance of payments. Small deficits of about $1 billion per year had existed during the early 1950s. In 1958 it increased to over $3 billion. This deficit persisted for several years, and during the period 1958–1962, it amounted on an average to $3.1 billion per year, causing, in connection with an outflow of gold, many worries for the American government and for economists much speculation on origin.

It could hardly have been caused by inflation. The activity level in the United States had, if anything, been lower than that of competing Western European countries and of Japan. The American price level had also not increased faster than that of other leading industrial countries. What, then, was the cause?

Some economists put forward explanations of a "structural" type. Steel prices in the United States had increased faster than other prices. This led to the intrusion into the American market of foreign steel exporters, who were able to capture a larger market share than before. At the same time U.S. steel exports had fallen off, and the lack of competitiveness of the American steel industry was the cause of the deficit.[1]

This may sound plausible, but it is a type of explanation expressed in partial terms, and we have been trained to think in terms of general equilibrium. It may now be useful to refer back to the models we set out in Part II, where we dealt with economic growth and international trade.

As we have stated, the general price level had not increased faster in

---

[1] See, for example, papers by G. Haberler and J. K. Galbraith in S. E. Harris (ed.), *The Dollar in Crisis*, Harcourt, Brace & World, New York, 1961; and E. Sohmen, "Competition and Growth: The Lesson of the United States Balance of Payments," in R. Baldwin *et al.*, *Trade, Growth and the Balance of Payments*, Rand McNally, Chicago, 1965.

the United States than among competing nations. Therefore, we might as well assume, for the sake of argument, that the American price level was stable. If steel prices then rose, other prices must have fallen. What are the implications of such a development for the balance of payments?

If, to begin with, we think in terms of a two-sector model, we find that if export prices rise, prices of import-competing goods will fall. The price development in this sector is also of importance for the trade balance. It is not possible to say what the net effect of this development will be.

In order to understand this, we think of a process of economic growth; for the time being we can disregard the causes of that growth and take it as given. We can think in terms of the model set out in Chapter 9. Prices are then the dependent variable, depending on growth and on the demand development induced by growth. Let us think in terms of a two-sector model with positive marginal propensities to consume both goods. If the growth is restricted to the import-competing sector, the demand for both kinds of goods will still increase. This leads to increased export prices and to a larger share of exportables being consumed within the country, creating, in other words, higher export prices and a decrease in the export share.

At the same time the supply of import-competing goods increases and their prices decrease. A larger share of consumption will be covered by domestic goods and there is a decrease in imports. It is not possible to determine if the decrease in imports is larger than the decrease in exports unless we have comprehensive information on propensities to consume, sectoral growth rates, price elasticities, etc. The only inference we may conclude is that the share of GNP traded falls.

This example shows that it is difficult to draw conclusions from partial evidence. It does *not*, however, show that an increase in export prices and a fall in the export share must go together with a deterioration in the trade balance, even though this might sometimes be the case.

If, in the example above, we used a three-sector model, with one export sector, one import-competing sector, and one sector for nontraded goods, and if growth had been concentrated to the sector producing nontraded goods, things might have turned out differently. Let us assume that the marginal propensities to consume all three types of goods are positive; export prices would then increase and exports fall. At the same time, the demand for imports would increase, and there would be a negative effect on the trade balance from the import side. This, then, is a case that satisfies the requirements of a decreasing export share, increasing export prices, and a deterioration in the balance of payments.

This simple exercise shows that explanations of a "structural" type for a deficit in the balance of payments easily become quite complicated. It is also difficult to get empirical information about sectoral growth rates, trends in demand, price elasticities, etc., which is necessary if one wants to test these types of models.

Simple causes for deficits, such as an excess in total demand, are often quite easy to identify. More intricate causes, such as changes in productivity, can be very difficult to establish. It would, for many reasons, be interesting if one could explain in detail the causes of deficits. This might have a bearing on the formulation of policies to restore external equilibrium. One should, however, keep in mind, that the policy instruments available are usually limited. Neither is there a one-to-one relationship between causes and means. Whatever the reason for a deficit, there are always policy means in existence to cure it, and the time has now come to discuss them and to look into how the adjustment mechanism works.

THE GOLD STANDARD: A CASE OF AUTOMATIC ADJUSTMENT

We said at the end of Chapter 13 that the international monetary system that now prevails under the guidance of the International Monetary Fund is characterized by fixed exchange rates and a fixed price of gold. This implies that every currency has a stable value in gold. This value might change, through a devaluation or a revaluation, but this does not happen often; the leading key currency, the U.S. dollar, has had a stable value in gold since the IMF was founded. The international monetary system, as it now exists, therefore resembles strikingly the traditional gold standard, the key feature of which was the fact that all currencies were kept, within narrow limits, at a fixed value in terms of gold.

The gold standard emerged slowly during the nineteenth century. It became more widely established about 1870 and was full fledged during the 40 years from the beginning of the 1870s to the outbreak of World War I. The leading countries tried to revive the gold standard in the 1920s. Great

Britain, for instance, went back on the gold standard in 1925 and other leading countries followed. This system collapsed with the Great Depression in the beginning of the 1930s.

As the international monetary system of today closely resembles the traditional gold standard, it is instructive to see how the gold standard worked (or was supposed to work). A suitable introduction to the study of the adjustment mechanism is therefore to see how deficits were cured " automatically " under the gold standard.

The main object of economic policy under the gold standard was to keep the balance of payments in equilibrium. The main instrument for this was monetary policy. The authority handling economic policy in those days was the central bank.

Under the gold standard a British gold sovereign, or £1, contained 113.0016 grains of pure gold. The U.S. dollar, in turn, contained 23.22 grains. As both currencies were tied to gold, it implied that £1 was worth $4.87 U.S. The dollar rate could fluctuate between an upper gold point of 4.90 and a lower gold point of 4.84. These rates were set by the cost of shipping gold from New York to London. The cost of shipping gold worth £1 amounted to 3 cents.

The stage is now set, and we can describe the workings of the gold standard. Let us assume that the United States had a deficit in its balance of payments. This implied that demand for foreign exchange in the United States was larger than the supply of foreign exchange and the price of foreign exchange tended to rise. It rose from 4.87, but it could not rise to more than 4.90, because the Federal Reserve Bank in New York had a commitment to sell and buy gold at a fixed rate. If importers found that they had to pay more than $4.90 for £1, they could, for $4.87, buy gold worth £1 in New York and ship it to London at a cost of 3 cents. Every pound sterling of gold which they shipped to London and which cost them $4.90 to buy and take there, they could sell to the Bank of England and acquire bank notes in exchange, which they could use to pay for their imports. Whatever the persistence of a deficit in the U.S. balance of payments, American importers knew that they would never have to pay more than $4.90 for £1.

What were the implications of a deficit for the U.S. authorities? Because of the deficit the country would lose foreign reserves and perhaps gold. This forced the authorities to pursue a restrictive monetary policy. The two most important means for this consist of raising the bank rate and decreasing the money supply. An increase in the bank rate has a general deflationary effect. It primarily discourages investment, because investors find it more difficult and expensive to borrow money, and if they believe particularly that the increase in the discount rate is temporary, they have good reason to postpone their investments and wait for cheaper money. The central bank also tried to decrease the money supply. The availability of credit in the banking system fell, and investors found it both more difficult and more expensive to obtain loans.

The increase in interest rates may also affect consumption, although this is less certain. The availability of all credits falls, including credits for consumption purposes, which will work in a deflationary direction. The effect of the increase in interest rates on savings, however, is less certain; it may lead to an increase in some savings because of the increase in returns, but it may also lead to a decrease in other savings, for instance, those for a fixed purpose (a given sum can be reached with less savings as the interest has increased). Therefore the effect on consumption and savings is less clear cut.

Thus a tighter monetary policy leads to deflationary pressure and to a lower level of activity. It will probably also give rise to some unemployment. The general price level will fall, and probably wages, too. This benefits export industries, which become more competitive, and import-competing industries, which then will be able to compete more successfully with imports.

This was the way in which the adjustment mechanism was supposed, by the participants themselves, to work in the days of the gold standard, when stress was laid on changes in prices. For modern economists it is natural to point also to income changes as important. The tightening of monetary policy will cause a reduction in nominal incomes, and national income will fall as unemployment grows, leading to a fall in imports. If prices are sticky, it might well be that changes in income, induced by the multiplier, are the most important factor for the adjustment mechanism.

If a country had a deficit, we would expect gold to flow out of the country. Historical evidence shows, however, that deficit countries quite often had an inflow of capital even in times of deficits. The causes for such an inflow of capital were usually of two kinds, one short term and the other long term.

The country with a deficit raised its discount rate, and this tended to attract short-term capital as interest rates went up. An even more powerful way to attract capital was by price changes on short-term bonds, which went together automatically with interest-rate changes. An increase in the short-term interest rate of, for example, 1 percent, may depress the price of a bond of short duration by, for example, 10 percent. A foreign investor may speculate in this and place $1 million in the deficit country, hoping that the bond price would go up, after perhaps a year, when the country's foreign reserves were plentiful and the deficit erased. If his speculation were successful, he could, on top of an interest rate of, for instance, 4 percent, make a gain of 10 percent because of the fluctuations in bond prices.

During the nineteenth century exchange rates were generally stable. With the exception of the period of the Napoleonic wars, the pound sterling had been immovable in terms of gold since 1717. Similarly, the dollar, apart from an adjustment in 1834 and the suspension of specie payments in connection with the American civil war in 1861–1865, had had a stable value in gold since 1792. Speculators were therefore not worried about changes in the exchange rate but usually acted promptly in connection with changes in interest rates.

Long-term capital movements also played an important part. As mentioned in Chapter 8, Britain and some of the richer European countries, notably France, acted as international bankers. They generated a surplus of savings which developing, "peripheral" countries could draw on. Many of these countries offered good opportunities for investment and had a long-term inflow of capital. These capital flows were autonomous and were in no way connected with immediate balance-of-payments considerations. They eased, however, the constraint that would otherwise have been exercised on the balance of payments, by making possible a higher rate of investment than that which domestic savings only would have permitted.

International capital movements were very important during the time of the gold standard. It can even be argued that without them the system would never have worked. The adjustment of real economic factors, especially price levels, which the system prescribed was often superfluous. The situation was temporarily eased by capital flows, and a mild dampening of the activity level sufficed for curing a disequilibrium. Several countries even had long-term capital imports stretching over decades. Economic policy was geared toward external equilibrium, but one did not have to obey the rules of the game too strictly, because capital movements eased the burden of adjustment to a large extent.

THE BALANCE OF PAYMENTS AS A POLICY PROBLEM

Today most countries are more ambitious than in the days of the gold standard. Equilibrium in the balance of payments is no longer the one overriding goal of economic policy but one of several aims. The stress is, therefore,
no longer on automatic adjustment. How to achieve external balance is
viewed as just one of many problems for economic policy. We shall, in
Chapter 18, discuss the problem of how to achieve external equilibrium
jointly with full employment and also say something about the general
problem of achieving a number of objectives of policy with a certain set
of instruments. In this chapter we shall start by describing the main policy
means at the disposal of a modern government and the way in which they
work.

If, for the time being, we exclude autonomous capital movements,
the balance of payments can be viewed as the difference between total
domestic output and total domestic expenditure. Using symbols, it can be
written

$$B = Y - E \qquad (16.1)$$

where B is the balance of payments (net) and Y and E stand for total domestic
output and expenditure, respectively.

If total output is larger than total expenditure, the country will have
a surplus in its balance of payments or if, vice versa, the country will have a
deficit, and if output equals expenditure the balance of payments will be in
equilibrium. If a country has a deficit it can, in principle, close the deficit
in one of two ways: by reducing expenditure or by increasing output. It is
often difficult to increase output in the short run, especially if the country
already has full employment. Therefore, the chief means for reducing a
deficit is usually an expenditure-reducing policy.

It is sometimes said that there are two main ways in which a deficit
can be cured: by expenditure-reducing or expenditure-switching policies. We
shall keep to this terminology and divide the policy instruments into these
two main categories. The terminology is somewhat inadequate, however, as
it suggests that expenditure switching could be substituted for expenditure
reducing. This is not the case. Given constant output, expenditure-switching
policies must also entail some element of expenditure reduction in order
to work. To put it more generally, expenditure switching must imply

either an element of reduction in expenditure or an increase of output to be effective.

EXPENDITURE-REDUCING POLICIES

We have seen, in connection with the gold standard, how monetary policies can be used to cure a deficit. Today expenditure-reducing policies can be divided into two broad categories: monetary policy and fiscal policy. Monetary policies today are in principle the same as under the gold standard, although the spectrum of policies is now broader. Fiscal policy was hardly used for this purpose before the 1930s; it has become an important policy weapon in connection with the growth of government expenditure which has occurred in most countries since World War II.

Changes in interest rates and open market operations are today the most important instruments for monetary policy. To cure a deficit the natural thing to do is to raise interest rates and sell bonds.

The primary effect of an increase in interest rates is on investment. As it becomes more expensive to borrow money and as the availability of credit becomes more scarce, producers borrow and invest less.

The effects of a tighter monetary policy on investment depend to a large extent on the general economic situation. If the country is in a boom period, the result of an increase in interest rates depends to a large extent on the expectations of producers. If they expect the interest rate to fall after some time, they may postpone investments. In such a case the increase in discount may have a considerable impact and through multiplier effects lead to a reduction in the national income or at least act as a brake in an inflationary situation. If producers, instead, expect prices to increase, they will also expect the higher interest rates to prevail in the foreseeable future. There is, therefore, no point in their postponing investment. They go ahead with their investment plans, and the effect of the higher discount is negligible.

Monetary policy became quite discredited in the 1930s, as it proved to be inefficient for domestic stabilization purposes during that deep depression. Even after World War II, in the late 1940s, many regarded it with suspicion. In the 1950s, when the overriding problem for many countries was that of inflation, monetary policy experienced a renaissance. It again became an important part of economic policy, and new variants of monetary policy were put into practice.

One aspect stressed was the availability of credit. In an inflationary climate investment returns were expected to be high. For conventional purposes interest rates were seldom higher than 7 to 8 percent. Nominal rates such as these were often not enough to discourage investors. Banks rationed credits, and availability arose as an important concept.

The standard means of regulating the supply of money and influencing the availability of credit is through open market operations. In open market operations the central bank sells or buys bonds and securities. If it sells bonds, bond prices will be decreased and the effective interest yielded will be increased. If the central bank wants to tighten the money supply, it sells bonds and other securities to commercial banks, insurance companies, households, etc. Commercial banks and other buyers of bonds will have to pay for them with liquid money. The liquidity of the banking system falls and the availability of credit decreases. The sale of bonds will also lead to a fall in their price and to an upward pressure on interest rates.

The decrease in availability of credit, together with an increase in discounts, can have a negative influence on investment; producers may now simply find it impossible to borrow money. If this is so, investment will obviously be curtailed.

The possibility of influencing the availability of credit by open market operations hinges on the fact that commercial banks keep a certain ratio between their liquidity and their loanable funds. If this is not the case, commercial banks may simply continue lending money, although their liquidity has decreased.[2] In some countries banks have not adhered to strict rules in this respect, and authorities have often used less subtle means for restricting credit. They have simply put a ceiling on credits, declaring, for instance, that the banking system can only lend 80 percent of the loanable funds available during a previous year.

New means for monetary policy were also put into practice during the 1950s. An increasing amount of funds went to finance the purchase of consumer goods, this being a natural consequence of the fact that an in-

---

[2] It is assumed in this argument that banks are already at this critical ratio when, with the intention of decreasing liquidity, open market operations start, and that if they keep a strict ratio, they will have to decrease lending as their liquidity decreases.

creasing proportion of consumption in industrial countries consists of consumer durables. Central banks have, in times of inflationary pressure, been able to restrict lending for purposes of consumption by forcing banks to ask for higher percentages in down payment and faster amortization, and to show greater selectiveness in granting loans.

Monetary policy has also proved to be a powerful instrument in the postwar period for correcting deficits in the balance of payments. The means aimed at curtailing investment have probably been most efficient. An increase in interest rates and a decrease in the availability of credit can hardly fail to affect investment. A decrease in investment will, through a multiplier effect, lead to a decrease in income and to a fall in imports. Analogously, policies that curtail consumption will also lead to a decrease in imports.

Thus a tighter monetary policy is one way of implementing a policy of expenditure reduction. It should also be stressed in this context that a " neutral " monetary policy will automatically work to curb a deficit, because a deficit implies that payments by residents of the country are larger than receipts by residents. This means that residents are depleting their cash balances. If the deficit continues, cash balances will eventually become depleted, and payments will be brought into line with receipts; the deficit will be self-correcting.

This, however, presupposes " neutrality " from the central bank, i.e., that it refuses to increase the money supply, even though cash balances are being depleted. Residents can only deplete their cash holdings by exchanging them for foreign reserves, and it is doubtful if the central bank has enough foreign reserves to be able to wait and let the self-correcting mechanism work itself out. One should also remember that as cash holdings become more scarce, the interest rate increases, which will also work toward curing the deficit. If, for some reason, the central bank does not want to tolerate an increase in interest rates, it must increase the money supply, and the deficit is no longer self-correcting.

Fiscal policy can also be used to reduce expenditure. We can divide the means of fiscal policy into two broad groups, depending on whether they are on the income or the spending side of the government budget.

The most important instrument on the income side is a change in taxation. An increase in direct taxes will reduce household incomes. Part of this decrease in income may lead to a reduction in savings, but part of it will most certainly lead to a reduction of consumption and a decrease in imports. An increase in indirect taxes, for instance, of sales taxes, will produce much the same effect; here the effect on savings may be relatively smaller, as indirect taxes, as opposed to direct taxes, are seldom progressive.

Many countries have also used taxes against investment in the post-war period, for instance, in the form of a flat-rate tax on certain types of investments. More subtle ways in which fiscal policy is used to regulate investment are in the form of so-called investment funds, which amounts to giving firms tax credits if they postpone investment. These means of fiscal policy have proved to be efficient in the curtailing of investment. A decrease in investment will, of course, through the usual multiplier effect, lead to a decrease in the national income and to a fall in imports.

Another form of expenditure-reducing policy is to cut government expenditure. The state budget comprises in many industrial countries 30 to 40 percent of total GNP. Some of these expenditures are of a transfer type (support of children, pensions, etc.), and some of them consist of public consumption and investment. A decrease in transfer payments will usually have an immediate effect on consumption, as the groups benefiting from transfer payments are on the whole low-income groups with a high marginal propensity to consume. A decrease in public consumption will, of course, also lead to a fall in total income. A decrease in public investment produces much the same effect on national income as does a fall in private investment and leads to a fall in national income and imports.

Fiscal policy can, therefore, be viewed as an efficient means of implementing an expenditure-reducing policy. In certain instances there is room for doubting the efficiency of monetary policy; there can be little doubt about the efficiency of fiscal policy. It may be difficult for a government to increase taxes and keep expenditures constant, or to decrease expenditures keeping taxes constant, but if it does, there is no doubt that total expenditures will decrease and imports fall.

The balance of the budget is sometimes taken as a measure of the effectiveness of fiscal policy. If the government permits a deficit in the budget, it pursues an expansionary policy, and if it has a surplus, its policy is deflationary. One has, however, to be very careful in applying such an argument, because the total effect of the budget depends not only on the sum of tax incomes and expenditures but also on the composition of taxes and expenditures. It is quite possible that a budget with a smaller deficit has a more expansionary effect on the economy than a budget with a larger deficit. To measure the total impact of the government sector on the economy, one has to take not only the deficit or surplus but also the composition of the budget into account.

In summing up, we see that monetary and fiscal policies are the chief means of implementing an expenditure-reducing policy. If a country has a deficit in the balance of payments, it can pursue a tighter monetary policy or a more restrictive fiscal policy. This will have a deflationary effect on the national income and lead to a fall in imports, or at least act as a brake on the increase in imports. It will also have a positive effect on exports and on import-competing industries. As the activity level falls, there will be downward pressure on factor prices, wages may fall or, at least, be stable or increase less than they otherwise would. This places the export and import-competing industries in a more competitive position. An expenditure-reducing policy will therefore have a positive effect on the balance of payments both by reducing imports and by creating space for an expansion of exports.

EXPENDITURE-SWITCHING POLICIES: DEVALUATION, THE ELASTICITY APPROACH

Expenditure-switching policies primarily work by changing relative prices. The main form for such a policy is a change in exchange rates, i.e., a devaluation or a revaluation of the domestic currency. Direct controls can also be classified under this heading and are usually applied to restrict imports. Consumers will then try to buy domestic goods instead of imported goods, and hence direct controls can be viewed as a switching device. We shall, however, concentrate on a discussion of devaluation for the time being, returning to direct controls at the end of this chapter.

We have already mentioned in Chapter 13 that a depreciation meant that the price of the domestic currency fell in terms of foreign currencies and that an appreciation meant that the value of the domestic currency increased in terms of foreign currencies. Devaluation is often used interchangeably with depreciation, and revaluation is often taken to be synonymous with appreciation. We will, however, make one distinction between the two sets of terms. Depreciation means a lowering in value with respect to other currencies, while devaluation means a lowering in value of a currency with respect to the price of gold. The same holds, *mutatis mutandis*, for appreciation and revaluation. If, as is the case with the present monetary system, the price of gold is fixed, depreciation of one currency implies devaluation of the currency in question. There exists, however, one possibility where devaluation does not imply depreciation. This is the situation where all currencies lower their value with respect to gold by the same percentage. Then there would be world-wide devaluation; i.e., the price of gold would increase by the same percentage in all countries but no currency would have been depreciated. For the time being, we are concerned with only one country, and as there can be no confusion we will use the two sets of terms interchangeably.

The immediate effect of devaluation is a change in relative prices. If a country devalues by, for instance, 20 percent, it means that import prices increase by 20 percent counted in home prices.[3] An increase in import prices leads to a fall in the demand for imports. At the same time, import-competing industries will be in a better competitive situation. Exporters will receive 20 percent more in home currency for every unit of foreign currency they earn. They can, therefore, lower their prices counted in foreign currency and will become more competitive. By how much they are able to expand sales abroad depends primarily on the foreign demand elasticities for their goods.

The traditional approach to the effects of devaluation on the balance of trade runs in terms of elasticities. We shall also start by giving an account of this view before going over to the more modern absorption approach.

The core of the traditional view is contained in the so-called Marshall–Lerner condition, which states that the sum of the elasticities of demand for a country's exports and of its demand for imports has to be greater than unity for a devaluation to have a positive effect on a country's trade balance. If the sum of these elasticities is smaller than unity, a country can instead improve its balance of trade by revaluation.

If we want to express this condition in terms of a formula it can be set out as follows:

$$dB = kX_f(e_{1m} + e_{2m} - 1) \qquad (16.2)$$

[3] This need not, strictly speaking, always be the case. This is a pedagogic simplification that will later be restated and refined.

where dB is the change in the trade balance, k the devaluation in percentage, X_f the value of exports expressed in foreign currency, e_{1m} the first (devaluing) country's demand elasticity for imports, and e_{2m} the second country's (the rest of the world's) demand elasticity for exports from the devaluing country. The theory behind the formula will be spelled out and the formula derived later in this chapter.

It is easy to see from expression 16.2 that the sum of the two critical elasticities has to be larger than unity for the trade balance to improve because of a devaluation. If the sum is less than unity, an appreciation should instead be used to cure a deficit in the trade balance.

We have already said that devaluation will lead to an increase in the price of imports. What the effect of this price increase will be depends on the elasticity of demand for imports. The larger it is, the greater will be the fall in the volume of imports. The value of the demand elasticity of imports depends, of course, on what type of goods the devaluing country imports. If a country primarily imports necessities, raw materials, and goods needed as inputs for its industries, the demand elasticity of imports may be very low, and a devaluation may not be a very efficient means of correcting a deficit. Some less-developed countries may be in this category. For most industrial countries one would expect the import elasticity to be quite high. This is especially the case if, as pointed out in Chapter 13, the country has a well-developed import-competing industry.

When the exporters, because of the devaluation, receive more for every unit of foreign currency they earn, they can lower their prices quoted in foreign currency. When they lower their prices they should be able to sell more. By how much the quantity exported increases depends on the demand elasticity confronting the country's exporters. Again, it depends to a large extent on the type of goods the country exports and the market conditions. If a country exports raw materials, for instance, and is the sole, or main, supplier of the product, the foreign demand elasticity for its exports may be low. If a country exports industrial goods in close competition with suppliers from other industrial countries, the demand elasticity for its products will probably be high.

There was a lively discussion among economists in the late 1940s and early 1950s about empirical measurements of demand elasticities. The first published studies, by Hinshaw and Adler, showed very low values for demand elasticities, around, or less than, unity. These studies were later criticized, mainly by Orcutt and Harberger, and two schools developed, one of " elasticity pessimists " and one of " elasticity optimists."[4]

The implication of low elasticities is that a policy instrument of a "liberal" type, such as devaluation, which presupposes a minimum of interference with trade, can hardly work, but that more direct means, such as trade controls, have to be used. Whatever the values of the demand elasticities may have been in the interwar and early postwar period, most economists seem to take the view that the relevant elasticities for most countries are now probably quite high, at least substantially higher than unity. Devaluation should then work according to the traditional elasticity approach.

Devaluation has also been used by some countries, for instance, by France in 1958, with successful results. It has, however, not been a very widely used policy instrument in the postwar period. Devaluation is viewed with suspicion, and it seems as if some economists and many politicians are of the view that it should be used only as a last resort. Devaluation has, in addition, some side effects that should be pointed out.

Devaluation can have an inflationary impact on the economy. We will deal with this question in Chapter 17, when discussing the effect of flexible exchange rates on the internal price level of a country. Suffice it to say here that the effects on the price level depend primarily on the economic policy accompanying devaluation. If a tight monetary and fiscal policy is pursued jointly with devaluation, the inflationary impact should be limited.

Another consideration to take into account is the effect of devaluation on the income distribution. It is often stated that real wages will fall because of devaluation and that there will be a redistribution of income away from the labor class to the nonlabor class. The effects on income distribution are, however, very complicated, and it is difficult to state general results. A devaluation should result in a reallocation of resources away from the sector producing nontraded goods and into the export and import-competing sectors. Thinking in terms of a model with linearly homogeneous production functions, and assuming that the sector producing nontraded goods is

---

[4] An annotated bibliography of the major contributions to the discussion of elasticities is to be found in Hang-Sheng Cheng, " Statistical Estimates of Elasticities and Propensities in International Trade," *International Monetary Fund Staff Papers*, vol. 7, no. 1 (April 1959).

labor-intensive, we ought to have the standard result that the labor class will receive a lower real income because of devaluation. The assumptions for obtaining this result are, however, quite arbitrarily chosen. In general we can say that the factors of production employed in the export- and import-competing sectors will benefit from devaluation. This holds especially true for factors that may be specific for the respective industries. In addition, the factors used intensively in these industries should receive a higher real income. In the full framework of general equilibrium we should also take into account the effects of consumption, and then the result will also hinge on the consumption patterns of labor or the specific factor of production in which we are interested. It is then almost impossible to draw clear-cut inferences. Neither should one expect that the effects of devaluation on the income distribution are any simpler or more clear cut than the effects of a change in monetary or fiscal policy.

The Marshall–Lerner condition set out in formula 16.2 is built on some drastic simplifications. It assumes, roughly, that the supply elasticities are large (approaching infinity) and that the trade balance is in equilibrium when devaluation takes place. The first may be true in times of recession, when capacity is not fully utilized, and supply can easily expand. It is, however, doubtful if it can be viewed as a close approximation to reality in times of full employment. If there were a large imbalance to start with, so that imports were much larger than exports, then imports would increase in domestic currency more than exports, although the sum of the demand elasticities is larger than unity. None of these two assumptions invalidate, however, the spirit of the Marshall–Lerner condition, which says that the larger the respective demand elasticities, the more favorable is the effect of a devaluation on the trade balance. For the sake of completeness we shall, however, also derive the complete formula for the effects of devaluation on the trade balance.

DEVALUATION AND THE TRADE BALANCE:
THE COMPLETE FORMULA

The reader with a weak background in mathematics need not follow the derivation in detail. It will suffice to take a look at the final result.

We start by setting out the following equation for the trade balance:

$$B_{1f} = x_1 P_{2m} - m_1 P_{2x} = X_{1f} - M_{1f} \qquad (16.3)$$

where B_{1f} denotes the first (devaluing) country's trade balance in foreign currency, where x_1 and m_1 are Country I's volume of exports and imports, respectively; P_{2m} and P_{2x} are the price of imports and exports in Country II; and X_{1f} and M_{1f} are the value of exports and imports in Country I, both denoted in foreign currency.

Differentiating equation 16.3 gives

$$dB_{1f} = dx_1 P_{2m} + dP_{2m} x_1 - dm_1 P_{2x} - dP_{2x} m_1$$

$$= X_{1f} \left(\frac{dx_1}{x_1} + \frac{dP_{2m}}{P_{2m}} \right) + M_{1f} \left(-\frac{dm_1}{m_1} - \frac{dP_{2x}}{P_{2x}} \right) \qquad (16.4)$$

We then define the following four elasticities:

$$s_{1x} = \frac{dx_1}{dP_{1x}} \frac{P_{1x}}{x_1} \qquad \text{elasticity of home export supply} \qquad (16.5)$$

$$e_{2m} = -\frac{dx_1}{dP_{2m}} \frac{P_{2m}}{x_1} \qquad \text{elasticity of foreign demand for exports} \qquad (16.6)$$

$$s_{2m} = \frac{dm_1}{dP_{2x}} \frac{P_{2x}}{m_1} \qquad \text{elasticity of foreign supply of imports} \qquad (16.7)$$

$$e_{1m} = -\frac{dm_1}{dP_{1m}} \frac{P_{1m}}{m_1} \qquad \text{elasticity of home demand for imports} \qquad (16.8)$$

We observe from the way in which these four elasticities have been defined that they will all be positive (barring Giffen goods).

We then assume that we have price equalization between the two countries through the exchange rate, r, so that we get

$$P_{2x} = P_{1m} r \qquad (16.9)$$

Differentiating equation 16.9 totally and adding in equation 16.9 gives

$$P_{2x} + dP_{2x} = P_{1m} r + dP_{1m} r + dr P_{1m}$$

$$= (P_{1m} + dP_{1m})r - k(P_{1m} + dP_{1m})r$$

$$= (P_{1m} + dP_{1m})r(1 - k) \qquad (16.10)$$

In equation 16.10 we have introduced the devaluation coefficient k, which shows the relative change in the exchange rate. We can define k in the following way:

$$k = - \frac{P_{1m}}{P_{1m} + dP_{1m}} \frac{dr}{r} = - \frac{dr}{r} \frac{1}{1 + \dfrac{dP_{1m}}{P_{1m}}}$$

$$\approx - \frac{dr}{r} \left(1 - \frac{dP_{1m}}{P_{1m}} \right) \approx - \frac{dr}{r} \tag{16.11}$$

From equation 16.10 we get

$$\frac{dP_{2x}}{P_{2x}} = -k + \frac{dP_{1m}}{P_{1m}} (1 - k) \tag{16.12}$$

In a completely analogous way we deduce that

$$\frac{dP_{2m}}{P_{2m}} = -k + \frac{dP_{1x}}{P_{1x}} (1 - k) \tag{16.13}$$

The relative changes in volumes and prices can now be expressed in terms of elasticities and the devaluation coefficient, k. Using equations 16.6 and 16.13 we get

$$\frac{dx_1}{x_1} = -e_{2m} \frac{dP_{2m}}{P_{2m}} = -e_{2m} \left[-k + \frac{dP_{1x}}{P_{1x}} (1 - k) \right] \tag{16.14}$$

but $dx_1/x_1 = s_{1x}(dP_{1x}/P_{1x})$. Substituting, we get

$$\frac{dx_1}{x_1} = e_{2m} k - \frac{e_{2m}}{s_{1x}} (1 - k) \frac{dx_1}{x_1}$$

From this follows

$$\frac{dx_1}{x_1} = \frac{e_{2m} k}{1 + (e_{2m}/s_{1x})(1 - k)} = \frac{s_{1x} e_{2m} k}{s_{1x} + e_{2m}(1 - k)} \tag{16.15}$$

In an analogous way we can derive

$$\frac{dP_{2m}}{P_{2m}} = - \frac{ks_{1x}}{s_{1x} + e_{2m}(1 - k)} \tag{16.16}$$

$$\frac{dm_1}{m_1} = - \frac{ks_{2m} e_{1m}}{e_{1m} + s_{2m}(1 - k)} \tag{16.17}$$

$$\frac{dP_{2x}}{P_{2x}} = - \frac{ke_{1m}}{e_{1m} + s_{2m}(1 - k)} \tag{16.18}$$

Using the last four expressions we get the effect of a devaluation on the trade balance:

$$dB_{1f} = k\left[X_{1f} \frac{s_{1x}(e_{2m} - 1)}{s_{1x} + e_{2m}(1 - k)} + M_{1f} \frac{e_{1m}(s_{2m} + 1)}{e_{1m} + s_{2m}(1 - k)} \right] \tag{16.19}$$

Expression 16.19 shows that the effects of the devaluation are somewhat more complicated than shown in equation 16.2; i.e., if we do not assume that supply elasticities are infinitely large, the situation becomes somewhat more complex. If, to take an extreme example, we assumed that the supply elasticities were equal to zero, there would be no improvement in the trade balance because of increasing exports but some improvement because of a fall in demand for imports. Generally speaking, we can say that if the elasticities are larger than unity, then the larger they are, both on the supply and the demand side, the larger will be the improvement in the trade balance.

The way to arrive at formula 16.2 from 16.19 is as follows: If supply elasticities tend to infinity, then

$$\frac{e_{2m} - 1}{1 + (e_{2m}/s_{1x})(1 - k)} \to e_{2m} - 1$$

If, furthermore, k is small, we get that

$$\frac{e_{1m}[1 + (1/s_{2m})]}{(e_{1m}/s_{2m}) + 1 - k} \to \frac{e_{1m}}{1 - k}$$

But if k is small and if we assume that trade is balanced before the devaluation, we get

$$dB_{1f} = kM_{1f}(e_{2m} + e_{1m} - 1) \tag{16.2}$$

We have now set out the main parts of the elasticity approach to devaluation. The dubious aspect of this approach is that it is built on a partial type of theorizing and that it does not take into account consideration of general equilibrium.

Demand and supply elasticities are conventionally defined *ceteris paribus*, i.e., other prices and incomes are supposed to be constant, but in devaluation prices and incomes will certainly change. Therefore, the use of partial elasticities in connection with devaluation can easily be misleading. What one would like to know is the value of the "total" elasticities, i.e., the value of an elasticity when all the factors involved in the devaluation change.

Such a total elasticity measures how quantities are affected by price changes when everything likely to change has done so. This is, however, not an operational concept, as it will never be possible to know in advance the values of such elasticities. The result of a devaluation depends not only on partial elasticities but also on the aggregate behavior of the economic system.

An alternative approach to the effects of devaluation formulated in macro terms is the so-called absorption approach. It was first developed by Sidney Alexander in a famous paper published in 1952.[5] As it gives a very useful complement to the traditional approach, we shall now discuss it.

DEVALUATION: THE ABSORPTION APPROACH

The absorption approach runs in macro terms. Its starting point lies in the fact that the balance of trade can be viewed as the difference between national income and total expenditure, or, as we have already stated,

$$B = Y - E \tag{16.1}$$

If we instead call total expenditure, or total demand, for total absorption, A, we can write

$$B = Y - A \tag{16.20}$$

It should be observed that total absorption includes the demand created for all purposes; in other words, it includes demand both for consumption and investment purposes. Using the simple national income identity we say that

$$A = C + I + G$$

Devaluation affects the trade balance by either affecting real national income, Y, or by affecting total absorption, A. We can write the change in the trade balance as

$$dB = dY - dA \tag{16.21}$$

[5] Sidney S. Alexander, "The Effects of a Devaluation on the Trade Balance," *International Monetary Fund Staff Papers*, vol. 2, no. 2, 1952, pp. 263 ff.

Total absorption can be decomposed in two parts. First, we say that any change in the real income will induce a change in absorption. How greatly absorption will change depends on the propensity to absorb, which we shall call c. Second, we can say that devaluation has a direct effect on absorption, depending, among other things, on the level of real income at which devaluation takes place. This effect we shall call the direct effect on absorption, D. We can then write

$$dA = c\,dY + dD \tag{16.22}$$

Combining equations 16.21 and 16.22 gives

$$dB = (1 - c)\,dY - dD \tag{16.23}$$

Equation 16.23 is useful because it directs our attention to three basic factors important for the outcome of a devaluation. It says that the effects of a devaluation on the trade balance depend first on how devaluation affects the real income (Y), second on the propensity to absorb (c), and third on the effect on direct absorption (D).

In order to deal with the effects of a devaluation we must distinguish between two main cases, one where there are idle resources (unemployment) and one where there is full employment. Let us begin with the first case.

If there are unemployed resources when the country devalues, then production can expand in the short run. We will expect the expansionary process to start by an increase in exports, giving rise to an increase in national income via the familiar multiplier process. By how much exports will expand depends greatly on whether, because of expansion, export prices in the devaluing country rise and on the capacity (and willingness) of the rest of the world to absorb exports from the devaluing country.

The net effect of the recovery or the increase in income on the balance of trade does not comprise the total amount of increase in production, but the difference between this and the induced increase in total absorption. This difference between increase in real production and real absorption can be called real hoarding. The effect on the trade balance is, then, equal to the amount of real hoarding which takes place in the economy.

Putting the effects on direct absorption aside, we see that the propensity to absorb, or the propensity to hoard, the other side of the same coin, is the all-important factor in this case for the effects of a devaluation on the trade balance.[6] As long as c is less than unity, some hoarding will occur, and hence there is a positive effect on the trade balance.

It may be, however, that c is larger than unity. Then a devaluation will have a negative effect on the trade balance, because the induced effects on absorption will be larger than the original effects on production. This case cannot be ignored. We have to remember that we are discussing the case of less than full employment. Devaluation will then have a positive effect on national income. Workers who are employed at this time will probably have a high propensity to consume. Further, the expansion in income may have a positive effect on investment. Together these factors can make the propensity to absorb larger than unity, and devaluation will then have a negative effect on the trade balance.

If the propensity to absorb is less than unity (or made less than unity by policy measures), devaluation is quite an attractive policy for a country in a depression, because it will have both a positive effect on the national income and improve the balance of trade.

That devaluation could have a positive effect on national income was recognized even before the breakthrough of Keynesian analysis. This was probably the main reason, together with balance-of-payments considerations, for the series of devaluations undertaken in the wake of the depression in the first few years of the 1930s.

A successful devaluation by one country will usually have adverse effects on other countries, primarily by outcompeting exports from the nondevaluing countries. That is one of the chief reasons devaluations tend to be competitive, and why, if one country devalues, other countries often feel that they must also. The International Monetary Fund has tried to avoid such situations by creating safeguards against competitive devaluations.

It is often argued that devaluation will lead to deterioration in the terms of trade. Exports are usually much more concentrated than imports, and if devaluation is to have a positive effect, a prerequisite is that export prices, quoted in foreign currency, are lowered. Imports are usually diversified, and import prices, again quoted in foreign currency, are seldom affected to the same degree as export prices. This is the main reason for the deterioration in the terms of trade.

If real income falls, because of adverse terms of trade, so will absorption, and this will have a positive effect on the trade balance. Let us

---

[6] The propensity to hoard is defined as $1 - c$.

denote by t the reduction in real income because of the deterioration in the terms of trade. Then the fall in absorption will equal ct. This does not constitute a net improvement in the trade balance, however, because the adverse terms of trade imply an initial deterioration in the trade balance with t. Hence the net effect on the trade balance is $t - ct$, or $(1 - c)t$. A deterioration in the terms of trade will, therefore, also normally entail a deterioration in the trade balance. Only if c is larger than unity will a deterioration in the terms of trade produce a positive effect on the trade balance.

We have now dealt with the unemployment case. We have now to deal with the case in which there already is full employment when devaluation takes place. In a situation in which the economy is already fully employed or the marginal propensity to absorb is larger than unity, the principal favorable effect of devaluation on the trade balance is through the direct effect on absorption.

The direct effect on absorption is not connected with any change in real national income. It depends on the fact that absorption out of a given real income may change as the price level changes. Let us show how the direct effect may work. Assume a country devalues by 10 percent and that it has an elasticity of direct absorption of 0.1. This means that a 1 percent increase in the general price level would induce a 0.1 percent reduction in absorption at a given level of real income. Let us assume also that the policy environment and substitution conditions in consumption and production between domestic and traded goods are such as to link export and import price changes to changes in the internal price level by a factor of 0.5. This means that a 10 percent increase of export and import prices in domestic currency leads to an increase of 5 percent in the general domestic price level. A 10 percent devaluation would, under these conditions, lead to a decrease in absorption of 0.5 percent. If the imports of the country consisted of 20 percent of its GNP, it would imply that the trade balance would improve by 2.5 percent, in terms of imports.

In conventional elasticity analysis it is often taken for granted that devaluation will improve a country's trade balance although the country has full employment. It can only do this by reducing total absorption. We have just given an example of how direct absorption can be reduced at full employment. This was, however, a very mechanical example. Now we have to look into the economics of that example and see which are the economic factors possibly producing an effect on direct absorption.

The most important of the direct absorption effects is the real balance effect. If the money supply remains unchanged, and if the holders of cash want to maintain cash holdings of a certain real value, they must, if prices rise, accumulate more cash. The only way they can do this is by cutting down on their real expenditures, i.e., by lowering their absorption.

A single individual may increase his cash by selling assets, but this is not possible for the country as a whole. We have also, by definition, ruled out capital movements. If the behavior of the economic subjects is such that they want to keep their cash holdings at a certain real value, and if the money supply is kept constant, then it follows that a rising price level will imply a fall in absorption.

We hinted that as the real value of cash holdings falls, individuals will try to sell assets to acquire cash. This tends to depress the price of assets and to increase the rate of interest. This is a process which will continue, while the money supply remains constant, until a new equilibrium is reached. It should be observed that the increase in interest rates will also affect investment and consumption, and we would expect the higher interest rates to reinforce the downward pressure on absorption. Hence the real balance effect will set in motion a whole chain of events, leading the economic system to a new equilibrium, at a lower level of absorption.

To illustrate the reasoning above, we give the following example. Assume that the money supply in Britain is £5 billion and that devaluation increases the price level by 5 percent, cutting the real value of cash balances by 5 percent, or £250 million. Suppose that before devaluation real balances stood in a desired ratio to real expenditures, and that for every £10 by which real balances were out of adjustment, there is a cut of £1 in expenditure in order to rebuild cash balances. Ignoring secondary effects through an increase in interest rates, there will be a cut in absorption of £25 million yearly, and hence an improvement by £25 million in the trade balance.

It should once more be stressed that the real balance effect is based on the assumption that the money supply remains constant. If this is not the case (if, for instance, the central bank increases the money supply to keep pace with the rise in prices—among other things in order to neutralize effects on interest rates and keep them stable), then the real balance effect will not come into play.

Other factors can influence direct absorption; one is connected with changes in income distribution. As already pointed out, it is not easy to derive clear-cut effects of devaluation on the income distribution, especially

not in the longer run when the effects of a devaluation have worked themselves out and a new equilibrium has been reached. In the short run it is
often assumed that devaluation will lead to an increase in profits at the
expense of wages. If this were the case, we would expect absorption to fall,
because the marginal propensity to consume out of profits can be expected to
be smaller than the marginal propensity to consume out of wages. One
should, however, keep in mind that an increase in profits may stimulate
investment. If a shift of income from wages to profits led to a strong stimulation of investment, the negative effects on absorption might be partially
or wholly offset.

Another factor that could lead to a decrease in direct absorption is the
presence of money illusion. If consumers spend less at higher prices, even
though their incomes have also risen, this will have a positive influence on
the trade balance.

An increase in prices and money incomes will lead to an increase in
government incomes. As taxes in most industrial countries are progressive,
the increase in government revenue will be more than proportional. The
government's marginal propensity to absorb is usually low, at least in the
short run. This mechanism will therefore lead to a fall in direct absorption.

Some of the effects of a devaluation leading to a fall in direct absorption may be of a temporary or transitory nature. They might also depend on
whether the devaluation is large or small. The real balance effect, for
instance, may initially be quite strong, but later the need for increased cash
balances may be met by an increase in the money supply. Wages may to
begin with lag behind and the money illusion could work for a time. A
small devaluation might take advantage of the money illusion, whereas a
larger one might shatter it.

We have already stated that the outcome of devaluation depends to a
large degree on the economic policy accompanying devaluation. The absorption approach brings out this fact very clearly. Our discussion of the absorption approach has so far consisted in looking into what in an economy are the
" automatic " factors which could lead to a decrease in absorption in connection with devaluation. These factors can, of course, be strengthened by a
conscious economic policy. In the unemployment situation the policy should
consist of trimming and expanding supply as fast as possible while restricting
expansion in over-all absorption. In the full employment situation the policy
has to be a more straightforward one of depressing absorption. The decrease
in absorption will then leave room for the necessary reallocation of resources,

leading to a fall in imports and an increase in exports. The absorption approach is somewhat portmanteau in nature, but it at least firmly keeps the emphasis on aggregated terms.

GENERAL REMARKS ON THE ADJUSTMENT MECHANISM

The time has now come to wind up the discussion about devaluation and to remark more generally on which are the important factors in the adjustment mechanism. What we shall do is comment on typical cases.

Let us start by dealing with a barter economy, a country, let us say, which has only one export good, one import good, and one domestic good, and where money or assets are not present. What would be the effect of a devaluation in this case, and in which way could such an economy achieve an equilibrium in its balance of trade?

In this case a devaluation would lead to a relative increase in the price of traded goods compared to the domestic good; i.e., the price of imports and exports would rise. This would lead to an increase in the production of both the export and the import-competing good and to a fall in demand for both exports and imports. On balance exports would increase, imports fall, and the trade balance improve in the process.

It is quite easy to see how the adjustment mechanism works in the case of the barter economy. Here the trick consists of a change in relative prices. The change in the relative price structure causes a change in production and consumption, which will erase the deficit in the trade balance and lead to a new equilibrium. It is important to note in this context that the larger the possibilities for substitution between traded and domestic goods both on the production and on the consumption side, the smoother the adjustment mechanism works. Essentially the same factors were at work in connection with the growth and trade models which we studied in Part II. Here the factors important for adaptability were captured by the so-called elasticity factor, set out in the denominators of expressions 9A.8 and 9.1.

Let us now assume that we have introduced money into the model. With a constant supply of money, a deficit in the trade balance implies that there is an excess demand for goods in the economy while people are trying to decrease their holdings of cash. This will have specific implications for relative prices. There will be a tendency for the price of money to fall compared to the price of goods. This tendency is reinforced by devaluation. Because of devaluation the price of traded goods will increase with respect to the price of money.

Money has become cheap because of devaluation, because its price in terms of goods (and especially traded goods) has fallen. Assuming that money has some positive utility for the consumers, devaluation will give them an impetus to acquire cash again. They can only do so by substituting cash for goods, i.e., by decreasing their demand for goods, especially their demand for traded goods. This will lead to a fall in total absorption and to an improvement in the trade balance. From the special viewpoint of monetary theory, this is an example of the workings of the real balance effect.

If assets were introduced into the model, their function would be much the same as that of money. Devaluation would decrease their relative price. As long as there is some substitution between consumed goods and assets, this substitution mechanism will work in the right direction and tend to restore the equilibrium in the trade balance.

We can now sum up the workings of the adjustment mechanism in the case of an economy where only goods are traded, where only domestic money exists, and where assets are not traded.

Devaluation will give rise to a change in the structure of relative prices. A fall in the relative price of money and assets will give rise to a fall in total absorption. This will have a positive influence on the trade balance. Furthermore, the price of nontraded goods will fall in relation to the price of exports and imports, giving rise to a substitution mechanism both on the supply and the demand side which will cause an expansion in exports and a decrease in imports. This in turn will strengthen the process toward an improvement in the trade balance that was started by the fall in total absorption.

It is obvious that this adjustment mechanism can be smoothened by economic policy measures. A deflationary monetary and fiscal policy will help to cut total absorption. Other measures may help to speed up the adaptability of the economy and bring about the necessary adjustment of exports and imports.

Another observation to make is that the development in the second country (or the rest of the world) will facilitate adjustment. The surplus in the balance of trade created here will lead to an increase in the money supply. This will have a positive effect on absorption, which will help the adjustment. It will also create a tendency for the relative price of traded goods to fall in this country, further reinforcing the adjustment.

If an international currency (for instance, gold) exists which is used in both countries, or if assets are traded internationally, the possibilities for adjustment are increased.

A deficit in the trade balance implies, as usual, an excess demand for goods. As money is now an international commodity, it will flow out of the country as it is used to finance the deficit in the trade balance. As money flows out, the wealth in the hand of the consumers diminishes. This will lead to a fall in total absorption that will help to close the trade deficit.

The existence of internationally traded assets will have much the same implications. To finance a trade deficit the consumers can now sell assets abroad. This will, of course, decrease their wealth, and that will eventually produce a negative effect on absorption.

The adjustment mechanism will also work in the usual fashion; the deficit in the trade balance will be connected with a change in relative prices, and the price of money and assets in terms of goods, especially traded goods, will fall. This will induce a substitution mechanism that will work to close the deficit in the trade balance. Devaluation will accentuate this mechanism.

The existence of an international currency, and the possibility of international mobility of assets, will, in short, further facilitate the workings of the adjustment mechanism as we have just described it.

DIRECT CONTROLS

The use of monetary or fiscal policy or of devaluation as a policy means to restore equilibrium in the balance of payments presupposes that there are possibilities for income and price adjustment. The implication is, in other words, that income is sensitive to policy measures or that price changes will lead to changes in consumption and production. This is not always the case. It may be that, even though adjustment through these channels could in principle take place, it would take too long. A country may have to resort to other means to reach equilibrium within a feasible time (before, for instance, the foreign reserves have been completely depleted). Direct controls are an example of other such means.

The word "control" has a somewhat ambiguous meaning in this context. It is often used in a wide sense to depict not only quantitative restrictions and exchange restrictions but also to include fiscal means such as taxes and subsidies and also tariffs. We have already dealt with fiscal policy in a general way and will discuss tariffs at some length in Part IV, so we shall here sketch only briefly the effects of direct controls, i.e., quantitative restrictions and exchange restrictions.

Direct controls can be roughly divided into two groups: commercial controls and financial controls. To improve the balance of payments, commercial controls can be used to increase exports and discourage imports. As there is very little that can be done to increase exports directly, commercial controls are usually applied to restrict imports.

The most obvious measure is to limit the volume of imports. This can be done, for instance, by applying quantitative restrictions. The government can, for instance, decide that only 80 percent of the previous year's volume of imports can be imported this year. Such a restriction of imports will make their internal value higher than their external value.

Let us say that in the previous year five cars were imported at a total value of $500. This year only four cars can be imported. What will be the price on the home market for these four cars? (Dollars are assumed to be the currency both abroad and at home.)

Let us assume that they each cost $100—and that their price is the same on the foreign market after the restrictions. If the demand is inelastic the price can now be increased to $125 for a car on the domestic market, and the same total amount will be spent on the cars after as before the restrictions, i.e., $500. The question now is: Who will reap the increase of price on the domestic market?

The government may try to pocket the increase by applying a special tax on imported cars. If import restrictions are applied to a wide variety of goods, and if the demand elasticity varies between goods, it will, however, be difficult to apply taxes efficiently. A quite probable outcome is that the whole, or part, of the price increase will go to the importers. This is, of course, especially the case if the government only introduces quantitative import restrictions without an accompanying means for dealing with the rents or monopoly gains which such restrictions imply.

A system of quantitative restrictions can also be combined with a system of import licenses. The price mechanism may then be applied in a roundabout way and these licenses auctioned off by the government to the importers; or the government can simply give them away (a system, however, easily giving rise to corruption). Alternatively, the government might try to introduce a system of rationing jointly with the import restrictions and establish a quota system for how much of every imported good the consumer can buy.

Another way of implementing direct controls is by the use of exchange restrictions. A government might try to hold complete control over all dealings in foreign exchange by stating that exporters have to sell their foreign earnings to a central board, and that importers have to buy their foreign currency from the same board.

If the government were completely successful in this undertaking, it would also hold complete control over foreign trade. It would then be able to cure any deficit in the balance of payments by selling foreign exchange only to an extent that corresponded to export earnings.

The government could also permit only those imports which it deems desirable (necessities, capital goods, military equipment) and not permit, for example, luxuries.

Import restrictions in the form of foreign exchange restrictions will also create a divergence between domestic and foreign prices on imported goods. This will give an impetus to circumvent the restrictions. A black market will probably be created and the exporters tempted to sell their export earnings on this market to obtain a higher price. Importers who are not able to obtain foreign currency legally may try to buy on this market. Importers who do obtain foreign currency for a specific purpose may try to use it for another purpose, and so on.

Controls of foreign exchange dealings have to be policed very thoroughly in order to be efficient. To neutralize some of these difficulties the government may try to introduce a system of multiple exchange rates.

Let us assume that the U.S. government wants to use exchange restrictions and to apply multiple exchange rates. There may be an official rate of, let us say, $4 to £1. This rate may be applied to American exporters, and some American importers that import necessities are able to buy British pounds at this rate. Other importers, however, who import goods deemed by the government to be less pertinent, may have to pay $6, $8, or $10 for £1, depending on how vital the imports in question are judged to be. The government can then pocket the difference between the selling and buying price of foreign exchange.

This, in essence, is how a system of multiple exchange rates works. Such a system is to a large extent afflicted by the same difficulties as an ordinary system of exchange control. Exporters still have to be induced not to sell their proceeds of foreign exchange to the highest bidder, and one has to control importers so that they use their allotted foreign exchange for the purpose specified. To work, the system has to be closely controlled.

This will suffice as a sketch of how trade controls work. One can, of course, also try to subsidize exports, but this will only have a positive effect on export earnings if the foreign demand elasticity of exports is larger than unity. If one jointly subsidizes exports and taxes imports in a nondiscriminatory fashion, one pursues, in effect, a policy that amounts to a devaluation.

The essence of direct trade controls is usually a wish to restrict imports. If imports are inelastic, such a policy may also be viewed as a tempting alternative to devaluation. It may also be a feasible solution in the short run. In the longer run its effect may often be harmful because of the distortion of prices that it creates and the harmful effects on the allocation of production and consumption that such price distortion implies. There is a degree of optimum trade intervention, as we shall see when we return to it in connection with the theory of tariffs. Most countries which apply trade restrictions have usually passed beyond this point. Direct trade controls can, under some circumstances at least, be quite a costly way of closing a deficit in the balance of payments. We will return to the question of quantitative restrictions in Chapter 20.

INTERNATIONAL CAPITAL MOVEMENTS

In this chapter we have been dealing with various ways of closing a deficit in the balance of payments. Before concluding the chapter it should be mentioned that it is quite possible for a country to continue with a deficit in its balance of payments and to cover it with capital imports.

We said at the beginning of the chapter that it was often difficult to specify the causes of a country's deficit. In a trading system with pegged exchange rates and convertible currencies, disturbances causing deficits will always occur. It is very difficult for a country to pursue a flexible-enough policy which will counteract any such disturbance and produce equilibrium in the balance of payments. This is especially the case if the country also pursues a policy of full employment, a point we shall return to in Chapter 18, where we shall discuss the problem of how a country can achieve external and internal equilibrium at the same time.

Given these circumstances, it may be preferable for a country to make some leeway by using capital imports to cover a deficit. One reason for this may be that the causes of the deficit may disappear and the country automatically return to equilibrium. Another reason may be that the expansionary effects among trading partners which a deficit in one country implies may, given time, work to correct the disequilibrium. The present trading system has, after all, a built-in steering mechanism that always works in the direction of equilibrium. One important aspect of capital movements is that they can give this international adjustment mechanism time to work itself out.

Another aspect of capital movements is that rates of capital accumulation and increases in activity levels may vary between countries. For such "real" reasons it is quite natural that international capital movements take place. Economic history contains several examples of such long-run capital movements between countries. If such a situation occurs, it is natural that a deficit in the trade balance is covered by capital imports.

Viewed from a different angle, it can be argued that the present international monetary system can only function well if it is supported by extensive capital movements. The central banks will play a critical role in this regard. Only if they manage to transform accommodating capital movements into some kind of autonomous capital movements can the present monetary system be expected to work well. Capital movements should not be viewed as exceptional but as a natural complement to other policy means. We shall return to the role played by capital movements in Part V, where we shall deal with the international monetary system.

SELECTED BIBLIOGRAPHY: CHAPTER 16

Classic works on the gold standard are:

W. A. Brown, Jr., *The Gold Standard Re-interpreted, 1914–34*, New York, 1934.

R. G. Hawtrey, *The Gold Standard in Theory and Practice,*
5th ed., London, 1947.

The standard work for a discussion of the effects of economic policy on the
balance of payments is:

J. E. Meade, *The Balance of Payments,* London, 1951, and its
Mathematical Supplement (published separately).

Another important paper is:

H. G. Johnson, "Towards a General Theory of the Balance of
Payments," *Economic Growth and International Trade,* London, 1958
(reprinted in *RIE*).

Early works on the elasticity approach are:

A. Marshall, *Money, Credit, and Commerce,* New York, 1924, app. J.

A. P. Lerner, *The Economics of Control,* New York, 1944, chap. 28.

J. Robinson, "The Foreign Exchanges," in *Essays in the Theory of
Employment,* London, 1937 (reprinted in *RTIT*).

One important essay is:

A. C. Harberger, "Currency Depreciation, Income and the Balance of
Trade," *JPE,* February 1950 (reprinted in *RIE*).

The first paper to elaborate the absorption approach was:

S. S. Alexander, "Effects of a Devaluation on the Trade Balance,"
SP, April 1951 (reprinted in *RIE*).

For a critical view of the absorption approach and a defense of the elasticity
approach, see:

F. Machlup, "Relative Prices and Aggregate Spending in the
Analysis of Devaluation," *AER,* vol. 45, June 1955.

For attempts to combine the two approaches see:

S. C. Tsiang, "The Role of Money in Trade-Balance Stability:
Synthesis of the Elasticity and the Absorption Approaches," *AER,*
vol. 51, December 1961 (reprinted in *RIE*).

S. S. Alexander, "Effects of a Devaluation: A Simplified Synthesis of
Elasticities and Absorption Approaches," *AER,* vol. 49, March 1959.

The derivation of the complete elasticity formula given in Chapter 16 follows
the approach developed by Alexander in the paper cited last.

Fixed versus
flexible
exchange rates

17

In Chapters 13 and 16 we discussed various aspects of flexible and fixed exchange rates. Chapter 13 described how the market for foreign exchange worked under a system of flexible exchange rates and the functioning of forward markets for foreign exchange and the main factors that determine the interrelationships between spot and forward rates. We learned that under a regime of flexible exchange rates, working ideally, markets would be cleared and the balance of payments automatically adjusted. Such a system therefore seemed to provide an elegant solution to the problem of external disequilibrium. A system of flexible exchange rates, however, might give rise to some problems hinted at in Chapter 13: It could make an economy prone to inflation and possibly introduce a degree of instability.

We know that flexible exchange rates have gained little ground in the world economy since World War II; no major country has used such a system (except Canada between 1950–1961). The dominant system in the world today is one of fixed exchange rates. We discussed in Chapter 16 various policy problems that such a regime gives rise to.

It is now opportune to compare the two kinds of systems, to try to evaluate gains and losses connected with either one of them. The relative merits and drawbacks of the two systems have long been a topic for discussion in international economics. This discussion has had a tendency, however, to become rather unfruitful. The debaters have had a tendency to talk past each other, each being concerned with a limited set of arguments that, although of relevance for the problem, presents only part of the picture. The proponents of fixed exchange rates usually assert that flexible rates will be detrimental to the volume of international trade and investment. The proponents of flexible rates usually argue that such a system would make it easier for a country to reach its domestic economic aims and free it of the constraints that concern about external balance could cause.

We will now take up some of the main issues. An important aspect of this chapter is the attempt to demonstrate that the problem is too complex for a straightforward solution to be possible. At a closer look the problem turns out to consist of several subsets of problems where functional relationships of very different natures are involved. We will take up four different aspects that all have an important bearing on the problem: uncertainty, speculation, inflation, and the macroeconomic costs for different exchange-rate systems.[1]

FLEXIBLE EXCHANGE RATES AND UNCERTAINTY

It is often argued that flexible exchange rates would create uncertainty and instability and that this would hamper foreign trade and investment. This would then be a factor to be counted against a system of flexible rates. At the same time, it is also often argued that movements in exchange rates under a system of flexible rates would only reflect changes in underlying economic factors and would therefore give exporters and importers correct signals to guide their behavior. Uncertainty and risk in connection with flexible exchange rates, however, is a very complex problem. That economists arrive at varying results seems to be because they deal only with limited aspects of this complex problem.

To elucidate the problems involved here, we could profitably start with two extreme examples. The first shows how flexible exchange rates decrease instead of aggravate the risks connected with foreign trade.

Assume a country where all prices move in common. Further assume that the general price level increases faster than it does abroad. This would, at fixed exchange rates, cause a deficit in the trade balance. The country, how-ever, is under a system of flexible exchange rates, and the exchange rate moves in complete harmony with the price level. If the price level increases by 50 per cent, the exchange rate depreciates correspondingly, which is, by assumption, enough to offset any disequilibria that could arise, and hence the balance of trade is kept in equilibrium.

---

[1] The author's views on this subject owe much to discussions with Anthony Lanyi of Princeton University, who has let him take part of two unpublished manu-scripts, "Notes on Inflation and the Case for Flexible Exchange Rates" and "The Case for Floating Exchange Rates Reconsidered." The latter has since been published as no. 72 in the series *Essays in International Finance*, Princeton, N.J., 1969. The author has also greatly enjoyed discussions with Guy Arvidsson of the University of Lund, Sweden, whose searching criticism has been most valuable.

What must be observed here is that money prices keep changing, but real magnitudes remain unchanged. An American exporter, for example, during one period exports goods to Great Britain for £100. If the exchange rate is $2 to £1, he will receive $200. Suppose that in the next period the American price level increases by 50 percent. He still exports the same amount as before contracted in pounds sterling and receives £100. His costs have increased by 50 percent, but the dollar has devalued *pari passu* and he now receives $300 for £100. Hence he is as well off as before and the change in price level and exchange rate will have no effect on the real variables in the economy.

A complication could arise here if there is a discrepancy between delivery of goods and receipt of payments and if the capital market uses contracts reckoned in monetary terms. The solution to this problem would be to have a capital market where contracts are governed by an index clause (stable-purchasing-power bonds), so that loans would have to be repaid in constant real amounts. Then a combination of flexible exchange rates and index loans would be the perfect solution to the problem of risk, as it would leave everyone in the same real position despite changes in the general price level. Granted the assumptions, this would, in short, solve the problem of inflation.

The assumptions of the above example, however, are quite restrictive. There is no reason to expect, in a dynamic world where economic growth occurs, that there is a direct relationship between changes in price levels and external disequilibria. Hence there is no reason to expect a direct and close relationship between changes in price levels and exchange rates. Furthermore, all prices in an economy do not move in the same way as the general price level. An institutional fact that we cannot disregard is that contracts in capital markets run in current prices; no major capital markets have so far developed index loans. Flexible exchange rates could conceivably reduce risks connected with foreign trade.

We shall now discuss the case where flexible exchange rates increase rather than reduce the risks of foreign trade. Assume a country where the general price level is stable. The country is under a regime of flexible exchange rates. To begin with, the balance of trade is in equilibrium, but after a time the demand for the country's imports decreases (for instance, because of a change in tastes abroad). This leads to depreciation of the country's currency. The general price level is stable, but importers find that import prices have risen. This leads to a fall in imports and marginal importers will

FIGURE 17.1

Flexible exchange rates under uncertainty

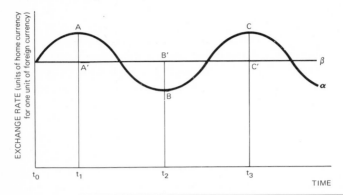

be unable to compete and will become bankrupt. At the same time, exporters will gain because of increased prices but will lose on a decrease in the volume of exports. What the net outcome will be depends on price elasticities, supply functions, and so on. Here we can see that a system of flexible exchange rates introduces an extra risk into the system compared with a regime of fixed exchange rates. The country's importers will be hurt by a change in the exchange rates to which they, through no faults of their own, have fallen victim. With fixed exchange rates, import prices would have been stable and the import volume would not have changed. Under flexible exchanges, import and export prices will show greater variation. An increased risk will be connected with foreign trade, and resources will be reallocated to a greater degree than under fixed exchange rates. Marginally profitable exports and imports will be outcompeted and the volume of foreign trade will be smaller than it would be under a system of fixed exchange rates.

Figure 17.1 should help to illustrate this argument. The α line shows how the exchange rate will fluctuate under a system of flexible exchange rates; the β line shows the exchange rate under a system of fixed exchange rates. At the beginning, at time t_0, the exchange rate will be the same regardless of systems. At time t_1 the currency will have depreciated under a system of flexible rates, as the rate is now at point A compared with point A' under a system of fixed rates. Under flexible rates, imports will therefore be discouraged, whereas exports (under normal market conditions) will be encouraged. At time t_2, however, the exchange rate will have appreciated under a system of flexible exchange rates, as it will be at B, whereas it would have been at B' had the country been on a system of fixed rates. At B, exporters will be worse off than they would have been had the exchange rate stayed at B'. Analogously, importers will be better off at B than at B'. The result of this is that the fluctuation of the exchange rate around a trend value as depicted in Figure 17.1 will cause an increased risk for exporters and importers that will have a dampening effect on foreign trade. Assume that this risk can be represented as a measurable cost.[2] How large this cost could be is difficult to say.

In principle, exporters and importers should be able to cover themselves against this risk by hedging, i.e., by buying and selling foreign exchange in a forward market as described in Chapter 13. This risk could then be approximated by the cost of hedging. Under the present system, when foreign exchanges are allowed to vary only within narrow limits, this cost is low. What it would be under a system of genuinely flexible exchange rates is hard to say. The cost of hedging in commodity markets, where price fluctuations are large, seems to be substantially larger than the cost of hedging in today's supervised and controlled foreign exchange markets. It should, furthermore, be noted that what is involved here is not only the risk connected with one single export or import transaction but with the export and import activities as a whole. It is certainly true that no market exists today that could ensure against all the risks connected with a system of flexible exchanges. It is doubtful if such a market could be established in the future if a system of flexible exchanges were introduced. A system of flexible exchanges might, therefore, have a considerably dampening effect on the volume of foreign trade.

From this point of view it might therefore be argued that a system of fixed exchange rates implies a subsidy to foreign trade, as it means that society as a whole carries part of the risk connected with foreign trade.[3] If the flexible exchange rate fluctuates in a fairly regular way around a trend value as in Figure 17.1, this subsidy goes to exporters and importers alike. We can observe, however, that if there is an upward or downward trend in the flexible exchange rate, then a system of fixed exchange rates could imply

---

[2] For a general discussion of risk problems, see K. H. Borch, *The Economics of Uncertainty*, Princeton, N.J., Princeton University Press, 1968.
[3] See Lanyi, "The Case for Floating Exchange Rates Reconsidered," pp. 6 ff.

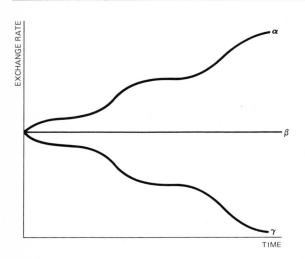

FIGURE 17.2

Flexible exchange rates
with appreciation
and depreciation trends

a subsidy to imports and a tax on exports, or vice versa. This is illustrated in Figure 17.2.

The α line shows an exchange rate with a depreciation trend in it. If the exchange rate was kept at the β level, this would imply a subsidy to imports and a tax on exports compared with what would be the case if the exchange rate were permitted to float. The γ line, conversely, shows a flexible exchange rate with an appreciation trend in it. In this case, the fixed rate at the β level would imply a tax on imports and a subsidy to exports.

From quite reasonable assumptions, it can therefore be argued that a pegging of the exchange rate means that a country will get a larger volume of trade than it otherwise would, as a system of fixed exchange rates implies a subsidy to foreign trade. We can then ask: Why should a country subsidize its foreign trade?

This question can be viewed from at least two angles. First we have the macroeconomic or stabilization point of view, from which it could be argued that one of the chief aims of modern economic policy is to stabilize variables such as national income, price level, and level of exports and imports. If pegging the exchange rate could facilitate attaining this aim, it could be worthwhile even though it would be bought at the price of subsidizing foreign trade. For the time being, we will just state the argument;

a proper discussion of it belongs to a later part of this chapter, where the macroeconomic costs of pegging the exchange rate will be discussed.

The second angle from which this subsidy can be viewed might be termed the microeconomic, or resource allocation, point of view. A subsidy to one sector of the economy means that resources will be drawn to that sector. Under a properly functioning price system and with properly functioning markets, there is no reason to engage in such a subsidy, which would merely lead to a misallocation of resources and a lowering of economic welfare.

If, however, imperfections or externalities are involved, the question has a different perspective. It could be, for instance, that foreign trade gives rise to external economies because a wide range of imports give rise to a wider range of choice for consumers. Life could become more varied and pleasant if the consumer had a wide range of goods from which to choose. The very presence of a large assortment of imported goods could increase the level of satisfaction. It could also be argued that a subsidy to foreign trade keeps a pressure on the domestic industry and increases the efficiency of the economy. In a wider calculus, we know that other factors, such as tariffs and taxes, also influence the volume of trade, often in a protectionistic direction. An offsetting subsidy in the form of a pegged exchange rate could then perhaps move the economy toward rather than away from an optimum position.

To sum up: It seems difficult to argue on a priori grounds that flexible exchange rates would either decrease or increase the uncertainty in an economy. This depends to a large degree on which factors produce the uncertainty, and whether one is concerned with real or monetary variables. One factor of critical importance is the correlation between export and import prices and the general price level. If there is a large degree of correlation in movements between foreign and domestic prices and if one is primarily concerned with real variables, it can be argued that flexible exchange rates would decrease uncertainty and that they would better reflect real conditions in an economy than would fixed exchanges.

With another set of assumptions it can be argued that a system of flexible exchange rates would introduce a greater uncertainty in the economy than a system of fixed rates. This seems highly probable if there is no high degree of correlation in the movements of foreign and domestic prices. Flexible exchange rates will then have a dampening effect on the volume of foreign trade.

In this respect, it therefore seems that one's views on fixed or flexible exchange rates must largely depend on the empirical characteristics of the economy in question.

Another question often discussed in connection with stability of the exchange rates is the effect of speculation on flexible exchange rates. We now turn to this problem.

SPECULATION AND THE STABILITY OF THE EXCHANGE RATE

Under a system of flexible exchange rates, many factors influence movements in exchange rates. The most important are connected with supply and demand of exports and imports. But speculation also plays a role. We learned in Chapter 13 that speculation influenced the movements of spot and forward exchange rates and made them move together. Speculation will also affect the supply and demand of foreign exchange. An important question is whether speculation is stabilizing or destabilizing, i.e., whether it tends to smooth out fluctuations in the exchange rate caused by trade or to make them larger than they otherwise would be.

It is often said that speculators see a decline in the exchange rate as a signal for further decline, and that their actions will cause the movement in the exchange rate to be larger than it would be in the absence of speculation. In such a case, speculation is destabilizing. It could be that political motives are also involved, causing capital to leave a country because of political instability or because the ruling class feels threatened by political reform. This has happened in some European countries; France during the popular front government led by Léon Blum in the late 1930s is an example, and the left-center coalition government of Papandreou in Greece in 1964–1965 comes close to being another example. Under such circumstances, speculation can easily be destabilizing.

The question of the role speculation plays in the stability of exchange rates is perhaps the most-discussed aspect of the subject. The empirical material that exists to illustrate the question now lies quite far back in time. It originates from the 1920s when several countries allowed their exchange rates to fluctuate. The most interesting example is probably France during the period 1919–1926.

The standard work for a discussion of the experiences of the interwar period in this sphere is Ragnar Nurkse's *International Currency Experience*, an investigation carried out for the League of Nations and published in 1944. Nurkse's own attitude is clear. His opinion is that the experiences of the free exchange rates of the 1920s were bad, mainly because speculation was predominantly destabilizing.

Later, Nurkse's interpretation of the development was criticized. Milton Friedman, for example, says without advancing any precise reasons that one can just as well interpret the material so that speculation appears as stabilizing.[4] The most interesting interpretation of the material is that by S. C. Tsiang in an article published in 1959 in IMF's Staff Papers.[5] He constructs an index of what he calls purchasing power and compares it with the development of the exchange rate. He then finds that the exchange rate fluctuated considerably more than was justified by real factors as measured by the purchasing-power index. He does not wish to explain it solely by speculation, but also advances other explanations such as the easy French monetary policy, the modification in the American monetary policy which forced American exporters to take home their export credits, political anxiety, etc.

It can suffice to say briefly that the experiences of the 1920s show that at that time, anyway, the fluctuations in the exchange rates under free price formation in the foreign exchange market were stronger than justified solely by changes in supply and demand of exports and imports. It can then be discussed whether this was due to speculation alone or was mainly based on other factors. The behavior of central banks is also of great importance. If they were to speculate against one another, speculation could easily become destabilizing. If, on the other hand, central banks choose to cooperate, this would certainly have a strong stabilizing influence.

Normally one would expect speculation to have a stabilizing influence on exchange rates. It should be noted that if speculation is destabilizing, it implies that the speculators lose money on their activity.[6] This, however, is

---

[4] M. Friedman, "The Case for Flexible Exchange Rates," in *Essays in Positive Economics*, Chicago, The University of Chicago Press, 1953, pp. 174 ff.
[5] S. C. Tsiang, "Fluctuating Exchange Rates in Countries with Relatively Stable Economies. Some European Experiences After World War I," *International Monetary Fund Staff Papers*, vol. 7, October 1959.
[6] This argument is put forward by Milton Friedman, *op. cit.*

not too strong an argument in favor of the stabilizing effect of speculation, as the speculators can consist of two groups: one professional, which usually makes a profit, and one a changing body of amateur speculators, which makes a loss.[7]

We should further note that the argument for speculation being stabilizing does not refer to the time period over which profitable speculation is stabilizing. If, for instance, speculation were stabilizing in the long run but destabilizing in the short run, it might be too costly an adjustment mechanism for a government to rely upon.

The question of the effects of speculation on exchange rates is very open. It is perhaps best, therefore, merely to outline the problem and to leave the drawing of inferences to the reader.

FLEXIBLE EXCHANGE RATES AND INFLATION

It is often argued by those who favor fixed exchange rates that flexible exchange rates will have an inflationary impact on an economy, because a depreciation of the exchange rate will cause a rise in the domestic price level. To elucidate this question, we shall begin the discussion with an example.

Depreciation of a currency means that import goods become more expensive, and the increase in import prices leads to an increase in the general price level. That is the argument. Assume that a country's imports amount to 20 percent of its national income and that its currency depreciates by 15 percent. This will lead to an increase in import prices of, say, 15 percent. If this increase is carried through completely, and no secondary effects occur, a general price index in the country will increase by 3 percent (20 percent times 15 percent). Here a depreciation produces an inflationary effect, i.e., causes an increase in the country's internal price level.

This example is based on several critical assumptions. For instance, we assumed that import prices increased by the same percentage as the fall

---

[7] M. Farrell, in the article "Profitable Speculation," *Economica*, May 1966, questions this argument and shows that it might be possible, under what seems to be fairly general assumptions, that speculation can be, at the same time, profitable and destabilizing.

in the exchange rate. This does not necessarily happen. The initial increase in import prices caused by depreciation will lead to a fall in the demand for imported goods. This fall in demand could force foreign exporters to lower their prices. If this happens, the rise in import prices caused by depreciation will be partially offset.

Another important factor to take into account is that as imports become relatively more expensive, they will be substituted by import-competing goods produced at home. This will also tend to restrict the rise in the general price level.

There are, however, several factors working in the opposite direction. Several industries, working for the home market or producing export goods, use imported goods as inputs. When imports become more expensive because of the fall in the exchange rate, the price of these inputs, and the cost of production, will rise. Another factor working in the same direction is an expected increase in the activity level as a result of depreciation. Exporters will receive more in home currency for every unit of foreign currency they earn. This will enable them to lower their prices, reckoned in foreign currency, and to expand production. Producers in import-competing industries will also be in an improved competitive situation, as outlined above. All this will give rise to an increase in the activity level in the country and produce upward pressure on the general price level.

It is sometimes argued by those who defend flexible exchange rates that a system of flexible exchange rates need have no inflationary impact— that a depreciation should not cause a rise in the general price level. This argument, however, hardly stands up to close scrutiny. Part of the general price level, the prices on import goods, will necessarily rise because of the depreciation. The only way in which the general price level could be kept unchanged would then be if other prices fell. Some substitution, as we have argued, will probably take place. But there is no reason to expect this effect to be so large as to outweigh the rise in import prices. This would, after all, imply (at least for fairly open economies) a drastic fall in the prices of domestic factors of production. But the interest rate cannot be expected to fall as long as the money supply is unchanged and there is little reason to expect a fall in wages. This argument can therefore hardly be sustained.

Another form that this argument sometimes takes is that an exchange depreciation cannot result in inflation if appropriately restrictive economic policies are pursued. In a limited sense, this argument is correct, but it disregards one critical factor: that in such a case, stable prices have to be bought

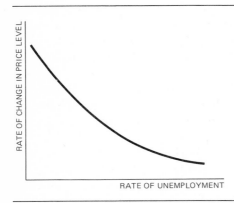

FIGURE 17.3

Relation between changes
in price level and unemployment

at the cost of a rise in the rate of unemployment. This will necessarily be the case if we assume that there is an inverse relationship between the general price level and the rate of unemployment. Such a relationship is set out in Figure 17.3. The curve in the figure is derived from the so-called Phillips curve, which shows the relationship between the rate of change of money wages and the rate of unemployment.[8, 9]

Empirical findings from different countries tell us that we would expect to find a relationship of this kind. The exact shape of the curve can naturally vary, but that there is a general relationship of this nature can hardly be doubted.[10] It is only where no predictable relationship between the price level and the rate of unemployment exists that economic policies which affected the price level would leave the level of employment unchanged. If this were so, the argument for flexible exchanges would be

---

[8] See Lanyi, "Notes on Inflation and the Case for Flexible Exchanges," *op. cit.*
[9] A. W. Phillips, "The Relation Between Unemployment and the Rate of Change of Money Wage Rates in the United Kingdom," *Economica*, November 1958.
[10] It is quite natural to think of the price level (P) as a function of the exchange rate (r) and the rate of unemployment (U). Then we can set out the following function:

$$P = f(r, U)$$

where $\partial P/\partial r > 0$ and $\partial P/\partial U < 0$. If this relationship holds, depreciation will increase the price level, and an increase in the rate of unemployment will decrease the price level.

greatly strengthened. However, such independence between exchange rate and price level is not to be expected.

In general it is true that the effect of a depreciation on the price level depends on the general economic policy pursued in the country. If a restrictive economic policy is pursued, a rise in the price level can be checked, and the recently mentioned figure for the increase in price level could be viewed as realistic, i.e., a fall in the exchange rate of 15 percent might give rise to an increase in the general price level of only 3 percent. If a restrictive economic policy is not pursued, depreciation could give rise to strong inflationary pressure on the economy. As the general price level increases, workers will probably press for higher wages. This is very understandable, as the immediate impact of depreciation is very likely to be a fall in real wages. If the workers manage to restore the purchasing power of their wages, this will again increase costs, and the country could fall into a wage–price spiral. If this happened, gains from depreciation would rapidly be destroyed, and there would be an increase in the general price level as large as the depreciation of the currency. A criterion for the success of depreciation is, as we know from Chapter 16, for it to lead to a fall in over-all demand (a fall in total absorption).

It is sometimes asserted that depreciation cannot lead to an increase in the general price level, because it gives rise to an improved allocation of economic resources. Before depreciation (or before the system of flexible exchange rates was introduced), quotas, import licensing, and other trade restrictions were employed in the economy to limit deficits in the balance of payments caused by the overvalued currency. In connection with depreciation, trade restrictions are dismantled, leading to improved allocation of resources and an increase in production. If this increase in production is large enough, depreciation can lead to an excess supply of goods at existing prices, although total absorption has not fallen, and the general price level will fall.

This type of argument, however, is built by stacking the cards in a very definite direction. A situation such as the one described could occur, but if we want to discuss the effects of flexible exchange rates, the logical thing to do is to compare a system of flexible exchange rates with another system (for instance, fixed exchange rates), assuming everything else to be equal. What we must do, in other words, is focus attention on what is relevant and not introduce factors that have no logical connection with a change in the exchange rates. That depreciation gives rise to a drastic change in the over-all efficiency of resource allocation is tantamount to introducing a specific argument into the discussion. (A change in relative prices caused by depreciation will, of course, always produce a change in the production pattern, but this is a different matter.)

A system of flexible exchanges will, under most circumstances, cause changes in the internal price level. If a country has difficulty in coping with inflation, or is averse to it, this could be a strong reason, also, to be averse to a system of flexible exchange rates, because depreciation can normally be expected to cause a rise in the general price level.

It must be stressed, however, that the way one views inflation is primarily a question of value judgments. A higher degree of inflation will probably follow from flexible exchange rates, but at the same time, flexible exchanges make policy makers less constrained by balance-of-payments considerations: it makes it easier to maintain a policy of full employment. How one views this question will therefore ultimately depend on how one values the unfavorable effects of inflation (undesirable redistribution effects and the like) compared with the benefits of a lower rate of unemployment.

Before concluding this section, we should touch on two more subtle effects in connection with inflation that flexible exchange rates might have. If we assume that flexible exchange rates produce greater movements in the exchange rate, this might produce an undesirable "ratchet effect."[11] A depreciation in the exchange rate will cause an increase in domestic wages and prices. But an appreciation will not cause a comparable fall in domestic prices and wages, because prices and wages are rigid downward. Hence an asymmetry will occur that produces an upward trend in the price level. Furthermore, if flexible exchange rates produce greater fluctuations in the exchange rate, this could result in overfrequent attempts at reallocation of resources. If there is a cost connected with reallocating resources, flexible exchange rates would perhaps produce a result in this respect that is worse than would be the case under fixed exchange rates.[12]

We have now looked into several aspects of a system of flexible exchange rates which tend to put such a system in a somewhat dubious light. We will now continue and take up a different aspect, one that might produce a more favorable result for flexible exchanges: the macroeconomic costs of pegging the exchange rate.

---

11 See R. Triffin, *Gold and the Dollar Crisis*, New Haven, Conn., Yale University Press 1961, pp. 82 ff.
12 See Lanyi, "The Case for Floating Exchange Rates Reconsidered," p. 13.

THE MACROECONOMIC COSTS OF FIXED EXCHANGE RATES

The macroeconomic costs of fixed exchange rates are of a somewhat elusive kind. The most important is connected with the fact that a pegged exchange rate will often render it difficult for a country to maintain both full employment and external equilibrium. As just indicated, there is a negative trade off between inflation and the rate of employment. A striving for full employment can easily create an inflationary pressure in an economy. Such a pressure easily leads to a balance of payments deficit under a system of fixed exchange rates. To restore external balance, the country might then have to tolerate a higher rate of unemployment. This increase in unemployment is the real cost of maintaining a system of fixed exchange rates.

It is important to remember that a flexible exchange rate will make it easier for the policy makers to attain several policy aims. It is not true, as we should realize by now, that a system of flexible exchange rates unconditionally frees the authorities of concern regarding the balance of payments. But a system of flexible exchange rates should at least make it as easy to achieve a certain combination of policy targets for the rate of employment and the external equilibrium as would a fixed exchange rate. The policy makers will at least be able to use the same combination of policy means as under fixed rates, and most of the time they should be able to do better.[13]

An important item in the assessment of the costs and benefits of the two systems is therefore the decrease in national product that unemployment might cause. The thing to do would be to try to measure the rate of employment under a system of fixed exchange rates and compare it with what it would be under a system of flexible rates. If this difference were known, an attempt could be made to use it to evaluate the national product foregone because of fixed rates. To this would also have to be added the indirect costs for social security, policing the unemployed, and so on. Unemployment is an important social phenomenon with many indirect effects which would also have to be taken into account. It would decrease the militancy of trade unions, increase the power of employers, weaken the position of housewives who would not dare to seek employment in a weak labor market, etc. In short, unemployment would have a powerful effect on the social balance of a

---

[13] We return to this problem in Chapter 18, which is devoted to an explicit discussion of aims and means in economic policy. How to reach external and internal balance under varying assumptions as to means is discussed there.

society. In the effect on the employment rate, the defenders of flexible exchange rates have a very strong card to play.

Another argument is that pegging the exchange rate might increase a country's need for foreign reserves. The holding of such reserves entails an opportunity cost for the country in question.[14] With flexible exchanges, these reserves could be reduced. Part of the reserves could be freed for domestic investment. The difference in yield between such investments and the yield on international reserves can be said to measure the opportunity cost of the reserves in question.

It is sometimes argued that the need for reserves would increase, not diminish, if a country under flexible exchange rates tried to intervene in the foreign exchange market to influence the rate.[15] This could conceivably be the case, but it seems that under most circumstances a system of flexible rates would decrease the need for foreign reserves.

We have now stated some of the arguments for and against flexible exchange rates. We will conclude this chapter by summarizing the main points. As the problem also has many essential political aspects, we will touch on some of them; although we have to concentrate on the economic aspects of the problem, it would be unwise to omit altogether the deep political aspects.

SUMMARY OF THE COSTS AND BENEFITS OF FLEXIBLE EXCHANGE RATES: POLITICAL ASPECTS

We have indicated some of the main factors that must be considered when discussing fixed versus flexible exchange rates. There are at least four important factors that no analysis of the problem can avoid. They can be grouped under four headings: (1) uncertainty, (2) speculation, (3) inflation, and (4) unemployment.

In principle, flexible exchange rates might increase or they might decrease uncertainty. For practical purposes, it seems that they would in-

---

[14] The nature of the opportunity cost is discussed more fully in Chapter 27 in connection with the problem of supply and demand of international liquidity.

[15] See R. Harrod, *Reforming the World's Money*, London, Macmillan, 1965, p. 51.

crease uncertainty for traders. This would have a dampening effect on the volume of foreign trade. A decrease in the volume of trade would have to be counted as a cost on the part of flexible rates compared with the benefit that a fixed exchange rate would entail in this respect. A pegged exchange rate could be regarded as a subsidy to those engaged in foreign trade. There can be different views as to who should carry the burden of this subsidy. It must be stressed that the question of exchange rates and uncertainty is very involved and that the implications of a certain exchange-rate regime can vary greatly for different economies.

When it comes to the effects of speculation, this must be deemed an open question to which no cut-and-dried answers can be given. The limited experience which exists from the 1920s seems to show that then, at least, speculation was destabilizing.

Regarding inflation, the problem is more clear cut. A system of flexible exchange rates will give an inflationary bias to an economy. A depreciation of the exchange rate will undoubtedly have a tendency to raise the price level. For most industrial countries, a " ratchet effect " will probably be at work, which will lead to a depreciation producing its full inflationary impact on the price level, although an appreciation will not have a comparable effect in a downward direction, as prices and wages can be expected to be rigid in a downward direction. To this must also be added the fact that flexible exchange rates might lead to an increase in frictional employment because of a tendency to " overreallocate " resources. Flexible exchange rates, therefore, can hardly avoid having an inflationary impact on an economy. This is especially true when there is a depreciation trend in the exchange rate.

If a system of flexible exchange rates has a definite weakness with respect to inflation, it has a strength over fixed rates when it comes to maintaining a high level of employment. As we saw in Chapter 16, a system of fixed exchange rates might make it very difficult for a country to attain both full employment and equilibrium in the balance of payments. Flexible exchange rates have a distinct advantage here as they automatically involve an element of expenditure switching which will make it easier for a country to reconcile the goals of a high level of employment with external equilibrium.

There is, as we have seen, no neat answer to the question of whether a country should go for a system of fixed or flexible exchange rates. The answer will depend on circumstances. It will depend on the characteristics of the economy, and it will change with time as the economy changes. Value judgments are also involved, and ultimately the answer could depend on values and views of a political nature.

One or two more general comments might be justified. The greater the openness of an economy and the more dependent on foreign trade it is, the larger are the risks connected with flexible exchange rates. The larger, then, will be the inflationary effect and the greater will be the losses connected with Triffin's "ratchet effect" and the resource-allocation effect. If there is no downward or upward trend in the exchange rate, the country might do well to stay on a system of fixed exchange rates.

If there is a trend in the exchange rate, things might turn out differently. If the cost level of one country rises faster than it does in other countries, this will usually mean that the country runs into balance-of-payments difficulties and that there is a depreciation trend in the exchange rate. If this is the case, fixed exchange rates could put an intolerable pressure on the economy, as a balancing of trade will mean a continually falling rate of employment. For countries that find it difficult to keep their cost level in line with the rest of the world, the attempt to maintain a fixed exchange rate could become a very frustrating undertaking.

This last point hints at a problem of great importance. In a world of fixed exchange rates, external disequilibria will undoubtedly arise. The rate and the pattern of economic growth vary among countries. Rates of inflation vary. Some countries are more ambitious than others as far as domestic economic goals are concerned. These factors will for some countries produce persistent depreciation trends in the exchange rate. These countries will basically have to choose between maintaining a fixed exchange rate until depreciation is forced upon them or going over to a system of flexible exchange rates.

If a country is unwilling to let the exchange rate float freely but still cannot afford to peg the rate completely, the solution might be to have a so-called sliding parity or crawling peg. This means that the exchange rate is allowed to vary but within broader limits than is the case with today's system of fixed exchange rates. Such a system can be regarded as a hybrid between fixed and flexible exchange rates and will permit expenditure-switching policies to play a larger role than is the case under fixed exchanges. We return to this problem in Chapter 26 in connection with a discussion of adjustment and the need for international liquidity.

This is a book about economics, and naturally the emphasis is on the economic aspects of a problem. The question of fixed versus flexible exchange rates, however, has many important political implications. Before concluding the chapter, we should at least mention some political aspects of the problem.

We have seen that the question of exchange-rate systems has direct political implications. Whether one prefers fixed or flexible exchange rates might depend on how one evaluates inflation compared with unemployment, for instance. The choice of system has another and perhaps even more important aspect: that of political workability and acceptability.

It is sometimes argued that the present system is very fragile—that "a breakdown of the system" could easily come about, or perhaps is even to be expected in the near future. What such a breakdown would mean is far from clear. To have any meaning, it would have to imply fairly far-reaching restrictions on international trade. The risk of such a breakdown does not seem to be very great. We return to this question in Chapter 28, after dealing with the international monetary system. There it is argued that the present system is quite workable and that minor reforms can be expected to keep it workable in the foreseeable future.

Given these premises, it might be easier to understand why politicians and practical men cling to a system of fixed exchange rates. It has proved acceptable, and it is difficult to argue that it is not workable. There is, for natural reasons, a bent toward conservatism inherent in the politicians' views on exchange-rate systems. Any change, for instance in the form of letting the market work more freely or giving increased authority to international organizations, will mean a decrease in the power of the national politician. The national state is still the dominant source of authority; there is little reason to expect politicians to further a system that would undermine their own sphere of influence. From this point of view, a system of fixed exchange rates has a definite attraction: It is the system that allows the largest scope of manipulation to the national politician.

An increased use of the adjustment mechanism might be forced upon the politicians; otherwise the system might not be workable. The alternative to fixed exchange rates is, therefore, probably a system of sliding parity or one that gives increased scope for discretionary exchange-rate changes. A system of flexible exchanges might in many instances be preferable from the point of view of an economist, but it might not be acceptable from a political point of view. And it is, after all, politicians and not economists who have the last word in these matters.

SELECTED BIBLIOGRAPHY: CHAPTER 17

The standard arguments in favor of flexible exchange rates are presented in:

> M. Friedman, " The Case for Flexible Exchange Rates," *Essays in Positive Economics*, Chicago, 1953 (reprinted in an abbreviated version in *RIE*).

Another work recommending flexible exchange rates is:

> E. Sohmen, *Flexible Exchange Rates: Theory and Controversy*, Chicago, 1961.

An older work, the implications of which are going in the opposite direction, is:

> R. Nurkse, *International Currency Experience: Lessons of the Inter-War Period*, Geneva, 1944.

Among numerous essays treating the subject, the following can be mentioned:

> R. E. Caves, " Flexible Exchange Rates," *AER*, May 1963.

> J. E. Meade, " The Case for Flexible Exchange Rates," *Three Banks Review*, September 1955.

> E. V. Morgan, " The Theory of Flexible Exchange Rates," *AER*, June 1955.

A good historical survey is given in:

> L. B. Yeager, *International Monetary Relations*, New York, 1966.

How jointly to achieve external and internal equilibrium

18

In Part III we have dealt with problems connected with the external balance of a country. We have seen in what sense the balance of payments can be in disequilibrium and in what sense it will always be in equilibrium, and we have studied the interrelationships among exports, imports, and national income. We have also dealt with the foreign exchange market and with how a country can cure a deficit in the balance of payments.

One of the most important economic questions of many countries is how to keep the external balance in equilibrium. We now know the chief means of economic policy for reaching this goal. External balance is important but is only one of the aims of a country. Most countries have several goals besides external balance. From an economic point of view, the most important one is usually full employment or internal balance. How a country can achieve jointly external and internal balance, and some of the policy problems connected with reaching these aims, is the subject of this chapter, which concludes our discussion of the balance of payments.

AIMS AND MEANS IN ECONOMIC POLICY

It is perhaps appropriate, before coming to the discussion of concrete cases, to say something about aims and means in economic policy in general.[1]

A country can have more or less specific aims for its economic policy. In capitalist, nonplanned economies, aims are usually stated in broad terms, such as "full employment," "stable prices," "equilibrium in the balance of payments," and "high growth rate." In planned economies the list of aims can sometimes be very long and very detailed. The aims of the economic policy may be stated in terms of tons and liters of commodities, for example. Here we are only concerned with the problem insofar as it bears on economic policy problems in the capitalist or mixed economies with which we are primarily dealing. Therefore, we shall limit ourselves to a few comments which bear on the problem of how to achieve jointly external and internal balance in those types of economies.

---

[1] The discussion of aims and means is based especially on Bent Hansen, *The Economic Theory of Fiscal Policy*, London, Allen & Unwin, 1958.

320

How jointly to
achieve external and
internal equilibrium

On an abstract level we could state the problem in the form of an "exact" model, consisting of n equations with m means or parameters that determine the values of the n unknowns:[2]

$$f_i(x_1, \ldots, x_n; a_1, \ldots, a_m) = 0 \qquad (i = 1, \ldots, n) \tag{18.1}$$

Here we have, in other words, a set of aims, symbolized by the x_i's, and a set of means or parameters, symbolized by the a_j's. We also have a functional relationship between aims and means, symbolized by the f_i's. If we knew what these functional relationships were, and if we determined some values to the means, then we would also know what values the aims would take.

This sounds simple. The principle involved is also simple. On a somewhat less abstract level, however, both deep theoretical problems and practical constraints are involved. Let us take a quick look at several of these, so as not to be completely unaware of some of the problems that engage those involved in economic policy.

Sometimes a model may be of such a type that the aims of the model are automatically fulfilled whatever values the means or parameters take. This is a feature quite common to economic models, especially those of a somewhat older date. We can think of a general equilibrium model of a Walrasian type, where all prices are flexible and where the exchange rate is also flexible. In such a model markets will automatically be cleared, and demand will equal supply. Hence there will always be full employment and external equilibrium, and these two goals will automatically be fulfilled as soon as the system has reached its equilibrium position. From the point of view of economic policy, such a world is the best of all possible worlds, because economic policy is unnecessary.

Another type of model is one where one of two aims is automatically fulfilled but the other is not. Here we can think of a Walrasian type of model for a closed economy, where the two aims are full employment and a constant price level. As prices are flexible, supply will always equal demand and markets be cleared. Relative prices are then determined within the system. Let us assume, however, that the absolute price level is determined by the total money supply.[3] A disturbance in the system, then, will never affect the

---

[2] We assume that the equations in the system 18.1 are independent and consistent and that the system has a unique solution in the x_i's.

[3] Whether or not this dichotomy is based on correct theorizing is of no consequence for the example.

level of employment—the system will always have full employment—but it may affect the general price level. Hence one means or one parameter is needed to control the price level. Given this parameter, it is possible to achieve the dual aim of stable prices and full employment.

Another case, somewhat resembling, although distinct from, the one just treated, consists of the following. Here neither of two aims is automatically achieved, but if one is reached, so is the other. We assume that price changes are a function of excess supply and demand of goods, that no savings or capital movements take place, and that the two aims are full employment and external equilibrium but that markets are not automatically cleared. Unemployment and disequilibria in the balance of trade are possible in this type of model, but once full employment is reached, external balance is automatically achieved. In this case only one means is necessary to achieve two aims, because full employment implies external balance.

In another type of model two means may be necessary to achieve two aims. In the usual Keynesian model, for instance, full employment does not imply external equilibrium. Here two means are necessary to achieve two aims. Fiscal policy may be used to achieve full employment, and commercial policy (exchange-rate changes) may be used to achieve external equilibrium.

This is, in fact, the general case. Only in specific circumstances can the means used be less than the number of aims. Generally, every aim requires a means. To achieve one aim, one means is required; to reach two aims, two means are required; for three aims, three means are needed; and so on. If there are more means than aims, an arbitrary combination of the means can be used to realize the aims.

Sometimes the aims are contradictory. In a logical or mathematical sense this can be thought of as a system of equations where no solution exists. Or to give a simple example, if, in a closed economy, the aims are for the national income to be $100 billion, investment $30 billion, and consumption $80 billion, then the three aims cannot jointly be achieved.

Usually the situation is less clear cut. If an economist says that the aims are contradictory, this is against a given economic background and with certain means in mind. It is sometimes asserted that the two aims of full employment and stable prices are not compatible. It is then asserted, assuming certain specific relationships between the economic variables, for instance, that wages are inflexible in a downward direction or otherwise assuming that the number of feasible means are restricted. It may also be asserted that external and internal equilibrium are not compatible. This might be done

322

How jointly to
achieve external and
internal equilibrium

against the background assumption that a means such as devaluation cannot be used.

If an economist concludes that aims similar to those just referred to are incompatible, it is always against a background of his knowledge of, or assumption about, economic relationships and his views on the feasibility of certain means. This state of affairs has deep political implications. What is impossible in a conservative economy (for instance, to reach and maintain full employment) may be possible in a liberal one. And what is impossible in a liberal economy may be possible in a planned socialist economy.

History shows that those means which are permissible change; what is "impossible" today may be routine tomorrow. If the conflict between aims and performance becomes acute, new means are usually introduced; in the meantime the character of the economy may also change.

Another important point concerns the relationship between aims and means. We have, throughout the book, used the approach of general equilibrium. This indicates, in terms of aims and means, that we cannot change one means or parameter without affecting all the aims; or, to use an example, if a disturbance occurs all the aims will, except in extraordinary circumstances, be affected. To restore the aims to desired levels, all the means normally have to be used. One should also remember that if one aim moves away from the target, when applying the designated means to achieve the desired level of the aim again, other aims will also normally be affected by the change in this parameter.

Against this background it is important to choose a combination of means and aims (to "pair them off") in an efficient manner. Let us say that the aims are full employment and a stable price level and that the means are fiscal policy and monetary policy. A change in any of the means will affect both aims. For a policy scheme to work, however, one means (for instance, fiscal policy) must take precedence with regard to one of the aims (for instance, full employment), and the other means must take precedence with respect to the other aim. When designing an optimal policy one must also take into account the secondary effects of a parameter.

In principle we can, of course, have models not of general equilibrium character, where a change in one aim, one variable, does not affect the other aims. In this case there may also be an isolated relationship between a means and an aim, so that one means only affects one aim without having any repercussions on other aims. In practice, it can also be the case that although a model is of general equilibrium character, the secondary relationships between one parameter and the aims to which it is not directly related are so unimportant that they can be neglected.

In a framework of general equilibrium, it is often necessary to use all means simultaneously to fulfill the aims. An approximative procedure, using one means at a time, may not lead to a stable solution because of secondary effects. Such a procedure may lead to an explosion of the system.[4] This can be of great practical importance if there is, for instance, one authority (the Ministry of Finance) handling one parameter (fiscal policy), but another authority (the central bank) handling another means (monetary policy).

After this introduction to means and aims in economic policy, it is time to discuss internal and external equilibrium in detail.

EXTERNAL AND INTERNAL EQUILIBRIUM WITH FLEXIBLE INCOME AND PRICES

How to achieve jointly full employment and equilibrium in the balance of payments is the most pertinent problem of economic policy in many countries. We shall discuss now some questions connected with this problem against the background of the earlier chapters. We will start with a model in which imports are a function of the national income and relative prices. The level of the national income can be changed by the use of a deflationary or inflationary policy (monetary and fiscal policy are both used to manipulate the income level), and the country has a system of fixed exchange rates. The country can, however, use devaluation and revaluation at discrete intervals to correct a deficit in the balance of payments. We shall disregard capital movements for the time being.

Figure 18.1 is used to illustrate the policy problems of a country in this situation. National income is measured on one side and imports on the other. At a certain level of the national income, Y_1, there is full employment, i.e., internal balance. As we only take the short run into account, the full employment level of the national income is constant. The vertical line shows

---

[4] See Hansen, *op. cit.*, pp. 16 ff.

324

How jointly to
achieve external and
internal equilibrium

FIGURE 18.1

Policy problems of fixed-exchange-rate countries

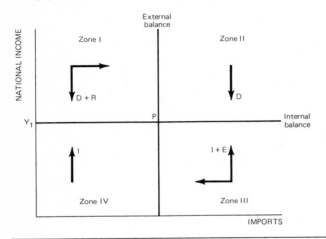

the amount of imports needed to produce equilibrium in the balance of payments. The line is vertical since exports are supposed to be a function of factors abroad (especially the foreign national income). The line shows the amount of imports that in the short run gives external balance.

The two aims of the economy are jointly fulfilled at the point in the diagram where the two lines intersect. This is at point P, which is the point of bliss in the economy. The two policy means are monetary plus fiscal policy, on the one hand, and variations in the exchange rate, on the other.

The diagram has been divided into four zones. For each zone a specific policy or policy mix has to be applied to achieve the two aims. D denotes deflation, I inflation, E devaluation, and R revaluation or appreciation.

In two of the zones only one means is needed to reach both aims. If the economy is at a point in zone II, there is both overfull employment (i.e., an inflationary pressure in the economy) and a deficit in the balance of payments. Then a deflationary policy is needed. A restrictive monetary and fiscal policy will then alone take care of both external and internal disequilibrium. It will assert downward pressure on money incomes and dampen inflation. As national income falls, so do imports; the scope for exports increases, and the balance of payments improves.

The arrows in the diagram illustrate the direction of the means: The vertical arrows show the direction of the means primarily influencing national income (inflation and deflation), and the horizontal arrows show the direction of the parameters that specifically have to deal with the balance of payments (devaluation and revaluation). The vertical arrow pointing downward in zone II thus shows that deflation is the correct policy if the economy is in that zone.

In zone IV inflation is the correct policy. In this case there is both unemployment and a surplus in the balance of payments. An easy monetary policy and an expansionary fiscal policy will lead to an expansion of national income. This will, of course, also lead to an increase in imports, but as the country has a surplus in its balance of payments, this need not give rise to any worries. Hence inflation alone can lead to a fulfillment of both aims in this case.[5]

In zones I and II both policies are needed to achieve the two aims. A point in zone I represents a situation with inflation and a surplus in the balance of payments. To eradicate overfull employment, a deflationary policy is needed. This will further increase the surplus in the balance of payments. To create external equilibrium, an appreciation of the exchange rate is necessary. This will increase imports and lower exports and thus work in the direction of equilibrium in the balance of payments.

The most problematic situation into which a country can fall is to be in zone III. Here the country has unemployment and a deficit in the balance of payments simultaneously. To be in zone I can also have its problems, especially as far as inflation is concerned, but a straightforward deflationary policy will cure it. The inflation will be cured at the price of a further increase in the surplus in the balance of payments, but this is a burden that most countries seem willing to endure. To be in zone III is, however, a situation which a country usually cannot accept with ease for more than a short period of time.

To get back to full employment an inflationary policy is needed. This will, however, further worsen the deficit in the balance of payments.

---

[5] It should be stressed, however, that to get exactly to point P two means might be needed. In zone IV, for instance, inflation will be the correct policy, as it will tend both to decrease unemployment and to reduce the surplus in the balance of payments. But it might be the case that the country will get full employment before it gets external equilibrium. Therefore, a combination of the two policy means might be necessary, even in zones II and IV, to get exactly to point P.

326

How jointly to
achieve external and
internal equilibrium

To get back to external equilibrium, devaluation is needed. Devaluation should improve the trade balance by decreasing imports and increasing exports.

Thus this situation requires a combination of an expenditure-increasing policy, to have full employment, and an expenditure-switching policy, to get external equilibrium. Did we not, however, say in Chapter 16 that an expenditure-switching policy such as devaluation needed an element of expenditure reduction in order to be successful? Here, instead, it is combined with an expenditure-increasing policy. How, then, can it work?

To solve this apparent paradox we have to invoke time and think in terms of sequences of time. In the first place we must remember that devaluation alone will have both an expansionary effect on the national income and lead to an improvement in the trade balance, provided the marginal propensity to absorb is less than unity. If unemployment is fairly deep and persistent, devaluation alone will probably not lead to internal equilibrium. Hence an inflationary policy is also called for. Timing is now important. The country should start with a devaluation, which would lead to an improvement in the trade balance, if the increase in internal absorption is checked for the time being. The trick consists of using devaluation as a switching device and to rely on the fact that a larger share of total world demand will be directed toward the country's exports. As exports increase, the foreign trade multiplier will work and the national income expand. At the same time, the country's balance of trade will improve, permitting her to use an inflationary policy in the next stage to bring the economy back to full employment. A careful use of devaluation combined with monetary and fiscal policy should thus enable the country to achieve both internal and external balance.

If a country is in a situation of disequilibrium, often a significant factor is the type of policy pursued by its trading partners. It is now useful to go back to the standard two-country model and see how two countries can coordinate their policies so that they can both achieve external and internal equilibrium.

The simplest situation is one in which the country with a surplus in its balance of payments tends toward deflation and unemployment and also one in which the country with a deficit has inflation. The first country (with the surplus) should now pursue an expansionary policy and try to reflate its income. As the country has a surplus in its balance of payments it can pursue such a policy and produce internal balance without worries for the external balance. Such a policy will help the second country as far as its external problems are concerned, because the demand for the second country's exports will grow. At the same time it will increase the inflationary pressure in this country. Therefore, this country has to pursue a definite deflationary policy, curbing the internal demand and thereby relieving the country of its inflationary pressure. Such a policy will also help to produce external balance, because it leads to an improvement in the balance of payments. This case requires, therefore, that the surplus country pursues a straightforward policy of reflation and the deficit country one of deflation. Thereby both countries can reach full employment and equilibrium in their balances of payments.

The first situation discussed above was one in which in some parts of the world the national income was too high and in other parts too low. At the same time disequilibria in the world economy were of such a nature that policies that cured the problem of internal stability also dealt with the external disequilibria. Let us now assume that there is a tendency toward world-wide inflation—that national income will be too high in both countries and that at the same time there are disequilibria in the balances of payments. This was a situation that characterized large parts of the world economy during the 1950s. What kind of policies should the two countries then pursue?

Here the deficit country is in a clear-cut position. It should pursue a deflationary policy. Such a policy will both cure the inflationary pressure in the economy and improve the balance of payments. It will at the same time dampen the inflationary pressure in the world economy and thereby also help the second country. This country will feel the deflationary effects primarily through a decrease in the demand for its exports. The multiplier will start working in a downward direction and through the fall in exports the national income will fall. Its balance of payments will worsen, but this will only be to the good, as the country has a surplus in its external balance.

Naturally the two countries have to adapt their policies and give them the correct dosage in order to reach both aims. If the external deficit is only slight in the first country but its inflationary pressure persistent, then it might reach external balance before internal. If this is the case, the prime responsibility rests with the second country, now the one with both a deficit and inflationary pressure. If this country now pursues a deflationary policy, it will help both countries to approach their two aims. By cooperation and the use of capital movements during the adjustment period, both countries should be able to achieve full employment and external equilibrium.

328

How jointly to
achieve external and
internal equilibrium

Let us now continue and treat what seems to be the dominating situation in the 1960s among the industrial countries. This is a situation with a tendency toward world-wide deflation with a certain amount of unemployment in many countries, combined with disequilibrium in the balance of payments. This is, from a historical point of view, not a new situation. It was the dominating feature of the world economy in the interwar period, especially during the 1930s. Then it led both to disastrous economic and political consequences and also to ominous forecasts for the survival of the capitalist system. The situation today is, of course, much less pointed, but some observers argue that the classic malady of the capitalist industrial countries is again appearing, although of a mild variety.

In this situation, it is the country with the surplus which should reflate. If circumstances are very favorable, this policy may solve all three problems, i.e., restore full employment in both countries and create equilibrium in the balance of payments. Such a lucky outcome would, however, be pure coincidence. If the surplus in the balance of payments were only small, the country would get a deficit before reaching internal equilibrium. Then it is the second country which should take over the duty to pursue an expansionary economic policy.

A more problematic situation is the one in which the first country reaches internal equilibrium but still has a surplus in its balance of payments. Then the situation is problematic for the second country, which has both unemployment and a deficit in the balance of payments. We shall return to this problem in a moment.

At this point we should comment on a situation that has had a certain relevance during the 1960s. This is the situation in which tendencies to a world-wide depression dominate, so that both countries have unemployment, but where the surplus country for some reason does not want to pursue a reflationary policy. There might be several explanations for this. One might be that the country values highly its external surplus and wishes to continue to build up its foreign reserves; another might be that it attaches fairly low weight to its unemployment. A third could be that the country, for some reason (for instance, because it wants to balance its budget or to keep the interest rate at a certain level), does not want to pursue an expansionary fiscal or monetary policy. That surplus countries with unemployment do not want to reflate seems quite common; one can mention, as examples, the United States during the 1930s and West Germany during the 1960s.

If this is the case, then the country with the combination of a deficit and unemployment will be in a difficult position. If the country sets a high priority on full employment, it will have to pursue an inflationary policy, but this will only aggravate its deficit and further increase the surplus of its trading partner. There are only two alternatives available to the deficit country if it is serious in its desire to reach full employment. It can try to convert the accommodating capital imports implied by the deficit into autonomous planned inflows, although this presupposes the cooperation of the surplus country. If the surplus country is unwilling to engage in capital movements of this type, the deficit country has to devalue. A devaluation should, rightly timed and used together with an inflationary policy, lead to an alleviation of the deficit country's problems, but again the behavior of its trading partner is important. It has to accept the correction of cost levels that the devaluation implies. If this is not the case, competitive devaluations can occur, with the probable result that world depression will continue. It is, therefore, very important that countries cooperate if they are to be able to reach a high level of employment and a continuous growth of world trade.

The situations with which we have so far dealt could all, in principle, be solved if the two countries used jointly, and to the appropriate extent, deflationary and reflationary policies. If the surplus country has an inflationary pressure in its economy and the deficit country has unemployment, no combination of monetary and fiscal policy in the two countries can do the job and secure both internal and external equilibrium in the two countries. To achieve internal balance the surplus country would have to deflate, but a deflationary policy in this country will only further increase the surplus in the balance of payments. Analogously, the deficit country would have to reflate to produce full employment, although such a policy would only worsen its external deficit. This situation shows that there is a fundamental disequilibrium in the cost levels in the two countries. The natural way out of this dilemma is for the deficit country to devalue its currency. Any other policy can act only as a stopgap.[6]

We have now seen how a country can achieve the two aims of full employment and equilibrium in the balance of payments using monetary and fiscal policy as the prime instrument for controlling the level of money income and exchange-rate changes as the prime instrument for adjusting

---

[6] One can add that long-run capital movements and structural changes (which require a long time to be carried through) can solve this as well as any other problem.

330

How jointly to
achieve external and
internal equilibrium

relative price levels. Given the appropriate instruments, a country should be able to achieve these two aims.

However, in the prevailing international monetary system, sanctioned by the International Monetary Fund, exchange rates are more or less pegged. A country can alter its rate of exchange by up to 10 percent without the sanction of the Fund, but any larger changes have to be sanctioned. Devaluations have taken place, the most conspicuous and important ones being the 1949 devaluation by Britain and most other West European countries, the French devaluation in 1958, and the second British devaluation in 1967. Some economists would argue that shifts in rates of exchange happen so infrequently that devaluations could be ruled out for solving short-run problems. If an important policy instrument is "frozen" in this way, the problem of how to achieve internal and external equilibrium may have to be posed in a different light. It will be instructive, before we end this chapter, to consider the problem in the context of a model with pegged exchange rates.

EXTERNAL AND INTERNAL EQUILIBRIUM IN A MODEL
WITH CAPITAL MOVEMENTS

If devaluation no longer can be used to correct a deficit in the balance of payments, some other means will have to be used to cure external disequilibria. Direct controls could be a possible means, although the trend in trade policy is against them. An important feature in the world economy after World War II is the establishment of common markets. These markets are based on free trade among members and a common tariff level against nonmembers; they can be said to have an element of protectionism in them. Otherwise the trend among the developed, industrial countries is toward a liberalization of trade. Therefore, direct controls or other discriminatory measures can hardly be used to correct external disequilibria. Yet there is no guarantee that a policy which provides full employment will also lead to equilibrium in the balance of payments. What other means can be used?

The answer is to divide the balance of payments into its two main parts: the balance of current account and the balance of capital account. Even if there is a deficit in the balance of current account, the country may

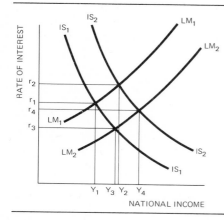

FIGURE 18.2

Hicks–Hansen *IS* and *LM* curves

have an offsetting surplus on the balance of capital account, i.e., an inflow of capital. We remember from Chapter 14 that the balance of current account was related to the flow aspect of a country's economy. A deficit related to the circular flow of income will then be covered by an inflow of capital, i.e., there will be a change in stocks. If a deficit in the balance of current account is covered by a surplus on the capital account, it implies that part of the ownership of the country's capital stock will be transferred abroad.

We shall now give an exposition of how to achieve internal and external balance under fixed exchange rates.[7] Figure 18.2 depicts *IS* and *LM* curves of the usual Hicks–Hansen type, with which the reader is probably familiar from elementary macro theory.[8] A given *IS* curve shows the combination of interest rate and national income which will give equilibrium in the national income for a given investment–savings behavior. The downward slope of the curve is based on the assumption that a fall in the interest

---

[7] See R. A. Mundell, "The Monetary Dynamics of International Adjustment Under Fixed and Flexible Exchange Rates," *Quarterly Journal of Economics*, vol. 74, May 1960, pp. 227 ff.; and "The International Disequilibrium System," *Kyklos*, vol. 14, 1961, pp. 153 ff. See also H. G. Johnson, "Theoretical Problems of the International Monetary System," *The Pakistan Development Review*, Spring 1967, pp. 1 ff.

[8] J. R. Hicks, "Mr. Keynes and the Classics," *Econometrica*, vol. 5, April 1937; and Alvin Hansen, *Monetary Theory and Fiscal Policy*, New York, McGraw-Hill, 1949. The reader may like to consult a textbook in macro theory; for instance, Gardner Ackley, *Macroeconomic Theory*, New York, Macmillan, 1961, pp. 359 ff.

332

How jointly to
achieve external and
internal equilibrium

rate gives rise to an increase in investment, producing an expansionary effect on the national income. If the interest rate falls from r_1 to r_3, for instance, the national income, in money terms, will expand from Y_1 to Y_3. This whole type of analysis is of a short-run character based on the usual Keynesian assumptions.

A shift in the IS curve, for instance from IS_1 to IS_2, symbolizes a change in the investment–savings behavior. It implies that the producers in the economy wish to invest more for any given level of interest rates. If there is, to start with, equilibrium at the interest rate r_1 and national income Y_1 and producers suddenly want to invest more (to take advantage perhaps of some new innovations), there will be an expansionary effect on the national income, increasing it from Y_1 to Y_2.

The LM curves show the interdependence among money supply, interest rate, and national income. A point on a given curve shows at what combination of interest rate and national income a given money supply will be demanded and hence equilibrium in the money market created. The positive slope of the curve is based on the assumption that if the national income expands, the demand for money will increase and hence the interest rate will increase if the money supply remains constant. If the money supply is increased, the LM curve will shift to the right. This implies that the availability of credit increases, having an expansionary effect on the national income in monetary terms and leading to a fall in the interest rate. This is illustrated in Figure 18.2 by the fact that if the LM curve shifts from LM_1 to LM_2 with a given IS curve, the national income increases from Y_1 to Y_3 and the interest rate falls from r_1 to r_3.

We can now combine Figure 18.2 with diagrams showing the interdependence between the national income and the trade balance and between the interest rate and capital imports. This is done in Figure 18.3.

The northeast quadrant (I) in Figure 18.3 reproduces the same IS and LM curves as those of Figure 18.2. We measure the national income both on the right horizontal axis and on the lower vertical axis. Hence we can project the national income Y_1 on to the latter axis as is done in Figure 18.3. The southwest quadrant (III) shows the relationship between national income and the trade balance, T. The trade balance is a function of national income. A surplus in the trade balance will fall if the national income increases. The reason is that an increase in national income in monetary terms gives rise to an increase in imports. The northwest quadrant (IV) shows the relationship between the interest rate and international capital movements.

FIGURE 18.3

External and internal equilibrium in a model with capital movements

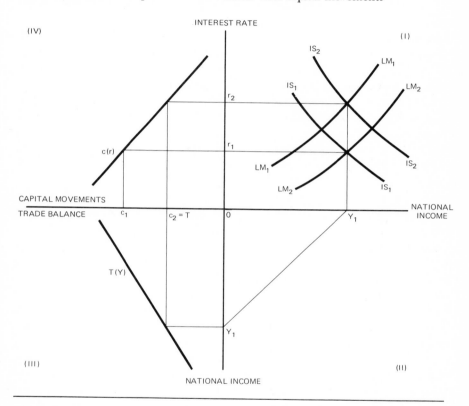

Capital movements are assumed to be a function of the interest level in the country. The lower the interest, the higher are the exports of capital. If the interest rate is r_1, capital exports will amount to Oc_1; if the interest level is r_2, capital exports will only amount to Oc_2. If the interest level in the country is high enough, the country will instead import capital.

We can now set the play in motion. Let us assume that we start with an investment behavior characterized by the IS_1 curve and a money supply characterized by the LM_2 curve. This generates a national income Y_1, the full employment income. This national income is connected with a trade

334

How jointly to
achieve external and
internal equilibrium

surplus of T. The interest rate is r_1. At this interest rate, there is an outflow of capital amounting to Oc_1. Hence there is a deficit in the balance of payments of $c_1 T$.

Given the investment–savings behavior depicted by the IS_1 curve, the money supply denoted by the LM_2 curve, and the interest rate r_1, the country will reach a level of full employment. As the capital exports are larger than the surplus in the balance of trade, however, the country will have a deficit in its balance of payments, reaching one of its policy aims, internal equilibrium, but not the other, external equilibrium.

To achieve external equilibrium, a change in monetary policy is required. Yet this alone is not enough. A change in monetary policy will also necessarily influence the level of employment. Hence an offsetting change in fiscal policy is needed to keep the national income at the full employment level. A new mix of monetary and fiscal policy has to be established, symbolized by a change in both the IS and the LM curves.

The supply of money has to be decreased, and we move from the LM_2 curve to the LM_1 curve. This will raise the interest rate to r_2. This will have a depressive effect on national income, and investment has hence to be stimulated by means of fiscal policy. Such stimulation may take the form of a lowering in taxes of corporations, for instance, or else the government may increase its spending. This will mean a shift in the IS curve from IS_1 to IS_2, and there will again be full employment but at the higher rate of interest, r_2. The surplus in the trade balance will again be equal to OT. At the higher interest level capital exports will decrease to Oc_2. Hence there will also be equilibrium in the balance of payments.

This argument shows how monetary and fiscal policy can be used together to give external and internal equilibrium in a model with fixed exchange rates. It should, however, be observed that no adjustment mechanism of the traditional type is at work here to create both external and internal equilibrium. There is nothing in the above situation which will eventually restore the relationship between foreign and domestic prices which could give the country external equilibrium at full employment with a more " neutral " policy mix; everything else being equal, the country will have to restrict its capital exports forever, or if it is an importer of capital, continue importing capital forever.

How to judge a situation such as the one above depends very much on circumstances. It may be argued, for instance, that if a country has a deficit in its trade balance and covers it with capital imports, it depends on the fact that the country's price level is out of control, that its wages and prices rise faster than its competitors'. If the country continues to cover its deficits with capital imports, the domestic price level will become more and more out of line with those of competing countries. The interest rate will have to increase more and more in order to attract foreign capital, and finally the country will fall into an untenable position. In this case a policy mix of the type discussed can be said to imply only a postponement of the necessary adjustment.

It may also be, however, that a policy of deficits in balance of trade and of capital imports leads to an increase in the rate of domestic investment within the country and to more rapid economic growth. If the growth is of a specific kind, it may after some time affect the balance of trade positively. Then the country will get equilibrium in its trade balance, enabling it to lower the interest rate and possibly become a capital exporter. In this case the policy mix has given the economy needed breathing space, permitting the economy to develop in such a fashion that equilibrium in the balance of current account will be reached without any immediate adjustment.

We have stressed earlier that capital movements are very important for a smooth functioning of the world economy. A policy that consciously tries to take advantage of capital movements and direct them into channels that will enable many countries to reach jointly external and internal equilibrium will therefore have an important role to play. We will return to this question in Part V, where we shall deal with the international monetary system.

We should also make a couple of more marginal comments in connection with the monetary–fiscal policy model for reaching external and internal equilibrium. We mentioned, in the discussion of aims and means, that it was important to combine aims and means efficiently. If monetary policy is used to achieve a desired level of capital imports, a change in this parameter will also affect the other aim, full employment. If one authority handles one means, if the central bank controls monetary policy and is responsible for external equilibrium while the Ministry of Finance controls fiscal policy and is responsible for internal equilibrium, it may be impossible to achieve both aims jointly if each authority takes action separately. If the system has some unstable features, the disturbing side effects of one means on the other aim can be so great that external and internal equilibrium will never be reached. Therefore it is necessary that either both authorities co-operate closely, or that one authority handle both means.

336

How jointly to
achieve external and
internal equilibrium

In the actual example we discussed in connection with Figure 18.3, the composition of domestic investment was changed, but its volume remained the same. At the same time external equilibrium was reached by a decrease in foreign investment, and hence total domestic savings decreased, which could imply a loss in welfare. By the increase in interest rate, private investors were bribed to invest more at home and less abroad. At the same time private investment fell and had to be supplemented by public investment. Because of the fall in total savings, the future national income (including returns on foreign investment) will be smaller than otherwise. The welfare loss will be apparent to future taxpayers who will have to finance a larger public debt than would otherwise have been the case. From this point of view, devaluation would have been a more appropriate policy, as it would have permitted a larger volume of domestic savings with joint external-internal equilibrium.

We have now seen how different means of economic policy can be used to achieve full employment and equilibrium in the balance of payments. We shall return to these problems and discuss them in a wider setting in Part V. As we should now have a reasonable grasp of the balance-of-payments problem from the point of view of one single country, we can then deal much more efficiently with the problems of the international monetary system.

Before coming to that, we also have to discuss problems of trade policy. We shall start with the theory of tariffs, continue with common markets and the theory of customs unions, and finally discuss some current problems of trade policy. We should be well prepared for this undertaking, as we have now studied both real and monetary aspects of international economics.

SELECTED BIBLIOGRAPHY: CHAPTER 18

For a general discussion of aims and means in economic policy see:

B. Hansen, *The Economic Theory of Fiscal Policy*, London, Allen & Unwin, 1958.

J. Tinbergen, *On the Theory of Economic Policy*, Amsterdam, 1952.

Important works discussing the problem of internal and external balance under different assumptions about which means are allowed to be used are:

M. Corden, "The Geometric Representation of Policies to Attain Internal and External Balance," *RES*, October 1960.

H. G. Johnson, "Theoretical Problems of the International Monetary System," *The Pakistan Development Review*, Spring 1967.

J. E. Meade, *The Balance of Payments*, London, 1951, chaps. 9–10.

R. M. Mundell, *International Economics*, New York, 1968, chaps. 11 and 14–18.

T. W. Swan, "Longer-Run Problems of the Balance of Payments," *RIE*, chap. 27.

PART IV

Trade policy

Tariffs under optimal market conditions

19

In Part IV we shall discuss questions of trade policy, and the first chapter will deal with the theory of tariffs under optimal conditions. We shall study what the effects of tariffs are, assuming that competitive conditions prevail in commodity and factor markets. Tariffs are, however, not the only means of trade policy that a country can use. Other important means are quotas and quantitative restrictions. They will be dealt with in Chapter 20.

Markets may not always be fully competitive. A time-honored argument for tariffs is the infant-industry argument, which states that tariffs may be needed to give an industry time to develop and become competitive. This argument will be discussed in Chapter 21, which will be devoted to tariffs under suboptimal conditions. Chapter 21 will also deal with the use of tariffs to foster economic development, and with a comparison of tariffs with other policy means for correcting distortions in commodity and factor markets.

Chapters 22 and 23 are devoted to a discussion of some current problems in trade policy. One of the central international organizations for trade policy is GATT (General Agreement on Tariffs and Trade). We will deal with the philosophy behind GATT and the results of the Kennedy Round in Chapter 22. An important element in postwar economic development is the growth of common markets. The most spectacular of these is the European Common Market. The development of regional trade groupings is also described in Chapter 22. The economic theory of customs unions is surveyed in Chapter 24. UNCTAD (United Nations Conference for Trade and Development) tackled some important issues of trade policy from the point of view of the less-developed countries at its conferences in Geneva in 1964 and in New Delhi in 1968. Examples of issues dealt with by UNCTAD are policies for stabilizing raw material prices and tariff preferences for developing countries. We shall look at these problems in Chapter 23.

Chapter 25, finally, is devoted to another important issue in international economics, that of direct investment. For some, direct investment is the most important way of speeding up economic development and bridging the gulf between industrial and less-developed countries; others view it as a vehicle of imperialism and neocolonialism. In Chapter 25 we shall deal with the economic significance of direct investment.

There are many reasons a country applies tariffs, and tariffs have long been used. Classical economics taught, as we have seen, the blessings of free trade. During the eighteenth and the beginning of the nineteenth century, tariffs were used primarily to raise government revenue. The taxing

341

of imports is probably the easiest existing means by which a government may acquire income. In the 1840s the teaching of the classical economists started to bear fruit in their home country, England. Income taxes were introduced, protection of agriculture was abolished, and the famous corn laws were repealed in 1846. Capitalists and workers joined forces against the landowning class, and the tariffs which helped English agriculture were abolished. England continued its course toward free trade and was, from the 1850s to World War I, a free trading nation for all practical purposes.

Other European countries, especially France and Germany, followed England's path and lowered already low tariffs in the 1860s. The United States alone stood as a fairly protectionist nation, although a trend toward the liberalization of trade was also predominant. World trade grew at an extremely fast rate during this period, as we learned in Chapter 8.

Soon, however, demands for a more protectionist policy were heard. There were two specific factors in the 1870s which helped protectionism. One was the invasion of the European Continent by cheap grain from the United States and Russia, made possible by railways, steamships, and innovations in agriculture. The other was the depression of 1873–1879, the longest and deepest period of stagnant trade the world had yet known. Distressed farmers in Germany and France started to ask for protection. At first Bismarck in Germany did not want to listen to them, but as the need for government income grew, he gave in, and during the 1880s tariffs on iron and food products were introduced. France revised her trade policy in the 1890s and increased tariffs.

The period between World Wars I and II saw a drastic increase in tariffs and other trade impediments; the 1930s especially was a period when protectionism increased. Since World War II the trend, especially among leading industrial nations, has been toward trade liberalization. Many impediments to trade have been abolished and the average level of tariffs has fallen.

We shall now examine the effects of tariffs.

THE THEORY OF TARIFFS: SOME PARTIAL ASPECTS

Tariff theory is quite complicated. To begin with, therefore, it may be useful to study the effects of a tariff in a simple geometric fashion in a partial way, i.e., disregarding all its secondary effects.

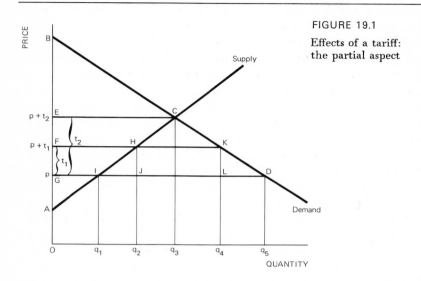

FIGURE 19.1

Effects of a tariff:
the partial aspect

The effect of a tariff is to raise the price of the good on which duty is levied. This is illustrated in Figure 19.1. Before the tariff, the price is p, and Oq_5 of the good is consumed; of this amount Oq_1 is produced within the country and q_1q_5 is imported. We then say that the tariff t_1 is levied on the good. This raises the price to $p + t_1$. Consumption falls to Oq_4, as the price of the good in the domestic market has increased. Domestic production at the same time increases with q_1q_2 to Oq_2 and imports fall to q_2q_4.

If a higher tariff, t_2, were levied on the good, the price would increase even further, to $p + t_2$. Domestic production would then increase to Oq_3 and consumption would fall to Oq_3. Hence consumption would equal domestic production and imports would fall to zero. The tariff t_2 is an example of a prohibitive tariff, i.e., a tariff high enough to curtail all imports of the good.

We have now seen that a tariff affects prices, consumption, production, and imports. It is now time to study the economic costs of a tariff. Implicit in the argument for free trade is a proposition that a situation with a tariff is worse than one with free trade. A tariff must then involve a cost for society, and we shall now examine the nature of this cost, the cost of protection, as it is often called.

We can use the tariff t_1 to illustrate the cost of protection. The increase in the domestic price of the good due to the tariff has caused a loss in consumers' surplus of $FKDG$.[1] This is a loss which the consumers of the good have to bear. Part of this loss in consumers' surplus goes to the government in the form of tariff revenue. This part equals $JHKL$. Another part of the loss in consumers' surplus goes to producers in the form of an increase in producers' surplus.[2] This part is $GIHF$. This leaves the two triangles IJH and KLD unaccounted for, and together these two measure the cost of protection for society as a whole.

The first of these two triangles, IJH, measures the production cost of protection. If the country had imported the amount q_1q_2 of the good, instead of producing it at home, its cost would have been $q_1q_2\,JI$. Now when the country chooses to produce it in its domestic industry the cost will be $q_1q_2\,HI$. The difference IJH represents a misallocation of resources brought about by the tariff. The economic reason for this is that if the country had used resources to a value of $q_1q_2\,JI$ in its export industry, it would have produced enough exports to buy q_1q_2 of the imported good. When it instead produces it at home in a protected industry, it has to devote a larger amount of resources, $q_1q_2\,HI$, to produce q_1q_2 of the imported good.

The second of the two triangles, KLD, measures the consumption cost of protection. The tariff introduces distortion in consumption. Because

---

[1] The consumers' surplus obtained from buying Oq_5 of the good at price p is represented by the triangle BDG. The idea is that the total satisfaction which consumers get from consuming Oq_5 of the good is represented by the whole area under the demand curve, i.e., BDq_5O. But they only have to pay the amount GDq_5O for getting this satisfaction. Hence the consumers' surplus equals BDG. Similarly, the consumers' surplus obtained from buying Oq_4 at price $p + t_1$ equals BKF.

This Marshallian concept of consumers' surplus has important limitations. It is based on the assumption that the marginal utility of money is constant—that the real income of consumers is not affected by the change in price and consumption of that commodity. It is a partial approach also in the sense that it disregards all cross effects on the demand for other goods from a change in the relative price structure.

[2] The cost for the domestic producers of producing the quantity Oq_1 is measured by the area under the supply curve, i.e., Oq_1IA. Their revenue equals Oq_1IG. The difference is called the producers' surplus. It consists at production Oq_1 of the triangle AIG. When production increases to Oq_2 the producers' surplus increases to AHF. Hence the increase in producers' surplus equals the area $GIHF$.

of the tariff, the value to the international producer of a unit of the good will be lower than the value to the domestic consumer. For the consumer, the tariff on the good will raise the price in comparison to other goods, giving rise to a distortion of consumption for the consumers. The size of this consumption cost of protection is measured by the triangle *KLD*.

It was assumed in the preceding analysis that the price of the good increased by the whole amount of the tariff. This is the same as assuming that the terms of trade are not affected by the tariff. This is an example of the partial aspect of the analysis, but it is hardly a realistic assumption.

When a tariff is levied on the good, we would expect its price in the domestic market to increase, decreasing consumption of the good and causing imports to fall. When imports fall, foreign exporters probably decrease the price of the good to try to recapture part of their lost sales. This means that the terms of trade of the country levying the tariff will improve, implying that the price of the good in the domestic market will increase by less than the full amount of the tariff. Only if the country levying the tariff is so small that a change in its demand will have no effect on international prices, or if the foreign supply elasticity is infinitely large, will the terms of trade not be affected by the tariff.

An improvement in a country's terms of trade implies an improvement in the country's real income. Cannot this gain from a tariff be so large as to outweigh the cost of protection we have just been discussing? Yes, it can be. We shall return to this question shortly when discussing the optimum tariff.

For the time being, however, we shall sum up what we have learned from a partial analysis of the effects of tariffs. The price of the good on which a tariff is levied will be raised in the domestic market. Imports will fall and the domestic production of the good increase. The government will receive an increased income in the form of tariff revenue. The national income of the country, however, will fall in the normal case because of the greater inefficiency in production and the distortion of consumption which the tariff entails.

All these results are by and large true even within the context of a more refined, general-equilibrium type of analysis, as we shall soon demonstrate.

Tariff policy has in most countries been a widely discussed political issue, because the tariff has been felt to have a very direct impact on the well-being of the citizens. If a tariff can save the livelihood of some citizens, it is understandable that they are interested in the existence or removal of that tariff.

Classical and neoclassical economists by and large advocated the virtues of free trade, but their success was limited. One of the reasons may have been that they did not fully understand the effects of a tariff on income distribution. Modern economics has achieved a very striking result in this respect, the so-called Stolper–Samuelson theorem, which is easily demonstrated with the tools at hand. As it is also the easiest result to verify in general-equilibrium tariff theory, we shall therefore begin to study the effects of tariffs in a framework of general equilibrium by looking into the effects of tariffs on income distribution.

TARIFFS AND INCOME DISTRIBUTION: THE STOLPER–SAMUELSON THEOREM

The Stolper–Samuelson theorem is best studied with the help of a box diagram. In Figure 19.2 we have the usual box diagram, with a contract curve OO'. (For the sake of convenience the isoquants are omitted.) Input of labor is measured on the horizontal axis and input of capital is measured on the vertical axis. Output of exportables is measured from the lower left-hand corner and output of importables from the upper right-hand corner. We start from a situation with free trade, when the country is producing at point P.

A tariff on the import good means, as we have seen, that the domestic price of importables rises. Domestic producers then change their production, increasing production of the import good and decreasing production of the export good. This is illustrated in the diagram by a movement from point P to point P'. What are the implications for factor prices?

We see immediately from the diagram that the production method in the export sector becomes more labor-intensive. Labor intensity also increases in the import-competing sector, the reason being that as producers start expanding production of importables (which are capital-intensive), they are especially eager to get more capital. Hence the relative price of capital is bid up. Producers then try to substitute labor for capital and the production methods become more labor intensive. The result is that the rent for capital

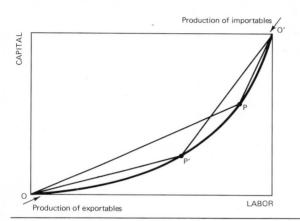

FIGURE 19.2

The Stolper–Samuelson theorem

goes up and the wage falls. The tariff causes income distribution to turn in favor of capitalists and against labor.

With a more general formulation we can say that a tariff favors the factor used intensively in the import-competing sector, because, as the tariff raises the price of the import good production of it will expand, and the demand for the factor used intensively in this industry will increase and its price will rise: The income distribution will unambiguously change in its favor.

We can also see this very clearly from looking into what happens to marginal productivities. When production moves from P to P', the marginal productivity of labor falls and that of capital increases. The explanation for this is that as factors of production are reallocated and moved from the labor-intensive export sector to the capital-intensive import sector, more workers tend to be allocated to each machine, with the result that the marginal productivity of capital increases while that of labor decreases. The wage and the return to one unit of capital is determined, however, by its respective marginal productivity. As there is full employment in both situations, it thus follows that labor's share of the national income has to fall while that of capital increases.

One of the assumptions in the analysis (and in the use of the box diagram) is that production functions are homogeneous of the first degree. This implies that the factor rewards exhaust the total product, in other words, that all the income generated in production is divided between the factors of production (in our case labor and capital) and that profits are zero, as they have been competed away in the equilibrium situation.[3]

Let us denote the total labor force by L, the total amount of capital by C, the wage by w, and the return to capital by r. The national income, Y, is then

$$Y = L \cdot w + C \cdot r \qquad (19.1)$$

Labor's share of the national income is then $L \cdot w$ and capital's share is $C \cdot r$. Let us say that equation 19.1 denotes the situation under free trade, i.e., the situation at P in Figure 19.2. The situation at P' can then be denoted by

$$Y^* = L \cdot w^* + C \cdot r^* \qquad (19.2)$$

where Y^* is the new national income and w^* and r^* the new wage and the new return to capital, respectively.

The marginal productivities, and hence the wage and the return to capital, are a function of the factor intensities alone. We know that with a tariff, at P', $r^* > r$ and $w^* < w$. From this follows that $L \cdot w^* < L \cdot w$ and that $C \cdot r^* > C \cdot r$, and that labor's share of the national income has fallen while that of capital has increased.

Yet could it not be the case that the national income has fallen because of the tariff, that Y^* is smaller than Y, and that although capital's share has increased, the capitalists will receive a larger share of a smaller national income and hence possibly suffer in absolute terms? But this is impossible. It is possible that the national income falls because of the tariff, a question to which we shall shortly return. But the return to the scarce factor, in our case capital, must increase in both relative and absolute terms. Because of the reallocation of resources, the methods of production will become more labor intensive in both lines of production, and the marginal productivity of capital will increase in both sectors. Hence, in whichever good we measure the return to capital, its reward will increase and the capitalists will receive a larger income in real terms.

The Stolper–Samuelson theorem demonstrates that the effects of a tariff are unambiguous within the context of the standard trade model. Following the Heckscher–Ohlin reasoning we can say that a country exports

---

[3] For a proof of this proposition see, for instance, R. G. D. Allen, *Mathematical Analysis for Economists*, London, Macmillan, 1938, pp. 317 ff.

the good which it produces primarily with the help of its abundant factor of production. A tariff will decrease production of exportables and lead to an increase in production of the import-competing good, and benefit the scarce factor—that used intensively in the import sector. Thus a tariff will benefit a country's scarce factor of production in an unambiguous fashion and cause the real income of the abundant factor to fall.

The Stolper–Samuelson theorem is based on some rather stringent assumptions; most of those needed to reach the Heckscher–Ohlin results, set out and discussed in Chapters 3 and 4, are also required for the Stolper–Samuelson theorem. Competitive conditions in commodity and factor markets are assumed, production functions are homogeneous of degree one, and there is always full employment. Furthermore, the theorem was only proved for the standard case with only two goods and two factors of production. But it can be generalized and some of the assumptions erased. The assumption of two goods is not critical. As long as we can classify the goods according to factor intensities, we are able to establish the results, although there are many goods. To increase the number of factors and still get the main result is more problematic; it is then difficult even to define what is meant by factor intensity. The assumption about linearly homogeneous production functions is also crucial. But the assumption about competitive markets can probably be released without the main result being more than at the most slightly changed.

In practice the theorem can therefore also be said to provide valuable insight into the effects of a tariff on income distribution. It is no longer possible to believe simply that free trade will benefit all groups of society. On the contrary, the presumption is that a tariff will benefit one of the factors of production at the expense of the other. History has many examples of economic groups which have tried to foster their cause by demanding tariffs. It is quite probable that they often were right in the sense that they had a correct understanding of the fact that tariffs would further their own economic interests.

Thus the general result of economic theory is that a tariff lowers the national income but benefits the country's scarce factor of production. We studied the dual result of this in Chapter 6 when we saw that free trade generally increases a country's national income but harms the factor of production used intensively in the import-competing sector of production.

In establishing the Stolper–Samuelson result, we assumed that a tariff will always increase the price of the import good in the domestic market. This amounts to assuming (as did Stolper and Samuelson) that the terms of trade are not affected by the tariff, which is a rather strong assumption, because in the normal case we would expect the terms of trade to improve through the tariff. Yet as long as the improvement in the terms of trade is no larger than the tariff, the domestic price of the import good will still increase, and this is the only factor necessary for the country to have a movement in the "right" direction along its contract curve, i.e., in the direction from P to P' in Figure 19.2. Could it not, however, be the case, that the improvement in the terms of trade is so large that it is larger than the tariff? This implies that a tariff will lead to a fall in the price of the import good in the domestic market, and the result for the income distribution would then be the opposite to the Stolper–Samuelson theorem. To deal with this question we have to study the effects of a tariff explicitly on the terms of trade and domestic prices.

TARIFFS, TERMS OF TRADE, AND DOMESTIC PRICES

We assumed in the beginning of this chapter that a tariff increased the domestic price of a good by the whole amount of the tariff, and it was later stated that this was hardly a realistic assumption. It is true that the immediate effect of a tariff is to increase the price of a good, but a tariff will also trigger a series of secondary events. It will affect not only the consumption and production of the good itself, but also production and consumption of other goods, thereby affecting all relative prices.

It is now time to study the effects of a tariff on prices in a general equilibrium setting, and for this offer curves are convenient. Figure 19.3 shows offer curves for Countries I and II in a situation of free trade. Country I has a comparative advantage in wheat and Country II in cloth. The free trade offer curves are given by I and II, respectively. Equilibrium is established at point P, and OC of cloth is exchanged for OW of wheat. The equilibrium terms of trade are given by the ray OP from the origin.

Country I now introduces a 50 percent tariff. This means that there will be a downward shift in the country's offer curve. The new offer curve is I'. As importers in Country I now have to pay a 50 percent tariff, they are only willing to give OW'''' of wheat for OC of cloth; the additional amount

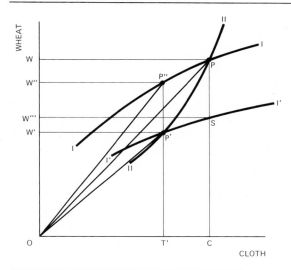

FIGURE 19.3

Effect of a tariff
on terms of trade
and domestic prices

PS $(= WW''')$ they will have to pay as a tariff. This amount, which is 50 percent of CS, and which formerly went to the exporters in Country II, will now go to the government in Country I in the form of tariff revenue. PS is one third of PC or 50 percent of SC. A 50 percent tariff will, analogously, cause all the points on the new, tariff-ridden offer curve to lie one third closer to the horizontal axis than a corresponding point on the free trade offer curve. In this way the exact shape of Country I's new offer curve can be derived.

After the imposition of the tariff, a new equilibrium is established. This is at point P', where Country I's new offer curve intersects Country II's offer curve. The volumes traded have decreased because of the tariff, and the terms of trade have improved for Country I. This can be seen from the fact that the ratio of exports divided by imports has decreased, as $T'P'/W'P'$ is smaller than CP/WP, which implies that Country I now receives more imports per unit of exports, also illustrated by the fact that the ray from the origin measuring the new terms of trade, OP', falls to the right of OP, the ray measuring the terms of trade under free trade.

This is also the standard result. Only if Country II's supply elasticity of exports were infinitely large, and the country's offer curve a straight line, would the terms of trade be unaffected by the tariff. Then the only result would be a decrease in the volume of trade, but at unchanged terms of trade.

Hence the terms of trade will improve for the tariff-imposing country, except in the limiting case in which the foreign country has a completely elastic offer curve, when the terms of trade are not affected by the tariff. In general it can be said that the larger the price elasticities of demand and supply in the foreign country, the smaller is the change in the terms of trade.[4] Large values on any one of these elasticities imply that either consumers or producers (or both if the two elasticities are large) are sensitive to changes in relative prices. If the demand elasticity is large, it means that consumers are easily able to substitute exportables for importables in consumption; if the supply elasticity is large, it means that producers can move factors of production easily from one sector to the other. In other words, the larger the adaptability in a country's economy, the smaller the chances are that it will suffer deteriorating terms of trade because of tariff increases in other countries.[5]

For the income distribution it is, however, not the effect on the terms of trade that is important but the effect on domestic prices. In the international market, the country will exchange OW' of wheat for OT' of cloth, but domestic importers will have to pay more in the domestic market: they will have to give OW''' of wheat to acquire OT' of cloth, because they must also pay a tariff amounting to $W'W'''$. Hence the price of the import good will increase in the domestic market as is seen from the fact that the fraction OW'''/OT' is larger than the fraction OW/OC, or from the fact that the ray from the origin representing the new domestic price, OP'', falls to the left of the ray OP. (Under free trade, before the tariff was introduced, the international terms of trade and the relative domestic price of the goods were, of course, the same.)

The result of our investigation so far is that a tariff improves the terms of trade for the country, but that this improvement in the terms of trade is not large enough to offset the tariff. Hence the domestic price of the import good will increase. This implies that the Stolper–Samuelson result holds

---

[4] See Bo Södersten and Karl Vind, "Tariffs and Trade in General Equilibrium," *American Economic Review*, June 1968, for a formal proof of this proposition.
[5] The reader may observe that essentially the same mechanism is at work here as in Chapter 9 in connection with the effects of economic growth on the terms of trade. The factors set out in the numerator of expressions 9A.8 and 9.1 play the same role here as they did in connection with economic growth there.

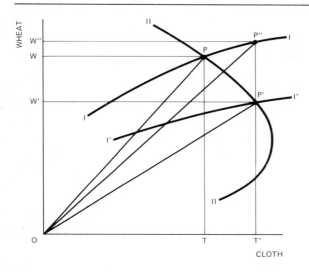

FIGURE 19.4

Effect of a tariff
on domestic prices:
inelastic offer curve

good, and that the tariff will benefit the factor of production used intensively in the import-competing sector.

The results just referred to for the effects of a tariff on the terms of trade and on domestic prices are standard. No one seems to doubt that a tariff will improve a country's terms of trade, or, in the limiting case, leave them unchanged. The effect on domestic prices is a more disputed question in economic literature. We will, therefore, go on to relate a case according to which the effect on domestic prices ought to be the opposite of the one just stated.

It is again convenient to use geometry to present the argument. Figure 19.4 illustrates offer curves for Country I and Country II, denoted by *I* and *II*, respectively. The difference is now that Country II has an inelastic offer curve. Under free trade the equilibrium is at point *P*. Country I still has a comparative advantage in the production of wheat, and exchanges *OW* of wheat for *OT* of cloth at the terms of trade *OP*. When Country I introduces a 50 percent tariff, there is a downward shift in its offer curve from *I* to *I'*. The new point of equilibrium is at *P'*, and *OW'* of wheat is traded for *OT'* of textiles. Because of the fact that Country II's offer curve is inelastic in the relevant range, a large improvement is produced in the terms of trade of Country I. The improvement is, in fact, so large that the country with the tariff receives a larger amount of imports for a smaller amount of exports. The new terms of trade are given by the ray OP' from the origin.

In the domestic market the relative price of wheat will be higher, and domestic consumers will have to pay OW'' of wheat for OT' of cloth; thus in the domestic market the relative price of imports has also fallen. This can be seen from the fact that the ratio OW''/OT' is smaller than the fraction OW/OT, and hence domestic consumers, even when the tariff is included in the domestic price of importables, will get more of the imported good for one unit of exportables than they did under free trade. This can also be seen from the fact that the ray from origin representing domestic price, OP'', is to the right of OP.

If the price of the imported good falls in the domestic market because of the tariff, then the effects on income distribution are the opposite to the ones suggested by the Stolper–Samuelson theorem. As the relative price of imports falls, the relative price of exports rises. This means that production of exportables will be more profitable because of the tariff, and resources will be transferred from the import-competing sector to the export sector. The factor reward of the factor used intensively in the export sector will increase and the income distribution will turn in favor of the country's abundant factor of production, i.e., the one used intensively in the export sector.

This is a quite striking result, first set out in a classic article by Lloyd A. Metzler.[6] He admitted that the result to be expected was a fall in the relative price of importables in the domestic market, but he argued that if the following condition were fulfilled, the relative price of imports would instead increase in the domestic market:

$$\eta < 1 - k \tag{19.3}$$

where η is defined as Country II's demand elasticity for Country I's (the tariff-imposing country) exports, and $1 - k$ is defined as Country I's marginal propensity to consume its export good. Condition 19.3 says, in other words, that only if the trading partner's (i.e., the rest of the world's) demand elasticity for the tariff-imposing country's exports is larger than that country's marginal propensity to consume exportables, will the price of the im-

[6] L. A. Metzler, "Tariffs, the Terms of Trade, and the Distribution of National Income," *Journal of Political Economy*, vol. 57, February 1949.

port good increase in the country which has levied the tariff. If the country's marginal propensity to consume its export good is larger than the foreign demand elasticity confronting its exports, the domestic price of imports will instead fall because of the tariff. We observe that the country's marginal propensity to consume its exportables can never be larger than unity. If the foreign demand elasticity (η) is larger than unity, an orthodox result always follows.

It is fairly easy to understand the economics behind Metzler's result. The larger a country's marginal propensity to consume exportables, the larger is the amount of its tariff revenue spent on demanding the good exported by the country. Hence an excess demand for exports may come from this source. If the foreign country's demand elasticity for the first country's exports is low, it means that its demand for this good will fall only slightly, although its relative price increases. Under such circumstances, a tariff could create an excess demand in the tariff-imposing country's market for its export good. If this happens, the price of imports will fall because of the tariff.[7]

However, the Metzler result has been disputed. Södersten and Vind argue that Metzler has posed the problem artificially.[3] If it is assumed that the tariff income is spent according to the same principles as all other income, the Metzler result cannot be produced, and the result is then clear cut. A tariff will always turn the terms of trade in favor of a country and cause the domestic price of imports to go up. This implies that the Stolper–Samuelson theorem holds unambiguously and that a tariff always will turn the income distribution in favor of the factor of production which is used intensively in the import-competing sector. Metzler's result depends on (still with reference to the above authors) the fact that he has introduced a question of income redistribution artificially, by assuming that the tariff income will be spent in ways different from those of other incomes. There is no reason, they argue, why the effects of a tax or a tariff should be made to hinge on the specific way in which the income from this tax or tariff is spent. If this is not the case, and the effects of a tariff are dealt with "neutrally" as suggested above, the results will be clear and unambiguous.

---

[7] Metzler refined his argument somewhat in a later article, "Tariffs, International Demand, and Domestic Prices," *Journal of Political Economy*, vol. 57, August 1949. The essence of the argument, however, remains unchanged. For a discussion and criticism of Metzler's two articles, see Södersten and Vind, *loc. cit.*
[8] Södersten and Vind, *loc. cit.*

We should now have gained a certain insight into the effects of a tariff on prices and income distribution in a general equilibrium setting. The time has now come to deal with another standard problem in tariff theory, the effects of a tariff on national income.

TARIFFS AND THE NATIONAL INCOME: THE OPTIMUM TARIFF

The effect of a tariff is to improve a country's terms of trade and to restrict trade by decreasing the volume of imports and exports. Often we would expect the negative effect of the misallocation of resources in production and of the distortion of consumption to be larger than the positive effect connected with the improvement in the terms of trade. There is then a cost involved in protection, the nature of which we discussed in the beginning of this chapter. It might, however, be that the positive effect on terms of trade is the larger; then there is a gain in protection. And if a country is in a situation of free trade it can always improve its welfare by applying the "right" tariff. This tariff, the tariff that maximizes a country's welfare, is called the optimum tariff. The optimum tariff is illustrated in Figure 19.5.

We start from a free trade situation where the curve I is Country I's offer curve and II is Country II's offer curve. Equilibrium under free trade is reached at point P, and the terms of trade are given by the ray OP (not shown) from the origin. There are also two sets of community indifference curves, $U_1 — U_1$, $U_1' — U_1'$, etc., for Country I and $U_2 — U_2$, $U_2' — U_2'$, etc., for Country II, which characterize the two countries' preference systems.

By applying a tariff, Country I will change its offer curve to I'. The new equilibrium will be at point P', where Country I's new, tariff-ridden offer curve cuts Country II's original, free-trade offer curve. The new terms of trade are given by the ray OP' (not shown) from the origin. This tariff, which changes Country I's offer curve from I to I', is the country's optimum tariff. This is shown by the fact that at point P' one of Country I's community indifference curves, $U_1' — U_1'$, is tangent to Country II's offer curve. This is the highest indifference curve that Country I can reach. The opti-

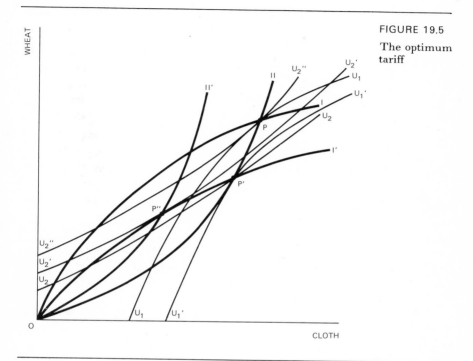

FIGURE 19.5

The optimum tariff

mum tariff is, in other words, a tariff that maximizes the real welfare of a country.

We should observe, however, that the optimum tariff only potentially maximizes a country's welfare. The optimum tariff will, like any tariff, affect the income distribution. It will make some better off but make others worse off. To increase a country's welfare in an unambiguous sense, therefore, the optimum tariff has to be accompanied by a redistribution policy to compensate those who are hurt by the tariff. As the optimum tariff by definition increases a country's total welfare, this will be possible and there will still be something left over for those who directly benefit from the tariff. It is in this sense that the optimum tariff is a proposition in welfare economics.

We can also see from Figure 19.5 that Country I's optimum tariff will have a negative effect on Country II. At point P, Country II was on the indifference curve $U_2'' - U_2''$. It will now be forced to point P' and will fall

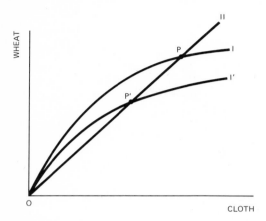

FIGURE 19.6

A case when a tariff
is not beneficial

on to a lower indifference curve, $U_2 - U_2$. The economic explanation for this is that Country II will both suffer deteriorating terms of trade and a decrease in its volume of foreign trade.

The only case in which Country I will not benefit from levying a tariff is when Country II's offer curve is a straight line from the origin, such as is illustrated in Figure 19.6.

Country II's offer curve is given by II and Country I's free trade offer curve by I. Under free trade, equilibrium will be at P and the terms of trade are given by OP. A tariff will change Country I's offer curve to I'. The new equilibrium will be at P'. The volume traded will be reduced, but the terms of trade stay unchanged. As Country I can only gain from a tariff if its terms of trade improve, its optimum tariff in this case will be a zero tariff. Hence free trade will maximize its welfare in this special case.

The economic explanation for Country II's offer curve being a straight line is that its price elasticity of supply for exports is infinitely large.[9] This means that the country without any cost or difficulty can shift factors of production from the export to the import-competing sector of production, and vice versa.

[9] In principle it could also be explained by the fact that the price elasticity of demand for importables is infinitely large, i.e., that exportables and importables are completely substitutable in consumption.

Leaving this special case aside, a single country can always improve its welfare by changing from free trade to a situation of optimum tariff, yet the restriction of trade that the optimum tariff implies will always hurt the second country. Both countries of course can play the tariff game, a convenient note on which to return to Figure 19.5.

Let us assume that Country I is the first country to introduce a tariff and that it levies an optimum tariff. That will take us to P'. The best that Country II can do in this situation is to levy a tariff that changes its offer curve to II'. The new trade equilibrium will be at P''. This will bring Country II to a new indifference curve, $U_2' - U_2'$, which represents higher welfare than the indifference curve passing through P' but a lower one than the indifference curve through P. This thus demonstrates that Country II can reach a higher level of welfare by retaliation, but that it cannot reach as high a level as that enjoyed under free trade.

Point P'' is not a stable equilibrium point according to the diagram. We would therefore expect the two countries to go on raising their tariffs until either all trade is killed off or a stable situation is reached, i.e., a situation in which both countries at the same time are levying what for each of them is the optimum tariff, taken the other country's tariff as given.

The moral of the story is that a country taken as a single unit can always gain by levying a tariff, provided that the other country does not retaliate. It could under specific circumstances gain, even if the other country did retaliate. From the individual country's point of view tariffs must therefore produce great attraction. It is only if both countries can jointly cooperate that we can hope for free trade. If we take both countries together, viewing them as a unit, free trade will be the optimal policy, since one country's gain from an optimum tariff will always be smaller than the other's loss from it. Free trade is in this sense the best policy, although it presupposes an internationalist point of view in order to be implemented.[10]

We should now have gained an insight into the meaning of the optimum tariff, although this concept can be still somewhat elusive. What determines, for instance, the height of the optimum tariff? To find an explicit answer to this question we would have to take a more formal approach and

[10] From the point of view of game theory, the optimum tariff is an example of the prisoner's dilemma. See R. D. Luce and H. Raiffa, *Games and Decisions*, New York, Wiley, 1957, pp. 94 ff.

develop a full algebraic model, and this would take us outside the scope of the present book.[11] We can, however, touch on some of the factors determining the height of the optimum tariff.

The higher a country's share of foreign trade, the larger is the scope for its optimum tariff, explained by the fact that the larger the share of national income which the country exports, the more effective will a given improvement in a country's terms of trade be. Otherwise the important factors stem from the second country (the rest of the world). Of the greatest importance are the effects produced by a change in relative prices on quantities consumed and supplied. The larger they are, the lower Country I should set its optimum tariff. A tariff in Country I will turn the terms of trade against Country II. If the second country's price elasticity of supply is high, the country has a flexible structure of production. Producers can easily switch their factors of production from one line of production to another. If this is the case, then the terms of trade will not change much because of the tariff and Country I will not stand to gain much by levying one. If the value of the supply elasticity is very large, there will be no change at all in relative prices because of a tariff, and Country I's best policy will be one of free trade. A high value of Country II's elasticity of demand for exports (or imports) with respect to a change in relative prices will play much the same role. It means that the goods are good substitutes and that consumers will easily adapt their habits of consumption to a change in relative prices.[12]

---

[11] For an explicit derivation of a formula for the optimum tariff, see Södersten and Vind, *loc. cit.* The formula they derive for the optimum tariff is

$$t_1^{\text{opt}} = \frac{\left(1 + t_2 \dfrac{\partial C_{2x}}{\partial Y_2}\right)(S_{1x} - C_{1x})}{(1 + t_2)\left[P(1 + t_2)\dfrac{\partial S_{2m}}{\partial P} + \dfrac{\partial C_{2x}}{\partial P} + S_{2m}\dfrac{\partial C_{2x}}{\partial Y_2}\right]} \tag{19.4}$$

where t_1^{opt} is Country I's optimum tariff and t_2 is Country II's tariff. Otherwise the symbols have the same meaning as in Chapter 9; i.e., $S_{1x} - C_{1x}$ is the exports of Country I, $\partial S_{2m}/\partial P$ and $\partial C_{2x}/\partial P$ are Country II's supply and demand elasticities with respect to relative prices, and $\partial C_{2x}/\partial Y_2$ is the marginal propensity to consume the export good of Country II. P is Country I's terms of trade and S_{2m} is the supply of import-competing goods in Country II.

[12] Quantity responses of supply and demand with respect to changes in relative prices play much the same role here as they did in connection with the effects of a tariff on prices and in connection with the effects of economic growth on the terms of trade.

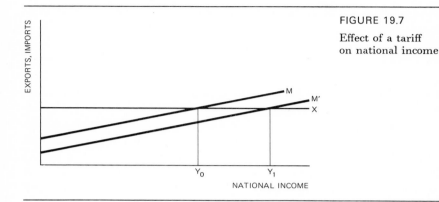

FIGURE 19.7

Effect of a tariff
on national income

Thinking in terms of developed and less-developed countries, we observe that industrial, developed countries usually have a high degree of flexibility in their economies both as far as supply and demand are concerned. Poor, less-developed countries often show a low degree of adaptability in their economies. This means that less-developed countries usually cannot expect to gain much from high tariffs and that their optimum tariffs are probably quite low. The developed countries might, from this point of view, have more to gain from exploiting a monopoly position by applying high tariffs. We could expect the optimum tariffs for these countries to be quite high at times; this applies especially to their trade with the less-developed countries.

The optimum tariff argument is important. Leaving dynamic considerations aside and assuming optimal market conditions, it is, from a welfare point of view, the only valid argument for a tariff. We have now seen how the main variables in a general equilibrium framework, i.e., prices, the national income, and the income distribution, are affected by a tariff. Before we conclude this chapter we will also mention in passing their effects on other variables.

OTHER EFFECTS OF TARIFFS

If a country has unemployment a tariff can be used to produce an expansionary effect on the national income. A tariff means, as we have seen, that imports will decrease and that the demand for home-produced goods will increase. This is illustrated in Figure 19.7.

Tariffs can be seen as a device switching demand away from international to home goods. We start, in Figure 19.7, with an export schedule X and an import schedule M, so that the national income will be Y_0. Because of the tariff the import schedule is moved down to M'. This implies that less imports and more home-produced goods will be demanded and that there will be an expansionary effect on the national income, which increases to Y_1. If there was unemployment at Y_0, it will obviously decrease as the national income expands.

The use of a tariff for eradicating unemployment is an example of what is sometimes called a " beggar-my-neighbor" policy. If there is unemployment in both trading countries, the country levying the tariff will export part of its unemployment to its trading partner, producing a negative effect on its national income and an increase in its rate of unemployment. It is therefore very likely that it will retaliate and in turn increase its tariff. Trade warfare could break out and the likely result be that no one will benefit from the gradual increases in tariffs.

It should be observed that only if the country levying the tariff has unemployment will the tariff produce a positive effect in real terms. Otherwise the tariff will only cause an increase in the national income in monetary terms.

If a country has unemployment, and provided that no retaliation occurs, a tariff can bring about a decrease in unemployment. The same effect can be brought about more efficiently, however, by means of monetary and fiscal policy.

A tariff will usually also have a positive effect on a country's balance of trade. The initial effect of an increase in tariffs is to cut imports but to leave exports unchanged, thus improving the balance of trade. At the same time the national income will expand, negatively affecting the balance of trade. Much now depends on the behavior of the trading partners. If repercussions are small and no retaliations occur, the trade balance may improve; but if imports in the tariff-increasing country go up very much because of the increase in income caused by the tariff, and if foreign repercussions are great, then the temporary improvement in the balance of trade may quickly be destroyed.

A more efficient way of improving a country's balance of trade is the appropriate use of monetary and fiscal policy, or devaluation, as described in Chapters 16 and 18.

SUMMARY

We have now studied some of the main effects of a tariff under competitive conditions. A tariff will improve a country's terms of trade and increase the domestic price of the imported good. This implies a reallocation of resources so that more home-produced and fewer traded goods will be produced. The import-competing industry will benefit and the income distribution will move in favor of the factor used intensively in the import-competing line of production.

A tariff will, at least if the starting point is free trade, lead to an increase in the income of the government. The national income will also be affected and an optimum tariff exists which will maximize a country's real income. A tariff will usually stimulate employment and lead to an improvement in a country's balance of trade.

SELECTED BIBLIOGRAPHY: CHAPTER 19

For a discussion of the concept "cost of protection," see:

> W. M. Corden, "The Calculation of the Cost of Protection," *Economic Record*, April 1957.

> H. G. Johnson, "The Cost of Protection and the Scientific Tariff," *JPE*, August 1960.

The standard essay on the effect of a tariff on the income distribution is:

> W. F. Stolper and P. A. Samuelson, "Protection and Real Wages," *RES*, November 1941 (reprinted in *RTIT*).

See also:

> J. Bhagwati, "Protection, Real Wages and Incomes," *EJ*, December 1959.

Two classical papers on the price effects of a tariff in a general equilibrium model are:

> L. A. Metzler, "Tariffs, the Terms of Trade, and the Distribution of National Incomes," *JPE*, February 1949 (reprinted in *RIE*).

L. A. Metzler, "Tariffs, International Demand and Domestic Prices," *JPE*, August 1949.

For a critical view of Metzler's results and a generalization and integration of the theory of tariffs, see:

B. Södersten and K. Vind, "Tariffs and Trade in General Equilibrium," *AER*, June 1968.

Concerning the optimum tariff see:

T. Scitovsky, "A Reconsideration of the Theory of Tariffs," *RES*, no. 2, 1942 (reprinted in *RTIT*).

For later works see:

J. de V. Graaff, "On Optimum Tariff Structures," *RES*, no. 1, 1949.

H. G. Johnson, *International Trade and Economic Growth*, London, 1958, chap. 2.

Quotas and
quantitative restrictions:
state trading

20

Tariffs are the most widely used means of trade policy for influencing prices and volumes in international trade, but there are other means. Quantitative restrictions and quotas are examples. We dealt with some implications of such means for the balance of payments in Chapter 16, under the heading of direct controls. We now give a somewhat more systematic account of their effects, and deal with the effects on " real factors " such as prices and volumes. We also touch briefly on another matter of interest in international trade: state trading.

THE USE OF TRADE RESTRICTIONS

We saw in Chapter 19 that the history of tariffs goes back to the beginnings of the national state. The principal reason for the use of the tariffs in its early days was the need for government revenue. The use of tariffs is probably the simplest means that a government has for raising revenue.

Quotas and other direct trade restrictions do not yield any income for the government, at least not directly. They came into practice later than tariffs. Direct trade restrictions are primarily used for protecting domestic industries and improving the balance of payments.

A brief summary of the history of trade regulations is far from easy. Wars and depressions seem to inspire an increase in protection. Otherwise, few generalizations are possible; regulations developed differently in different countries.

By and large, it can be said that the period from 1750 to 1850 saw a decline of trade restrictions. After World War I, the trend was in the opposite direction; the interwar period especially was characterized by an intensification of trade restrictions. After World War II, the international organizations for dealing with international trade and monetary policies, GATT and IMF, have sought to turn the tide. The developed, industrial countries have agreed not to use restrictive trade practices as an ordinary policy measure. The less-developed countries, however, use them frequently to deal with the balance-of-payments problems created by their own development efforts.

The attempts at liberalizing world trade and at dismantling trade restrictions have been quite successful since World War II; world trade has also grown at an unprecedented rate. Trade restrictions, however, are to a considerable extent still used. Several industrial countries have resorted to them on occasion when pressed by balance of payments difficulties. For less-developed countries, quotas and quantitative restrictions are very important policy means for controlling imports. There is no sign that these countries will change their policies in this respect.

THE EFFECTS OF QUOTAS

The effects of a quota have almost exclusively been analyzed under partial conditions, so we start with the partial case. As the effects of a quota have important similarities to those of a tariff, it is convenient to follow the analysis of tariffs quite closely, and Figure 20.1 is like Figure 19.1.

The world market price of the good is p. At this price, the country demands Oq_5 of the good and produces Oq_1. Thus, imports amount to q_1q_5. The country now decides that it will have to lower imports of the good. The authorities decide that imports will have to be reduced from q_1q_5 to q_2q_4.

A quota that reduces imports to q_2q_4, as in our example, will in many respects be equivalent to a tariff such as the one in Chapter 19, which increased the domestic price of the good from p to $p + t_1$ (the reader should note that the price p' in Figure 20.1 equals the price $p + t_1$ in Figure 19.1). The effect on domestic production and consumption will be the same, the effect on the home-market price and the international terms of trade will be the same, and the effect on imports will be the same. In one important respect, however, there is a difference: a tariff will give rise to a tariff revenue that will go to the government, whereas the quota will give rise to a gain of equal size that will go to the quota holders. If we assume that competitive conditions prevail in the import industry, a monopoly profit will accrue to the quota holders.

If the effects of a tariff are equivalent to those of a quota that limits imports by the same amount, why should the government use a quota instead of a tariff, only to deprive itself of tariff revenue?

Part of the answer is that the equivalence depends in a critical way on market conditions. Only on condition that there are competitive market conditions abroad, that there is free competition in the domestic import-competing industry, and that there is perfect competition among quota

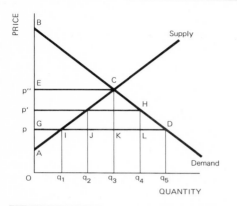

FIGURE 20.1

Effects of a quota: the partial aspect

holders, will a tariff be equivalent to a quota that limits imports to the same amount as the tariff.

But competitive conditions do not always hold in all the relevant markets. Quotas have typically been used to limit imports of agricultural products. They especially flourished in the 1930s because the supply of many products was very inelastic then. A country confronted with an inelastic supply of exports of certain goods would find it difficult to limit imports of the goods by way of a tariff. Under these circumstances, a tariff would primarily give the tariff-imposing country a large improvement in its terms of trade, but it would fail to protect domestic production of the goods by a limit of imports. A tariff would have little or no effect on the domestic price of the goods, which would remain low despite the tariff, and domestic production would be outcompeted.

The foreign export supply of agricultural products is often inelastic, especially in the short run. In this situation, a quota is often the only way by which imports can be limited and the domestic price of the goods upheld. An important aspect of domestic agricultural policy in several countries is price support for agricultural products that guarantee farmers a " fair income," so agricultural products are typically the ones for which import quotas have been used. The French were pioneers in the use of quotas in the 1930s, and since World War II quotas have been an integral part of the agricultural policy of the United States, where they have been used to limit and control imports of such products as sugar. The United States has an important domestic sugar production, but for various reasons it has wanted to import from abroad. The question whether to use quotas or tariffs to control imports from less-developed countries has been debated in recent years. We return to this in Chapter 23 in connection with a discussion of UNCTAD.

It is therefore important to remember that if markets abroad and at home are not perfectly competitive, the effects of tariffs can be quite different from quantitative restrictions. Another important aspect of a quota is that it can have important repercussions on the market structure in the country that imposes it.

Assume that there is an emerging industry in a country and that the authorities decide to help it by establishing a quota on imports that compete with the products of the industry. This secures a market for the domestic industry, and a domestic monopoly could be established, one profiting from the higher domestic price that the quota implies. Had a tariff been used instead, imports would have been permitted freely at the tariff-inclusive price. If the foreign supply is quite elastic, the domestic industry would eventually be in a perfectly competitive situation. If quantitative restrictions are used, a domestic producer can benefit from them to establish a domestic monopoly, whereas if tariffs had been used, he would have had to accept full international competition.

Besides limiting competition in domestic markets, quantitative restrictions attach a scarcity value to imports, and the scarcity value gives rise to an economic rent. Who will capture this rent? It depends on market conditions and on the way the quantitative restrictions are organized.

If the government merely introduces a quota, and if domestic producers are organized, and foreign producers are not, the domestic producers will capture the rent by increasing profits and prices. But if foreign producers are organized and domestic ones are not, then the foreign producers can get a substantial part of the rent by increasing their prices and turning the terms of trade against the country.

The government, however, might not be content merely to announce the introduction of a quota without further ado. It might want to capture the rent for itself, which it can do by auctioning off import licenses. If the auctioning is done efficiently, and if market conditions are fully competitive, the effects of a quota can be precisely the same as those of a tariff, including the revenue going to the government in the form of an income from auctions.

This is a theoretical possibility that is difficult to put into practice. Quantitative restrictions invariably seem to benefit some specific groups in society. Who benefits largely depends on how the system is organized. In India, for instance, import licenses are divided into established importers (EI), actual users (AU) and capital goods (CG). EI licenses, used for imports of consumption goods and other commodities, are allocated to traders. AU licenses are allocated to producers, and CG licenses to investors with approved investment projects.

The reason for using quantitative restrictions seems to be that they give a sense of certainty. With them, a country can then be sure it can limit imports of the good. But this certainty is often bought at quite a high price and often at the cost of introducing uncertainties of other kinds, for instance, the effects on the production and cost structure within the country.

QUANTITATIVE RESTRICTIONS AND THE BALANCE OF PAYMENTS

We have already dealt with some implications of quantitative restrictions for the balance of payments under the heading of direct controls in Chapter 16, so we can be brief here.

It is true that quantitative restrictions are often introduced to improve a country's balance of payments. They have an immediate visible impact on a country's imports. But they also have secondary effects. When these are taken into account, the total impact of quantitative restrictions could be considerably less beneficial than an untrained observer might suppose.

In a general way, quantitative restrictions might be thought of as an expenditure-switching type of policy. It is useful, when dealing with them, to think in terms of the absorption approach that we elaborated in connection with the discussion of devaluation in Chapter 16. Like any other expenditure-switching type of policy, quantitative restrictions will improve a country's balance of trade only if they decrease a country's total absorption. (Or, given unemployment, if they increase total production.)

The most important ways in which this can be done are as follows. The general price level of the country will in all probability increase because of the restrictions. If the supply of money is kept constant, a real balance effect will come into play as consumers and firms try to restore the real value of their cash holdings. This will lead to a fall in total absorption in the same way as happened in connection with a devaluation. Savings can also be affected in several ways. The restriction of imports might lead to forced savings, for instance through purchases being postponed if the public expects the restrictions to be temporary. The income distribution might be changed in favor of profits (if entrepreneurs and traders reap the rent connected with the restrictions). If savings out of profits are less than savings out of wages, total absorption will fall. Investment too might be affected, for instance if imports of capital goods are curtailed.

All these effects, however, are quite subtle in character. Quantitative restrictions cannot be expected to lead to an improvement of the balance of payments equal to the amount by which imports are cut. In all normal circumstances, they will lead to a change in demand: goods that were earlier exported will now be demanded by domestic consumers. The net effect on the balance of payments of quantitative restrictions is therefore often much smaller than the amount by which imports are originally cut.

It should be stressed, however, that all ways of curing a deficit in the balance of payments contain some costs and painful adjustments. Expenditure-reducing policies can sometimes be regarded as too costly in terms of unemployment. If for some reason a country cannot or will not devalue, quantitative restrictions can be the best solution.[1] It must be realized, however, that in such a case the equilibrium in the balance of payments is bought at the expense of a certain misallocation of resources.

STATE TRADING

The state also plays a direct role in international trade by making its own purchases and sales. It is difficult to define state trading precisely; it can take many forms. It can take the form of a government agency or monopoly operating more or less according to the same principles as a private firm, or it can be a ministry or an organization that completely controls the country's international trade, as in most Communist countries.

---

[1] A very interesting case for the use of quantitative restrictions is made by R. N. Cooper in *The Economics of Interdependence: Economic Policy in the Atlantic Community*, New York, McGraw-Hill, 1968, pp. 227 ff.

The government sector is increasing in most developed, industrial countries, so state purchasing for direct government use is increasing. Thus one would expect states to become more and more directly engaged in international trade, but most governments tend to be quite chauvinistic in this respect: they prefer to buy at home.

This tendency was especially strengthened during the depression in the 1930s, but it is still prevalent. Governments pay no tariffs. A certain preference for domestic producers (say 10 percent of the price) can therefore seem natural, to enable the domestic producers to compete on the same terms as foreign producers. In recent years, much larger preferences have been granted to domestic producers by certain governments. The United States, for instance, had during the interwar period a 25 percent preference which was lowered to 10 percent during the 1950s. For balance-of-payments reasons, however, this preference has during the 1960s been increased to 50 percent. One result of this is that the effects of the Vietnam war on the U.S. balance of payments has been astonishingly small. In this war, American troops have been supplied with American goods down to the last can of beer. The economic effects on neighbor countries have also been limited. Countries whose exports have been boosted by the war, such as Formosa and South Korea, have often had to accept payments that can be used only to finance imports directly from the United States.

In times of balance-of-payments pressure, governments often introduce rules about buying home products, so that government officials are urged to use only domestic airlines, embassies to serve only domestic wines, etc. Thereby a double standard is used: no tariffs or quantitative restrictions for balance-of-payments reasons for the private sector, but near autarky as far as government purchases are concerned. This might be understandable, but it is hardly rational economically.

Some products, such as tobacco and alcohol, are frequently handled as government monopolies. In Sweden, for instance, the state liquor authority is the sole importer of wine and liquor and the largest single buyer of French wines in the world. In many countries, a tradition of state trading has long existed. State trading expanded greatly during the 1930s when several countries started to engage in direct trading in connection with schemes for supporting domestic industries, especially agriculture. Nazi Germany pioneered some new arrangements in this field, especially in its trade with the Balkan countries. So-called bulk buying was one example of this. It meant that Germany imported all, or the larger part, of a country's export crop, for instance tobacco from Greece. Arrangements of similar kinds were also discussed after World War II. The thought was that if the seller had an assured market, he could plan production, utilize economies of scale, and lower costs. The benefits reaped could then be shared with the purchaser by a lowering of prices.

State trading has also played an important role for many less-developed countries in recent years. These countries have often tried to organize market boards for important agricultural products. This has been done with the double intention of rationalizing the internal market structure and helping to improve agricultural technique. Another important objective has been to get some control over the country's foreign trade and to improve the terms of trade by taking advantage of monopoly power.

It is difficult to give a fair assessment of the significance of state trading. It was estimated that in 1964 as much as 15–20 percent of world trade was conducted by various state agencies. For many less-developed countries the figures are substantially higher. The United Nations Economic Commission for Asia and the Far East estimated that in the early 1960s 70–80 percent of Burmese exports and 30–40 percent of imports were conducted by state agencies. The share of state trade imports in Ceylon was estimated at 25–30 percent, in India at 40–50, in Pakistan at 30–50, and in Indonesia at around 45 percent.[2]

Thus state trading is quite important. It is difficult to prophesy its future development. It has diminished in importance in the developed, industrial countries of the West since World War II. It plays an important role in many of the developing countries, however, where the trend toward state trading might very well continue.

SUMMARY

Under competitive market conditions there are important similarities between quotas and tariffs. If imports are curtailed by the same amount, the

---

[2] UN Economic Commission for Asia and the Far East, *State Trading in Countries of the Ecafe Region*, New York, United Nations, 1964, p. 7.

effects on prices and volumes will be the same. An important difference is that a quota will not give the government any tariff revenue but will instead give rise to an economic rent.

Under monopolistic market conditions, the effects of quotas and tariffs will differ. An important effect of a quota might be to help establish a domestic monopoly.

The advantage of quotas and quantitative restrictions is often claimed to be certainty: using a quota, a country can be certain that its imports will fall. When all secondary effects are taken into account, the certainty proposition is less valid. The balance of payments will improve only if quotas lead to a fall in total absorption.

State trading used to be confined to certain state monopolies, such as tobacco and alcohol. It usually increases in times of wars and emergencies. It is nowadays on the upsurge primarily in less-developed countries.

SELECTED BIBLIOGRAPHY: CHAPTER 20

For the theory of quotas, see:

J. Bhagwati, "On the Equivalence of Tariffs and Quotas," in R. E. Caves, H. G. Johnson, and P. B. Kenen (eds.), *Trade, Growth and the Balance of Payments*, Chicago, 1965.

For an illustration of the problem of economic rents in connection with quotas, see:

R. P. Manes, "Import Quotas, Prices and Profits in the Oil Industry," *Southern Economic Journal*, July 1963.

Other interesting contributions are:

J. M. Fleming, "On Making the Best of Balance of Payments Restrictions on Imports," *EJ*, March 1951 (reprinted in *RIE*).

R. Frisch, "On the Need for Forecasting a Multilateral Balance of Payments," *AER*, June 1947.

M. W. F. Hemming and W. M. Corden, "Import Restriction as an Instrument of Balance of Payments Policy," *EJ*, September 1958.

B. Tew, "The Use of Restrictions to Suppress External Deficits," *MSS*, no. 3, 1960.

The use of auctions in connection with quotas is discussed in:

J. Bhagwati, "Indian Balance of Payments Policy and Exchange Auctions," *OEP*, no. 1, 1962.

On state trading, the literature is sparse. A somewhat older work is:

J. Viner, *Trade Relations Between Free Market and Controlled Economies*, Geneva, League of Nations, 1943.

Tariffs, subsidies, and distortions in commodity and factor markets

21

We learned in Chapter 19 that from a welfare point of view the only valid argument for tariffs is the optimum tariff. In arriving at this result we assumed that both the factor and commodity markets worked under fully competitive conditions. But this might seem to be quite a drastic assumption. In many countries, especially perhaps in the less-developed ones, markets do not work under optimal conditions. Distortions of different kinds exist.

Distortions may exist in commodity markets, and examples of such are external economies. It can be the case, for instance, that farmers do not realize that, through their farming methods, erosion takes place and the soil is destroyed. The private cost of producing agricultural goods may therefore underestimate the true social cost. Another factor which could complicate matters is the existence of economies of scale which for some reasons are not reaped. Distortions in the factor market could also exist. Producers in industry may have to pay a higher wage than agricultural producers, for instance. If such distortions existed, free trade would no longer be the optimal policy.

We will now discuss these problems. We should, however, note that this part of tariff theory differs not only in its assumptions from the tariff theory which we dealt with in Chapter 19. It differs also in the questions asked. In Chapter 19 we asked what the effects of tariffs were on prices, income distribution, etc. Here we are concerned with less ambitious questions. This type of tariff theory evaluates, on the one hand, the effects of tariffs compared with free trade on the welfare of a country and, on the other hand, compares tariffs and other means (subsidies, taxes) available for best correcting distortions.

THE INFANT-INDUSTRY ARGUMENT FOR PROTECTION

The oldest existing argument for protection is the infant-industry argument. It was forwarded in the 1840s by the German economist and politician Friedrich List.[1] The core of the infant-industry argument is the existence

---

[1] Friedrich List (1789–1846), professor of economics at Tübingen University. In 1841 he published his main work, *Das Nationale System der Politischen Oekonomie*, containing his thoughts on the need for a protective tariff for less-developed countries.

376

Tariffs, subsidies, and
distortions in commodity
and factor markets

of some kind of internal economies. A firm cannot compete if it is small. It
has to be large before it can harvest all the economies of scale in production
and become competitive. Therefore, it has to be protected for some time and
be permitted to grow, without meeting immediate competition from abroad.
When the firm has become fully developed, the tariff can be dismantled and
free trade can be allowed. This is the essence of the argument.

The country List had in mind when he developed the infant-industry
argument was Germany of the mid-nineteenth century. Great Britain was
then the leading industrial state and German industry had difficulty competing with the older, more established British industry. List was modern
in his views insofar as he saw industry as a prerequisite of progress. On this
score he had no doubts: "Manufactories and manufactures are the mothers
and children of municipal liberty, of intelligence, of the arts and sciences, of
internal and external commerce, of navigation and improvements in transport, of civilisation and political power."[2]

Free trade was good for Britain whose position was already established. For young, emerging German industry, however, tariffs were necessary. The infant-industry argument soon won acceptance, and even the dean
of classical economics in the 1850s, John Stuart Mill, gave it a niche in his
exposition of classical economic theory.[3] List was, in other words, the first
successful German economist.

Figure 21.1 is a geometric illustration of the infant-industry argument for protection. To start with, the country has the production possibility
curve SS. The international terms of trade are given by the line P_i-P_i,
which is tangent to the production possibility curve at P. The country produces at P and moves by trade to T. This depicts the country's situation
under free trade.

The country now wants to protect its industry. It introduces a tariff
(assumed to be prohibitive) so that the price for domestic consumers and
producers now becomes P_h-P_h. This price line is tangent to the production
possibility curve at P', and under protection the country will produce and
consume at this point. Protection lowers the country's welfare, as seen from
the fact that P' is to the southwest of T.

---

[2] Friedrich List, *Das Nationale System der Politischen Oekonomie*, Jena, 1928,
p. 230.
[3] John Stuart Mill (1806–1873), English philosopher and economist. His main
work in the economic field is *Principles of Political Economy*, published in 1848.

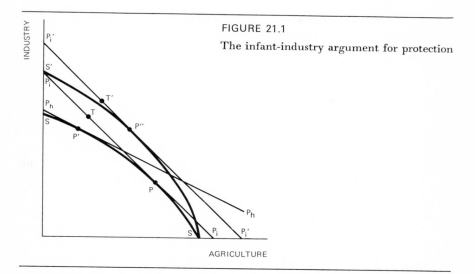

FIGURE 21.1

The infant-industry argument for protection

This is, however, only what happens in the short run. Protection gives rise to a substantial increase in production of industrial goods. Thereby internal economies can be reaped, industrial skills can be learned, etc., and this will lead to an increase in productive capacity; i.e., there will be an outward shift in the country's production possibility curve. After some time of protection, the new production possibility curve will be $S'S$. The country can then start free trade again. If the same international terms of trade prevail as before protection, the country will produce at P''. ($P_i'-P_i'$ is parallel to P_i-P_i.) Through trading, the country can then move to T'. As T' is to the northeast of T, it represents higher social welfare. By nurturing an infant industry for some time, the country has thus been able to reach a higher level of welfare than would have been possible if it had been engaged in free trade all the time.

A protectionist policy initially implies a lowering of welfare. In the usual manner a tariff will cause a production and consumption cost. For protection to produce social benefits, the infant industries must grow up. They must eventually be able to compete at world market prices. They must pass what is sometimes called Mill's test.[4] Not only, however, do they have to

---

[4] See M. C. Kemp, "The Mill–Bastable Infant Industry Dogma," *Journal of Political Economy*, vol. 68, February 1960.

Tariffs, subsidies, and
distortions in commodity
and factor markets

grow up; for a protectionist policy to be profitable, they will also have to be able to pay back the losses due to protection during the infant industry period. They will have to pass what is sometimes called Bastable's test. Only then is there a clear-cut case for infant-industry protection.

We now have to look somewhat more closely into the circumstances causing an industry to be of an infant-industry type. We did not say why the production-possibility curve in Figure 21.1 expanded. One reason could be the existence of internal economies. Let us say that the production function in the industry shows increasing returns to scale. This means that as production expands, the unit cost will fall. Investment will have to take place at some period and production expand until the optimum size is reached. During this time the industry will have to be protected. This, therefore, is the main argument.

In reality this argument is less convincing than it may at first sound. It is not enough to show that present losses have to be incurred if future gains are to be had. This is, in itself, no argument for protection, because if a capital market exists and functions properly, and if domestic producers have a correct view of the profitability of the investment, they will invest in the industry even without a tariff. The existence of internal economies is not, by itself, a sufficient reason for protection. The infant-industry argument has to be built on a more intricate case than this.

It might be the case, for instance, that the capital market does not function properly. This is a common feature to many less-developed countries. They have small and poorly developed credit markets, and it can be difficult for a single investor to raise the money needed to make the investment. Or it could be that investors are not properly informed about the prospects of investment. They might be unduly pessimistic about the future or unwilling to take chances in an unprotected market. The case for infant-industry protection will then be strengthened.

An important reason the social return of the investment in an infant industry may exceed the private return is connected with education. This phenomenon is usually of special importance for less-developed countries. One of the results of the investment may be the acquisition of knowledge, for instance, in the form of experimenting with a suitable technique of production. Once acquired by one firm, this technique can usually be bought at minimal cost by competing firms. Another factor is that part of the cost of the investment may comprise instructing workers, for instance, in the form of on-the-job training. Once the workers have gained these skills they can go to another industry and use them there. These could contribute to the reasons an investment, although socially profitable, may not be undertaken by a private firm in an unprotected market. Protection, therefore, can give the added incentive necessary for undertaking the investment.

We have now shown examples of the economics behind the expansion of the production-possibility curve as illustrated in Figure 21.1. We now have to ask the question: Is a tariff the most suitable policy means for achieving this increase in productive capacity? We have to admit that there are cases in which protection for some time will give better results than free trade. Are there, however, other policy means which would be more efficient than tariffs for promoting the desired increase in productive capacity?

The answer is yes. On a somewhat abstract level we say that an optimum solution implies equality between the foreign rate of transformation (FRT), the domestic rate of transformation in production (DRT), and the domestic rate of transformation in consumption (DRS).[5] From this point of view we can say that if a country has "monopoly power" in trade, i.e., can influence its own terms of trade, the situation under free trade will be that $DRS = DRT \neq FRT$. Hence there is scope for the optimum tariff. Only that can give $DRS = DRT = FRT$.

In the presence of infant industries, the true domestic rate of transformation in production is not equal to the domestic rate of transformation in consumption. Hence we have a situation where $DRS = FRT \neq DRT$, although a tariff cannot here bring equality between all three rates of transformation. It would give equality between DRT and FRT but inequality with DRS. In this case only a policy combination of taxes and subsidies can produce equality between all three rates of transformation.

This means that tariffs are not the most suitable means of dealing with the problem created by infant industries. It is always possible to reach a better solution by using subsidies, perhaps in combination with taxes.

In the case first discussed, internal economies were present. If the entrepreneurs were not able to reap them because of risk aversion or an imperfect capital market, the state should deal with these imperfections directly. It could, for instance, help the entrepreneurs to acquire correct information or underwrite some of the risks. Or it could give loans on

[5] For a penetrating discussion of these problems see J. Bhagwati and V. K. Ramaswami, "Domestic Distortions, Tariffs and the Theory of Optimum Subsidy," *Journal of Political Economy*, vol. 71, February 1963.

380

Tariffs, subsidies, and
distortions in commodity
and factor markets

favorable conditions. Thereby the private rate of transformation in production can be made to coincide with the true social rate of transformation, and no disturbance on the consumption side will occur. A tariff would always distort consumption by making the home market price higher than the international price of tariff-ridden goods.

Analogous conditions hold if external economies in education exist. If private entrepreneurs are unwilling to undertake some investment because they cannot get profitable returns on their investment in education, the state should subsidize them. This the state can do in the form of starting trade schools or by compensating the entrepreneurs for the costs of on-the-job training. The appropriate policy in this connection is some sort of subsidy or tax concession, not a tariff. Tariffs are only efficient if, for some reason, the country also wants to decrease its dependence on foreign trade.

The infant-industry argument for protection is essentially dynamic.[6] It is an argument for a tariff (or if properly formulated a subsidy) during a transient period of time. For some reasons original free trade will not permit a country's true comparative cost situation to develop. Therefore, trade has to be protected for a period of time to enable the country's real pattern of comparative advantage to be established.

Sometimes the existence of external economies and diseconomies are given as reasons for infant-industry protection. These are, however, better dealt with in connection with distortions in commodity markets. We will now discuss this case.

DOMESTIC DISTORTIONS IN COMMODITY MARKETS

If external economies or diseconomies exist, they could cause the private cost of production to differ from the social cost. If monopolistic or oligopolistic market conditions prevail in parts of the industry, they may have the same effect. External economies is probably the most interesting case. Let us, therefore, deal with that.

---

[6] It could also be applicable to a situation with two stationary states of an economy, where in the first state some internal economies were not reaped and the tariff was used to shift the economy over to another stationary state, where these internal economies were then reaped but nothing else had happened.

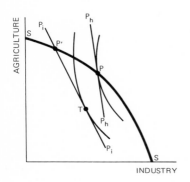

FIGURE 21.2

Domestic distortion in the market for agriculture: a tariff increases welfare

Economists often speak about the importance of external economies. Some even go as far as to say that they are the most important basis for state intervention in markets: The theory of socialism should be based on them. Be that as it may, it is often difficult to visualize them and find good examples of external economies. Bees and flowers could do, but somehow they convey no sense of urgency.

Let us think in terms of a two-sector economy, with one agricultural and one industrial sector. An example of an external diseconomy in agriculture could be that farmers do not realize that they impoverish the soil by their farming methods—that, for instance, erosion and soil destruction could be the consequences. This implies that the private cost of producing a certain amount of agricultural products is lower than the social cost, because farmers in their calculations of price do not reckon on the impoverishment of the soil. Then relative prices in the domestic market will not reflect the true marginal cost of transformation in production.

Figure 21.2 is a geometric illustration of this fact. Production of agricultural goods is measured on the vertical axis and production of industrial goods on the horizontal axis. The "true" production-possibility curve reflecting the social marginal rate of transformation is given by SS. Because of the distortions in the commodity market caused by the external diseconomies in agriculture, relative prices in the domestic market are given by the price line $P_h\text{-}P_h$. At these prices the country will produce at point P. The international terms of trade are given by the price line $P_i\text{-}P_i$. This shows that the country has a comparative advantage in agriculture (at

382

Tariffs, subsidies, and
distortions in commodity
and factor markets

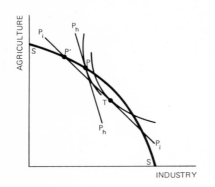

FIGURE 21.3

Domestic distortion in the market
for agriculture: a tariff decreases welfare

distorted prices), as agricultural products are more expensive on the international market than in the distorted domestic market. With free trade the
country will produce at P'. It will trade according to international terms of
trade and consume at T. As T is to the southwest of P (and lies on an indifference curve representing a lower level of welfare), the country will be
worse off because it is trading.

Figure 21.2 exemplifies the possible detrimental effect of trade on a
country when domestic distortions exist in the commodity market and shows
how the country specializes in the wrong commodity. If all the external
effects were taken into account, the country would have exported industrial
goods instead of agricultural products. Free trade accentuates the importance
of the external diseconomies. In this case, a policy of protection would stimulate production of the industrial goods, in which the country's true comparative advantage lies, and lead to an improvement in welfare.

The tariff introduces a distortion of the usual kind for consumers, because the domestic price will differ from the world market price. This will
entail a loss of welfare for consumers. At the same time it will lead to an
improvement in the allocation of resources, because it will curtail the production of agricultural goods and decrease the impoverishment of the soil.
In the case illustrated in Figure 21.2, gains on the production side are larger
than losses on the consumption side, and the tariff leads to an improvement
in welfare.

This outcome is, however, not necessarily so. Figure 21.3 illustrates
the opposite possibility. The assumptions and the situation in this case are

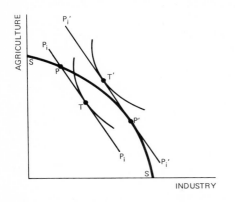

FIGURE 21.4

Domestic distortion in the market for agriculture: the optimal policy

the same as in that illustrated in Figure 21.2. To start with, the country produces at point P. With trade, production will move to P', and trade will take the country to T. Even in this case the country specializes in the wrong commodity. Trade will lead to a worsening in resource allocation and a loss on the production side. But consumers will gain and the gain on the consumption side will outweigh the loss on the production side, as seen from the fact that T lies on a higher indifference curve than P.

The result of the discussion so far is thus that protection can improve a country's welfare if distortions exist in a country's commodity market. This is, however, not a definite outcome. It could also lead to a deterioration in a country's welfare. Whether it does, or does not depends on the relation between production gains and consumption losses.

A tariff is not the optimal policy instrument if distortions exist. By applying the general principles exposed earlier in this chapter, we find that better results can be reached by a combination of subsidies and taxes. This is illustrated in Figure 21.4. Under free trade and with no interventions in the market, the country will produce at P and consume at T. At point P, however, the international terms of trade are not equal to the country's social cost of transformation in production. Because of distortions, the real cost of producing agricultural goods is underestimated. A tariff might make the country better or worse off, depending on conditions just outlined. The best policy is a combination of taxes and subsidies. A tax on agriculture combined with an industrial subsidy should make the private cost of transformation equal to the social cost of transformation. Such a policy takes the

384

Tariffs, subsidies, and
distortions in commodity
and factor markets

country to point P', where the social cost of transformation equals the international terms of trade. (P_i'-P_i' is parallel to P_i-P_i.) Then the country can engage in free trade at undistorted prices, thus taking the country to T', the best point the country can reach with the given technique, preference system, and international prices. This point can never be reached by means of tariffs. Hence a policy of subsidies *cum* taxes is superior to tariffs when dealing with distortions in commodity markets.

DISTORTIONS IN FACTOR MARKETS

It is often argued that industry in less-developed countries has to pay a higher wage than agriculture in order to get labor. This may be a reason why industry in these countries is placed at a disadvantage and why it should be protected. We then have a distortion in the factor market. We now have to examine whether protection is an appropriate policy or not for the case where distortions in the factor markets exist.

One sometimes hears the assertion that in underdeveloped countries the marginal productivity of labor in agriculture is zero. Yet the peasants and agricultural workers earn a positive wage. If this is the case, then there will always be a distortion in factor markets, as long as the marginal productivity and the wage in industry is positive. Whether the marginal productivity in agriculture is in reality zero is a question which we shall not discuss here. We shall simply assume that some distortion in the factor market exists.

One cannot, however, from the simple existence of a wage differential between industry and agriculture, draw the implication that a distortion exists. There may be many rational explanations for such a wage differential. One could be that workers prefer to work in agriculture, where they are therefore willing to accept a lower wage. Another could be that work in industry requires specific training and that the higher wage reflects a return to this investment in human capital. A third reason may be that work in industry requires a movement for which the worker has to be compensated. All these, and several other reasons, are examples of wage differentials with rational economic foundations. Hence no distortions are involved.

One can also find examples that reflect a true distortion. One could be that labor unions exist in industry but not in agriculture and that they

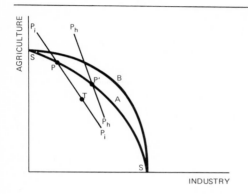

FIGURE 21.5

Distortion in the factor market: a tariff increases welfare

force the employers in industry to pay a certain minimum wage. Another could be that employers in industry pay "decent" wages on humanitarian grounds. If this is the case, labor will not be optimally allocated between industries and total production will be lower than it would otherwise be.

There are also other more intricate factors that could entail distortions. One could be that industry might have to pay a higher wage because of "dynamic" reasons to get labor. Another may be that industry cannot give employment to the nonadult members of a family the way agriculture can. Hence a higher wage for the head of the household is needed, in order to make him move.

Despite the fact that all that may look like distortion is in reality not distortion, one can certainly think of conditions reflecting true distortions. We will now go on and give a geometric illustration of factor market distortions and see what the effects of protection will be, given that such distortions exist.

Figure 21.5 illustrates the case where distortions exist in the factor market. The production-possibility curve in the prevailing distorted market is given by SAS. If the distortions did not exist the production-possibility curve would be given by SBS. Factor market distortions lead, in geometric terms, to a position where the production-possibility curve is pulled in toward the origin. The reason for this is that factors will not be optimally allocated if distortions exist. The relation between marginal productivities in the two industries will not be the same. The marginal productivity of labor in industry, for instance, will be higher than the marginal productivity of labor in agriculture. This means, in geometric terms, that the country will

386

Tariffs, subsidies, and
distortions in commodity
and factor markets

not be on the contract curve in the box diagram. (The country will produce on the contract curve only if it is completely specialized, i.e., only if it is producing at one of the two ends of the box diagram.) In general, the country will produce somewhere off the contract curve. The production-possibility curve which could be derived if the country were producing along the contract curve in the box is SBS. The production-possibility curve that can be derived from the combination of points where the country will produce under distortions is SAS.

Let us assume that we start off with free trade. The country is then producing at P and consuming at T. Protection in the form of a tariff on industrial goods would take the country to P'. This point is obviously preferable to T, and hence protection is advantageous for the country.

This is, however, not a necessary result. The situation here is completely analogous to the one with distortions in commodity markets. Protection might give a better result than free trade, but it might also lead to a lowering of welfare. It all depends on the specific case and the relationship between production gains and consumption losses implied by a tariff if distortions exist in commodity or factor markets.

If distortions exist in the factor market, a tariff can, however, never be an optimal solution. This is illustrated in Figure 21.6. The international terms of trade are given by the three parallel price lines. Under free trade the country will produce at P and consume at T. Because of the distortion in the factor market, the social marginal rate of transformation will not coincide with the terms of trade. The real cost of producing agriculture at P will be higher than that shown by the market price. A tariff may in this case lead to an improvement, or it may not. (The student can easily convince himself that a combination of tariff-ridden price lines and indifference curves can lead to a deterioration in welfare.) A tariff can, however, never bring the true domestic marginal rate of transformation in production to coincide with the international terms of trade.

A subsidy could do that, in a specific sense. It could bring the marginal rate of transformation along the distorted curve to coincide with international prices. A subsidy to industry could take the country to P'. Through trade it could then move to T', which is obviously superior to T. Hence a policy of subsidies on production is better than free trade, if factor market distortions exist.

A subsidy on production is, however, not the best policy. It is still the case that the relation between marginal productivities in the two lines of

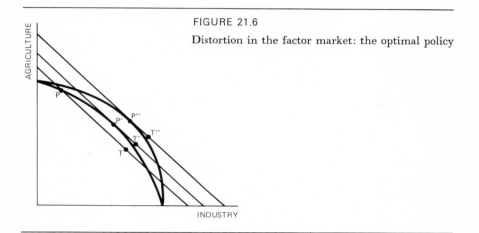

FIGURE 21.6

Distortion in the factor market: the optimal policy

production differs. What is needed is a tax or subsidy on the use of the factor of production. A subsidy to labor in industry could lead to greater employment within industry and to the equalization in both sectors of the marginal productivity of labor. A tax on the use of labor in agriculture would have the same effect. Only by such a policy could the country reach its undistorted production-possibility curve.

This would mean, in our case, that the country would produce at P'' and through trade could move to T''. This point is obviously superior to T' and represents the best the country can do, given its production possibilities and the international terms of trade.

To sum up: If distortions in the factor markets existed, protection might give a better result than free trade or a worse result, but it will never be an optimal policy. Subsidies and taxes on production are more efficient means of economic policy, but neither will they be optimal. The best policy means are taxes and subsidies on the use of the factors of production. Only these will lead to optimal results.

TRADE POLICY FOR DEVELOPMENT: FIRST COMMENTS

We now have met two serious arguments for tariffs. The first was the optimum tariff argument which we met in Chapter 19. The second, or rather

388

Tariffs, subsidies, and
distortions in commodity
and factor markets

second group of arguments, is that dealt with in this chapter. In a nationalistic world a protectionist policy will always hold appeal. It is quite natural that protectionism has been tried by less-developed countries as a means of speeding up their economic development. The difficulties involved in fostering economic growth are now well known. Many countries are in desperate situations, and their possibilities of meeting population pressure with increased production are limited. There are cases where the per capita income is stagnant or even falling.

Against this background it is easy to understand why protectionism is a tempting alternative. It is usually heavily backed by certain domestic interests; a policy of increasing tariffs is also often easy to implement. Protectionism seems to give a lot of mileage for a little effort.

A protectionist policy also contains very real dangers. It is doubtful, as we have already hinted, whether the optimum tariff argument has much relevance for most underdeveloped countries. A tariff can only increase a country's welfare if the adaptability of supply and demand for the country's exports in the rest of the world is low. This is probably not the case for most of the less-developed countries. This implies that the value these countries can derive from a tariff must, on this score, be limited. Consequently, the relevance of the optimum tariff argument for less-developed countries is probably small.

The infant-industry argument can very well be applicable in some instances to underdeveloped countries. Distortions in commodity and factor markets also presumably exist. These could be reasons for using a protectionist policy. In both these cases, however, tariffs are not the optimal means of economic policy. Yet tariffs are often easy to implement, as they are usually easier to use than taxes and subsidies. This argument, incidentally should not be carried too far. Even most underdeveloped countries have a set of taxes, which can be dimensioned to deal with the distortions.

Protectionism could, however, be a defensible policy under these circumstances, at least as a second-best solution. If tariffs are used to correct distortions and foster development, they should be used with great discrimination and against the background of a carefully worked out policy. Many less-developed countries have used tariffs to implement a policy of import substitution. Such a policy of inward-looking industrialization seems rarely to have produced any significant results. On the contrary, it seems to have led to stagnation in several cases.

The countries which have perhaps most intensively engaged in a policy of import substitution are the Latin American states. For instance, Argentina started on such a course in the early 1930s. This led to the neglect of the export sector, and exports thus fell. The domestic industry grew but did not expand on an efficient enough scale and thus could not compete in international markets. The policy of discrimination against the traditional export sector led to a slowing down of international trade and to a balance-of-payments deficit. The over-all result was one of near stagnation. It is difficult not to have the impression that the main result of the policy of import substitution was a lowering in the rate of economic growth. It seems that for most Latin American states import substitution created more problems than it solved.

One of the reasons for the failure of a policy of import substitution was probably that the policy makers and bureaucracy had a weak understanding of the complexity of input–output relationships characteristic of modern industry. A tariff on an import good will usually increase the price of this good. If the good is used as an input in the production of other goods, their prices will rise. Protectionism will, therefore, not only change the prices of the goods directly involved but change all prices. If a country imports large amounts of raw material, intermediate goods, machinery, etc., a policy of protectionism can easily become self-defeating. To achieve a deeper understanding of this problem we have to study the theory of implicit tariffs, one of the most fashionable subjects in international economics during recent years.

IMPLICIT TARIFFS

Implicit tariffs have been quite widely discussed in recent years. It is a relatively new concept which has caught the eye of the economist, has given hope to many a prospective Ph.D. candidate, and been viewed as a concept having an important bearing on economic policy. From a theoretical point of view, a discussion of implicit tariffs does not properly belong in Chapter 19 but neither does it really belong in this chapter. The theory of implicit tariffs has not yet been developed in the context of a general equilibrium model, and it also has nothing to do with distortions or market imperfections. However, it might as well be dealt with here as in any other chapter.

390

Tariffs, subsidies, and
distortions in commodity
and factor markets

The theory of implicit tariffs is so far quite rudimentary, one reason it is difficult to deal with and why it is hard to ascertain its policy implications. A general, and quite critical discussion of the concept will be given here. In the appendix to this chapter a formula for the implicit tariff will be derived.

The idea of the implicit tariff is that if inputs are taken into account, the manifest tariff or the final tariff on a good may differ widely from the rate of protection given to the value added in the production of the good; and it is the protection given to the value added that is important, according to the proponents of the theory of the implicit tariff.

Let us assume, for instance, that the manifest tariff on a good is 10 percent, and that inputs (raw materials, intermediate goods, etc.) used in the production of the good amount to 50 percent of the value of production and that these inputs are imported without duty. The implicit or effective rate of protection accorded to value added is then 20 percent, not 10 percent as the manifest duty implies.

The value added is created by the factors of production. (We disregard profits, for simplicity's sake.) The purpose of a tariff is to protect the factors of production, and hence the implicit tariff is a more meaningful concept than the manifest tariff. This is the argument of the proponents of the implicit tariff.

It might be assumed that capital is available for industries in different countries on more or less the same conditions. What a tariff then really aims at protecting is labor. Let us assume, in the above example, that half of the value added was created by capital and half by labor, and that we deduct capital and take labor to be the only original factor of production to be protected. The effective rate of protection for labor in the above example is then 40 percent. Hence a manifest tariff of 10 percent in reality gives an effective rate of protection to labor of 40 percent. Using this argument it is easy to see that the implicit tariffs, especially if calculated in the form of the effective rate of protection given to labor, can differ very significantly from nominal or manifest tariff rates. Empirical calculations have also shown large discrepancies of this kind.[7] It should be observed that, everything else being

[7] See B. Balassa, "Tariff Protection in Industrial Countries: An Evaluation," *Journal of Political Economy*, vol. 73, December 1965, and G. Basevi, "The U.S. Tariff Structure: Estimates of Effective Rates of Protection of U.S. Industries and Industrial Labor," *Review of Economics and Statistics*, 1967.

equal, the smaller the value added in an industry, the larger will be its effective tariff (provided it is positive).

This indeed sounds interesting, but interesting results sometimes depend on defective or partial theorizing. We must now try to see if this is the case with implicit tariffs.

First we might observe that the theory of implicit tariffs is completely static. The calculations of effective tariff rates which have been made also build on a mechanical use of input–output tables, and what has been done is simply that an input–output table has been taken and the tariff rates calculated. (The formula used is set out in the appendix.) What can possibly be the economic significance of such an undertaking?

To understand the theoretical importance of effective tariff rates it is useful to restate a couple of the claims which have been made for them. The following quotation from a paper by H. G. Johnson is illustrative:

> Suppose that advanced countries permit free entry of a certain raw material, but impose a 10 percent duty on it after it is first processed; and that one quarter of the value after first-processing represents the cost of (value added in) first-processing. To be able to compete in the advanced country market for the first-processed product over the 10 percent tariff, the underdeveloped country would have to be able to produce that product for $\frac{10}{11}$ (=91 percent approximately) of the advanced country price. But since 75 percent of the advanced country price is the cost of raw materials, the same in both countries, the cost of first-processing in the underdeveloped country must be only 16 percent of the advanced country price, as compared with 25 percent in the advanced country, for the underdeveloped country to be able to supply the first processed product competitively. In other words, the cost of value added can be up to $\frac{9}{16}$ (over 50 percent) greater in the advanced country, or down to $\frac{9}{25}$ (over $33\frac{1}{3}$ percent) less in the underdeveloped country, without the latter being able to overcome the competitive disadvantage imposed by the 10 percent advanced country tariff on first processing. Nor is this all: the cost of value added includes both labour costs and capital charges, and presumably capital is internationally mobile, so that the competitive position of the underdeveloped country depends on its relative labour costs. If half the value added in the advanced country ($12\frac{1}{2}$ percent of the price) is capital costs, and these would be the same in both countries, the underdeveloped country must have labour costs of $3\frac{1}{2}$ percent of the advanced country price as

392

Tariffs, subsidies, and
distortions in commodity
and factor markets

compared with labour costs of $12\frac{1}{2}$ percent of the price in the advanced country: to be able to compete over a tariff of 10 percent on first processing, the underdeveloped country must have labour costs less than 30 percent of those in the advanced country.[8]

This is good enough but we are still only within a static framework. W. M. Corden has made the most clear claim for the theory:

> One must ask what the purpose of the effective-protection rate-concept is. The answer is that it should shed light on the direction of the resource-allocation effects of a protective structure. If we have calculated that tradable industry X has 10 percent effective protection and tradable industry Y has 20 percent, we should be able to conclude that resources will be drawn from X to Y and into both from non-protected tradable industries and from those non-traded industries where prices have stayed constant.[9]

And furthermore, he says:

> Ordinary *nominal* tariffs apply to commodities, but resources move as between economic activities. Therefore, to discover the resource-allocation effects of a tariff structure one must calculate the protective rate for each activity, that is, the *effective* protective rate. This is the main message of the new theory of tariff structures.[10]

To deal with these claims and evaluate their importance we first have to formulate our problem in a meaningful way. It might be useful to connect to Corden's reasoning and first ask the following question: Let us assume that we start from a situation with free trade and that we then introduce a differentiated tariff structure; what will be the effects on production and resource allocation?[11]

The tariffs will affect the prices in different ways; some prices will rise and some will fall.[12] After the new equilibrium has been reached we will

---

[8] H. G. Johnson, "The Theory of Tariff Structure with Special Reference to World Trade and Development," *Etudes et Travaux de l'Institut Universitaire de Hautes Etudes Internationales de Genève*, vol. 4, 1965, pp. 21–22.

[9] W. M. Corden, "The Structure of a Tariff System and the Effective Protective Rate," *Journal of Political Economy*, vol. 74, June 1966, p. 227.

[10] Corden, *loc. cit.*, p. 222.

[11] It does not make any difference if we start from a situation with free trade or from one with tariffs and then make a change in the established tariff structure.

[12] We deal here with the general case where a change in tariffs will affect both the international terms of trade and the home market prices; the general equilibrium implications of this case were explored in Chapter 19.

have a new set of prices, and resources will have been reallocated. What can be said about production and resource allocation changes?

First we might observe that the new set of prices will not simply be the old prices plus tariffs. Substitution possibilities differ between goods both on the demand and supply side. Can it at least be said that the goods having the highest manifest or nominal tariffs will have the highest price increase? No, this does not seem to be the case. A good with, for example, a 20 percent nominal tariff might have very good substitutes while a good with a 10 percent tariff might have poor substitutes. This being the case, it is possible that, in the new equilibrium, the price of the good with the 20 percent tariff will have increased by, say, 5 percent, while the price of the good with a 10 percent tariff will have increased by, say, 8 percent. Hence there is no one-to-one correspondence between nominal tariffs and new equilibrium prices. Nor can there be a one-to-one correspondence between implicit tariffs and the new equilibrium prices.

What then, will determine the changes in production and the flow of resources? Production of those goods will increase whose relative price has increased because of the tariff, and production of those goods will fall whose relative price has fallen. There does not seem to be any unambiguous, one-to-one relationship between nominal tariffs and changes in relative prices, and there is certainly no such relationship between relative price changes and implicit tariffs. We have, therefore, to reject Corden's statement that resource-allocation effects are determined by implicit tariffs as an unfounded assertion, at least for the general case of a change in the terms of trade.

There is a basic ambiguity in the theory of implicit tariffs concerning the treatment of factors of production which should be observed. In usual tariff theory labor is a homogeneous factor of production. Those who have written about implicit tariffs are not explicit on this point but they seem to think of factors as specific to each industry. If this is not the case, an example such as that of Johnson just referred to can hardly have any meaning.

Were it the case that labor (or broad groups of labor) was homogeneous, then there would be no point in calculating implicit tariff rates. For then we know that in equilibrium, the wage would be equalized between industries and to calculate the effective tariff rate for labor in any specific sector would be a spurious undertaking. If, however, factors of production are divided up in noncompeting groups, where each industry or

394

Tariffs, subsidies, and
distortions in commodity
and factor markets

sector has its own specific factor, the concept of implicit tariffs can be more meaningful.

The dilemma which this gives rise to is most clearly seen in Basevi's work, so far the most ambitious empirical study of implicit tariffs. Basevi tries to measure the effective rate of protection for labor. He comes to the somewhat puzzling conclusion that labor has the highest rate of protection in capital-intensive industries.[13]

This is not, however, a very astonishing conclusion if one takes into account the way in which the effective rate of protection of labor is calculated. The higher the capital intensity in an industry, the smaller will be labor's contribution to value added, and the smaller this is, all else being equal, the higher will be the effective protective rate, i.e., the higher will be the implicit tariff effect of a given nominal tariff rate.

This result, however, contradicts the standard tariff theory. The Stolper–Samuelson theorem states that labor will be protected only if it is the intensive factor in the import-competing, protected industry. Basevi's result, however, says that the less labor-intensive an industry is, the more protected it will be.

It is difficult to give economic meaning to Basevi's results if one thinks in terms of a model where factors of production are reasonably homogeneous within broad groups and substitution possibilities exist in production and consumption. In other words, if one thinks of an economy exhibiting broadly the neoclassical features, Basevi's results seem to be nonsensical. One can always measure certain facts but to claim that these facts have a deep economic significance is something altogether different.

More meaning could possibly be given to the concept of implicit tariffs if one assumed that factors of production are specific to each industry and that substitution possibilities are limited. It might then be of interest to try to measure the effective rate of protection given to each such factor. It might also be the case that the notion of implicit tariffs could be interesting from some other point of view, because it is fully possible that changes in tariffs on inputs can have important economic consequences.

Such a theory of implicit tariffs would, however, have to be worked out in a much more careful way than is the existing theory for effective protection. This theory, and the claims that have been made in its name,

---

[13] Basevi, *op. cit.*

hardly stand up to closer scrutiny. So far, the effective rate of protection is little more than an interesting concept in search of a theory.

We will discuss some of the policy implications that have been claimed for this theory in Chapter 23 when we deal with the question of tariff preferences for less-developed countries.

21-A

The idea behind the notion of implicit tariffs is to take intermediate goods into account. If this is done, the nominal tariff rate on a good can differ from its implicit or effective tariff rate. Let us think in terms of an input–output system. Then the implicit tariff can be derived in the following way:

$$v_j = 1 - \sum a_{ij} \tag{21A.1}$$

where v_j is the value added (or income earned by the factors of production) in the jth industry and a_{ij} is the value of the input from the ith industry into the jth industry, all at world market prices.

If there is a system of tariffs, domestic prices and values will differ from the international ones. The value added in the domestic industry is then

$$v_j' = 1 + t_j - \sum a_{ij}(1 + t_i) \tag{21A.2}$$

where v_j' is the domestic value added in the jth industry, t_j is the nominal tariff in that industry, and t_i is the nominal tariff in the ith industry.

Let us now define the implicit tariff (the rate of protection of value added), or the effective rate of protection, as

$$v_j' = (1 + \tau_j)v_j \tag{21A.3}$$

Then we obtain

$$\tau_j = \frac{t_j - \sum a_{ij} t_i}{v_j} = \frac{t_j - \bar{t}_j \sum a_{ij}}{v_j} = t_j + \frac{(t_j - \bar{t}_j) \sum a_{ij}}{v_j} \tag{21A.4}$$

where $\bar{t}_j = \sum a_{ij} t_i / \sum a_{ij}$ is the weighted average tariff rate on inputs of commodities into the jth industry.

We can observe from equation 21A.4 that if $t_j = \bar{t}_j$, then the nominal tariff rate and the effective tariff rate are the same. If $t_j > \bar{t}_j$, then the effective rate of protection is higher than the nominal tariff rate. If $t_j < \bar{t}_j$, then the implicit tariff is smaller than the nominal or manifest tariff rate. If $t_j < \sum a_{ij} t_i$, then the effective rate of protection is negative. This is usually the case with exports, but it can also happen with imported goods that have a positive nominal tariff.

SELECTED BIBLIOGRAPHY: CHAPTER 21

Two works trying to prove that protection is to be preferred to free trade are:

M. Manoilesco, *The Theory of Protection and International Trade*, London, 1931.

E. Hagen, "An Economic Justification of Protection," *QJE*, Nov. 1958.

A classic essay discussing tariffs versus free trade under different market imperfections is :

G. Haberler, "Some Problems in the Pure Theory of International Trade," *EJ*, June 1950 (reprinted in *RIE*).

An excellent paper on tariffs and subsidies as means to correct market imperfections, on which the exposition in Chapter 21 draws quite heavily, is:

J. Bhagwati and V. K. Ramaswami, "Domestic Distortions, Tariffs, and the Theory of Optimum Subsidy," *JPE*, February 1963 (reprinted in *RIE*).

Among other works in this field are:

P. K. Bardhan, "External Economies, Economic Development, and the Theory of Protection," *OEP*, March 1964.

H. G. Johnson, "Optimal Trade Intervention in the Presence of Domestic Distortions," in R. E. Caves, H. G. Johnson, and P. B. Kenen (eds.), *Trade, Growth and the Balance of Payments*, Chicago, 1965.

J. E. Meade, *Trade and Welfare*, London, 1955.

H. Myint, "Infant Industry Arguments for Assistance to Industries in the Setting of Dynamic Trade Theory," in R. F. Harrod and

T. D. C. Hague (eds.), *International Trade Theory in a Developing World*, London, 1963.

W. P. Travis, *The Theory of Trade and Protection*, Cambridge, Mass., 1964.

Concerning the theory of implicit or effective tariffs, see:

M. Corden, "The Structure of a Tariff System and the Effective Rate of Protection," *JPE*, June 1966.

H. G. Johnson, "The Theory of Tariff Structure with Special Reference to World Trade and Development," in H. G. Johnson and

P. B. Kenen (eds.), *Trade and Development*, Geneva, 1965.

H. G. Johnson, "A Model of Protection and the Exchange Rate," *RES*, 1966.

For empirical estimates of effective rates of protection, see:

B. Balassa, "Tariff Protection in Industrial Countries: An Evaluation," *JPE*, December 1965 (reprinted in *RIE*).

G. Basevi, "The U.S. Tariff Structure: Estimate of Effective Rates of Protection of U.S. Industries and Industrial Labor," *RE&S*, December 1966.

GATT, EEC, and the Kennedy Round

22

In the period between World Wars I and II there was marked deterioration in international economic relations. In the 1920s an attempt was made to go back to "normal" conditions. This meant the gold standard, as far as international monetary cooperation is concerned. An attempt was also made to organize world trade on a liberal basis.

This system did not function well. Great Britain, for instance, had difficulties because of an overvalued currency, and when the depression came in the beginning of the 1930s, the system broke down. Competitive devaluations followed, and trade restrictions were introduced. Many countries reverted to an autarkic pattern of production, and trade on a bilateral basis was introduced.

At the end of World War II, the interwar period was still fresh in memory. When the victorious countries (especially Britain and the United States) started to plan for new, more viable relations in the international economy, they were determined to avoid the mistakes of the past. The Bretton Woods conference (named after the meeting place, Bretton Woods, New Hampshire) held in 1944 was the starting point for a new order. The world economy would be organized around three cornerstones: the International Monetary Fund (IMF), the International Trade Organization (ITO), and the International Bank for Reconstruction and Development (IBRD).

The IMF was designed to take care of short-term problems in connection with international liquidity. It would help to smooth out and to solve difficulties that the respective countries would perhaps have with their balances of payments. ITO, on the other hand, would deal with the "real" side of trading relations. It would help to create a liberal system of regulations governing world trade; it would, in the long run, be the vehicle that carried the world toward a system of free trade. IBRD would help to channel international investments along desired lines. It would especially help the countries most in need of capital, the less-developed countries, to get capital from the more-developed, industrial countries.

The attempts at reforming the world economy have not been completely successful. The problem of international liquidity is more acute than at any time since World War II. The debate about trade policy is intense, and the opinions between nations are sharply divided. The International Bank has made only marginal contributions toward solving the problems of the less-developed countries, and the larger parts of international investments have been done outside the Bank.

We will deal with some of the main problems that the three organizations were given to solve. In Part V we shall deal at length with the international monetary system. Chapter 25 will be devoted to direct international investments. This chapter and the next will deal with some of the most pressing problems of trade policy.

GATT AND THE PRINCIPLE OF NONDISCRIMINATION

The International Trade Organization was the least successful of the above-mentioned three organizations; it never actually came into existence. A conference in Havana in 1947–1948 established a charter for ITO. This charter, however, was never ratified by the U.S. Senate. Nor did any other country ratify it; thus ITO was never established. Instead, GATT came into being. GATT was a less ambitious organization with headquarters in Geneva. It would serve as a sort of clearinghouse between nations. Instead of bargaining on a bilateral basis, the member countries of GATT would meet in Geneva and negotiate jointly at the same time on matters of trade policy. Thereby, it was hoped, a more orderly and just result could be achieved.

There are today more than 70 countries that are contracting parties to GATT and approximately 10 more that belong to GATT on a somewhat provisional basis. All the main industrial countries in the Western world are members, as are most less-developed countries; the latter group constitutes roughly two thirds of the membership. The Communist countries do not belong to GATT. About 80 percent of world trade is carried on between members of GATT.

The basic principle of GATT is that of nondiscrimination. Countries that belong to GATT accept the so-called most-favored-nation clause. This means that a country agrees not to give better treatment to any single nation than it gives to all the contracting parties of GATT. The clause of most-favored nation in principle rules out any preferential treatment among nations as far as trade policy is concerned.

The United States in particular has shown an almost fanatical attachment to the principle of most-favored nation in its trade policy. This goes back to the 1930s when Cordell Hull, Secretary of State in the Roosevelt administration, made it the leading principle in his crusade against the rising tide of protectionism and for a more liberal trade policy. It seemed to be a principle characterized by justice and equality, it harmonized with high-minded American principles, and it gave the American line an air of moral superiority. This principle also played a large role in the planning of a postwar trade organization.

Principles that might appear simple and just from a moral or legal point of view often fail to give the same impression when viewed from an economic angle. That is the case with the most-favored-nation principle. What appears just and equitable is not necessarily anything of the sort.

If the United States, for instance, has a certain tariff structure and applies it equally to all countries, it means that the country does not discriminate between producers, but it does not necessarily follow that the United States does not discriminate between nations. If it has a high tariff on cacao but a low one on Scottish sweaters, it means that Britain is given better treatment than Ghana. Any change in a tariff structure can also be geared so that it favors some countries over others. It avails the African states little if the United States makes tariff concessions on industrial goods only, if these nations cannot produce and export industrial goods. Then what is a nondiscriminatory policy in principle becomes for all practical purposes a policy of discrimination. It should also be borne in mind that a change in a given nominal tariff rate can differ widely in effects, depending on circumstances. The discussions in Chapters 19 and 21 have indicated that the effects of a change in tariffs depend on the interplay of all the economic forces in the general-equilibrium framework. The lawyer's play of equal treatment can turn out to be something quite different when studied from an economist's point of view.

The principle of most-favored nation is also somewhat peculiar if regarded from a more general, political point of view. It is a case of extreme nationalism. It lumps all foreigners together in one big pack and contrasts them to the members of one's own nation. The home producer, for some reason, has a moral right to be protected. And all foreigners, regardless of neighborhood, political ties, common cultural background, etc., should be treated equally; i.e., all foreign producers should have a right to enter the country's home market on the same conditions as all other foreign producers. If anything, the principle of most-favored nation seems to build on a combination of extreme and opposing political philosophies.

Experience has also shown that a policy built on the most-favored-nation clause has not been very realistic. Little progress has been made along its lines. GATT has also made important exceptions from the principle of nondiscrimination. Customs unions and free trade areas are thus permitted among groups of countries. A customs union means that a group of countries renounces all tariffs between the members of the union but has a common outer tariff wall. A free trade area means also that no tariffs exist among the member countries but that they each have different outside tariff rates; i.e., these exceptions imply that discrimination within GATT is allowed provided it is a 100 percent discrimination.

We can also observe that, even in principle, there is nothing specifically advantageous about a policy of nondiscrimination. It could well be that a discriminatory trade policy is more efficient and leads to a larger improvement in welfare than a nondiscriminatory one. We will return to this point in this chapter and also in Chapter 24.

GATT was slow in getting started and played little role in the immediate postwar period. Apart from nondiscrimination, the leading principle of GATT was that only tariffs would be tolerated as a means of trade policy. The reason was that tariffs are an "honest" means of protection. If exporters in foreign countries know what the tariffs are and if these are kept stable (or perhaps lowered) they know what they have to deal with. Other forms of trade restrictions, especially quotas, exchange controls, etc., are more difficult to deal with and their effects are often very hard to calculate and to foresee; usually they are also prone to frequent alterations and should therefore be avoided.

The difficulties that many GATT members encountered in the first postwar years, however, were so great that the GATT rules could not be strictly kept. The countries in Western Europe, especially, had to be granted exceptions; they used different types of direct controls to deal with their balance-of-payments problems. Frequent rounds of trade negotiations took place under the auspices of GATT, but to begin with it seemed as if the United States and Canada had to grant genuine tariff reductions and in return mostly got empty gestures from the Western European countries. The United States, however, obtained a very important concession: the granting of a waiver that agricultural policies and trade in agricultural goods should be exempted from the GATT rules. This was a time when the United States pursued a policy of extensive farm subsidies that kept American agricultural prices high, a policy that led to a development of very considerable farm surpluses. By the GATT waiver, the United States ensured that this policy would not have to be complicated and endangered by competition from foreign producers of agricultural products.

The negotiations within GATT seemed to produce meager results. The exceptions for agricultural goods also implied a trend in a protectionist direction. But apart from that, some improvement took place, especially concerning the dismantling of direct controls. Trade expanded rapidly in the 1950s, and the trend in trade policy was in a liberal direction. The relatively slow and painstaking development toward a lowering of tariffs through non-discriminatory tariff changes on a world-wide basis, however, soon became overshadowed by the very rapid development of regional trade groupings.

THE DEVELOPMENT OF REGIONAL TRADE GROUPINGS

The state of Western Europe in the late 1940s, after World War II, gave no cause for optimism. The productive machinery of the countries had been greatly damaged by the war. Many problems were encountered when trying to rebuild the economies, not least those concerned with external imbalances. A general feeling was that the reconstruction could not follow traditional national lines, but that cooperation on a wider scale was necessary.

Soon, two competing lines for a Western European integration developed. One argued for close and compact integration of a small group of countries. The other approach aimed at cooperation among a larger group of countries on less specific terms.

Already in the beginning of the 1950s, the proponents of the first approach made some substantial progress. France in 1950 took the initiative in bringing about an economic integration of the steel and coal industries in Belgium, France, Italy, Luxembourg, the Netherlands, and West Germany. The year after, in April 1951, the European Coal and Steel Community (ECSC) was created. The aim of the ECSC was to regulate the production of steel and coal in a way that would benefit the six countries. By close cooperation in an area such as this, the six countries demonstrated a new view on common problems; a war among these countries would now be impossible.

The other approach worked for closer cooperation among the group of countries belonging to the Organization for European Economic Cooperation (OEEC), founded in 1948. The OEEC comprised all the European countries outside the Communist Bloc. It was first created in connection with the launching of the Marshall Aid program, and then was an important forum for economic cooperation between the United States and Western Europe in the first half of the 1950s. Britain was the leading proponent of this approach, which aimed at a less far-reaching cooperation in the form of a European free trade area.

The conflict between the two approaches became manifest in 1955. In this year, the foreign ministers of the six countries belonging to the European Coal and Steel Community met in Messina, Italy. At this meeting Paul-Henri Spaak, the Belgian foreign minister, proposed an enlarged economic cooperation among the six that would lead to a comprehensive common market among them.

A period of intense, prolonged, and nerve-wracking negotiations now followed. The British argued for a European free trade area for industrial goods. Their interests, at this time, lay primarily outside Europe. They wanted close cooperation with the United States and also to have a comparatively free hand in dealing with the overseas members of the British Commonwealth. This approach suited the Scandinavian countries, too, which were primarily interested in free trade but cared less for a close political cooperation with central Europe.

France, especially after de Gaulle came to power, was less interested in larger, more loose cooperation, but preferred closer cooperation among the six. Negotiations were pursued and the French showed great skill in raising unforeseen difficulties while keeping the conferences going and their partners hopefully and enthusiastically bargaining through days and nights, until the bitter, French-determined end.

The result was the establishment of the European Economic Community (EEC). The inaugural date for EEC, or the Common Market, as it is often called, can be set at January 1, 1959. The document in which the six member countries declare their intention to form a common market and in which the ground rules are laid down is the so-called Treaty of Rome, which the six member countries signed in 1957.

The core of the Common Market is the customs union. The partners started immediately to dismantle the tariffs between one another. The progress was rapid in this respect. By January 1966, the internal tariffs on industrial products were abolished. The EEC also aimed at establishing a joint outer tariff wall, set at the arithmetical mean of the 1957 joint tariffs of the six countries. This meant, by and large, an increase in the West German and Benelux tariffs and a decrease in the French and Italian tariffs.

An attempt was also made to harmonize agricultural policies. This proved more difficult. All six members agreed that their agriculture had to be protected. The French, who had the most competitive agriculture, argued for low subsidies, thereby hoping that the French farmers would be able to out-compete the others, especially the German farmers, and get a larger share of the total market. The Germans, on the other hand, wanted a policy of high subsidies that would keep West German agriculture alive; that this would be at the expense of French farm surpluses was not primarily their concern. After protracted negotiations an agreement was reached on a policy of joint prices for farm products to be introduced in 1967. The price policy seems to lean primarily in the West German direction, i.e., to be a policy of high prices. This policy for internal prices is supported by a protectionist policy with regard to nonmembers, so that duties are levied on imports of agricultural products. These duties are to be adapted with the object of avoiding competition from foreign producers.

In Chapter 24, the economic theory of customs unions and their effects on economic policy are discussed.

Other important aspects of the EEC is that the member countries will harmonize their social and economic policy. They will also extend the co-operation to encompass factor movements. Labor will be permitted to move freely between the countries by 1970 and free capital movements within the community will be allowed. Citizens of EEC countries will have the right to establish a business in whichever of the countries they choose.

The negotiations for a broader European free trade area broke down definitively in November 1958. The seven countries outside the Common Market, Austria, Denmark, Great Britain, Norway, Portugal, Sweden, and Switzerland, then started to negotiate the formation of a trade grouping among themselves. In November 1959 they signed the Stockholm treaty, whereby they formed the European Free Trade Association (EFTA). The countries belonging to EFTA, sometimes referred to as the Outer Seven, decided to take away all tariffs among themselves but that each country would have its own, separate tariff wall to the outside world. The decrease in tariffs started in January 1960, and a program of rapid tariff decreases was implemented so that by January 1967 all tariffs on industrial goods among the EFTA countries were abolished. The EFTA countries have not tried to harmonize their social and economic policy or to pursue a joint agricultural policy. The aims of EFTA are limited to free trade in industrial products. EFTA was, from the start, conceived as a basis for bargaining between the Outer Seven and the Six. The most important EFTA country, Great Britain, has also applied for full membership in the Common Market.

The United States played an important role behind the scenes for the development of European economic policy. It favored the concept of a Common Market over the looser cooperation in the form of a free trade area. It is doubtful whether the EEC could have been established at all but for the good will of the United States, which saw a close economic and political cooperation between the Western European countries as a prerequisite for a strong Western Europe that would be able to offer effective resistance against Communist forces.

It is difficult, however, to try to solve short-term problems by long-term structural reforms. One of the ironies of recent history is that the policies of the EEC, which the United States helped to create by a great deal of effort, have proved to be one of the main obstacles to American foreign policy. Once given power, de Gaulle knew perfectly well what he wanted to do with it; his first object was to get rid of American domination.

Europe was not the only continent where regional cooperation developed. Because of the high growth rates of the EEC countries, an annual average 5.5 percent from 1950 to 1963, economic integration looked like a remedy for a variety of sicknesses. It was also tried in Latin America, where 10 countries formed the Latin American Free Trade Association (LAFTA).[1] LAFTA was formed in June 1961. So far, the method used in EEC and EFTA, linear tariff reductions, has not been tried. Instead, a fairly complicated method of bilateral bargaining among lists of products has been tried. Each country has promised to reduce a weighted average of tariffs by an annual 8 percent. After 6 years, 50 percent of all trade within LAFTA should be free; after 12 years, in 1973, the countries comprising LAFTA should have complete internal free trade. So far, however, progress lags behind expectations.

Another interesting regional organization is the Central American Common Market (CACM), consisting of Costa Rica, El Salvador, Guatemala, Honduras, Nicaragua, and Panama. Here integration has made rapid progress, and in 1966 almost all internal trade was on a free trade basis. An

---

[1] The members of LAFTA are Argentina, Brazil, Chile, Colombia, Ecuador, Mexico, Paraguay, Peru, Uruguay, and Venezuela.

almost complete coordination of external tariffs had also been achieved. The period from 1955 to 1965 was one of rapid economic development in this region.

Regional cooperation has also started among other less-developed countries, for instance, in East Africa. So far, these trade groupings are at an embryonic stage.

Regional cooperation has been a dominant feature in the development of trade policy after World War II. GATT did not play the role expected of it. The most important developments were of a discriminatory nature and took place outside GATT. The United States, the most important member of GATT and the main sponsor of a policy of nondiscrimination, did not object to the formation of customs unions such as the EEC; on the contrary, it gave them considerable encouragement. But customs unions usually have a protectionist aspect. If they became too successful, they could prove detrimental to outside interests. This was a risk encountered with the EEC. The United States saw this risk and tried to revitalize a policy of nondiscrimination. This led to the important trade negotiations which took place inside GATT under the name the Kennedy Round.

THE KENNEDY ROUND

The United States had been generous in helping to establish the European Common Market. The EEC was certainly not built on the principle of nondiscrimination, and the GATT rules had to be amended to permit customs unions. This could never have been achieved if the United States had not granted its approval of the procedure.

As the EEC developed into a full-scale customs union, the United States began to feel its protectionist slant. As a reaction to this development and to take the sting out of it, the Kennedy administration in 1962 introduced a bill aimed at vast reciprocal tariff reductions. The idea was contained in the so-called Trade Expansion Act put before the Congress in that year. From a political point of view, the bill was presented as necessary if the United States was to keep up the Atlantic Alliance with Western Europe that had been the cornerstone of American foreign policy. It was also argued that it would improve the U.S. balance of payments; although why joint tariff reductions should improve any particular country's balance of payments was never explained. When American industry showed reluctance to adopt the idea, the Kennedy administration argued that it could now live up to its ideal of competition as the best foundation for a free economy.

The economic content of the Trade Expansion Act was that Congress would grant the administration the right to make a 50 percent tariff reduction on all commodities. On top of this came "the dominant-supplier authority." This said that on commodity groups in which the United States and the Common Market accounted for 80 percent or more of the trade among noncommunist countries, tariffs could be cut to up to 100 percent. Tariffs could, moreover, be completely eliminated if the U.S. tariff rate were less than 5 percent, and on tropical products, provided the Common Market countries reciprocated. The countries' agricultural policies should also be discussed, as would be other nontariff barriers to trade.

The concept behind the Trade Expansion Act was a bold and grand one. Since World War II five tariff-cutting conferences had been held under GATT's auspices. They had all been essentially performed on a bilateral basis and had consisted of bargaining on an item-by-item basis. Progress had been limited. Now it was desired to achieve a great leap forward that could match the achievement of the EEC and EFTA for Europe on a regional basis.

Naturally, the self-interest of the United States was also involved. This was perhaps best seen in connection with the dominant-supplier arrangement. Although phrased in a nondiscriminatory manner, it was hardly so in spirit, as it would allow the largest tariff cuts to be concentrated to goods that were especially important for trade between the United States and the EEC. The less-developed countries would be appeased by the fact that unilateral tariff cuts by the industrial countries were foreseen on certain tropical primary products.

The Trade Expansion Act was adopted by the U.S. Congress in 1962. The enthusiasm of the European countries was less than the Americans had expected, but the negotiations, the Kennedy Round, got under way slowly in 1963.

Soon difficulties arose. The dominant-supplier arrangement was the first casualty. This had built on the belief that Britain would be allowed into the Common Market. When France vetoed British entry in 1963, the dominant-supplier arrangement became, for all practical purposes, void; the eligible commodity groups shrank from 25 to 2, vegetable oils and aircraft, neither of which offers much scope for trade liberalization.

Another difficulty arose in connection with agricultural policy. The EEC countries were at this time, as already stated, involved in a violent internal discussion about what kind of agricultural policy the Common Market should pursue. The Americans wanted the EEC countries to settle this dispute before the Kennedy Round began; they even threatened that no negotiations could start until this matter had been settled. The United States wished for a liberalization of trade in agricultural products. What kind of agricultural policy the EEC chose would therefore be of vital interest to the United States. Eventually the Common Market chose quite a protectionist policy in this respect. The United States could not very well object to this, as the American agricultural policy could be seen as a precedent for the European policy.

The Kennedy Round was thus off to a slow and limping start. Soon other differing views also became evident. The French, especially, did not subscribe to the idea of flat, across-the-board tariff reductions. They argued instead for a " rationalization " of tariff structures. The French view was that tariffs should be low on raw materials, somewhat higher on semimanufactured goods, and high on finished manufactures. Why such an arrangement should be deemed a " rational " one is not easy to see. (The reader might observe, however, that such a tariff structure will have a " cascading " effect and will make the effective rates of protection, as calculated in Chapter 21, very high.) Another objection that the Common Market countries, especially France, raised, was that flat, across-the-board reductions would especially benefit the United States. The average American tariff structure did not seem to differ much from that of the EEC, but it was less even than that of the Common Market. Some American tariffs were unnecessarily high, they " contained water," and even if they were lowered, their protective effect would not be greatly diminished. The low-tariff countries, therefore, should not have to cut their tariffs as much as the high-tariff countries. Another complication was that both the United States and the EEC had lists of goods that they did not wish to introduce into the tariff bargaining for, *inter alia*, defense reasons.

All this led to the negotiations dragging out for several years. By July 1, 1967, the special powers given to the American administration by Congress would be revoked. It was therefore critical for an agreement to be reached by then if the Kennedy Round was to achieve anything. The situation in the spring of 1967 did not allow for much hope. By late May, however, an agreement was reached.

The tariff cuts were smaller than had been envisaged when the Trade Expansion Act was first introduced; there was no question of 50 percent over-all cuts and more. Nonetheless, progress was substantial. Trade covered by the tariff cuts approached a value of $40 billion. It mostly involved trade between the developed countries of the world. The tariff cuts, to be spread over five years, average, on an arithmetical basis, roughly 30 percent. The results of the Kennedy Round are far more substantial than any of the results achieved during the five preceding tariff-cutting conferences held under the auspices of GATT during the postwar period.

The U.S. tariffs on most industrial goods will be about 10 to 20 percent when the results of the Kennedy Round have been fully carried out. Britain's tariffs will be about the same, perhaps slightly higher, whereas those of the Common Market countries will be somewhat lower, probably around 10 percent, and also have a smaller spread. The tariffs of the Scandinavian countries will be lower still.

The Kennedy Round will probably be the last attempt at large tariff reductions in a nondiscriminatory fashion. In a way, it can be regarded as the epitaph of GATT; there is probably not much more to be gained in the way of nondiscrimination. There are those who argue that tariffs now are so low that they can no longer play any crucial role in curtailing trade. GATT, however, can still play an important role in connection with regulating and controlling other impediments to trade, such as quotas, taxes, subsidies, and administrative measures of different kinds that could be used to regulate imports. Tendencies in that direction have not been absent during recent years; if they were to grow, they could of course, cancel the effects of the tariff reductions. GATT can serve a useful purpose in acting as a watchdog in checking those tendencies.

Both the regional cooperation in Europe and the development within GATT's framework have primarily been of concern to developed industrial noncommunist countries, i.e., the United States, Japan, and the countries of Western Europe. The development toward liberalization of trade has been of less significance for the less-developed countries, "the third world." To focus attention on their problems, the countries of the third world pressed the United Nations to convene a special trade conference in Geneva in 1964. Out of this conference developed the United Nations Conference on Trade and Development (UNCTAD). Chapter 23 will be devoted to UNCTAD and to some of the problems it has tried to deal with.

SELECTED BIBLIOGRAPHY: CHAPTER 22

For accounts and discussions of GATT, see:

G. Curzon, *Multilateral Commercial Diplomacy*, London, 1965.

G. Patterson, *Discrimination in International Trade: The Policy Issues, 1945–65*, Princeton, N.J., 1966.

On European trade policy problems and the development of regional trade groupings, see:

Miriam Camps, *Britain and the European Community, 1955–1963*, Princeton, N.J., 1963.

S. Dell, *Trade Blocs and Common Markets*, New York, 1963.

L. B. Krause (ed.), *The Common Market: Progress and Controversy*, Englewood Cliffs, N.J., 1964.

On Latin America:

S. Dell, *A Latin American Common Market?* New York, 1967.

V. L. Urquidi, *Free Trade and Economic Integration in Latin America*, Berkeley, Calif., 1962.

M. S. Wionzek (ed.), *Latin American Economic Integration: Experiences and Prospects*, New York, 1966.

For some aspects of the Kennedy Round, see:

R. E. Baldwin, "Tariff Cutting Techniques in the Kennedy Round," in R. E. Baldwin *et al.*, *Trade, Growth and the Balance of Payments*, Chicago, 1965.

R. N. Cooper, *The Economics of Interdependence: Economic Policy in the Atlantic Community*, New York, 1968, chap. 9.

See also:

B. Balassa, *Trade Liberalization Among Industrial Countries*, New York, 1967.

B. Balassa (ed.), *Studies in Trade Liberalization*, Baltimore, 1967.

UNCTAD and trade policies for less-developed countries

23

The problems of the less-developed countries have now been in the forefront of public discussion for a considerable time. In the years immediately after World War II, when the public generally began to realize the importance of the problem, many economists had a sanguine view of the question. Capital accumulation was asserted to be at the root of the problem. If only capital could be inserted into the underdeveloped economies, they would start to grow. After years of dubious development efforts and depressing experiences, one is now less ready to offer panaceas. There are those who argue that the problem of economic development will be with us, not for years, but for decades and perhaps centuries.

We have seen that the main developments in trade policy have had little relevance for solving the problems of less-developed countries. It is quite natural for the representatives of less-developed countries to feel frustrated by the work done within the framework of GATT and to feel that more consideration ought to be given to their specific problems. It was the efforts roused by such feelings that led to the establishment of United Nations Conference on Trade and Development (UNCTAD).

UNCTAD AND THE QUESTION OF TRADE PREFERENCES

In 1961 the General Assembly of United Nations designated the present decade as United Nations Development Decade, a period in which "member states and their peoples will intensify their efforts to mobilize and sustain support for measures required on the part of both developed and developing countries to accelerate progress towards self-sustaining growth."

Representatives of less-developed countries soon started to press for a special trade conference within the UN's Economic and Social Council. Despite certain opposition their efforts were successful, and in 1964 the first UNCTAD conference was convened in Geneva. One tangible achievement of this conference was the establishment of UNCTAD as a permanent organization with a secretariat employing about 200 persons stationed in Geneva. A second UNCTAD conference was held in New Delhi in 1968.

411

412

UNCTAD and
trade policies for
less-developed countries

The two main problems that have come to dominate the discussions at the conferences and the work of UNCTAD are those of trade or tariff preferences for less-developed countries and of stabilization of international commodity prices. The latter problem will be discussed in the next section. We will now deal with tariff preferences.

The demands from the less-developed countries for trade preferences have grown out of their desire for industrialization. A stabilization of raw material prices might be deemed necessary, but it is not sufficient. "Trade not aid" has been a popular slogan. It is not perhaps meant to be taken literally, but it points to a course which the less-developed countries want to take. A policy of import substitution has not been very successful either, for reasons sketched in Chapter 21. The idea has gained ground that an "outward-looking industrialization" is necessary. This means promoting exports, especially exports of industrial products.

It ought, parenthetically, to be stressed that aid and trade are not substitutes for each other as is sometimes suggested in popular discussion. Aid provides resources for development in the receiving country without the country having to make any efforts of its own. Trade does not in itself create any new resources for a country; it merely provides an opportunity for converting domestic resources into foreign exchange by means of exports. The confusion of the effects of trade and aid usually stems from superficial balance-of-payments considerations; they both provide foreign exchange. From a real economic point of view, it is usually more appropriate to regard aid and trade as complements instead of substitutes, as far as a country's development effort is concerned.

There are two strong reasons exports of manufactured goods could play a critical role in the economic development of most countries. The first is that, for most countries, industrialization is the natural means of development. The second is that, in order for the development effort to be successful, the country in question needs to increase its exports, and the type of export that it can most profitably promote is that of industrial goods. But it has proved difficult for most less-developed countries to gain a foothold in the import markets of the industrial countries. To achieve this one has felt that some kind of new policy is needed. The idea of exports as an "engine of growth" has come back into the discussion. Many believe that in tariff preferences they have found the policy means that could make such an export expansion possible.

The idea behind tariff preferences was primarily developed by Raúl Prebisch, the Secretary-General of UNCTAD, who is also the *spiritus rector* of the organization.[1] Prebisch makes a distinction between "conventional" and "real" reciprocity in trading relations between nations. In this view, conventional reciprocity, when an industrial and a less-developed country make concessions to each other, leads to the less-developed country becoming dependent on an archaic trade pattern, where it will be deemed to go on exporting primary products. Real reciprocity, on the other hand, means that the developed countries grant unilateral tariff reductions to the less-developed countries. Thereby the export capacity of the latter countries will grow, their demands for imports from industrial countries will increase, and world trade will expand. There is no need for close scrutiny of this line of reasoning. We can simply accept that the demand for tariff preferences is built on political and economic wishes of the less-developed countries to increase trade.

The arguments for tariff preferences proposed at the first UNCTAD conference centered to a large degree around the idea of infant-industry protection. Preferences would be granted for a limited time, during which infant industries would be able to grow up by having access to large markets.

It should be observed, however, that this argument differs from the ordinary infant-industry argument. In the ordinary case, the consumers of the country in question will have to pay higher prices and subsidize the producers to enable them to learn skills that will make it possible for them later on, to compete at world market prices. In the case of tariff preferences, it is the consumers of the foreign country, the one granting preferences, who will have to subsidize the producers of less-developed countries, so that they will eventually be able to compete at world market prices.

Even if such an arrangement worked, we must as usual ask whether it is the most efficient means for industrialization in less-developed countries. Would it not be better if the consumers of the developed countries were taxed and a certain amount of taxes given as aid? From a purely economic point of view, it seems that this would be a more rational policy, as it would avoid the distortion of consumption that a tariff preference necessarily

---

[1] The philosophy behind UNCTAD is explained in an important document written by Prebisch, *Towards a New Trade Policy for Development*, Geneva, United Nations, 1964.

414

UNCTAD and
trade policies for
less-developed countries

implies. Against this, it can be argued that what the less-developed countries need is to get some experience of industrialization, and that this can be facilitated by their having access to the markets of the industrial countries.

Another important question in this regard concerns the choice of industries that should be given preferences. Presumably, those industries would be chosen in which the less-developed countries had, or could be expected to have, a comparative advantage. It would be hoped that these would also be the industries in which the industrial countries have substantial tariffs. This would not necessarily be the case, but, if it was, there would perhaps be scope for substantial tariff preferences. There is nothing, however, that says that these industries would also be those that are of an infant-industry type.

Two different principles for granting trade preferences can be imagined. One would be of a fairly nondiscriminatory nature, at least as far as the preference-receiving countries are concerned. Here would be chosen broad groups of industries, in which the less-developed countries would be expected to establish a comparative advantage, and to grant the same preferences to all less-developed countries. This would amount to a general subsidy from the developed countries to industrialization in the less developed countries. Apart from the dynamic effects in the learning of skills and so on that it could have, it can also be said broadly to have the same effect as a combination of transfer of aid from the developed countries and a devaluation by the less-developed countries. However, we should not disregard the political difficulties that such an arrangement could create in the developed countries: Industries that are weak and highly protected in these countries are often supported by strong political pressure groups. Such an arrangement would have the advantage of being easy to comprehend and fairly easy to implement.

The other principle would be to pick the industries that would be given preferential treatment according to their prospects of becoming infant industries. To pick the right industries to qualify in this respect, to determine the duration of protection, etc., would probably be a most cumbersome undertaking. To this must be added that one cannot be sure that tariffs in industrial countries are so high, and hence a preferential treatment so effective, as to provide enough stimulus for industrialization in the less-developed countries. Tariff preferences must then be accompanied by subsidies. We know from tariff theory (Chapter 21) that subsidies are a more efficient policy means than are tariffs. It can then be argued that it would be more efficient to forget about tariff preferences and to concentrate on subsidies altogether if the problem is to promote infant industries.

The idea about tariff preferences also met with criticism and resistance at the UNCTAD conference. One line of argument was that tariffs on most industrial goods are so low in the leading industrial countries that the scope for tariff preferences is limited.[2] The tariff rates seem to average between 10 and 15 percent. If tariff preferences of 50 percent were granted, the price of a less-developed country over competitors from a developed country would be about 5 to 7 percent. Such a small price advantage, it is argued, would not be decisive. If the less-developed countries are unable to compete without a trade preference, they will not, under these circumstances, be able to compete given a preference.

This line of argument perhaps sounds plausible; it does, however, have some weaknesses. First, it must be stated that even though average tariff rates are not too high, tariffs on individual products could be substantially higher. Second, it is quite arbitrary to presume that tariff preferences would be limited to, for instance, 50 percent. A complete preferential treatment of certain sensitive products could perhaps give much higher price advantages than 5 to 7 percent.

A more important objection is that what really counts is not the final or manifest tariff rates but implicit rates or effective rates of protection. Here we must refer the reader to the discussion at the end of Chapter 21. Fairly low final rates could conceal much higher effective rates of protection. If that is the case, the question of tariff preferences, it is argued, would have to be viewed in a completely different perspective.[3]

Most countries have a "cascading" type of tariff structure; i.e., tariffs on raw materials are lower than tariffs on semimanufactured goods which in turn are lower than tariffs on final products. This usually means that the effective rates of protection on final goods are substantially higher than the nominal tariff rates.[4] On most consumer goods of export interest to

---

[2] This argument is presented in Gardner Patterson, *Discrimination in International Trade, The Policy Issues,* 1945–1965, Princeton University Press, Princeton, N.J., 1966.

[3] This argument is put forward by H. G. Johnson in *Economic Policies Toward Less Developed Countries,* Washington, D.C., The Brookings Institution, 1967.

[4] For empirical estimates of effective rates of protection, see B. Balassa, "Tariff Protection in Industrial Countries: An Evaluation," *Journal of Political Economy,* vol. 73, December, 1965; and G. Basevi, "The U.S. Tariff Structure: Estimates

416

UNCTAD and
trade policies for
less-developed countries

less-developed countries, the final tariff rates in the United States, Western Europe, and Japan seem to be about 20 to 25 percent, whereas the effective rates on the same goods seem to be more than double that figure, in the 50 to 60 percent range.[5] This would indicate that there could conceivably be substantial scope for tariff preferences on these goods.

We have to bear in mind, however, the objections raised in Chapter 21 against the use of effective rates of protection. For several reasons raised there, the vagueness about what effective rates of protection are really supposed to protect, the disregard of substitution possibilities, etc., we must be quite skeptical in trying to assess the value and implications of the empirical evaluations of effective rates of protection. Pending further research, primarily of a theoretical nature, we must leave its relevancy for the question of trade preferences very much open. It has in no way been proved that taking effective rates of protection into account will pose the problem of tariff preferences in a new light.

In general, it can be said that the theory of tariff preferences is a branch of the theory of discriminatory tariff changes, as it has primarily been developed in the form of the theory of customs unions. This is a very complex branch of general equilibrium analysis which has been developed since 1950, and the results of a more general nature which this branch of theory has, so far, arrived at are few and not very deep. The theory of customs unions will be surveyed in Chapter 24; the ambitious reader can then try to assess the validity and relevancy of those results for the question of tariff preferences. The immediate relevancy of the results of the theory of customs unions for the question of tariff preferences, however, is probably not too great.

Broadly speaking, it can be said that discriminatory tariff changes give rise to two types of effects: trade creation and trade diversion. Trade creation means that because of the preference, low-cost goods from the preference-receiving country will outcompete high-cost goods produced at home. This effect is beneficial, as it will mean an increase in welfare. Trade diversion means that, because of the preference, goods from the preference-receiving country produced at relatively high cost will outcompete goods from a third

---

of Effective Rates of Protection of U.S. Industries and Industrial Labor," *Review of Economics and Statistics*, December 1966.
[5] See Johnson, *op. cit.*, pp. 174 ff.

country produced at lower cost, but which will now be at a disadvantage because they are being discriminated against. Trade diversion will generally lead to a lowering of welfare, as it results in a misallocation of resources in production.

The results of tariff preferences can therefore be said to depend on whether they cause trade creation or trade diversion. If the former, they are beneficial; if the latter, they will lead to a lowering of the world's welfare (and most likely also of the welfare of the trading partners).

Two examples of possible effects of tariff preferences could be useful. One is where the preference-receiving country produces only a small part of the preference-granting country's total imports of the goods in question. After it has been granted the preference, the less-developed country can increase its price of this export from the world market price up to the tariff-included price in the preference-granting country. This means that the producers in the less-developed country will get a windfall gain. If they can expand production at not too steeply rising costs, it would possibly yield a handsome profit, which they can reinvest for further expansion and so on. If they can acquire factors of production, for instance, labor, at only substantially increasing costs, their profits would perhaps not increase much but, in the long run, the country would get a substantial increase in its volume of trained labor, and so on. In this event, the tariff-granting country would gain nothing; all the gain would go to the preference-receiving country.

An example at the other extreme is that where the tariff-receiving country is the dominant world producer of the goods in question. Then, no matter what happens in the tariff-granting country, the tariff-receiving country will have to go on selling the product at the world market price. This means that producers in the tariff-receiving country will take over the whole market in the tariff-granting country, but this will in all likelihood be only of marginal concern to them, and they stand to gain little. Here the gain is concentrated to the tariff-granting country, which will benefit in two ways. First, because the consumers can buy the goods in question more cheaply; second, because the country will get the goods at a lower opportunity cost by importing it than by producing it at home. Both these effects are of a trade-creating nature.

These are two examples of how the theory of discriminatory tariff changes can be applied to throw some light on the effects of tariff preferences. Generally speaking, we might say that the former types of effects, which are

418

UNCTAD and
trade policies for
less-developed countries

primarily beneficial to preference-receiving countries, would probably prevail, as in most cases the less-developed countries would not be large producers of the goods in question. A policy inference to be drawn is that there would be no great point in granting preferences for primary goods and raw materials in which the less-developed countries already have a dominant share of world trade.

From a strictly economic point of view, it is difficult to argue either firmly against or firmly for trade preferences. The question is also sensitive viewed from a political angle. Some countries tend to view the problem from a primarily protectionist point of view. They do not see anything unnatural in discriminating against foreigners, and some countries could be regarded as more foreign than others. This means that they can use tariff preferences to discriminate against these countries while tying other countries closer to their own sphere of influence by granting them tariff preferences.

Other countries could view the problem from what can be predominantly termed a free trade angle. They could argue that a discriminatory policy would, during a certain period, be used as an instrument for achieving freer trade. But tariff preferences should then be used in as little a discriminatory fashion as possible. Especially poor or weak countries could be given extra preferential treatment, but otherwise preferences should be granted equally to all underdeveloped countries and should encompass broad commodity groups in which the less-developed countries could be expected to develop a comparative advantage.

So far, not much progress concerning tariff preferences has been achieved at the two UNCTAD conferences in 1964 and 1968. This is perhaps natural, taking into account the large economic and political complexities involved. Ultimately, the strongest argument for tariff preferences will perhaps have to be of a very pragmatic nature. The need for an increase in the rate of economic development in most of the less-developed countries becomes more pressing each year. It is obviously very difficult to find and implement any policy means that foster development. Against this background it is natural to try to see if tariff preferences could not be an efficient means for accelerating development. This could in the end be the strongest reason for trying to work out a scheme for tariff preferences that would prove viable.

STABILIZATION OF INTERNATIONAL COMMODITY PRICES

The other big problem with which UNCTAD has been concerned is that of stabilization of international commodity prices. Exports of primary products are by far the most important source of earnings of foreign exchange for most less-developed countries, accounting for 85 to 90 percent of their export earnings. But prices on primary products fluctuate widely. This leads to instability in the export earnings. The instability gives rise to many problems, including difficulties in planning development, and hampers the development process seriously. If commodity prices could be stabilized, an important obstacle to development could be eliminated. Hence the stabilization of commodity prices must be given high priority. This is the argument.

Here the ground is slippery and we must tread carefully. It is otherwise easy to perpetuate old dogmas and go on mechanically repeating old half-truths. The traditional view just paraphrased sounds convincing, but we must examine it more carefully. First, we might observe that it is not quite clear what is to be stabilized. Stabilizing prices is not the same thing as stabilizing earnings, and stabilizing export earnings is not necessarily the same thing as stabilizing real income.

One line of argument is that the terms of trade between broad groups of commodities, such as primary products and industrial goods, ought to be stabilized and that the purchasing power of a certain amount of exports of primary goods in terms of imports of industrial goods should be preserved. This line of argument has been pushed by Raúl Prebisch for years and traces of it are also evident in the 1964 UNCTAD report prepared by Prebisch.[6]

This argument, however, is primarily an act of wishful thinking and can claim no foundation in rational economic reasoning. We know from earlier reasoning, especially from our study of economic growth and trade in Part II, that international prices must be viewed as endogenous variables in an economic system. Variations in the terms of trade depend in a complex way on changes in production and consumption and on other basic economic variables. An aspiration to control the long-term development of the terms of trade is the same as an aspiration to control all variables in the economic system. To be effective, it would imply perfect economic planning on a world-

---

[6] *Towards a New Trade Policy for Development*, pp. 11 ff.

420

UNCTAD and
trade policies for
less-developed countries

wide scale. It is difficult to see how anyone who has grasped the core of the problem could support schemes of such a utopian nature.

To claim that a certain amount of primary products should have a stable purchasing power over industrial products in the long run is about as unrealistic a claim as that of stabilizing terms of trade. There is no reason whatsoever to expect such a development to take place, nor is there anything specifically "just" about it. It is impossible to understand why one should try to keep stable, in the long run, a certain relation between volumes and relative prices given at an arbitrary historical moment.

We then come to more reasonable views about what to stabilize. One view is that we should try to stabilize prices on some well-defined primary products. Another is to try to stabilize export earnings of the less-developed countries. These two proposals do not amount to the same thing. Stabilization of prices will not lead to a stabilization of export earnings if the supply changes. This is an important point to bear in mind, as output changes seem to be a prime cause of fluctuations in export earnings. Another point worth making is that a stabilization of money proceeds or money incomes is not the same as a stabilization of real incomes if the general price level changes.

We can take a more reasonable proposal to be that commodity prices should be stabilized in order to stabilize export earnings. This demand for stabilizing prices derives from the proposition that unstable prices cause difficulties for development policies and for plans to manage the domestic economy in a successful way.

Instability per se need not, however, have such disastrous consequences. In principle, the governments in these countries should be able to plan around trend values for prices and incomes and help to overcome the difficulties of lean years by building up reserves during fat years. Governments of less-developed countries could for several reasons experience difficulties in doing this. Then a demand for price stabilization could be viewed as a demand from weak governments to stronger governments to help solve problems that should primarily concern only the weak governments.

It could perhaps be argued that the governments of less-developed countries are afflicted with especially difficult problems in this regard. The reasons usually given for this is that supply and demand vary greatly for individual primary products, that supply and demand elasticities are low, that the exports of the less-developed countries are specialized to a few products, and that, on the marketing side, they have to rely on market conditions in a few industrial countries.

These factors could potentially cause fluctuations in prices. In reality, prices on primary products do not seem to have been particularly unstable. The thought of instability has been one of the most cherished beliefs of development economics. This belief does not seem to be borne out by the facts.

A British economist, Alisdair MacBean, published in 1966 a major econometric investigation about fluctuations in prices of primary products.[7] When MacBean started his investigation, he thought that the prevailing views were correct. He merely wanted to study what policy means could be used to dampen the fluctuations in export proceeds and to see how their adverse effects on the growth process could be eliminated.

But soon he started to question the basic facts. His findings can be briefly summarized as follows: Less-developed countries have only insignificantly greater fluctuations in their export incomes than industrial countries. Three causes that could have been expected to result in instability—commodity concentration of exports, proportion of primary goods in total exports, and geographical concentration of exports—all have little value in explaining the fluctuations that have taken place. One extremely important finding is also that it is not fluctuating prices that have primarily caused the fluctuations in export incomes. The prime causes are on the supply side. MacBean chose 12 of the less-developed countries that had had especially large fluctuations in their export incomes: Argentina, Bolivia, Ghana, Haiti, Indonesia, Iran, Iraq, Korea, Malaya, Pakistan, Sudan, and Vietnam. In four of these, Malaya, Indonesia, to a certain extent Pakistan, and Vietnam, price fluctuations have had an important bearing on the fluctuations in export incomes. But in the others, and also to a large extent in the four countries, the primary cause of fluctuations in export proceeds is the fluctuation in output produced. The main difficulty of the less-developed countries in producing primary products lies in controlling supply. It is the variations in output produced that is the prime cause of fluctuations in export incomes.[8] Part of the cause of supply changes among the 12 countries referred to also lies in political disturbances, but this does not change the main picture.

---

[7] Alisdair MacBean, *Export Instability and Economic Development*, London, Allen and Unwin, 1966.

[8] It is interesting to note that Cuba has understood this dilemma. It is now making great efforts to promote agriculture, to concentrate exports to a limited number of products, and to take great care in trying to control supply conditions by implementing scientific agricultural methods.

422

UNCTAD and
trade policies for
less-developed countries

Another of MacBean's findings worthy of note is that the changes in export incomes that have taken place have not led to such adverse effects for the growth of the economies as could have been expected. Built-in stabilizers and high marginal propensities to import seem to offset fluctuations to a large extent. Therefore, fluctuations in national incomes are not so large as could be expected.

Empirical and theoretical considerations thus lead to the scope for stabilization schemes being more limited than at first sight thought likely. Much care must be taken in defining the objective of a stabilization scheme and in studying what the causes of instability could be. If the cause is irregularity of supply, a stabilization of prices will usually aggravate instability by holding prices down when supply is short and by keeping prices up when supplies are plentiful. Stabilization schemes are usually costly to carry out. Therefore, it could be asked whether or not other means, such as provision of money reserves or borrowing facilities, could be more efficient in dealing with the problems that instability gives rise to.

International commodity agreements have been attempted ever since the 1920s, but with limited success. Since World War II, agreements have been concluded for only five commodities: wheat, sugar, coffee, tin, and olive oil. Two of these, the agreements on olive oil and sugar, do not currently influence international trade. The sugar agreement broke down in 1962 when trade between Cuba and the United States ceased, and the olive oil agreement is primarily concerned with the coordination of domestic national policies; trade in olive oil comprises only 5 percent of the total world production. The wheat agreement has been of little importance; the price-maintaining policies of the two main suppliers, the United States and Canada, have instead played the dominant role. Nor do the other agreements seem to have been particularly successful. The coffee agreement, made in 1963, has encountered serious difficulties, such as numerous requests for change in basic quotas, but it is still too early to say anything more definite about its usefulness.

It is not surprising, against the theoretical and practical difficulties that commodity agreements entail, that they have been in little use. Instances could arise, however, in which they would serve a useful purpose. Some of the theoretical considerations that will probably have to be taken into account when constructing stabilization schemes will now be discussed.

There are several types of stabilization schemes that can be constructed. One is the use of buffer stocks. The operators of the scheme own a stock, either of money or of a commodity. They use this stock to mitigate fluctuations in prices by selling from the stock when prices are high and buying the commodity when prices are low.

This scheme is only possible for certain products with low storage costs. There is always a cost involved in the form of interest on the capital invested in the stock. If additional costs, such as costs for warehousing space, refrigeration, and pesticides, are high, a buffer-stock scheme is obviously impracticable. The main difficulty with a buffer-stock scheme (as with stabilization schemes in general) is in foreseeing the long-term equilibrium price. If the operators are too optimistic about prices (or pressed into being too optimistic by producer interests), they will try to maintain too high a price, and the stocks will keep growing. This cannot go on indefinitely; eventually the stocks will have to be disposed of at a loss. If the price should be set too low, which is more unlikely, the stocks will instead be sold out and the price can only be kept down for a limited time. Buffer-stock schemes can only be used to mitigate short-term price fluctuations; they cannot be used to offset the damaging effects of trends in prices.

Another type of stabilization scheme is a restriction scheme. This means that less-developed countries agree to restrict production or exports of the commodity in question in order to maintain its price. Restriction schemes can be useful, especially if competition among producers is keen and demand inelastic. Then the price might be driven down very low if nothing is done. Under these circumstances, prices can be maintained and the total revenue increased by a restriction of exports.

Restriction schemes, however, have certain drawbacks. One is that they are usually difficult to enforce for any long period. There is always a temptation for a single producer to break away from the scheme, thereby being able to sell a larger quantity at a good price. Tendencies to overproduction, which usually follow from the price-maintenance policy, can easily cause a breakdown of the system.

If the price is maintained at a high level for some time, this can also create difficulties on the demand side. The demand elasticity could be low in the short term, but it could be substantially higher in the long run. A policy of high prices could then mean that demand for the product will not expand as much as it otherwise would. It could also lead to the development of competing products, for instance, of a synthetic kind, that can prove very damaging in the long run. What has happened to rubber is an illustration of this danger.

424

UNCTAD and
trade policies for
less-developed countries

Restriction schemes, moreover, easily give rise to a misallocation of resources. They tend to conserve a given production structure both among and within countries, and established but inefficient producers will prevail over new and more efficient ones. Restriction schemes could be useful to alleviate short-term problems, but they are rarely efficient in the long run. They build on an intrinsic conservatism and will probably eventually prove detrimental to economic growth.

Other schemes could be more useful. An interesting multilateral price-compensation scheme was proposed at the 1964 UNCTAD conference by James Meade.[9] Let us assume, says Meade, that there are two countries, Ruritania and Urbania, and that Ruritania exports a primary product, Commod, which Urbania imports. The two countries now agree on a "normal" volume traded and a "standard" price. The countries then devise a sliding scale whereby if the price falls below the "standard" price, Urbania pays Ruritania a compensation which equals the shortfall of the "standard" price on the "normal" amount traded. Conversely, Ruritania pays Urbania an amount equal to an excess over the "standard" price times the "normal" volume if the price is above its normal level.

The main idea behind the Meade proposal is to try to separate the distributional effects of the price mechanism from its allocative effects. When the price of a product falls, this is a signal to producers to produce less and to consumers to consume more. This is the efficiency aspect or allocative aspect of the price mechanism, and this we usually do not want to interfere with. But price changes also have distributional implications. When the price falls, producers get hurt, because their incomes fall. So do workers in the less-developed country; the tax base of the government shrinks, and so on. This can, at least partially, be avoided by a scheme à la Meade. It is most natural to think of the scheme as one between governments. If the price falls and the producers in Ruritania get lower incomes, the consumers in Urbania will benefit by lower prices. But they will now have to pay more in taxes, and this increase in taxes will be transferred to the government in Ruritania. The government there can then dispose of this income as they see fit. They can directly subsidize producers of Commod, or they can invest it for development purposes.

---

[9] J. E. Meade, "International Commodity Agreements," *Lloyds Bank Review*, vol. 73, July 1964.

So far the scheme has been sketched on a bilateral basis. But it can easily be extended to a multilateral basis. Then a "normal" volume of imports is designated for each importing country and a "normal" volume of exports for each exporting country. A "standard" price has to be agreed upon. Then if the actual price differs from the "standard" price, the respective countries will have to pay and receive compensation according to "normal" volumes.

A difficulty with this scheme, as with others, is that of forecasting the price correctly. If the price is set too high, the scheme amounts to a transfer of resources from the industrial to the primary producing countries; conversely, if the price is set too low. One could think of an arrangement whereby initially the price was set too high, but then would be gradually lowered. Then the compensation scheme would also entail an aid arrangement which could help the primary producing countries to develop other sectors during a transitory period.

The Meade scheme is both simple and elegant, but it has certain drawbacks. An important one is connected with its aggregated nature. If a producer is small and a change in his output does not affect the world price of the goods, it could well be that even though the output of this producer is very low one year, prices would not exceed the "standard" price. The country would then get no compensation, even though its export proceeds fell considerably. A scheme such as Meade's has difficulties in dealing with fluctuations caused by changes in the supply of single countries. This is a serious deficiency, as we have seen that the primary cause of fluctuations in export earnings seems to be difficulties in controlling supply conditions in the primary producing countries themselves.

CONCLUDING REMARKS ON TRADE POLICIES FOR LESS-DEVELOPED COUNTRIES

So far the result of our discussion has tended to be on the negative side. It seems that the trend in the thinking among experts is away from commodity agreements. The theoretical and practical difficulties that they entail seem to be so great that the costs of implementing them would be greater than the eventual benefits.

426

UNCTAD and
trade policies for
less-developed countries

Another possibility is compensatory financing of fluctuations in export earnings. Such schemes can be of two kinds. They can either be straight-forward insurance schemes designed to stabilize a country's earnings over time without altering its total receipts, or they can, on top of the insurance part, also involve a transfer of real resources from the developed to the less-developed countries.

The most important scheme so far is that devised by the International Monetary Fund. This is a scheme to help less-developed countries whose export earnings decline to get easier loans than usual. A country can temporarily borrow 25 percent of its IMF quota, subject to the approval of the Fund if the export earnings fall below a certain moving average. This scheme was criticized at the UNCTAD conference for being too limited and conservative. The less-developed countries wanted to have more medium-term credit available in times of declining export earnings.

Any scheme of compensatory financing will probably prove unsatis-factory from the point of view of the less-developed countries. This depends on fluctuations not being their main problem, which instead is lack of resources. To get some degree of approval, a scheme of compensatory financing has to have some element of aid in it. But to tie aid to fluctuations in export earnings could easily be arbitrary and create a weakness in this type of scheme. Countries that strive successfully to control supply condi-tions could get the smallest amount of aid. Under such circumstances, resources could easily be transferred to countries where they are least efficiently used.

The most efficient type of trade policy that the developed countries can for the time being pursue is probably to extend protectionist preferences to less-developed countries. Such a policy can take different forms. The two most promising ones seem to be either levies in the developed countries on products from the less-developed countries which are then reimbursed to these latter countries, or established quotas in the developed countries for products from the less-developed countries.

The first line has been taken up in a French plan for organization of markets. On goods that both countries produce, a tariff can be levied on the imports from the less-developed country. This will make prices on imports and domestically produced goods coincide. A part, or the whole, of the tariff revenue can then be reimbursed to the less-developed country. If the goods are a primary product not produced in the developed country, a tariff can be viewed as a tax on consumers taken up by the government in the developed country on behalf of the government in the less-developed country. This could be a way for the less-developed country to exploit a monopoly situation in the market of the industrial country.[10]

Another line, favored by the Americans, is to give quotas or quantitative guarantees of access to markets in developed countries for producers in less-developed countries. This has the advantage of giving control to the importing country of how much it will accept, and the exporting country at least knows that it can sell a certain quantity to the industrial country. This is a policy that has been used by the United States, in its imports of cane sugar, for instance.

None of the policies sketched above is ideal. For a believer in international competition and division of labor, they have obvious shortcomings. A policy of manipulating prices by tariffs leads to featherbedding for producers in both developed and less-developed countries. Under the guise of a working price system, competition is eliminated or greatly restricted, and consumers are exploited by the use of monopolistic practices. A policy of quota arrangements will, in all probability, lead to a control of markets and the conservation of inefficient production structures. Prices will also be kept artificially high and consumption be curtailed.

Still, in a world of protectionist practices, measures like these are perhaps the only practicable ones. An American economist, John Pincus, has made some estimates of gains to be had along these lines.[11] According to several criteria, he found that coffee, tea, cocoa, bananas, and sugar would be suitable products for support. In 1961, export earnings of these commodities amounted to $4.3 billion. Monopoly pricing would have raised export earnings by a little more than 15 percent, to over $5 billion. This might be taken as a rough measure of the gains to be had from policies of a protectionist nature.

Our discussion has not given too much reason for hope. There are perhaps some gains to be derived for the less-developed countries from a

---

[10] It should be observed that producers in less-developed countries in general should not try to maximize revenues and thereby earnings of foreign currency. This is a fallacious view reached by confusion of balance-of-payments considerations with real-income considerations. Provided that resources used in primary production have some alternative opportunity cost, an optimum policy implies that output should be restricted below the level that would maximize total revenue.

[11] John A. Pincus, *Economic Aid and International Cost Sharing*, Baltimore, The Johns Hopkins Press, 1965.

428

UNCTAD and
trade policies for
less-developed countries

revision of trade policy in the developed countries. These gains, however, seem to be limited. In the immediate future, export earnings of the less-developed countries will have to come primarily from exports of primary products. A revision of trade policies, especially of agricultural policies in the developed countries, should be of help to the less-developed countries, but this help will be limited. Many less-developed countries will have to try to get their industrialization under way. Tariff preferences could help in this respect, but how efficient they would prove is an open question. A certain skepticism is probably not unwarranted.

Trade policies are not unimportant, but they will have only marginal effects unless supplemented by other means. What is needed is the application of scientific methods in agriculture that can lead to control of supply conditions and give the less-developed countries a firm and reliable export base in products in which they have a natural comparative advantage. Furthermore, industries will have to be built and managed rationally. Whether this can be done within the existing structure of society is an open question. Large vistas open up in which trade policy is only a detail.

SELECTED BIBLIOGRAPHY: CHAPTER 23

Two interesting documents prepared for the two UNCTAD conferences by R. Prebisch (then Secretary General) are:

Towards A New Trade Policy for Development, United Nations, Geneva, 1964.

Towards A Global Strategy of Development, United Nations, Geneva, 1968.

For a book dealing especially with the political and institutional aspects of the 1964 conference, see:

A. S. Friedeberg, *The United Nations Conference on Trade and Development of 1964*, Rotterdam, 1968.

See also:

G. Patterson, *Discrimination in International Trade: the Policy Issues 1945–65*, Princeton, N.J., 1966.

For a neat presentation and concise analysis of trade policy questions in connection with less-developed countries, see:

H. G. Johnson, *Economic Policies Toward Less Developed Countries*, Washington, D.C., 1967.

For discussions of commodity arrangements see:

J. W. F. Rowe, *Primary Commodities in International Trade*, Cambridge, 1965.

J. D. Coppock, *International Economic Instability*, New York, 1962.

A. I. MacBean, *Export Instability and Economic Development*, London, 1966.

For tariff preferences see:

H. B. Lary, *Imports of Manufactures from Less Developed Countries*, New York, 1968.

S. Weintraub, *Trade Preferences for Less Developed Countries*, New York, 1967.

The theory of customs unions

24

We have seen that one of the major aspects of international trading relations during the postwar period has been the development of regional trade groupings, primarily in the form of customs unions. This development naturally aroused the attention of trade theorists. Standard trade theory had only been concerned with the effects of nondiscriminatory tariff changes, the type of tariff theory we have studied in Chapters 19 and 21. But customs unions are by definition discriminatory. They mean a lowering of tariffs within the union and an establishing of a joint outer tariff wall. They combine free trade with protectionism.

This makes customs unions difficult to deal with from a theoretical point of view. We have seen that ordinary tariff theory is quite complicated when general equilibrium considerations are taken into account. The theory of customs unions is even more complex.

To begin with, one tried to formulate general propositions about the welfare effects of a customs union. The free trade aspects of customs unions were stressed, and the general consensus seemed to be that customs unions would increase welfare. This was disputed on several grounds as the theory developed; economists tended to oscillate between broad generalizations and agnosticism.

Still, the theory is quite intuitive in character, and its results tend to take the form of some propositions of the type "if these conditions prevail, customs unions will lead to an increase (alternatively a lowering) of welfare." These propositions are generally not very deep. No precise, neatly established theorems, built on explicit models of a general equilibrium character, have so far been derived. It is characteristic that the discussion runs in terms of "welfare effects"; it has not been possible to derive precise results for the effects on all the different variables in the general equilibrium setting, terms of trade, domestic prices, volumes, national incomes, etc. Instead, an intuitive kind of reasoning has been used. The main results in customs union theory, as it stands today, will now be surveyed.[1]

TRADE CREATION AND TRADE DIVERSION

The pioneering study of the theory of customs unions was made by Jacob Viner.[2] In the beginning, customs unions had been viewed favorably. The

---

TABLE 24.1

Production cost of commodity X in three countries

Country	A	B	C
Production cost	50	40	30

---

reasoning was: Free trade maximizes welfare. Customs unions are a move toward free trade. Therefore, they will increase welfare even though they might not maximize it.

Viner showed this conclusion to be incorrect. He introduced, instead, the key concepts of trade creation and trade diversion. They might best be illustrated by Table 24.1. The table measures the production cost of a commodity in three countries. Let us disregard transportation cost, markups, etc., so that production cost completely determines the supply price of the good, and tariffs are the only source of diversion between price and cost. If Country A has a tariff of 100 percent on X, there will be no imports of the good, but domestic producers will dominate the home market. If A had levied a lower tariff, say 50 percent, and it was nondiscriminatory, it would have imported the good from the lower-cost source, Country C, and the price in A's home market would be 45.

Let us now assume that A and B form a customs union. A will then, instead, import X from B, and the price in A's market will be 40. Imports will be switched from the low-cost supplier, C, to the high-cost supplier, B. This is an example of trade diversion. Trade diversion takes place when imports from a more efficiently producing country are switched to a less efficiently producing country because of the customs union. Trade diversion will lead to a lowering of welfare, as it entails a less efficient allocation of resources.

We must mention here that this analysis assumes that the countries involved are fully employed both before and after the formation of the customs union. In this sense the analysis is of a neoclassical type. This being the case, it is natural to let the analysis primarily be concerned with the

---

[1] This chapter builds primarily on R. G. Lipsey's celebrated article "The Theory of Customs Unions: A General Survey," *Economic Journal*, vol. 70, September 1960.

[2] J. Viner, *The Customs Union Issue*, New York, Carnegie Endowment for International Peace, 1953.

FIGURE 24.1

Complementarity and overlapping production structures

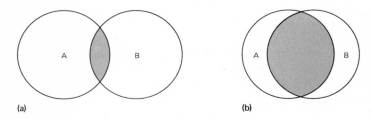

(a)   (b)

effects on the allocation of resources and the welfare implications of these effects.

This kind of analysis gives rise to three possibilities. First, neither of the two countries forming the union produces the good in question. The customs union would then be of no significance, as both countries would import the good from a third country just as they did before forming the union. Second, one of the countries forming the union produces the good inefficiently, i.e., is not the lowest-cost available source of supply. The union partner would then import from the cheaper source and there will be a case of trade diversion. Third, both countries forming the customs union produce the good, in which case one of the countries would be more efficient than the other. The market in both countries will then be secured for the more efficient industry, and there will be trade creation.

This analysis suggests that if a customs union primarily leads to trade creation, it will lead to an increase in welfare; and if it primarily gives rise to trade diversion, it will lead to a lowering in the world's welfare. In this case, it will certainly lead to a lowering in the welfare of the third country (the rest of the world). Whether it will also lead to a lowering in the welfare of the countries forming the customs union is less certain; we will shortly return to this case.

The implication of this analysis is that customs unions will lead to detrimental effects if the countries are complementary in the list of goods they produce. If, on the other hand, the group of commodities that both countries produce under tariff protection is large, the scope for positive welfare effects is large. Figure 24.1 illustrates these facts.

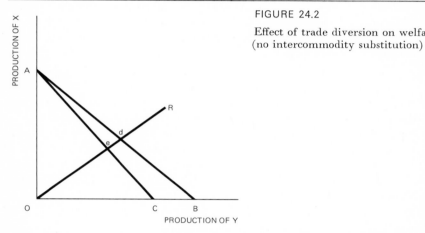

FIGURE 24.2

Effect of trade diversion on welfare
(no intercommodity substitution)

Figure 24.1a illustrates a situation where the two countries are primarily complementary. The area where the two economies overlap, shown by the shaded union of A and B, is small. Figure 24.1b shows a situation where the two economies are primarily competitive. The area of overlapping production, shown by the shaded union of A and B, is large.

Intuitively, one might think that an agricultural country ought to form a union with an industrial country. This is not the case. Agricultural countries should form customs unions with each other, and an industrial country should form a union with another industrial country. The scope for trade creation is then largest, and so is the scope for an improved allocation of resources and an increase in welfare. The countries within the European Common Market are all primarily industrial countries. Therefore, we would expect them to make substantial gains from their union.

We can also observe that the larger the cost differentials between the countries in the union on goods they both produce before the union, the larger the scope for gains. We will shortly return to this point.

The Vinerian analysis of trade creation and trade diversion is useful, but it is only a beginning. Viner assumed that there are no possibilities of substitution in consumption—that all price elasticities of demand are equal to zero. On the supply side, on the other hand, he supposed the supply elasticities to be infinitely large, so that all products are produced under constant returns to scale. It is easy to understand why Viner chose these assumptions.

If goods are consumed in constant proportions irrespective of prices and if costs are constant, then the only interesting thing left to study is the shifts in production between countries as given by trade creation and trade diversion. Then trade diversion, for instance, will always cause a lowering of welfare. This is illustrated in Figure 24.2.

Country A is completely specialized in production of X. It produces at point A on the X axis. It exchanges X for Y on the world market at the best terms of trade possible. They are given by the line AB. Consumers in the country consume the two goods in a constant proportion given by the ray OR from the origin. The point of consumption is then at d.

A now forms a customs union with Country C. This leads to trade diversion. Country A is still completely specialized in production of X, which it exchanges for Y from C. Because of the customs union, A's terms of trade deteriorate. The new terms of trade are given by the line AC. The country still consumes along the ray OR and consumption now will be at point e. This point is clearly inferior to d as it represents a smaller amount of both goods.

This analysis shows that, on the Vinerian assumption of no substitution in consumption, trade diversion will necessarily lower A's welfare. But Viner's assumptions are very strong and quite unrealistic. A customs union will normally lead to a change in all relative prices. Will not, then, substitution take place? This is what we would normally expect. We will now look into some of the effects that substitution in consumption might give rise to.

INTERCOUNTRY AND INTERCOMMODITY SUBSTITUTION

If a country enters a customs union and trade diversion follows on some goods it means that the country will have to pay a higher price in acquiring these goods. But at the same time the domestic consumers will no longer have to pay a duty on the goods, and its domestic price will probably fall. This will lead to an expansion in consumption of the goods, provided substitution takes place. This implies an improvement in the welfare of consumers. There are then two contradictory forces: a deterioration in the terms of trade, implying a lowering of welfare; and increased consumption, implying an increase of

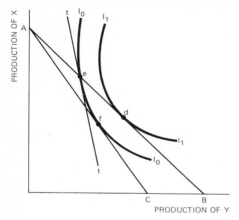

FIGURE 24.3

Effect of trade diversion on welfare
(with intercommodity substitution)

welfare. The result of trade diversion is then no longer given. This case is illustrated in Figure 24.3.

Country A is completely specialized in production of good X and produces at point A on the X axis. Before the union it imports good Y from the cheapest possible source, Country B, at the terms of trade AB. If free trade were permitted, consumption would be at point d, where an indifference curve I_1–I_1 is tangent to the price line AB. Now, the country prefers to have a steep duty on Y, and the domestic price ratio is indicated by line tt. Consumption is then at point e, where another indifference curve, I_0–I_0, is tangent to the price line tt. The tariff leads to a fall in consumption of Y which is substituted by X and to a lowering in consumers' welfare. The terms of trade AB are assumed not to have been affected by the tariff.

Country A now forms a customs union with Country C. This leads to trade diversion and to a worsening of A's terms of trade. The country still produces at A and exchanges X for Y. The new terms of trade are given by line AC. This need not necessarily lead to a lowering in welfare for consumers, because the price ratio AC will now be ruling in A's domestic market and Y is now cheaper than at the tariff-inclusive price ratio tt. Y will therefore be substituted for X in consumption and consumption will move to point f. Point f is on the same indifference curve as e. Hence consumers are as well off after the customs union as before. This shows that a customs union, even though it leads to trade diversion, could result in consumers being as well off as before. If the deterioration in the terms of trade had been less than what is shown by AC, and the new price line had been somewhere between AB and AC, the customs union would have led to an increase in consumers' welfare and would have put them on a higher indifference curve than I_0-I_0. Then the customs union would have increased consumers' welfare even though it was of a trade-diverting kind.[3] This demonstrates that if substitution in consumption takes place, it implies that a customs union can lead to an improvement in welfare even if it is of a trade-diverting nature.

Thus we can speak about intercountry and intercommodity substitution. Intercountry substitution is Viner's trade diversion and trade creation. Intercommodity substitution is the usual substitution that takes place between commodities, both on the supply and the demand side, because of changes in relative prices. A customs union will give rise to both kinds of substitution. If both kinds are taken into account, the situation becomes more complex and the possibility of drawing inferences becomes more limited.

On a somewhat abstract level we could say that a situation with tariffs is a nonoptimum situation, where the relation between home market prices differs from international price ratios. If free trade were introduced, it would imply an improvement, as the real rates of transformation at home and abroad would be the same, and this would imply an increase in welfare. The formation of a customs union means that, as tariffs are taken away on imports from the union partner, the relative price between these imports and domestic goods is going to coincide with real rates of transformation. This tends to increase welfare. The relative price between imports from the union partner and imports from the rest of the world, however, is moved away from equality with real rates of transformation. This will tend to lower welfare. A customs union thus has both a free trade side and a protectionist side. The welfare effects of a union depend on which is stronger.

It is important, in this connection, to bear in mind that it is not primarily the size of the imports from the union partner that is of interest, as they are involved in both a gain and a loss. What is important is the size of domestic trade in relation to imports from the outside world. The larger and more important domestic trade is, the more likely is the union to bring a gain. The reason is that then "correct" price relations will be established on a large and important number of goods. Conversely, the smaller trade is

---

[3] It should be observed that this gain takes place because the initial tariff was not optimal; otherwise d could have been reached initially.

with the rest of the world, the better, because then only a few and unimportant price relations will be disturbed by the formation of the union.

Suppose, for example, that the only import from the rest of the world is rucksacks. Then the price relation between rucksacks and imports from the union partner will be distorted, a not very important consequence, presumably, whereas prices of imports from the union partner are brought into harmony with prices of all domestically produced goods. If the country, instead, only produced rucksacks, it would be the other way around. Then "correct" price relations between rucksacks and union imports would be established, whereas price relations between all outside imports and union imports would be distorted. The most important consequence of this reasoning is that countries heavily dependent on each other in their trade should form customs unions with each other. There are no gains to be had by forming unions with countries that, economically speaking, are of only marginal importance. Another consequence is that countries which have only a small part of their national product going in international trade can safely form customs unions. Then domestic trade is dominant and the scope for gains from a customs union substantial. Countries with a large foreign trade quota must be more careful, as they might risk important distortions in their trade with the rest of the world.

We have now seen some of the factors that are important when assessing the economic gains and losses of a customs union. The gains are primarily connected with trade creation, the losses with trade diversion. But how are these gains and losses to be measured? By volume only? Here the height of the tariffs comes in as an important factor.

THE HEIGHT OF TARIFFS AND TARIFF REMOVALS

In a competitive world, the supply price of a good indicates the cost (marginal) to the producer and thus the opportunity cost, and the demand price indicates the utility of the good to the consumer. If no tariffs, taxes, or other distortions exist, the supply price of a good will be the same as the demand price. If taxes or tariffs exist, this is no longer the case. Suppose there is a 50 percent tax on a product: if the cost of production of the good is $2, then

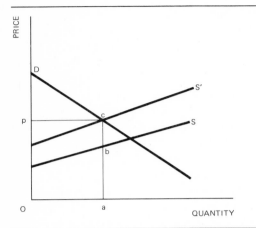

FIGURE 24.4

Effect of tariff removal on welfare

the producer of the good will get $2 for it, but the consumer will have to pay $3 for it.

Since the producer is living in a competitive world, it means that the last unit of the product must be worth $2 to him—that it must cost $2 worth of resources to produce. Similarly, since the consumer is willing to pay $3 for a unit of the goods, it means that it must be worth $3 to him. A discrepancy in utility for producers and consumers thus exists, and if trade in the product could be increased, this would lead to an increase in welfare.

A tax or a tariff has completely analogous effects in this respect, and we can illustrate the effect of a tariff in a geometric fashion (Fig. 24.4). A tariff, or a tax, can be thought of as shifting the supply curve to the left. The pretariff supply curve is S and the tariff-inclusive supply curve is S'. Equilibrium is established at c, with p being the price and Oa the quantity consumed. The tariff rate in Figure 24.4 is cb/ba percent, and the supply price differs from the demand price by this amount. An increase in trade of this good would, on the margin, mean an increase in welfare of an amount equal to cb.

This kind of analysis implies that the higher the initial tariffs between the countries forming the customs union, the larger the scope for gain. Conversely, the lower the tariffs with the outside world, the lower should be the losses due to trade diversion.

Assume that $100 million worth of trade is created because of the customs union and that $50 million worth of trade is diverted. Say that, before the union, the tariff was 100 percent on the goods in which trade has been created. A rough estimate of the net gain on the trade created is $100 million. Consumers were spending $200 million on the goods before the union; now they need only spend $100 million on the same amount of goods. Suppose the tariff to the outside world is 10 percent. The loss on trade diversion could then be approximated to $5 million. The country will now pay $50 million on imports of these goods when buying from the union partner; if they bought from the cheapest possible source, they would only have to pay $45 million.

These are very rough examples, but they should help to illustrate the main principle involved. The higher the tariffs between the union partners before the union, the larger is the scope for a reallocation of production according to comparative advantage. The lower the tariffs to the outside world, the smaller are the risks that the countries will have to pay a high premium because of subsidizing union partners at the expense of the rest of the world.

When we take the heights of tariffs into account we can no longer try to estimate gains and losses by simply taking trade creation and trade diversion at face value. We also have to weigh the values of trade created and diverted with the heights of the tariffs involved.

In practice, customs unions, such as the Common Market, reduce tariffs gradually. The largest gains are to be had initially when tariffs are high and the distortions are important. As time goes on and tariffs become lower, so does the possibility for prospective gains. Finally, taking tariffs away completely could even entail a loss.[4]

EMPIRICAL FINDINGS AND DYNAMIC CONSIDERATIONS

We have now studied some of the main elements of the theory of customs unions. Now we must briefly look at some empirical estimates of gains and

---

[4] This follows from a proposition in the theory of the second best which says that under nonoptimum conditions, a complete removal of some taxes or some tariffs might move the economy away from instead of closer to a second-best optimum. See R. G. Lipsey and K. J. Lancaster, "The General Theory of the Second Best," *Review of Economic Studies*, vol. 24, no. 1, 1956.

losses in connection with customs unions. Not too many empirical studies have been made. The best known is probably one by the Dutch economist Verdoorn, later used and commentated upon by Tibor Scitovsky.[5] Another study was made by H. G. Johnson.[6] All these studies used the type of theory outlined in this chapter and tried to estimate the gains and losses from trade creation and trade diversion. There is no need here to go into any detail of how the measurements were made. It suffices for our purposes to report on the main results.

The common feature of these empirical findings is the smallness of the estimated gains. Verdoorn, for instance, estimated that trade between the countries of the Common Market would increase by 17 percent. These estimates of trade increases were then weighted with the respective tariffs. It turned out that the welfare effect of the prospective union amounted to about one twentieth of 1 percent of the sum of the national incomes of the six countries. We quote Scitovsky's comment on this result:

> The most surprising feature of these estimates is their smallness. . . . As estimates of the total increase in intra-European trade contingent upon economic union, Verdoorn's figures are probably under-estimates; but if, by way of correction, we should raise them five- or even twenty-five-fold, that would still leave unchanged our basic conclusion that the gain from increased intra-European specialisation is likely to be insignificant.[7]

Other findings, for instance those of Johnson, tend to go in the same direction. He finds that Britain, by joining a European Free Trade Area, can expect at the most to gain 1 percent of the national income.[8]

These results are surprising. The question of whether to join the Common Market was *the* leading political question in many European countries in the late 1950s and early 1960s; it is still a question of great importance for Britain and the Scandinavian countries. One would, therefore, expect that some very tangible economic gains or losses were at stake. Can the above results be taken seriously, then? Do they not have an inherent bias,

---

[5] T. Scitovsky, *Economic Theory and Western European Integration*, London, 1958.
[6] H. G. Johnson, "The Gains from Freer Trade with Europe: An Estimate," *Manchester School of Economic and Social Studies*, vol. 26, September 1958.
[7] Scitovsky, *op. cit.*, p. 67.
[8] Johnson, *op. cit.*

either by being directly wrong or by putting the question in too narrow a framework?

We then need to understand what type of economic theory that of customs unions is. It is of a comparative-static nature. It starts from an equilibrium with a given tariff structure. Then a discriminatory change in this structure is made, and the effects on economic welfare are estimated. The above-mentioned estimates are based on this kind of comparative-static theorizing, and no one has been able to show any serious defects in them as far as they go. Traditional economic theory would therefore tend to support the view that the welfare effects of customs unions are small.

One could argue, however, that there are other effects of a " dynamic " or perhaps institutional kind that are more important. One such dynamic effect is the presence of unutilized economies of scale. Because of the segmentation of markets, European industry has not been able to reap the fruits of economies of scale: that is the argument. This argument, however, has the character of an unproved assertion, and it is perhaps not as convincing as it appears at first sight. First, most European industries where economies of scale could be expected are already export industries and have a larger market than the national one. Second, even though there are perhaps unused economies of scale on the production side, administration and selling costs could be rising, causing the total unit cost to rise also. For such reasons the argument for unreaped scale economies is perhaps not too valid.

Another argument of a dynamic character is that a customs union will lead to enforced competition. This argument has been applied to the European Economic Community.[9] Large parts of the French industry, it is argued, consist of, on the one hand, some large efficient firms, and, on the other, several small inefficient firms, often family businesses. French big business does not want to be ruthless, so the small family firms are kept alive, competition is minimal, and economic growth is not so fast as it otherwise could have been.[10] The German pattern is different, and here competition is vivid and strong. When French industry enters into closer competition with German industry because of the Common Market, it can no longer afford to be complacent and lenient. To survive it will have to adopt

[9] See Scitovsky, *op. cit.*, pp. 110 ff.
[10] For a vivid description of French business behavior see D. S. Landes, "French Business and the Businessman: A Social and Cultural Analysis," in E. M. Earle (ed.), *Modern France*, Princeton, N.J., Princeton University Press, 1951.

the German pattern. Competition will be enforced on French industry, and economic growth in France will be speeded up.

This could be a plausible argument. However, it is very difficult to get numerical estimates of effects such as these. Therefore, the way such an argument is evaluated is largely a matter of belief.

Other institutional aspects which could be important are those connected with increased factor movements and with rights to establish businesses within the union. Movements of labor and of capital could increase the productivity of the factors in question and foster growth. A greater freedom in establishment rights would perhaps lead not only to a greater personal freedom and increased well-being, but also to a faster spread of knowledge and thereby to faster growth. Factors such as these could be important, but it is difficult to say how important.

The establishment of the European Common Market has perhaps created an optical illusion. For several reasons, the EEC countries happened to have very high growth rates during the 1950s and the beginning of the 1960s. This was thought, at the time, to be because of their forming a customs union, but primarily other reasons caused the rapid economic growth. By a coincidence in time, the effects of the European economic integration were thought to be much more splendid than they actually were. The last few years have also demonstrated that economic integration does not guarantee rapid economic growth unless other factors are also favorable.

SUMMARY

We finish this chapter by summarizing some of the main results of the theory of customs unions. The basic conclusion is that it is impossible to pass any judgment on customs unions in general. Having said this, we find that the basic concepts of the theory are those of trade creation and trade diversion. Trade creation will lead to an improvement of welfare, whereas trade diversion generally leads to a lowering of welfare. A customs union is more likely to lead to an increase in welfare if the union partners are actually competitive but potentially complementary. The larger the cost differentials between the countries of the union in goods they both produce, the larger is the scope for gains. The higher the initial tariffs between the union partners, the greater is the scope for an increase in welfare. The lower the tariffs to the outside world, the smaller are the losses on trade diversion. The larger the part of trade originally covered by trade between the union partners, the greater is the scope for gains from the union. If a union leads to a realization of dynamic effects such as reaping of economies of scale and enforced competition, it could be important, and these effects will have to be added to the effects of a comparative-static nature.

SELECTED BIBLIOGRAPHY: CHAPTER 24

A classic work which started the modern discussion of the theory of customs unions is:

J. Viner, *The Customs Unions Issue*, New York, 1953.

Two standard contributions to the theory of customs unions are:

R. G. Lipsey, "The Theory of Customs Unions: A General Survey," *EJ*, September 1960 (reprinted in *RIE*).

J. E. Meade, *The Theory of Customs Unions*, Rotterdam, 1955.

Other interesting contributions are:

C. A. Cooper and B. F. Massell, "A New Look at Customs Union Theory," *EJ*, December 1965.

C. A. Cooper and B. F. Massell, "Toward a General Customs Union Theory for Developing Countries," *JPE*, September 1965.

F. Gehrels, "Customs Unions from a Single Country Viewpoint," *RES*, no. 63, 1956–57.

H. G. Johnson, "The Gains from Freer Trade with Europe: An Estimate," *MSS*, September 1958.

T. Scitovsky, *Economic Theory and Western European Integration*, London, 1958.

J. Vanek, *General Equilibrium of International Discrimination: The Case of Customs Unions*, Cambridge, Mass., 1965.

Direct
investments

25

We touched on capital movements from various points of view in earlier parts of the book. In Chapter 8 we studied the importance of capital movements during the nineteenth century from a historical standpoint. For several countries, imports of capital played an important role in their development process. For the lending countries, exports of capital were an important outlet for savings, which helped to smooth out business cycles and led to, if not a more rapid, at least a more stable, pattern of economic growth.

In Part III we saw the significance of capital movements for balance-of-payments purposes. Accommodating capital movements are unavoidable under a system of fixed exchange rates. Capital movements have an important role to play in the adjustment mechanism.

In this chapter we shall deal with a specific type of capital movements: direct investments. By direct investment is meant an investment in a foreign country where the investing party (corporation, firm) retains control over the investment. A direct investment typically takes the form of a foreign firm starting a subsidiary or taking over control of an existing firm in the country in question.

Direct investments are increasing in importance in the world economy. They have always attracted a good deal of attention and given rise to heated controversies; this, perhaps, is not astonishing in a world of nationalism. The Marxists saw them in the beginning of the twentieth century as the natural consequence of a maturing capitalism: the logical fruits of an ever-hardening competition, the last manifestations of a doomed system before its collapse. During recent years they have attracted renewed interest both in underdeveloped and developed countries. It is significant that one of the international best-sellers of the 1960s, *The American Challenge* by Jean-Jacques Servan-Schreiber, is devoted to the effects of direct investments on the European economy.

We shall now briefly discuss the differences between portfolio and direct investments.

PORTFOLIO AND DIRECT INVESTMENTS

As already stated, the main distinction of direct investments is that the investor retains control over the invested capital. Direct investments and

444

management go together. With portfolio investments, no such control is exercised. Here the investor lends his capital in order to get a return on it, but he has no control over the use of that capital.

We saw in Chapter 8 that foreign investments played a large role in international economy in the period leading up to World War I. The largest part of these investments consisted of portfolio investments. Great Britain provided more than 50 percent of the total international capital outstanding in 1914. About 90 percent of British investments during this period were of a portfolio type. These investments were primarily governed by interest differentials. Britain during this period generated savings that were much larger than domestic investments (25 to 40 percent of gross domestic savings were invested abroad), and these foreign investments were primarily invested where the return on capital was high. This also applies to the other two major lending countries, France and Germany. They were also primarily engaged in portfolio investments. During a period when exchange risks were negligible and the political situation from this angle was stable, international investments were primarily governed by interest-rate differentials. Young expanding economies, which offered high returns on capital invested, could borrow money from the major lending countries.

The United States was the only country which already differed in this respect. American investors seem to have been of a more dynamic type, not content merely to reap a fairly small interest-rate differential. Even before World War I, a dominant share of U.S. capital exports consisted of direct investments.

We know from Chapter 8 that capital imports were of limited importance during the interwar period. The role and pattern of capital movements have changed considerably since World War II. The importance of private portfolio investments have decreased; instead, the role of government gifts and loans and of direct investments have increased. This is illustrated in Table 25.1, which shows long-term capital movements to less-developed countries from the so-called DAC countries, i.e., the countries which belong to OECD's Development Assistance Committee: Western Europe, North America, Australia, and Japan. These countries together generate 90 percent of the total capital outflow to less-developed countries.

We can see from Table 25.1 that official capital movements are today the most important between industrial and less-developed countries. Private portfolio investments are negligible, whereas private direct investments still play a fairly important role. The most important capital movements today

TABLE 25.1

Capital outflow from DAC countries to less-developed countries

	1956–1960		1961–1965		1966	
	Billions of dollars	Percent	Billions of dollars	Percent	Billions of dollars	Percent
Bilateral gifts	3152	43	3974	43	3761	38
Bilateral loans	635	9	1566	17	2158	22
Multilateral gifts and loans	397	5	502	5	513	5
Sum of official gifts and loans	4184	57	6042	65	6432	65
Private direct investments	1989	27	1864	20	1955	20
Private portfolio investments	706	10	572	7	346	4
Private export credits	417	6	758	8	1132	11
Sum of private investments	3112	43	3194	35	3433	35
	7296	100	9236	100	9865	100

SOURCE: T. Gårdlund, *Främmande Investeringar i u-land*, Stockholm, Almqvist & Wiksell, 1968, p. 44.

are those between developed countries. Here the role of direct investments are even more important, as we will shortly demonstrate.

Portfolio investments are primarily governed by interest-rate differentials. The British and French invested abroad in the period before World War I because the interest rate was higher abroad. If the interest rate was 4 percent in London but 5 percent in South Africa or Argentina, it meant that the British investor got a 25 percent higher return on his investments. In the atmosphere of stability that reigned during this period, the risks on such portfolio investments were not regarded as very large, and even fairly modest interest-rate differentials acted as an important stimulus for attracting capital from old European countries.

The situation after World War II has been quite different. Few of the less-developed countries can offer the combination of attractive investment opportunities and stability that could attract foreign portfolio investments. Moreover, most developed countries have had tendencies for inflation and for domestic investment opportunities to be larger than domestic savings. Under such circumstances, there is little scope for private capital exports of a portfolio type.

When it comes to capital movements between industrial countries, the picture is different. Here the political stability has been considerable. But there has been no persistent difference between countries regarding investment demand and domestic supply of savings that could warrant an interest-rate differential. This being so, there has been no foundation for long-term portfolio investments. Most capital movements which have taken place between the developed, industrial countries have been either short-term or direct investments. Direct investments between the United States and Western Europe have been especially important. Later, we will discuss them at some length. First, however, we shall touch on a problem common to all capital movements, the so-called transfer problem.

THE TRANSFER PROBLEM

The transfer problem is of long standing in international economics. It is essentially a matter of international adjustment in the balances of payments. It is easy to see why the transfer problem has attracted so much interest: It arises in connection with many different types of international transactions.

If a country lends $100 million to another country, it means that the lending country puts resources to the value of $100 million at the disposal of the borrowing country. The lending country will have to free resources valued at $100 million in order to export them to the borrowing country, which will import goods for $100 million more. To be successful, any long-term capital movement will have to be accompanied by a transfer of resources of equal size. This implies a change in the trade balance between lending and borrowing countries. How this comes about is studied under the heading of the transfer problem.

W. F. Taussig of Harvard University and a group of his students first studied the transfer process and the adjustment mechanism in connection with the long-term capital movements to countries such as Canada, Argentina, and Australia, which took place during the latter part of the nineteenth and the earlier part of the twentieth centuries.

The transfer problem, however, is not only connected with capital movements; it also played a prominent role in connection with reparations payments for war damages. Such payments occurred, for instance, after the Franco-Prussian War in 1870–1871, when France had to pay indemnities to Prussia, and after World War I, when Germany had to pay indemnities to France. In connection with the latter payments, a heated theoretical controversy arose between Keynes and Ohlin. It is obvious why payments for war damages give rise to a transfer problem.

More recently, the transfer problem has arisen in connection with international aid programs. One example was the Marshall Aid Program. Other examples of transfer processes are those connected with aid programs from industrial to less-developed countries. The theory of the transfer process therefore has wide applications. First, we will set out the main results of this theory and then study its implications in connection with direct investments.

The transfer theory has been developed within the context of two theoretical models. The earliest discussion of the problem was formulated in "classical" terms. The results of these investigations are very important. The more modern version of transfer theory is formulated in Keynesian terms. For reasons that will soon become clear, we will concentrate the exposition to the classical transfer theory and then see how this can be supplemented by taking some considerations of a Keynesian type into account.

The classical analysis cast the reasoning in the form of the standard trade model with two countries trading, producing, and consuming two goods. It worked on the assumption that both countries were fully employed and that the balance of payments of both countries was in equilibrium before the transfer took place. The question now is: How could the transfer be affected and a new external equilibrium be created, given these assumptions?

Let us begin by discussing the following example. We can assume that Country A lends Country B \$100 million. The immediate effect will be to decrease Country A's income by \$100 million and to increase Country B's income by that amount. What will be the effect on the balance of trade? This will depend on the marginal propensity to import in the two countries. Let m_a and m_b be the marginal propensities to import in the respective countries. If $m_a = 0.3$, it means that Country A will decrease its imports by \$30 million when the income decreases by \$100 million. If $m_b = 0.4$, it means that \$40 million of the income increase in Country B will be spent on imports from A. This means that the transfer will be *undereffected*.

The meaning of this term is: Because of the transfer, Country A will have to put resources to the value of \$100 million at the disposal of Country B, i.e., will have to increase its exports by \$100 million. The income changes connected with the transfer will decrease A's imports by \$30 million and increase B's imports from A by \$40 million; i.e., Country A's trade balance will improve by \$70 million because of the immediate effects of the income changes connected with the transfer. But an improvement of \$100 million is needed to take complete care of the transfer. Hence Country A will have a deficit in its balance of trade of \$30 million after the transfer has taken place.

Both countries are fully employed both before and after the transfer. The only way in which the deficit in Country A's trade balance can be corrected is by a change in relative prices. Country A's terms of trade will have to deteriorate. Such a change in the terms of trade leads to an adjustment in the balance of trade in two ways. First, it implies a fall in the real income of Country A and an increase in the real income of Country B. This will lead to an increase in imports in Country B and a fall in imports in Country A. Second, the change in relative prices will lead to substitution. As imports become more expensive in A, exportables are substituted for importables and vice versa in Country B. This will further improve Country A's balance of trade, and equilibrium will again be achieved but at worsened terms of trade (for A).

Provided that the transfer is undereffected, it implies a secondary burden for the lending country. At given incomes and prices, there will not be equilibrium in the balance of payments. Prices will have to adapt, and the real income of the lending country will have to fall for a new equilibrium to be reached.

This is, however, not a necessary outcome. The critical factors are the marginal propensities to import. If the sum of the marginal propensities to import had been unity, the transfer would have been completely affected. Say that $m_a = 0.4$ and that $m_b = 0.6$. Then a loan from A to B of \$100 million would decrease imports in A by \$40 million and increase imports in B by \$60 million. The net effect on A's trade balance would be an improvement of \$100 million, exactly enough to take care of the transfer. Thus the transfer would be completely effected and there would be no secondary burden.

If the sum of the marginal propensities to import is larger than unity, the transfer will be overeffected. This means that it will lead to a surplus in A's balance of trade. To restore equilibrium the terms of trade will have to turn in favor of A, and part of A's fall in income connected with the transfer will be restored by an increase in the real income due to improved terms of trade.

We have now set out the basic results of the classic version of the transfer theory. We have seen that the critical factors for the effects on trade balance, terms of trade, and real income are the changes in import spending induced by the transfer. We have set out the simplest version of this theory, with only two goods and involving no transport costs or impediments to trade. The theory can be extended to more complex cases, but the main drift of the argument is still the same.

If, for instance, transport costs and tariffs are introduced in the two-sector model, the transfer will be affected even though the sum of the marginal propensities is less than unity. In the case with three goods (two traded goods and one domestic, nontraded good), the result also depends on the possibilities of substitution between traded and nontraded goods in the two countries. The relative price of domestic goods will fall in the lending and increase in the borrowing country. The change in the terms of trade and the secondary effects on real incomes will therefore also depend on substitution possibilities between traded and nontraded goods. The larger these are in the lending country and the smaller they are in the borrowing country, the greater is the probability for a favorable development of terms of trade for the lending country, and the smaller should the eventual secondary burden be.

We have now studied the main results of classical transfer theory. An essential element of this approach is that equality between income and expenditure is assumed at a level of full employment. The modern, Keynesian transfer theory is built on very different assumptions in this respect. This model is based on the assumption of underemployment: Each industry in each country has an excess capacity. Commodity and factor prices are therefore fixed. Hence there can be no adjustment via prices. The adjustment instead takes place by changes in national incomes (which change both in nominal and real terms).

The main finding of this type of analysis is that the result will depend on the income changes induced by the transfer. If the marginal propensities to save in the two countries (call them s_a and s_b) are positive, income changes will not suffice to take care of the transfer and it will be undereffected. If, as the term goes, each country is stable in isolation (i.e., $s_a > 0$ and $s_b > 0$), income changes alone will not suffice to take care of the transfer.[1] Another point worth noting is that if the marginal propensity to save is larger in the lending than in the borrowing country, the transfer will have a depressive effect on world income. It is easy to see why this is so: Then the induced deflationary effect on Country A's income will be larger than the inflationary impact on Country B's income.

For most purposes it seems that the classical formulation of the transfer problem is of more interest than the Keynesian approach. Since World War II most of the world's industrial countries have had almost, if not quite, full employment. And the type of employment problem that most less-developed countries have does not seem to be very well approximated by the Keynesian model. This should not cloud the fact that a certain insight can be gained by combining the insights from the Keynesian transfer model with the perhaps more relevant classical model. In doing this, a certain caution must be used, as the two models are based on different, not easily reconciled, assumptions.

Summing up the discussion so far, we can say that there are powerful mechanisms at hand working for a smooth adjustment in the balance of payments in connection with transfers. The initial income changes induced by the transfer will give rise to changes in the demand for imports in the two countries. This will automatically take care of a good deal of the transfer. If the sum of the marginal propensities to import is large enough, the transfer will be completely affected by this mechanism. In most cases, however, one would expect the transfer to create a deficit in the trade balance of the lending country. Then the terms of trade will have to deteriorate for the lending country. This should work along much the same lines as a devaluation and should lead to a new external equilibrium. Income changes might also play an important role in this context. The transfer ought to have a

[1] This result was first derived by L. A. Metzler, "The Transfer Problem Reconsidered," *Journal of Political Economy*, vol. 50, June 1942. For further references to the literature see the bibliographical notes at the end of this chapter.

deflationary impact in the lending country and an inflationary impact in the borrowing country. This mechanism, then, will also make for a smooth adjustment in the balances of payments of the countries taking part in the transfer.

Historical experiences also show that the adjustment mechanism works smoothly in connection with transfers. Taussig and his students found that the transfer process worked even more smoothly in the real world than the classical view would have predicted. The classic verification of the transfer process in connection with international lending is Jacob Viner's *Canada's Balance of International Indebtedness, 1900–1913*. His thorough and ingenious study showed that the terms of trade really played the role it was expected to play according to the classical model.

One can also find counterexamples to the rule of a smooth working of the transfer mechanism. The outstanding one is connected with Germany's reparations payments in the 1920s. The difficulties, however, were primarily created by the consistent deflation policies pursued in the receiving countries, especially in Britain and France, which shows that if strong countervailing policies are pursued, the transfer mechanism can, of course, be made not to work.

Under normal circumstances, the transfer mechanism can therefore be expected to work smoothly. The transfer theory has been presented in its ordinary two-country version. In a multicountry framework, the interrelation between the transfer and the transferee country might be complicated by the presence of other countries; we should then normally expect the sum of the marginal propensities to consume by the two countries directly involved in the transfer to be less than unity. On the other hand, we have to take into account the possibility of part of the transfer being tied to exports from the transfer-giving country. Even if no such formal ties are connected with the transfer, this is still what one would expect in connection with, for instance, direct investments. Capital movements of an autonomous kind, such as direct investments, have important implications for the balances of payments of lending and borrowing countries. Under normal circumstances, the transfer mechanism should work and the external balances adjust so as again to create equilibrium after the capital movements.

Having now dealt with some of the main aspects of the transfer problem, we will continue and discuss some determinants of direct investments.

THE THEORY OF DIRECT INVESTMENTS

We have already observed that direct investments have played an increasingly larger role since World War II. The United States is by far the most important country engaging in direct investments. An increasing share of U.S. direct investments goes to other developed countries; most direct investments today go to Canada and the EEC countries of Europe. Table 25.2 illustrates this.

Canada, for natural reasons, has always been a big recipient of U.S. direct investments; the Canadian market has always been adjunct to the large U.S. market. In the early 1950s, some less-developed markets, especially in Latin America, were important outlets for *las ambiciones norteamericanas.* Since about 1958, Western Europe, especially the EEC countries, have become increasingly important as receivers of direct investments from the United States.

We have stated that portfolio investments are primarily governed by interest-rate differentials. In short, capital flows from where it is plentiful to where it is scarce. Concerning direct investments, it is more difficult to discern what the causes are of these. No well-established theory of direct investments exists today. We shall not attempt to develop a rigorous theory here but suggest some possible causes and motives.

We have already observed that one of the distinct features of direct investments is that the investor wants to retain control over his investment. Control, however, is a legal concept, not too useful for economic analysis. It might be better to say that one of the main determinants of direct investments has to do with technological superiority or superior managerial skills.

A firm or corporation, say in the United States, working under monopolistic or oligopolistic market conditions has developed some new product or new production technique. It wants to generalize the use of its innovation and to increase its possibilities of making a profit from its superior technology. Therefore, it wants to enter foreign markets. The natural way to do this and to enjoy the benefits of its superior technology is by direct investment.

To understand the determinants of direct investments, it could be useful to set out the following production function:

$$Q = f(L, C, M) \tag{25.1}$$

TABLE 25.2

New U.S. direct investment abroad ($ million per year)

	Total		Europe		EEC		United Kingdom		Canada		Japan	
	Net outflows	Retained earnings	Net outflows	Retained earnings	Net outflows	Retained earnings	Net outflows	Retained earnings	Net outflows	Retained earnings	Net outflows	Retained earnings
1950–1952	660	716	60	69	32	68	15	86	317	189	19	2
1953–1955	742	830	74	197	43	64	15	112	388	306	13	6
1956–1958	1858	1158	322	261	116	113	172	130	567	359	2	8
1959–1961	1555	1132	724	308	246	129	325	128	397	349	20	17
1962–1964	2015	1373	1056	404	627	109	167	156	305	467	66	26
1965	3418	1542	1479	388	857	−3	317	242	912	540	19	49
1966	3543	1716	1805	434	1140	105	384	190	1087	539	31	49

SOURCE: U.S. Department of Commerce, *Survey of Current Business.*

where Q denotes the output produced, L and C labor and capital, and M managerial skills or organizational technique. The difference between this formulation of the production function and the formulation used in earlier parts of the book and formally set out in Chapter 3 is, therefore, that we now take management or organization explicitly into account as an argument in the production function. This is explained by the fact that we now regard management as one of the essential variables needed to explain the phenomenon we are studying.

Speaking in terms of factor endowments, we could say that the United States has a large amount of M compared to other countries. This leads to the marginal product of managerial skills, $\partial Q/\partial M$, being lower in the United States than in other countries. The United States, therefore, ought to export products which are intensive in the use of managerial skills. This might also be the case. However, we are not now primarily interested in explaining trade but in explaining factor movements. We can say that we live in a world where factors of production are at least partially mobile. Some factors, however, are more mobile than others.

The least mobile factor is labor. For legal, institutional, and sociological reasons such small parts of the labor force are mobile that we can presume labor to be, for all practical purposes, immobile. Capital is more mobile than labor, but the conditions of supply of capital are not so different between countries as to make capital movements all that important. Furthermore, capital is a joint factor of production often paired with management. The most mobile factor of production is management.

Executives, or members of the technostructure as Galbraith calls them, can fairly easily move between countries.[2] The sociological milieu of executives in developed industrial countries is not all that different; to be a director of an oil company or a computer corporation in New York, Paris, London, or Frankfurt does involve certain differences in the way of life, but the resemblances in general cultural outlook, family life, and, above all, in general working conditions are also great. It might even be argued that making an executive career in an international corporation today implies a willingness to spend one's life in different parts of the world. This is also true, although to a somewhat lesser degree, for the interchange between industrial and the less-developed countries of a capitalistic type.

---

[2] See J. K. Galbraith, *The New Industrial State*, Boston, Houghton Mifflin, 1967.

The main cause of direct investments is hence a willingness to increase profits by taking advantage of some technological superiority or superior organizational form. This theory will enable us to explain several facets of direct investments. First, however, we should comment on the somewhat inadequate term "direct investment."

As we can see, it is not so much a movement of capital involved in a direct investment as an international movement of technique or organization. This improved technique or organization is often embedded in capital, but the main thing to keep in mind is that capital, most of the time, is only the complementary factor of production in a direct investment.

We should now have a better understanding of some main aspects of direct investments. It is only natural that the United States, as the world's leading industrial nation, is the main direct investor. For a country to become a portfolio investor, the main prerequisite is that it be able to generate a savings surplus. France did this, for instance, during the last quarter of the nineteenth century, even though the country was not one of the leading industrial innovators at that time. To be a direct investor, a country has to have a technical or organizational comparative advantage in at least some field.

It is not necessary, however, that the country as a whole have positive net savings and in this sense a surplus in its balance of payments. The situation of the United States since 1958 well illustrates this point. The country has had direct investments amounting to $3–5 billion per year but at the same time had deficits in its balance of payments and a short-term inflow of capital. In reality, some countries have by short-term lending to the United States financed U.S. direct investments that have taken place in their countries.

Another point worth mentioning in this connection is that the amount of direct investment which shows up on a country's balance of payments is often only the tip of the iceberg. This also holds for U.S. direct investments in Europe in recent years. The big corporations undertaking direct investments are very credit-worthy firms. Therefore, they can easily raise the money needed for their investments in the local credit markets. It has been estimated that as little as 10 percent of American direct investments in Europe has been financed by American capital.[3]

The United States is the largest direct investor, but it is not the only

---

[3] J.-J. Servan-Schreiber, *The American Challenge*, New York, Atheneum, 1968, chap. 2.

country making such investments. Direct investments are often a two-sided affair. Not only does the United States make direct investments in Western Europe, but Western European countries also make direct investments in the United States. In 1964, for instance, the United States made direct investments of $807 million in the EEC countries, and the EEC countries made direct investments of $165 million in the United States during the same year.[4] This is easy to understand against the background of the model just developed.

It is true that, generally speaking, the United States has the most developed technology. But the technological level within any one country varies between sectors. Some sectors are the leading ones, whereas others are relatively backward. This is true in varying degrees for all countries. Therefore, some parts of the German industry or the Swedish industry are technologically more sophisticated than the corresponding parts of American industry. This being so, there is a *prima facie* case for German or Swedish direct investments in the United States. Empirical facts also show that, between industrial countries, direct investments flow in both directions. The U.S. direct investments in Europe are much more important than European direct investments in the United States, but there are still flows going in both directions. No such correspondence principle holds, however, for the relations between developed and less-developed countries. Here it is a one-sided relation whereby the developed countries make direct investments in the less-developed countries without any offsetting direct investments being made by the less-developed countries in the industrial countries. The capital flows from less-developed to developed countries are exclusively of a portfolio type.

Another observation we can make concerns the interrelations between the inputs in the production function set out in equation 25.1. An increase in any one of the three inputs, L, C, or M, will increase the marginal productivity of the other two factors.[5] It is quite easy to see why this should be so. The production function is of an ordinary neoclassical kind. The three factors of production can to a degree be substituted for one another. The more of the third factor two of the factors have to work with, the more efficient they will become.

---

[4] R. N. Cooper, *The Economics of Interdependence: Economic Policy in the Atlantic Community*, New York, McGraw-Hill, 1968, p. 87.

[5] We assume, in other words, that $\partial^2 Q / \partial L\, \partial M$ and $\partial^2 Q / \partial C\, \partial M$ are positive.

The essence of direct investments is that it brings one of the three factors of production, managerial skills, or organizational efficiency (M), to work with the other two. Hence the marginal productivity of labor and capital increases in the country where the investment is made. This will lead to an increase in wages for the workers and to an increase in the return to capital because of the foreign investment.

In the simple model we have set out, managerial or technological superiority is the key variable. Such an explanation of direct investment presupposes that the market forms should not be purely competitive. Under free competition there is no room for product differentiation, brand names, etc., and the scope for technical improvement is limited. The representative firm is small; it cannot differentiate its product, and it has little resources to devote to research and development. Direct investments are also not very prevalent in branches such as farming, retailing, textiles, etc., where the markets seem to approach pure competition. The most important industries engaging in direct investments are typically those where monopolistic or oligopolistic market conditions prevail. The auto industry, the petroleum industry, and the computer industry are typical examples. This is what we would expect: These are areas in which advanced technology plays a large role and where the scope for innovations, both of a technological and managerial kind, is large.

The fact that, typically, the corporation undertaking the direct investment is trying to exploit a new innovation under monopolistic or oligopolistic market conditions also helps to explain why most such corporations are so averse to partnership or joint ventures. Many of the multinational corporations refuse on principle to take part in any kind of joint venture.

Direct investments are a very complex affair. It is only natural that, in outlining the basic theory, we seek to focus attention on some simple explanations that can take us a long way toward an understanding of the subject. However, several other factors are important. One is protectionist policies; another is closeness to the market.

The effect of protectionist policies is quite obvious. Many countries are averse to imports of industrial products. Governments with a protectionist slant often think that such products could, or should, equally well be produced by national firms. They then seek to foster domestic industries by using tariffs and other protectionist means. What such policies cannot do, however, is to deprive the foreigner of his technological or managerial advantage. Such policies, therefore, often induce foreign corporations to undertake direct investments and go directly into the protected market to which they earlier, instead, exported their products.

It is not difficult to find examples of direct investments that have been undertaken for such reasons. Countries such as Argentina and Brazil offered examples of protectionist policies that stimulated direct investments in the late 1940s and early 1950s. Some of the upsurge in direct investments which took place in the EEC countries during the latter part of the 1950s could be explained along similar lines.

Protectionist policies (or beliefs about the alleged effects of such policies) were not the only reasons for the steady increase in direct investments, especially from the United States, which took place in Western Europe from the mid-1950s onward. Western Europe had experienced an unprecedented economic growth. This made the European market attractive to many American corporations. Western Europe, especially the EEC countries, had emerged as politically stable industrial countries with mass markets for consumer goods. Currency restrictions were removed and full currency convertibility for nonresidents was established for most European currencies at the end of 1958. All this naturally encouraged American direct investments.

Another factor worthy of note concerns size—the fact that most leading American corporations are much larger than their foreign counterparts. Not only is it true that in most fields the American firm represents the most advanced technology, it also typically commands much larger personal and financial resources. In many industries, the petroleum, electronic, and computer industries, for instance, American corporations could take over some very promising and prosperous European firms for defensive reasons—to make sure that there could be no unnecessary competition from foreign firms. It seems that a fair amount of direct investment has consisted of such placement buying of already existing assets—"picking the plums," to use Joan Robinson's colorful phrase.[6]

We have discussed some theoretical aspects of direct investments, some of the factors that could explain the reason for direct investments. We now discuss the effects of direct investments on the two partners involved: the investing (home) country and the host country.

---

[6] J. Robinson, *The New Mercantilism: An Inaugural Lecture*, Cambridge, England, Cambridge University Press, 1966.

SOME EFFECTS ON THE INVESTING COUNTRY

Most of the debate about the merits and demerits of direct investments has treated the effects on the host country; we return to that shortly. Much less attention has been paid to the problems that could arise for the authorities in the investing country. We will briefly touch on some of them.

One problem is concerned with the balance of payments. We would expect, as we know from transfer theory, that a direct investment would lead to a worsening of a country's balance of payments. The extent depends on several factors, primarily on the interrelations between transferer and transferee, as expressed in the marginal propensities to import. For a typical American direct investment, a study by The Brookings Institution yields the figures given in Table 25.3. These figures suggest that the link between the investing and the host country is rather weak and that the direct effects on the two countries' balances of payments are small. Such conditions create a strong immediate negative effect on the investing country's balance of payments.

The time perspective plays an important role for the balance of payments of the investing country. If the investment in the example given in Table 25.3 was one injection, it would take 6 years for it to pay off, in the sense that the balance of payments of the investing country would again be positive. If the direct investment, instead, consisted of a steady flow of $100 million per year, it would take 11 years to reach equilibrium; if the flow of direct investment increased by 22 percent per year, it would never pay off.

Against this background it is easy to understand that a large and growing volume of direct investments could be problematic, from the standpoint of the investing country's balance of payments. Part of the fairly large and persistent deficit that the United States has had since 1958 can also be explained by the outflow of long-term capital; we return to this problem in Chapter 26.

The United States also tried to restrain direct investments in 1965. In February 1965, a Voluntary Credit Restraint Program was imposed. Nine hundred corporations were asked to pursue policies aimed at producing a 5 percent improvement in their impact on the balance of payments. This need not necessarily be done by curtailing investment; it could also be done by increasing exports, decreasing imports, increasing the remittance of dividends, shifting finance to foreign sources, etc. Further restrictions were introduced in 1968.

TABLE 25.3

Balance-of-payments effects of a direct investment

Balance of payments improving		Balance of payments worsening	
Export stimulus	10.6	Capital	100
Remitted dividends	8.1	Import stimulus	6.5
Royalties and fees	2.3	Loss of exports	None

In the long run, direct investments ought to have a positive effect on the investing country's balance of payments. This is especially the case if the flow of direct investments is steady or decreasing. We can see this effect today on investments from the United States and some other developed countries in their dealings with several less-developed countries. If the flow sharply increases, there could be marked adverse effects on the balance of payments. Direct investments undoubtedly strained the United States' external position in the late 1950s and early 1960s.

Other problems that could arise are more concerned with real factors. With the increasing internationalization of firms, the possibility of any single country to pursue its own independent economic policy becomes circumscribed. Corporations could gather in one country to work out pricing and market arrangements for another country. As long as there is no international legislation concerning taxes, restrictive business practices, etc., any single country will have difficulties in efficiently implementing its own laws.

Differing tax laws could create specific problems for investing countries. Switzerland had exceptionally low taxes and favorable treatment of foreign firms in the 1950s. (This seems still to be so even if a certain harmonization of tax regulations has taken place.) This led to many American firms routing their sales from all over the world through sales offices located in Switzerland. This also led to exceptionally high earnings on investments in Switzerland. This is illustrated in Table 25.4.

In 1962, the United States changed its tax laws. Earlier, taxes on earnings from subsidiaries abroad were deferred until they were repatriated. In 1962 this provision was changed so that earnings on holding companies and so-called tax-haven operations became taxable when earned. This had an immediate effect on location of new service and sales offices: in 1961–1962, 40 percent of these were located to Switzerland; in 1963 this figure fell to 10 percent.

TABLE 25.4

Earnings on U.S. Direct Investments abroad[a]
(percentage of book value at the beginning of year)

	1958	1962	1966
MANUFACTURING			
Europe	16	12	11
EEC	17	14	11
Switzerland	36	11	15
TRADE AND OTHER[b]			
EEC	20	18	6
Switzerland	42	40	16
PETROLEUM			
Europe	5	3	−2
Middle East	60	71	60
Venezuela	21	18	19

[a] After foreign taxes.
[b] All direct investments other than mining and smelting, manufacturing, and petroleum.
SOURCE: U.S. Department of Commerce, *Survey of Current Business*.

This is an example of how the investing country could try to counteract undesirable effects of direct investments by changes in its legislation. The possibilities for such countervailing measures, however, are limited. Several countries, especially well-developed ones with big taxes and highly developed social services, could find their tax base shrinking as a result of direct investments. Their possibilities of implementing economic policies could also become circumscribed by the operations of multinational firms.

There are several ways in which an international corporation could take out its profits in the most suitable place. The most important is perhaps by intracorporate pricing practices. These seem to explain the fact demonstrated in Table 25.4 that the big oil companies show such small profits in Europe, where taxes are high, and such huge profits in the Middle East, where taxes are low.

The cases referred to above will perhaps suffice to illustrate the principle that national economic policy will encounter difficulties in a world where economic integration becomes increasingly important but where the national state is still the dominant political entity. Direct investments certainly give very tangible advantages to firms in the investing countries, but they also lead to policy complications for governments of these countries.

SOME EFFECTS ON THE HOST COUNTRY

The problems created for the host country by direct investments have aroused by far the most intense feelings and discussion. The reason is not difficult to understand.

Consider first the balance of payments. It is obvious that in the short run the host country will under normal conditions improve its balance of payments and possibly also its terms of trade. This follows from a straightforward application of transfer theory.

In the long-term things will turn out differently. Then, remittances of profits, etc., will be a negative post in its balance of payments. If the direct investment is of a once-for-all nature, or if the flow of direct investments into the country diminishes, the negative effects on the host country's balance of payments will soon be larger than the positive effects. This is natural; it does not imply that the investment has proved detrimental to the country. Broadly speaking, as long as the positive effect on the host country's economic growth is larger than the negative effect on its balance of payments, the investment has benefited the country.

Most of the critique raised against direct investments has been concerned with factors of a real nature, not with the monetary aspects of the question. An essential factor is that of control.

We have already noted that the essence of direct investment is management control; this factor distinguishes it from other forms of capital movements. If direct investments take place in a country, it means that part of its industry will be controlled by foreigners. Many host countries find this difficult to accept; it has led to countermeasures in many countries.

The problems have become most acute probably in Canada. Here 59 percent of the total capital in manufacturing is controlled by foreigners (40 percent by Americans). Efforts have been made from time to time to increase Canada's control over foreign direct investments. In 1963, for instance, a new tax law was introduced requiring firms of less than 25 percent Canadian ownership and with less than 25 percent Canadian representation on the board of directors to be taxed at a somewhat higher rate than Canadian corporations.[7] Some developing countries, such as Mexico, require 50 percent of ownership and directorship to be in domestic hands. France has also attempted to check foreign control of its industry. The Soviet Union pointed out, as a reason for its intervention in Czechoslovakia in August 1968, fear of direct investments in the country from capitalist firms in Western Europe.

Host countries fear direct investments for several reasons. Various types of charges are levied against foreign control. One is akin to balance-of-payments considerations. It says that the foreign firms do not export enough and that they give preference to firms in their home country or abroad (perhaps other subsidiaries of the parent corporation to which the firm in question belongs). Other charges are that foreign firms ignore local employment practices. Moreover, they could interfere with or upset domestic economic policies, for instance in the field of fiscal and monetary policy, or they could render national planning difficult. They are also often accused of having a negative effect on research and industrial development in the host country.

Before we consider the validity of these charges, advantages that direct investments can bring to the host country will be mentioned.

Some of these are implicit in the treatment we have already given to the matter when dealing with the theory of direct investment. The classical advantage is that direct investments raise world output by moving capital and managerial skills from regions where they are plentiful, and thus earn a low return, to regions where they are scarce, and thus earn a high return. We also learned that the normal effect of a direct investment is to increase the marginal productivity of both labor and capital in the host country and hence to have a positive effect on both the real wage and the real rate of return to capital. Comparative static theorizing will undoubtedly tend to stress the beneficial effects of direct investments; the negative effects are concerned with more elusive arguments of a dynamic type or connected with various types of external effects.

It can also be added that a firm behaving rationally and maximizing its profits has no reason to behave differently whether it is located in its own or a foreign country. A Canadian-owned Canadian firm, for example, should

---

[7] See A. E. Safarian, "Foreign Ownership and Control of Canadian Industry," in A. Rotstein (ed.), *The Prospect of Change: Proposals for Canada's Future*, Toronto, McGraw-Hill, 1966.

behave in the same way as an American-owned Canadian firm.[8] On the contrary, it can be argued that an international firm will act in a more rational, a less discriminatory, way than a domestic firm, because it has broader horizons and better information about possible markets, supply conditions, and points of location.

We can now revert to our main line of argument and consider other, more important, complications that direct investment could create for the host country. Perhaps the most important argument against direct investments that a host country can raise concerns its effects on domestic research and development.

Foreign ownership of important parts of a country's industry can stifle scientific research and development work in the host country. We have seen that the main determinant of direct investments is superior technology or managerial skills. Direct investments, especially U.S. direct investments in Europe, tend to be made in technologically advanced industries whose importance for economic development is great. The research for further development of these key industries tends, however, to be located in the investing country, i.e., primarily in the United States. Thereby the host countries are deprived of the important stimulus given by research in these industries.

Hence research tends to be concentrated in the home country. This country started with a comparative advantage in the production of goods which are intensive in research and innovating capacity. By the cumulative effects related to direct investments, this comparative advantage tends to become even more pronounced, and the host countries, in Europe and elsewhere, tend to sink into a position of second-rate economic powers.[9]

Another important point in this connection concerns external effects. It is widely believed that expenditures on research and development have important external effects. In the process of developing a certain product or improving production techniques, scientists and technicians are stimulated;

---

[8] This is a well-known point, often quoted by American economists, made by two Canadian economists, I. Brecher and S. S. Reisman, in *Canada-United States Economic Relations*, Ottawa, 1957, written for the Royal Commission on Canada's Economic Prospects.

[9] This, in concentrated form, is the main message of Jean-Jacques Servan-Schreiber's *The American Challenge*, which presents an intelligent and well-reasoned argument, even though it is somewhat amateurish from an economist's point of view.

new applications valuable outside the immediate project will be discovered; encouragement for, and incentives to, research in universities and other organizations outside the industry will be provided; etc. A rational attitude geared toward experimenting will be fostered, competent scientists will be trained, etc., and all this will have positive effects on the whole intellectual climate of the country.

If foreign firms via direct investments take over control of important parts of a country's industry, they will tend to shift research to their home country. This could be entirely rational from the point of view of the international firm, which is simply taking advantage of the economies of scale connected with the research activity. It can even be argued that this behavior is rational from the world's standpoint, because it maximizes world income. It still can have very detrimental effects on the host country, which is deprived of research activities that are perhaps comparatively inefficient but which, to the country itself, can be of great importance. How this question is viewed is largely a matter of values. It depends, in technical language, largely on the kind of preference function used, whether international, for the home country, or for the host country. Before pursuing this, we will touch on a closely related question, that of the "brain drain."

The tendency, inherent in direct investments, to lead to a reallocation of research activities could also induce scientists and technicians to leave their home countries—to what has popularly been called the "brain drain." According to this argument, the United States will induce a "brain drain" from Canada and Europe; Britain and France, too, will tend to siphon off scientific and technical talent from their formerly dependent areas.

It should be pointed out that such movements of educated and skilled people from the periphery to the center can be explained in rational economic terms. Education is a time-consuming activity, and teaching is a labor-intensive activity. It could therefore be expected that human capital (to use the existing jargon) should be produced in low-cost locations, as presumably the less-developed or semideveloped countries are, being rich in labor. This is probably to some extent what happens. Several less-developed and semi-developed countries have probably, in relative terms, quite a large supply of certain types of educated people who might have difficulty finding adequate work in their home countries. As wages are higher in the developed, industrial countries, the educated people will naturally move away from their home countries to more developed countries; i.e., a "brain drain" will take place. This type of migration is also encouraged by laws and institutional factors, as most countries tend to favor immigration of educated persons rather than those with less training. To this should also be added the important fact that these skilled immigrants will be provided with more material capital to work with as the ratio of material to human capital is often much higher in the rich countries. Hence an English scientist will often be more efficient in the United States, and an Indian doctor will be more highly productive in England. The migrating scientist can often truthfully argue that what attracts him to move, to take part in the " brain drain," is not the increased salary but the opportunity to work with better equipment and more assistance in more congenial surroundings.

How one views the effects on scientific activity induced by direct investments and the consequent " brain drain " is largely a matter of values. From the world's standpoint, it can be argued that both of these effects are beneficial, as they tend to increase world income. But world income is a fairly abstract concept. There is also little reason why anybody should want to maximize world income irrespective of the effects on the world income distribution. Measures that only make the rich richer and the poor poorer can certainly be questioned.

How we view these problems, therefore, primarily depends on what type of welfare function we use. From the investing country's point of view the secondary effects on research and migration could be all to the good. From the host country's point of view it could be quite another matter.

The host country could welcome the immediate effects of a direct investment but be highly reluctant toward the secondary effects on research activity and the " brain drain " that could be induced. If it means, for instance, that a highly promising computer program is abandoned because a domestic firm is being bought up and some very able scientists are induced to move abroad, the negative external effects are obvious. Then the country could, instead, choose to engage in a scientifically oriented infant-industry protection in the hope that, after a certain amount of development aid, the firm will become competitive on a world scale.

We cannot in this context go deeper into these interesting and many-faceted problems of direct investments. We must be satisfied with the hope of having been able to point out some of the very real problems in connection with direct investments facing a host country.

Before concluding this chapter, we should also remark briefly on another emotive aspect of direct investment, that of direct investment and exploitation.

DIRECT INVESTMENTS AND EXPLOITATION

Direct investments have in the Marxian tradition played a double role, and in both roles they have had important political implications.

In the first variant, direct investments are necessary to postpone the collapse of the capitalist system, and in the second and milder variant they are merely one of many forms of capitalist oppression.

The first line of thought was started by J. A. Hobson and taken up and developed by Lenin.[10] The essence of the argument is that capitalism needs new markets to survive. The inner forces of capitalism, primarily the relentless pursuit and application of new innovations, make it expand to new territories to find new markets and new consumers to postpone the collapse that history, according to Marx, has in store for it. The drive to technical progress also makes capitalists look for cheaper sources of raw material in distant countries. Imperialism, according to Hobson and Lenin, is simply the logical consequence of the economic forces inherent in the capitalist system of production.

Marxists of later vintages have some difficulties in explaining this theory in its strict Leninist formulation.[11] The Marxian theories of impending collapse of the capitalist system, impoverishment of the workers, etc., are not easy to uphold in the light of the development of the capitalist system. The strong version of the Marxian theory of direct investments, which argues the necessity of these investments for the survival of the capitalist system, can hardly be sustained.[12] That capitalist countries derive profits from their

---

[10] J. A. Hobson (1858–1940), British economist. His book *Imperialism* was published in 1902. Lenin's views are contained in *Imperialism: The Highest Stage of Capitalism*, written in 1916 in Zürich and published the following year in Leningrad.

[11] This could be concerned with the eminence of the exposer of this theory. Even such a sharp analyst as Oskar Lange becomes unusually vague and elusive when dealing with Lenin's theorizing. See Lange, *Ekonomisk Utveckling och Socialism*, Stockholm, Rabén & Sjögren, 1966, pp. 121 ff.

[12] An interesting attempt at rescuing the strong version of the theory has been made by an American economist, Harry Magdoff, in "Economic Aspects of U.S. Imperialism," *Monthly Review*, November 1966. His argument is, essentially, that on the margin, foreign operation of American firms is very important, and that it is from the marginal production and sales that profits are primarily derived.

direct investments abroad is one thing; it is quite another thing to argue that the industrial, capitalist nations are so dependent on the territories they in some sense dominate via direct investments that their economies would break down without them. It is hardly correct to argue that the United States, Britain, France, etc., are so dependent on their direct investments (or their trade with third countries in general for that matter) that their economic systems could not be sustained without them. A certain lowering of U.S. economic welfare would follow if, to take a drastic example, all their foreign investments were nationalized overnight by the countries in question and no compensation paid. But there is no doubt that the effect of such an action would imply marginal changes in the American economy rather than a collapse of its capitalist system.

The Marxian-Leninist view of direct investments in its strict interpretation must therefore be refuted. This does not mean that a milder version of it also lacks credibility. In its milder version, however, the theory becomes much more pedestrian and diluted. Then it does not amount to much more than pointing out possibilities that, under certain circumstances, exploitation could occur, much in the same way as it was stressed in the preceding section that sometimes direct investments could have undesirable consequences for the host country.

Exploitation is an emotive word, more suitable for political purposes than for economic analysis. When speaking about exploitation in connection with direct investments, we must therefore state each time, more or less, what we mean by the term in order to make a meaningful statement.

That the investing country takes some advantage of the host country, i.e., that exploitation in some sense takes place, is most common in connection with direct investments in less-developed countries. Edith Penrose maintained, for instance, that the American-controlled Iraq Petroleum Company had exploited Iraq because it had earned a higher return than the minimum it would have been willing to start the Iraq venture for.[13] It can also be maintained that what the big American corporations really strive for is monopolistic control over foreign sources of supply and foreign markets.[14]

[13] E. T. Penrose, "Profit Sharing Between Producing Countries and Oil Companies in the Middle East," *Economic Journal*, vol. 69, June 1959.
[14] See P. A. Baran and P. M. Sweezey, *Monopoly Capital*, New York, Monthly Review Press, 1966, pp. 178 ff.

Once this has been established, the corporations can exploit their monopoly power.[15]

It is not difficult to find examples of exploitation in some sense of the word. If one country has a strong economic influence over another, and couples that with an allegiance with certain ruling forces of the host country and maintains a close military cooperation with those ruling forces, the host country could be in a difficult position. Then it certainly can be maintained that both a political and economic exploitation occurs.

An attempt to deal with a situation such as that just sketched would, however, quickly take us beyond the scope of the present work.

Suffice it to say that in general, we would expect direct investments to benefit both the investing and the host country, for reasons set out earlier in this chapter. But we cannot disregard the fact that direct investment is a very complex subject and that there are instances where direct investments could have undesirable consequences for the host country.

SUMMARY

Direct investments involve international movements of technology and management rather than movements of capital. International flows of capital are also involved, but they are not the essential feature. The main determinant of direct investments is superior technology or superior skills.

A firm possessing superior technology or management will naturally seek to increase profits by expanding its horizons and investing abroad. Direct investments primarily take place under monopolistic or oligopolistic market conditions. Among developed countries it is often a two-sided affair, even if it is natural that the United States, as the leading industrial country, is also the largest direct investor.

The principal advantage of direct investments is that they raise world output by moving managerial skills and capital from regions where these factors are plentiful, and thus earn a low return, to regions where they

---

15 It could be argued that the exploitation in this instance is measured by the difference between monopoly pricing and the price that would be charged under competitive conditions.

are scarce, and thus earn a high return. Normally, direct investments will benefit both the investing country and the host country.

The immediate impact on the investing country's balance of payments can often be adverse, even though the transfer mechanism usually works smoothly. The investing country could have difficulties in controlling domestically located firms operating in international markets. National economic policies could be difficult to implement, and attempts at economic planning could be thwarted.

For the host country, the immediate impact of a direct investment will usually be an improvement in the balance of payments. In the long run, the effects could be negative. From a "real" point of view, the effects are beneficial as long as the positive effects on the country's economic growth are larger than the negative ones on the balance of payments.

There are some effects of a secondary or external type that could be detrimental to the host country. The most important one is that direct investments could stifle scientific research and development work in the host country.

Direct investments could conceivably lead to exploitation, primarily of less-developed countries. The meaning of the terms, however, has to be well defined and the circumstances carefully scrutinized before any such charge can be meaningfully leveled at direct investments.

SELECTED BIBLIOGRAPHY: CHAPTER 25

The important theoretical papers on the transfer problem are:

> P. A. Samuelson, "The Transfer Problem and Transport Costs: The Terms of Trade when Impediments are Absent," *EJ*, June 1952 (reprinted in *RIE*).

> P. A. Samuelson, "The Transfer Problem and Transport Costs, II: Analysis of Effects of Trade Impediments," *EJ*, June 1954 (reprinted in *RIE*).

The two Samuelson papers cited above both treat the problem on "classical" assumptions. For a treatment on Keynesian assumptions, the standard paper is:

L. A. Metzler, "The Transfer Problem Reconsidered," *JPE*, June 1942 (reprinted in *RTIT*).

For a partial reconciliation of the two approaches see:

H. G. Johnson, "The Transfer Problem and Exchange Stability," *JPE*, June 1956 (reprinted in *RIE*).

Two major empirical studies of the transfer problem are:

J. H. Williams, *Argentine International Trade Under Inconvertible Paper Money, 1880–1900*, Cambridge, Mass., 1920.

J. Viner, *Canada's Balance of International Indebtedness, 1900–1913*, Cambridge, Mass., 1924.

For a reworking of the Canadian material see:

J. A. Stovel, *Canada in the World Economy*, Cambridge, Mass., 1959.

There is little to be found by way of systematic treatment of the theory of direct investments in the literature. An interesting but, alas, unpublished contribution is:

S. H. Hymer, "The International Operations of National Firms: A Study of Direct Investment," doctoral dissertation, Massachusetts Institute of Technology, 1960.

An interesting discussion is also contained in:

R. N. Cooper, *The Economics of Interdependence: Economic Policy in the Atlantic Community*, New York, 1968, chap. 4.

For monographs on specific countries see:

D. T. Brash, *United States Investment in Australian Manufacturing Industry*, Canberra, 1966.

A. W. Johnstone, *United States Direct Investment in France*, Cambridge, Mass., 1965.

M. Kidron, *Foreign Investment in India*, London, 1965.

A. E. Safarian, *Foreign Ownership of Canadian Industry*, Toronto, 1966.

A. Stonehill, *Foreign Ownership in Norwegian Enterprises*, Oslo, 1965.

The problem of the brain drain is discussed in the following anthology, with interesting contributions by H. G. Johnson and Don Patinkin.

W. Adams (ed.), *The Brain Drain*, New York, 1968.

This and other aspects of direct investments are discussed in:

J.-J. Servan-Schreiber, *The American Challenge*, New York, Atheneum, 1968.

The Marxian point of view is presented in the works by Lenin and Rosa Luxemburg referred to in Chapter 25. For a neo-Marxian treatment of direct investments and imperialism see:

P. Baran, *The Political Economy of Growth*, New York, 1957.

P. Baran and P. Sweezey, *Monopoly Capital*, New York, 1966.

E. Mandel, *Marxist Economic Theory*, London, 1968, vol. 2.

PART V

The
international
monetary
system

International liquidity: the setting of the problem

26

This final part of the book is devoted to the international monetary system. Chapter 26 begins by elucidating the concept of international liquidity. To do this, we must deal with the development of the U.S. balance of payments. The dollar is used as the main key currency in the world today (the other key currency being the pound sterling). The supply of international liquidity is intimately bound up with the supply of dollars, which, in its turn, is a function of the external balance of the United States.

Apart from the dollar, gold is the main internationally used store of value. The role that gold plays for international liquidity is also described in this chapter.

The problem of international liquidity is often dealt with in simple quantitative terms. It is frequently argued that the international monetary system does not function well because it cannot provide enough of international liquidity. But when dealing with the supply of and demand for international liquidity, the price at which it is supplied must also be taken into account; perhaps the excess demand for international liquidity is simply caused by a too low price. This, and some other theoretical problems in connection with the international monetary system, will be dealt with in Chapter 27.

Many economists and politicians are dissatisfied with the present system for providing international liquidity. The reasons for dissatisfaction are different and diverse. Some argue for going back to a pure gold standard. Others, on the contrary, argue for the establishment of an international central bank. Some of the main proposals for reform of the international monetary system will be analyzed and discussed in Chapter 28.

THE U.S. BALANCE OF PAYMENTS

The United States had a very strong competitive position in the world economy at the end of World War II. This led to the country having a very substantial surplus in its balance of payments. The strong external position was founded in a very strong balance of trade. The United States had for a long time been exporting more than it imported. This was especially the case in the late 1940s. Table 26.1 gives a clear indication of this.

477

478

International
liquidity: the setting
of the problem

TABLE 26.1

U.S. merchandise trade
($ billion: average per year)

Years	Merchandise exports	Merchandise imports	Merchandise export surplus
1947–1949	13.8	6.8	7.0
1951–1956	14.0	11.3	2.7
1958–1962	18.5	14.7	3.8
1963–1966	25.7	20.6	5.1

SOURCE: U.S. Department of Commerce, *Survey of Current Business*, June 1967, pp. 22–23.

At the end of World War II, the most important trading partners of the United States, Western Europe and Japan, had severely damaged economies in need of restoration. To build up their productive capacity, these countries needed to import both consumer goods and capital equipment. The dominant supplier of these goods was the United States. Hence a huge export surplus of $7 billion evolved during the first postwar years. If services are included, the surplus is even larger, as shown in Table 26.2.

The large surplus on current account of over $8 billion could not be maintained for long. Once Western Europe and Japan had built up their damaged economies, their import surpluses decreased. An important correction of cost levels between some of the leading industrial countries also took place in 1949, when the most important countries in Western Europe, including Britain, France, and Scandinavia, devalued their currencies by roughly 30 percent. The United States still had a substantial surplus on current account throughout the 1950s, a surplus that has continued during the 1960s.

The United States also had an outflow of private capital that partially offset the surplus on current account. The magnitude of this outflow of capital is given in Table 26.3.

The outflow of private capital from the United States was fairly limited until 1955. Then a change took place, and during the latter half of the 1950s it increased to over $3 billion annually. It was primarily American investment in Western Europe that sharply increased. We have discussed

TABLE 26.2

U.S. balance of current account
($ billion: average per year)

Years	Merchandise export surplus	Services export surplus	Net balance on current account
1947–1949	7.0	1.6	8.6
1951–1956	2.7	1.8	4.5
1958–1962	3.8	2.1	5.9
1963–1966	5.1	3.5	8.6

SOURCE: U.S. Department of Commerce, *Survey of Current Business*, June 1967, pp. 22–23.

some of the reasons for this increase in Chapter 25. Here we can add that the establishment of the European Common Market, the easing of exchange restrictions, and the return to convertibility, plus a climate buoyant with profitable expectations all made for a rapid increase of American investment in Europe. As can be seen from Table 26.3, a large volume of American investment abroad has also continued during the 1960s. Canada and Western Europe are still the main recipients; roughly two thirds of the net outflow of American capital goes to these countries.

An important role has been played by government transfers. Since World War II, the American government has given aid and military support to many nations, either by placing foreign currency at the disposal of the foreign government or by providing it with American goods. In both cases it puts a strain on the American balance of payments. The magnitude of the American government transfers is given in Table 26.4.

In the immediate postwar years, government grants and loans played the most important role. These were the years when the Marshall Aid Program was introduced to help the Western European countries to rebuild their economies. In the 1950s, the emphasis shifted to the military field. This was the era of the containment policy practiced by the Eisenhower administration. Half of the government transfers during this time consisted of military aid and half of loans and aid for civilian purposes. During recent years, the emphasis on military aid has increased in connection with the war in Vietnam. Surprisingly little of these military efforts show up in the balance-

480

International
liquidity: the setting
of the problem

TABLE 26.3

Net private capital flows
($ billion: average per year)

Years	Net flow of private long-term capital	Net short-term capital outflows	Net private remittances	Total
1947–1949	— 0.8	0.0	— 0.6	— 1.4
1951–1956	— 1.2	— 0.2	— 0.5	— 1.9
1958–1962	— 2.6	— 0.8	— 0.5	— 3.9
1963–1966	— 4.1	— 0.6	— 0.6	— 5.3

SOURCE: U.S. Department of Commerce, *Survey of Current Business*, July 1967, pp. 22–23.

of-payments statistics. Some of the aid for civilian purposes is, however, quite directly a fruit of the war effort. The total value of government transfers is very substantial, about $6 billion in recent years.

A summing up of the different parts described so far, with the object of presenting a total view of the external position of the United States is given in Table 26.5.

During the immediate postwar years, the huge surplus on current account was partially offset by government transfers, while the net outflow of private capital was small. However, the United States still had a surplus in the balance of payments of about $1 billion. This situation put a great strain on the economies of Western Europe. They had large deficits in their external balances, which caused them to lose already low reserves of foreign currency. The situation would in all probability have led to a collapse of the international trading system had it not been for the aid from the American government, which was very substantial during these years, as can be seen from Table 26.5.

At the beginning of the 1950s, a change took place. The American surplus on the balance of current account started to decrease; it was less than $5 billion. About the same amount was transferred abroad by the American government to foreign governments. The outflow of net capital increased to almost $2 billion. This meant that the surplus in the American balance of payments was transformed into a deficit. The average deficit up to 1956 was not very large; it amounted to roughly $2 billion per year.

TABLE 26.4

Government transfers
($ billion: average per year)

Years	Government grants and loans	U.S. military expenditure abroad	Total government transfers
1947–1949	5.6	0.6	6.2
1951–1956	2.3	2.3	4.6
1958–1962	2.6	2.7	5.3
1963–1966	3.5	2.3	5.8

SOURCE: U.S. Department of Commerce, *Survey of Current Business*, July 1967, pp. 22–23.

The American deficit during this period caused no worries. On the contrary, it was regarded as essential for the proper functioning of the international monetary system. The most important of the U.S. trading partners, the countries of Western Europe and Japan, showed a rapid economic growth and world trade also grew at a rapid pace. International liquidity was necessary to finance world trade. The main reserve currency was the dollar. To help the other leading industrial nations build up their reserves of foreign currency, i.e., dollars, the United States had to run a deficit in its balance of payments so that its trading partners could transform part of their export surpluses into liquid dollar holdings. This was what took place during the earlier part of the 1950s.

A change in this pattern occurred in 1958. The surplus on current account was still large, about $6 billion. But government transfers amounted to roughly the same figure. At the same time, American direct investment abroad, especially in Western Europe, increased sharply to over $3 billion. The deficit in the balance of payments therefore increased to over $3 billion.

This still need not have caused too much worry; the deficit amounted to less than half of 1 percent of the U.S. GNP. But at the same time an outflow of gold took place. The United States had since the 1930s accumulated a very large stock of gold. It had guaranteed a stable price of gold. It bought and sold gold at $35.0875 per ounce. This had led to gold being dug up in South Africa and buried at Fort Knox.

482

International
liquidity: the setting
of the problem

TABLE 26.5

Balance of payments
($ billion: average per year)

Years	Balance of current account	Private net capital transfers	Government transfers	Over-all surplus (+) or deficits (—)
1947–1949	8.6	— 1.4	— 6.2	1.0
1951–1956	4.5	— 1.9	— 4.6	— 2.0
1958–1962	5.9	— 3.9	— 5.3	— 3.3
1963–1966	8.6	— 5.3	— 5.8	— 2.5

SOURCE: U.S. Department of Commerce, *Survey of Current Business*, July 1967, pp. 22–23.

In 1958, some Western European countries also started to acquire gold instead of dollars, and the United States lost about $2.3 billion worth. This greatly disturbed parts of the American business and financial community. The outflow of gold focused attention on the underlying cause, the deficit in the American balance of payments.

The deficit has persisted during the 1960s. The picture has been remarkably stable. A surplus on current account of over $8 billion has been offset by government transfers of some $5 billion, to which a net outflow of private capital of more than $5 billion has to be added. This gives rise to an over-all deficit in the balance of payments of approximately $3 billion. During some of the earlier years of the 1960s, it was somewhat lower, but in 1967 it grew to $4 billion.

The outflow of gold has continued. In the beginning of the 1950s, the value of the American gold stock amounted to $25 billion. In 1958 its value was $22 billion; at the beginning of 1968, it had sunk to $10.5 billion.

Now we shall look at the reverse side of the coin, the position of Western Europe and Japan, and see what role gold plays in their external reserves.

TABLE 26.6

Official holdings of gold and foreign exchange
($ billion)

	Gold holdings				Foreign exchange			
	1953	1958	1963	1967	1953	1958	1963	1967
Belgium	0.8	1.3	1.4	1.5	0.3	0.2	0.4	0.6
France	0.6	0.8	3.2	5.2	0.2	0.3	1.3	0.6
West Germany	0.3	2.6	3.8	4.3	1.6	3.7	3.3	2.6
The Netherlands	0.7	1.1	1.6	1.7	0.5	0.4	0.3	0.4
Italy	0.3	1.1	2.3	2.4	0.4	1.0	1.1	1.9
Sweden	0.2	0.2	0.2	0.2	0.3	0.3	0.5	0.6
Switzerland	1.5	1.9	2.8	2.8	0.3	0.1	0.3	0.4
Japan	0.0	0.1	0.3	0.3	0.8	0.8	1.6	1.5
Great Britain	2.5[a]	3.1[a]	2.5	1.7	—	—	0.2	1.2

[a] Including convertible currencies (prior to 1958, U.S. and Canadian dollars only).
SOURCE: United Nations, *Monthly Bulletin of Statistics.*

THE ROLE OF GOLD AND THE RESERVE POSITION
OF WESTERN EUROPE AND JAPAN

Japan and the industrial countries of Western Europe all had small reserves of gold and foreign exchange in the early 1950s. The attempts to rebuild the economies after the war put a strain on the balance of payments. External deficits, which were already small, tended to decrease still further. Direct controls over foreign trade were introduced to avoid deficits in the balance of payments.

Soon the economic resurgence took place and the external balance of most countries improved. This process is illustrated in Table 26.6. As early as 1953, West Germany, for instance, had built up fairly large dollar holdings. Switzerland had also a substantial gold reserve.

Most countries, however, had small reserves at the beginning of the 1950s. Naturally, the leading industrial countries outside the Communist bloc, which together with the United States dominate world trade, tried to rebuild their depleted reserves of gold and foreign currency. Table 26.6 shows that they were successful. West Germany, Belgium, and Switzerland, for instance, had acquired ample reserves in 1958. In the late 1950s and

484

International
liquidity : the setting
of the problem

TABLE 26.7

Gold as a percentage of total official gold and
foreign exchange reserves, September 1966

Over 90 percent	United States, Switzerland
80–90 percent	France, South Africa, the Netherlands
70–80 percent	Belgium, Spain
60–70 percent	West Germany, Italy, Venezuela, Great Britain, Portugal
40–60 percent	Austria, Canada
20–40 percent	India, Mexico, Sweden, Denmark
1–20 percent	Japan, Australia, Norway

SOURCE: First National City Bank, New York, *Monthly Economic Letter*, January 1967.

---

early 1960s, Italy and France generated large export surpluses that enabled them to rebuild their gold reserves.

The deficits in the American balance of payments formed a prerequisite for this development. It was only because the United States was running deficits that its main trading partners could generate surpluses which could then be transformed into holdings of gold and foreign exchange.

An important feature in this development is the division of the reserves between holdings of dollars and holdings of gold. Parts of the reserves consist of working balances. A country needs a certain amount of reserves to carry on the daily transactions and to meet seasonal fluctuations. These are usually held in the form of dollars or pounds sterling. When these needs are covered, a country can choose between holding gold or holding dollars.[1]

The central bank is the institution that handles a country's foreign reserves. Central banks vary widely in this respect. Some, such as those in Japan and the Scandinavian countries, have only a small ratio of their reserves in gold, whereas others, for instance the central banks in Switzerland

---

[1] We disregard in the future discussion the pound sterling, the minor key currency. Including it would not change anything essential in the discussion.

and the EEC countries, have a high ratio of their total reserves in gold. This is clearly illustrated in Table 26.7.

It should be added that the reserve countries, the United States and Britain, naturally have a high percentage in gold as they cannot count their own currency as part of their foreign reserves.

The reason for holding dollars as reserves is that dollar claims usually give some interest. Treasury bills or other short-term dollar claims usually yield an interest of 2 to 3 percent. Gold gives no interest at all. The reason for holding gold could be that the central bank in question fears a devaluation of the dollar that would cause a loss on its stock of dollar reserves. The price of gold, on the other hand, is expected to be stable or even to increase. A central bank that would be a profit maximizer as far as its foreign reserves are concerned would thus have to weigh the interest earnings on dollar reserves against the probability of the dollar being devalued or of the price of gold rising. There could also be political reasons for choosing one or other form for foreign reserves. This question is discussed further in Chapter 27.

We have now described some of the main features of the external position of the main industrial countries, without which the question of international liquidity cannot be understood. We now examine some of the policy implications of this situation.

INTERNATIONAL LIQUIDITY AND THE PROBLEM OF CONFIDENCE

With the single exception of 1957, the United States has been running a deficit in its balance of payments since 1950. During the first part of the 1950s, up to 1958, it seemed to go mostly unnoticed; nobody seemed to be concerned about it. On the contrary, it was viewed as a necessity for providing the world economy with international liquidity. The American liabilities were also amply covered by its gold holdings. As late as the end of 1960, the United States had short-term liabilities of about $18 billion, of which $10 billion were claims held by foreign central banks. Against this stood assets of $24 billion, of which U.S. gold holdings amounted to $18 billion.

As the American deficit in the balance of payments continued, its short-term liabilities also continued to grow. The first warning had been the

486

International
liquidity: the setting
of the problem

TABLE 26.8

Changes in world gold reserves 1934–1968[a]
($ billion)

| | Change | | Stock |
	Jan. 1934– Dec. 1949	Dec. 1949– Feb. 1968	outstanding Feb. 1968
United States	17.7	−14.1	10.5
Great Britain	−0.2	−0.1	1.3
France	−4.6	4.7	5.2
West Germany	−0.2	4.1	4.2
Switzerland	0.8	1.3	2.8
Italy	−0.4	2.1	2.4
Netherlands	−0.4	1.5	1.7
Belgium	0.1	0.8	1.5
Canada	0.4	0.5	1.0
All other countries	1.0	3.0	6.9
International institutions	1.5	0.8	2.3
	15.7	4.6	39.8

[a] The Soviet Union, China, and other Communist countries are left out, as no official figures for gold reserves and changes in gold stocks are published for these countries.
SOURCE: First National City Bank, New York, *Monthly Economic Letter*, April 1968.

run on gold in 1958. In the early 1960s, the American authorities tried to induce the surplus countries, especially the EEC countries, to hold dollars instead of gold. West Germany cooperated for some time with this policy, whereas other countries, especially France, did not wish to cooperate with the American authorities but instead continued to hoard gold. The flow of gold from the United States to Europe continued.

The central banks of the European Common Market countries had for several decades had the habit of holding the bulk of their foreign reserves in gold. As their reserves grew, it was only to be expected that they would acquire more and more gold. The United States had a requirement that 25 percent of the domestic currency should be covered by gold. Approximately $12 billion worth of gold was earmarked for this purpose. As could easily be foreseen, the international monetary system was heading for a gold crisis. This came in March 1968.

At this time, the U.S. gold stock reached the critical $12 billion figure. Private speculators joined the central banks of the EEC countries in bidding for gold. From October 1967 to March 1968, almost $4 billion worth of gold went into private hands. The price of gold on the Paris market (the only one open during the critical days) was bid up from the guaranteed price of $35 per ounce to almost $45 per ounce. The pressure against the dollar and for a world-wide devaluation, i.e., a rise in the guaranteed price of gold, had reached a climax.

The change in the world gold reserves from 1934 to 1968 and the distribution of the stock of gold in February 1968 are shown in Table 26.8. The most striking feature of Table 26.8 is the decline in the U.S. share of the world's gold stock. In the late 1940s, the United States had 75 percent of the total gold stock. In 1968 its share had fallen to 25 percent. At the same time, the EEC countries and Switzerland held over 40 percent of the total gold stock. The United States and these countries between them still had more than 75 percent of the gold stock.

During the 1930s and the 1940s a large amount of gold flowed from Europe to the United States. The last 15 years have seen a reversal of this trend. What primarily has taken place is a change in the distribution of gold between the United States and the Common Market countries; the gold that was earlier hoarded by the United States is now being hoarded by the EEC countries and Switzerland.

The importance of this development is that the dollar, not the currencies of the EEC countries, is the key currency of today's international monetary system.

The accumulated value of the outstanding dollar liabilities is now at least twice as large as the American gold stock. As long as the United States had all its liabilities covered by gold, there was no need to worry about the deficits in the American balance of payments: Anyone having dollar claims could be sure that he would be able to convert them into gold. This is no longer valid. It is this situation that has created a problem of confidence in the American dollar and fears for an American devaluation. The persisting American deficits will reinforce the lack of confidence in the dollar. This is perhaps one reason for some European central banks transforming part of their dollar holdings into gold.

488

International
liquidity: the setting
of the problem

On the other hand, however, there are many who argue that there is not enough international liquidity. As world trade grows, more liquidity is needed. The net increase in the gold stock is only about 2 percent per year and the increase in liquidity has to be larger if the international monetary system is to function efficiently: that is the argument. The only way international liquidity can grow under the present setup is by an increase in dollar holdings. But that presupposes deficits in the American balance of payments.

The dilemma in which the present international monetary system is caught is thus that more international liquidity is needed, but more liquidity cannot be created without impairing the confidence in the main key currency, the dollar. The present international monetary system builds on an internal contradiction. Unless some thorough reforms are carried out it will be heading for a collapse.

This sounds disquieting indeed. Before we tackle some important theoretical aspects of the problem of international liquidity, it might be useful to comment briefly on gold hoarding.

We have seen that the problem of confidence is intimately linked with the question of gold hoarding. It is not the American deficits per se that create a lack of confidence in the dollar. The prime reason for disquiet lies in the fact that a larger share of the dollar claims are not backed by gold.

The gold crisis in March 1968 was triggered off by private speculators, but the real gold hoarders are the central banks in Switzerland and the Common Market countries. If they could be induced to hold dollars instead of gold, the problem of confidence would be greatly minimized.

It can also be argued that it is irrational for these central banks to hold gold as they thereby forsake interest earnings on dollar holdings. At a 3 percent interest rate on dollar holdings, a 35 percent devaluation of the dollar every 10 years would be necessary for gold to be as profitable a source of reserves as dollars. As devaluations of the dollar are very rare, it seems that central banks, acting out of profit motives, ought to hold dollars instead of gold. This, in fact, is what the central banks in Japan and the Scandinavian countries do. Why, then, do the central banks of the Common Market countries hold gold?

On a somewhat superficial level, the answer could simply be that these banks, because of inherited traditions and routine, hold a high ratio of their reserves in gold. Gold is regarded as a guarantee of stability, central banks do not see profit maximization as an important aspect of their function; therefore, they prefer to hold gold even if this implies foregone earnings of interest. From the point of view of the directors of the central banks, another aspect perhaps also plays some role. If the dollar was to be devalued, a central bank with large holdings of dollars could easily come under attack because of the large losses on the stock of dollars that a devaluation would create. This could easily cost the head of a central bank his position; nobody, however, has heard of a director of a central bank being fired on account of the bank's holding gold.

On a deeper level, the answer is perhaps that central banks hold gold for political reasons. The central banks in the Common Market countries would probably argue that the United States pursues an economic policy that is too inflationary. This creates difficulties for the European countries and forces them to accept more price increases than they like. By hoarding gold, they can exert pressure on the United States and so force the American authorities to pursue more restrictive policies in order to close the deficit in the balance of payments. Hoarding gold, in this view, is therefore primarily a measure of trying to implement more deflationary policies in the world.

Another aspect of gold hoarding is that it could be a way of declaring dissatisfaction with the present international monetary system. The French government under de Gaulle declared that it would like to see the world go back to a pure gold standard, without reserve currencies. To move in this direction, the French central bank hoarded as much gold as it could. The French saw no reason not to accentuate the problem of confidence in order to make the world ready to accept a reconstruction of the international monetary system *à la française.*

Is there any risk of the problem of confidence becoming so acute that the present international monetary system will collapse? At this juncture, no attempt will be made to answer that question directly. The whole discussion in this part of the book is an attempt to elucidate this question. For the moment, we will merely add that the problem of confidence is in no way inherent in the present international monetary system. It is very largely created by the central banks themselves. So far, they have always proved willing to come to the rescue of the present system when it is under pressure; this was last demonstrated at the meeting of the Ten[2] in Stockholm in March

---

[2] The Ten consists of the following industrial countries: Belgium, Canada, France, Great Britain, Italy, Japan, the Netherlands, Sweden, United States, and West Germany. This group of countries, at the meeting in Stockholm, decided to create a double world market for gold (the central banks will buy and sell to each

490

International
liquidity: the setting
of the problem

1968 at the time of the most intense gold crisis since World War II. The question is therefore not so much whether the present system can be maintained but whether the leading industrial countries outside the Communist sphere wish to maintain it. Chapters 27 and 28 will be devoted to the question involved in that problem.

THE ROLE OF THE INTERNATIONAL MONETARY FUND

We have so far described the development of the two main forms international liquidity can take: U.S. dollars and gold. There is also a third form, drawing rights on the IMF, which have played a less important, although not altogether negligible, role. We have already referred to the IMF in Chapters 16 and 22. We now briefly describe the workings of the IMF and examine its role in the international monetary system.

The IMF was established in 1944 at Bretton Woods. Its primary aim was to help solve the short-term balance-of-payments problems that might arise in the world economy after World War II. From an original membership of 44, the IMF has expanded to 107.

Each member of the Fund is allotted a quota, the size of the quota varying according to the importance of the country. The sum of all quotas was established at $8.8 billion in 1944[3]. This can be compared with the figure for total world liquidity, which at the time amounted to approximately $38 billion. It should be noted that each country's quota determines its voting rights, and thereby the influence of the country. The United States was dominant. Its quota at the beginning amounted to 36 percent of the total holding of the IMF. This quota has since decreased to 22 percent, but the United States, together with England and some other Western European countries, still retains a controlling influence over the Fund. This is also

---

other at the established price of $35 per ounce and the price of gold on the second, free market will be governed by market forces) and in addition to establish so-called special drawing rights. The meaning of this last act will be discussed in Chapter 28.

[3] This includes $1.2 billion from the Soviet Union which, however, never joined the Fund.

witnessed by the fact that the Soviet Union and the Communist countries of Eastern Europe are not members of the IMF. The general quotas have since been increased twice; by 50 percent in 1959 and 25 percent in 1966. Including new members, the second increase brought total IMF quotas to $21 billion.

A detailed description of how IMF works is not necessary for our purposes. We outline its main functions and give a brief evaluation of its role in the postwar period.

A country's quota has three important aspects. First, it specifies how much the country must subscribe to the Fund. Of this subscription 25 percent must be paid in gold, and the rest in the country's own currency. Second, the quota defines a country's drawing rights, i.e. how much a country can borrow from the Fund. Third, it indicates the country's voting power.[4]

The most important aspect, from our standpoint, is the drawing rights. Each country's drawing right is divided into five parts. The first is called the gold tranche, because it corresponds to the country's subscription in gold. The next four are called the first, second, third, and fourth credit tranches. The importance of the drawing rights lies in the fact that a country can make drawings on the IMF and use the currency it thereby obtains to cover deficits in the balance of payments. Under IMF practice, a country can automatically make use of its gold tranche. Also, it can usually use its first credit tranche without much difficulty. Thereafter, drawings on the Fund depend on approval by the Fund. The conditions of approval become more and more stringent as a country applies to go beyond its first credit tranche. Usually, a country must repay the Fund within three to five years, and there is an increasing scale of interest on drawings that go beyond the gold tranche.

The IMF began its operations in 1947. It had been foreseen at the Bretton Woods conference in 1944 that normal conditions in the international monetary field would not be achieved until some time after the war was over. It was 1961 before "normalcy" returned.

From the first, IMF played a conservative role. The Fund feared that its resources would be used for reconstruction purposes and not for solving short-term balance-of-payments problems. Therefore it laid down stringent conditions for its lending operations; for instance, the rule that a country must repay the Fund within 3 to 5 years. It also increased charges on its outstanding loans. For a country to get help, it had to convince the Fund

---

4 There is no nonsense about "one country, one vote" in the IMF. Each member has 250 votes plus one vote for each $100,000 of its subscription.

492

International
liquidity: the setting
of the problem

that its balance-of-payments problems were temporary, and that it could over-come them within a fairly short time.

All this led to the IMF playing quite a passive role during the 1950s. In the late 1940s it stressed the necessity of adjustment in the exchange rates, and took a positive view of the devaluations by Britain and most other Western European countries in 1949. Later, it took the view that changes in major exchange rates were undesirable. According to the regulations of the Fund, a member country can devalue by less than 10 percent without consulting the Fund. If a country wishes to devalue by more than 10 percent, it must prove to the satisfaction of the Fund that it has a "fundamental dis-equilibrium" in its balance of payments.

Instead of devaluation, IMF stressed the importance of internal measures, i.e., expenditure reduction for keeping the balance of payments in equilibrium. In the view of the Fund, it was more or less each country's own responsibility to maintain a balance in its external transactions. In 1952, for instance, it stated in its Annual Report: "It is important, therefore, that countries follow commercial policies that will enable them to build up re-serves in periods of prosperity which would provide a first cushion to absorb the shock of a recession."[5] The argument that a country should primarily rely on expenditure reduction was continually reiterated on behalf of the Fund.

This argument, however, never had to meet a real test. It did not happen that, of the three main types of "adjustment" (expenditure reduc-tion, expenditure switching, and provision of liquidity), only the first was relied on. On the contrary, international liquidity grew quite fast, as evidenced in this chapter. But it was not primarily the IMF that provided this liquidity. It was, instead, provided by the United States' balance-of-payments deficits.

Table 26.9 illustrates the development of international reserves during the postwar years. The table again confirms that the two most important sources of increase in world liquidity have been gold and U.S. dollars.

Developments in the 1950s and the first half of the 1960s tended therefore to bypass the IMF. In times of crisis the central banks tended to cooperate directly, outside the IMF. Of importance were so-called swap arrangements between the Federal Reserve System of the United States and

---

5 IMF, *Annual Report*, 1952, p. 46.

TABLE 26.9

International reserves
($ billion, end of year)

	1945	1955	1965
Gold	33.3	35.8	41.4
Foreign exchange	14.3	17.0	23.0
Gold tranche position at the IMF	—	1.9	5.4
	47.6	54.7	69.8

SOURCES: *Federal Reserve Bulletin* and *International Financial Statistics*.

the central banks of some Western European countries and Japan. The "swaps" consist of an exchange of currencies between countries. They are, in fact, short-term credit arrangements. As the two countries taking part in the swap exchange each other's currencies, the foreign reserves of both countries will increase. By early 1968, these swap facilities amounted to over $7 billion. They were available at very short notice and played an important role in staving off particularly speculative movements of currencies.

By such direct credit arrangements, the central banks of the leading industrial countries (the members of the Group of Ten) helped each other when there was a run on a country's currency. Examples of assistance between central banks are the case of Canada in 1962, that of Italy in 1964, and that of France in 1968. In each of these cases, credit possibilities of more than $1 billion were created. Britain has also been helped on several occasions.

The cooperation between central banks is also becoming closer. The heads of the most important central banks meet each month in Basle, Switzerland, to discuss matters concerning the external balance. There is also a section within the OECD that continuously watches the development of the balances of payments of the member countries. Consultations also take place within the Group of Ten.

These arrangements have reduced interest in the IMF. It can be argued that, so far, the Fund has not played the central role that some of its creators at Bretton Woods envisaged. Some would even argue that the Fund ought to play a secondary role, that it should primarily concentrate its energies on helping the less-developed countries, and perhaps assist occasionally when an industrial country is under particular stress. The implication

494

International
liquidity: the setting
of the problem

of this line of thought is that "the club of the rich countries" can manage their own affairs by more direct cooperation.

Lately, however, the tendency has been for the IMF to play a more active role again. This is best witnessed by the creation of the so-called special drawing rights at the IMF meeting in Rio de Janeiro in 1967. This might be characterized as the most far-reaching reform so far made within the sphere of the IMF. It might also be argued that more far-reaching, structural reforms are best made with the help of the IMF. We return to the special drawing rights and other plans of extension of the IMF in Chapter 28, which is devoted to reform plans for the international monetary system. Before concluding this chapter, however, we should also discuss whether it is possible, and if so in what way, to eliminate the deficit in the U.S. balance of payments. This question is not without importance for the functioning of the international monetary system.

CAN THE DEFICIT IN THE U.S. BALANCE OF PAYMENTS BE ELIMINATED?

We have seen that the United States has been running a deficit in its balance of payments of about $3 billion every year since 1958. This has created a problem of confidence in the dollar and has given U.S. authorities cause for worry. We can now ask: What has caused the deficit? How can it be cured?

Little can be said about the causes of the deficit. The balance on current account has shown a large surplus, averaging more than $6 billion per year. The U.S. economy seems therefore to be quite competitive. Nor has the degree of inflation in the United States been any larger than the degree of inflation in the main competing countries in Western Europe. On the contrary, it seems that the price increases in Western Europe (and Japan) have been higher during most of the period.

To find a reason for the deficit, we must take the other two main items on the balance into account; the balance of government transfer and the balance on capital account. First, government transfers: We have seen that they almost equal the surplus on current account. Are they the cause of the deficit?

Here we must first make an important observation. Most of American aid is tied. This means that American aid and assistance is given in the form of American goods. Even if aid was *not* tied, we would still expect an American grant to be spent, at least partially, on imports from the United States and hence have a positive effect on American exports. Ordinary general-equilibrium considerations tell us that there ought to be a link between a country's aid and its exports.

This is a well-known problem in international trade literature, usually dealt with under the heading of the transfer problem. We gave a fairly thorough discussion of some theoretical aspects of this problem in Chapter 25. We learned there that using the two-country model, we can say that a transfer is going to be completely effected, i.e., cause no disequilibrium in the balance of payments and have no effects on the terms of trade, if the sum of the marginal propensities to import in the two countries equals unity. If, as is perhaps to be expected, the sum of these critical propensities is less than unity, the donor country would perhaps have some difficulties with its balance of payments and could suffer deteriorating terms of trade. There could still be no question, however, that the eventual deficit in the balance of payments would be much smaller than the sum total of aid and assistance.

It has been estimated that 80 percent of American aid is tied. If we take this as a rough measure and disregard the finer points of transfer theory, we can say that if the American aid was decreased by $5 billion, the net improvement of the balance of payments would be only $1 billion. It is therefore difficult to say that the transfers of the U.S. government are the main cause of the deficit. Even if the United States stopped all transfers to other countries, there would still be a deficit in the American balance of payments.

It could be argued that the policy of aid and assistance boosts American exports and helps to create a surplus on the balance of current account. At the same time, it could be said that the United States has to have an export surplus to pursue the type of foreign economic policy the country engages in. The American dilemma is that even though the surplus on current account is substantial, it is still not large enough to permit the country to engage in a policy of aid and assistance to the extent it would like to. In this sense it can be said that the American competitive situation is quite weak.

The other main item that makes for a deficit in the American balance of payments is the outflow of American capital. The net outflow amounted during the last 10 years to an average of over $4 billion per year. Most of

496

International
liquidity: the setting
of the problem

this outflow of capital is composed of direct American investments in Europe.

Could this outflow be halted? We have seen in Chapter 25 that there are several complicated reasons for this outflow. Freedom of capital movements between countries is one of the basic beliefs of the free market system. It is difficult to see how anything of a substantial nature could be done to limit the outflow of capital without impairing this principle. American direct investments abroad also have great advantages to offer the main investors, the large American corporations. They get both a good return on their investments and control over important parts of foreign industry. It can also be added that the European central banks help, by holding dollars, to finance the American acquisition of European industry.

Small measures, such as harmonization of tax laws and interest-rate equalization, can be used to reduce the American outflow of capital. But it is difficult to see how anything more substantial can be done. The freedom of international capital flows is an integrated part of a liberal trading system. It is also in the interest of the business community. It is therefore unlikely for the outflow of American capital to be stopped as a result of balance-of-payments considerations.

The deficit in the American balance of payments is centered around the transfer and capital accounts. The result of our discussion so far, however, is that very little can be done concerning these two accounts to cure the deficit. To reduce the government transfers would mean a complete reversal in American foreign policy. Even so, it is quite unlikely that any substantial result would be achieved, as most of the help and assistance is tied. It is not likely that the United States will make a drastic reversal of its foreign policy and stop giving military and other aid to its allies because of balance-of-payments considerations; it is more rational to cure the deficit by more direct means. Nor is it easy to reduce the outflow of capital without drastic changes in the rules of the game; such changes, however, could be a possibility.

The means available to the United States for curing its deficit are the standard ones: restrictive monetary and fiscal policies, devaluation, or direct controls.

The U.S. authorities also began in 1967 and 1968 a more cautionary fiscal and monetary policy, to a large extent because of considerations for the external balance. The gold crisis in March 1968 focused the world's attention on the American balance-of-payments situation. An immediate effect was a raise in the American discount that was already very high.[6] Tax increases and cuts in government spending have also been carried out. Whether the effect of this restrictive economic policy will be large enough to cure the deficit remains to be seen.

If the deficit should persist, the risk is that the United States will revert to a more protectionist policy and introduce various kinds of direct controls. Nor can the threat of a devaluation of the dollar be completely neglected if the deficit continues.

What the future course of the U.S. balance of payments will be is, of course, impossible to tell. It might well happen that the United States will again have an equilibrium or a surplus in its balance of payments.

We have, however, now gained a certain amount of insight into the position of the main key currency and the development of the international monetary system during the 1950s and the 1960s. We will now go on to deal with some theoretical aspects of the problem in the next chapter.

SELECTED BIBLIOGRAPHY: CHAPTER 26

The literature in this area is very voluminous. It is difficult to single out any items at the cost of others; much depends on personal judgment. Useful surveys of the development of the international monetary system and the supply of international liquidity are given in:

R. N. Cooper, *The Economics of Interdependence: Economic Policy in the Atlantic Community*, New York, 1968, especially chap. 2.

R. Hinshaw (ed.), *Monetary Reform and the Price of Gold*, Baltimore, 1967.

For an overview of problems in connection with international monetary reform, see:

F. Machlup and B. G. Malkiel, *International Monetary Arrangements: the Problem of Choice*, Princeton, N.J., 1964.

---

[6] The American discount was raised to its highest level since 1929.

498

International
liquidity: the setting
of the problem

For a discussion of the supply of liquidity with an emphasis of the defects of the present system, see:

> R. Triffin, *Gold and the Dollar Crisis*, New Haven, Conn., 1960.

> R. Triffin, *Our International Monetary System: Yesterday, Today and Tomorrow*, New York, 1968.

Other interesting contributions are:

> O. L. Altman, "The Management of International Liquidity," *SP*, July 1964.

> C. P. Kindleberger, "The Prospects for International Liquidity and the Future Evolution of the International Payments System," in R. F. Harrod and D. C. Hague (eds.), *International Trade Theory in a Developing World*, London, 1963.

> W. M. Scammell, *International Monetary Policy*, 2nd ed., London, 1961.

For a useful survey of the development of the U.S. balance of payments and an interpretation of the facts, see:

> L. B. Yeager, *International Monetary Relations*, New York, 1966, chap. 25.

For a survey of the discussion of dollar shortage and dollar glut, see:

> M. O. Clement, R. L. Pfister and K. J. Rothwell, *Theoretical Issues in International Economics*, Boston, 1967, chap. 8.

For a discussion of how to measure the U.S. balance of payments, see:

> R. N. Cooper, "The Balance of Payments in Review," *JPE*, August 1966.

A useful but now somewhat dated discussion of U.S. balance-of-payments problems is contained in:

> S. E. Harris (ed.), *The Dollar Crisis*, New York, 1961.

See also:

> P. A. Samuelson, *Stability and Growth in the American Economy*, Stockholm, 1963.

Useful information on the actual state of the system and differing views on how well it functions can be obtained from various sources. The International Finance Section of the Department of Economics at Princeton University publishes *Essays in International Finance*, a series that contains much useful information. Several papers published in connection with hearings held by the Joint Economic Committee of the U.S. Congress contain excellent information and views expressed by leading professional economists. Publications like *The Economist, The New York Times,* and *The Wall Street Journal* can prove useful to anyone who wants to obtain information about the subject.

Useful information is also provided by IMF in its annual reports and staff papers. The *Federal Reserve Bulletin* usually gives very good descriptions of various international financial operations.

The adequacy of international liquidity, the price of international liquidity, and the adjustment mechanism

27

In Chapter 26 we studied some basic facts of the international monetary system. We saw how the supply of international liquidity has grown in the postwar years and how it is distributed. We now deal with some more theoretical issues in connection with international liquidity. We can, with profit, start by discussing a question that has attracted much attention, that of the adequacy of international liquidity.

THE ADEQUACY OF INTERNATIONAL LIQUIDITY

One important school of economists argues that international liquidity grows too slowly. World trade has since 1950 grown at the annual rate of 7.5 percent. Total gold reserves have grown at 1.4 percent per year, and over-all liquidity has grown at 2.7 percent per year. Table 27.1 illustrates the growth of international liquidity. The table shows that the gold reserves have grown steadily during the 1950s and the 1960s at a rate of 1.7 percent. World liquidity grew at the same rate, 1.7 percent per year, from 1954 to 1959. During the first part of the 1960s, the growth rate of world liquidity almost doubled: It increased to 3.3 percent per year.

However, the development of different countries has varied greatly. Some, such as the United States and Britain, have had a decrease in their international reserves, whereas others, especially members of the Ten apart from the United States and Britain, i.e., Belgium, the Netherlands, France, Italy, West Germany, Japan, Canada, and Sweden, have had a rapid increase in their reserves. The table illustrates this.

While over-all liquidity has grown slowly, the reserves of some important industrial countries, such as the eight just mentioned, have grown very rapidly. During the 1950s, the growth of reserves of this group of countries could be explained by their wish to rebuild reserves drained by war and reconstructions. During the 1960s, the increase in their reserves has been differently inspired—to some extent, it could even have been involuntary. We can also see from Table 27.1 that other developed countries and less-developed countries had significantly larger reserves in 1965 than they had in 1960.

500

TABLE 27.1

Changes in total official reserves

Areas and years	Gold reserves		Foreign exchange reserves		Reserve positions with IMF	Global reserves	
	Aggregate change ($)	Annual rate of increase (%)	Aggregate change ($)	Annual rate of increase (%)	Aggregate change ($)	Aggregate change ($)	Annual rate of increase (%)
ALL COUNTRIES							
1954–1959	3,560	1.7	740	0.8	1,360	5,660	1.7
1960–1965	4,045	1.7	6,350	5.7	2,125	12,520	3.3
THE TEN AND SWITZERLAND							
1954–1959	3,455	1.8	1,035	3.0	1,165	5,655	2.4
1960–1965	2,595	1.3	3,900	8.2	1,615	8,110	2.9
THE TEN, EXCLUDING THE UNITED STATES AND BRITAIN							
1954–1959	5,785	12.7	1,100	3.3	595	7,480	9.1
1960–1965	8,285	9.6	2,600	6.0	3,075	13,960	9.9
OTHER DEVELOPED COUNTRIES							
1954–1959	415	4.7	395	2.0	155	965	3.4
1960–1965	1,530	11.2	1,110	4.8	330	2,970	7.6
LESS-DEVELOPED COUNTRIES							
1954–1959	−310	—	−690	—	40	−960	—
1960–1965	−80	—	1,340	3.3	180	1,440	2.4

SOURCE: R. Hinshaw (ed.), *Monetary Reform and the Price of Gold*, Baltimore, The Johns Hopkins Press, 1967, p. 28.

502

The adequacy of international liquidity,
the price of international liquidity,
and the adjustment mechanism

The argument about inadequacy of reserves can therefore be regarded from several angles.[1] One is straightforward: that from a global point of view international liquidity grows too slowly. Another is that the distribution of liquidity is too uneven. Some countries have too much liquidity, whereas others have too little; and, perhaps more significant, there is no mechanism inherent in the present system that allows an orderly provision of a steady increase in international liquidity.

This argument is basically a variation of the question of confidence raised in Chapter 26. The growth of liquidity has been made possible only by the United States running balance-of-payments deficits. However, this cannot continue indefinitely. Therefore, it is argued that the present system for providing international liquidity is inherently unstable.

It will perhaps be useful to begin the discussion of adequacy by taking the global aspect first. It rests on three postulates: (1) that world trade is expected to grow at 6 to 7 percent annually and that reserves should grow at approximately the same rate, (2) that monetary gold reserves are expected to increase at a maximum of 2 percent annually, and (3) that foreign dollar reserves then must grow more rapidly than this, which is considered impossible.

We must now inspect this line of reasoning somewhat more closely. The first part of the argument, concerning the growth of world trade, could simply be taken as a desirable target. If world trade grows at this rate, it can be taken as a measure of an efficient international division of labor. The growth figure given for gold reserves is also apparently realistic. It is the third point that is debatable and, with it, the whole concept of adequacy of international liquidity. We could simply ask the innocent question (as several economists have done): What is an "adequate" reserve of international liquidity?

Sometimes adequacy of international reserves is measured by their size in terms of yearly imports. In this view, a country would have adequate

---

[1] Robert Triffin is the economist who has most persistently and most cogently argued that the present international monetary system cannot provide enough international liquidity in the long term. Among Triffin's books can be cited *Gold and the Dollar Crisis*, New Haven, Conn., Yale University Press, 1960; *The Evolution of the International Monetary System*, Princeton, N.J., Princeton Studies in International Finance, no. 12, 1964; and *The World Money Maze*, New Haven, Conn., Yale University Press, 1966.

reserves if they are large enough to finance imports for 3 to 5 months.[2] Apart from the fact that a country can hardly come into a situation where she can export nothing but will import as usual, this is an arbitrary measure.

Two countries, both having foreign reserves large enough to cover 3 months of imports, could still be in very different circumstances. One could be in a weak external position and not dare to pursue an expansionary policy, whereas the other has no hesitation in using its reserves, as it regards its deficit as temporary in nature.

It is sometimes argued—especially by bankers and economists dealing with practical matters—that adequacy of reserves is a matter of "feeling." If the authorities of a country feel that reserves are adequate, then they *are* adequate. This, however, is hardly a useful approach for judging whether international liquidity grows at a pace that can be judged adequate.

It is perhaps not very useful to discuss the adequacy of international liquidity merely in terms of volumes and divorced from the adjustment mechanism. To come to grips with the problem we must adopt a more analytical approach. We could begin by stating the problem in terms of supply and demand for liquidity and include the price of liquidity. If the supply of liquidity is too small compared with the demand for it, could it perhaps simply be because the price is too low? We then must discuss the adequacy of international liquidity in terms of its price.

THE PRICE OF INTERNATIONAL LIQUIDITY

International liquidity is a somewhat elusive concept. It takes primarily two forms: gold and holdings of foreign currency. The price of international liquidity can, in a direct sense, be said to be the price of gold expressed in home currency and the price of the foreign currency (for instance, dollars) also expressed in the home currency (i.e., the exchange rate).

It would probably be more useful, however, to think in terms of opportunity costs. Then the price of international liquidity equals its opportunity cost; the price of international liquidity is the difference between

---

[2] Triffin is one economist who has used 3 to 5 months as a criterion for adequate reserves.

504

The adequacy of international liquidity,
the price of international liquidity,
and the adjustment mechanism

the rate of return on gold and foreign currency and the rate of return that other investments give.

When we take the price of international liquidity into account, the problem will perhaps change its character. If the demand for international liquidity is larger than its supply, it could be that the price of international liquidity is set too low. If demand and supply are elastic with respect to price, an increase in the price of international liquidity could easily create an equilibrium. If demand and supply are very inelastic with respect to price, it could be more difficult to reach equilibrium, and then price changes would probably play only a minor role.

We must bear in mind that the market for international liquidity is a very special one. The holders of international liquidity are primarily central banks and, to a lesser degree, commercial banks. The central banks, especially, will perhaps not behave according to usual economic rules. This could limit the usefulness of an analysis that runs in terms of price. It could also happen that the price of international liquidity is determined by political reasons. But this should not stop us from trying to pursue an analysis in ordinary economic terms.

Let us begin by looking at the supply of international liquidity. The supply of gold should be determined by the price of gold in an obvious way: If the price of gold goes up, the supply of gold should increase.

Gold is used broadly for three purposes: by central banks as reserves, hoarded by private persons and used as a (safe) store of value, and by industry (for jewelry, dental purposes, etc.). During the last 20 years, about 40 percent of the increase in total supply of gold has gone to central banks, 40 percent has gone to private hoarders, and 20 percent has been used by industry. This development is illustrated in Table 27.2.

If the price of gold increased (by a world-wide devaluation), it is highly probable that the supply of gold for central bank purposes would increase. The total supply would certainly increase, as gold mining would become more profitable. The demand from industry would in all probability decrease; this would leave a larger share of the total supply for other purposes. The main difficulty lies in getting information about private hoarders. Here it could go either way.

If the increase in the price of gold were large enough and hoarders believed that no further price increase would come in the foreseeable future, they would probably start releasing their hoards, and gold available for monetary reserves would increase substantially. But a price increase could

TABLE 27.2

World gold supply and distribution, 1946–1966
(millions of ounces)

	1946–1955	1956–1966	1966	Total (1946–1966)
SUPPLY				
Production (excluding USSR)	241.1	350.2	41.7	633.0
Sales by USSR to rest of world	8.0	90.8	—	98.8
	249.1	441.0	41.7	731.8
DISTRIBUTION				
To official monetary reserves	123.1 (49.4)[a]	167.0 (37.0)	—	290.1 (39.6)
To industry, jewelry, and the arts	55.1 (22.1)	86.3 (19.6)	14.5 (34.8)	155.9 (21.3)
To traditional hoarding centers (net)	70.9 (28.5)	86.9 (19.7)	15.0 (36.0)	172.8 (23.6)
Other private holdings		100.8 (22.8)	12.2 (29.2)	113.0 (15.5)
	249.1 (100.0)	441.0 (100.0)	41.7 (100.0)	731.8 (100.0)

[a] Figures in parentheses are percentages.

SOURCE: R. Hinshaw (ed.), *Monetary Reform and the Price of Gold*, Baltimore, The Johns Hopkins Press, 1967, p. 116.

also be interpreted as an indication that the gold price would no longer be fixed in the future but be subject to changes. This could result in further hoarding by private persons and the gold available for monetary purposes could thus even decline.

It is extremely difficult to form any positive opinion about the effect of a devaluation on private hoarding of gold on a priori grounds. As Table 27.2 indicates, private hoarding has been very substantial since World War II. The value of the 732 million ounces of gold that have been added to the world's gold supply since 1946 can be estimated at $25.6 billion. Of this, 40 percent has gone to private hoarders. These have thus acquired gold valued

506

The adequacy of international liquidity,
the price of international liquidity,
and the adjustment mechanism

at roughly $10 billion. Most of it has gone to "traditional hoarding centers" (Middle East, India, Far East, and France). Gold hoarding in these countries seems to have deep psychological roots and would probably continue even if the price of gold increased. A certain increase in the supply of gold from this source is to be expected, but how long it would take before hoarding would start again at a renewed rate is impossible to say.

The supply of international liquidity in the form of foreign exchange is in the main equal to the supply of American dollars. This is again determined by the U.S. supply of short-term dollar assets, which is primarily a function of the American balance-of-payments situation. As long as the United States is running a deficit, there will be a supply of dollars that can be used for liquidity purposes. This was analyzed in Chapter 26.

It should be observed, however, that an American deficit is not strictly a prerequisite for an increase in foreign holdings of U.S. dollars. One could think of a situation where the American balance of payments was in equilibrium but where offsetting capital movements still helped to create international liquidity.

Assume, for instance, that the balance of payments between Europe and the United States is in equilibrium. At the same time, Europe is lending short to the United States, acquiring short-term dollar assets that can be used for liquidity purposes, whereas the United States is making long-term direct investments in Europe to the same amount. In this way, Europe can go on increasing its international liquidity, i.e., its holdings of dollars, everything being in balance. In this sense it is not strictly necessary for the United States to be running a deficit in order to increase liquidity.

Monetary policies can be geared in such a way as to create liquidity. By pricing its short-term assets in a way that makes them attractive for other countries to hold, the United States can help to increase international liquidity. This, however, has definite implications for U.S. monetary policy in general. One of the difficulties of U.S. monetary policy in recent years, when trying to induce European central banks to hold dollars instead of gold, has been the limitations on possible increases in interest rates that domestic policy considerations have enforced.

Summing up concerning price effects on the supply of international liquidity, we can therefore say that the price mechanism can only be expected to work in a limited way. As far as gold is concerned, a certain increase in the supply should follow from a price increase. As far as the supply of dollars is concerned, it primarily depends on factors other than the price of short-term dollar assets. Price increases on these assets, however, could have a role to play.

Price changes do probably play a larger role in the demand for international liquidity. There are several reasons a central bank might want to hold assets that are internationally liquid. One is the transactions motive. Even if receipts and payments were to balance in the long run, there is little reason to expect them to balance every day or every month. To bridge the gap between payments and receipts, a country needs reserves. How large these reserves need to be depends on the nature of the country's trade and also on stochastic factors. The theory of inventory holding can help to calculate the amount of reserves that a country needs for transaction purposes.

When the volume of trade grows, the necessity for increased reserves also grows. It is known, both from the theory and practice of cash holding, that the volume of reserves need not grow as fast as the volume of trade. Under certain simplified conditions, it can be shown that the volume of reserves need only grow in proportion to the square root of the increase in the volume of trade. If trade grows at 6 percent per year, the demand for international liquidity for transaction purposes would only have to grow at approximately 3 percent per year.

This is obviously an important fact to keep in mind when discussing adequacy of international liquidity. The demand for transaction cash is most certainly sensitive to price changes and to conditions in the credit market. Much of the reserves needed for transaction purposes are held by commercial banks. The percentage of total reserves held by commercial banks could therefore hint how large a share of the total reserves are needed for transaction purposes. In Sweden, for instance, it seems that about 15 to 20 percent of total reserves are kept by commercial banks, although at times it has been as high as 30 percent.

The holdings of working balances in foreign currency are sensitive both to changes in interest rates and to availability conditions in the credit market. Holdings of foreign currency can sometimes be a substitute for holdings of domestic currency. If the domestic credit market becomes tighter, commercial banks will perhaps shift out of foreign currency to increase availability of domestic credit. If foreign short-term interest rates are increased, banks would perhaps be induced to hold larger cash balances in foreign currency, etc.

Thus it seems reasonable to conclude that a certain amount of a country's international reserves are held for transaction purposes. This part

508

The adequacy of international liquidity,
the price of international liquidity,
and the adjustment mechanism

will grow as world trade grows but at a lower rate. Cash holdings of this type are sensitive both to changes in interest rates and to availability conditions in credit markets.

Other reasons for demand for international liquidity could be termed the speculative reason and the policy reason. The speculative motive in ordinary Keynesian liquidity analysis is primarily concerned with expectations about changes in interest rates and asset prices. The speculative motive has many dimensions in connection with international liquidity. It can have an effect on demand both for over-all liquidity and for the composition of liquidity.

The role of the speculative motive for the composition of liquidity is obvious. If a reserve currency is under speculation—if there is a risk that it will be devalued—this is a strong reason for other countries to shift out of the currency and into gold and other currencies instead. This has been a strong motive for many central banks not to have too-large holdings of pounds sterling and U.S. dollars, the two main reserve currencies of today. We have already seen examples of this in Chapter 26.

Price can play an important role in the composition of reserves. If countries become averse to holding dollars, say, U.S. authorities will perhaps try to counteract this development by an increase in short-term interest rates on dollar assets. As gold gives no return whatever, the relative margin on holdings of dollar assets increases, and the opportunity cost of holding gold goes up. It will also have indirect effects, as it will be taken as a signal that the key currency country is determined to defend its currency by the use of a restrictive monetary policy. The problem of confidence that we treated in Chapter 26 is essentially one of composition of reserves. As the price of international liquidity can play an important role for the composition of reserves, it can also play an important role for dealing with the problem of confidence in the dollar, which is one of the main issues at stake.

Changes in interest rates can also influence the over-all demand for international liquidity. There are several ways in which a key currency country can manipulate the structure and levels of its interest rates so as to induce other countries to hold a desired amount of its own currency and thereby of international liquidity. If it wished to decrease the amount of international liquidity available—for instance by inducing countries to decrease their holdings of short-term dollar assets—it could do so by a relative increase in long-term interest rates. This will lead to a fall in prices of long-term assets and to an increase in the effective rates of return on these assets. This will induce reserve holders to buy long-term assets and decrease their speculative cash holdings.

If, on the contrary, the central bank of the key currency country wished to increase international liquidity, it could do so by increasing the rate of return on short-term holdings of the reserve currency. This will act as an inducement to central and commercial banks abroad to hold more of the reserve country's short-term assets that are counted as part of international liquidity.

So far, we have discussed the demand for international liquidity in terms analogous to those used by the standard Keynesian analysis for holdings of cash. But central banks do not act exactly as private businesses; they have other interests to pursue apart from the profit motive. Another motive influencing holdings of international liquidity can be termed the policy motive.

We have already seen in Chapter 26 that the composition of the holdings of international liquidity differs very substantially between countries. Table 26.7 showed that the percentage of gold in total reserves varied widely between different countries. These differences can hardly be explained either by the use of the transactions or by the speculative motives, at least not completely. Here we must take into account policy motives of a type already discussed in Chapter 26. Some countries prefer to hold a high proportion of their reserves in gold because of tradition or because they want to put pressure on the reserve currency countries into changing their policies with respect to international liquidity.

The policy motive can also play a role for the total amount of reserves that a country wishes to hold. Some countries with a nationalist outlook, which want a free hand in determining their foreign policy, could strive to pursue an economic policy that will ensure the country having large reserves. Other countries, which value economic growth highly, could be inclined to decrease their reserves and pursue expansionistic policies even at the risk of crises caused by too low an amount of international liquidity.

Holdings of international liquidity are also determined by a wealth effect. As countries grow richer, we can expect them to hold larger amounts of international reserves. This can be seen, for instance, from Table 27.1, which illustrates the fact that less-developed countries usually have very low reserves.

To sum up, part of the demand for international liquidity, especially the part governed by policy considerations, cannot be expected to be very

510

The adequacy of international liquidity,
the price of international liquidity,
and the adjustment mechanism

sensitive to price changes. Other parts of the demand—those influenced by transactions and speculative motives—should be quite sensitive to price changes. It is therefore an oversimplification, when dealing with the adequacy of international liquidity, to think only in terms of volumes. To disregard price can lead to quite erroneous conclusions.

THE QUESTION OF SEIGNIORAGE

Another problem in connection with international liquidity that we should briefly touch upon is what is sometimes referred to as the problem of seigniorage. The essence of the problem is as follows: If a commodity, for instance gold, is used as money, it takes some real resources to produce it. To increase its money supply a society will have to renounce real resources to produce more of the commodity used as money. If changes in the price level are intimately linked to the money supply, the use of commodity money could act as a stabilizer of the price level.

Historically speaking, we know that commodity monies have been supplanted by paper monies in all advanced national states. The reason is that paper money can be created at no (or very low) cost.[3] It fills the need for liquidity the same way as commodity money does, but it fulfills this need at a lower social cost. From this fact stems the basic advantage of paper money over commodity money.

The social saving achieved by using paper money instead of commodity money can be approximated as the value of the resources that are freed from the need to create the increase in the stock of the commodity used as money. Let us suppose that the money-printing facility is given as a monopoly to the central bank. The central bank can now extract a monopoly profit from its printing of paper money which is approximately equal to the difference between the resources used in creating the commodity money and the resources used in printing the paper money. This monopoly

---

[3] It is often assumed that the cost of providing paper money is negligible. This might not be completely true if indirect costs such as precautions against forgery, etc., are also taken into account.

profit we could call seigniorage.[4] This monopoly profit is made possible because holders of money are willing to forego the interest on their holdings of money, as they get in return a means of payment that is fully liquid. Therefore the central bank that issues the paper money does not have to pay interest on the real resources it gets in return for the paper money. The central bank is free to invest these resources as it sees fit. This discrepancy in behavior between private persons or institutions and the central bank is the real source of seigniorage.

In connection with the international monetary system, the question of seigniorage arises from the fact that the country issuing the reserve currency (or currencies) has a certain monopoly power to extract seigniorage in a way analogous to that of a central bank.

A country that wants to increase its international liquidity by getting dollars can only get those dollars by creating an export surplus; i.e., it will have to give up real resources in exchange for the dollars. The rate of return on such dollar holdings is zero if the dollars are held in the form of bank notes or currency. If they are held in another form, they might give some positive rate of return but still very low. The central bank of the United States, however, can invest at a higher rate of return the resources it has got in return for the bank notes it has issued to foreigners. The seigniorage created by this process accrues to the United States because it is the main reserve country of the world.[5]

It is understandable that other countries object to the United States being able to extract seigniorage. Some countries, for instance France, which favor a system of commodity money, could argue that it is one more of the features which they dislike in a paper-money system. Other countries, which in principle favor a system of paper money, will perhaps object to seigniorage accruing to only one country (or two countries).[6]

History reveals that systems of paper money have been able to out-compete systems of commodity monies within the national states. There are

---

[4] Seigniorage is the difference between the cost of a mass of bullion and the value as money of the pieces coined from it, usually claimed by a sovereign or feudal superior as a prerogative.

[5] Great Britain will also be able to extract seigniorage because the pound sterling is used as a key currency.

[6] This is one of the reasons underlying the so-called Hart–Kaldor–Tinbergen proposal for an international commodity reserve money. We shall return to this proposal in Chapter 28.

512

The adequacy of international liquidity,
the price of international liquidity,
and the adjustment mechanism

powerful reasons for believing that this will also happen on an international level. Then the question of to whom should accrue the seigniorage created within the international monetary system will have to be faced. It is perhaps not one of the crucial questions of international monetary reform, but it is sufficiently important to be kept in mind when dealing with plans for international monetary reforms.

We will deal with plans for reforms of the international monetary system in Chapter 28. First, however, there is one more very important problem of a basic theoretical nature that must be tackled: the nature of the adjustment mechanism needed to take care of the disequilibrium in the international monetary system.

THE ADJUSTMENT MECHANISM AND THE INTERNATIONAL MONETARY SYSTEM

We know from Part III that the present international monetary system ruling among the developed non-Communist countries builds on a system of fixed exchange rates. There is no reason to suppose that the external balances of the different countries will automatically be in equilibrium under such a regime. When disequilibriums occur, some kind of adjustment has to take place. In Chapters 16 and 18 we studied quite intensively different ways through which adjustment can occur.

International liquidity is needed to provide time for deficit countries to adjust. Nevertheless, it is not meaningful to discuss problems of international liquidity except against a background of possible ways of adjustment. International liquidity cannot be discussed apart from the adjustment mechanism. Much of the discussion of international liquidity is futile because the problem of liquidity is discussed in the abstract, without due attention being paid to what the explicit policy goals are and to the possible means of adjustment that are available.

One important issue, perhaps the most important of all, is that concerned with the flexibility of exchange rates. Under a system of flexible exchange rates, external balances would, ideally, always be adjusted, and international liquidity would only be needed for transaction purposes. We do not live in such a world. We know that exchange rates are pegged. Even so, within such a system, there is great scope for changes of exchange rates.

To start with, even IMF permits countries to adjust their exchange rates up to 10 percent without consultation. If a country can prove that it has a "fundamental disequilibrium" in its balance of payments, it will be allowed to depreciate its currency by more than 10 percent. As we know from the discussion in Chapters 16 and 18, several countries have devalued their currencies, and two countries, West Germany and the Netherlands, have appreciated their currencies during the postwar period. Exchange-rate changes are therefore still important policy means.

It could be argued, however, that changes of exchange rates have not been used as frequently as have been needed. Devaluations are still looked upon as a measure of last resort. This is unfortunate and has put the international monetary system under unnecessary strain.

Fairly large devaluations, say 15 percent and more, could be viewed as unnecessarily drastic policy means, which, not least politically speaking, are too risky to undertake except under very special circumstances. A way of increasing the role of adjustment of exchange rates without dramatizing such changes is by widening the gap within which an exchange rate can normally fluctuate.

Today, an exchange rate can fluctuate but within a very narrow range. The Bank of England, for instance, permits the rate of £1 in terms of dollars to fluctuate between \$2.38 and \$2.42. This range could be broadened; it would automatically encourage adjustment. If the price of the pound sterling tended to fall, i.e., if it depreciated somewhat, this would have a dampening effect on British imports, while British exporters would be in a better competitive situation, as described in Chapter 16. As both exports and imports can be expected to be price-elastic, such changes in the rate of exchange might have substantial effects on volumes of exports and imports, thereby giving rise to important adjustments in the balance of payments. If, at the same time, exporters and importers know that the exchange rate will not fluctuate except within these set margins, at least for some time, they might not be unduly worried by such fluctuations. Besides, they can always cover themselves by buying and selling exchange forward, as described in Chapter 13.

This would perhaps be an efficient way of letting the price mechanism help to bring about adjustment in the external balance. If after some time, say 2 years or so, the currency in question should prove to be overvalued and that therefore the price tended to stay at the upper margin (reckoned in

514

The adequacy of international liquidity,
the price of international liquidity,
and the adjustment mechanism

terms of units of the home currency that would have to be paid for one unit of foreign currency), then the mean of the interval could be changed in an upward direction. In this way, the country would be approaching a system of "sliding parity." This would mean that an adjustment could take place by a change in exchange rates. Changes in exchange rates, however, would be relatively small and would take place gradually. Thus the risk for speculation could be minimized and exporters and importers would know exactly what the exchange rate would be (possibly by using the forward market).

This is one way in which adjustment of external balances could be facilitated. Another way is by using appreciations and depreciations more frequently than is done now. Much would be gained if exchange rates could be changed without drama. It would obviously lead to a great improvement in the possibility to adjust if the exchange rate could be looked upon as an ordinary policy weapon, similar to the discount rate or the rate of taxation.

True, a change in the exchange rates has inconvenient side effects. Depreciation could have inflationary tendencies and the income distribution could be affected, as discussed in Chapter 16. But changes in discount rates and taxation can also have such side effects; they can also cause inflation or affect the income distribution in seemingly undesirable ways. If the exchange rate can be used as an ordinary means of economic policy, the arsenal of possible means increases and, as described in Chapter 18, the efficiency of economic policy increases.

It must also be noted that it is not only depreciations which should be used. Appreciations can be equally important for a smooth working of the adjustment mechanism. Surplus countries should also play their part if the adjustment mechanism is to function well. Surplus countries have been extremely reluctant to appreciate or to pursue expansionary policies during the 1950s and 1960s. The small appreciation of West Germany and Holland (5 percent) in 1961 is the only example. The surplus countries in Europe (mainly the EEC countries) have preferred, instead, to accumulate large reserves. This, of course, unquestionably increases the strain on the international monetary system and aggravates the need for reserves.

Changes of exchange rates involve a "true" adjustment. A second factor plays a very important role in this connection: capital movements. We have already discussed the role of capital movements at some length, both their role for creating equilibrium in the balance of payments (Chapter 14) and their role for adjustment (Chapters 16 and 18). We studied, for instance in Chapter 18, how capital movements could be induced by the use of monetary policy to offset a deficit in the balance of current account. In a way, however, capital movements there did not bring about a "true" adjustment in the sense that a depreciation would have done.

Even if capital movements do not always imply the same type of adjustment as expenditure-reducing or expenditure-switching policies do, they still have an extremely important role to play.

We have already demonstrated, for instance in Chapter 16, that it can be difficult to identify the causes of a deficit in the balance of payments. There are also instances where it is impossible for a country to reach, at the same time, external and internal equilibrium. Under such circumstances, capital movements can be a necessary means for facilitating the burden of adjustment.

Under a monetary system such as prevails in the world today, capital movements play a critical role. Even if the adjustment mechanism can be made to work more smoothly than it has done so far, external imbalances will be frequent. In that context, capital movements can play two important roles.

First, capital movements can provide a breathing space. Even if a deficit country has decided that it must adjust its balance of payments, this can take time. The country could, for instance, wish to adjust gradually. During some period, the country could then need to import capital to cover the deficits that will occur until a complete adjustment has been achieved.

Second, capital movements can act as a substitute for a traditional type of adjustment. This is discussed at the end of Chapter 18. If a country has a deficit on its balance of current account, this could be covered by an inflow of capital on the capital account. Such an arrangement need not be viewed merely as a temporary phenomenon, it can easily go on for a decade or two.[7] During this time, basic conditions can change, so that the country's situation as far as the external balance is concerned also changes and the deficit country becomes a surplus country.

Imbalances are often of a somewhat accidental nature; it is then unwise to insist on adjustment at any cost. Too much stress on balancing foreign accounts can easily lead to too much precaution and deflationary policies, which will spread from one country to another and lead to slow growth of the world economy.

In today's international monetary system, it is natural for the capital movements between countries to be managed by the central banks. Central

---

[7] The reader should consult Chapter 8 for historical examples.

516

The adequacy of international liquidity,
the price of international liquidity,
and the adjustment mechanism

banks have also engaged in capital movements during the postwar period. Britain, for instance, has on several occasions been able to borrow on a short-term basis from other members of the Ten to cover deficits in its balance of payments. So-called swap arrangements between central banks have also been used; they are essentially arrangements for short-term lending whereby a central bank in acute need of foreign funds can borrow from other central banks.

A difficulty with arrangements such as these is that they are too ad hoc by nature; they are usually intended only to cover very immediate needs and involve only transactions on a short-term basis.

But the underlying causes of imbalances are rarely of a short-term nature. They often persist for some years (5 to 10, perhaps). Imbalances need not be of a long-term nature, but they are not generally of a short-term one, either; perhaps the term *medium term* could be used to characterize most imbalances. France's deficits in the early 1950s, U.S. deficits since 1958, Germany's surpluses during the 1950s and 1960s are obviously not short-term in character; in these cases it seems appropriate to speak of medium term.

The capital movements between central banks which have been organized so far hardly seem to be appropriate to handle cases such as those just mentioned. It could also be argued that the deficiencies of the International Monetary Fund to a large extent stem from the fact that the IMF is built on the concept that imbalances usually change in a cyclical, short-term fashion.

What is needed is some arrangement whereby medium-term capital movements can be organized. Surplus countries might not want to appreciate their currency, but they might be willing to engage in foreign lending. Thereby short-term accommodating capital flows could be turned into planned, autonomous flows of a medium-term nature. This could obviously relieve the pressure on the external balance of a deficit country. If capital movements could be organized along lines like these, the international monetary system could be made to function in a more coherent and stable fashion than it does today. In such a system, the need for international liquidity would diminish.

SUMMARY AND CONCLUSION

We have seen that the concept of adequacy of international liquidity is elusive. It hardly seems meaningful to refer to the need for international liquidity in simple quantitative terms. There is no valid mechanical rule that says that international liquidity has to grow by an annual percentage figure.

If the price of international liquidity is taken into account, it becomes clear that the problem is many-faceted and that price changes can play an important role in determining the supply and demand of liquidity.

International liquidity cannot be discussed except in the broader context of the adjustment mechanism. It can very well be argued that there is no lack of international liquidity per se but that insufficient attention is paid to the functioning of the adjustment mechanism and the role of international capital movements.

Chapter 28 is devoted to a discussion of reform plans for the international monetary system. The exposition in Chapters 26 and 27 can be viewed as preliminaries to that discussion.

SELECTED BIBLIOGRAPHY: CHAPTER 27

An interesting discussion about international liquidity from a theoretical point of view is contained in:

American Economic Review, Papers & Proceedings, vol. 63, no. 2, May 1968.

Among contributions to that discussion are:

R. Clower and R. Lipsey, "The Present State of International Liquidity Theory."

R. N. Cooper, "The Relevance of International Liquidity to Developed Countries."

J. M. Letiche, "International Liquidity: Synthesis and Appraisal."

For a discussion of international liquidity in terms of supply and demand, see:

B. Hansen, *International Liquidity*, National Institute of Economic Research, Occasional Paper 1, Stockholm, 1964.

518

The adequacy of international liquidity,
the price of international liquidity,
and the adjustment mechanism

See also:

F. M. Machlup, "The Need for Monetary Reserves," *Princeton Reprints in International Finance*, no. 5, October 1966.

W. M. Brown, "The External Liquidity of an Advanced Country," *Princeton Studies in International Finance*, no. 17.

H. R. Heller, "Optimal International Reserves," *EJ*, June 1966.

For a discussion of seigniorage, see:

H. G. Johnson, "Theoretical Problems of the International Monetary System," *Pakistan Development Review*, 1967.

Plans for reform
of the international
monetary system

28

The discussion of reform plans for the international monetary system has been very intensive during the past 10 years. An immense literature exists on the problem. We shall discuss in this chapter what we regard as the main issues.

We shall first discuss briefly two proposals that seem rather unrealistic. The first is to introduce a regime of flexible exchange rates; the second is the plan for turning the present gold-exchange standard into a pure gold standard.

We shall then deal with the group of proposals that involve more or less far-reaching reforms of the present system. They accept the logic of the present system but wish to improve it. They could be called revisionistic proposals, as opposed to the others, which are either revolutionary or reactionary (using an ideological vocabulary). Here belongs the plan for a World Central Bank, which is the most utopian proposal of this kind. At the other extreme come what might be termed plans for ad hoc solutions. In between are plans for a reformation and extension of the International Monetary Fund, proposals connected with the names of two American economists, Robert Triffin and E. M. Bernstein.

The discussion in this chapter will be carried on against the background of the description of the present international monetary system and the analysis of liquidity problems that have been made in Chapters 26 and 27.

FLEXIBLE EXCHANGE RATES

Many economists argue that a system of fixed exchange rates is an anomaly. Such a system will always be accompanied by external imbalances. An international monetary system based on such a regime will always balance on a knife-edge. Sooner or later the strains on the system must become too great. Then various impediments to trade will be introduced by deficit countries to balance their trade, and the possibilities of gains from trade will be curtailed.

This part of the book deals with practical, immediate problems. Whether one prefers a system of flexible or of fixed exchange rates is largely a matter of belief. Having already dealt with the theoretical pros and cons of flexible exchange rates in Chapter 17, we can be brief here.

519

520

Plans for reform
of the international
monetary system

Ideally, a system of floating exchange rates should solve a country's balance-of-payments problems. The need for international liquidity would be minimum, and the international monetary system would work like a servomechanism. These are obviously great attractions. On the other hand, a system of flexible exchange rates might have undesirable side effects such as destabilizing speculation or an inflationary impact on domestic price levels. (These well-known problems were dealt with in Chapters 13 and 17.)

The point here is that there is little prospect of getting a system of flexible exchange rates in the immediate future. Whatever the theoretical attractions of such a system are, there is no chance of it being accepted in the near future by practical men, i.e., men who have power. This chapter is devoted to more mundane problems; therefore, we shall merely mention that a system of flexible exchange rates does not lack its proponents; then we can go on to plans of more immediate concern.

THE GOLD STANDARD: AN INCREASE IN THE PRICE OF GOLD

There are various arguments for a return to a gold standard. There are those who simply argue for an increase in the price of gold, without necessarily implying that the dollar and the pound sterling should be abandoned as reserve currencies. Then there are those who, while also arguing for an increase in the price of gold, primarily see this as a step on the way back to a pure gold standard, where no reserve currencies will exist but all international liquidity will take the form of gold.

Take the first line of reasoning. Its proponents argue that a substantial increase in the price of gold would solve the problem of international liquidity. If, for instance, the price of gold was doubled, i.e., raised from $35 to $70 per ounce, the value of the monetary stocks of gold would also be doubled. This would obviously lead to a large increase in world liquidity.[1]

---

[1] The economist who most energetically and most cogently has argued for an increase in the price of gold along these lines is the British economist Sir Roy Harrod. His argument is presented in *Reforming the World's Money*, London, Macmillan, 1965.

The countries that would especially benefit would be the United States and the EEC countries of Western Europe, which, as we saw in Chapter 26, together hold 75–80 percent of the world's known monetary gold reserves.

That the value of the existing stocks would increase is obvious. The proponents of an increase in the price of gold also argue that the long-term growth of the world supply would increase. This, however, as pointed out in Chapter 27, is a more debatable point.

Mining of gold would be more profitable and would undoubtedly lead to an increase in the supply of gold. The vital point is the effect of a price increase on hoarding. The proponents of a world-wide devaluation argue that a dishoarding would follow and that gold would therefore come out of various hiding places and flow into the central banks as hoarders and speculators took advantage of the price increase. This line of argument is also supported by historical evidence. The last general increase in the price of gold, in 1934, when it was raised from $20 to $35 per ounce, did produce a considerable dishoarding of gold.

What effect on hoarding would a price increase have today? This is much less certain. For the United States it would be the first revaluation of gold since 1934. But for Britain it would be the third since 1949 and the second since 1967. For France it would be the eighth, the first since 1969. For some other countries it would be the tenth or the twelfth.

Against this background, it is doubtful whether a world-wide devaluation of currencies and revaluation of gold would be looked upon as a once-and-for-all phenomenon. There could be those with good memories, who would have a feeling that, in the future, gold would be revalued again and therefore would continue to hold on to it. In this case, no dishoarding of gold would take place, and there would be no increase in the amount of gold available for monetary purposes.

An increase in the price of gold also has some obvious drawbacks. The increase in the value of the stocks of gold could have an inflationary impact on the world economy. As we have seen, stocks of gold are very unevenly distributed among countries. A world-wide devaluation would benefit only a small group of countries, which, it could be argued, already have large enough reserves. Against this, it could be argued that what matters is the total amount of reserves. If this is increased, any country can, by appropriate policy measures, determine what reserves it desires to hold.

Another point worth mentioning is that a revaluation of gold would penalize those countries which have most loyally cooperated in sustaining the

522

Plans for reform
of the international
monetary system

present system by holding reserve currencies instead of gold. Provided the reform is carried out within the context of the present system, it can also be argued that it will in the future increase the confidence problem discussed in Chapter 26, as it will teach the world that speculation against a reserve currency is profitable in the long run.

We mentioned that an increase in the price of gold will increase the supply of newly mined gold. The world's two largest gold producers are South Africa and the Soviet Union. These two countries would then benefit from an increase in the price of gold. How this effect is evaluated is obviously a political question. As the problem is hardly of primary importance, there is no need for us to dwell on it here.

The main issue at stake in this connection is therefore the effect on the growth of gold reserves. It is, as we have seen, highly doubtful whether any increase in the increments of the world's stock of monetary gold would take place because of a gold revaluation. Even if one were willing to accept (or disregard) all the side effects that we have touched upon, it is, therefore, doubtful whether an increase in the price of gold could be judged a rational policy. This is especially the case if the revaluation of gold took place in small steps, say 4 percent per year, instead of a large revaluation of a once-and-for-all nature. If a revaluation of gold were truly to be of the latter kind, one would, of course, in the long run, still be left with the problem of how to increase world liquidity.

We have now dealt with the arguments of those who support an increase in the price of gold within the framework of the gold-exchange standard, i.e., within the framework of the present system. There exists also a school of economists whose views are more radical in this respect. This school argues for a return to a pure gold standard, to a system where gold would be the only means of international liquidity and where no reserve currencies would exist. Prominent members of this school include the French economist Jacques Rueff, an advisor to de Gaulle, and the Swiss economist Maurice Heilperin.[2]

---

[2] Rueff's views are presented in his books, *The Age of Inflation*, Gate Regnery, 1963, and *The Balance of Payments*, New York, Macmillan, 1967. A neat presentation of his views is given in R. Hinshaw (ed.), *Monetary Reform and the Price of Gold*, Baltimore, The Johns Hopkins Press, 1967. Heilperin's views are given in "The Case for Going Back to Gold," *Fortune*, September 1962.

The main point of this latter school is: If gold was revalued and the price increased from $35 to $70 per ounce, for instance, the value of U.S. dollar holdings would increase from approximately $10 to $20 billion. The value of U.S. outstanding dollar liabilities is roughly $20 billion. The United States could then use the bulk of its gold holdings to pay off the dollar balances in gold. The United States would perhaps not be able to pay off the total amount of its outstanding liabilities at once, but assume that it at least paid off $10 billion worth (the equivalent of its windfall gain of revaluation), it would then retain the same cash position in terms of dollars as before the revaluation, but it would be in a greatly improved position as a debtor country.

Britain, according to this view, should act in an analogous fashion. Its situation, however, is somewhat more complicated. Britain's gold balances amount to approximately $2 billion. After a revaluation they would be worth $4 billion. The outstanding sterling balances, however, are worth about $12 billion. The recipe that could be applied to the United States thus could not be applied to Britain, at least not in the immediate future.

Measures such as these could be expected to have a deflationary bias. The United States, for instance, could no longer rely on other countries being willing to accept dollars to finance the deficits in its balance of payments. It would have to close the deficit in its balance of payments and presumably would have to create a surplus in its external balance so as to be able to repay its outstanding dollar liabilities. To perform such an act it would certainly have to pursue a stringent deflationary policy or to carry out a depreciation of the dollar, which would to some extent entail a dose of deflation. Such policies could not avoid having a deflationary impact on its trading partners. A strong impetus to a world depression would follow.

The logic in the case of Britain is somewhat harder to understand, but in essence it would have to be the same as in the case of the United States. Britain would have to pursue a policy of rigorous deflation that, over the years, would build up surpluses in the balance of payments which would permit Britain gradually to pay off all the outstanding sterling liabilities.

Needless to say, the proponents of a return to the gold standard see no reason for an increase of international liquidity. The implication of our analysis in Chapters 26 and 27 is that the need for a long-term growth of international liquidity is perhaps less obvious than is often stated. But from there to the argument that no increase is necessary in the foreseeable future

524

Plans for reform
of the international
monetary system

and that strong deflationary policies really are what is needed is a long step indeed.

This, as far as we can see, more or less takes care of the proposal of going back to a pure gold standard. Unless we are willing to face strong deflationary policies we cannot argue for a return to *l'ancien régime* in this respect.

Other points of criticism can be raised against such a scheme. One is connected with the question of seigniorage. Production of gold requires the use of real resources. The creation of paper money involves practically no cost. Therefore, the use of gold for monetary purposes entails a social waste, as it builds on a refusal to use a more efficient means of payment. Efficiency in the use of the world's resources presupposes the use of an international paper money instead of gold and that the resources used for production of gold are instead used for production of useful commodities.

To sum up, an increase in the price of gold would hardly solve the problems of the international monetary system in the long run. Its effects on the supply of gold are highly debatable. If a considerable revaluation in the price of gold was undertaken, it could easily have an immediate disruptive influence on the world's price level. A return to a pure gold standard would most certainly have a deflationary impact in the long run. To leave the supply of international liquidity to the vagaries of gold production is hardly rational. A pure gold standard would also entail a social cost in comparison with an international credit money.

A WORLD CENTRAL BANK

A return to a pure gold standard is the most far-reaching proposal at the conservative end. The most radical, or utopian type of proposal is that of a World Central Bank. The idea of a World Central Bank is an old dream of students of foreign exchanges.

The analogy naturally comes from the central banks of the national states. On an abstract level the analogy is also perfectly valid. If a World Central Bank were created and only one currency established, there would hardly be the risk of a liquidity crisis. A World Central Bank would be able, by lending, open market operations, etc., to create the amount of liquidity it thought necessary, and this should cause no great problems or concern.

The problems associated with the idea of a World Central Bank are of a different order. First, there are the obvious ones. The idea, of course, is premature. States are not willing to give up their independence in this vital area of economic policy. A coordination of world monetary policies in the hands of a World Central Bank would presuppose coordination of fiscal and other types of economic policies; otherwise, we cannot expect efficient policies to be implemented. But hardly any country can be expected to agree to such a handover of sovereignty in the crucial area of economic policy. This, in itself, is sufficient to explain why the idea of a World Central Bank cannot be regarded as a realistic policy proposal.

However, another important point must be considered, one that is sometimes overlooked. Assume, for the sake of reasoning, that the various states could agree on creating a World Central Bank. Someone would still have to decide what policies the Bank should pursue. How much liquidity should be created? Should the Bank help countries in need of liquidity even if this were to cause inflationary pressures in the world economy? Or should it implement deflationary policies? Should it engage in countercyclical activities? If so, to what extent and at which level?

Questions such as these cannot be avoided. No mechanical rules about "normal" increases of world liquidity or such things can replace reason: Mechanical rules always prove to be hindrances for rational policies. The main point to keep in mind is that the creation of a World Central Bank does not, in itself, solve any problems. It simply postpones the real issue one step, so to speak. The real issue is still which policies should be pursued.

World trade has grown at a fast rate, more than 7 percent per year, since World War II. This might be taken as a sign that, after all, the international monetary system has perhaps not worked so badly. A World Central Bank that had implemented a more cautious policy in monetary matters would possibly have been able to force the growth rate down to, say, 5 percent. Such a development, had it happened, could hardly have been regarded as a great sign of progress.

The idea of a World Central Bank is perhaps primarily an example of too-naive idealism, which substitutes vague and high-sounding schemes for an analysis of real problems.

526

Plans for reform
of the international
monetary system

THE KEYNES PLAN

Now to turn to more immediate and practical plans for reform of the international monetary system. The proposals in this group are all revisionistic; all aim at reform and development of the present monetary system. The most interesting ones aim at an extension of the International Monetary Fund. However, we shall begin with a plan of somewhat earlier date, the so-called Keynes Plan, which can act as a useful relief for later plans.

The Keynes Plan was proposed in 1943 as a background for the discussion of how the international monetary system should be organized once World War II was over.[3] A central feature of the plan is the establishment of a clearing union. In this sense, the Keynes Plan aims at the creation of an international central reserve bank. This will be done as follows.

A new international currency unit, called bancor, with a fixed value in gold will be created. At the same time, holdings of foreign currency will be abolished. Gold, however, will still be used for international monetary purposes. Thus, when the system is fully developed, only two means of international payments will be in use: gold and bancor.

According to this plan, a single country can acquire bancor in two ways: It can sell gold or use its overdraft facilities with the clearing union. The exchange of gold and bancor, however, is one way. Gold can be used to acquire bancor, but bancor cannot be used to buy gold.

The essence of the Keynes Plan is the clearing union. The plan builds on the concept that deficits and surpluses in the balance of payments change in a cyclical fashion. A deficit country needing liquidity can borrow from the clearing union by using the overdraft facilities. Each member country has a quota in the union. The quota depends on the sum of each country's exports and imports. If a country uses more than one fourth but less than one half its quota, it will have to pay a charge of 1 percent per year on its borrowings with the union; if it uses more than one half its quota, the charge will be 2 percent.

An interesting feature is that surplus countries too will have to pay a charge if they are excessively liquid. If a surplus country has a credit balance with the union of more than one half its quota it will have to pay a charge of 1 percent per year.

---

[3] *Proposals for an International Clearing Union*, presented by the Chancellor of the Exchequer to Parliament by Command of His Majesty, London, 1943.

A basic part of the philosophy behind the plan is the view that external imbalances are of a cyclical, short-term nature. For a year or two a country might be in deficit, during which time it should be able to borrow from the union. Similarly, a country might have a surplus in the short term, but if it accumulates too great a reserve of bancor it should be penalized.

Connected with this view of the nature of imbalances is the belief that the adjustment mechanism works or should be made to work. Imbalances are (or should be) of a short-term type, and economic policies, presumably both expenditure-reducing and expenditure-switching policies, should be used for the rapid creation of a new balance. Surplus countries should also play their role by inflating or appreciating, thereby trying to eliminate the surplus.

It should also be observed that adjustment can take the form of capital movements. The only way deficit and surplus countries can avoid paying charges to the union is for a deficit country to borrow from a surplus country and for a surplus country to lend to a deficit country. Capital movements between countries are therefore encouraged by the Keynes Plan. It is envisaged that accommodating capital movements can be turned into autonomous capital flows and that they can play a role both as a form of adjustment and as a creator of breathing space while other measures of adjustment are being prepared.

The Keynes Plan has several attractive features. It is modest in scope, in that it only relies on the creation of a clearing union and a new international currency. To that extent, it goes in the direction of a World Central Bank, but it does so only to a realistic and very modest degree; there is no question of the creation of a full-fledged World Central Bank and of coordinating world monetary policies. It is also a sound proposal in that it (at least implicitly) stresses the role of adjustment and capital movements. However, it is somewhat naive in its conception of the nature of imbalances, and it is far too sanguine in its belief in the possibilities of the various countries to keep their external balances in equilibrium. Another interesting aspect of the Keynes Plan is that it makes no provision for a gradual, long-term increase in international liquidity. The perfect state it envisages is where all external balances are in equilibrium; then no international liquidity is needed.

528

Plans for reform
of the international
monetary system

AN EXTENSION OF THE INTERNATIONAL MONETARY FUND:
THE BERNSTEIN PLAN

We now deal with the actual discussion of the present international monetary system and with those proposals that argue for an extension of the International Monetary Fund. The two best known and most carefully worked out of these plans are those connected with the names of Bernstein and Triffin. We first discuss the Bernstein Plan.[4]

The leading idea of the Bernstein Plan is to give the IMF a more central place in the present international monetary system. The member countries now hold quotas in the IMF. The quota of the United States, for instance, amounts to over $5 billion, that of Sweden $225 million. These quotas, however, are not regarded as "first-line reserves."

At present, members have automatic access to the first 25 percent of their quotas (their gold subscriptions to the Fund). Moreover, they have almost automatic access to another 25 percent. Thereafter, drawings from the Fund are subject to increasingly stringent conditions of Fund approval.

The first suggestion of the Bernstein Plan is that the IMF quotas should be integrated into each country's working balances. Thereby the amount of international liquidity should increase.

The second suggestion of the Bernstein Plan is the creation of a Reserve Unit Account within the IMF. This is the central feature of the plan. A member country of the IMF could be allotted, say, $300 million of reserve units. This would mean that the country would deposit an equivalent amount of its own currency with the Reserve Unit Account.[5] The allotment of reserve units could, for instance, be in proportion to the respective country's quota in IMF. These reserve units would then be used in settlements of deficits and surpluses in the balances of payments.

The creation of the Reserve Unit Account would be a way of institutionalizing capital movements. Deficit countries would be able to cover their deficits by borrowing reserve units from the Account and using these

---

[4] E. M. Bernstein (1904–) has served for many years as a U.S. Treasury official. He was the first director of research and statistics at the IMF. He is the founder and president of EMB (Ltd.), a firm of research economists in Washington, D.C.
[5] It is not completely clear whether all member countries of the IMF or only a select group of the largest and most developed industrial countries should subscribe to the Reserve Unit Account. Under all circumstances, the bulk of the currencies of the Account should be those of members of the latter group.

in settling their deficits. An advantage for the deficit countries would be that they would not have to negotiate with central banks of various surplus countries but only with the IMF directly. If the system came to be accepted, it would presumably mean that deficit countries could more or less automatically count on acquiring a certain amount of reserve units. This in effect would mean that deficit countries, at least for some time, could count on turning accommodating capital imports into autonomous, controlled inflows.

Another important aspect of the Bernstein Plan is that it provides for an increase in international liquidity. When the plan was first set out in the 1950s, Bernstein hardly viewed the amount of international liquidity then available as insufficient. Today, he would probably argue that there is need for an increase in liquidity and that this need will be accentuated in years to come.

The growth of reserves could simply be handled by an increase in the total amount of reserve units. Bernstein suggests that new reserve units should be issued each year to " provide for an adequate but not excessive increase in total monetary reserves."[6] To avoid abrupt changes of policy in this respect the amounts of reserve currencies to be issued could be determined at 5-year intervals.

The Bernstein Plan has several attractive features. It builds on existing institutions and does not imply any great changes in this respect. The reform of the IMF that the plan entails would perhaps be viewed as radical by some, but it can hardly be argued that it would be impracticable. Furthermore, it recognizes that what really counts in international monetary matters is the behavior of a handful of the leading industrial countries. If they could get together in creating a Reserve Unit Account within the IMF, there is no doubt that this could be done. Another important point is that the plan explicitly recognizes the need for organized international capital movements as support for the international monetary system.

The main drawback of the Bernstein Plan is that it does not solve the confidence problem. On the contrary, it could be argued that it introduces new complications into this problem. Gold would still be used within the system. The reserve unit would have a guaranteed gold value. It is somewhat unclear whether or not the reserve unit would be freely exchangeable with gold. If it was, the confidence problem of the present system is left

---

[6] R. Hinshaw (ed.), *op. cit.*, p. 66.

530

Plans for reform
of the international
monetary system

intact: There is no guarantee against a run on gold and away from reserve units. If reserve units are not freely exchangeable with gold, one can easily envisage a situation where surplus countries would refuse to accept reserve units. Then the system could break down.

There are also other facets to the confidence problem under a Bernstein type of plan. As time goes by, the composition of the backing of the reserve units could change and increasingly come to consist of "soft" currencies. Devaluations could cause trouble, with arguments about who is going to make up the loss, incurred by those (including the Reserve Unit Account) who holds the devaluing currency. If a holder of reserve units wished to redeem them prematurely and instead wanted, say, pound sterling, and Britain's lending capacity was already used up, this again could cause problems.

There are also problems connected with interest rates charged on reserve units to lenders and borrowers which could be difficult to solve.

The way increases in liquidity should be handled would also have to be solved. The Bernstein Plan only creates a mechanism through which increases can be made; it does not solve the essential problem: What rules should govern the creation of liquidity? The plan could in this respect easily turn into a scheme for special assistance to deficit countries.

We shall return to some of the problems dealt with by the Bernstein Plan in the concluding section of this chapter. But now to the Triffin Plan.

THE TRIFFIN PLAN

The Triffin Plan resembles the Bernstein Plan to the extent that it also builds on the idea that international monetary reserves should be centralized.[7] It also takes the IMF as the starting point of reform. The Triffin Plan, however,

---

[7] Robert Triffin (1911–) is professor of economics at Yale University. He has also worked with the Federal Reserve Board and the IMF. He is the author of *Monopolistic Competition and General Equilibrium Theory*, Cambridge, Mass., Harvard University Press, 1940, and of several books on international monetary problems, including *Gold and the Dollar Crisis*, New Haven, Conn., Yale University Press, 1961, and *The World Money Maze*, New Haven, Conn., Yale University Press, 1966.

is more ambitious than the Bernstein Plan; it involves a more direct attack on the gold exchange standard. It also goes further toward the creation of an international central bank.

Triffin has been a relentless critic of the present international monetary system. He has attacked the irrationality of a system so dependent on gold and has argued that sooner or later a system of paper money will have to replace the present hybrid system with its element of commodity money. He has also argued that a system of one or two reserve currencies cannot last forever: The problem of confidence will be sharpened and the threat of collapse will always lurk in the background.

The basic solution, according to Triffin, lies in a centralization of world reserves. Member countries of the IMF will have to start opening deposits with the IMF which will act as the central banks' central bank. These deposits will originally be created by a transfer of existing reserves from the central banks to the Fund. Thus the IMF will get reserves and the central banks will be credited with deposits with the IMF in return.

An important point in this connection is that the deposits with the IMF will carry a gold guarantee. If this should be insufficient as an inducement for the member countries to convert their reserves into deposits with the IMF, Triffin suggests that member countries be required to hold at least 20 percent of their total reserves as deposits with the Fund.

The IMF will then gradually expand its activities in this direction and eventually will acquire all international reserves in the form of foreign currency. It will be permitted gradually to liquidate its holdings of these foreign currencies so that in the end there will be only two means of international liquidity: deposits with the IMF and gold.

Perhaps the most distinguishing feature of the Triffin Plan is that it suggests that the Fund be empowered to engage in open market operations and thereby regulate the amount of international liquidity available. If the Fund wished to increase the amount of international liquidity, it could do so by buying securities from private persons, commercial banks, or the central bank of a member country. The IMF check thus obtained by any of the mentioned groups is cashed with the central bank of the member country in question, which deposits it with the IMF to be credited to the account of the central bank in question. If, say, the Fund bought securities for $100 million, international liquidity is increased by that amount by the Fund operation.

The background of this part of the plan is the need for a long-term increase of international liquidity, which Triffin views as one of the essential

532

Plans for reform
of the international
monetary system

tasks that any reform plan should solve. If the IMF recognizes a need for a secular growth of international liquidity, its open market purchases will exceed its open market sales. The amount of reserves held by the central banks with the IMF will then increase as the securities portfolio of the IMF increases and the amount of international liquidity increases.

This part of the plan has naturally aroused criticism. To appease the critics who fear that his plan will be inflationary, Triffin has suggested that an upper limit for the annual rate of increase of monetary reserves should be proposed, something like 3, 4, or 5 percent per year. To lay down a mechanical rule could be unwise; it is better, argues Triffin, to set an upper limit for possible increases of liquidity and leave the rest to the discretion of the Fund.

A number of minor objections have been raised against the Triffin Plan. One is that it does not provide for a substantial increase of international liquidity in the short term; another, that it might even lead to an immediate decrease of liquidity if countries treat their deposits with the Fund as less liquid than dollars and gold; a third, that it might unduly favor industrial countries because open market operations would be concentrated in these countries.

Relevant as these objections perhaps are, however, we shall concentrate on a more fundamental kind of criticism. The essential weakness of the Triffin Plan is that it builds on a peculiar contradiction. On the one hand, it is too conservative, too pragmatic; on the other hand, it is too utopian.

Triffin will retain gold as a means of international liquidity. He even goes so far as to have a gold exchange clause so that gold can be exchanged for deposits with the Fund, and vice versa. This amounts to preserving the confidence problem that haunts the present system (dealt with in Chapters 26 and 27). If a central bank (or a series of central banks) wished to exchange their IMF certificates for gold, there is nothing in the Triffin Plan that could stop them. This could, of course, create a confidence problem of much the same type as that connected with a run on gold and away from dollars. It seems that the only measure that could save such a situation would be the cooperation of a sufficient number of strong central banks. We are then back to precisely the type of conditions now prevailing. This kind of confidence problem was well illustrated by the happening of March 1968 and the gold crisis which then occurred. Chapter 26 described the nature of this crisis and the development leading up to it.

In this respect, the Triffin Plan is conservative. The utopian aspect of the plan is the one connected with the extended functions of the IMF, more precisely its power to control liquidity by open market operations. Triffin wants here to transcend the possibilities of the present system and to move in the direction of a World Central Bank. Basically, the same kind of criticism that can be raised against the idea of a World Central Bank can also be leveled against Triffin's extended version of the IMF.

On a pragmatic level, it can be argued that there is little reason to believe that countries will be willing to abstain from sovereignty over an important part of economic policy and let some directors of the IMF decide for them. On a deeper level, one can doubt the wisdom of empowering the IMF with such policy means. Single governments acting under democratic responsibilities would perhaps be more powerful in implementing policies than a board of governors of the IMF performing the somewhat dubious and vague role of high priests of international monetary policy.

If the management of international economic policy was a purely technical task, one could argue for a solution à la Triffin. But we have seen, for instance in Chapter 26, that opinions in these matters differ strongly between countries. Some want more of deflationary policies and a restriction of the growth of liquidity; others hold the opposite opinion. Placid people perhaps regret that such policy differences exist. They rest, however, on deep-seated differences in views on economic policy, and little can be done about them. To try to sweep them under the rug would be very unwise.

To sum up: Triffin deserves credit for his insistence on pointing out the inherent difficulties and contradictions of the present system. His diagnosis of the present international monetary system points to its essential weaknesses. Triffin's role as a critic is not diminished by the fact that he was perhaps the earliest and has been the most insistent critic of the present gold exchange standard. His plan for international monetary reform, however, is a halfway house. It is at the same time too conservative and too extravagant. It would leave the confidence problem virtually intact. At the same time, it rests on far too sanguine a view of the possibility and desirability of implementing a far-reaching reform of the IMF. Triffin's plan does imply a radical institutional reform in this regard, but from a policy point of view it leaves too much to be decided at the discretion of a few directors of the IMF; in this regard, it only postpones the real problem one step.

Our review of plans for reform of the international monetary system has so far left us fairly empty-handed. This could be due to the problem having so far been posed somewhat inefficiently. The reform plans that have

534

Plans for reform
of the international
monetary system

been discussed up to this point have all rested on the implicit presumption that far-reaching reforms are needed. But the present system does not, perhaps, function so badly. Possibly only marginal reforms, interventions of an ad hoc nature, are needed? We shall return to this question in the concluding section. First, however, we will touch on a problem that we have not so far dealt with: the implications for less-developed countries of international monetary reform.

THE LESS-DEVELOPED COUNTRIES AND THE INTERNATIONAL MONETARY SYSTEM

Two of the great problems facing the international economy in the last decade have been how to reform the international monetary system and make it function properly, and how to channel external resources to help the less-developed countries to speed their economic growth. It is only to be expected that several economists and politicians would try to work out schemes that would solve these two sets of problems jointly. We shall now briefly look at different kinds of such schemes. It is often argued that the problem of international monetary reform is primarily one for the developed, industrial countries. The essence of this argument will be elucidated at the end of this section.

The first type of scheme builds on the concept of an increase in international liquidity in the form of the creation of a new international paper money.[8] This could take the form of the IMF issuing a new currency (call it bancor) or reserve units à la Bernstein. If this were to be the only international currency in existence (and gold were to be replaced) there would be no limit to the amounts of currency the IMF could issue and to the assets it could acquire for the outstanding amounts of its currency.[9] Then the IMF could lend or give away the new currency to less-developed countries. The developed countries in their turn could earn units of this international currency from the less-developed countries by exporting real resources to them,

[8] There are several variants of this scheme, but we are only concerned here with the basic principles involved, so we limit the exposition to the elucidation of these principles.

[9] This would, of course, imply that the IMF would be transformed into a full-fledged World Central Bank.

which they could use in their development efforts, while the developed countries on their part would acquire international liquidity.

In a less-radical variant of this scheme, where gold, for instance, would be kept as a safeguard and the new currency would be convertible into gold, the IMF would have to be more careful about what assets it acquired to back its liabilities, but it would, at least to some extent, be able to buy, say, securities issued by the International Bank for Reconstruction and Development (IBRD) or issued by the growing number of regional development banks. Thereby at least part of the savings implied by an international paper money could be channeled to the less-developed countries.

A scheme of this kind perhaps sounds attractive. However, it has serious drawbacks. The scheme, in its more radical form, which implies the development of the IMF to a World Central Bank, encounters criticism of the kind that any variant of the idea of a World Central Bank encounters; we have already dealt with this. It is, of course, also completely unrealistic.

In its less-radical forms the scheme would not amount to a great deal. Suppose the world monetary reserves amount to $70 billion. If they grow at 3 to 5 percent per year, it would amount to $2.1 to $3.5 billion yearly. Only a smaller part of this amount could be expected to go to the less-developed countries, and that in the form of loans. This would obviously be of only marginal importance to the less-developed countries.

Furthermore, the scheme builds on the idea that the left hand does not know what the right hand is doing, or that the developed countries would leave their forms of aid untouched even though this scheme would amount to a tax on them to increase the amount of international liquidity, which is in no way necessary for this very purpose. This, however, is a debatable proposition. If the developed countries act rationally and dimension their assistance to the less-developed countries according to more objective criteria, this scheme would leave the total amount of aid unaffected. It would then only be an unnecessarily clumsy way of increasing international liquidity.

The second type of scheme suggests the introduction of a commodity-reserve money of a kind to be specifically beneficial to the less-developed countries. An ingenious reform proposal along these lines is contained in the so-called Hart–Kaldor–Tinbergen Plan.[10]

---

[10] Albert G. Hart, Nicholas Kaldor, and Jan Tinbergen, "The Case for an International Commodity Reserve Currency," UNCTAD, E/Conf. 46/P/7, February 17, 1964.

536

Plans for reform
of the international
monetary system

According to this plan the IMF should issue a new international currency backed by a bundle of primary commodities, primarily those produced by the less-developed countries. By sales and purchases of this group of commodities and by open market operations in commodity markets, the price level of this bundle of commodities should be stabilized. Thereby prices in general would also be stabilized, which the proponents of the plan regard as one of its main advantages.

They also argue that it would promote world economic growth. Their argument in this respect is somewhat doubtful, but it seems to rest on an assertion about asymmetry in the growth of production of industrial goods and primary goods. A growth in the production of industrial goods stimulates prices and production of primary goods. An increase in production of primary goods does not evoke any analogous increase in the production of industrial goods. Instead, it leads to a depression of prices on primary products, to lower incomes for primary producers, and to a fall in demand for industrial products. A stabilization of primary prices would, it is argued, lead to an increase in demand for industrial products and promote world economic growth.

This scheme, too, can be severely criticized. Let us start by taking the basic idea of the scheme, that about the beneficial influences of a stabilization of money prices of a group of primary products. We have dealt with several aspects of a stabilization of international commodity prices in Chapter 23 and with the basic theory of growth and trade in Part II. We can therefore be brief here. First, even if the scheme succeeded, it would only stabilize prices, and this is not equivalent to stabilizing export earnings or money incomes, or real incomes. Furthermore, it is the average price of a bundle of commodities that should be stabilized; this could easily mean destabilizing price changes for particular commodities induced by the scheme. Sharp price changes for particular commodities could easily be induced by the open market operations that the IMF is supposed to engage in in commodity markets. Nor, as we are well aware of from earlier parts of the book, could the scheme be expected to do much about the alleged long-term tendency for the terms of trade to deteriorate for less-developed countries. The long-term development of relative prices cannot be controlled unless one is prepared to engage in complete world-wide planning of production and consumption.

Even judged on its own merits, the Hart–Kaldor–Tinbergen Plan therefore leaves much to be desired. There are also several other drawbacks to the plan (and to any commodity-reserve currency) that could be pointed out. One is that it would involve a social waste in the form of seigniorage, which a paper money does not. Furthermore, a commodity currency built on perishable commodities and not on a metal such as gold will always require extra costs for storage, handling, etc., which will be substantial. The Hart–Kaldor–Tinbergen Plan also implies the development of the IMF in the direction of a World Central Bank to which objections can, as we know, be raised both on theoretical and practical grounds.

The Hart–Kaldor–Tinbergen Plan can hardly be taken seriously. The very prominent economists who have proposed the plan have indulged in a flight of fancy. In this, among their many reports for international organizations and various governments, they have preferred to enjoy themselves in a purely academic fashion.

Reform plans that would at the same time solve the problems of the international monetary system and help the less-developed countries have not seemed very efficient. This is due primarily to the fact that two different problems can rarely be solved by one means. A more efficient way is to design one policy for one of the problems and another policy for the other problem. In this sense, it could be argued that the problem of international monetary reform is not primarily a problem for the less-developed countries. As shown in Chapter 27, less-developed countries also have small reserves of international liquidity. There is always an opportunity cost involved in holding reserves. Less-developed countries are in general too poor to be able to afford to hold more than a minimum of reserves. Also in this sense the problem of international liquidity can primarily be said to be one for the more well-to-do, industrial countries.

Against this background, it is reasonable to argue that the problem of international monetary reform is primarily one for the developed countries. It is also of great importance to the less-developed countries, but mostly in indirect ways. Many of the trade and aid policies of the developed countries are hampered by balance-of-payments considerations, which in their turn are aggravated by deficiencies in the present international monetary system. Most developed countries prefer to give aid and assistance along bilateral lines and to tie their aid. A conspicuous example of this is the United States, which, to an increasing degree, has tied its assistance to the purchase of American goods. This has been done mainly out of concern for the balance-of-payments situation. International monetary arrangements are, of course, of great importance in this connection. If the United States should

538

Plans for reform
of the international
monetary system

be forced to pursue more rigorous policies to close the deficit in its balance of payments, this would most certainly affect the ability and willingness of the United States to give aid and assistance in a negative direction.

In an analogous fashion, balance-of-payments difficulties of the developed countries, which would be enforced by a poorly functioning international monetary system, would most certainly lead to increasing protectionist practices on the part of the developed countries which would affect the less-developed countries in negative ways. Increased protectionism of this kind would hamper both the export possibilities of the less-developed countries and their possibilities to import capital and technical assistance. The less-developed countries can hardly expect plans for reform of the international monetary system to be geared to a direct solution of their own problems. But they certainly have a very direct interest in that the reform plans are of an expansionist kind, so that they help the developed countries to maintain full employment policies and foster economic growth. From the point of view of the less-developed countries, it is important for international disequilibriums to be solved by the help of expansion in surplus countries instead of contraction in deficit countries. If this should imply an inflationary bias to the world economy, it should not unduly worry the less-developed countries. On the contrary, it would rather help facilitate growth in these countries and make them more competitive than they otherwise would be. The representatives of the less-developed countries therefore have to judge plans for international monetary reform with a cool eye as to their practical economic consequences.

REFORMS WITHIN THE EXISTING ORDER:
THE SPECIAL DRAWING RIGHTS

We shall now return to the main line of argument and discuss plans for reform of the international monetary system which are of a more immediate concern. The plans we have discussed so far have all had serious drawbacks. They have all had tendencies of being too far-flung; they have all been on the extravagant side. It could be argued that the present international monetary system functions fairly efficiently and that only smaller improvements and reforms are needed, at least in the immediate future. Such reform plans, however, should be designed to be capable of development, so that the international monetary system can be gradually adapted to take care of the future needs that could arise. In this way, the IMF could in due course develop some more definite traits of an international central bank.

It is difficult to get a precise measure regarding how efficient the international monetary system has been. We cannot scrutinize this system in isolation. We have to keep in mind that it is only a means to an end: an efficient allocation of resources on a world-wide level and a rapid development of the world economy. World trade has grown at the rate of more than 7 percent per year since World War II; it seems difficult to deny that this is quite a good record. In this perspective, it can be argued that the international monetary system has served its purpose quite well.

It must be said that this has only been achieved at the cost of a substantial amount of strain and stress. The problems inherent in the present system (described in Chapters 26 and 27) have been accentuated in recent years, and several acute conflicts over confidence, liquidity, and the place of gold have had to be met and solved, often in an atmosphere of crisis-like urgency. Many students of these questions argue that such a state cannot be perpetuated. Others point to the fact that, somehow, the problems are always solved and argue that the real issues at stake are being overdramatized. According to this view, the system could do with some minor reforms but is basically perfectly viable.

It is important to stress, as was done in Chapter 27, that possibilities of adjustment must exist if the need for international liquidity is to be kept within reasonable limits. There are several ways in which the workings of the adjustment mechanism can be improved. Some of these are discussed in Chapter 27. The basic mechanism is simple: Surplus countries ought to appreciate and deficit countries should depreciate. This can be done both in a gradual, sliding fashion and by using larger, discretionary changes of exchange rates. Whichever method is used, substantial effects on export and import volumes can be expected, at least as far as trade between industrial countries is concerned. An increased use of changes in exchange rates should also help to make speculation stabilizing and to induce capital movements that help to ease the burden of adjustment.

Capital movements need not, of course, be only of this market-oriented type. Central banks can do much, as is pointed out in Chapter 27, to facilitate adjustment, to give room for adjustment, and even to act as a "pseudo-adjustment" mechanism, as described in Chapters 18 and 27.

540

Plans for reform
of the international
monetary system

Improvements in these areas should lead to the international monetary system functioning more smoothly and the need for liquidity being minimized. It also seems as if exchange-rate changes are becoming more of an accepted means of economic policy and that countries are becoming more willing to regard it as a regular policy weapon. The most important international monetary project of reform of recent years, the introduction of the so-called special drawing rights (to which we will return shortly), can from one standpoint be characterized as a way of institutionalizing capital movements.

There are also other relatively small measures that can be undertaken which can help to avoid or at least mitigate the importance of the threats that have been haunting the present international monetary system. An increased use of markets and of the price mechanism could both help minimize the dilemma implicit in the confidence problem and regulate the need for international liquidity, so that the amount available appears as "adequate"; how this could be done is discussed in Chapter 27.

The confidence problem is, as we know, essentially a question of distribution of reserves. It arises from the fact that some central banks prefer to hold gold instead of dollars. The United States could, at least to some extent, alleviate this problem by introducing a gold guarantee, to the effect that the holders of dollars would be compensated were the dollar to be devalued. It is not easy to understand why the United States has not agreed to introduce such a measure. One sometimes meets the argument that such a guarantee could inflict huge future losses on the United States. This is nonsense. All it could do would be to prevent the United States from gaining a profit on its short-term liabilities through the depreciation; it has, after all, acquired the assets corresponding to the liabilities at predevaluation prices and can now liquidate them at postdevaluation prices, thus making a gain if no gold guarantee exists.

If a gold guarantee were introduced, it is difficult to see why any central bank would want to hold gold. Dollar assets would still give a positive return and there would be no risk in holding dollars. Hence central banks which acted rationally ought to sell out their gold and acquire dollars instead. Gold would flow back to the United States and a much larger share of the outstanding liabilities of the United States would be covered by gold than is the case at present. This would solve the confidence problem. This problem is, after all, one of liquidity, as no one can doubt the solvency of the richest country in the world.

The United States has so far not been willing to give a gold guarantee. It is difficult to interpret this in any other way than that the United States does not view the confidence problem as very pressing, because a reserve currency country cannot require other countries to have full confidence in the exchange rate of its currency and at the same time insist on having its hands free to change the exchange rate at liberty. This is not a tenable position.

In this light, it is difficult not to view the confidence problem as a much exaggerated problem, when it seems that such a simple measure as a gold guarantee could more or less take care of it. It is also difficult not to infer that the present system, in this respect, is much more stable than its critics like to admit.

We have seen that the concept of adequacy of international liquidity is an elusive one. The supply and demand of liquidity can to a large extent be determined by price policies, as is discussed in Chapter 27. To increase the availability of international liquidity can still be deemed a pertinent problem. An important step in this direction was taken in the form of the creation of the so-called special drawing rights.

The Plan for Special Drawing Rights was approved at the joint meetings of the IMF and the World Bank in Rio de Janeiro in September 1967. The essence of these special drawing rights is that they create a new international reserve asset. They can be used unconditionally by the participating countries, and they are not backed by any assets.

The new reserves, i.e., the special drawing rights, are allocated to all member countries of the IMF, irrespective of their current balance-of-payments situation. The criterion used for allocation is the quota in the Fund that the respective countries now have. A country in deficit can then use its special drawing right, and a country whose currency it wants to acquire will have to accept the special drawing right in return for its currency.

An important feature of the special drawing right is that it is unconditional. We know already that countries now have immediate access to 25 percent of their basic quota in the Fund but that increasingly stringent conditions of approval are needed if a country wishes to use more than the 25 percent. The special drawing rights thus differ in this respect. They have an automaticity that will lead to international liquidity being automatically increased when needed (at least within the limits given by the special drawing rights).

542

Plans for reform
of the international
monetary system

Another important factor is that this scheme recognizes the fact that international reserves can be created without the need for assets to back the new international liabilities. The use of any money depends ultimately on its acceptability in settlements. This fact has been used in connection with the special drawing rights. The "resources" of the new scheme is not a pool of currencies or line of credit. It is simply the obligation of the participating members to accept the special drawing rights for settlement of payments between the member countries.[11] A national money could require convertibility into some better (i.e., more widely acceptable) form of money; it could, for instance, need to be convertible into an international currency. But the acceptability of an international currency must ultimately rest on the faith that the creditors, i.e., those who have acquired real resources with the help of the money, will honor their commitments.

It is still too early to say how important the special drawing rights will become. It all depends on the practical use of the scheme. However, the special drawing rights have the potentiality of becoming a revolutionary improvement of the present international monetary system. The great weakness of this system is probably, in the final analysis, its inherent deficiency in providing an adequate amount of international liquidity. If the special drawing rights were to be used extensively and to become an established means of international liquidity, it could overcome this deficiency.

If this system failed, some other way of broadening the present system will most likely have to be tried. This could be either the creation of reserve units, for instance along the lines suggested by Bernstein, or the introduction of a multiple-reserve currency scheme, whereby not only the U.S. dollar but several of the currencies of the leading industrial nations would be used as reserve currencies. The need for such a scheme, however, is not imminent. The resources of the present system are as yet far from being exhausted.

To sum up, the present international monetary system has worked quite well during the period since World War II. It has, on the whole, provided an adequate monetary framework for the growth of world trade. The crises that, especially since 1958, have accompanied the development of world trade do not seem to have led to any substantial increase in the degree of protectionism or any curtailment of the growth of real factors.

---

[11] Not to strain the system unduly at the beginning, this obligation is, incidentally, set at twice a country's allocation.

This should not disguise the fact that some strains on the present system should be alleviated. The adjustment mechanism should be improved and changes of exchange rates ought to be regarded as an ordinary means of economic policy. Capital movements should be encouraged and organized systematically by central banks. The price mechanism should be used to regulate the need for liquidity. Cooperation within the IMF, as in the case of special drawing rights, should be undertaken.

If policies such as these are carried out, it seems that the present international monetary system could be made to work in a perfectly satisfactory manner for the foreseeable future. It is only if reforms such as these prove inadequate that more messianic measures will have to be tried.

SELECTED BIBLIOGRAPHY: CHAPTER 28

A small book that gives a very good survey of reform plans for the international monetary system is:

> F. M. Machlup, *Plans for Reform of the International Monetary System*, rev. ed., Special Papers in International Economics, no. 3, Princeton, N.J., 1964.

A good overview of the problem with contributions from some of the best-known proponents of reform, Bernstein, Rueff, and Triffin, is given in:

> R. Hinshaw (ed.), *Monetary Reform and the Price of Gold*, Baltimore, 1967.

Another useful collection of essays is:

> H. G. Grubel, *World Monetary Reform: Plans and Issues*, Stanford, Calif., 1963.

An excellent discussion of policy issues in connection with the present international monetary system is given in:

> R. N. Cooper, *The Economics of Interdependence: Economic Policy in the Atlantic Community*, New York, 1968.

Other interesting contributions are:

> R. F. Harrod, *Reforming the World's Money*, London, 1965.

> M. A. Kriz, " Gold: Barbarous Relic or Useful Instrument? " *Princeton Studies in International Finance*, no. 60, June 1967.

544

Plans for reform
of the international
monetary system

R. V. Roosa, *Monetary Reform for the World Economy*, New York, 1965.

R. V. Roosa, *The Dollar and World Liquidity*, New York, 1967.

L. B. Yeager, *International Monetary Relations*, New York, 1966, chaps. 26–28.

For a discussion of international monetary reform and the less-developed countries, see:

H. G. Johnson, *Economic Policies Toward Less Developed Countries*, Washington, D.C., 1967, chap. 7.

The question of the adjustment mechanism and sliding parity is discussed in:

G. N. Halm, *The "Band" Proposal: The Limits of Permissible Exchange Rate Variations*, Special Papers in International Economics, no. 6, Princeton, N.J., 1965.

J. H. Williamson, *The Crawling Peg*, Essays in International Finance, no. 50, December 1965.

Index

70 71 72   9 8 7 6 5 4 3 2 1